P9-CFR-141

THE
COMPLEX SECRET
of BRIEF
PSYCHOTHERAPY

A NORTON PROFESSIONAL BOOK

THE COMPLEX SECRET
of BRIEF
PSYCHOTHERAPY

James Paul Gustafson, M.D.

PROFESSOR OF PSYCHIATRY
UNIVERSITY OF WISCONSIN

W · W · NORTON & COMPANY

NEW YORK · LONDON

Copyright © 1986 by James Paul Gustafson. *All rights reserved*. Published simultaneously in Canada by Penguin Books Canada Ltd, 2801 John Street, Markham, Ontario L3R 1B4. Printed in the United States of America.

FIRST EDITION

Excerpt from *The Inferno*, by Dante Alighieri, translated by John Ciardi. © 1954, 1982 by John Ciardi. Reprinted by arrangement with New American Library, New York, New York and the estate of John Ciardi.

"Bums, on Walking," from *Helmets*, by James Dickey. © 1963 by James Dickey. Reprinted by permission of Wesleyan University Press.

"Praise for an Urn, In Memoriam: Ernest Nelson," from *The Complete Poems and Selected Letters and Prose of Hart Crane*, edited by Brom Weber, by permission of Liveright Publishing Corporation. Copyright © 1933, 1958, 1966 by Liveright Publishing Corporation.

"Evening Song," from *Mid-American Chants*, by Sherwood Anderson. Copyright by the John Lane Company, renewed 1945 by Eleanor Copenhaver Anderson. By permission of Harold Ober Associates, Inc.

Excerpt from Homer, *The Odyssey* translated by Robert Fitzgerald. Copyright © 1961 by Robert Fitzgerald. Reprinted by permission of Doubleday & Co., Inc. and William Heinemann Ltd.

Excerpt from "The Waste Land," in *Collected Poems 1909–1962* by T. S. Eliot. By permission of Harcourt Brace Jovanovich, Inc. and Faber and Faber, Ltd.

"Uncle Bungle," from *The Queen of Eene* by Jack Prelutsky. Copyright © 1970, 1978 by Jack Prelutsky. By permission of Greenwillow Books.

Excerpt from "The Second Coming" by W. B. Yeats. Reprinted with permission of Macmillan Publishing Company, from *The Poems of W. B. Yeats*, edited by Richard Finneran. © 1924 by Macmillan Publishing Co., renewed 1952 by Bertha Georgie Yeats. Worldwide use granted by permission of A. P. Watt on behalf of Michael B. Yeats and Macmillan London, Ltd.

Excerpts from *Mind and Nature: A Necessary Unity* by Gregory Bateson, © 1979. Reprinted by permission of the publisher, E. P. Dutton, a division of New American Library, and John Brockman Assoc., Inc. on behalf of the Bateson estate.

Library of Congress Cataloging-in-Publication Data
Gustafson, James P. (James Paul)
    The complex secret of brief psychotherapy.

    "A Norton professional book" — P.
    Bibliography: p.
    Includes indexes.
    1. Psychotherapy, Brief. I. Title.
RC480.55.G87   1986   616.89'14   86-12422

ISBN 0-393-70028-3

W. W. Norton & Company, Inc., 500 Fifth Avenue, New York, N.Y. 10110
W. W. Norton & Company Ltd., 37 Great Russell Street, London WC1B 3NU

1 2 3 4 5 6 7 8 9 0

To my parents Jane and Paul,
my wife Ruth,
and my children
Ian, Caitlin, and Karin

Contents

PART III

A Theory for a Method of Methods

PART IV

A Sequence for a Method of Methods

PART V

Learning Problems

Acknowledgments

I F SOME OF the poetry of the midwest becomes part of the poetry of science, I shall be glad. I have gone to both coasts for my education in psychiatry, where I was blessed at Harvard and Mount Zion with the best of teachers, John Nemiah, Les Havens, Elvin Semrad, Ed Weinshel, Joe Weiss, and Hal Sampson having been the most important, although I cannot name them all. I have gone on to travel to other teachers now living and many back in time who are described in this book. Little of this journey would have seemed possible without the example of Les Havens before me. I have had the best of conversation, moral support, and readership foremost from my wife, Ruth, but also from Lowell Cooper, Steven Stern and Mike Moran, and Robin Skynner, Myron Sharaf, Mike Wood, Yi-Fu Tuan, Joe Kepecs and Fred Wamboldt.

The faithfulness and skill of my secretarial help from Kay Corwith and Dee Jones, also Terese Bailey, Rosalie Breitenbach, Lori Thornton, and Jan Montgomery, have been essential to me; I am especially grateful to Kay Corwith for her help down the stretch when I depended greatly upon her. The same with Jan Martinson all along for his expert help with the television apparatus so vital to study in our clinic. Nor could I have done any of this work without the room and time given me by my department all along to proceed in my own way, without the curiosity of the students who come eagerly to this place to learn, without the patients presented here who have shared their lives with us so generously. I thank Kathleen Sigrist and Randy Thompson for help in reading through the proofs of the entire manuscript. I also thank Dr. J. D. Kabler and his fine staff of the University of Wisconsin Health Service, who have provided a home and referrals for our Brief Therapy Clinic for the last five years. I thank at last Susan Barrows, who has the great gift as editor to know what is significant and what can wait.

This is a terribly dangerous time. Two superpowers, as Le Corbusier wrote (1947),

transgress the law of nature—of human nature, which is eminently alternating and not continuous. . . . The American potential which has sprung up in the course of the century, which has drawn an unimaginable profit from the two wars, is an event overflowing and exceeding the present limits of material and moral control, just as, at the other end of the world also, in the USSR, an equally powerful but different potential has begun a series of events whose repercussions are unpredictable. Thus far neither the one nor the other of these forces is clear-sighted; they are quite simply on the march, getting under way. . . . For the philosophic spectator, the end of the road quickly appears: as things are, the cycle of the actions of life is not carried out, or not fully, or with pain and loss, in the irremissible period of time of each day. That is the judge, that is the touchstone: daily life. And here is the verdict: incompleteness, dissatisfaction, written into the overcrowded solar day, recurring each day and impoverishing each day, and consequently into the whole life of men. (pp. xvi–xvii)

If this book is to last in a world which is not destroyed by nuclear war between these superpowers, we shall all be in debt to those who have faced the problem head on, the International Physicians for the Prevention of Nuclear War, the Union of Concerned Scientists, the Center for Defense Information, the *Bulletin of the Atomic Scientists*, and all those others who realize and work against our peril. For the time being I have given myself to this book, but every tornado siren tells me of the incredible end of the world which lies over our horizon, unless we become responsible. Books mean nothing without a world to receive them.

There is something extreme about juxtaposing my personal world in which this book has arisen and the gross simplification of the world of the superpowers; however, I believe this is necessary. Social coordination is gross simplification. We all point west together, or east, or whatever. This generates Americanization at everything, including Wisconsin football crowds and my department of psychiatry.

But individual persons are full of themselves and will not allow themselves to be reduced for long or forever to such social coordination. The resulting organization of the individual, therefore, becomes quite complex, to coordinate being full of oneself with the social marching which is obligatory. This was a difficult problem in the relatively small world of Homer, worse in the much larger, late medieval Christian world of Dante, and extremely difficult for us in the enormous impinging world of the twentieth century. To understand how we and our patients operate in such a world is something of a complex secret.

Sing in me, Muse, and through me tell the story of that man,
skilled in all ways of contending, the wanderer, harried for years
on end, after he plundered the stronghold on the proud height
of Troy.

He saw the townlands and learned the minds of many distant
men, and weathered many bitter nights and days in his deep
heart at sea, while he fought only to save his life, to bring his
shipmates home. But not only by will nor valor could he save
them, for their own recklessness destroyed them all—children
and fools, they killed and feasted on the cattle of Lord Helios,
the Sun, and he who moves all through heaven took from their
eyes the dawn of their return.

— *The Odyssey*

PART I

A Method of Methods

1. *A Proposal*

I WRITE at once for the broadly educated reader, the newcomer to the practice of psychotherapy, and the would-be expert in brief psychotherapy. All know something about local tradition and its troubles, for the same fate awaits all traditions, whether they be literary, scientific, or those of families and individuals. Eventually all run aground with problems which are unsolvable in the familiar way of observing, feeling, acting, and thinking. All become stuck.

I am interested in what people do when their local tradition stops working for them, leaving them in doubt and fear.[1] What is their method when their method no longer helps? I want a method of methods (Selvini Palazzoli, 1985, p. 32) which is extremely reliable, which has held up against the most severe tests of time. Schools, methods, and local traditions come and go fast. This is all the more true in the multiverse (Maturana, 1985) in which we live, where traditions collide frequently with their neighbors. What is the average life of a school of brief therapy? Twenty years at best, I think. A line of success appears brightly, but soon discovers its own failures. Freud (1937, p. 228) admired a witticism that fits the schools of therapy well: "Every step forward is only half as big as it looks at first." Even this is optimistic.

Fortunately, I do not have to invent a method of methods. I only have to see that we have had such a method of methods in Western civilization for more than 25 centuries, a method which has stood the shocks of time very, very well.[2] I refer to an idea which allows us to have art and science. Allow me to explain.

Whatever large differences may appear between one kind of art and another, or one kind of scientific theory and another, there is a way that discussion may go on. Any work of art or explanation of science concerns some local difficulty. Now the particular work or explanation may fail to evoke that difficulty or fail to generate a mechanism to explain how it occurs. But failures may be more interesting than success for those of us who follow, for these failures become our problems. We too will run aground, perhaps in the same place, perhaps somewhere down the line. So we have art and science as tradition insofar as we accept this cycle of problems, solutions, and new problems.

But there is one other element that makes all the difference. When a solution is stuck, we may borrow outside of the local domain in which we have posed the problem. To borrow well it is useful to have had a liberal education in the related domains of art or science. Thereby we have a potential set of perspectives available to us when we get in trouble with our local method. This is the method of methods which has built our civilization. This is an introduction to our complex secret.

So I propose a way to use psychotherapy as a tradition of varying local traditions which will allow us to be as brief as possible. My technical aim follows a remark made by Sullivan: "I think the development of psychiatric skill consists in very considerable measure of doing a lot with a very little — making a rather precise move which has a high probability of achieving what you're attempting to achieve, with a minimum of time and words" (1954, p. 224).

Many of the cases in this book are taken from the teaching practice of the Brief Therapy Clinic at the University of Wisconsin, which routinely offers about a semester of once-a-week sessions to its individual patients. But since I see few major differences in principle between brief and long-term therapy, individual and family therapy, the reader will also find illustrations from all these domains. This book could rightly be described as being about *briefer* therapy.

At times I have been tempted to say there is some universal style to follow.[3] I have wanted to recommend Freud or Winnicott or Sullivan or the Milan team to all my students as a single exemplar for all of them to follow, for the very same reasons T. S. Eliot could recommend Dante to all writers:

For the science or art of writing verse, one has learned from the *Inferno* that the greatest poetry can be written with the greatest economy of words, and with greatest austerity in the use of metaphor, simile, verbal beauty and elegance. When I affirm that more can be learned about how to write poetry from Dante than from any English poet, I do not at all mean that Dante's way is the only right way, or that Dante is thereby *greater* than Shakespeare or, indeed, any other English poet. I put my meaning into words by saying that Dante can do less *harm* to any one trying to learn to write verse than can Shakespeare. Most great English poets are *inimitable* in a way in which Dante was not. If you try to imitate Shakespeare you will certainly produce a series of stilted, forced, and violent distortions of language. The language of each great English poet is his own language; the language of Dante is the perfection of a common language. In a sense, it is more pedestrian than that of Dryden or Pope. If you follow Dante without talent, you will at worst be pedestrian and flat; if you follow Shakespeare or Pope without talent, you will make an utter fool of yourself. (1932, p. 213)

I do believe that some styles in psychotherapy are *more* to be recommended than others because they have "the perfection of a common language."[4] The array of ways that I admire as relevant to the practice of brief therapy, described in Part II of this book, will, I believe, go some way to meeting this literary ideal. But I think none ought to be recommended as a universal method of brief therapy. I see each of them as recommending a position for observation with both virtues and hazards.

A HISTORY OF DECENTERING

Consider what has happened in the last 90 years from the stem of psychoanalysis. I know it well, as I was trained in the psychoanalytic paradigm, only to be driven to shift my position successively through many of the major observing positions that have succeeded one another. Therefore, I think my idiosyncratic path may tell the reader something about the virtues and hazards of different methods of brief therapy in the broad analytic tradition. With such a history, I would not be one to espouse a universal method.

I had a strict psychoanalytic unbringing at Harvard Medical School and at Mt. Zion Psychiatric Clinic, for many years the teaching clinic for many of the analysts of the San Francisco Psychoanalytic Institute.[5] I had successful cases, in which powerful, unconscious stories came to light. Five years after my residency, when I began to explore the technical possibilities for individual, brief dynamic therapy, my interest in a very vigorous analytic technique was renewed, particularly through the work of David Malan (1963, 1976, 1979), which is so close to that of Freud in his original *Studies on Hysteria* (Breuer and Freud, 1895).

The difficulty for Freud and for Malan and for me was that certain findings kept cropping up on the periphery of the success. The recurrent anomaly was that many patients appeared to have attitudes which kept the therapist at bay. So long as these "constant attitudes" were not put right in the center of interest, they kept reappearing. Freud found this out to his chagrin with Dora. Once he accepted the necessity of an analysis of the constant attitude of the character, Freud got the extraordinary result of the Rat Man. Reich then worked out the consistent technique for the analysis of the constant attitude in the 1920s.[6] Recently, Davanloo found ways to confront even more forcefully than Reich. I too studied Freud and Reich and Davanloo, getting some breakthroughs which had not been possible for me before (Gustafson, 1984).

But certain findings disturbed my content with this powerful method. Anomalies began to show again. While some patients seemed to welcome being delivered from their enclosures, others did not. A battle seemed to strengthen their resolve. Still others seemed to yield in the battle of trial therapy, only to return to zero once they discussed the experience with their families. Finally, I did not like how I was acting with my students—too much the way Freud, Reich, and Davanloo all became with their students. I was confronting them as well. While some enjoyed this spirit, others snapped back. This method seems to pull everyone into interpersonal tangles.

How to get out of the clinch? I began reading Winnicott and Sullivan, hoping to find a way out (Gustafson and Dichter, 1983 a, b; Gustafson, Dichter, and Kaye, 1983). Their reply was clear: you can become an observer of interpersonal interactions, to see which ones are destructive or useless, which ones more promising. Since every patient has his or her own repertoire, the job is to see which recurrent interactions have reliable possibilities, which are extremely likely to wreck things. From this perspective of interpersonal interviewing, brief therapy seemed to have a wider domain than did psychoanalysis or the vigorous analysis of the constant attitude.

After many successful experiments along the interpersonal line of sight, I began to notice trouble again with my peripheral vision. Always the anomalies. Noticing the hopefulness of ordinary solutions often seemed to bring a halt, while noticing the destructive maneuvers often seemed to make them worse.

Fortunately, these difficulties had been faced before by the systemic thinkers, who placed the stabilization of social relations in the center of their observations. From their perspective, the interpersonal maneuvers which might be hopeful would be sacrificed when they threatened stability. Manifestly destructive maneuvers might have to stay because they helped social stability. The systemic perspective, especially of the Milan team, appeared most powerful of all the perspectives. Now I felt I had the technique with the widest possible range for brief therapy.

I became troubled by this latest position for observing when I saw that some of its most capable practitioners were being seduced into being gods. They were becoming richly joined to the conference networks, appearing everywhere, losing themselves. I thought the extraordinary guile of this method might be dangerous.

Indeed it is. Notice that the three shifts of perspective I have followed from psychoanalysis are all moves to decenter from self-interests. Piaget (1967) believed that growing up is the capacity for such cognitive decentering. Now it appeared that the technical advances which seemed most powerful and helpful to me were also of this kind. Psychoanalysis sees the hidden demands of the animal in us. The analysis of character sees the "constant attitude" which protects the animal from without. Interpersonal interviewing sees the interactions which tie us into trouble with other people. Systemic interviewing sees these interactions in the service of stable social relations.

It may be that these subsequent movements to decenter perspective lead to more and more powerful interventions, but they also jeopardize therapists who are tempted into the fascination of solving labyrinths. Thus, I find that the return back to the interests of psychoanalysis is helpful. After all, we may become capable of great guile, decentering, but we all put our heads down on our pillows every night, having the needs of children for simplicity, for our nice dream screens, for seeing our big friendly tree out back as the center pole of the world tent. So I think we need to retain the way back or round to the observing position of psychoanalysis, to reckon with our own simplicity.

So I also find that "constant attitudes" are quite amazing in their own right, such as the unforgettable patient of Reich who had the unconscious movements of a trout (1948). I am glad to keep such observations from the perspective of the analysis of character. I also find the attention to inter-personal maneuvering so acute in Sullivan, Alexander, Winnicott and Balint that I would not give up this observing position either.

So I conclude that systemic thinking is only the most powerful perspec-tive when the richness of observations from the earlier positions is conserved. Perhaps systemic thinking is too dangerous if one cannot stay with one's own simplicity, one's own constant attitude, and one's own perceptions of how people are maneuvering.

RECOMMENDATIONS

Therefore, I say there is no universal method of brief psychotherapy, no Dante to follow for everyone. Every observing position has its advantages, its successes, and its dangers. Every position has a periphery, where impor-tant phenomena will occur and be missed, because of the center of interest of that position.

I suggest that every student should be allowed to begin from the observing position most natural to him or her. It will prove to have its difficulties, whereupon teachers may help. When they run aground in their local tradition, students will be in less trouble if they have had a liberal education in the various observing positions. This book contributes to such a liberal educa-tion, to the use of the tradition of psychotherapy which has decentered from psychoanalysis and yet comes back round to appreciate its helpfulness.

I am aware that many derivations from psychoanalysis are possible other than those I will describe in the array which follows in Chapters 2 through 17, which I see as *a* history of decentering, both of the tradition and of myself. I know that other histories are equally possible and powerful, for I see that my friends and colleagues who have learned so much from Jung or George Kelly or Milton Erickson, and so forth, give exceptional help and fine think-ing. I trust that they will not take offense that my array, which I find I need to explain the field of brief therapy, can only be as long as it is long. I may only integrate so much, or I will weaken myself. I think this may be ap-preciated. I have borrowed only as I have had difficulties that I felt impelled to overcome.

I find no difficulty talking with my friends who have different methods of thinking when we share a method of methods, that is, a broad interest in criteria of explanation that are scientific, as well as a delight in descriptions which have literary virtue, which are memorable.

I am also aware of a second weakness of my book, for which I have no remedy but the tolerance of the reader for my limitations. I believe that long-term follow-up, conducted by an impartial research team, is an important test of any method of brief therapy, but I can only provide short-term follow-up interviews, conducted by myself, for my more recent case presentations.

My Method

Having granted the weaknesses of any position and the limitations of my own, having given recommendations for students to begin from the position most natural to themselves, I still have my own preference for my own practice. I describe my practice chiefly from a systemic perspective, because I can reach all the other positions most easily from the most decentered of positions. Part III, "A Theory for a Method of Methods," explains how I do this, how I attempt to conserve the virtues of the previous positions. The universal style I seek, therefore, is no method, but a relatively simple way to give each method, each student, the best chance. Part IV, "A Sequence for a Method of Methods," describes the opening, middle, and end games that I see in brief therapy. Part V, "Learning Problems," discusses the difficulties for us in this multiverse of the Brief Therapy Clinic. After all, we must not "leave ourselves out of the equation" (Skynner, 1981).

A few final words on the use of this book. I view it as relatively dangerous for those of us who already have a way of practicing which works for us, more or less. If we add a second eye to the one we have, we may become worse. We may get double vision. We may get cross-eyed. All virtuoso skills are unstable. It is usually better to leave them as they are until they get in trouble. When the first eye is well trained, but stuck, then casting about for a second eye is timely.

Therefore I suggest the reader find his or her own perspective in the array of Chapters 2 through 17. If troubled by its limitations, a neighbor perspective may be enlightening. If other perspectives may be looked over without having to borrow them, then a liberal education might not jeopardize practice. Young therapists may take this risk more lightly.

Many pragmatic readers will want to know as soon as possible what the author proposes to do in his own work with patients. They could go straight for Part IV, "A Sequence for a Method of Methods." When they try out the procedure for themselves, they may become more interested in deeper study of its components and theory, which they will find in Parts II and III. Often the clinical work in the last years of medical school inspires the most serious interest in the medical sciences which were taught previously.

Parts IV and V could be safely read without immersing oneself in the array of Part II or the theory of Part III. This allows a deceptive simplicity which need not be overly troubling, since the plain spoken method of methods is apt to jibe well with general scientific and literary training. Readers with such a background who are not therapists might read anywhere they please, amusing themselves with the stories and ideas, having no difficult patients to face, having to risk no stance at all. Like gods they may enjoy it all.

For, as Professor Agassiz used to say, one can see no farther into a generalization than just so far as one's previous acquaintance with particulars enables one to take it in.

—William James, 1902

PART II

An Array of Observing
Positions

I shall therefore adopt the method of Little Jack Horner, pulling out plums one after another and exhibiting them side by side to create an array from which we can go on to list some fundamental criteria of mental process.

—Gregory Bateson, 1979

2. *Freud and Breuer: Double Appreciation*

ELISABETH VON R.

We BEGIN WITH HINTS. Elisabeth von R. was an attractive 24-year-old woman who reported "great pain walking" and being "quickly overcome by fatigue, walking or standing" for two years (Breuer and Freud, pp. 135–181). She was referred to Freud in the autumn of 1892 by a doctor who suspected hysteria, noted misfortune. Freud himself got three leads from hearing the woman tell her story. She took to bed for a day and a half with pains in the legs, in the last months of nursing her father before he died four years previous. She got the pains back and kept them for the two years prior to her visit to Freud after nursing her mother through a serious eye operation. The final hope of her family, which had been the very happy marriage of her sister to a delightful and thoughtful man, was smashed by the unexpected death of this sister in pregnancy. For 18 months, Elisabeth dwelled on this and her leg pains.

But the recounting of this story did not help at all. Freud wrote: "During this first period of her treatment she never failed to repeat that she was still feeling ill and that her pains were as bad as ever; and, when she looked at me as she said this with a sly look of satisfaction at my discomfiture, I could not help being reminded of old Herr von R.'s judgment about his favorite daughter—that she was often 'cheeky' and 'ill-behaved.' But I was obliged to admit she was right." Most physicians would have quit right here.

But Freud had learned from Breuer that such patients can tell more than they appear to know. Freud decided to "put a direct question to the patient in an enlarged state of consciousness," that is, by putting her head between his hands and asking, "What came to her mind's inner eye in connection with the first occasion of pain in the legs?"

The inner eye saw a different story, which was told to Freud over the next nine months. This story began with the thought of a young man who had seen her home after a party. Finding her father worse, she felt awful about her desire for the young man and did not go out like that again. He drifted away. She lost hope of marrying him. Now she could tell Freud that the pain in her thigh was exactly where her father's leg rested on hers.

Now it appeared that the relating of this painful story relieved the pain in the leg, for a while, until an adjacent pain appeared, which would be relieved by another confession, and so on. The patient began to get better. Freud wrote: "It was as though she were reading a lengthy book of pictures, whose pages were being turned over before her eyes." Standing reminded her of "standing alone." "Walking" reminded her of a walk with her sister's husband. "Sitting" reminded her of sitting in a lovely place on a hill she had enjoyed with her sister and her husband, when they had gone and she had had a "burning wish she might be as happy as her sister." "Lying" reminded her of the agonizing train trip back home, when she feared, rightly, that her sister might die.

Now a "chance occurrence" allowed Freud to make the critical observation in the case: "One day while I was working with the patient, I heard a man's footsteps in the next room and a pleasant voice which seemed to be asking some question. My patient thereupon got up and asked that we might break off for the day; she had heard her brother-in-law arrive and inquire for her.[1] Up to that point she had been free from pain, but after interruption her facial expression and gait betrayed the sudden emergence of severe pain." Now Freud was able to put together the hidden, sly story: "She succeeded in sparing herself the painful conviction that she loved her sister's husband, by inducing physical pains in herself instead; and it was in the moments when this conviction sought to force itself upon her (on her walk with him, during her morning reverie, in the bath, by her sister's bedside) that her pains had come on, thanks to successful conversion. . . . The recovery of this repressed idea had a shattering effect on the poor girl. She cried aloud when I put the situation dryly before her with the words: 'So for a long time you have been in love with your brother-in-law.'"

Finally, Freud had her recall how her love for the brother-in-law had been aroused and he even talked to Elisabeth's mother about whether there was any hope for Elisabeth to marry the man.[2] Finding this to be impossible for the time being, he encouraged her to accept the uncertainty as calmly as she could. She was furious with Freud for talking to her mother, got her pains back for a little while, but then recovered splendidly, as Freud described: "In the spring of 1894 I heard she was going to a private ball for which I was able to get an invitation, and I did not allow the opportunity to escape me of seeing my former patient whirl past in a lively dance. Since then, by her own inclination, she has married someone unknown to me."

Two Views of the Method

It is tempting to see this method in the very straightforward way that Freud himself offers. It is no more than a series of successive approximations to a secret, shameful story. The story is gotten by looking for more, insisting, receiving well what is revealed, interpolating, and so forth. The "illness" is a set of somatic allusions to the secret story. The patient will remain "ill" because she is devoted to impossible hopes. The feeling about these hopes is being "strangled." Only when the "mortification" of these feelings can be faced can the patient go on. Indeed, in German, mortification and illness are closely related ("kränkung" and "krankheit").

It is possible to make this operation into the whole of psychotherapy. Of the three successful cases in *Studies on Hysteria*, Katherina needs but one session, Lucy seven, and Elisabeth an unknown number for nine months. All give up something impossible, to resume a path which is usual. We will see, later in this book, that David Malan (Chapter 11) will make all of psychotherapy into the discovery, and interpretation, of such hidden stories. He will begin from the more familiar and acceptable secrets, like the jealousy in these cases, gradually introducing secrets which are more violent, stranger, more primitive.

We would be misled by this unifying idea. We may check ourselves by two considerations. First, we could take notice of the two other cases in the *Studies on Hysteria*, Anna O. and Frau Emmy von N. It appears from these two that *some* patients have no healthy interaction to return to, once they have given up their fall into mortification. Freud could ignore this characterological interaction with Katherina, Lucy, and Elisabeth, who were so vigorous and loving when they were not "ill." Therefore, illness as "mortification" has this limited domain. It works like grieving, when there is something quite good to take up again. Indeed, this is the simplest idea of brief psychotherapy.

But even this idea is misleading. It reduces the job to a single description, of finding the hidden story. I doubt if this is any better than accepting the first story at face value. We doctors like single-minded procedures, so that we have had great difficulty understanding that Freud and Breuer were offering a double description[3] of these patients. Consider, for example, this description by Freud of the conclusion of his work with Elisabeth. He saw her as concealing, but he also saw her as loyal:

As we worked through these recollections it became clear to Elisabeth that her tender feeling for her brother-in-law had been dormant in her for a long time, perhaps even from the beginning of her acquaintance with him, and had lain concealed all that time behind the mask of mere sisterly affection, which her highly developed family feeling could enable her to accept as natural.

And again, he reminded that her loyalty was as important as her deviation.[4]

But it was a long time before my two pieces of consolation—that we are not responsible for our feelings, and her behavior, the fact that she had fallen ill in these circumstances, was sufficient evidence of her moral character—it was a long time before these consolations of mine made any impression on her.

Freud had the same double attitude in the beginning with this young woman. He admired her, and he suspected her. On the one hand, he wrote:

Here, then, was the unhappy story of this proud girl with her longings for love. Unreconciled to her own fate, embittered by the failure of all her little schemes for reestablishing the family's former glories, with those she loved dead or gone away or estranged. . . . If we put greater misfortunes on one side and enter into a girl's feelings, we cannot refrain from deep human sympathy with Fraulein Elisabeth.

On the other hand, Freud also saw a girl "with a sly look of satisfaction at my discomfiture." "I could not help," he wrote, "being reminded of old Herr von R.'s judgment about his favorite daughter—that she was often 'cheeky' and 'ill-behaved.'"

So Freud got two stories—one of family loyalty, another of sly hopes. He appreciated both. Some readers might want to introduce the later analytic idea of "conflict" to explain the findings, but I do not think it is at all necessary to the method in the *Studies on Hysteria*. Freud himself wrote of the secret story as being "incompatible" with the apparent story—hence, its disappearance. But once both stories have been fully appreciated, there is no apparent discussion of their relation. Evidently, in some cases, no more than this double appreciation is needed. Mann realized this much later, as I shall describe in Chapter 12. There is something quite extraordinary about someone's realizing that one has tried so hard to be what the family has needed, yet, in spite of one's best efforts, one has had other feelings, which would appear to be incompatible. Yet there they are.

I use Bateson's term "double description" here, because I think it most simply refers to what the therapist has to do. He has to grasp the patient's situation from two *incompatible* perspectives, feeling and thinking how the two belong together. This would be missed by nearly everyone who knows the patient, because most people are incapable of more than one perspective. Therefore, the therapist would place himself much closer to the center of the patient's world than the patient would think possible. This is extremely relieving. Feelings can be let down.

The idea of "conflict" is not as powerful here. We are talking about "incompatible" feelings, rather than "conflicting" feelings. We are talking about something "impossible," not something possible. Elisabeth would go to extreme lengths to look after her father, her mother, and her sisters, yet in spite of all this effort she could covet her sister's attractive husband. Indeed, the more she sacrificed, the more this sly desire for her own gratification might be impossible to keep in bounds. The more she got out of bounds, the more she might try harder to deny herself. Freud did not go so far as this, to think in terms of circular events. This would take another 60 years, with the introduction of Bateson's thinking into psychotherapy by the Palo Alto project and, later, by the Milan analysts. But this is not necessary in some cases. Sometimes it will do quite nicely to appreciate the incompatible feelings, which appear to be paradoxical. Some patients find this enough. Perhaps, it is the discovery, confirmed by another person, that the organization of the family has a dark side, that is, a variation of its structure that might be quite surprising to anyone unable to fully appreciate the situation. Once appreciated, the individual can live with the discovery.

AN INADMISSABLE ROAR

There are many patients we see now who are like Katherina, Lucy, and Elisabeth in their potential to resume a very healthy and vigorous life once some difficulty is fully faced. The job is to see both the health and the difficulty. It is amazing, with such patients, to see how the pieces come together. Children who have been loved do not require disguises which are that difficult to read. They have confidence in being found out.

A young woman in her first month of graduate school came to our clinic complaining of a terrifying, recurrent dream she had had since the third grade. She had had the most frightening version in many years the night before her classes in the university were to begin. Interestingly, she had been extremely happy the week before during registration, settling in with a group of new friends. In the dream she was enjoying her new friends at a party in the dormitory when a "yellow ooze" began to come through a crack in the wall. She then took a ride to another place, which was quite mysterious, with its large doors, high ceilings, and an open door in the back. There her mother appeared, handing her "my baby self." At this point, she found a "roar" coming out of her own mouth and awoke in terror.

This very pleasant young woman could not, at first, believe that she would ever want to roar at her mother. Indeed, she felt so deeply grateful to her mother, who had been the one to stand by her, while her less responsible father had gone off with other women, breaking up the marriage when our patient was in third grade. We felt this young woman to be so loyal to her mother that she seemed to be just like her mother in her matronly, neighborly way with us.

So we appreciated that, while she was deeply grateful to her mother, she also had something to roar about. We didn't know why, but there it was. She seemed very relieved after this first session. Her semester with one of our residents not only kept this double view of herself, but also new versions of the same dream. The next session the resident learned that her mother had once overlooked that our patient had broken her leg, dismissing the pain as exaggerated. Soon he also learned that her mother had allowed her father to take her to the movie in which the "yellow ooze" had terrified her. We began to see that, for all her love of her mother, there was something to roar about as well. This young woman began to dress more like someone her own age than like a mother of the 1950s. She began to be less completely accommodating to her boyfriend, someone with something to roar about at him.

In her final session, she reported the same dream, the blob, and so forth. Only this time she was only a little afraid, instead of terrified. She said that instead of roaring, her teeth fell out! Hearing about this in supervision, I, of course, wondered about whether she would have to take the "bite" out of her anger in the future. Certainly, our resident did not get bitten in this final session, where we might expect him to hear some grievance. I was more reassured to hear that she laughed very heartily in describing what had occurred to her teeth in the dream. My point is not that the treatment was as good as it could be. Rather, I am saying that it could be a good treatment based on a rough idea, which a young therapist could keep in mind. Here was a young woman, devoted to her mother, yet with something to roar about. This is the kind of double description introduced by Freud and Breuer, which remains so useful when the patients are relatively well.

3. *Freud, Ferenczi, and Rank:*
Return to a Childhood Structure

The Young Croatian Musician

HERE IS a grateful part for us, as musicians might say. The patient was a young Croatian woman, a musician, "who suffered from a host of phobias and obsessional states," reported by Ferenczi in 1921. "Of her endless symptoms," Ferenczi describes two graphic ones. The first was stage fright. "If she was asked to play in front of others at the music school, she became scarlet in the face; finger exercises . . . seemed to her prodigiously difficult; she made mistakes on every occasion and had the obsessive idea that she must disgrace herself, which she accordingly did pretty thoroughly in spite of her unusual talent." The second was also stage fright, only the stage was the street, where she felt constantly observed because of her "voluminous breasts." Walking in the street, she was alternately covering them by folding her arms in front of her, then thinking this was even more conspicuous. "She was unhappy if in spite of her marked beauty no attention was paid to her, but was no less disconcerted when actually spoken to by someone who misunderstood (or, rather, correctly interpreted) her behaviour" (1921, pp. 202–203).

She came to Ferenczi after an analysis of many months, which was prolific but useless—many memories, much theoretical insight, no change. For weeks it was the same with Ferenczi, until, "at one interview, a street song occurred to her that her elder sister (who tyrannized her in every way) was in the habit of singing." After long hesitation, she was willing to recite the text of the song, became silent, and admitted what Ferenczi suspected, that it was the *melody* of the song which ran through her mind.

Ferenczi asked her to sing the song out loud to him. This took two hours, before she could overcome breaking off, singing softly, leaving out gestures, and so forth. Finally, Ferenczi asked her to get up and repeat the song "*exactly* as she had seen her sister do it," whereupon "she showed herself to be a perfect chanteuse." From now on, she came to use the analytic hours for these little productions, whereupon Ferenczi could tell her that "we knew now that she enjoyed displaying her various talents and that behind her modesty lay hidden a considerable desire to please. . . . It was astonishing how favourably this little interlude affected the work" (p. 204).

Now he could take his technical measure one step further, constraining her "to carry out the activities of which she had the greatest fear. . . . She conducted in front of me (while at the same time she imitated the sounds of an orchestra) a long phrase from a symphony: the analysis of this notion led to the discovery of the penis jealousy by which she had been tormented since the birth of her brother" (p. 204). Similarly, playing the difficult piano piece for Ferenczi, over which she had feared disgrace in the examination, led to her "disgraceful" pleasures as a child touching herself, her love of showing her breasts and even passing flatus. After she became fond of revealing these activities to Ferenczi, making what had been useful into exaggeration, he forbade this, which also helped her improvement. He concluded his mention of this case by describing how she was flooded by voluptuous sensations at the piano when she played, which he advised her to give up. She did, and they now knew very well what had made her performance so impossible.

Return to the Experience of Childhood

If we recall Elisabeth von R. here, if we remember the essential idea in her analysis in the *Studies on Hysteria*, we may see clearly what changed from early to middle, or classical, psychoanalysis. Elisabeth von R. appeared to suffer from the impossible, strangulated hopes of an adult, while the Croatian Musician those of a child.

This change in the definition of neurotic "illness," from an adult to a childhood experience, was resisted as much by analysts as by patients. Hence, psychoanalysis could easily become a watered-down, intellectual procedure, which made adults comfortable, but which did them little good. This is what Ferenczi and Rank thought in 1925, when they wrote their little treatise, *The Development of Psychoanalysis*. They argued that any useful psychoanalysis has two technical phases. The first is to analyze resistance to free association, so that the ability to *experience* as a child can be regained. The analyst is entirely vigorous and forceful here. He is "the champion of the infantile." But his success in the first phase will bring about a fully aroused child, demanding satisfaction from the analyst himself, as if he were the very parent of that child. This "transference" is to be welcomed, for no weaning from the excessive demands of childhood can be arranged until those demands are presented. This weaning is the second phase of analysis, in which the patient must find substitutive satisfactions in his adult life, to replace the pleasures of childhood, that is, the pleasures of analysis. He may not be willing to do this unless the analyst gives him a time limit, within which his pleasures in the analysis will come to an end.

This procedure is an analogy to that described 50 years later by James Mann as "time-limited psychotherapy" (see Chapter 12). Here it was being described by Ferenczi and Rank as the essence of an analysis.[1] Ferenczi and Rank emphasized that the realm of the infantile is not easily talked about.

Talk is something else, usually later in life. The patient may only be able to *enact* what he once experienced. Therefore, the *"language of gesture"* is likely to be more important than the language of words. The first aim of the analysis, therefore, is to bring about an *enactment* of what is being missed from childhood. This is what Ferenczi did with the Croatian Musician when he got her to sing like her sister. Enactment is now being rediscovered 60 years later by Strupp and his colleagues (Binder, Strupp, and Schacht, 1983) as the decisive event in brief psychotherapy.

What patients will respond so beautifully to having "infantile experience"? It is not so easy to tell if such an experience will be too little or too much. The Croatian Musician shows one kind of success which we see from time to time. This is the situation where a child has had a very satisfying life as a small child, then given it up suddenly to become an abnormally "good child." This can be reversed, allowing the patient to get back the original vitality. When Ferenczi fought the resistance of his Musician to performing her sister's song, he put her back to her earlier experience, which he described as follows:

It was astonishing how favourable this little interlude affected the work. Presently memories of her early childhood, of which she had never spoken, occurred to her, memories of the time when the birth of a little brother had had a really unholy effect on her psychic development and made of her an anxious, shy, and abnormally good child. She remembered the time when she was still "a little devil," the darling of all her family and friends, when she displayed all her talents before people and generally showed an unrestrained pleasure in muscular movement. (1921, p. 204)

The latter half of the treatment may then wean the patient from this complete happiness less suddenly than occurred when her brother was born. She will have time to arrange substitute satisfactions, a compromise rather than a renunciation, which worked so badly.

Often, however, such an experience in psychoanalysis is too little. The patient has an exceptional, childlike experience, but there is no room in his or her adult life to carry on with such pleasures. This is why, as Greenson (1967) suggests, that "working-through" is the "time-consuming element." The system of actual, present relationships, or interactions, makes the generalization of the "breakthrough" impossible or very, very slow. Therefore, the classical procedure has gotten longer and longer. Perhaps, the performance demands of adult life have left less and less room for being a child.Could this have been easier in the 1920s? When one had had a breakthrough, and some weaning, was it easier to go on with adult life? It still works, nowadays, for some patients, such as I will presently describe.

However, before we come to the Case of the Murderous Medical Student, I would like also to say that the procedure described by Ferenczi is sometimes too much. As Michael Balint (1968), the great student of Ferenczi, would later emphasize, there are some patients who enter into a "benign regression" like the Croatian Musician. They are willing to give up their demands, when they are fully appreciated, so that their regression may be said to be "in the service of recognition." Other patients have a "malignant regression," where no giving up appears to be possible. The demands upon the analyst become worse and worse, more and more dangerous, completely "in the service of gratification."

Finally, I would emphasize that many patients fear the regression too much. When no one knows whether it would be benign or malignant, they are entirely set against it. The entire attitude, what Reich (1933) has called the "constant attitude," is dedicated to stopping a disinhibition. Therefore, the technique of Freud, Ferenczi, and Rank, for these neurotic characters, is at once too much and too little: too much feared by the patient, too little that the classical procedure can do about it. Therefore, the analysis becomes lame. We will see how Reich takes on this technical problem in the next chapter.[2]

THE CASE OF THE MURDEROUS MEDICAL STUDENT

This was an extremely nice young man, so very accommodating to everyone, until he felt he would explode or stab someone. This is why he came to me, since what had been occurring on and off for several years had become an obsession — that he would murder a bystander who happened to cross him. He described himself as having been a "mindless lackey" in the service of his father. Such a service made him an excellent medical student, not to mention a fine helper for the research of a professor. He ran from one diligent job to the other.

But then he found himself wanting accommodation to his every need from his girlfriend. He felt like stabbing her for the smallest slight of her inattention. He was quite shocked. Perhaps, the first important intervention that I made was to tell him that he sounded quite as self-centered, quite as crude about that, as his father.

He literally choked on this, grabbing himself by the neck as if to cut his own throat. I told him he found his own crude aims so entirely unacceptable that evidently he would kill himself first. Now it appeared that it was me he wanted to do in. He resented having to see me, quite all of a sudden. He wanted to barge in on his girlfriend. Both of us were to accommodate him.

This base, murderous feeling was not directed right at me. But it was also true that a flurry of defenses kept him busy and off my neck. At this time, after six sessions of one hour once a week, his girlfriend dropped him. He spent most of the session sobbing. He was amazed I could tolerate his "vile emotion."

He was now moving very fast. Between the sixth and the seventh sessions, he conducted an experiment on his own in behavioral flooding. He stood near a girl who enraged him, a knife near by, until the urge to stab went away.

He was exultant. Now that we had had our first phase of the experience of infantile demands, he was arranging, himself, for the second phase of prohibition, of weaning. In this seventh session, I confronted him again about his deference to me, which allowed him to tell me more about his rage at me.

He came in for the eighth session, what he had decided would be the final one, with a long independent discovery, which he spent most of the session describing to me. I suppose his father was prone to long speeches too. He told me he finally realized how like his own father he had become. He was excessively responsible, and then forced others to do his bidding. Very much of a doctor, indeed. He realized how he had overwhelmed his girlfriend. No wonder she had dropped him. He visited his parents, where he decided he did not, after all, have to do his father's bidding anymore. It only made him force others. I was quite impressed by his discovery. I told him he might want to try out his success for a while. We could see how it held up. Fifteen months later, I got a letter inviting me to his marriage. He had met a woman whom he loved deeply. He was no longer working a second job. He was enjoying his emotionality, and he felt full of confidence. He felt the eight sessions had changed his life completely.

Here again, as with the Croatian Musician, we see a person who had become abnormally good. The more he had trouble, the more he would try to be even better, the more his tension became unbearable. No wonder he felt like stabbing someone. Such a way to get relief! Thankfully, he had been a very happy, passionate child, who could become this child again. Of course, he couldn't have everything he wanted, but he found in me someone who could take his tears and rage about standing in his way.

4. *Freud and Reich: The Constant Attitude*

THIS MAN APPEARED to be giving Reich (1933, pp. 81–113) everything he might want. He was a 24-year-old bank employee who came in for help with anxiety, specifically fears of syphilis that began when he saw a hygiene exhibit one year prior to treatment. He began by offering some exciting material about his attraction to his mother: how "he had often thrown his mother on his bed to which she had reacted with 'bright eyes and flushed cheeks,' . . . , " etc. Reich was not impressed by this. We should say he was not tempted by this provocation to pursue the patient's "sexual interests," which offer a dramatic confirmation for analytic ideas about loving one's mother, etc. Reich simply told him that "his whole attitude indicated he was hiding something (else)." He explained to his readers that deeper material is often used to hide actual difficulties closer to the surface.

Reich was not misled by content; it was the form of the patient's communication to which he paid attention. This patient was so eager to please. His whole manner was eagerness to do the right thing, including telling Reich things that he estimated might confirm Reich's theories. Reich made this attitude his single object of analysis, as he wrote:

I told him that not only was he distrustful of analysis; that furthermore, by his behavior, he pretended the exact opposite.

Upon this, the patient became highly excited, and through six sessions he produced three different hysterical actions:

1) He thrashed around with arms and legs, yelling: 'Let me alone, don't come near me, I'm going to kill you, I'm going to squash you!' This action often changed into another:

2) He grabbed his throat and whined in a rattling voice: 'Please let me alone, please, I'm not going to do anything anymore!'

3) He behaved not like one who is violently attacked but like a girl who is sexually attacked: 'Let me alone, let me alone!' This, however, was said without the rattling voice and, while during the action of the second type he pulled up his legs, he now spread them apart. (1933, pp. 88–89)

Again Reich was being tempted to get caught up in this dramatic content, but again he kept his eye on the form, not the content. He told the patient "that he was producing his actions so frequently in order to please me. . . . " Why did he, continually, have to please? Keeping to his vertical focus, the unwavering Reich and his patient were led deeper by the dream of the following night, in which the patient openly distrusted Reich. He confessed he cheated Reich on the fee.

This was the first breakthrough of the constant attitude of pleasing, and the patient was now very afraid. Reich became interested in the nature of the threat: "I only remarked that his tendency to economize must have something to do with his fear of catastrophe, that apparently he felt more secure when he had more money" (p. 92). The patient replied that his father once took his savings without asking and spent them, for which the patient had never forgiven the father.

The patient now dreamt openly of being attacked by various male figures, making it entirely clear that he feared Reich was a robber. The negative transference was no longer frozen. The patient had to placate Reich by giving him money. Reich insisted that he and the patient must find out what the patient was afraid of. They found that the patient felt that Reich and other men meant to harm him in quite a variety of ways. The patient now began to dream of cruel acts of his own, becoming more or less free to bring out his own aggression, without cowardice. The childhood neurosis had now unfrozen as well, that of the little boy as a frightened robber himself.

There is a great deal more detail, but the first six months of the analysis kept entirely to a focus on the patient's "constant attitude" of having to please. The patient used several defenses, such as telling Reich what he wanted to hear about sex or acting hysterical. Reich kept to the "attitude" that utilized these individual defenses. This yielded the "breakthrough" of open mistrust, the negative transference of Reich as a robber, the patient's dread of this and of his own cruel intentions. There was scarcely a word of interest from Reich in the sexual content offered.

The final seven months continued mainly with an emphasis from Reich on why it was the patient was still afraid, which led into the patient's archaic, sexual notions. Reich emphasized that the "resolution" occurred in two ways: 1. by getting to what the fears actually were; 2. by keeping open the "breach" to this deep level. The patient feared that women were "wounded" in lacking a genital, making him fear for his own. He had such an archaic, egocentric idea about "wanting to get everything from a woman, the mother, without giving anything himself" (p. 110). He feared the excitement of giving something himself, as he imagined ejaculation to be disaster. However, each time Reich was about to get to one of these essential archaic fears, the patient reverted to the pleasing attitude, which Reich then had to remind him about. This kept the breach wide open for the necessary intense and complete *experience* of the desires and fears. Thus, the "constant attitude" continued as the *focus* to the very end, albeit intermittently toward the end.

The result, upon five-year follow-up, was that the patient's aggression and sexuality remained free. This was the "dynamic change," as Malan (1963, 1976) would say. Also, he no longer had the symptoms which brought him for analysis. This was the "symptomatic" change (Malan, 1963, 1976). The reader will note that Reich had been careful in the resolution phase to attend to the patient's archaic, egocentric ideas about sexual gratification. The result was not someone who simply let go with his instincts, unmindful of others. The patient was then free to love and to hate, without anxiety.

LAME AND CHAOTIC TREATMENT

Some patients, like this man, are entirely set against a return to childhood. They are dedicated *not* to have a regression. Indeed, Reich (1930) argued that the disturbed child gets over his misery by adopting the attitude of some admired or feared adult. No wonder he is not about to give it up.

We can see why many patients adopt an attitude of some adult and do not let go. This man had to please and submit. Perhaps he borrowed the attitude from his mother. If he didn't act this feminine part, his inclinations to become a robber could not be contained. Since he felt men like his father and his doctor, Reich, to be even bigger robbers than himself, he would be cornered. The doctor, Reich, might pretend to be helpful, just as the patient might pretend to be giving the doctor everything he needed to be helpful. A single slip could drop the patient back into the deep well of childhood. Having given the hint of his own difficulty with being a little robber, he would have a worse one sitting over him.

We do not have someone here hoping we will get through to them. We do not have a Croatian Musician, who was a beloved devil, hoping we can find her out again (Chapter 3). Such a person welcomes the "analysis of resistance," brought by the "champion of the infantile." Such a person is ready to spring out from hiding.

No, we have a patient here who is systematic in his procedures for defending himself from access. He has some hope of being discovered, but the "champion" who would deliver him must be more systematic in his advance than the patient is in defense (Reich, 1933). There is so much to lose. The dedication of the doctor will be proven by his appreciation of the wonderful fortification. John Donne described such a helpful assault in one of his famous sonnets:

> Batter my heart, three-personed God; for You
> As yet but knock, breathe, shine, and seek to mend;
> That I may rise, and stand, o'erthrow me, and bend
> Your force, to break, blow, burn, and make me new.
> I, like an usurped town to another due,
> Labor to admit You, but oh! to no end;
> Reason, Your viceroy in me, me should defend,
> But is captived and proves weak or untrue. . . .

In such a situation, the "analysis of resistance" is too weak. Everything the patient does is misleading.

Free association is misleading, because it offers a content opposite to what is of actual concern. The passive feminine character offers sexual excitement for his mother, because he believes Reich will be pleased by such an offer. This content is offered, just when the patient is actually preoccupied with robbing Reich and being robbed by him.

Analysis of the resistances or single defenses is misleading, because they can appear to yield, one to another, endlessly, as long as the doctor does not identify how they work together in the service of an attitude. This man could shift from pleasing offers to hysterical thrashing to hypochondriacal illness to any number of other maneuvers—and back again. But Reich was able to see the consistent attitude, the "cardinal character resistance," the cardinal deploying the troops, if you will. When he conveys his appreciation of the inner consistent logic of the defenses, he gets tremendous access.

If he does not appreciate the defenses as a remarkable system, or organization, he will be kept at a distance, where he can be watched. The "analysis of the transference" then will also be misleading, because the transference will not set a foot upon the field of battle. One cannot identify something which is not present.

Therefore, these neurotic characters are too much for the classical technique of Freud, Ferenczi, and Rank. "Chaotic analysis" occurs, as the content and defenses switch around, governed by a purpose that cannot be deciphered. "Lame" analysis occurs, as the transference of the dreaded past never comes stalking into the room (Reich, 1933).

It is not that the various technical maneuvers of the analyst are wrong in themselves. What is crucial is seeing the organization of these maneuvers, which makes the analyst ready for his formidable, organized antagonist. This organization is what Reich is about. This is his loyal revolution. He realizes the hierarchy of the defenses. This is a different kind of looking.

It is not easy to get the feel of a constant attitude from the defenses which operate upon spoken free association. They can be quite mechanical, quite similar from one person to another: such as undoing, depersonalization, somatization, etc., etc. In themselves, they give away little of the attitude behind them, as *any* patient can utilize them for *some* defensive purpose. What gives away the attitude is the *gesture* Reich found.[1] He watched for the attitude in these moves, as, for example, in the first meetings with the passive-feminine character. "He kept apologizing for the most trifling things; on arriving and on leaving he made several deep bows. . . . When he asked for something, he would stroke the analyst's arm" (p. 83).

Keeping to this "constant attitude," one would not be misled by talk and individual defenses. One would follow the attitude like a "red thread" and be led to the center of the labyrinth. Here is a "vertical focus" which leads into disturbance, through whatever layers of content. A "horizontal focus" of keeping to some period of difficulty in the patient's life, even such as an oedipal preoccupation, would be likely to mislead.

One has so little force, after all, so it must be applied in one place only, with all the power one can bring there. This is, therefore, a treatment which is entirely consistent and which uses its power in the largest dose possible. This revolution was not acceptable.

Most analysts believed the contrary. By interpreting resistances fully and patiently, they hoped to allow some affect in, eventually to mobilize the transference bit by bit — "an immense number of minute steps" of interpretation, as Strachey argued in defense of the orthodoxy: "For the mutative interpretation is inevitably governed by the principle of minimal doses. It is, I think, a commonly agreed clinical fact that alterations in the patient under analysis appear almost always to be extremely gradual" (1934, p. 144).

Reich did not accept the "clinical fact" of "extremely gradual alterations." He believed a "breakthrough" was necessary and that this "breach" needed to be kept open. Reich did not accept that "mutative interpretation is inevitably governed by the principle of minimal doses." He thought that potent doses were required. He wrote: "Many neuroses are not accessible to mild measures." These methods are "as potent as they are unpleasant for the patient" (1933, p. 146).

Notice also how the "illness" has been redefined. The illness is no longer a "secret story" of "incompatible feelings." Nor is it a childhood story, put away too soon. Both of these elements are there all right, but not in the center. Now the patient is ill because his *system* has stopped working right. Every neurotic character has a system which has a weakness, when what it is designed to prevent returning, returns anyway. The passive-feminine character could not be introduced to sexuality, at age 23, without arousing his urges to steal a woman for himself. Appearing to please others had been set up to deny this. Freud's Rat Man (1909) was beautifully organized to carry out his exacting loyal duties, preventing urges to advance himself as would a greedy rat. When he was offered a job that he needed very much to start his law practice, he was tempted to give up his beloved. His greed was overly aroused. Illness, therefore, occurs when a dreaded stimulation takes place, before the early warning system of the *eye* of the constant attitude has time or room to get its routine in order. A neurotic illness, for Reich, is therefore a signal of the breakdown of the careful, systematic operations of a neurotic character. Once it breaks down, it may indeed stay in a state of breakdown, because this can be a new steady state, with its own routine.

It is not so easy to demarcate the workable domain for this idea, since a case can almost always be made for working in this way. It is perhaps easier to say where this idea is *not necessary* or *not useful*. Cases like Elisabeth von R. and the Croatian Musician show a constant attitude, but there is enough confidence in other people to show the dark story or the devil, with confidence of being accepted. Some children want to be found out more than they dread it. So here the diligence of following the red thread of the constant attitude is not necessary.

In the chapters which follow, we shall see that the constant attitude not only operates to contain one's own dreaded possibilities by keeping others out and away, but also operates externally in a more active sense to bring about painful situations over and over. Other people not only are kept out, but also are gotten to do the wrong things. The interpersonal revolution will be necessary to bring this into focus (Chapters 5–8). Secondly, the constant attitude may be a necessary and desirable attitude which serves the purposes of the people vital in the patient's life. The systemic revolution will be needed to see this (Chapters 15–17).

When the doctor is working only with the constant attitude in the relationship with himself, as Freud and Reich did so well, he may have these remarkable breakthroughs of the transference.[2] What he may not get to see, and may not, therefore, do anything about, is that this same patient keeps arranging for other people in his life to do him harm as they always have before, and he keeps arranging for other people to put him back in old, comfortable places where he has been so useful. On the other hand, it does happen, sometimes, that the breakthrough to these dreadful transference experiences and the assimilation of that instinctual power allow the patient to take on his previous negative relations, his family, and other powerful organizations, in a very different way.

University is a propitious time for this to happen, because the binding ties to family of origin are loosened. The new binds to marriage, family, and career have yet to be fastened. Thus, the revolution of a character analysis finds its most receptive patients in those who are between commitments. As this is true of the university student, it is also true of the newly divorced or separated, and of those changing careers.

A "Modern Passive-Feminine Character"

I got a breakthrough with this young college student within a half hour of his first long, two-hour trial therapy with me in our clinic. The reader must think that this young man wanted to be found out. After all, Reich took seven months of daily analysis to get his breakthrough with the passive-feminine character. My patient, a modern passive-feminine character, may have shared an attitude similar to that of Reich's patient, but he must have been much more secure, much more ready to reveal himself as a child. His readiness to return to his childhood ferocity would be more like that of the Croatian Musician.

While I would readily concede this argument, I would also suggest that my analysis of his "constant attitude" was quite telling. Some of the reason that it worked faster than what Reich did was that I was not slowed down by using "free association" as the vehicle of our conversation. I was asking a series of probing questions, to clarify what had brought him to me. These questions brought his "constant attitude" directly into collision with our "focal inquiry." Such a collision could be postponed by free association even though Reich was noticing the "constant attitude," since the patient could persist in his free association, whatever Reich was saying to him. With my "inquiry," we soon located the patient in a spot where there was no place to run away. We shall see later how Davanloo put these two ideas together in analysis of the "constant attitude" in the service of a "focal inquiry" (Chapter 14). The technique described here is this modern version of Reich. I describe the case in this chapter, because it illustrates how misleading a "constant attitude" can be unless one is able to bring it directly into focus.

What is most amazing to me about the interview with this young man is how he changed his chief complaint so many times in such different ways. He was so ready to offer what he thought the doctor wanted to be finding and prescribing for. I hate to think what might have happened to him had he wandered into a different clinic.

Why had he come for help? Because he was depressed over spring break. His friends were away, which made for a lonely week. What got him down about this? He might always be lonely. Why was that? Because they had girl-friends and would marry them, leaving him behind. So far, an offer of depression, but the next question changed all of that.

But why wouldn't he have a girlfriend too? "Because," he said, "I have no sexual attraction to women! Did your head jump up when I said that?" I told him, "No, I was just paying attention," but he surely seemed to think that I had a powerful, startled reaction. What was that about? "It's sick, isn't it, not to have sexual attraction to women?" I said, "No, not necessarily, it isn't all that unusual for young men to be quite inhibited." He relaxed a little. "Oh," he said.

Now, he made his third offer of "illness." "I am attracted to men." I said, "Oh, what do you mean?" He meant that he often saw strong-looking men walking down the street. He wished he could be them. Now, I could have taken up this offer to look into his "homosexuality." Students of mine who have looked at the videotape of this session have often advised me that this would have been best, to follow his lead. I didn't think so, given his "attitude" of offering illnesses that doctors might want.

Rather, I said to him that we didn't know how his attraction to women had disappeared, but we could have a look at that. That was fine with him. "So," I said, "well, let's see, how might we find this out?" Perhaps we could find out what occurred when he took a girl out. Had he dated? Yes, he had a girlfriend in high school named Sue. She was a good girl. His parents approved of her. They went out a lot, but he never felt any sexual desire for her.

Could he describe Sue to me? "Well, yes, she was very nice." The way he said that she was nice made me think she was not exciting. Here he was telling me what his parents might want to hear, but I was not going to accept this misleading account. I said, "Tell me more about her." He said, "Well, she was flabby . . . " broke off and flushed. He worked very diligently to get rid of this sentence, which was so inconsistent with his entirely pleasing and submissive outlook, but I would not let go of it. He started to remind me how nice she was, and so forth, and so forth, to which I replied, "but she was flabby." I must have cut him short four or five times here, as he attempted different maneuvers to pretend he had not criticized Sue. Each time I came back to, "but you said she was flabby."

After a while, he was very restless in his seat, obviously uncomfortable, and flushed. I wondered aloud if he resented my questions. He said, indeed, he had been resenting them for quite a while, flushed again, and began his usual back-peddling, denial, change of subject, smile, etc.

By now I was ready to make my counteroffer, that he had a fourth illness, which he had not mentioned, although I didn't use the word illness. I told him he was very uncomfortable criticizing either Sue or me; even a word of criticism would not do. He looked like he had been hit. He could not talk, he was so choked up. He didn't know why. I told him we didn't know why, but here he was crying. He began to cry and continued, silently, for quite a while.

Indeed, he didn't know for a long while why he was crying so deeply, but we gradually made some sense of his associations, when he was able to speak. One association was to his best friend in childhood. Somehow, they had been wrestling, in a friendly way, but the other boy got rough and pinned him down and wouldn't let go, so my patient, in desperation, bit the boy. The boy's family was unforgiving. My patient lost his best friend. Another association was to the yelling between his parents, who broke up their marriage when my patient was in high school. A third was how his friends keep him waiting, for example, to go running, but however annoyed or angry he may be, he will not say a word of protest. I began to see why.

To make a long story short, I told this young man we would be glad to help him with his painful problem, that he could begin with one of our psychologists, for a semester at once a week. I can only say here that the later sessions were about the same difficulty as the first one, with varying intensity. I was quite startled to see a videotape of one of the last meetings. I hardly recognized the soft, rounded, soft-spoken man I had once interviewed. I saw a strapping, assertive man who looked more like a wrestler. I saw a man with angular and sharp features, sitting in a T-shirt too small for him, so that it barely covered his bulging shoulders, telling his doctor what he had in mind and what he wanted.

Now that he could wrestle again, as he once had as a child, with this aggression returned to him, his sexual feelings had also appeared. He had not gotten a girlfriend yet, but he had become a powerful man. Only the long-term follow-up will tell us if he got enough from our treatment. It certainly was in the right direction, but, of course, sometimes one semester may be too little; sometimes it gives a start that the patient can carry through on his own without further psychotherapy. Malan's follow-up studies (1976) bear this out clearly.

I would just add a few more words about this analysis of the constant attitude, from a pedagogic standpoint. It is not easy to teach, because it requires the doctor to give complete attention to what would be mere details for another doctor, such as the way in which this man talked about his girlfriend. It is something like Sherlock Holmes coming upon the tracks of a crucial suspect, from just a few strains or shreds. He could smell and then imagine his quarry. Many people cannot learn to do this. Reich was quite extraordinary about it. There are some movements a person makes which give him away, that is, reveal his essential attitude about himself. One has got to be willing to get down to these details.

The second reason this is difficult to teach is that you need a sense of rhythm. Perhaps that could be felt by the reader in our back-and-forth questions and answers. The patient's defenses break up the rhythm. More exactly, the patient's constant attitude makes sure that the gathering rhythm is stopped, before the patient can begin to flow instinctively. It's too dangerous. The doctor gets a sense of where to challenge, and locate, this breakup of rhythm, by being able to establish a rhythm with the patient that will be disrupted.[3]

The Interpersonal Perspective

(CHAPTERS 5 THROUGH 8)

*R*eich and Alexander had opposite ideas about character. Reich would find ways to break it down, to let the instinctual rhythm through. Alexander would find ways to strengthen the character, so that it could bear the old feelings in a new context. Both ideas are very useful.

Alexander's idea is the beginning of a perspective on character entirely different from that of Freud, Ferenczi and Rank, and Reich. No longer are we concerned with getting inside to the hidden story of the instincts. Now the eye is on the relation between the person and the environment, the success or failure of that adaptation. Instincts or feelings have not disappeared, but what is more important is how the person uses the environment to bear the strain.[1]

Alexander, Sullivan, Winnicott, and Balint all saw the different possible relationships inherent in a person's situation, and deftly managed the music.

The first two, the Americans, pulled for the unrecognized line of simplicity of adaptation. They are the pragmatists, continuing that American tradition. The second two, the English, were interested in another line of solution, the notion that going forward often required going backward first, into some kind of regression. This tolerance and interest in regression are what made Winnicott and Balint alike, despite being quite different in temperament and in use of the English language.

5. *Alexander and French: With the Grain, Against the Grain*

An INDIVIDUAL CASE can demarcate a different perspective about psychotherapy, like a proof for a new geometry. The lines and points come together so beautifully, in a way no one ever quite saw before. A new set of principles allows the proof to be extended to countless related cases. Anna O. was such a case for psychoanalysis, while the Rat Man was the proof of the possibilities of character analysis (Gustafson, unpublished).

Alexander's Case B (1946, pp. 146–155) is, I believe, one of these single cases that demarcate a new geometry. The proof is a stunning argument, which lasted but two sessions and yet contains all of the major ideas that were to follow later from Alexander and French. It was the first in the series of 292 cases treated by their group between 1938 and 1946, reported in *Psychoanalytic Therapy* in 1946.

CASE B, THE SCIENTIST

The patient was a 51-year-old scientist who came to Alexander weeping, agitated, and exhausted. He had made great progress for three years upon a research project of "considerable importance to humanity," but for six weeks he had been unable to solve a complex mathematical problem that would complete the work, despite renouncing all other interests, despite feverish activity, and despite taking only three hours sleep a night. Now he told Alexander he could work no longer. He refused to present a paper on the work at an important scientific convention in a few weeks and would not even allow his name to be included in a report by his junior colleagues.

While the man emphasized his devotion to serving humanity through his science, Alexander could not help noticing that he took "unmistakable satisfaction" in the fact that his colleagues would never complete the mathematics without him. So Alexander began his response by calling attention to this contradiction. The man avowed his service, but was obviously pleased that only he could do it. Why did he have to deny this selfishness? Yes, the major motive was helping through science, but didn't he have the self-serving need that we all have? The man left the first session shaken, but relieved.

The man appeared for the second session much improved, very favorably impressed by Alexander's response, no longer confused, and no longer severely depressed. He was getting back his self-confidence and thinking about participating in the convention. "He said that as a scientist he had been impressed by the therapist's approach to emotional problems, that he had not realized they could be treated in such a rational manner" (p. 148). He had not seen his self-deception before. He had seen quite suddenly that "his whole life seemed to center around competition." This had been a revelation to him, yet Alexander had made this acceptable.

At this juncture in his narration, Alexander tells the story of the man's life, which he pieced together in the two sessions. The first marriage had been awful, the second marriage now in trouble, since the man's sexual power had markedly declined in the last three years, at the same time he was throwing himself into research. He had been the child of a second marriage, preceded by 12 stepbrothers and stepsisters. "Treated as a weakling by the whole family, he had felt that only by some extraordinary achievement could he bridge the hopeless gap between himself and his older brothers" (p. 149). This achievement he found possible in his talent for mathematics. "With a great deal of emotion he recalled a scene in which he had embarrassed the teacher before the whole class by solving a problem which the teacher had messed up on the blackboard. In high school he once solved in twenty minutes a geometrical problem which had never been solved before in that school" (p. 149).

Now Alexander began to move "against the current."[1] So, if the man withdrew from his work, no one could solve the problem! The man now realized he had begun the research desiring to prove the existing theory to be a fallacy. Not very different from his high school performances! Alexander remarked that the "patient's work could not have been dictated exclusively by the wish to serve humanity" (p. 150).

Gathering momentum, Alexander plunged on to *his* proof. He told the man that his "old pattern, his need to prove his powers" must be "reinforced" by his sexual decline, his failing second, as well as first, marriage. Worse, he was scared of his young colleagues. The man contradicted Alexander for the first time. That was impossible. "His supremacy was unchallenged. Everyone admired and loved him because of his devotion to research and teaching. His colleagues came and begged him to return to his work; they were all concerned about his condition. How could he be afraid of them? That would be pure insanity" (p. 150).

Now Alexander gathered up all his evidence and put it before this doubting scientist. He had competed with father, brothers, his teacher, suitors of his wives, and now the younger generation of scientists. This was his "ingrained pattern." Was not his whole research to prove a theory wrong? To prove his superiority? Sure, it was for humanity, but:

because his old insecurity had been revived, his research no longer served merely his scientific interest, it was also a means of proving his superiority at the cost of others. Therefore he now made the sulking gesture of leaving his collaborators in the lurch at the last moment—as if to say, "Well, go ahead, you young giants. Do it without me, if you can. But you cannot. You need me!"

The analyst mentioned in a dramatic fashion, "And they come and beg you. But you remain adamant. You say, 'No, I am going to retire; I have had enough of fight and struggle. You do it yourself!' You are taking a malicious satisfaction in their impotence to solve the mathematical equations. In your own eyes you are fully rehabilitated. You can say, 'I may no longer be a great hero in the field of sexuality, but I am still better than this younger generation. I am better in what really counts.' All this you cannot permit yourself to feel frankly. You must have some alibi, and this you receive from your illness. You are depressed, you cannot sleep, you cannot stop weeping, you do not want any recognition. Why should you feel guilty? In this way you can have satisfaction and still not feel bad about it because at the same time that you hurt others you also hurt yourself. But would you be so generous if you were not sure they could not accomplish your work without you? Sure that even if they could, they would certainly give you the credit? Your martyrdom is only a cover for a vindictive triumph over your colleagues—whose only crime is that they are younger than you!" (p. 151)

The patient took this very well. His "only reply was that all this opened up a new world for him; that this was the first time in his life that he could talk about himself freely with someone. He said he now felt quite different about the whole affair and would consult the therapist again whenever he felt the need" (p. 151–152).

The patient later described the two interviews to a friend as follows: "The analyst picked out of my life's history little pieces, assembled them in the same way that you put a jigsaw puzzle together and made a picture, a vivid picture which I could see plainly—namely, that I was exceedingly vain and yet at the same time I hated vanity (and I do), that I often did things to punish that vanity without any recognition on my part of the motivating cause or compelling factor." (p. 152)[2]

The man completed the mathematical work in a few months, having presented the paper before this at the convention in its imperfect form. In two follow-up interviews eight years later, the therapist learned that the patient had had some mild depression on several occasions, but it did not seriously interfere with his work. There had been no further periods of morbid hyperactivity. He had coped with not being needed in his retirement by rewriting his thesis so that people could derive more benefit from it.

EXPERIMENTAL ATTITUDE

You can always recognize a major shift in scientific theory by its surprising predictions. Certain events are anticipated which previous theory could not expect or explain (Kuhn, 1957, 1962). Alexander was definitely operating in this Case B of the Scientist with a shift in theory that would be of major proportions for the field of psychotherapy. We notice, with some anxiety, that Alexander is responding to this patient in two ways which strike us as wrong according to traditional psychoanalytic theory. First, an extremely depressed man who has come in for help weeping, agitated, and exhausted has been hit extremely hard by Alexander about his destructive envy and competition. Surely, we would not want most doctors to respond like this to most of their extremely depressed patients! This could kill people. Secondly, this man has been given a picture of his difficulty, in the form of a tour de force, a proof gathering momentum and ending in a brilliant display of mimicry, wit, and dramatic intensity. Surely, this also breaks the rules that most of us follow. God help most patients if they should be lectured like this, for few of them would want to come back.

This is why Alexander and French are so hard to follow. If you take some of their maneuvers literally and use them across the board with a variety of patients, you will do great harm. If you are going to follow them with profit, you have to understand the major shift in theory that they are using to derive their specific interventions for specific patients. Such interventions are often counter-intuitive and, as we see in Case B, counter to what is usual good practice.

Therefore, let us walk through this two-session case very carefully, to understand the theory, the essential ideas of Alexander and French, from which specific interventions are derived, very different from one case to another.

Alexander and French are like great generals summoned to the front lines to take over a battle that is being lost. Their first aim is to survey the entire scene, from the best vantage point. They will look for the two essential findings. First, what is the best fighting strength of their own army? What is the "ingrained pattern" which has been successful up until now? They understand that a comeback is always made from native, enduring strength which has become temporarily weakened, not from some new, unfamiliar capability which has seen little of battle. Second, they look for where the "ingrained pattern" is failing, where it has been asked to do more than it can do, so that it is collapsing, that is, the weakest point of the defenses. So, in brief, they are looking for the best news and the worst news. They will not make a move, but sit calmly on horseback, until they reckon with the overall field in the broadest possible strokes. Given such a bold and clear-sighted view, they will act decisively when the time is ready. Notice that the metaphor of the military generals is mine. They themselves refer to the doctor more modestly as a "traveler" coming upon "the country through which he is about to journey" (p. 109). The general will appear at first as an interested traveler, before he takes off his coat, and gives some orders:

> First of all, it is very often easier to get a clear picture of the patient's problem and life history as a whole during the first few hours of an analysis than it will be at any time later until the analysis is almost completed. It is preeminently during the period before the patient has become deeply involved emotionally in relation to the analyst that it is easiest for the analyst to gain an adequate perspective upon the patient's problems as a whole. The analyst during this period may be compared to a

traveler standing on top a hill overlooking the country through which he is about to journey. At this time it may be possible for him to see *his whole anticipated journey in perspective.* When once he has descended into the valley, this perspective must be retained in the memory or else it will be gone. From this time on, he will be able to examine small parts of this landscape in much greater detail than was possible when he was viewing them from a distance, *but the broad relations will no longer be so clear.*" (my italics); Alexander and French, 1946, p. 109)

So what does Alexander see from the first hill with Case B, the Scientist? He sees a man whose "ingrained pattern" has been to save himself from humiliation by feats of mathematical skill, by thinking of himself as "saving mankind" with his talent. No wonder the man is weeping, agitated, and exhausted. For this one vanity could not be expected to win every battle in life, and yet the man has been forcing his one talent to carry that load. Which leads to the other crucial question. Where is the "ingrained pattern" now being defeated? What is the weakest point of the adaptation, which is terrifying to this man because he fears to lose the entire battle of life? Here, Alexander shows a terrific eye for the unspoken, for the most hidden weakness which is *most* frightening to this great scientist. The ingrained pattern *always* obscures the most serious weakness, by its own prominence, so the eye for the fatal weakness in the arrangement depends on considerable sense about what people are up to, what they are hiding the most. Alexander figures that the ingrained pattern of this man picturing himself as a talented scientist far more skilled and generous than all other scientists has to be so *desperate* because the *opposite* is true: He feels his young colleagues will soon show him up! So he is making a desperate move to destroy their promising start by withdrawing his contribution. A brilliant stroke of perception by Alexander! This talent for not being misled by the ingrained pattern which is so prominent, but finding the obscured (developmental) weakness, is also characteristic of Sullivan, Winnicott, Balint, Gedo and Havens (Chapters 6–10).[3,4]

How will the ingrained pattern be strengthened before the turn to its weakest point? It will be admired. Its overall success in the battle of life will be appreciated. The tone and attitude and words chosen will fall in entirely with this dominant adaptation of the patient. The doctor will become isomorphic with the ingrained pattern of the patient. Notice how exactly Alexander is able to join this patient, the Scientist; consider especially his opening move (p. 147).

Even while he is beginning to move "against the current," very early, he does so with a tone and attitude and words that have to be very comforting to his patient. He calls attention to "contradictions" in the patient's attitude. He appreciates the man has been "devoted" to his work, though now he has an "extreme distaste" for it. "He avowedly wished to serve humanity," but he gets "gratification" in feeling "he alone could complete the present task." But, of course, all "human actions are overdetermined," so that "many different motives (are) all active at the same time":

Emphasis upon an acceptable motivation often serves to hide the unacceptable. . . .
Why did he have this exaggerated need to prove his complete unselfishness, if not to
deny his very selfishness? The emphasis on his altruism, the therapist pointed out,
was obviously a way of defending himself against self-accusation. The therapist stressed
his belief, however, that the patient's *major* motive was indeed to help humanity. He
said authoritatively that the patient must also have selfish motives, probably unconscious, of which he did not approve but which are *universal*. Then the therapist
spoke in general terms of the standards of our competitive culture, *deploring* the fact
that a competitve spirit has unfortunately invaded all fields of activity. He remarked
that scientific advancement requires *devotion* to knowledge for its own sake, a *quality which the patient obviously possessed to a high degree.* (my italics, p. 147)

This first response by Alexander in the initial session concludes with his deep
appreciation of the man's ingrained pattern. Although Alexander opens with
pointing up the man's weakness, his terms hold the weakness in a scientific
framework of "contradictions," of "devotion" to work and humanity, and
of "overdetermined motives" within which "gratification" and "selfishness"
can be contained. All of this "moving with the current," allows the beginning
of the counter-movement "against the current," which will gather great momentum in the second session.

I would like to have written that the two movements, with and against
the ingrained pattern, were separable. That would be easier for the reader.
But we have seen already how the opposite movements begin together, the
movement "against the grain," however, being smaller at the beginning than
the movement "with the grain," which concludes with such a beautiful tribute
to the patient's devotion. But this is only preparatory for the stronger move to
weakness and disarray. Why must this weakness be faced so forthrightly?

A little theory is necessary to understand the second movement. The
weakness, the dread of losing in this man, pulls him to redouble his deploy-
ment of his one considerable talent, his mathematical ability, beyond its power
to succeed. As that ability falters, the dread of losing altogether overwhelms
him, which makes him force the talent even more desperately. This is the
"vicious cycle" whereby the weakness drives the exaggerated use of one talent,
whose apparent limitation makes the patient feel more exposed, which drives
more forcing, etc. The deterioration is, therefore, very extreme, after three
months of working on the single mathematical feat for 21 hours a day. The
patient arrives at Alexander's office "weeping, agitated and exhausted." Therefore, having appreciated the man's devotion to science and his great skill,
Alexander must move against this dominant current to confront him with his
decline. Until this is faced and accepted, the patient's desperate feats will be
driven.

This will be what Alexander and French call an "emotional adjustment"
for the patient. The "decline," the possibility of being beaten by colleagues,
will be bearable because the patient is no longer the weak child humiliated
by 12 stepbrothers and stepsisters, but rather a very successful scientist ap-

preciated by a very successful doctor. The *unbearable strain* (of inferiority) is tolerable in a *strengthened context*: This is the precise meaning of the "corrective emotional experience." If the strain can be borne in this way, it will no longer require more compensatory effort, that is, for the man in question, to appear as an extraordinary altruistic mind, when such compensatory effort has already been extended to the breaking point.

This phrase "the corrective emotional experience" has been a misfortune for Alexander and French, because its precise meaning tends to become a diffuse meaning, of somehow making up to the patient his childhood, of somehow giving the patient a parenting that has been missed. Once the meaning is diffuse, just about anything would and could be justified in the name of "corrective emotional experience." Probably, most people who have heard of Alexander and French have heard little more than this unfortunate phrase, whereupon they have one of two responses: They are glad to justify whatever they are doing in this name or they are glad to dismiss Alexander and French as making psychoanalysis into a trivial theory. Both responses betray a failure to read the cases in question, as well as a failure to understand their precise experimental theory, whose logic is much more demanding than that of the standard technique. With the theory of Alexander and French, one has to do a lot *more* thinking about the individual patient, not less. With a precise idea about the ingrained pattern and the weakness which is becoming unbearable, one can take precise action to provide a strengthened context, whereupon the weakness will be faced. With such a theory requiring such exact adaptation to the individual patient, *nothing but this exact adaptation* can be justified in the name of "corrective emotional experience." I would throw out the phrase, for it seems only to invite foolishness, for and against.

Alexander and French believed that "in historical perspective, our work is a continuation and realization of ideas first proposed by Ferenczi and Rank" (1946, p. 23). They thought that Ferenczi and Rank were entirely right that "emotional experience should replace the search for memories and intellectual reconstruction" (p. 23). Their improvement on Ferenczi and Rank is to argue that it is not possible to have the patient experience again the most unbearable strain from childhood, unless there is a strengthened context in which to bear that strain. Hence, their idea of moving "with the grain" before moving "aginst the grain." Ferenczi and Rank had only proposed moving against the grain, i.e., against the resistances, "to unwind the libido."

One way to strengthen the present context we have already described is this moving "with the grain." But there is a second way to strengthen the context, which is for the doctor to act in ways which *separate* him most decidedly from the negative transference expectations. This gives the patient much more confidence in the relationship with the doctor. This idea explains much of what remains puzzling about Alexander's behavior, for example, with the Scientist. Why does the man take so well to such rough handling? Why does he appreciate an overwhelmingly powerful proof by Alexander rather than resent it as a damnable lecture? These anomalies can only be understood with reference to the negative transference.

This man had been looked upon and "treated as a weakling by the whole family." Alexander will separate himself from the family, most decisively, by giving him a rough time, which proves his respect. It is bold to tell him what a powerful and generous scientist he actually has been; it is bolder to give him a very rough time as well. The man appreciates it very much. So what makes the big proof work as well? Here is a man who fears that his one talent, for scientific demonstration, will fail to encompass and protect him from decline and defeat. Alexander demonstrates it is possible to face the decline and possible loss in competition, yet place it in the powerful context of a scientific demonstration where it can be borne. One can be frightened in the context of being powerful. This demonstration by Alexander, which gathers such sweep and momentum, also, decisively, separates Alexander from a past which regarded the man as either a weakling or completely powerful. For his family, he was weak. For the teachers, he was so intimidating. For Alexander, he is neither. Thus, Alexander provides a strengthened context to make the old pain more bearable, because the man will see Alexander neither as holding him in disrespect nor as being swamped by the power of his destructiveness. Both will be borne, because the relationship is with a man who regards the patient as worthy of respect, but not too much to handle.[5]

But generals who turn around a failing army have to provide more than the right relationship. They must get the proportions right, about how much to support the ingrained pattern, how much to put the army into the difficulty it must eventually handle. Generals are like mothers, helping a child to learn to walk. If they stand too close, the kid does not extend himself and take the necessary chances. If they stand too far away, there are too many crashes to the floor. How much dependency to allow depends on the needs of each case. For example, in Case Y of Alexander and French (pp. 119–125), a desperate, demanding girl who is pregnant and feels she has nowhere to turn will be allowed a haven with the doctor, with no challenge for a while, before she is turned to face her predicament. Yet in this Case B, a famous scientist can be confronted in the first session, even as his considerable virtue is being recognized.

Alexander and French thought that most psychotherapy allowed too much dependency, so that a long middle phase of "couch diving" was permitted before the patient was brought back to face his failures. Therefore, they thought that treatment could be much more to the point if the patient were allowed no more dependency than he needed for the strength to cope with the strain. Freud, and then Ferenczi and Rank, had had the idea of interfering with these defensive dives into the couch by setting an ending date for treatment. As Alexander and French point out, this is only one of many possible devices for pulling the patient up short from dependency he does not need, probably not the best choice either, since it can merely bring about a panic or some kind of neurotic flight. Interruptions with the opportunity to return are usually better. "It is advisable to make the interruption not too short. The patient should have the opportunity to struggle with his problems alone and should not be encouraged to turn to the analyst at the first sign of relapse. On the other hand, he should have the assurance that if he really needs his therapist, he can always return to him" (Alexander and French, 1946, p. 36).

Thus, Alexander and French were always gauging how much dependency was actually useful to the case at hand. They appreciated that there could be errors either way. Many of their patients were hard-driving, competitive persons, like the Scientist, who were very frightened of being needful. It would be very useful to help them allow for being taken care of a little, but they would want to return to the battle soon on their own. One might need to hold them back a little. Others would be clinging in their ingrained pattern, and it would be important to interrupt this. One would be interfering with their inclinations to dive into the couch. The most elegant example of this titration of dependency reported by Alexander and French was the case of a patient who had become psychotic in a previous therapy because of extreme feelings of either abandonment (too little dependency) or intrusion (too much). So, their plan was as follows. When the patient felt abandoned, an appreciation of this was followed by an appointment the next day. When the patient felt intruded upon, this was appreciated and followed by a longer interval until the next meeting. This is very much what Winnicott (Chapter 7) would call being available "on demand" or careful "adaptedness to need."

In summary, then, the doctor is to give just enough that the patient successfully negotiates a difficult problem of his life. To continue our military metaphor, the patient wins a battle he thought was lost. The ingrained pattern which was failing is adapted to the fight. He has been helped to negotiate this reversal of fortune by a technique which: 1. gets an overall view of the ingrained pattern and its current failure or weakness; 2. shores up this ingrained pattern by an isomorphic relationship and 3. by a relationship which is decisively separated from the negative transference; 4. moves then against the grain to face the weakness, in this strengthened context; 5. accurately gauges the difficulty that the patient has to be carried over; 6. allows enough dependency for strength, but less when the patient is judged ready to handle the trouble; 7. finally, reckons carefully with what the environment is likely to do in response to the patient, for without this reckoning it is difficult to know what to supply.

A nice example of the final principle is Case K (Alexander and French, pp. 234–244), a 21-year-old woman who had been her mother's best friend. She became acutely anxious, so that she had to stay with her mother at home, after a successful visit to the parents of her new boyfriend. The therapist appreciated that this new sexual relationship threatened the close tie to the mother. While putting the patient in touch with her resentment, the doctor was equally careful to appreciate the girl's deep loyalty to her mother. The doctor reckoned that the problem was to "slow down" the girl's movement away from the mother towards the boyfriend to what *both* could tolerate. Therefore, the doctor met with the mother to judge what speed the mother could tolerate. As it turned out, the mother welcomed some room for her own life. Still, the doctor kept the girl from making a move too fast.

It is quite amazing how close this intervention is to many of those made by the Milan team in recent years. How far Alexander and French were ahead of their time! They realized that if the doctor were setting himself to the problem of successful adaptation, he had better get an adequate idea of the social environment into which the patient was trying to fit herself. Hence, the talk with the mother. Hence, the idea of loyalty to the mother and the need to slow down the pace of the development of the girl's sexual interest to conserve the relationship to the mother.[6]

THE DOMAIN OF THIS TECHNIQUE

Before Alexander and French, character or ingrained pattern had been seen as interfering with getting to the hidden story of difficult feelings. It put up resistance, or even, according to Reich, was one highly organized posture set against what the doctor needed to find out. Therefore, in both classical analysis and character analysis, the patient was challenged about his resistances or entire posture. This threatened him with having fewer defenses and feeling highly vulnerable for the time being. Many people cannot tolerate this. Therefore, the domain of classical analysis or character analysis is smaller than allowed for by the technique of Alexander and French.

Alexander and French, by moving first to strengthen or shore up the ingrained pattern, before moving against the grain to confront the weakness, made their procedure much more tolerable for a wider domain of patients. Among the 25 cases described in *Psychoanalytic Therapy*, taken from the 292 treated by their group between 1938 and 1946, are many precarious and desperate people who would never have tolerated any further descent into vulnerability at the start of treatment. They were far enough gone already. We have already seen such a state in the Scientist, Case B, but the remainder of the list includes many cases of similar difficulty. Case N was a chronic alcoholic of ten years' duration. Case F was a businessman with a peptic ulcer, who dreaded his need to be taken care of, Case Q a medical student with asthma, who became ill when his dependency was interfered with. Case Y was a desperate young woman who became pregnant out of wedlock, who came to the first session with a volley of demands to force others to become responsible for her. And so forth. Clearly, if you know how to move "with the current," to strengthen or shore up the ingrained pattern, you can take on people who are terrified of their emotions. This is the great advantage introduced by Alexander and French.

I could never quite understand before my last reading of Alexander and

French why they infuriated so many people and were so completely excluded by psychoanalysis. I attributed the exclusion to the overwhelming tendency
of psychoanalysis to defend the standard technique against any alternative.
But I began to see that there were weaknesses in Alexander and French that
invited the attack. Their presentation in *Psychoanalytic Therapy* tempted me
to call this chapter, "Fairy Tales." All 25 cases are too good to be true. Could
the other 267 be so wonderful? But it was not only that. I found it difficult
at first to remember the different cases, because they were like psychoanalytic
fairy tales, in which some familiar psychoanalytic idea was verified and ex-
emplified. The individual patient disappeared, for me, into the idea he or she
represented. The cases seemed to be mere occasions for expounding some
truth I knew already, such as that some patients become asthmatic when their
dependence is threatened. The patients all respond so beautifully. I thought
I had been given a sample of "star cases," such as Malan would describe much
later, people who are determined to get better with a minimum of help. Out
of 292 patients, we could expect about 25 of these determined people. Perhaps
the technique was not so decisive after all, only the selection of cases presented!

But after a struggle with my resentment, I was able to keep reading and
finally let myself admire the depth and complexity of the strategic understanding of Alexander and French. They really did have a gift for this. I began
to see that part of my difficulty learning from them was envy. Why could
they pull off fairy tales, when I could not? No wonder they were hated. They
could have given as much thought to coping with their colleagues as they did
with their patients. We all could have accepted their brilliance more easily if
they allowed us to see more of their failures. This would have been more in
the scientific tradition. Malan (1976) was later to appreciate this need for hearing both sides of the story.

Having overcome my resentment and envy, and admiring the coherence
of Alexander and French's planning, I became able to appreciate this as a set
of moves which is quite lovely, but with only one set of possibilities. Fairy
tales seem complete until one has wider experience. We will see that the men
who followed Alexander and French had many such different experiences.
Sullivan would discover that the situations described by patients are not often
like fairy tales in which it is soon evident what the bad parent did wrong and
what the good doctor must do. Indeed, if matters were so clear, the patient
probably would have known what to do by himself. Often patients are in
situations which are quite obscure or which are obscured by the patient's ingrained pattern, which offers such a "selective inattention" to the environment. Sullivan's technique will be necessary to "an adequate account." Winnicott and Balint discovered that the rigid, automatic forms of character, the
ingrained patterns, often can be given up only if the patient can go back to
a very unorganized relationship with the doctor, to a very primitive, fluid object relationship. Dependency need not be so negative; it might even be

necessary for a "new beginning." The Milan team discovered that the systemic demands of the environment may be extremely powerful, requiring a sacrifice of individual development. Alexander's little talk in Case K with the mother about her tolerance for a move towards sexual independence by her daughter is but a small step in the direction of understanding the full force of systemic requirements that can hold a person in a tight knot for a lifetime, whole families for generations.

Therefore, the technique of Alexander and French, like most offers, is "not half so good as it first appears," as Freud (1937, p. 228) remarked about his own work, because of these limitations: The good/bad picture given by the patient of his relationships is often the work of the patient's selective inattention. It is not an adequate account, upon which the doctor can reliably gauge what the patient needs from him. Dependency and regression into an unorganized relationship may be more often necessary than Alexander and French could allow for, given their inclination to allow as little dependency as possible. The systemic context for which the patient loyally holds back his or her development may require much more thorough delineation than Alexander and French were prepared to look for. Still, the domain of their technique is a wider domain than that of classical psychoanalysis or character analysis.

Besides these inherent limitations to this technique, there are many limitations in doctors which would make it difficult for them to follow Alexander and French this far. Doctors like standard technique. They like experiments less. But Alexander and French propose to make every case an experiment! Freud had this attitude in the early and middle phases of his career. Ferenczi was always up to his grand experiments; Reich was also. Indeed, perhaps all of the writers described in this book take this experimental attitude about psychotherapy. Certainly we shall see it in the following chapters about Sullivan, Winnicott, Balint, Gedo, Havens, and the Milan team. The modern, well-known brief psychotherapists, Mann, Malan, Sifneos, and Davanloo, had some of this experimental attitude, but all were ambitious as well to define a standard technique of their own. All became defenders of their own dogma. The experimental attitude makes life as a psychotherapist much more interesting. Perhaps it is an attitude which makes brief therapy possible for many patients, since they may borrow some of this daring and get on with the experiments necessary to their lives![7]

In summary, Alexander and French offer wider possibilities for working with and against the currents of strength and weakness in the patient. The chief danger is that the doctor will accept or construct a standard story which has too little to do with the patient at hand. Then the doctor's attempt to influence the story to a fine outcome will be improbable.

This danger can be reduced if the doctor will continue to "work the opposing currents" (Havens, 1976, Chapter 3), even after he or she has gotten a first view of the patient's strengths and weaknesses. Second, third and fourth pictures may be very different from the first picture. Hopefully, there is a "successive approximation."[8] Alexander might hit it right the first time with his Scientist, but this is unusual.

Notice that I have to work against the speeding current of the young businesswoman in the case which follows, to feel the danger for her of the slow current which she fears will take her back to the depths of her childhood unhappiness. Then I may appreciate the necessity of her speeding project. This is a relief for her.

THE CASE OF A YOUNG BUSINESSWOMAN ON THE MOVE

The reader may well feel after I have presented this excerpt from a case of my own that "the mountains are in labor; a mouse is born" ("Parturient montes; nascetur ridiculus mus"—Horace). The excerpt is a small and modest piece of work, next to the mountain of Alexander and French which we have reconstructed. So be it. Everyday clinical experience is a shadow of greater things.

This young woman set up her own small business in a very original way. Her dedication was extreme. Her complaint to her medical doctor and to me was hoarseness.

One day in the middle of her brief psychotherapy with me, she came in to discuss the most recent episode in which her voice had given out. She had been at a meeting in Chicago in the morning, during which another young businesswoman had made an inspiring speech about what women could accomplish in business. Overstimulated, she "barreled" back to Madison, reaching her desk on the run and tearing through the usual stacks of documents, before she raced off to Milwaukee with her secretary for an evening meeting with a client, all the while giving an ear to the secretary's run-down on her own difficulties. By evening, she had quite a sore throat.

I got her to slow down a little, just to go through this narrative of the day. This helped her get hold of herself. She sat back a little. This gave her room to have a little thinking of her own, an independent discovery that she might have "stolen" an hour for lunch.

Then she joked to me, "But a good person doesn't do that." What did she mean by a "good person"? "Of course, someone who works as long and as hard as they can." Where did she get that idea? Well, her mother was like that, her mother who died of a stroke in her fifties. Grandmother was the same. Here was an ingrained pattern over several generations.

The sequence here is interesting. I slow the patient down, which is certainly my working against this speedy current. The patient has an exceptional thought, about taking a break. Then she is propelled out of fear of this thought back to the ever-working ingrained pattern of herself, her mother, and her grandmother.

I now moved against the speeding current again. I asked her what her mother would think of the idea that a good person could have 20 more years to get work completed. Could she take a long-range view of looking after herself? This might include stopping at noon. She said that never would have occurred to her mother. She just worked.

Again, the exceptional thought, about taking a long-range view of taking care of yourself, got the current running fast again so that we could see it more clearly. She offered, "Perhaps I can take it easier when I've proved myself. Now I cannot. I feel gripped by responsibility."

I asked her what this "proving" was about. She said she never fit in as a child. She felt lonely and worthless and excluded. Her job in the university was more of the same. Then, five years ago, she had an experience which changed her life. She had set up a conference for business people at the university, where she met some other young women who had been successful in constructing their own enterprises. She got the idea that since she did not fit into organizations in her world, she would build an organization into which she could fit herself. She would make her own home. Her eyes filled with tears as she told this to me. Of course, she resumed speed within seconds, but the significance of her communication was not lost on me. She seemed surprised that I understood this deeply held idea, of creating your own medium.

Having appreciated her project for her life, moving deeply with her current, rather than skimming with her at the surface, I could now double back with few minutes remaining against this forceful current. "All right," I said, "then how long will it be for you to prove yourself?" "Two years," she replied, "when the business has its own momentum!" Running out of time, I asked her with a faint smile, "So then it will be possible to have a break for lunch, when you are overstimulated coming back from Chicago . . . in two years?" She smiled, "We'll see. Maybe next week, who knows?"

Only by my appreciating her devotion to her project could I come close to helping her let up on it, since she fears any slowing will make her lose the momentum necessary to building this medium (home) (mother) she is constructing for herself, and she would fall into the abyss of her forlorn childhood. As she gathers her own strength, and the strength and competence of her passionate project are recognized, she can let up a little and not be so hoarse.

6. *Sullivan: Dependable Hypotheses*

THE CASE OF THE HOUSEWIFE-ECONOMIST

A YOUNG MARRIED WOMAN, bogged down after a few months of therapy, was presented to Sullivan with the hope of getting her moving again (1956, pp. 371–376). She was described to him as being "extremely tense, apprehensive and inarticulate." She had described herself as "an inefficient housekeeper who 'lazes' most of the day away."

She had been deserted as a child by her mother, then again by her father, then used by the maternal grandparents "more or less as a servant." However, because she was gifted intellectually, she was allowed to finish college. Somehow, she went on to get a Ph.D. in economics. She married a fellow student there, only to become his housewife. He was extremely critical of her housekeeping. He also frequently told her of his "romantic entanglements" with other women, who were presented as "romantic ideals." After ten years of this relationship, two children, and the husband talking about divorce and immersing himself in his work, she had become increasingly inactive and isolated.

What, then, had Sullivan to say about moving this case out of a bog? "I would start therapy," he said, "by asking, 'Well, why haven't you a maid?' And I want to *know*, in a fashion that makes it perfectly clear to me why they don't have a maid. If there isn't any adequate explanation, I would then ask, 'How about getting one?'" No doubt he would have her attention! There would be more alertness in this bog than there was yesterday.

Now he would go on "by saying that her training seems to be rather exceptional for a person who has accepted a purely domestic role all these years and that, under the circumstances, her feeling of helplessness to get going in the morning rather encourages me than otherwise. Has she never heard of a woman who preferred something else to domestic preoccupation?" Sullivan would be one hundred and eighty degrees from the husband. He would be "encouraged" by her "helplessness to get going in the morning" to housework. Of course she felt helpless. Who wouldn't? He would suggest this is a good sign. She had better things to do.

Now he would want to know what happened to her economics? "Since women economists are not the most common thing in the world, I would point out that it looks to me as if she must have followed some natural bent. Now of course it may come out that she did it because great-aunt Catherine recommended it, something of that kind, but that immediately excites me about great-aunt Catherine, who seems to have had ideas, you know." Sullivan was looking for something worthwhile that was given up or lost. Where had she given up? What had she given up? He had a hunch. He would play it.

"What I am attempting to do here is to get her mind open a little bit to the fact that not only is she in a disagreeable situation, but she finds it disagreeable. And by sort of hounding her to prove that she is an exceptional woman with an exceptional education—and an exceptional inclination to go on suffering an impossibly silent domestic involvement—I am simply hoping to crack the shell that surrounds all her feelings. . . . if I get her to wondering what the hell she has been doing all this time and why she has never felt entitled to object to any of it—then I can anticipate that she will be equal to feeling some very real anger at times."

He wanted to rouse her a little, to get a little "outward movement of her interest, a beginning suspicion, 'Well, this really wasn't all necessary and inevitable.'"

I would lead her to talk a little bit about how she explained this tacit ban on her developing ordinary relationships, and I would expect that she would then hint of her acceptance of her unworthiness for a free life. At this point I would ask, "Well, now, how do you explain college and the rather original choice of subject that you carried through so well?" Then, after I had listened to a good deal of that, I would come down like a ton of bricks on economics. "Well, how about economics? Why has that interest vanished from your life without a trace? You take a Ph.D. in economics, marry an economist, and as far as I can discover, from then on research in economics has been left exclusively to him. Did that suit him? Was that what he insisted on? Did you just accommodate his feeling that it was awkward to have a wife who knew something about his business, or what?"

So he would get a little resentment going. But it would be located back there in what Sullivan called "the middle distance," between present and childhood, which is less explosive. He would start her education there, to "close in on areas that inevitably must open her mind to a reassessment of what has been taken more or less for granted as a continuing act of God."

Having gotten her underway "by that remote route," he would turn a corner, in his usual surprising way.

The thing I would be determined that this woman should tell me sometime or other is that she has discussed with her husband just what he had in mind in advising her in long, ecstatic letters of his great love for another woman some years back, and I would try to get her to look at that simply as a piece of research or investigation. "Now here is a very interesting research problem," I would say. "One's husband goes off and becomes terribly enamored of some goddess and writes his wife all about it. Now what was he doing? What did he think he was doing?" She doesn't know, of course, she hasn't had any experience in being anybody's husband. Then I ask her, "But why not find out?" Here again, I hope that I would be pushing on something far enough away and essentially intriguing enough so that she will rather calmly ask him a few questions. I think they will be profoundly embarrassing questions.

Sullivan reckoned this would be interesting for the wife, disconcerting for the husband, but not a roughhousing which would drive him away. Rather it would teach her she could manage him and have some fun. Hell, life might be more fun for both of them.

THE METHOD AND ITS DOMAIN

A Believable Picture

The reader will recognize many moves here in common with Alexander and French. There is movement with the grain of her potential for "research" interest, against the grain of the "continuing act of God" that she be subservient. Sullivan takes an overall view, shores up her natural bent, separates himself from the criticizing attitude of the husband, gauges her need for starting carefully in the "middle distance," and figures what the husband might tolerate. All of this can be put in terms of what we have learned from Alexander and French, even though Sullivan knew next to nothing of their work. He had a similar freedom of movement in "fine disregard for the classical rules" (White, 1952), to set up rules of his own.

But the reader should not be misled by the comparable movement, for the purpose of the movement in Alexander and French would not have been acceptable to Sullivan. Sullivan did not like doctors to presume they were "therapeutic" in acting upon the patient as an object either by "interpretations" or by "interventions" (1976, pp. 210–212). He felt this was often foolish or even dangerous. I believe he would have admired the adroit maneuvers of Alexander and French, while he would have rejected their being organized to provide "corrective emotional experiences." Perhaps Alexander did hit it right with the Scientist, but this would be unusual in its accuracy.[1]

Sullivan believed it was much more reliable for us to think of ourselves as working for an *accurate picture* of the patient's trouble. So much of what the patient will do, and what the doctor will follow, will be misleading. This patient led her doctor into her bog of self-disparagement, and he got in with her. This went nowhere. So Sullivan asks a series of relevant questions. He wants to understand what will give this patient what she wants in life. When had she had it before? Why shouldn't she have it again? He wants dependable hypotheses. He has hunches. The questions will see whether he is in the right direction.

He will take care to keep his inquiry from making her too anxious. *She* will then do the experiments.[2] If the patient feels worthwhile about some start in life, goes after where she left off, and is clear about what will get in the way, she will be extremely adaptive. She gave up, previously, because she must have felt it was too dangerous not to be subservient. That was the security she knew as a household servant. Sullivan will help her resume her inquiry, getting it underway with him, setting it on a useful, practical course with a high probability of results. He keeps her away from a sequence which will be explosive and therefore too anxious for both her and her husband.

What It Takes for Expert Inquiry

Sullivan is deceptively simple. He intended that. If you don't come across simply, the patient can't follow you and give you the findings you need. But since illness is a roundabout and complicated way to do something, the doctor has to catch on why patients go around the barn, when they could go in the front door. Since patients can take forever with these performances, a good doctor can be recognized by his ability to do "whatever was required by the patient and the patient's needs in the shortest possible time" (Gustafson and Dichter, 1983, p. 633). Let us then look a little more closely at his consultation on the Housewife-Economist. This country boy, the American doctor, bears watching.

The patient has made what Sullivan would call a "damaging admission" (1954, p. 226). Her husband is right. She is a lazy housekeeper. She is failing to earn the ticket which admits her to the human race. The prosecution has the upper hand, and the defendant is in a hopeless bog. Sullivan enters the courtroom. He finds the admission encouraging. A little wave of surprise goes through the crowd. The defendant turns hopefully towards this new doctor. She is less afraid of him. She'll tell him more than the others. He finds her all right.

The courtroom metaphor is no accident. This is the kind of little world that Sullivan thought we all live in, where every feeling or idea or action of the individual has its audience.[3] Since every patient plays to some such courtroom with considerable anxiety, a doctor's interview could improve or worsen the judgment of the patient by these "other people in the room" (Havens, 1976, Chapter 2). How could the doctor get an "adequate account" (1956, Chapter 3) in front of all these people? Nowadays, how could we get an "adequate account" when the trial will be even recorded on videotape? Sullivan shows how. The "damaging admission" has been looked at wrongly. Almost always it is something "ordinary." Here it is even "encouraging." Sullivan will put it in an acceptable perspective. You have to do this or you will get "convenient fiction."

Next he asks why she hasn't a maid? Why not the "ordinary solution"? "How about getting one?" The patient gets hopeful right away. Something useful and ordinary may come from this talk. That kind of hope is the only way that painful disturbing situations can be faced, that poor performances can be revealed. Darn it, I may learn something from this man, fool though I have been, painful as my recall may have to be. Without such hopefulness in the patient, the doctor will get to know very little. The "ordinary solution" is a surprise to the patient, also. Most people who have gotten tangled up in some complicated, indirect route have what Sullivan called "selective inattention" (1956, Chapter 3) for the ordinary, direct route. It makes them too anxious, given their past, so they don't even see it. So the idea of "Why not a maid?" comes as hopeful, and surprising.

People who have been in bogs for too long forget that they used to walk forward quite well. "Everything begins" (1976, p. 29), as Sullivan would say. He'll look for that worthwhile past. At some time and place, development got off course. He'll go back to that. This patient was exceptional. "Women economists are not the most usual thing in the world."

He will protect this worthwhile sense of herself, once he's got it. He will "hound" her about it with his questions. How do you explain this success? "How do you explain college and the rather original choice of subject that you carried through so well?" Sullivan is constructing what is useful and worthwhile in her life, what elsewhere he calls putting up a "buttress" (1976, p. 120). He wants this in place before he widens the field to what is most frightening. Meanwhile, she is trying to prove she isn't worth the trouble, that she is not a going concern. He will "kick out the props" of this negative perspective (1976, p. 167). Hounding her with evidence in her favor, he will finally come down "like a ton of bricks" on economics. He will "hit this hard" (1976, p. 172). So there is a double movement here: a construction of what is useful and worthwhile in her and a destruction of her self-disparagement.

But when Sullivan was helping a patient build up something useful, he wanted something not too difficult. The simplest, ordinary thing to do, which would not be too much for her environment, would be for her to take up a little "research," at a "middle distance." He didn't want her to attack a difficult current problem until she had the "underpinning" to cope with it (1976, p. 164). Heterosexual difficulties are often impossible, because the patient lacks some simpler capacities. She'd better think of herself as worthwhile first. With that "buttress" in place, the husband will not pin her down defending her right to exist. He'll have to explain his own behavior. Therefore, Sullivan would have a sequence in which to take the complaints.

But then, there is a sudden transition. This gets a very alert and aroused patient. So what did the husband have in mind with these tales of romance? After the "remote route" which has prepared the woman, there will be some difficult questions for the husband to answer.

All of this involves bold moves, like Alexander and French, but all proofs are questions: What about this? What about that? The hunches are not apt to get far off, since they invite the patient to bring up findings that could change the picture. Hence, the procedure is likely to bring about "a genuinely communicative situation." Sullivan wanted reliable communication more than anything. The psychiatrist is an expert who "deals primarily in information, in correct, unusually adequate information" (1954, p. 13). This is the only reliable way to go fast.

Why Help Becomes Necessary

Human beings need confidence to operate at all, to be able to connect with their fellows to get needs met, to be able to defend themselves from their fellows being harmful.[4] We are a profoundly interdependent species. Immature human beings get confidence when the family adapts to their needs, allowing the child to feel powerful in this smaller sphere. But as the child moves out into wider and wider circles of experiment, he or she will need to become more skillful to get what he or she wants, as the environment becomes less adaptive to the child, more indifferent or even hostile. More and more skill must take the place of relying on being looked after for confidence to persist.

If the individual has no environment ready to meet his need and no skill to get it for himself, he will be anxious. When parental passions seem to abandon him, when peers do not accept his movements, when the organization he belongs to wants to use him without concern, he will be anxious. Worse, if these audiences object to his performance as being unacceptable, he will be extremely anxious.

What happens? The need to belong is more critical. It is more necessary to feel secure, to have that anxiety reduced, than to get what one needs. So people utilize "security operations" to get rid of the developmental problem, so that their anxiety about belonging is manageable. They pretend, like our Housewife-Economist, for example, that being a servant is all they have in mind. Having minimal expectations is one common operation for feeling secure. The developmental experiment is given up; it is not accepted because it is too dangerous and makes her feel too anxious.

Sullivan thought that the psychoanalytic perspective was apt to take up a lot of unnecessary time, given the kind of ordinary situation I have just described. If you allow such a patient to run along in so-called free association, taking on resistance to that wandering, you can get a picture of the person that has little use for improving his relation to the environment. With the Housewife-Economist, you got a train of self-disparaging remarks, sinking into a bog. This will make the patient feel somewhat secure with you, but dissociated from what is occurring between her and her environment (husband), which you won't know much about. Indeed, this is the tendency of most patients to make therapy itself into a security operation. So the patient feels more secure in the doctor's office, but, somehow, keeps having unforeseen collisions with her environment, which set her back even further. This is unreliable help.

The twofold problem of helping a person is therefore: 1. finding something worthwhile in the patient to feel secure about, while, 2. getting increasingly clear and sharp about what is happening between the patient and others who matter very much, so that skill in managing these essential situations is forwarded. The patient needs to know more and more about the ordinary, simple ways that people get on with each other. If it's too complicated, it's apt to work badly (1954, p. 220).

SULLIVAN'S PROCEDURE

I can give an outline of Sullivan's scheme for interviews, which he took an entire book to describe, his *Psychiatric Interview* (1954). The reader hopefully will turn to that book for close study, perhaps reading backward from its clear and powerful statement in Chapters 10 and 11, "Problems of Communication" and "Conclusion."[5] Then, having that scheme well in mind, the reader is likely to derive a huge profit from seeing the scheme at work with a specific case in *A Harry Stack Sullivan Case Seminar* (1976). What, then, do I take to be essential to his routine for bringing about a "genuinely communicative situation"? It is a ritual in four stages.

First is what Sullivan called the "formal inception." The doctor has to present what he is there for in a clear way, for the patient to know what to do with him. He is there as an expert to untangle the patient's "problem." His first job in every interview, therefore, is to establish what the patient wants his help with. What is the patient's question? Only with clarity about the patient's question can he decide what data bear upon the situation. What is the patient trying to do that he cannot do?

Even at the outset, defining this agreement between himself and patient, the doctor must also be keeping the patient's anxiety bearable, for the patient may already have asked himself whether he is worth the help that might be given to him. So the doctor must also be defining and establishing "the worth of the patient as a person. That is, not that he is a marvelous person, but that he is enough of a going concern to be very worth the effort that it will take to get well" (1976, p. 213).

The subsequent movement of the doctor, his transitions, mostly need to be clear to the patient, if he is to give responses that are to be understood. Conversely, confusing movements give confusing data, e.g., when the patient wonders what in the world the doctor had in mind in asking about such and such. The quality of the data will also go down when the patient's hopes for the session being useful to him are weakened. It will improve when his hope is strengthened by the doctor's developing with him some findings which bear on his being worthwhile and upon his hopes for the session. A doctor with good hunches gets a more eager and responsive patient.

This expert relationship is something like Kurosawa shows in his movie, "The Seven Samurai." There the villagers seem hopeless about defending their village from bandits, until they see that the Samurai seem to have approaches to their defense problem which make sense. Their own resourcefulness then comes into play. Samurai were experts in warfare and defense. Psychiatrists are experts in untangling problems about living, without making their patients feel too anxious.

Second is what Sullivan called the "reconnaissance." We soon need a rough sketch of the landmarks in the patient's life, but again we need to get this map without upsetting the patient. "We say that the skill of the psychiatrist is to some extent manifested not by his avoiding anxiety, but by his mapping the areas which are colored by anxiety, and showing some reasonable discretion when he is stomping around there" (1976, p. 206). Who is this person who has come for help? What is his work? Where does he live? Who are the important people? How has his education come along? What was his childhood like? Who lived in the house in the early years? In other words, what has he been up to? Since his first guise is likely to be misleading, we need to begin to correct our first impression. The landmarks will revise the picture, which would be way off. We begin the work of what Havens (1976) calls "successive approximation."

Third is the "detailed inquiry" about the patient's problem. This depends on two necessary ideas. The first is that "everything begins." We need to get back to where the patient did *not* have this problem, to get a clear picture of how he got off. The second is that our picture of how he got off depends on comparing the patient's picture with ordinary progress or ordinary development for a person in the patient's particular neighborhood or class. Sullivan would be asking the patient and himself just how most people he knows would be managing the problem. If the patient has little or no idea, Sullivan would be saying so and so and asking what kept the patient from the ordinary thing. "Why not a maid?" Also, if the patient had not done the usual thing at the time, why not later? Why not the "corrective experience" (1976, p. 121) later, where school or peers or friends could remedy something sensible missing in the family? This line of inquiry tends to develop useful findings.[6]

Of course, the detailed inquiry is full of possible complications. Often a patient cannot manage a later problem in life, such as a heterosexual relationship, because he lacks the "underpinnings" for intimacy. He may have so little ability to connect or protect himself, such that the attempt is sure to fail. Sullivan would not take on impossible aims. What in the hell makes women so damned important anyway? Hasn't the patient got something better to do? (1976, p. 75).

Or the patient may entertain "transcendental aims" (1976, pp. 215-6) for the relationship with the doctor. A little understanding from him might beget the patient's having to make him into God Almighty. This sets up a crash. Sullivan would not take on "great expectations." He might say, "What the hell do you expect from spending twenty years in psychiatry? Do you expect me to know nothing?" (1976, p. 77).

"Another grave limitation to the smooth and easy progression of inquiry appears when you have become so involved with patient's self-esteem that you are being sold an extended piece of goods — that is, being misinformed by the minute, which is very expensive to the patient. In this case, an easy progression of inquiry will merely keep up an unfortunate motion" (1954, pp. 224-225). For this and other situations, the doctor must be the one to make the *transition* to something more useful.

Sullivan was very skillful at making the kind of transition he wanted. A "smooth (and well-defined) transition" is necessary for the patient to follow the doctor's line of inquiry. An "abrupt transition" throws the patient out of something impossible, because of the kind of "great expectations" described in the previous paragraph or because of a flood of anxiety bearing down on the discussion. An "accented transition" is necessary to tell the patient to cut out what he is doing. Sullivan felt you had to do this in your own way. His way would be something like this: "I may not change the subject, but I do change the communication by showing traces — sometimes very glaring amounts — of satire, boredom, restlessness, annoyance, or something of the sort" (1954, pp. 224–225).

So half of one's job in the detailed inquiry is to keep to a decent aim for the work and to be bringing in relevant and important findings bearing on this aim. This gives hope and an aroused partner for the job. The other half is to help protect the patient from too much anxiety, which always threatens to cut things off. Anxiety will break up the communication when the patient feels he is coming across as less than a worthwhile person. He will forever be assuming that your thinking agrees with his, which is often that he is not worthwhile, given what he has to reveal (1976, pp. 32–33). Sullivan was forever tearing up such misconstructions, "knocking the props out" from under them, as he would say.

"Damaging admissions" cannot just sit there. We have already seen how Sullivan would take care of such a thing as the Housewife-Economist's being "lazy." Also, the doctor must not give "tacit consent to delusion or very serious errors on the part of the patient."

In these cases, you should first confirm, by asking the most natural questions that would follow, that the patient intended to say what he did, and that there was no misunderstanding on your part. Having made sure that the patient's statement was as bad as it sounded — that he is entertaining an idea which is not only wrong, but also, in a sense, does violence to the possibility of his living in a social situation among others — you do not then say, "Oh, yes, yes. How interesting!" You rather say, "I can scarcely believe it. What on earth gives you that impression?" You note a marked exception. That is all you need to do, in my experience, in order to go on with the interview. If something seems terribly off the beam, you register your amazement and ask about it. (1954, p. 235)

A third kind of misconstruction to be torn up by Sullivan, besides the "damaging admission" and the idea "terribly off the beam," was what he called the "routinely futile" operation. Crazy, nonsensical talk and self-disparagement are two common futile operations. Marital relationships are often weakened on a daily basis by such variations as tuning out into the television, or crying, rather than talking. Sullivan put it this way:

I think that insofar as I can prevent a person doing, shall I say, routinely futile things, that even that is an attack on his anxiety. It works something like this, that anxiety prevents you from saying what you need to say. When you look back and cannot be impressed by what you did, it again reflects on self-esteem and in its way means that the level of chronic anxiety is raised; it is for that reason that I set about trying to educate this boy that there is no use of thinking that nonsensical use of speech kids me or serves its purpose. It still leaves his anxiety about what he is trying to express but it does not add continuously failure after failure. It emphasizes that I don't feel it is necessary any longer. The "any longer" in itself is an expression of hope. (1976, pp. 123–4)

The other way to protect the patient from too much anxiety is to find what is worthwhile, as opposed to what is wrecking him. We saw how Sullivan would do this for the Housewife-Economist. If she was so insignificant and lazy, what the hell was the Ph.D.? Thus, Sullivan would "buttress" a construction of what made the patient worthwhile with actual findings from his history, never with generalizations. Only when some kind of positive construction like this had a reliable "underpinning," as he would say, could one risk certain topics which would give the patient a "jolt" of anxiety. One wouldn't want to open up a wide field of failure with its sweeps of anxiety without a fort to fall back upon. Notice the metaphors of construction and deconstruction here. Sullivan believed that anxiety could be kept tolerable by careful attention to positive, reliable constructions, and by taking apart negative constructions.

In the fourth and final stage of the interview, the "termination," the job is to keep the work open, so more can be accomplished between interviews by the patient on his own (1976, pp. 74, 227). It is important that the patient feel he comes away from each interview with something useful. A summary may help him hold onto what has been constructed. An abrupt transition out the door may keep the patient from mucking up something useful which has been achieved (1954, p. 228). At the end, as along the way, one is backing constructions which are useful and making it tough for the patient to get away with wrecking things.[7]

THE DOMAIN OF SULLIVAN'S PROCEDURE

This procedure of Sullivan's allows us to contend with a continuous distortion of communication. Sullivan assumes that all stories are continuously played to an unseen audience, continuously altered to suit its unseen demands. Therefore, we do not get a "genuinely communicative situation" unless we can contend with the distortion line by line.

We may well ask if all situations between doctor and patient are so distorted that they require this procedure of Sullivan. This must not be so, for the methods described in the preceding chapters have been somewhat successful. I am inclined to think that patients may still be candid with their doctors on occasion, just as they may still be indiscreet among friends. I agree with Winnicott (Chapter 7) that some patients still give themselves away, when well received.

Yet I am also inclined to think that Sullivan is right about most communications from patients to doctors. Why do I think he is right? Why is it so difficult to have a "genuinely communicative situation" with a patient?

Sullivan's answers would be, were, the following: First, the "stream of generalities" (1976, p. 24) that passes for communication between patient and doctor is damn near useless.

Second, people tend to find some point of correspondence between what they are saying or thinking and what the other person is saying or thinking and assume an overall correspondence which is completely unjustified (1976, p. 19). The patient does this regularly and believes the doctor shares his own distorted views; then, he becomes alarmed or despairing, or foolish in his "transcendental expectations" (1976, p. 216). The doctor does this regularly, and thinks he is in touch. Most people do not understand that every element in a person's communication contains every other major element in his perspective. Any element is part of a gestalt or system (Ollman, 1971). Therefore, you do *not* understand what a person is saying, ever, because you could not possibly share all the major elements in his perspective. All you can do is get "successive approximations" to his view (Havens, 1976, pp. 113–114). You do not assume you know what the patient means. Rather, you get him to tell you more about just what he had in mind when he said such and such. This is the business of what Sullivan calls "getting an adequate account" (1956, Chapter 3). This is an unusual ability, for someone to be able to follow someone else so closely.

Third, the patient is never going to give you reliable information if he has little or no hope you can be useful (1954, pp. 126, 106–107). Everyone has a sharp need to look good, to get an acceptable appraisal by another person. The hopeful patient will take the risk of being thought a good learner, someone with promise, in place of being thought already successful. Many doctors do not know how to keep the inquiry in touch with the patient's hopes which are sensible. There are so many ways these can be smashed. If the patient is able to ascribe the negative views of himself or crucial other people in his life to the doctor, this defeat can occur in the first minutes of the interview (1976, pp. 32–33), without the doctor knowing it has already happened. Sullivan saw that right away with the Housewife-Economist, who offered through her doctor such a defeating view of herself.

Fourth, even if the patient has hope you can be useful, the patient is going to hide the weakness in his development which you have to know about. You've got to be able to go looking for it, against the grain, if you will, of the patient's coverup, the patient's security operation. Alexander did this with the Scientist, who hid behind his prestige. Sullivan did it with the Housewife-Economist, who hid behind her minimal expectations. You've got to be able to make hunches of your own (1976, pp. 23, 78). This means you need to look at every presentation against the background of what an ordinary solution would look like. This yields the "overwhelmingly probable hypothesis" (1956, Chapter 3). The patient will have complete or "selective inattention" for what's missing. So you cannot expect him or her to tell you. Quite the contrary. You can expect him to make hints, but mostly to mislead you.

Fifth, your "overwhelmingly probable hypothesis" may be overwhelmingly probable, but wrong. Therefore, you do not have a "genuinely communicative situation" unless whatever *you* think can be corrected, as easily and as soon as possible by the patient (1954, pp. 61–62). Thus, interpretations are always "approximate hypotheses," questions to be answered (1976, p. 210). The feedback loop from the patient must be as open as possible, or the data are not dependable.

Sixth, I would add something implicit in Sullivan, but not so clearly stated by him. You are on better ground when you are answering the patient's questions, rather than vice versa. The communications become distorted when the patient is answerable to you, rather than you being answerable to him. You may have *your* questions, but they have to be in service of the patient's central question, that is, why he cannot have what he wants.

THE CASE OF A MODERN PASSIVE-FEMININE
CHARACTER RECONSIDERED

Now we may also come to appreciate how Sullivan's technique leads naturally back and through the technical possibilities described by Reich, Ferenczi and Rank, and Freud, described in the perspectives of character analysis and psychoanalysis. But I think Sullivan's description is the more powerful description, in which the others are contained as special cases. Special cases will get us in trouble when we take them beyond their limited domain.

Therefore, I will redescribe in Sullivan's terms a case which I presented in Chapter 4 as a modern version of Reich's Passive-Feminine Character. There, I gave what I thought could pass as a description of a very consistent challenge to the man's "constant attitude," which brought about a breakthrough of deep emotions held back by the man's "passive-feminine attitude."

I have watched many of my students try to follow this example and get it quite wrong. It is very easy to get in trouble with Reich's description in mind. Many patients will rightly ask themselves how the doctor's challenging could be in their interest. Many doctors will think that this activity is all they need to do. Many stalemates result. Therefore, let me explain why it is more *reliable* to see this interview as a clear *inquiry* about what ails the patient, while protecting him from anxiety about not being a worthwhile person. The challenge to the constant attitude then will occur in passing.

The reader may recall that this was the young man whose chief complaint changed about five times in the interview, from "depression", to "being unable to ask a woman out," to "having no sexual feeling," to "being attracted to men," to being unable to "criticize" anyone. His anxiety to find a complaint which would get him approval was quite evident. We may see from this overview that we are in the domain which Sullivan described. Notice also that the interview proceeds entirely from questions.

Why had he come for help? Because he was depressed over spring break. His friends were away, which made for a lonely week. Notice how fast this moves. Already we have the *basis* for the *work*, which is to understand why he became depressed, and we already know when it sharply *began*.

It was a lonely week. What got him down about that? He might always be lonely. Why was that? Notice I do not take being "lonely" in some *general* sense. I am asking what is in *his* mind about loneliness. He might always be lonely, because his friends had girlfriends and would marry them, leaving him behind. But then I am thinking, and then asking, why would he not also do the *ordinary* thing?

But why wouldn't he have a girlfriend too? "Because, he said, "I have no sexual attraction to women! Did your head jump up when I said that?" I told him I was just paying attention, but he surely seemed to think I had a powerful, startled reaction. What was that about? "It's sick, isn't it, not to have sexual attraction to women?" I said, "No, not necessarily, it wasn't all that unusual for young men to be quite inhibited." Here is one of those crises in the interview where the patient felt he had made a "damaging admission." He *assumes* my thinking agrees with his, that he is sick, which gives me the chance to tell him his missing sexual feelings are not unusual. He relaxed a little. "Oh," he said. Now we go on.

Now he made his third offer of illness. "I am attracted to men." I said, "Oh, what do you mean?" He meant that he often saw strong-looking men walking down the street, and he wished he could be them. I showed no further interest in his so-called "homosexual" interests here. "Why not follow this?" I am always asked by those who have watched the videotape. Sullivan's thinking is very clear here. I have a man who has come for help with depression because he fears being left behind by his men friends. I am most interested in why he too cannot seem to do the *conventional* thing! This, as Sullivan argues, is always the simplest way, if it is possible for the person. This man is desperate for the conventional solution, so I want to see with him whether it is not indeed possible. Why not? Why shouldn't he have what he wants?

So here I scratched my head for a minute, and proposed a way we might see how his attraction to women had disappeared. This is one of those "accented *transitions*" in the interview, where he sat waiting nervously for my proposal. I could not have had a more attentive patient.

So, I said, let's see, how might we find out what had happened to his attraction to women? I thought to myself that we could look for the ordinary *development* of attraction to women in the ordinary way. Perhaps we could find out what occurred when he took a girl out. A little excitement might be expected there, I thought. Had he dated? Yes, he had a girlfriend in high school named Sue. She was a good girl. His parents approved of her. They went out a lot, but he never felt any desire for her.

I had a *hunch* hearing about this Sue, what a nice, good girl she had been. Of course, he had no sexual feeling for her! Who would? But this man had a mistaken idea that here was an occasion he should expect himself to be aroused. This was interesting.

Could he describe Sue to me? Getting a more exact picture of her I figured would confirm my *hypothesis* or not. "Well, yes, she was very nice." Here was the kind of thing his parents might want to hear about Sue, but I was not about to let this generality pass for "an *adequate account*." I said, "Tell me more about her." He said, "Well, she was flabby . . . " broke off and flushed. He worked very diligently to get rid of this sentence, which was so inconsistent with his entirely pleasing and submissive outlook, but I would not let go of the sentence. He started to remind me how nice she was, and so forth, and so forth, to which I replied, "but she was flabby." I must have cut him short four or five times here, as he attempted different maneuvers to pretend he had not criticized Sue. But, as Sullivan would say, I came down like a ton of bricks on his phrase, "but you said she was flabby."

Before I had presented this little difficulty with this little word as throwing his "constant attitude" into the clearest possible light. It did that. But notice also that it is a critical finding in his favor, that, of course, he would not have sexual feelings for someone unattractive. I have seized this finding, and will not let go, because I have found some decisive *evidence* to upset his self-disparaging views. This is why the challenge, here, is difficult for him to dismiss. The "constant attitude" gets challenged not for itself, but as it happens to stand in the way of this evidence. In other contexts the challenge would be of little use. That is why taking the analysis of the constant attitude as the central technical idea gets a therapist very unreliable results.

After a while of my "*hounding*," as Sullivan would say about this phrase, he was very restless in his seat, obviously uncomfortable, and flushed. I wondered aloud if he resented my questions. He said, indeed, he had been resenting them for quite a while, flushed again, and began his usual back-peddling, denial, change of subject, smile, etc.

My hypothesis now was appearing to be what Sullivan would call the "*overwhelmingly probable hypothesis*," as I could see his difficulty saying a critical word about me as well as Sue. When I put this difficulty to him, he looked like he had been hit. He could not talk, he was so choked up. He didn't know why. I told him we didn't know why, but here he was crying. He began to cry and continued, silently, for quite a while. As the reader will recall, the next half hour of the interview brought in his associations to this crying, all about how a little sharpness had been extremely painful in his life, in losing his best friend from childhood, in the breakup of his parent's marriage in high school.

I have also described how we accepted him for brief therapy and how well he could use the help we gave him. One more idea here from Sullivan was crucial to our success with him. I thought it would only make him *anxious*, unnecessarily, to go back to the missing sexual attraction to women. My *hunch* was that he was like most men, who cannot have sexual excitement until they are capable of some fight or other aggressive behavior. Once that capability was in place, I felt his sexual excitement would emerge on its own. Therefore, the *sequence* in which to take his problem mattered. Getting it backwards would only have made him very, very anxious and feeling quite a failure at being a *worthwhile* man. That could have held up his work a long, long time.

Perhaps it is now clearer to the reader why I believe Sullivan's thinking and technique provide a reliable way to proceed with brief psychotherapy.

7. *Winnicott: Therapeutic Consultations*

W
HILE WINNICOTT could fit patients into a traditional schedule of psychoanalysis, one hour a day, five days a week, every week save vacation of the year, for many years, he also became interested in an idea which is the very opposite. Perhaps *he* could fit into a time frame dictated by the needs of the *patient*? Therefore, he ventured into giving two- or three-hour meetings at intervals as long as once in several months or even "on demand" (Winnicott, 1971b; Gustafson and Dichter, 1983a). One of the experiments in "adapting to need" was his long series of single hours of consultation. Here the single hour he gave was set in advance but the willingness to repeat the single hour would be elicited when the patient rang back to ask for it again. Most of the cases in *Therapeutic Consultations in Child Psychiatry* (1971b) are of small or latency-age children, with a few adolescents; there is one case of a 30-year-old mother, called Mrs. X., reported there. It is a remarkable piece of work which sets up a whole world of possibilities for "therapeutic consultations" with adults.

When I had an interview in 1981 with Masud Khan, Winnicott's editor and friend for many years, Khan told me that Winnicott got better results with brief psychotherapy sessions with adults than with his long analyses of adults. Winnicott never wrote of this, because he was very careful to appear as accepting as he could manage with respect to psychoanalytic theory (Gustafson and Dichter, 1983a). Certainly, Khan would know better than anyone about Winnicott's practice, but in a way, it doesn't matter whether his "therapeutic consultations" with adults were unusual for him, or frequent and striking in outcome. If we understand what he did, and what he thought, as with Mrs. X, we can carry on this remarkable tradition of "therapeutic consultations" with adults ourselves.

THE CASE OF MRS. X.

This 30-year-old mother of a six-year-old daughter was "constantly bringing her daughter for one doctor or another to examine her and to treat her for ailments the severity of which was not as great as the mother's anxiety would seem to indicate" (1971b, p. 331). When Winnicott got word from the social worker that the mother at last might be ready to talk about herself, Winnicott conducted the interview I will describe from *Therapeutic Consultations*. "The result of this interview was favourable from the point of view of the clinic's efforts to give suitable help to the child since the mother, having communicated about herself, was now able to do a new thing, which was to hand over the management of her daughter to the case-work organization" (p. 331). The girl was "carried through" the next several years quite well in a special school, while keeping daughter and mother in contact. This mother "became better able to manage her own affairs following the interview and its sequel: the proper care of the daughter" (p. 332).

I am obliged to quote much of the back and forth between Winnicott and this Mrs. X., for this is what the consultation is about, this way in which Winnicott finds his way into her world. A little overview of the interview might help, to keep our bearings. Here is a woman who, as Winnicott puts it, "insisted on her own badness, and in this she persisted to the very end of the consultation" (p. 332). Winnicott, from his side, accepted what was "terrible," but always went looking on for the something "worthwhile" that made it possible for her to "manage it all." With this only "companion," his theoretical knowledge of emotional development, he went in search back there for what made it possible for this woman to live. Always, Winnicott wanted to go as far back as necessary to find a place *from where a person could start, from where a person could live in a positive sense*. He was done with an interview when he had made his *transition* from what was most *worthwhile* to what was most *terrible*, and back again. Here the transition was made the other way, from the terrible to the worthwhile.

Winnicott always seemed to open with an off-hand remark, which was telling:

I saw Mrs. X. alone.
I said: "Hello! You look rather thin."
She said: "As a matter of fact I am fat and I can't get my clothes on." She was looking serious and worried.
I said: "Let's talk about Anna—it will break the ice."
Mrs. X. said: "She is really good, you know, She does not have a very nice life—I never talk to her, for instance, simply because no one ever talked to me when I was a child." (p. 332)

Oh, my, what a plunge into a miserable life! But Winnicott would not be knocked over by this. As she made the case against herself, something like the Housewife-Economist of Sullivan, only worse, Winnicott held out for the good in her. While the patient confessed that she failed exams for becoming a nurse, was thought "amoral" at 20 by a doctor, took all affection as a sexual event, wrecked all relationships by becoming totally jealous and possessive, had two lesbian affairs, and so forth, Winnicott was saying: "I can't think how you managed. . . . Children are often like that—probably Anna has been? . . . Well, all that is terrible. Something good has happened to you elsewhere but it has got lost. I am sure of that because you can recognize good things in Anna. . . . Perhaps mother may have been all right at the beginning from your point of view" (pp. 332–333).

This first attempt by Winnicott to "reach back" for what was worthwhile got only more desolation. "She said: 'She (my mother) could not have been (a good mother) if she was so cruel that I had to be taken away from her' " (p. 333). The woman then spoke of her desperate loneliness and jealousy of girlfriends who seemed to have something. So she could not reach her mother yet in the interview. In a way, that would be Winnicott's aim, by the conclusion, for it would make the woman's life more bearable to have back a good piece of her long lost mother. She would be less desolate, therefore less destructive in the usual antisocial way of forcing the environment (here the clinic) to make it up.[1] Winnicott thought he could reach her, because he always thought that antisocial activity is a sign of hope, that the child-adult is in protest of something having been lost, and hasn't given up yet (1958). He also noticed here something else hopeful about her that "she kept her normal self going in the personality of her friends, of whom (in consequence, perhaps) she is inordinately jealous" (pp. 333–334).

Asking for her knowledge about her childhood, Winnicott got more of the desolation. She knew from her birth certificate that her parents' last names were "Y" and "Z," while hers was "X." She suspected the orphanage changed her name to "X" to save her from shame, perhaps a crime in the family. She was placed in an orphanage with 150 children, later smaller places. Her only single memory of kindness was one visitor who let her choose something out of a bag of gifts, and she chose a mirror. Then she became ill and was sent to the hospital.

Here Winnicott did something else, which he always did with these antisocial presentations.[2] He *acknowledged* how the woman was let down: "I spoke of the awfulness of being taken from an orphanage, which was different from being taken from one's own home, because of the uncertainty of returning. . . . I made a remark here about the ward having dealt with her body but seemed to leave out the rest of her" (p. 335). The patient responded: "I feel that people owe me things, but of course it is *me* who is wrong." She would wreck what little she got.

Winnicott knew this territory very well. He knew about the destructiveness to expect here.

I said: "It must be very difficult for you to know what to be angry with, and yet there must be violent anger in you somewhere."

She said: "Yes, but it takes an odd form—I feel a shudder going through me. It is a feeling as if *for a split second* (she found it very difficult to describe this) *I might go mad*, but I remember where I am, and it's over." I said: "You mean you *do* go mad, only it is done so quickly that it is all over. Your fear is that you will find you have done something awful while you have been mad." (p. 335)

Of course, Winnicott is letting her know, as Sullivan would, that the worst could be received all right by him, and she then gave it to him. "She told me something which she said she had 'never told anyone,' and she was very distressed" (p. 335). It was about nearly strangling a child who was screaming and got on her nerves. "She took it by the neck and shook it, but then stopped. . . . On another occasion she would hug children hard in order to get sexual feelings." This was when she worked in a nursery.

"This is horrible and dirty—do any other women ever do anything like this? Sometimes Anna gets into bed and hugs me and I feel sexy. Has *any* mother *ever* felt this? Of course in the nursery school I was given all the dirty jobs, including cleaning up the babies, I was never allowed to do anything of the kind that would be important for a baby."

Those babies in the nursery were all going to be collected by their parents and so I suggested that this could be one reason why she nearly murdered this child, she herself having never had a home to go back to. (p. 336)

Again, like Sullivan, Winnicott handled the "damaging admission" as something ordinary for her circumstances. "She then went on." Now they would plunge deeper.

Mrs. X. now confessed about stealing a pound note at 18 from her young mistress "to buy herself something pretty," which got her sacked. She went on about her craving for sweets. Winnicott asked then about the mother again, and was told that her mother

" . . . never came near me in all those years from 3 to 16. A friend said to me, though, 'You are always searching for something.' . . . I interpreted here about the link between the compulsive stealing and searching for something, perhaps for a lost bit of good relationship with her mother. She said she does not steal ever now but she still has a terrible urge for sweet things. At any minute she may have a desperate need and have to rush out and buy a cake, even when giving Anna a bath" (p. 337).

Here we see a *transition* that Winnicott himself discovered, not a transition that Sullivan knew about so far as I can tell, though he knew about so many other transitions. That is the transition from the "bad", antisocial forcing of the environment by the child-adult to the good relationship which was taken away. Having reached the two ends together, Winnicott now made another kind of *transition* which was typical of him, and original to him. He knew the *right time* to reach deeper, which he would almost always do by asking for a dream.

First he got a dream about a rat eating the child's orange, so she could starve or eat where the rat had bitten. Winnicott "withheld using this dream." She then offered others, including being chased by thousands of little people with little bodies and huge heads, which reminded her of the lice.

"The lice in my head would run over the pillows and I felt compelled to touch my head, although it was all terrible. I have always wanted someone to love or cuddle me, but I was never kissed until I was 19. Auntie never kissed any of us good-night. I am all the time ashamed of the orphanage." Here she put in an illustration that showed her sense of fun. She said: "Once on a bus the conductor said to Auntie (who was a nun): 'Are all these your kids?' Auntie was flustered and said: 'Yes, but they have all got different fathers.'" (p. 338)

After this little oasis, "she quickly returned to the desert," with more desolate remarks about the orphanage with Auntie, and how she could get a little from seeing the queen had children, from sweets, from substitute helpers for Auntie, from daybreak fantasy for two hours with her hand between her legs, and from rocking with her thumbs in her armpits.

Now Winnicott knew it was *time* to make his last move, to reach the good mother, as he would not get another chance: "It seemed to me that we had nearly had enough, each of us, and I must do some work. I must act now or not at all" (p. 340).

I said: "You know, it may be that these rats and mice are in between you and the breast of the mother that was a good mummy. When you get back to infancy and you think of your mother's breasts the best you can do is rats and mice."

She seemed shocked, and she shuddered and said: "How can that be!" I said dogmatically that the rats represented her own biting, . . . I related this to the fact that her own mother failed her during the time she was dealing with the new problem of the urge to bite in her personal development. She accepted this and immediately started looking for something in the relationship to the mother which could be carried over. She said she had never had a nice dream. . . . Then a significant thing happened. She said she remembered something—being carried—it had to do with the time before the orphanage. (p. 340)

She now "reached back over the gap," and to some extent recovered the memory of her own "good" mummy. One thing was a cereal food from her country home called "pobs"; the other a frightening episode of how the home was lost:

She tried very hard to get it.

"There is a voice—feet are running—I know doors are opening—there was a man there—people are shouting and someone has a bag or case." This was the moment of being taken from home to the orphanage.

This was a memory which was extremely precious to her and she felt sad to be losing it, although it never quite got her back to the early days as the word "pobs" did. (p. 340)

Winnicott now could end, "by saying that it would be quite possible for the relationship between her mother and herself to have been good at the start, although from the point of view of people observing, the mother was said to be cruel to her. We had to leave things in this state" (p. 341). "She said, however, that if I really liked she would show me her birth certificate, which she never shows to anyone as she keeps it locked up. Once she could have got married to someone very nice, but at the last minute her birth certificate had to be produced so she ran away from the whole thing" (p. 341). Winnicott has reached her most precious possession, her beginning.

As was said in the preamble to the case presentation, Winnicott had waited for confidence in the clinic to allow this interview. After the interview, "she stopped using the daughter as ill and in need of medical care. The child went into substitute care, and the good relationship between her and her mother was maintained and enriched. Anna is now almost an adult" (p. 341).

A Contrast to Sullivan

Before we walk through this consultation to Mrs. X., let us remark the contrast to Sullivan. What is common to Sullivan's "psychiatric interview" and Winnicott's "consultation" is how both allow the patient to make herself known very fast. "Terrible" revelations are received as terrible, but ordinary. The worthwhileness of the patient is sought after, steadily, in spite of the negative findings. So both men could get both the worst and the best. Both were after this kind of accurate picture, where at least the extreme dimensions would be gotten right.

But the emphasis falls differently. Instead of the "formal inception" of Sullivan, we see the informal, offhand remark from Winnicott to begin: "Hello, you look rather thin." This is an easy, unforced atmosphere, offered by this kind of beginning. We will get to Winnicott's theory about why this atmosphere gives a "natural method of history taking" (1971b, p. 161). For now, simply notice the informality, in contrast to the sharp presence of Sullivan.

There is something like Sullivan's second stage of the interview, the "reconnaissance," in that Winnicott also goes after a rough sketch of the landmarks—what happened to her mother and father, and so forth. But in other cases Winnicott did little of this.

I saw the child without first seeing the mother who brought her. The reason for this was that I was not at this stage concerned with taking an accurate history; *I was concerned with getting the patient to give herself away to me*, slowly as she gained confidence in me, and deeply as she might find that she could take the risk. (my italics; 1971b, Case XIII, Ada, p. 220)

Sullivan's routine was to go after the rough sketch, using history to make a connection with the patient (1976, p. 38). Winnicott might use history or not. What was more important to him was this "getting the patient to give herself away to me." The word "play" has something to do with this atmosphere, this kind of interaction, but it is one of those generalizations which can hardly tell us very much. We need a more accurate description of what Winnicott did. I would say that he and the patient would *fall in together* into something both wanted to do. You can't leave yourself out—how you are feeling that day, that hour — but, on the other hand, you don't want an impingement. You cannot dance leaving yourself out, but neither must you force yourself on the other person. The two of you fall into what you need to do, and, hopefully, the patient gives herself away. Another example may help:

Hesta and her mother seemed friendly, and after a few minutes in which we all talked together about the family the mother decided to go for a walk in the district. I was left then with a rather heavy 16-year-old girl, potentially hostile and a bit dressed up, so that one felt she had been told to put on her best things because she was supposed to see the doctor. It was a very hot day. I was in a mood in which I was reluctant to work; I let her know about this and it seemed to suit her very well. . . . (1971b, Case XI, Hesta p. 177)

Winnicott got them both out of a stiff start. Soon they were having some fun, passing drawings back and forth in his "squiggle game." He stayed with her. He writes:

You will see here again *how I give myself away freely* in this sort of interview. (Drawing number 7) Hers. She *knew what it looked like to her, but wanted me to have my own way of working it out*. Eventually I tried to draw her idea. It was a baby dinosaur. "It's stupid." Later she named it Cyril. She was very pleased indeed with this drawing and thought it might be the best we would do. (p. 182)

Really, is it so unfamiliar? I don't think so. It's what we do following a child's lead in a game. They tell us. We play along. Playing along means you do have to show some of your "own way of working it out," but you also have to let the child direct the play. They quit when you direct or divert. With adults, it is about the same: "There is no essential difference between an interview with a parent and an interview with a child except that with adults, as with older adolescents, it is unlikely that an exchange of drawings would be appropriate" (p. 331). So usually there will be a back and forth over the adult's *sketch of her own history*, as with Mrs. X. This is the second part of the consultation, getting to know "where the patient lives." In the Case of Mrs. X., this part is very prolonged, because she will only tell desolate, terrible things for the longest time.

For the third part of Sullivan's interview, the "detailed inquiry," we get in Winnicott the *transition* down deep, almost always by asking for a dream, at the right time when the patient is ready.[3] We saw he did this with Mrs. X., after linking up her stealing with searching for the good mother. So this third movement in Winnicott is down deep and inside, whereas the third movement in Sullivan is towards the problem with the environment, why the patient can't do the "ordinary thing."

The fourth movement, the termination, is quite similar in both — a little summary, or a sharp end to keep the patient from wrecking something good. Here with Mrs. X. we see a little summary, and then a sharp period: "We had to leave things in that state."

THE THEORY BEHIND THIS APPARENTLY OFFHAND METHOD

I believe we need a little of the theory behind what Winnicott did, or we will not see how well conceived is the consultation. Then we can take on Mrs. X. As with Sullivan, Winnicott's scheme is deceptively simple, but deep.

Let us start with "anxiety." Sullivan saw anxiety as the threat of disapproval or humiliation in the social world. Therefore, his job was to see why the individual could not find an ordinary, simple way to get what he wanted, without risking too much of this disapproval or humiliation.

Winnicott did not see "anxiety" in such an external way, as the anticipation of threats "out there." Neither did he want to accept the psychoanalytic emphasis on anxiety as an "internal event" or "intrapsychic" experience. What interested Winnicott was the possibilities *for playing the internal onto the external* (1971a). This is a *"transitional area"* where he thought we all live most of the time. Neither inside, nor outside—rather, seeing what we can do to map inside onto outside. This is culture, this is *preoccupation*, this is where we live.[4]

Anxiety for Winnicott occurs in this attempt to map inside onto outside. The most primitive kind is whether a self can be at all, or whether it will be *annihilated*, bowing in futility and helplessness to external impingement. Mrs. X. is one of those people who *appears* nearly dead, or desolate, whom the world had failed too much, but in whom a hidden spring of life runs. Of course, getting this precious secret of hers wrecked would do her in altogether. Notice how she ran from having to show her birth certificate, so she didn't get married. So Winnicott has to work, in this case, against a strong current of anxiety about annihilation.

A less primitive, though still primitive, kind of anxiety for Winnicott is what he called "depressive anxiety," following Melanie Klein. Here there is a response to the self which is good enough for the self to take risks, to be a going concern as Sullivan would say, but look out when that self is let down! There will be destructiveness. The depressive anxiety will be: "I am wanting to smash what is good to me when I get less. Will I make holes in what is good to me? Will I destroy it?" With individuals like Mrs. X. who got something, then lost it, the destructiveness will run very strong, in an attempt to *force* the environment to make up the loss. But the individual will be very anxious about wrecking what little good there is. Mrs. X. was forcing the clinic, which could have destroyed her ability to get care from the clinic, and she was very anxious about her daughter's need for doctors, probably given her own destructiveness to this one good object in her life. We could say that the self-disparagement of Mrs. X. then controls both her anxiety about annihilation and her depressive anxiety. It hides her wellspring, even from herself, and it blunts her destructiveness from being inflicted on others, by inflicting it more on herself.[5]

The reader also needs to understand a little piece of original theory from Winnicott about the "antisocial tendency," since this theoretical understanding of this tendency governs many of his moves in the interview.[6] When a child-adult *has* something good, which is lost or taken away, the child gets destructive, *to force the environment to take notice.* For example, when Malcolm X's father was murdered when Malcolm was a child, he began stealing fruit. If the environment did not take notice, the destructiveness can become chronic and hopeless, although it is difficult to say in any given case when the possibility of reaching the child-adult is over.

As a therapist you do three things. You *acknowledge* the letdown. You *face* the destructiveness squarely. You then *reach* back to recover the goodness that was lost. These are three necessary *transitions* that the doctor will need to make for the patient so that she will have the necessary *experience* to bring the parts of herself back together — the pain, the destruction, and the good. Notice how this procedure gets the patient through the two major anxieties that concerned Winnicott. The acknowledgment of the letdown, that it *objectively* occurred, protects the patient from thinking herself crazy, from this kind of chronic self-annihilation. The facing of the destructiveness helps the patient get a handle on the actual danger of destroying what is good in the environment, a risk the person may run to dangerous extremes, hoping to be noticed. The reaching back to the good that was there before gives back the source of most help against annihilation, a source that could not be reached for fear that it too would be endangered. That *would* be annihilation.

We also need to understand Winnicott's theory of ordinary development to appreciate what he did with Mrs. X. He thought that infants, and small children, first need the "preoccupation" of the mother, so that what is inside the infant or child is met dependably by the mother.[7] The child will locate herself or himself in the mother's response, will literally find herself or himself in the mother's face. In her expressions she or he will get herself or himself back (Chapter 9, 1971a). This is why Winnicott "will give himself away" (p. 182), as he said with Hesta, and why Hesta would say to him, "She [Hesta] knew what it looked like to her, but wanted me [Winnicott] to have my own way of working it out" (p. 182). Here is an idea that the Milan team would take up later — that we become ourselves in the eyes of others, so that we can be refound in our view of what others see in us.

As primary maternal preoccupation fades, the child gets different frustrations, and gets destructive. But — here is a difficult idea which the reader should ponder carefully — *externality* can only be created by the attempts to destroy it (Chapter 6, 1971a). This is how the child learns what is *not* him, according to Winnicott, by trying to destroy something and not being able to. It *survives* him; therefore it is *out* there, not *in* him. This is the continual experiment of growing up. This is why Winnicott wrote, "In the unconscious phantasy, growing up is inherently an aggressive act. . . . If the child is to become an adult, then this move is achieved over the dead body of an adult (unconsciously)" (1971a, pp. 144–145).

The trouble is that the necessary destructiveness will make the child fearful of actual destroying, which can occur if the parents are weak. This is the depressive anxiety. How does the child learn it is not necessarily so? *Over time* he learns, by being *carried through* episodes of his own destructiveness. Then he can give back (reparations) to the environment-mother. This is then a benign cycle, as the giving back gives him confidence that instinctual letting go can be survived and made up for. Perhaps the reader can now appreciate how Winnicott will be doing just this with Mrs. X. — carrying her through a spate of her own destructiveness, which he will survive, only for them to reach something good finally, and for her to give something to him at the end, showing her precious memories and her birth certificate.

Winnicott had little to say about progression beyond this, except that the child attempts to play his dream onto wider and wider social circles of external, material reality, where he is subject to increasing dangers and setbacks, which his earlier accomplishments must comfort him through. For his view of development, two kinds of anxiety will do: either anxiety about being hurt or annihilated oneself or about destroying the good environment.

This developmental perspective takes Winnicott out of the psychoanalysis he wanted to stay in. He preferred to blur the dichotomy between his thinking and conventional psychoanalysis; in doing so he actually made a transitional zone *for himself* while being loyal to the convention.[8] He was actually President of the British Psychoanalytical Society twice. But he did think that psychoanalysis got caught up in the intrapsychic, behaving as if the environment could be dismissed. His view was that the "good enough" dependability of the environment makes all the difference to the well-being of the child. The same may be said of what he gave the patient as an environment for the consultation. A good enough environment for a consultation will *be* there to find the patient "where he lives" and *be* there to survive his destructiveness.[9]

WINNICOTT'S CONSULTATION WITH MRS. X.

Perhaps the reader now has some of the "backbone . . . of theory . . . of the emotional development of the individual" which grew up with Winnicott, which is the basis of the consultation. The aim is to give "the child [adult] some hope of being understood and perhaps even helped" (1971b, p. 5).

Winnicott believed that first visits gave the doctor a terrific chance, because of the intensity of the anticipation of the child-adult. One indication of this opportunity is the "frequency with which *the children had dreamed of me the night before attending.* . . . Here I was, as I discovered to my amusement, *fitting in with a preconceived notion.* . . . What I now feel is that in this role of subjective object, which rarely outlasts the first or first few interviews, the doctor has a great opportunity for being in touch with the child" (1971b, p. 4).

This "dream of the doctor" indicates the "very great confidence which children can often show in myself (as in others doing similar work) on these special occasions, special occasions that have a quality that has made me use the word sacred. Either the sacred moment is used or it is wasted. If it is wasted, the child's belief in being understood is shattered. If on the other hand it is used, then the child's belief in being helped is strengthened" (pp. 4–5).

The consultation then may give the hope of being understood and, therefore, the readiness to go forward with treatment. Some will be so deep that "whereas a child was caught up in a knot in regard to the emotional development, the interview has resulted in a loosening of the knot and a forward movement in the developmental process" (p. 5). The hope of being understood and the further loosening up of development depend upon the child-adult's having an experience of herself as a going concern and making the transition back to what is most disturbing, but also further back to a positive starting point from which a person can live. When the child-adult can get back and forth between what is most terrible and what is most reliable, when the child-adult can *use the enviornment* to support this back and forth, then a coming together or integration of the child-adult has begun to move forward. The consultation discovers how this *use* of the environment will work for this particular patient. The first interview may need to be repeated a few times, or "on demand," to remind the patient or the parents how the "good enough" use of the environment works for *this* patient. "No two cases are alike." Then the patient and the environment can continue their work of meeting the patient's needs.

Now let us see how Winnicott did this with and for Mrs. X. He opened spontaneously, as always, giving himself away, hoping for the same back from the patient. "'Hello, you look rather thin.' She said: 'As a matter of fact I am fat and I can't get my clothes on'" (1971b, p. 332). This is the kind of reply Winnicott was up against until the very end of the interview, the presentation of herself as a bad or objectionable person. The misery ran on, with an absence of spontaneous gesture. The patient would *not* "give herself away."

What kind of an environment is needed by this kind of person? Well, Winnicott will show us. First, what is needed is an environment which will not give up, which has an eye for what is hopeful in a person despite the attempts of the person to appear either dead or desolate or hopeless. "I can't think how you managed. . . . Well, all that is terrible. . . . Something good has happened to you elsewhere but it has got lost. . . . " When this first attempt did not get there, Winnicott made a second attempt, through his theoretical understanding of the antisocial tendency.

He acknowledged how the woman had been let down: "I spoke of the awfulness of being taken from an orphanage, which was different from being taken from one's own home, because of the uncertainty of returning . . . "

and so forth. The patient responded: "I feel that people owe me things, but of course it is *me* who is wrong."

He knew what to do here next. He had reached her about being "let down," but she had gotten twisted up in her own destructiveness, turned back upon herself. The destructiveness now had to be acknowledged, also. "She said, 'Yes, but it takes an odd form — I feel a shudder going through me. It is a feeling as if for a split second . . . I might go mad.' I said: 'You mean you do go mad only it is done so quickly that it is all over. Your fear is that you will find you have done something awful while you have been mad" (p. 335). Now he has acknowledged "being let down," destructiveness, *and* madness. This brings out the most distressing, the most terrible part of her, how she nearly murdered a child. This being accepted, this being understood in her circumstances of "having never had a home to go back to . . . " (p. 336), Winnicott would now look for a transition to what was good in her.

He got the transition to the good from the stealing and craving for sweets which she now introduced. A friend had said she seemed to be "always searching for something." Winnicott told her it was for the lost bit of the good mother. This was a standard move for Winnicott, at this point, to "reach back for the good object," having gotten the letdown, destruction (and even madness). Another standard move for Winnicott, when he felt the right time had come for getting deep, would be to ask for a dream. What is complex here is that Winnicott did both at once, so he was reaching for *both* the good object and for the depths, for a good object he knew was in the depths, given how difficult the job had been of locating it at all. This is a virtuoso move.

So is the final and decisive "last chance" for Winnicott with Mrs. X. Even getting deep in her unconscious looking for a good mother, he got rats and mice eating the child's orange, lice in place of someone to hold her. A little hint of encouragement came, however, from her joke about Auntie having so many husbands. He could not have made this final move without his theory. He took her dream material of rats and mice as the last veil to be put aside: "When you get back to infancy and you think of your mother's breasts the best you can do is rats and mice." This reaches her, when she comes right through with the memory of "pobs," the long lost childhood country home, and the terrifying memory of being taken away from there.

The ending is very much like Sullivan, a little summary about the good mother she had reached, and a sharp end — "We had to leave things in this state" (p. 341) — which prevented her from wrecking what she had gotten. Winnicott liked to give back what he got in this way, so the person would have something positive to go on with or back to as he or she needed. Often, he would go over the series of drawings, so the transition into the disturbance and out of the disturbance was as clear as possible.[10] This meant that there was a road back and a road forward. This is what the "good enough" environment has to do for a person with a problem — to give him or her the road backward and forward. This gives him or her a transitional area, more room to maneuver, to live in, a loosening of the knot, and hope.

Notice how Winnicott used his theory, "his only companion" for a journey like that of Orpheus into the depths.

The only companion that I have in exploring the unknown territory of the new case is the theory I carry around with me and that has become part of me and that I do not even have to think about in a deliberate way. This is the theory of the emotional development of the individual which includes for me the total history of the individual child's relationship to the child's specific environment. One could compare my position with that of a cellist who first slogs away at technique and then actually becomes able to play music. (1971b, p. 6)

His theory always gave him, as with Mrs. X., a probable map of the depths. In her case it gave him the idea of looking for what was worthwhile that was hidden, the idea of taking up the letdown, the destructiveness and the madness, the reaching back for the lost, good mother, and the idea of the rats and mice as the final veil to be swept aside. But probable maps never fit an individual, and Winnicott was entirely flexible about having the patient set him right. Interpretations with him were for letting the patient know what he *did* understand, but also what he did *not*. He and Sullivan were both inviting the patient to say where they got it right, where they got it wrong. Thus, Winnicott showed his flexibility over being kept away from anything positive for almost the entire interview, over taking the reach for the good mother and the dream dive simultaneously, and over being ready for the final veil of rats and mice, without dismay. A virtuoso has a backbone of theory and technique, but is also ready for taking the surprising variation. Here is a musician giving himself to the music.

The Domain of this Technique

No one really knows how far you can go with therapeutic consultations. It appears one can take on much more disturbance than is conventional for brief therapy, given what Winnicott did with Mrs. X. Winnicott did insist that you do *not* do this kind of interview when there is not a good enough environment to carry the patient back over the ground traversed by the interview. You do not do this with strangers riding on the bus. The context for the interview with Mrs. X. is the holding environment of her relationship to the clinic. Winnicott waited for her to have confidence in the clinic, before he felt the time was right for the interview.

Also, Winnicott was prepared "on demand" to see the patient over again, as needed, so the patient would not be let down altogether if the environment was not quite carrying the patient forward. Winnicott would be there as a backup, knowing the success of the first interview could be repeated, as needed, once reached. The road backward and forward could be replowed, as necessary.

Winnicott's consultations in the book are about more than "talion" or oedipal fearfulness. Most often, they were about depressive anxiety, where the person (child) fears he will destroy the good object with his savagery. This is what makes the "good enough" environment so necessary for his work, as it must be able to hold on and survive the onslaught.

The other kind of case in the book is of people who have not found a self, and dread to begin to have a self, for fear of annihilation. Mrs. X. had this problem, as we saw, but there are others who are more difficult to reach than she was. These others require an extension of the technique described with her, which is further described by Winnicott, especially in *Playing and Reality* (1971a),[11] as a return to formlessness, to a completely non-impinging, receptive relationship. An adaptation to this need is necessary for some patients.

Of those patients who have a self which can be reached, whose difficulty lies with some interruption of a relation to good objects or a good enough environment, the extent of what therapeutic consultation plus adjustment of the environment can do is unknown. Often with patients showing the antisocial tendency, a lot of holding environment was necessary, while in others very little.[12] Each of Winnicott's cases was some kind of experiment. His attitude was to improvise as best he could, giving time for consultation as he had time he could give and as the patients could get to him from all over the country.

LIMITS TO THE DOMAIN

Since no technique is a panacea, even for the realm of neurotic patients, I am sure, and Winnicott was also, that therapeutic consultations have their limits as well. First, as Reich argued and demonstrated, some patients will do everything possible to avoid a regression, their entire bodily attitude being dedicated to this. Winnicott's use of the counterproposal, in play, will not draw some child-adults out of their holes or poses. He just got to Mrs. X., this woman so dedicated to proving how bad she was, in his final move. He gave up with George, the last case in the book, who was too far gone, "a nothing," where reaching him would have required an enormous involvement from Winnicott and a boarding setup, which could not be provided.

Winnicott himself also said that you do not do this kind of consultation without a good enough environment to take up what you get going.

I rely on an 'average expectable environment' to meet and to make use of the changes which have taken place in the boy or girl in the interview, changes which indicate a loosening of the knot in the developmental process. . . . Where there is a powerful continuing adverse external factor or an absence of consistent personal care, *then one would avoid this kind of procedure.* (1971b, p. 5)

As Sullivan made so clear, some people live in hateful environments, often built up by themselves gradually over time. Given such predicaments, a perspective like that of Sullivan for clarifying the muddled, obscured, hateful interactions may be necessary to find the relatively simple, ordinary adaptations which are possible. Bad obsessionals, for instance, routinely need something like this of Sullivan, because a more free, playful, original slant may just reap the hatred generated by past interactions of the obsessional.

No doubt there are other person-environment situations, requiring different adaptations to need by the doctor. Winnicott would have welcomed such differences which meet the need as it actually appears. For him, it was the technique that needed to be adapted, not the patient fit into the standard procedure.

A Word about the Doctor

My discussion about the domain of this technique would be missing something important without a word about what this technique is like for the doctor. My experience is that Sullivan's technique is a strain, because of the sharp demand for expertise at all times. It is a terrific challenge, to be this acute, but more anxiety is therefore carried by the doctor.

Winnicott's consultation relies more on the informal atmosphere and the ability to enter in oneself, freely, into something quite disturbing. It is much less of a strain, but it also requires a healthier person to go in easily to big trouble without the defense of a formal stance.[13] You play into the patient's direction in your own way, which is quite exciting. As Winnicott wrote, "the test of these case descriptions will hang on the word enjoyment" (1971b, p. 6). There is great pleasure and excitement in inviting the patient to take a risk, which is what Winnicott asked for, and in "hanging fire" as he would say, to see if the patient takes the risk. Not every doctor is up to this kind of adventure.

The Case of the Daughter of a Saint

What follows is a report of my consultation to a patient whose love is more easily reached. The emphasis here will fall on bearing the destructiveness—not so easy for the daughter of a saint. My patient wanted to know why the thought of her boyfriend sleeping with another woman should disturb her so much. She was in a panic. This was our fourth consultation, of two hours each, a month apart. After a lovely, calm, self-reliant bike ride in the country, she was driving home, contemplating seeing Sam again for some fun, when she hit this thought about his sleeping with other women. Their relationship had been good, but not exclusive.

I was a little elaborate here, wondering whether this indeed was what she most wanted to talk with me about. She had gotten me to take over the previous talk, so I wanted none of that. She was anxious to please. Was this new offer another variation on pleasing me? No, it appeared this subject was quite for her.

So, all right, what was this experience about driving back? She hated to say. She felt she would be unproductive for days, unable to get rid of the experience. She felt it would take her over for hours at a time. She cried. She was angry. I said it sounded dangerous, the way she talked about this state of mind. She said, "Yes, my loving feelings can disappear for the longest time." I said, "Yes . . . and then?" She seemed to be hinting at what harm she could do feeling destructive, but I did not know yet what she had in mind. I would have to wait.

Her answer was indirect. She said that she had had an affair when married, which she told her husband about. Actually, she had only "made out" with a man, but felt obliged to confess. Her husband was very hurt and very angry, having been neglected by her as well for several years. That had been the beginning of the end of their marriage. I said, "Well, so telling can do damage." She nodded sadly. "But," I said, "Somehow you could not bear to contain this emotional burden . . . of having done some wrong. You had to get it out." I had now gotten a second hint, of a developmental problem concerning being able to hold and feel something destructive. This could explain the panic, driving home, thinking of her boyfriend having sex with another woman. Perhaps she could not contain her urges to destroy him or their relationship.

She was thinking along the same line, for she then asked me, "But why should I be preoccupied with men having sex with other women?" This, I thought, was the right time to dive deeper. We had two powerful stories of her inability to feel something destructive, and I knew very well what had happened to her as a child that would make bearing something destructive into a big problem for her. Why not state the ordinary explanation? So I did. I said, "I suppose it has to do with losing mother when you were five, losing possession when you had had her all to yourself." I knew her mother had remarried then, several years after her father died. She responded by starting to cry. She said, "Sex and possession are all tied up for me, a blow to who I am. When mother remarried, it destroyed the happiness of her and me, grandma and grandpa."

I said, "So you could bring out your hurt and anger then." She said, "No, mother's husband was in a near rage most of the time. Mother was a kind of saint herself, quite fragile. If I had declared my feeling, I would not have had her affection for my dear little self. How irrational." I said, "No, not necessarily. It could have been so." She could well have been let down. I wanted that acknowledged.

She felt better. Perhaps she would be all right now about her boyfriend sleeping with other women? I thought to myself, "Not so fast!" I said, "Perhaps this perspective on being five helps, but there could still be a problem at 35 because 'instincts' can *still* make holes in relationships, damage them — either sexual instincts or hurt and angry feelings. I am beginning to see why you had to confess your sexual feelings before to your husband, as you think sex is quite destructive to relationships." She said, "Oh . . . I am having trouble feeling much in my vagina, and I do not come to orgasm. Could we talk about that?"

I said, of course, but before we took that up next time, a big subject, I had one more question. Why had the little girl, who could not tell her feelings to her saintly mother, not told them then to someone else who was important? Where was grandma? Where was grandpa? Well, she told me grandma was warm, but idealizing of her. For grandma, it was you and me against the world, you who can do no wrong. How could she talk to grandma about feeling destructive towards mother? Grandpa was awfully kind. She palled around with him on the farm. He was very nice. So I said, "So neither might be able to receive your hurt and anger about mother." She began to cry. She told me grandpa died a year after mother remarried.

I told her, ending, that we had found someone very important to her whom I had not known about. She said, "So if instincts can do damage, why am I always hopping into bed with men?" I said, "Well, they aren't always . . . " She said, "I have trouble finding out when." I said, "Yes, it seems so." Notice how I end by holding to something good in her. This allows her to introduce her uncertainty about when she is good and when she is bad. She gets mixed up.

This was quite an outpouring. I recognized early in the consultation that her trouble was about her own destructiveness, hence the depressive anxiety, a sudden panic on the road. I was glad for Winnicott's map of this problem. I would "carry her through" the outpouring of feeling which she had felt that no one could bear. Hence, her depressive anxiety about destroying what good was there for her: her boyfriend, and before, her mother and grandparents. The transitions are simple, but they are decisive to what we accomplish. The first is to be sure the subject is hers. The second is to go right into these two destructive experiences with her, noticing she finds them so dangerous. The third is to say to her that she had this same problem very much as a child. This is the dive into the depths that Winnicott would take after being well underway. She then came up to say that had helped very much. I took her down for another time, to ask how it was that no one had been there to receive her hurt and anger at her mother. Finally, I say, "Enough," despite an invitation into another big subject, her inhibited sexuality. I am willing to hear this music of children fearing their own destructiveness. I want to know the context in which she had to contain her destructiveness. I want to know how her environment had let her down before. I made a road back to where she had to hold up herself, to become such a pleasing person, and I carried her through and along another road of her own outbursts, a road forward, but a road she had to be careful about. You can wreck what you've got, even now. This is all Winnicott.

8. *Balint: Regression for the Sake of Recognition*

THE CASE OF THE STATIONERY MANUFACTURER

I WILL ONLY DESCRIBE how Balint got this case underway on what we might call a useful drift. The later moves were quite powerful also, but they were variations of the orientation that Balint discovered early on. Also, I have described the case from start to finish before, and I have no interest in repeating myself (Gustafson, 1981). I think I have something new to say about how Balint "organized" the case, as he would say, pivoting on the third session. The reader may refer to a little book (Balint, Ornstein, and Balint, 1972) devoted completely to a description of this interaction over 27 sessions.

The patient, Mr. Baker, was a 43-year-old director of a stationery firm and a father of three teenage children who became preoccupied with the rival suitor for his wife from 20 years previous. He never entirely forgot about this rival, but it only became an obsession on three occasions: when he was ill in India and his wife-to-be left off writing him because of interest in this other man; 6 years prior to treatment with Balint when he had a breakdown; then 18 months prior to treatment when he got onto this preoccupation again, very badly for the two months prior to his seeing Balint for the first time. Despite these breakdowns, he had been very successful as the "driving force" in the family business, taken over from his father and run by himself and two brothers. He married his Turkish wife, despite the rival, and was apparently quite happy with her. They had three children, who are very much in the background of the report of this case.

In the first session, Balint "hit it off" with the man by "brushing aside" his complicated story about his wife's interest in another man and about how he had ground her down about the details, saying that what mattered was how he felt about it. Balint offered to be his "sounding board."[1] The man was tearful, and very grateful. Balint did not yet formulate the case. Already, Balint showed his ability to manage the possible relationships offered by the patient. With his hand, as it were, he "brushed aside" the destructive pattern of wearing down the wife (and potentially the analyst), while his ear picked up the man's need to be taken care of, namely, to have a "sounding board."[2]

In the second session Balint got the crucial information that the first breakdown followed moving into a new house after the father-in-law's death and that the second breakdown followed taking control of the family business with his brothers from his own father. Balint "saw" a relation here, which was undoubtedly accurate, that the man had difficulty with his two victories over the fathers. But "seeing into" a very paranoid patient is something to be very careful about. The "ear" is more accurate here. But Balint fell into telling the patient that he could "look into" the timing of his disturbance, how the idea of the wife's infidelity had taken him over but recently. The patient then didn't show up for 15 weeks! — until such a worsening of his condition got him sent back to Balint by the wife and GP.

Balint got the message. He thought he was right about the difficulty with victories over father-in-law, father, and rival suitor. He therefore proposed two focal aims for this relationship: 1. that the man be able to *have* his victory over other men; 2. or, if not that, at least to *share* his victory with other men. But he had been wrong about "looking into" the man. Something else would need to be devised.

So the patient got back to Balint, thanks to the wife and the GP, looking haggard and near to a paranoid breakdown. He had deteriorated after the wife had gone to unburden herself to the GP because she could not bear any more cross-examination by Mr. Baker about the rival from 20 years previous. She confessed to Mr. Baker that many stories she had told him were inventions to get him off her back, and that the true story was the first one. Mr. Baker was shook, as Balint noted, for two reasons: one, because he could see what unbearable pressure he was putting on his wife, and two, because it was apparent the wife did do some lying.

I now want to draw attention to the moves made by Balint in this third session, which retrieve his previous error and a dangerous, pending breakdown. The patient will leave on a new course, which will be the drift of the treatment, whatever its ups and downs. I count five crucial interventions in this third session.

The first is another movement of the hand, another "brushing aside." Who has ever taught us to "brush aside" certain destructive activities of the patient? Only Sullivan, I would say, who would refer to such activities as "routinely futile operations" (Chapter 6). Balint wrote:

I brushed to one side all the external events and interpreted his cruelty and ruthlessness to his wife. He had obviously felt very badly hurt by her and ruthlessly took revenge for it. (pp. 30–31)

This is much better for a paranoid patient than "looking into" him! Some severity with these people, as Sullivan recommended also, is much more tolerable. Few besides Sullivan and Balint would realize one could be so rough here. "This he accepted without any difficulty and went on describing how badly he was hurt . . . " (p. 31), how his wife "let him down," how he could not stop himself from tormenting her.

Balint's reply is the second move:

Here I intervened and said that the hurt cannot be undone or escaped from, the only thing that can be done is to accept the fact and live with it; but this apparently is what he cannot do, and here I repeated that he must have this revenge. (p. 31)

Again, like Sullivan, Balint is all ordinary sense here. The hurt must be accepted, but the patient cannot do this ordinary thing. Balint gave the paradox back. One can be in no hurry here. Winnicott would have understood this "hanging fire" altogether. The patient's response took them deeper. He suggested that this "hurt" must have special significance, as he had been hurt before.

Balint accepted this clarification, yet he wanted to move the blame off of the wife, so he "added that this means that the hurt started well before Farah (his wife) appeared on the scene" (p. 31). Balint was determined to get in the way of what the patient was doing destructively, which would only make his situation worse. He did not want this patient to drive his wife way past the point of (her great) toleration.

The patient readily agreed that he had been hurt before his wife appeared on the scene and went on to talk about how "inferior" he had been to every man, including the suitor he defeated. Every detail showed the virtue of the other man.

Balint made his fourth move:

I then picked it up and showed him that the same details admitted just the opposite interpretation, namely that Mr. Baker was superior to the other man. He was greatly surprised but could not escape its impact. (p. 31)

Here is one of Balint's surprises. Not only did he stand against the man's ruthless attacks, but he refused to accept the opposite, that the man wanted to offer himself as a humiliated, inferior fellow. After all, this latter would only drive him back into his cruelty.[3] Neither would do. Balint had learned something from "looking into" the man in session two. It wouldn't do. Since the man degraded himself, he would assume Balint's thinking to agree with his own. Balint made this impossible by assuming the opposite tack. The man was "superior." Notice how similar this move was to Sullivan's tack with the Housewife-Economist, whose lack of interest in starting the day's housework "encouraged" Sullivan "more than otherwise."

Mr. Baker then went on to describe running away from a number of previous relations with women, from "easy meat" prostitutes and girls he might get pregnant. Time being overrun, Mr. Baker asked for treatment. Balint offered a few more sessions to see what could be done this way or whether the patient needed analysis. But should he, the patient asked, go on or refrain from churning over these incidents with his wife? The patient was giving Balint another version of the paradox. Balint could not support the churning up (grinding up) of the wife; nor could he forbid it. So he finishes:

I told him I could give him no instructions; he must do what he's got to do, but the only thing I would like would be that he should report it truthfully during the next session. (p. 32)

From here to the final, twenty-seventh session, there are few intervals of smooth sailing, but the drift has been set which will carry them through. The patient has offered a number of possible relationships for himself and Balint. Balint has opposed the two which are very destructive: his humiliating himself to others or his ruthlessly cross-examining and punishing others. In other words, Balint opposed the two "routinely futile operations" (Sullivan, Chapter 6) of the man's family — what his mother did to his father, what his father did to his mother.[4]

Balint also identified two other actual relations which the patient is capable of and which have a constructive drift. Balint allows that the patient had to feel hurt and that the patient has won. The job is to allow these constructive relations while standing in the way of the destructive relations.

In the next session the patient tempted Balint into hearing about his homosexual, degraded relations, which Balint countered again. Indeed, Balint declared the man had won. Mr. Baker then became relatively secure, curling up in a dream with a big snake, which Balint interpreted as himself.[5]

When Balint attempted to "tail off" treatment, the patient tried to rip up Balint as he had his wife. Balint survived the onslaught, barely. Balint was taken deeply into a dive into despair and destructiveness. This second half of the treatment mended together the man's capacity for success and his previous desolation of childhood. Here was a father who could tolerate both extremes of the patient. The result was a spectacular success on four-year follow-up.[6]

CHARACTER ANALYSIS IN A NEW LIGHT

If one is going to get in the way of destructive relations or routinely futile operations, one had better have an adequate idea of what can take their place. As early as the beginning of the 1930s, Balint saw that the idea of Reich and of his teacher, Ferenczi, often worked out poorly. Balint spent the next 40 years working out his own solution, which is summarized in his book, *The Basic Fault* (1968).

Reich and Ferenczi both believed that many forms of rigid character have no further possibilities. The rigidity can only generate more destructiveness or futility. The only way to go forward is to go backward first, giving up the hopeless rigidity for a more primitive developmental state with more plasticity or fluidity. From that more primitive state, the patient may go forward again with a greater wealth of possibilities. This is the basic idea of a therapeutic regression.

Balint realized that you could think of this regression in terms of the psychoanalytic perspective or the interpersonal perspective. He followed John

Rickman's characterization of the two perspectives as either "one-body" or "two-body" psychology, that is, involving only the one-body, intrapsychic idea of psychoanalysis, or the two-body relation of the interpersonal scheme. Balint thought that it made an enormous practical difference which of the two perspectives you took to think about regression (1968, p. 159).

In terms of one-body psychology, regression is a return to primitive gratification. In terms of two-body psychology, regression is a return to a primitive relationship. For example, Ferenczi described his Croatian Musician as needing to get back to her primitive desires for voluptuous sensation. This is a one-body idea. But we could equally describe the regression in two-body perspective as a regression to a relationship in which she showed herself off. For a second example, Reich described his Passive-Feminine Character as needing to get back to his ferocious desires. This is also a one-body idea, which we could equally describe as a need for a primitive relationship in which he had the upper hand.

Both Ferenczi and Reich saw these two patients, and all other patients, in one-body perspective, as being able to recover their own vitality from repression as primitive gratification. Often they were able to see such patients through the dangers of such an experiment, so that the full force of the instincts could become available to their patients, and then become tamed.

The risk of this kind of experiment is not negligible, however. Balint followed many of Ferenczi's cases before and after Ferenczi died in 1933. Balint found that many got better temporarily, but returned to a "regression for the sake of gratification," which had a "malignant" course, with more and more grand looking after being required to quiet the violent demands. This is the kind of situation many of us would remember from Blanche in *Streetcar Named Desire*. Balint, therefore, thought that "regression for the sake of gratification" was quite dangerous and only workable for some patients.[7]

Balint thought that it was much more promising to think of regression to a primitive *relationship*; this offered little but ordinary gratification, but wide latitude for the *display* of primitive attitudes, feelings and conceptions. He called this "regression for the sake of recognition." He gradually worked out over 40 years the rules for conducting such a regression, which he presented then most clearly in *The Basic Fault* (1968). Not all patients are capable of such a "benign regression," which only gets into demands to have primitive states *recognized* and then allows the patient to go forward from the primitive, plastic, fluid regression. However, the following rules make benign "regression for the sake of recognition" much more likely. These rules can be summarized in three principles.

First, the doctor should offer a *minimum of interpretation*, so there is no pretension to omniscience. Rather, the doctor ought to be more interested in the interpretations or "independent discoveries" made by the patient. This stance will make the doctor and patient into roughly *equal* partners in this job of "recognition." In the Case of the Stationery Manufacturer, this stance would work against the tendency of this patient to degrade himself, as he acted more and more of an equal partner as the case went along. While his "independent discoveries" were very few in the first third of the case, and more in the second third, they were equal in number to Balint's interpretations in the final third (p. 131).

Second, the doctor should put up a *minimum of resistance to being used* by the patient as he needs to use him. The doctor is to be like a "primary substance," like earth, air, fire or water, there to be made use of, to carry the patient along. Balint recognized that this man needed to use him as a "sounding board." This was in the right direction. But when Balint proposed to "look into" the patient, he violated this second principle. The patient is to *use the doctor, not vice versa.*

Third, the doctor is to *avoid any* suggestion or *promise of omnipotence*, such as the unfortunate idea that he might be able to bring the patient out of the regression. Rather he must only be there, be reliable, be *indestructible*. Balint had to have believed in this principle to get through the second half of this treatment with Mr. Baker, which would otherwise have been intolerable. The patient came out of his regression when he had put Balint through enough, so both recognized what intolerable loneliness he had endured in childhood.

Two other brief, lovely examples might give the reader a little more feel for these principles. The first is Balint's waiting 30 minutes for a patient to speak in a session:

The silence was eventually broken by the patient starting to sob, relieved, and soon after he was able to speak. He told his analyst that at long last he was able to reach himself; ever since childhood he had never been left alone, there had always been someone telling him what to do. (1968, p. 142)

Words are not as important for this method as the relation which the patient must get from the doctor. Words can lead up to a possible relation, but the doctor must be ready to receive what then can be displayed. Consider the second example:

At about this time, she was given the interpretation that apparently the most important thing for her was to keep her head safely up, with both feet firmly planted on the ground. In response, she mentioned that ever since her earliest childhood she could never do a somersault; although at various periods she tried desperately to do one. I then said: "What about it now?"—whereupon she got up from the couch and, to her great amazement, did a perfect somersault without any difficulty. This proved to be a real breakthrough. (1968, pp. 128–129)

Balint believed that many patients have been failed by their environment before words were available to the child-adult or in ways words can never describe. The closest he could come himself in words was to say that these patients have been defaulted upon by their environment, or that a fault existed in the environment which now existed in the patient or in the patient's relation to his environment. Given this kind of situation, one can lead up to the fault with words, but it can *only be traversed by relations*. Such relations are the confidence of the doctor in the patient's somersault or the doctor's waiting a half-hour without telling the patient what to do. In the Case of the Stationery Manufacturer, we are talking about the doctor's becoming first a sounding board, later in a dream a big snake with whom the patient could snuggle, and finally someone or something indestructible to take back with him into the desolation of his childhood.

The overall movement hoped for was described by Balint in the same Kleinian language used by Winnicott. The first problem is to get back to a very primitive relation, this "primary relationship" in which one is used by the patient as a "primary object," as earth, air, fire or water, so to speak. The "paranoid position" of the patient stands in the way. For example, Mr. Baker seemed to be allowing Balint to become his "sounding board" because of Balint's brilliant intuition that this man who was ruthlessly tormenting his wife with jealousy might need such an object. But one wrong sentence from Balint about "looking into" the patient and their relation was disrupted for 15 weeks. This is the "paranoid position." A series of moves from Balint from the third through the ninth session were necessary to allow Mr. Baker to believe in Balint's reliability. In the ninth session the patient reported that the week before had been "one of the best weeks of his life" and asked to talk from notes about his fear of "utter loneliness," his dread of being "forgotten and abandoned," and his father's behaving towards him with "utter unconcern" (p. 50). Balint's final move here was to appreciate the man's "marked dependence" on his father and on Balint himself, which explained "why he so easily accepted any homosexual approach." After this final move, the patient offered the "most pleasant dream in which a big snake, a very friendly creature, snuggled up to him and put his head in his lap. He was not afraid at all" (p. 50). This is what Balint meant about overcoming "the paranoid position" to reach actual dependency.

Once dependability is gotten, the second major problem to be expected is that of the "depressive position," which is that the patient's destructiveness is actually aroused by any interference with his primary relation, so that the patient needs to acknowledge that parts of himself are actually bad and need to be "above all mourned for . . . and buried with full honours" (1952, p. 255).

For this man, Mr. Baker, the depressive problem is how ruthlessly he would punish anyone giving him less than he wanted. Balint and Mrs. Baker got it again and again in the second half of the treatment, when Balint attempted to "tail off" treatment. The second half of Balint's effort was chiefly involved in bringing up to Mr. Baker his destructiveness, as something to be given up. A very fine statement of this is in session 15, where Balint could take him to task for flaunting the use of prostitutes to his wife:

I summed up the situation that apparently Mr. Baker's liberation has to be paid for by Mrs. Baker's pains and that there is a real problem to be solved: how much liberation is to be achieved at the price of how much suffering? (p. 63)

At the same time Balint had to be "adamant" against this destructiveness, he had to accept, for the time being, that it was necessary to the patient. There is a fine passage in session 18 along this line:

He went on questioning why it is that he must relentlessly persist with his questioning. After some time I proposed that he cannot tolerate any disharmony between himself and an important person in his environment . . . that perhaps this was one of the reasons for his recent bad period, that he felt we two did not understand each other and that was more than he could tolerate. (p. 75)

This struggle went many rounds, until the patient was able to emerge in session 23 with his own notes, acknowledging his profound insecurity about being let go as a child and continuing as an adult, which drove this destructiveness. Balint nearly had given up. He wrote: "Although the therapist tried to remain steadfast, he could not escape completely from the emotional impact of this almost unbearable turmoil" (p. 91).

I do not see very much acknowledgment by this patient of his own destructiveness. I do not see a mourning of his ruthless questioning. But he did appear to give it up. This is what Balint was after, and this theoretical idea about the "depressive position" was what guided the second half of the management of the case.

This outline of the rules for the "regression for the sake of recognition" fits Winnicott's method as well as Balint's. Winnicott would have put the matter in his own words, but I think the reader will get to the same technique by either language. It is useful to have both languages, since for individual reasons we sometimes are more accessible to one than the other. Winnicott would have said that he went back for a "starting point" where the patient could "live from," then "carried the patient through the necessary destructiveness." Whatever the words, both depended on the elastic, primitive relationship as the temporary alternative to the rigid, destructive or futile pattern which had no way to go forward.

What is a little different in Balint is his explicit concern for the dangers of the procedure, which he knew so well from Ferenczi. Winnicott had little to say about this. Therefore, we get from Balint a more explicit set of rules for heeding the dangers of "regression for the sake of gratification," for getting a "regression for the sake of recognition." Both men followed these rules, but Balint was clearer about them.

THE DOMAIN OF THIS TECHNIQUE

What gave this technique such latitude was Balint's freedom in adopting such a range of possible relationships that could be defined between a patient and a doctor. He was wonderfully adaptive to the terms needed by the client. He could even adapt to medical doctors. When he worked with general practitioners, he appreciated that they needed to see themselves as objective, descriptive doctors. Therefore, he offered the study of their difficult relations with their patients as the study of "the pharmacology of the drug 'doctor'," "the most important drug in the pharmacopeia." When he got going with them working in the GP Group, he would prove himself even more careful and cautious than they were! As he described in his famous article in the *Lancet* (1955b), the foremost English medical journal, he would show doctors how little was known about "prescribing oneself," such as: "When to start?" "When to stop?" "What are the unexpected consequences?" As I have described in my previous writing on Balint (Gustafson, 1981), which I will not repeat here, Balint could also recognize and appreciate all the different, useful kinds of doctoring that can be offered. His GPs were objective-descriptive, psychoanalytic, existential, or interpersonal, and that was all right with him, and well recognized (Balint, 1957). Very few of us have this kind of latitude for appreciating different kinds of adaptive behavior.

He did the same for patients. Myerson (1982) noticed how Balint picked up on the "special circumstances" of Mr. Baker's successful adaptation and would not let go of this finding. The man had won. He could learn to have his victory, or he could learn to share it with another man. Few of us can keep our eye on the special virtue of this adaptation when overrun by the patient's maladaptation.

Few of us also can "brush aside" destructive or futile operations, as Balint did the ruthless questioning in the first session and over and over again later. Balint was willing to make up his mind that some such operations are indeed destructive or futile and stand "adamant" against them, while understanding they are necessary to the patient for the time being.

Finally, few of us can then allow ourselves to be used in a nonverbal primitive relation, to be at ease in something which is not organized by words, in which the atmosphere is almost all that matters. To bring up a favorite phrase of Balint, doctors have to be allowed "the courage of their own stupidity" for patients to be allowed to have the same.

In other words, who else could be so catholic about potential adaptation, so trenchant when necessary, and yet so unorganized when necessary? Only Balint, Winnicott, and Sullivan that I know, which makes them my favorite trio in the realm of psychotherapy. This trinity of virtues is no recent discovery, however, for their recognition by Homer in Odysseus stands at the very beginning of nearly 30 centuries of Western literature.[9] Such virtues in a doctor give him or her great latitude. We have only begun to see how far this can be taken with brief psychotherapy, since Balint, Winnicott, and Sullivan did some brief psychotherapy of adults but were mostly preoccupied with other serious clinical problems.

But every technique has it limited domain, no matter how impressive. I see two major limitations for the technique of Balint. First, like Winnicott,

Balint had very little idea of the systemic field which surrounds an individual patient, how it might be clarified or reckoned with. In the Case of the Stationery Manufacturer, he never reckoned with the tremendous loyalty of Mr. Baker to his own parents, whose most destructive relations the patient was reenacting.[10]

Since Balint did not reckon with the systemic field, he depended on this surrounding environment being "good enough" to be more helpful to the patient than otherwise, if only the patient could contain his own mistrust and destructiveness. I use Winnicott's phrase here of the "good enough" environment, because he and Balint both depended on this background. Indeed, in the Case of the Stationery Manufacturer, Balint relied over and over again upon the helpfulness and tolerance and even tremendous devotion of the patient's wife and GP. Avery (1982) is right to say this picture could not be other than an idealization, that there must be some circular interaction between Mr. and Mrs. Baker, where she unconsciously threw him off his stride to maintain some kind of equilibrium for herself. He noted some evidence for this hypothesis. Yet Balint could get away, in this case, with paying this systemic interaction no attention, because the environment was "good enough" to allow the patient's drift towards improvement. It is doubtful whether he could have gotten away with this assumption, and his technique, if the man had had only his destructive relations with his parents. Mr. Baker would never have come back for his third session, after Balint misstepped in the second, but for the wife and GP, and he would never have had the wife who could both weather his pounding and indicate when she could not bear it anymore. With only his own parents, he would have gotten neither. He would not have been "carried through" his own destructiveness between sessions and he would not have been "looked after" when he needed that. As Winnicott stated outright, you do not do this kind of work when there is not a good enough environment to carry the patient back over the ground traversed by the interview.

When the environment is more thoroughly hostile, it must be read very accurately, as provided for in the technique of Sullivan (Chapter 6) and that of the Milan team, which I will describe in Chapter 16. There are many environments where a more positive emergence of the patient would be destroyed by the collective action of others who needed him to stay the same for the sake of system stability. In such situations, the technique of Balint is not sufficient. When Mr. Baker was a child, such would have been the situation, where Winnicott would have declined a therapeutic consultation. He was so used by both parents. When Mr. Baker was grownup and successful, the necessary assistance in the environment was in place for Balint's technique to be successful.

The second limitation of Balint's technique is related to the first. Not only did he require a good enough environment, but he also required a patient with some kind of successful adaptation. The patient may have been slipping very badly into a paranoid psychotic break, but there was strength to build on, to build back. This man was the driving force in his family business, a good husband when not crazy, and the able father of three children. If the technique is going to come up against enormous dread and longing for dependency, as well as enormous destructiveness, there had better be something in the patient which is actual strength, if the doctor is going to get in and get out in 15 months with 27 sessions! Both the "good enough" environment and the patient with considerable strengths are necessary for a brief psychotherapy with very disturbed patients with this technique of Balint.

THE FOREST RANGER

We first saw this young man in our clinic when he was in his first year of the university and could not tell his high school girlfriend that their relationship was over. He got quite down about himself. He would go home to placate her even when he did not want to absent himself from the exciting life at the university. He would make a stand against being with her and become anxious that he was breaking her heart. And so forth.

He seemed to be a very friendly kid. He looked healthy. There was a very winning smile, and the color rose to his cheeks easily. You could see right away that he would have many friends, and so he did. He was full of good intentions. He hoped to study in the university so he might do something about protecting the environment.

We offered him brief therapy about his girlfriend problem, which he used, apparently, quite well. He got better at asserting himself with the girlfriend, broke up with her, and yet seemed to feel all right about himself. I did not see him then for several years, until he telephoned me one winter morning to say he felt an urge to throw himself off the top of a building.

I saw him right away, of course, and found myself with an altogether different patient. I was quite alarmed. He described being cornered by several people who had decided he was their friend. He could never say no. He was forever going along with dinners and dates and bicycle rides and what have you — indeed, whatever was proposed to him. He would try to slip away as often as he could. He did not allow himself to resent any of this. He hated himself for preferring to be alone, for getting away from his well-meaning friends. He only loved his dog. He felt nothing for other people. This seemed terribly wrong to him. Maybe he ought to kill himself, since he had always felt this way, and always would. He would never belong.

I managed to get him through this dangerous time, when I was concerned about him as ever I have been about a patient. I believe what was essential from me was my conveying to him that he was a worthwhile person, whatever he might find unacceptable about his own responses to other people. After several months of self-berating, and rather constant suicidal thinking, he came out of this morbid state and began to be interested in his studies and in outdoor activities. He still seemed incapable of saying no to his friends, but he got better at making excuses and looked forward to getting away from several of them at graduation. I was relieved he was better for the time being, and did not stand in the way of his going east for the summer after graduation.[11]

The young man came back to me that fall, having spent the summer in the east as a forest ranger. He was feeling suicidal again, but he had some confidence that he and I would find a way out. Now we come to where Balint has been so useful.

My problem all along had been finding a map that would explain the psychological territory of this young man. We had taken him first for a relatively healthy young fellow with some depressive anxiety about assertion. This appeared right at the time, but then the second look had been much, much worse. Still, even when I had gotten him through his beating himself up, I understood little more than his own cruelty to himself.

Fortunately, I came upon Balint's paper from 1955, "Friendly Expanses — Horrid Empty Spaces," where he described the following patient:

The other patient, also a young woman, a doctor, never wanted to have a home. Since her late student days she had gone from one resident post to another, feeling all her possessions to be a burden. Finally, as a generous compromise, she agreed with herself to tolerate as many personal belongings as two suitcases could hold. They were suitcases of very moderate size, because one condition of the agreement was that in any emergency she should be able to pick them up herself and walk away with them. . . . She had an uncanny power of winning people's affection, confidence and deep gratitude; she was really a perfect listener, saying only the right word at the right time. Many people, from royalty to railway porters, from professors of medicine to laboratory stewards, called her their friend and would have done anything for her if she had but asked them. Several men asked her to marry them; she always got out of it, but remained the trusted friend of them all for life. . . . So she developed an admirable skill in dealing with people who needed her, but only so that she might be left at peace afterwards. . . . Objects, both human and physical, were a nuisance to her. . . . She accepted her success with some pride and satisfaction, and then got away as painlessly and speedily as possible. . . . It is true that both these women were ill, even very ill. (pp. 225–226)

Thanks to Balint, I now had a map. My forest ranger was one of these people so sought after because of the skill to give others what they want. I could see now how we had thought he was relatively well, only needing a little help with assertion. I could also see why he was so glad to be alone:

For the philobat [Balint's term], the whole world is quite different. Provided the elements are not too cruel, e.g. no storm or gale is raging, the pilot is quite safe in the sky, the sailor on the high seas, and the skier on the slopes, the driver on the open road, the parachutist in the air. Danger and fear are evoked only if an object appears that has to be negotiated; the pilot has to take off or land; the sailor has to take his ship in or out of harbour; the skier has to negotiate rocks, trees or crevasses; the driver other cars or pedestrians on the road; the parachutist has to jump off or land. We may therefore say that the philobatic world consists of friendly expanses dotted more or less densely with dangerous and unpredictable objects. One lives in the friendly expanses, carefully avoiding hazardous contacts with potentially dangerous objects. (p. 228)

Now this is indeed how the world looked to my patient, the forest ranger, but he had never gotten any understanding about it. On the contrary, he was forever being told by his family and friends that "being close" to other people was the most important thing in life. Given that his feelings ran to the opposite conclusion, he was forever thinking something was wrong with him. No wonder he was in such despair. He was being encouraged to follow a line of development which was, actually, impossible for him. He could only get worse and worse. At best, I had only been able to keep him from being completely destroyed by this point of view. I had had no alternative. I will describe one hour, in which Balint helped us find another route, a route that will be very difficult but possible for this man.

He began this session, the 183d between us, by saying he didn't understand life at all. How was that? He felt people were silly, jabbering to one another about little things. It didn't seem real to him. He felt like someone sitting in the darkness watching a play that made no sense. Why do people do what they do?

I asked him what was bringing up this subject. He said his best friend, Jack, had been angry at him the evening before for "never confiding." He had felt at a loss for his reply. Why do people want to talk to him? Why do they want to know him? He shook his head, "Do people really want to do these things?"

I knew my patient had been comparing himself with Jack as long as I had known him, always thinking that Jack was a proper man, and he was not. Many of his self-beatings had followed conversations like this one with Jack. It was about time that I replied. I told my patient that there are two kinds of people in this world: those who feel secure when close, like Jack, and those who feel secure in the wide open, lovely spaces, like himself.

He replied that he had been very lonely, and he would like to think there was some way that he could have some relation to people. Somehow, he'd like people in his life, but he always felt cornered by people who wanted to be close like Jack. I asked him if there had not been exceptions to this rule?

Indeed, there had been a girl with whom he took long walks, who liked to sit with coffee and say very little. He had felt very comfortable with her, for most of a summer. She made no demands. They were easy and fun together, so very much alike. However, she had taken up with his best friend. He found them in bed together one fine afternoon, and had been very, very hurt.

I then said to him that I could see how he had felt little or no hope of having people in his life. He had known two alternatives, both bad for him. Either he would get cornered, crowded and trapped by these people who insist on being close. Or he would find someone like himself who wanted room, but he had not learned which of these people could be relied upon. He had known this girl's reputation for promiscuity. He had liked the room she gave him, but really he had been very hurt by her.

I was interested in why he had not gone after other relations like the one with this girl? He said actually there was another girl he was very fond of, who likes distance and roaming about, but Jack had been extremely critical of this friend. My patient felt condemned by Jack, because what Jack said of this girl could be equally said of my patient. Jack said to forget this girl and spend more time with him. The propaganda went on and on. Other friends agreed with Jack.

I said I didn't agree with Jack. Jack had his way, which was fine for him, but not for my patient. I said it only made him feel worse and worse not to be able to follow this advice. He could only think, "What the hell's wrong with me?" He said this was very interesting and he left.

Now I do not mean to say that this single session made all the difference. What I did for my patient was to recognize a direction which had been hopeless, which could only make for more and more despair. This direction was being urged by the patient's friends and family, who probably conveyed to my patient the terrible idea that psychotherapy would help him learn to be close and involved. He would have to fail at that, which would rob him of his last hope. Balint, and Sullivan also, were very clear when some "routinely futile operation" like this was being attempted. One could not go along with such attempts.

On the other hand, one has got to have some notion which one can convey to a patient like this that there is some other possible way he could live. Thanks to Balint's map, I was able to discover that this man *already* had been successful along altogether different lines from closeness and confiding. He had had a problem with the relationship with the girl, but we could help him learn to be more discerning about people like himself. He had been too fast to see her as *just* like himself, just as reliable as himself, when they had only shared a common feeling of how to be comfortable. He could learn to be more discerning. So there was hope for him. I had borrowed successfully from Balint's keen sense of the "special circumstances" (Myerson, 1982) that make possible *different* kinds of adaptations.[12]

This case also introduces the subject of the next two chapters, that is, the occasions in which long-term psychotherapy is necessary. The case of the Forest Ranger could not be brief for two reasons. First, he was not a relatively healthy, secure individual who could become intensely involved and leave with something useful. Second, he did not have a good enough environment which could understand whatever we might traverse in the hours. Sometimes a more disturbed patient, like the Stationery Manufacturer, can get away with a brief therapy because of the capability of the patient and the supporting environment. The Forest Ranger will only get his "regression for the sake of recognition" in a very long series of sessions with me which will take years to conclude.[13] Fortunately, the therapist's office can become a "friendly expanse," and the therapist can become part of that territory, less and less of a treacherous object (Balint, 1955a). There is a way forward for this man. We will now see from Gedo and Havens, two of the leading writers of our time about long-term psychotherapy, when this kind of long procedure is necessary. If we are clear about long-term needs, we can be more decisive about what can be done briefly.

Brief Therapy from the Perspective of Long-Term Therapy

Simplification can be a fairy tale. If the simpler, briefer job is not to be a deception, we need to be able to recognize the complex, long job. Only then can we reckon whether the long route has to be taken. For this reckoning, we need adequate accounts of what the complex, long job looks like. After all, that too could be wishful thinking, that the long "couch dive" is worthwhile. The dive could be little more than a vacation. I find Gedo and Havens the most plausible about long-term therapy. I include them in my array of ideas relevant to brief therapy because these opposites may keep us honest.

Gedo continually invites skepticism because he presents the patient, his mother, or his grandfather as brilliant, beautiful, extraordinary, splendid, gifted, and so forth. Conversely, the spouse or the father is cruel, jealous, ill, pathological, and so forth. The patient will be admired, the spouse renounced. Fairy tales can be long as well as brief therapy! But Gedo is useful, nevertheless, because he describes what his patients are able to manage and not manage in their daily, practical lives. We get a picture of actual deficits being directly addressed by the analyst. We also get a clear theoretical framework about the "hierarchy of personal aims" which has gotten tangled up, which Gedo will help the patient put in order. We also get a clear description of how different identifications may give several, contradictory "constant attitudes."

Gedo, therefore, may be useful to challenge the prevailing tendency of brief therapy to see a single constant attitude and a single hitch in development. He has described so well how patients may be held back by more than one constant attitude, how these different identifications can bring about a string of developmental deficits and a very confused hierarchy of personal aims. With this description of the entire house, we are in a better position to assess what a brief repair can set right — and what it cannot.

Havens provides even more useful correction on the perspective of brief therapy, because he gives us views of the entire canvas of methods in psychiatry. We see how the different schools have had such partial views of the patient that psychiatry has been more often fooled than understanding. The patient is not so easy to find. The patient is not open to view like a house. Gedo has described the hierarchy of personal aims as if you could see it before you. As Havens likes to remark, the brain is in the cranium, but the mind may not be in the room. We are more likely to get some kind of show, whereby the patient gives the doctor what he wants to get. Havens gives an adequate account of the methods for finding the patient with less chance of deception and increasing reliability.

We have a chance of being less foolish about brief therapy if we grasp the complexity of the entire hierarchy of personal aims and if we have methods for locating where the patient actually lives.

9. *Gedo: A Hierarchy of Personal Aims*

A Character out of Toulouse Lautrec

H ERE IS A FINE CASE for introducing long-term work. A previous therapist had attempted psychotherapy for a year with this young man of 25, but gave up to refer the man to Gedo for an analysis. In the initial consultation, Gedo recognized him as a "likeable and enormously talented young man immobilized by the very multiplicity of his goals, none of which did he experience as truly his own" (1979, p. 39). Listen to the complications set up by this young man:

He said he was a graduate student, but he had in fact dropped out of school, in so complicated and gradual a manner and with such an accumulation of unfinished obligations that he could not even reregister without having first met these old commitments, a task that would take many months of effort. On the other hand, he definitely did not consider himself to be a part of the adult world; he continued to live on the campus of the university he had formerly attended, very much part of the student community, undecided about what he might wish to be "when he grew up"—all this in spite of the fact that he had been completely self-supporting for several years and was a full-time *employee* of the university, playing an important, albeit self-taught, technical role in a long-term project involving the administration of the institution. Moreover, he felt himself to be completely isolated from the *students*, who were then almost uniformly caught up in the facile political enthusiasms of opposition to the Vietnam war, an issue he tended to view with the moral detachment and sense of tragedy of a Thucydides scholar. On the other hand, he expressed his distaste for mid-America and its constraints by adhering to such manifestations of the counter-culture as a consuming interest in rock music, underground films, and taking various drugs, and by adopting a manner of dress which was both theatrical and eccentric. (1979, pp. 39–40)

How was Gedo to entertain the multiplicity of this existence without becoming lost himself? A very nice technical problem for long-term therapists.

Gedo challenged this young man's living arrangements as suddenly as Sullivan took on the Housewife-Economist. While Gedo has never mentioned Sullivan in his books, listen to the similarity of the opening moves:

It was in connection with these (theatrical and eccentric) behaviors that we succeeded in establishing our mode of working together; when he asked me what my attitude to his drug-taking would be, I replied that I doubted whether he could afford to pay for drugs as well as analysis at the same time—a statement that made him laugh with surprise and delight and one that was literally borne out by subsequent events. As for his clothing, within a few days of starting our work, and in response to his own declarations about feeling a lack of authenticity, I told him that his dress made me feel he was impersonating someone else, like a character out of a Toulouse Lautrec poster. With a glow about being understood, he confirmed somewhat sheepishly that he had copied the costume of the star performer in the most celebrated of these works. (p. 40)

And on they went, with Gedo asking of one arrangement after another: Why not do the ordinary thing? You can't pay for analysis? Why not have the university pay you for the value you are giving them? You don't want to take money from your mother? Hell, she can't stop you paying her back, even if you have to pay her estate! Gedo could see like Sullivan into complicated arrangements for the missing ability. He could read what was missed growing up. The young man had been the favorite of a devoted, intrusive, and very well organized mother. Unfortunately, his mother also applied her "genius" to looking after the patient's father, a cranky, jealous, paranoid man, and to her own father, an "outstanding figure" in the musical life of their city. Both of these latter projects were at the patient's expense, since father hated the precious son, and since mother gave herself over to nursing the dying grandfather when the patient was four. The boy was left in the lurch.

He did what Reich (1930) described so well. He lifted himself out of the childhood neurosis of unmet needs by identifying with the attitude of someone he admired. He could be *above* his own needs with such a "constant attitude." Although Gedo has not mentioned Reich in his recent books, he has improved on Reich by showing that the "constant attitude" can be several "constant attitudes," based on variations of the admired adult or based on several different admired adults. For this man, there was mostly his mother's attitude of making the extraordinary try. But he also borrowed from his grandfather, Einstein, Toulouse Lautrec, the opera, and even his father.

But placing himself above his own needs by taking himself to be a version of his extraordinary mother had a series of effects on his growing up. First, he did not learn to protect himself from being assaulted, as, for example, by his older brother. "Instead of fighting back, he had turned to the manipulation of a toy microcosm he had constructed inside a small box" (p. 42). The attitude of contempt for the brother stood in place of the missing ability. "Secondly, he could never calm himself sufficiently to go to sleep when she (mother) was out, but immediately fell asleep when he heard the parents' car coming into the garage. This inability to manage his own tensions was still troubling him, and the only way he could get along was to be utterly without scheduled obligations . . . when he was bound to the clock, his disrupted diurnal rhythms caused him to lose track of the schedule and fail in whatever he undertook" (pp. 43–44). The attitude of the extraordinary try to do many things stood in place of the missing ability to calm himself. Thirdly, he never learned to tell when his capability was actually remarkable and when it was foolishly exaggerated. He could not recognize his own worth to the university, but then he would exaggerate his power to save his girlfriend the pop singer. He could not make these distinctions, which would have permitted him to be sensible. The attitude of the extraordinary try stood in place of sense.

What we are discussing are failures at Level I, II, and III in Gedo's scheme of the hierarchy of personal aims. This man lacked the ability to calm himself (I), to defend and organize himself in a coherent way (II), and to understand what was illusion and what was capability (III). The virtue of Gedo's scheme is that one can say what is missing, just like that, in one sentence, or in a diagram on a single page (e.g., Figure 11, p. 195). Sullivan could be right to the point about missing capabilities in the patient, like this, but he was not as succinct in his theoretical statement about the critical developmental steps. Sullivan's *Interpersonal Theory of Psychiatry* (1953) is a rambling book. The "hierarchy of personal aims" in Gedo's *Beyond Interpretation* (1979) is so clear and concise that one can readily keep in mind what deficits to be concerned about.

Gedo then could go directly to work on helping the patient construct a good enough "holding environment" for himself. Like Winnicott, he was willing to adapt himself to recognizing and meeting these early needs:

He had given his mother many cues that he required her guidance, as he was now cuing the analyst that he needed the availability of a calm person who could keep track of a program arranged in accordance with the relative importance of its various parts. The analyst's statement that getting his head examined was for the patient the most crucial of his current enterprises and that all else had to be subordinated to coming to his sessions at the correct time made sense to him, and he gradually gained the ability to make some order out of the chaos of his previous drifting, at least during the working week. (p. 44)

Perhaps there is even an improvement on Winnicott (1965a), in that the specific needs for a "holding environment" are better defined, which allows us to think about whether they are being met or not. The specific needs are for calm (Level I), for organization which can be defended (Level II), and for less illusion about strengths and weaknesses (Level III). This young man *sacrificed* all of these profound needs to his archaic ambition to be extraordinarily helpful like his mother. He was above such needs. Therefore, he was subject to extreme overstimulation, chaos, and illusions that were then rudely punctured.

Gedo's interest in the "holding environment" missing from this man's life had three major effects in the first year of the analysis. One was that Gedo got a clearer picture of how the man sacrificed these needs to be extraordinarily helpful like his mother:

On the one hand, everywhere he went the patient felt drawn into attempts to rescue or to help needful people. . . . This was of one piece with his general attitude of having to be above mundane matters. . . . He also showed lack of moderation in his choice of women, getting involved in an affair with a rising pop singer whose frenetic lifestyle was hardly compatible with his felt need for order and calm. When her infidelities and general unreliability drove him into wishing to disengage from her, his sense of values did not permit him to drop her, no matter how bothersome she had become, so long as she expressed a need for him. (p. 48)

The second effect was that the

analytic experience had become essential for him if the patient wanted to maintain his sense of direction and purpose. Every interruption of the schedule of appointments, at first even that of an ordinary weekend break, disorganized him. After he had learned about this pattern, which he conceptualized as being equivalent to the necessity of utilizing a program in computer work, he became able to bridge the gap from one scheduled appointment to the next. (p. 49)

The third effect was that the analyst who had become this essential self-object was idealized.

How then did the patient get better from the second through the fourth year of the analysis? An incident from the second year may serve as a telling example. The patient thought he saw his previous female therapist with an infant. This misidentification suggested to Gedo that the young man might have felt deserted by his mother when his younger sister was born. Several months after that, it turned out, the grandfather had become ill, and the mother had thrown herself into nursing him.

The patient's principal early memory was that of riding his tricycle all alone, back and forth on the sidewalk in front of the grandparents' house . . . his mother had been under great stress because her husband absolutely could not tolerate any sign of mourning; it was from this period that the patient's feeling nothing was right anymore actually dated: if mother was not perfect, nothing could be right. As the emotional climate of this period of his childhood was being reconstructed . . . the patient realized that his paramour was a psychotic woman, and he grasped the impossibility of his grandiose quest to repair her pathology through the magic of personal contact. He also realized that such efforts were in identification with his mother's caretaking attitude toward everyone, especially with her success in coping with her husband's paranoia—even at the cost of relinquishing her deep emotional need to mourn for her father. (p. 50)

It is a series of episodes in analysis like this one which permits giving up an adopted attitude, so that the patient can meet his own needs for calm, for organization, and for clarity about his own actual power. When he became able to provide his "holding environment" for himself, he no longer had to idealize Gedo as his infallible self-object.[1] This passed with the man's gathering up his own strength.

Gedo's Technique, Summarized

I have built up Gedo's technique for myself and for the reader in familiar terms, using what we know of Sullivan, Reich, and Winnicott (see Chapters 6, 4, and 7). But something disconcerting and even strange occurs to this picture once you grasp the "hierarchy of personal aims." This frightening effect is not described by Gedo himself, who writes of theory in the usual bland, latinate, psychoanalytic style:

I have offered a hypothesis which views the effectiveness of treatment as a result of the correction of the unfavorable outcome of various developmental crises. A corollary of this theory is the inference that different modalities of intervention are indicated to deal with the consequences of pathogenic experiences at varying developmental levels. At the archaic end of this continuum, analysis must supply for the patient a "holding environment," the provision of which is made possible only by the analyst's accurate perception of the analysand's objective needs through empathy. By contrast, at the more mature end of the scale, the principal issues center on the conflicts around the analysand's subjective wishes. (1979, pp. 261–2)

I find the "hierarchy of personal aims" disconcerting, because it allows us to see how a move at one level of the self may upset arrangements at all other levels. What is most strange for us who think of ourselves as having neurotic conflicts (Level IV) is that looking into such events may show us lost in some illusion, defending a lopsided organization, and unable to sleep because of overstimulation (Levels III, II and I disturbed). We can be shaken to our boots. We can feel all too well what troubles our most disturbed patients. Gedo is saying that *all* analyses will arouse these more primitive needs and weaknesses, and will have to meet them to be helpful. Now if we can tolerate the frightening implications of his knowledge, we may be able to use it. It can organize what we can do with the methods of Sullivan, Reich, and Winnicott.

Now I may summarize Gedo's technique more simply by starting from its center in the hierarchy of personal needs. How did Gedo know right away to challenge this young man about the organization (Level II) of his finances and the illusion (Level III) of his "costume" from Toulouse Lautrec? The answer is that the man himself was complaining about these deeper levels being out of control. He could not pay for analysis and he felt inauthentic. When the doctor sees that gross illusions, shoddy organization, and overstimulation are setting a person up for a bad fall (Levels III, II, and I) and the individual is asking for help about this, then we may ask why in the hell the person is doing things that way? Why not the ordinary solution? Sullivan's line of questioning can be put to a very relieving use!

This has two major effects. One is that the person may become very dependent on the doctor for a more reliable solution to these essential, objective needs. Winnicott's adaptation to need is therefore very relieving. Once the patient has merged into this kind of relationship, he may then make clear his devotion to previous parenting. Here, Reich's description is the original map. The patient adopted the parent's constant attitude to dismiss his own unmet needs. In childhood this made him less tense (I), organized to suit the parent (II), and sharing of the illusion of the parent (III). But this local success often works poorly in the larger world. Now it is possible to demonstrate the *sacrifice of the essential needs* (I, II, and III) that *occurs in continuing to adopt* the parental attitude. The young man became able to see his rescue of the pop singer was an impossible job, which destroyed his calm, the organization of his life, and his ability to tell illusion from capability. Of course, many further lessons of this kind were necessary over the next two years of the man's analysis, since the man had so little experience in keeping himself well, and since so many situations invite the familiar sacrifice. Modern culture is a maze of overstimulation, overextended organization, and invitations to illusion. It is difficult for any person to stay well, let alone those who have little experience along this line.

What Is Useful from Gedo for Brief Therapy

The reader should understand that Gedo is no proponent of brief therapy. Quite the contrary. He thinks most neurotic characters have these different identifications which hide many developmental deficits. All are very complex. All do best in analysis. Brief therapy is allowable and useful only for "current developmental crises" (Gedo, 1964, 1981, personal communication).

Yet I find in his work some contributions which are very useful to the field of brief therapy. The first two are confirmations of the interpersonal revolution. They rid us of dogma, very succinctly. First, Gedo tersely describes the shift of attention of psychoanalysis, from the study of "isolated compromise formations" (wishes, slips, dreams, symptoms) to the "patterns of human adaptation we have designated as *character*" (1979, p. 165). The latter needs to be our concern. Secondly, Gedo confirms the idea of Winnicott that the "*holding environment*" is necessary to helping many neurotic characters. Only when this kind of patient feels "held" in this background of the archaic good relationship can he show how unable he is to calm himself, to organize himself, and to give up limiting illusions. Only then could the risk be taken to show how ill one has been. Only then may the patient give up the "constant attitudes" which have obscured the illness.

The other three contributions are useful for orienting ourselves to possible complexity: of deficits, of identifications, of levels of disturbance. First, the possible deficits are now familiar to us from the Character Out of Toulouse Lautrec. Some progress might be made with such a young man in brief therapy, but it would soon be destroyed by some agitation, some contradiction in his boggled plans, or some disaster unforseen through his lenses of illusion. Most of my failures in brief therapy have occurred when I have overlooked the patient's inability to provide a "good enough" environment for him or herself. The patient got temporarily better, until the weaknesses at Level I, II, or III were demonstrated by subsequent events. Gedo's description of these weaknesses can alert our selection for brief therapy.

The second kind of complexity that we need to be concerned about in brief therapy is the possibility of several or more "constant attitudes," which may pin the patient down from showing what is wrong. Gedo describes these "disavowed" worlds, especially in his Case Two (1979). This was a very masochistic woman, who lost her Maronite nurse at age two, when her family left Lebanon for the United States. The needs tied up in the nurse were disavowed by taking on her own mother's superior, blue-blood outlook. This attitude, in turn, was hidden by the patient's appearing to take the attitude of her modest, saintly father. Both attitudes removed the child from her needs with the nurse, but both kept the child-adult from ever making up the failure. Imagine taking this patient into brief therapy, thinking one might get her over this attitude of modest, saintly denial of her assertion. Imagine her scorn! Gedo's more complex description of these plural constant attitudes may help us to be skeptical of what appears to be a simple formulation.

Finally, there is the running together of levels of disturbance. All too often in the field of brief therapy, we are asked to believe that the patient has some particular neurotic conflict (Level IV). Gedo's description of the accompanying disturbances at the deeper levels may help us. We may be prepared to see as well that the patient feels deeply disillusioned (Level III), or unable to defend herself (Level II), or full of unbearable tension (Level I). Now, these latter disturbances down the hierarchy of personal aims may be secondary, but they may be deeply felt by the patient. The doctor may give too little when he only gives an understanding of the patient's conflict (Level IV). He may also need to appreciate: that the lost illusion is tolerable only when the actual strengths of the patient are recognized (Level III); that the patient may need to think about defending herself better (Level II); that her overstimulation may call for the doctor to be unruffled (Level I) despite provocation. Such a theory as we get from Gedo could keep us from overlooking the holding environment that may be needed as much as the accurate understanding of the conflict.

The Domain of Gedo's Technique

If we acknowledge the theoretical importance of the stable adaptation of character to environment, of holding environments, and of possible complexity of deficits, identifications, and levels of disturbance, then what do patients need from us? Gedo's reply is that everyone needs analysis, with the exceptions of those who are in danger of regression into psychosis and of those who need to be in the hospital: "Accordingly, I believe that psychoanalysis is now the treatment of choice not only for the neuroses, but for the whole array of characterological problems, however archaic their genesis" (1981, pp. 12–13). He means *analysis*, and *not* long-term psychotherapy, for he thinks that regression into symbiosis with the "holding environment" can only occur with the daily couch of analysis, and not in long-term psychotherapy.

If this prescription could be afforded, if every little town in Wisconsin could have its bevy of psychoanalysts, I still think it to be a mistaken idea. I think Gedo has made a number of mistakes in his thinking about the domain of his technique.

First, while it may be true that "holding environments" are necessary for the improvement of many neurotic characters, it is not true that analysis is the only way this can be provided. Winnicott and Balint, as I described in Chapters 7 and 8, demonstrated that this could be done for some patients in brief psychotherapy. Havens, as I will describe in Chapter 10, has a reliable technique for providing a "holding environment" in long-term therapy. Winnicott thought that some family environments are "good enough" so that the patient may only need brief consultation to gain confidence to use that environment again, to give it a second chance to provide what it can provide. The treatment need not *make up* what the child has missed, but only *recognize* this gap, so the child feels understood. This understanding may give the child confidence to proceed to ask for what he needs to learn from the "good enough" environment. Maybe it is also more important for adults to get this kind of confidence from brief therapy, to use the worlds that lie outside of psychiatry, than to stay for long stretches in a world of analysis. No one knows which is more probable, for the study has never been conducted.

Secondly, Gedo exaggerates the domain of his technique by overlooking its negative effects. For one thing, patients in his reports often seem to improve by dismissing the "ill" spouse. Of course, the spouse could be a heavy stone around the neck of the patient, which needs to be cut loose. But the spouse may be no more ill than the patient! In some cases, Gedo is likely to be overlooking how both may get better together, if their interaction could be appreciated. That appreciation would require a systemic perspective which Gedo does not have.

Another negative effect, I think, is the pull from Gedo for grandiosity, in both patient and doctor. He congratulates himself on his objectivity, as if his admirable theoretical description of the hierarchy of personal aims allows him to look the patient over as a skillful architect would overlook a house. We will see from the next chapter on Havens why patients are unlikely to allow themselves to be looked over like this. Now it is quite true that admiration will open many doors to many of the rooms. Havens began one of his recent papers with an explanation from Nietzsche: "How poor the human mind would be without vanity! It resembles a well stocked and ever renewed ware-emporium that attracts buyers of every clan: They can find almost everything, provided they bring with them the right kind of money—admiration" (1984a, p. 385). But Havens is right to say, a little later, that many people are stocked with garbage and worse things. From reading Gedo's grand descriptions of his patients, I can think of many things about myself I wouldn't want to tell him. They wouldn't do.

The third kind of error Gedo makes about the domain of this technique is to confuse possible complexity with actual complexity. Another way to state his argument about possible complexity is to say that the mind can be compartmentalized in respect to its depth and width. Horizontal lines of splitting may give us a view of certain levels of difficulty while hiding others; for example, we may see the patient's conflicts (Level IV) but not see his illusions (Level III). Vertical lines of splitting may give us a view of certain sides of the patient, while making it impossible to see others that are disavowed or dissociated or just held back out of shame or dread; for example, we may see the patient's modest attitude, like that of her father, while we are barred from seeing her blue-stocking pride, like that of her mother (Gedo, 1979, Case Two). Of course, Gedo is right to say that such compartmentalization of attitudes and levels, vertical and horizontal, is entirely *possible*. When it is actually the case, the potential for the therapist to be deceived by a partial picture is great. There are labyrinthine characters, to be sure. For these neurotic characters, it will surely take a long time to figure and find them out. I will grant readily that such patients will take years to discover. They will need analysis or long-term therapy. The error of Gedo, in prescribing analysis as necessary for every neurotic character, is to presume so much splitting, compartmentalization, and complexity in the average patient. Sullivan surely would not have agreed, as he saw many people having characters which are quite sketchy. I would add that a central issue in many patients, such as Mann's "present and chronically recurring pain," often pulls together an amazing range of the average patient's experience, as if the "'me' over time" is the "red thread" which pulls all the other threads together, just as Reich had hoped. This convergence of some characters is what makes a brief therapy in great depth possible, and analysis or long-term therapy unnecessary.

Still, with these three kinds of limitations to the domain of Gedo's technique of analysis, he is still right to say that many neurotic characters need two to five years of treatment. Because of the several crippling identifications which many patients carry, they have indeed been unable to make up early deficiencies by later education. It can take a long time to gain confidence in oneself as a worthwhile person and to gain the calm that goes with such confidence. It can take a long time to learn to defend and organize oneself so that one's aims do not trip each other up, so one's organization of personal aims is simple and clear enough to be workable. It can take a long time to clear certain very limiting illusions. While one can start a patient right away on the road to progress in these several kinds of deficits, often there is no one to sustain him in a deep, archaic bond but the therapist. Often no one else could keep an eye on the continual drift back towards the early identifications, which work so poorly but are so familiar and comforting. Often there is no one who could see and address what is off about the patient's management of his environment.

If the patient's family could provide these aspects of the necessary holding environment, then the therapist might only be needed to set the reeducation going and be available "on demand" (see Chapter 7 on Winnicott). If the patient's family (or spouse) were in therapy with him then the therapist might only be necessary to set the family on a better course, as in family therapy. But since neither of these latter situations may obtain, or because neither may be able to provide but a fraction of the necessary holding functions, then long-term therapy may be necessary. No one knows how often. I would say that half of the neurotic characters referred to me seem to need such a long haul with me, as opposed to brief individual therapy or family therapy, but this is not a figure to be generalized, as it is only indicative of my assessments with my referrals, at my present state of capability with brief and long-term individual therapy and family therapy. In other words, the need for long-term therapy depends very much on what can be gotten from the patient's environment, or not. I supply what is missing.

Gedo is also right that the weaknesses at earlier levels of development will eventually cause mischief, if overlooked. We must be looking for them. When we fail to take up these weaknesses, sooner or later our patient will fall apart, because of unbearable tension (Level I), because his aims contradict or cancel one another or because he cannot defend himself (Level II), or because one of his illusions of power leaves him wide open to successful attack (Level III). Think of any serious adult job which has serious demands. Think of writing, for example. Sooner or later, you come to a passage which falls to pieces. The fifth version of a sentence is as poor as the first. The different abilities to provide your own holding environment will be called upon. You have to give up the illusion that you could make sense in this passage, for the time being (Level III). You have to think about how this part relates to the whole of your essay. Perhaps you don't know (Level II). Finally, you may have to quit for a few hours, before your tension gets so extreme that you smash your typewriter (Level I).

Perhaps it is evident to the reader why these specific abilities to provide for one's own holding environment are so critical to adult success. Most serious tasks fall apart without them. Most success in brief therapy falls apart when an incapacity to sustain a holding environment for oneself is overlooked in the assessment. Sooner or later such a person will wreck himself. Or he or she will resort to "security operations" which get rid of anxiety and possible weakness by confining him or herself to defending a smaller territory. Utilizing the example of writing again, we can see why writers drink so much, in the light of Gedo's scheme. Intoxication sustains illusion, simplifies organization, and reduces tension. It is a familiar security operation for writers. Gedo is right that brief therapists will overlook such weaknesses, at their own peril. He has given us a map to beware of.

The Case of the Policeman's Daughter

This young woman came to talk with me about being in love. In the spring, a young man had fallen for her. She had been interested, but cool about their affair, her mind on her summer in New York City. There she had become terribly lonely, whereupon she had confessed her devotion to him in long letters. In the meanwhile, he had drawn back, so her confessions were met at arm's length. She grew very angry and told him all about her anger. He withdrew further. By fall, he was pursuing another woman, and she was dropped. What, she asked me, was she to do now? She loved him, but it appeared hopeless.

This is the kind of opening that could lead just about anywhere in psychiatry. This could be the story of any ordinary young woman, who, sooner or later, will have a disappointment in love. But at the extreme, this could be the prelude to a schizophrenic break. In between, the entire range of levels of disturbance is possible. Falling in love, and getting hurt, tests how we are put together.

I was more than a little interested in her story, as I had seen her three years before in a brief psychotherapy that had been extended to 38 hours. Here I was now writing this chapter on Gedo. Perhaps I would get a view of some complexity which I had overlooked in my first attempt at brief psychotherapy. I had practiced more naively before, but it was evident I had helped her. She seemed vigorous and full of feeling now, compared to the shy and clumsy girl I had seen three years before. What then was the extent and depth of her difficulty? Perhaps very little. I did not know at the end of the first hour. I was quite impressed by her directness and deep feeling. Maybe this was all that was needed? Pouring out her story to her therapist so well, maybe she was only showing how much her brief psychotherapy had helped her to know her "true feelings." Such follow-up visits are not unusual.

I arranged to call her when I got a free hour, as she wanted to talk a little more. In the second hour she seemed more reconciled that her love for the young man was hopeless. She forgot him sometimes, seeing two other men now. But occasionally she found herself looking him up in his familiar place in the library, and feeling tormented that she could not have him. Again, I thought, quite an ordinary story. Who hasn't had this experience?

Therefore, I asked her what she thought the ordinary solution to her dilemma might be? I hoped from this angle to see if she could get on in the ordinary, simple way that people do when hurt in love. She knew very well what she could do. She could either throw herself into one last try for him, or she could give him up resolutely. I told her I agreed. Either A or B, but not AB, this seeing him and not seeing him, which only prolonged her torment. This reached her. She said, "But it's so hard to give him up." I said, "Please describe him to me." If mourning him could be begun, I thought this would set it going. It did. Her description halted when she got to his "radiating smile." There were tears in her eyes. I said gently, "It reaches back down deep, his smile, like a beacon . . . something you lost, his smile you miss." She began to sob. "No one else has filled me like this," she was able to get out after a while. It being late in the hour, I said: "I don't think this is just John. You think it is him, so you stay away from him, go near him, stay away again. But I think he has touched something deep in you, which you need to know about. When you reach this something in you, I think he will be less important. You will feel more in control." This calmed her, and made sense to her. We agreed to have a two-hour session, after her exams, to see if we could reach this something in her which was so important.

She appeared for her long session in a lovely purple blouse. I noted to myself, "royal purple," and thought of the royal wishes of children. So how would we get back to what her sobbing was about? She seemed cool. She said the last session seemed very distant. There seemed to be several royal roads down to her loss, but all seemed blocked — not unusual, after a session which had gotten so deep, so unexpectedly. I said, "Well, we could get back where we were by several roads. There was this smile? Perhaps you have had dreams lately?" She shook her head at both. She said that we could also talk about some other occasions when she saw him, as the other night when she saw him again and felt ripped up.

I said, all right, there are these three roads. Which did she want to take? She laughed and said, "None." I asked her if she would remind me about her family. She did. Now I was reminded of how she had been the youngest, the favorite, who had come along when her brother and sister were in their teens. Mother and sister had been quite devoted. Mother had hoped to see her "on the cover of *Time Magazine*." Father had been more difficult to please, more critical.

We did not get very far in the first of the two hours. Every time something got going, she stopped it. I did learn something important, however. She did not want to be "upset." She feared "loss of control." Her father, the police-man, did not "respect" crying. She would not be "vulnerable." She shared his cool attitude. After all, how would she make it in the tough world of career in New York City unless she could keep her cool? Her mother was more emotional. She did not want to be like mother. She started to cry. She remembered her mother's words, "No man is an island. . . . " She caught herself. Would I see her next semester? She had big plans. She was determined to be an outstanding student again. She could do terrific work. She would go to New York City and beat everyone in her field.

This is where Gedo began to be useful to me. I thought to myself: Here is a young woman who is alternating before my eyes between her father's constant attitude of being cool, to get respect, and her mother's constant attitude of direct emotionality and connectedness. The two attitudes were not integrated, but alternating. No wonder she had been cool with the young man, and gotten his love, and then very emotional, and lost it. She was like two different people. I could see where this could be awkward for her. So I said to her, "Look, last time you were sobbing, which seemed to be all right. This time you are trying very hard to stay cool. The moment you start to let loose, you tell me how hard we can work and what you will achieve, and, I suppose, get my respect." She said, "Yes, I want to be a big success. I feel this feeling in me to be disquieting, childish and giving way. But how do I bring these two attitudes of mine together? I really do want both, my logic and my feeling." I said, "Yes, really, you are quite lucky to have both in you. It is a gift." I told her we'd take a break for five minutes, and then we could have the last of the two hours.

She came back in and remarked about Christmas cookies, how nice to have them from her cousin. She liked fudge too. I said, "Maybe you can acknowledge that you want to be taken care of. . . . It is nice to get the Christmas cookies." She smiled and said, "I'd like to tell you the dream I had last night." I smiled to myself, remembering she had denied having any dreams to tell when I had asked her in the beginning of the first of our two hours. In her father's compartment, there was no such dream to tell. In her mother's compartment, there it was!

The gist of the dream, which was very long, was as follows: She was driving a taxi. When she spotted three men standing in front of a theatre, she threw the taxi into reverse, and roared back down the alley to pick them up. They jumped in, and she took them to a party. One gave her a kiss for a tip. She followed him into the party, wanting more kisses, but he ignored her.

The next she knew she was being asked to drive another guy somewhere else. He was a Mafia type, with flashy jewelry, and obviously mean. She was amused. She had, curiously, taken her cab meter with her into the party (which defies the laws of physics, given the size of cab meters). The meter showed $107! The guy had a gun, and ordered her to take him where he wanted to go. She did. My telephone call this morning offering the session had then woken her up. Was she scared? Oh no, quite cool. She had been amused.

She and I now walked through her associations to the dream, quite in the classical way. I will abbreviate our findings, to give what was striking. There was a very "pleasant contrast" between the late, dark, cold night . . . and the warmth of the three men getting in the cab. She felt secure. When one of the men kissed her, for a tip, she didn't want to stop. She had been amused. Now it hurt . . . like a pang. I said (thinking of the Christmas cookies which had reminded her of the dream): "You were hungry for more kisses. Your appetite was whetted." She now began to cry, and then she got mad, saying, "You bastard, John, you bastard . . . I can't believe it." We were back to the loss.

Halfway through the dream, she now explained to me how she had figured that falling in love with John would be all right. But she was tricked! She had thought they could tell each other their "true feelings." Both had promised to be honest. (I thought to myself here: So much for brief therapy, which invites telling your "true feelings!") But John had let her down. When she was away in New York City, he hid his turning away from her. But she was so lonely in the City. Why couldn't he see it? Just when she needed him! When she was most vulnerable. I said, "Just when you needed someone to depend on!" She was fearful. I said, "Maybe you didn't know John all that well?" She described how she had some premonitions about him in the spring. He seemed so judgmental in putting down some of his friends, who were a little different. I said, "But your hopes were up. You overlooked this." She said, yes, that was so.

We were running down on time. I took her back to completing her associations to the dream. The Mafia guy reminded her of her racy competitors for John. The $107 of her phone bill, calling him from New York! She smiled, "The guy wasn't going to pay me, but I kept my meter running anyway." I said, "He ignored your need to get something back." She smiled, "I wouldn't turn it off." I said, "You are a woman of considerable hopes." Interesting! She now remembered another piece of the dream! Evidently I had to acknowledge her hopefulness before she could find this piece. The Mafia guy offered her any of ten pills! She had replied: "Buddy, you owe me $107." Her associations were to a gay guy she knows who gets young boys to sleep with him by giving them pills. She was quite disgusted.

We now had very few minutes left. It was time for me to pull together a little for her. I had been given a remarkable description of what her difficulty or deficit was, which had allowed her to be so hurt this past summer. I thought it was time to acknowledge this and give it back to her. I saw now why she had had difficulty protecting herself, why a brief therapy which had invited her pouring out her true feelings had pulled her into her mother's world and left her at the mercy of the cold world. I was glad I had Gedo's map. In her mother's world, she would connect, naively, suddenly. This identification, this constant attitude, robbed her of her judgment, needed to evaluate men. In her father's cool world, you got awfully lonely, though you could keep others at arm's length. Your loneliness built up, as in New York City. You then might switch back into mother's world, because father's leaves you so very tense. Then you'd get the warmth, the relief from the dark, cold, late night, but you'd fall too fast, overlooking how well you knew the man, and so forth. I could see how alternating between her two worlds of identification left her with deficits, of tension (Level I), of organization to defend herself (Level II), and illusions (Level III) about how men and women get to know each other well.[2]

So I said to her: "The second world, the second half of the dream is so degraded. But your meter keeps running. You want something. Who can you trust? It's damn difficult to defend yourself. . . . So you see a man you want. You speed backwards." She interrupted me here: "You have to. When you get your chance, you have to take it! The competition is fast too." I said, "Yes, and you get a painful lesson. Hell, it happens. You get too excited, you go too fast. You get hurt. Then you correct, to this cool, logical, detached and amused view you take in the second half." She replied, "Yes, I overcorrect! . . . Do you think I went so fast, because my folks are fading fast, in their seventies?" I said: "It could be . . . it could be." Our time was up. She wished me a Merry Christmas, and asked where I was from. I told her. She asked if I would see my folks. I said, no, not this year. As she left, she was flushed and quite happy. I had the feeling she trusted me. Perhaps I would hear from her again. Perhaps she had gotten a lesson right on the mark. Perhaps she would need a little more, but I think we both knew we could continue if she needed. I would be here. I had to thank Gedo to myself for what I was able to do for her. His ideas about possible complexity had allowed me to see her double constant attitude and the specific weaknesses their alternation had left in her. I could tell her directly what made looking out for herself get compromised. Some cases, after all, are not so simple that the patient can get where she wants to go when she knows her "true feelings." Nor are they so labyrinthine that you need five years of analysis. Many are in between, where a map of complex possibilities allows an accurate reading of a modest complexity. This is what you need for driving taxis.[3]

10. *Havens: Reliable Findings*

Havens wrote of Sullivan that his technique was "ear to ear," by which Havens meant that intonation and accentuation make all the difference, as in poetry.[1] Havens builds on Sullivan, so let us listen carefully, line by line, without the interpolating comments you will find in Havens' text (1976, pp. 73–75). The first patient is a young woman writer who came to the clinic because she could no longer write at all, not even in her own journal.

PATIENT And I'd say, this is stupid, Anne, nobody's going to read this except you, I mean, you don't have to be a perfectionist here, at all. Relax. And I couldn't do it.

THERAPIST As though somebody else was reading it all the time.

PATIENT Always. That's really a good way of putting it 'cause I always feel like somebody was looking over my shoulder or eavesdropping on my mind.

THERAPIST It's probably not hard to get to that way.

PATIENT Well, what do you mean? There were several people.

THERAPIST Several people?

PATIENT It was my advisor who I really respect a lot and is very, very good. She's brilliant, and an excellent writer. I felt like I could not sit down to write anything without her being there correcting my punctuation, my thoughts.

THERAPIST Because she was such a big cheese in all this.

PATIENT Yeah. She's very good. I've always thought I was a perfectionist; I've never met anybody that was (laughter) such a perfectionist.

THERAPIST This is really not good news, to put it mildly.

PATIENT Right. I felt whatever I did for her was wrong. But then it extended into other kinds of writing.

THERAPIST You mentioned the journal.

PATIENT Yeah, reading the journal, it didn't even sound like me. I'd read them a day or two later and say, who wrote that?

THERAPIST They weren't only looking over your shoulder; they were guiding your pen!

PATIENT I hated them, I didn't like what I wrote at all. It just seemed artificial, not only bad writing, but not my writing.

THERAPIST The teacher even, for all her good qualities, was probably a little filtering or censoring.

PATIENT Well, yeah, she is just extremely critical and a fine eye for detail and I don't know, she very rarely praises you for anything and when she does, well I feel really good.

THERAPIST But she's probably not so easy to tell to get lost either.

PATIENT Oh, I can't no. My degree hinges on her approval of my thesis. I'm in no position to tell her to get lost . . . I did at one point . . .

Notice the one line sentences of the therapist, which fall in, responsively, to the longer passages of the writer.

So you need a musical ear for this work, or you will be singing too long, in the wrong places, or out of tune. Intensity depends on this accompaniment, for it builds, by back and forth, by responsiveness. Narrative depends on encouragement, as any story teller could tell us. Above all, Havens wants the patient to tell her story.

But some other people don't want the patient's story told. They are looking in, so they've got to be dismissed. The invisible "other people in the room" which Sullivan taked about. Havens knows they are there, before we do. I doubt the reader knew this from the patient's first statement about her own perfectionism. She said it was her own. Havens said: "As though somebody else was reading it all the time." Soon, the teacher was that somebody, and next she was a "big cheese . . . guiding the pen" and who could tell her to "get lost"? Notice how he moves her, escorts her, separates her slowly from the patient, slowly from himself, one sentence at a time, until she is almost out the door! Havens did not want the distortion of her presence. Hell, the patient first pretended the perfectionism was her own! Individuals will twist themselves into knots for other people. If we want to unravel the knot, we must see what is distorted for "them." Otherwise, we have very unreliable communication.

The teacher nearly sent packing, the patient is now able to tell Havens about her try to break free of the confinement: the five-page letter to the teacher. She had explained how she had always had confidence in herself before in school, in writing, until now when she was stopped altogether. The teacher replied that the letter was very touching. The narrative is coming along.

THERAPIST She found it touching.

PATIENT Meant to evoke your sympathy.

THERAPIST She found it kind of moving or touching.

PATIENT Yeah. Look, in a way, I was glad that she responded at all (laughter).

THERAPIST Thank God for little favors. I mean, what more could a poor student expect?

PATIENT Yeah, exactly. That is what keeps occurring to me. It didn't at the time, but subsequently it has. I've gotten to the point where . . . my schoolwork I'm grateful for any little crumb I get.

THERAPIST Any little crumb that is thrown to you from the great teacher. Yeah, well, God forbid you should be a patient under those circumstances.

PATIENT Well, frankly, I'm a little suspicious about that.

THERAPIST After that experience I wouldn't be surprised. So the great lady was at least willing to be touched by it. This communication. (1976, pp. 76–77)

Notice how the conversation about the teacher allows the therapist and patient to adjust to each other. As the two gaze outward at this third person, they compare notes, make marks, erase, remark, adjust, drawing pictures together. Each may correct the other, easily. The therapist suggests that the teacher being "touched" was no favor; the patient says, no, it was better than nothing. Her sketch of the teacher has a little color that the therapist missed on the first try. But then the therapist suggests that the clinic will be little different from the teacher. Because the patient has broken down on a regime of crumbs, she has to wonder if the clinic will be any different. Havens is beginning to get her to see his sketch of the clinic.

The patient has suggested that her five-page letter was mistaken by the teacher for a call for sympathy. The patient has little confidence in getting across. Five pages! And it was received all wrong. Havens has no confidence in long statements either. Every line is a chance for misunderstanding. Therefore, he will offer her chances for revision, line by line: of her picture of the teacher; of his picture of the clinic. This is why the doctor has to talk so much, so he can be corrected.[2] His offhand remarks invite correction. When distortion is rampant between the patient and her environment, this is the only chance for reliable communication. Every sentence is pounded by waves of distortion. Doctor and patient are standing in the surf, which is rough and booming, trying to exchange a few pebbles in the wash at their feet, trying to get a few things across to each other.

Given that they have corrected each other about the teacher, a little, and the clinic, a little, the patient can go on with her story.

PATIENT This was towards the end of January, going on February, and I thought something's got to give, and nothing ever did. I mean by spring I'd finally managed to get a twenty-page outline which normally I would have written in ten days. And it took me two to three months. And it is lousy.

THERAPIST You were down and out.

PATIENT So then after spring vacation I came back actually to do the research on this thing and as long as I was doing the research in the library I was fine, but as soon as it became time, about the end of January to begin writing it up, I just blanked again and I couldn't write anything and, all the physical things started returning, I mean I started throwing up and my heart . . .

THERAPIST Your heart?

PATIENT Racing, racing, racing all the time and my stomach, and that was what first got me going to the counseling center last fall 'cause one day I almost fainted and I thought, this is just stupid.

THERAPIST . . . you needed a doctor.

PATIENT Something's got to stop, but another thing too. I keep wondering why I'm doing this, a couple weeks ago I sat down to write one morning and I didn't feel particularly nervous or anything but I did . . . all at once, I'd no sooner sat down than my stomach started going bluh bluh and I'd keep gasping for breath all the time and um, so I went away from the typewriter to sit down and read and before my eyes and I could feel my heart and then it sort of occurred to me that anybody else would have said to hell with this thing a long time ago.

THERAPIST But not you.

PATIENT But why am I?

THERAPIST There's this teacher.

PATIENT There was the teacher, the pressure from home. There was the fact I had completed ten years. . . . (pp. 78–79)

Here's the other problem, besides the pounding waves. She feels terrible. Will anyone share that with her? If the doctor is willing, he will get quite a feel for her torment. Here, he is willing: "You were down and out." "You needed a doctor." He will even admire her endurance. Anybody else would have said to hell with this thing long ago. "But not you." The sharing, of torment and devotion, prepares both for another move outwards, to see what else in the environment had impinged and broken the patient's confidence. "But why am I (still trying)?" "There's this teacher." Havens points outward again. The patient revises. No, there's the parents, too. Out of the blur of criticism, once only that of the patient's own "perfectionism," have stepped two more sources of trouble, besides the patient herself and the teacher. Now we get the parents. The narrative is coming along.

The reader may want to pause for thought about the first conversation, before switching over to snatches of two conversations with two other patients. I want to give a little more feeling for what Havens is able to do in a line or two. Apparently massive structures, like swamps or mountains, can be given the slip.

Sometimes patients have so little expectation that they give up before the clinic has a chance. Thus, Havens had to lift the sights of the young writer out of her swamp, to something a little hopeful. Sometimes, patients have great expectations; this is every bit as bad, for the crash will come for great hopes that no treatment could sustain. Either of those roads, the low road into the swamp or the high road over a cliff, is no way to allow the patient to begin treatment. Havens wants to start off the long journey of the treatment on a road that leads somewhere, eventually. A journey of a thousand miles begins with a single step. Morale is sound, when that first step is in the right direction. So Havens is not about to allow someone to get off wrong at the outset.[3] Listen to how he calls off a megalomanic adventure.

PATIENT My father asked if I was through the treatment.
THERAPIST Something troubled him.
PATIENT Maybe you didn't give him enough hope.
THERAPIST Maybe not.
PATIENT I blew it last night. It was a wonderful evening. I really enjoyed that couple, you know the Br.'s. I was feeling so hopeful. Then at the end I got all excited and grandiose.
THERAPIST Well so much for hope.

*   *   *

PATIENT Why don't you clarify this? You know me very well, I'm confused.
THERAPIST That's right.
PATIENT I can't do this alone.
THERAPIST Neither your boss nor the girlfriend have clarified things either.
PATIENT They haven't.
THERAPIST Everywhere you look: No one helps.
PATIENT But you're supposed to.
THERAPIST I suppose your parents were, too.
PATIENT They didn't.
THERAPIST No wonder you want someone to take their place. (1980, pp. 59 and 61–62)

Havens knows that great expectations cannot be contradicted. This will make them worse, for you are failing to accept the patient as he demands to be accepted. So what you do is accept the naturalness of great expectations – only they belong elsewhere. So these protests barreling at the therapist, "You didn't give him enough hope . . . But you're supposed to (help) . . . ," become: "So much for hope (from the couple) . . . " and "I suppose your parents were too (supposed to help). . . . No wonder you want someone to take their place." What appears to be massive structures . . . can be pointed elsewhere. Who needs them?

The third and final conversation I want to present from Havens brings in something as important as the reliable road forward. It is that the patient has to believe he or she is someone worth traveling with at all. Some patients are so self-critical

that almost any statement to them becomes a fresh criticism. For example, a genuinely devoted and hardworking young female patient was subject to a virtually constant barrage of self-recriminations. She remarked that she could not recall leaving a conversation without spending sometimes hours in review of what seemed like her stupid remarks during the conversation. Often, the content of the self-recriminations close-ly resembled comments she recalled her mother making. It appeared that her mother, an editor for an academic press, extensively edited her children's utterances. More-over, the patient did not protest against these judgments of herself. In fact, she sought them out by her meticulous reviews of conversations. . . . the patient was essentially supine. One result was that the therapist's attempt to highlight this dependence and self-critical hegemony was seen as evidence of still another failing. "You shouldn't be so self-critical" was then added to the list of her other inadequacies. This was not a trivial blow because the patient felt that the self-critical review of her behavior was a strong point, that only by such means was she being kept free from a still worse fate. (1984a, p. 393)

Again, another of those situations which appear to be huge and awful. Notice how Havens got out. Who would think of it?

For a period I was reduced to smiling at her, which, for all I know, reinforced the self-critical behavior. The idea of performative statements was saving. The task be-came not to critique her for being self-critical but to admire what she was generally critical of. She accused herself of being garrulous, when actually her comments were brisk and to the point; so I said as much. Very gradually, this and other performa-tives created states of being admired; the recriminations decreased. (1984a, p. 393)

What have we seen in these three conversations with three patients? A young writer lost in her own perfectionism has been found to be beset by "the other people in the room," her teacher and her parents. Her torment has been shared. Therefore, it has been possible to get her story, and modest hope. A megalomanic young man has been pointed on a more sensible road. An-other beset young writer has been found to be "brisk and to the point," that is, worthwhile. This is what Havens is about: finding a story that is to be be-lieved, a road which is to be believed in, and someone worth the trip. De-spite so many deceptions, something reliable can be found. But isn't it curious what apparently offhand remarks can do? Perhaps one must be offhand when one intends to slide massive structures off the patient's back or off one's own neck.[4]

THE FULL RANGE OF AVAILABLE METHODS

Havens had for his teachers two of the best interviewers ever seen in Boston, Ives Hendrick and Elvin Semrad, but they moved in opposite ways. One pursued the patient and tracked him down. The other got close by waiting and sharing. Both subscribed to the theories of psychoanalysis. Both were analysts. But what each man did with patients was a world apart from the other. What Havens was learning from carrying around books by Harry Stack Sullivan was a third world of methods, which no one approved of in Boston.

Havens knew these differences of method all were powerful in their own way, but it was not so easy to say how each was pulled off. He wanted to be capable of carrying out the methods of all three of his principal teachers, and he wanted to provide an adequate account, as Sullivan would say, of the technical requirements necessary to each method. So long as it is left vague and unclear what the different schools of psychiatry actually *do* with their patients, so long as theorizing can run on apart from *action*, then the schools can dispute as they did in the Middle Ages. Thus, the disputing in psychoanalysis could tell Havens next to nothing about the serious differences in method among his three teachers. What could be done about this? Havens decided it was time to sharpen the description of the tools of psychiatry and to set aside the woolly theorizing.

This is no small job. Havens set himself to studying all the major schools of psychiatry which emerged from 19th century medicine. But he did not want to get swamped in irrelevant details. One could easily be lost in trivial scholarship.

What he did was to borrow the pragmatic method. We Americans like to think of ourselves as pragmatic, by which we mean practical. We like to think of ourselves as "getting the job done." Often, this means reducing "the job" to something crude and single-minded. Winning, making money, losing weight, being "number one" (of something!), and reducing anxiety are typical aims for us. So we move towards a psychiatry with very reduced aims. Behavioral programs will shape the action in the single direction we shoot for. Psychopharmacological programs will subdue the feelings we want to be rid of. One way to be practical is to be single-minded, but this is not what Havens has had in mind—nor William James when he described the pragmatic method. Both thought it very important to be practical about complex aims. Philosophy and ecology and psychiatry are in deep trouble if complex aims result in woolly thinking.

But this has been the great problem of philosophy and of psychiatry, according to James and Havens. The great schools of philosophy and of psychiatry become metaphysical. They have the virtue of broad consideration, but this sacrifices the ability to get things done. Could we not have *both* the complex aims and the practical ability?

Yes, we can have both, but we need a very clear method. This method is pragmatism, which James described as follows:

The pragmatic method in such cases is to try to interpret each notion by tracing its respective practical consequences. . . . Whenever a dispute is serious, we ought to be able to show some practical difference that must follow from one side or the other's being right. . . . the tangible fact at the root of all our thought-distinctions, however subtle, is that there is no one of them so fine as to consist in anything but a possible difference in practice. (1907, p. 23)

Havens set himself to the job of reinterpreting all of psychiatry according to these "differences in practice."

. . . the present day fragmentations and disputatiousness not only confuse practice but also obscure the extraordinary advances that have been made. One of my contentions in the book is that these advances concern *methods* of investigating human nature more than they do theories of human nature. . . . The emphasis of this book is on methods and facts, seldom on theories. The nature of psychiatric information and concerns encourages theorizing. The result is that psychiatric theories lie around us like fogs. It is time, in Emerson's sharp language, to "pierce this rotten diction and fasten words again to visible things." (1973, pp. vii–viii)

The Center of Havens' Method

The principal difficulty with following Havens' revolutionary project is that we can become lost in the welter of possible methods. This is better than becoming lost in theorizing. We learn so much about what we *might* do with our patients, but we can lose our bearings about what we *will* do, case by case, day by day. Havens' work of the last 20 years is like a very large canvas, where the painting has begun in four or five places. Many of us have gotten from him a clear sight of these fragments of the overall design of the picture. But who has been able to utilize this wealth in a concerted way?

For this use to occur, I think we need to locate the central organizing idea of the painting. It is only recently that this center has become clear to me. This is probably because in the last few years Havens has become much more clear himself about where the center of perspective lies in his work. Then the pieces begin to fall into place. How then do we decide what to do with our patients when we have all the different methods so well described? What comes first, according to Havens? And second, and third? We have to decide what is most important, what is less, or we cannot act.

The picture that comes out from Havens' canvas is one of psychiatrists of each school becoming taken with the partial picture of the patient that they can get from their method of investigation. They become badly deceived, thinking that they have found the patient. This story, over and over, is like John Donne's poem about finding "a woman true and fair":

> If thou find'st one, let me know;
>   such a pilgrammage were sweet.
> Yet do not; I would not go,
>   Though at next door we might meet.
> Though she were true when you met her,
> And last till you write your letter,
>   Yet she
>   Will be
> False, ere I come, to two or three.

This is the most difficult practical problem. How not to be deceived? How to find where the patient actually lives, not yesterday, but in the session today? Sullivan also appreciated that this was much more difficult than it first appears, which he also described in his own characteristic way:

. . . people go into any interview with quite mixed motivations; they wish that they could talk things over frankly with somebody, but they also carry with them, practically from childhood, ingrained determinations which block free discussion. As a result, people often expect that the psychiatrist will be either a great genius or a perfect ass. (1954, p. 9)

Since the psychiatrist is in continual danger of being "a perfect ass," according to Sullivan, Donne, and Havens, this takes precedence over all other practical problems. If you do not get reliable findings, you help for the patient is apt to be futile, stupid or destructive, or it will work by accident. You will not know what the patient is trying to do. When what is worthwhile to and for the patient cannot be located, it also cannot be protected and advanced. When what is routinely futile or destructive cannot be determined, it will continue to wreck the patient's worthwhile aims.

Therefore, all methods in psychiatry need to be subordinated to this first aim, which is to find where the patient lives. Balint put this as follows:

It happens so rarely in life that you have a person who understands what you are up to and openly faces it with you. That is what we can do for our patients, and that is an enormous thing.

Reliable Findings

How then are we to get reliable findings, hour by hour? This is as crucial for brief psychotherapy as for long-term psychotherapy. Brief psychotherapy is apt to become a "convenient fiction," a fairy tale of simplification. Long-term psychotherapy is apt to become a different "convenient fiction," a domestic tale of settling into what is merely comfortable.

There are two prevailing, overwhelming tendencies that are apt to get us to accept fiction, which is our defeat. Can we make measurements without distorting the findings? Our problem is very much like that of modern physics (Havens, 1982b). There is both a particle phenomenon and a wave phenomenon. The particle phenomenon is that the patient is like a hidden particle. She is self-absorbed, but she has little faith in being found out there. How to go looking for her? There is also the wave phenomenon. The patient plays to the social field, giving what is expected. Everything she says is shaped by these social waves. How to find the patient in these distorting waves?

Attempts at precision are apt to fail. Objective-descriptive psychiatry will place the patient on its coordinates of "illness"—every case is defined by the "syndrome," its cluster of expected symptoms, its natural history, epidemiology, prognosis, and standard treatment. One might get a rough idea about the patient, by a protocol which can be repeated with precision, but what patient wants to be caught in this matrix? The brain may be subjected to precise measurement, because it can be found in the cranium, but the mind need not be in the room. Of course, some patients *appear* to be willing to be subjected to this kind of precise study, but this is likely to mean they see some advantage in presenting themselves as "ill."[5]

Psychoanalysis may be an improvement. It too sets up "standard conditions" for observation, namely, its strict "standard technique" of free association and keeping only to the analysis of resistance and transference. This is to allow the past to come into the present. But the same kind of distortion is possible with psychoanalysis as with objective-descriptive psychiatry. The past will come into the present as the patient finds this advantageous. What kind of past does the analyst want to hear about? What kind of past is advantageous to the patient to construct? Whose past are we getting? It is very difficult to know.[6]

If precision cannot force us into reliable observations, what is more promising? Havens believes that "loose holding" is more likely. This is possible with the methods of both the interpersonal and existential traditions. They are the corrections for the wave and the particle phenomena (Havens, 1982b). If the patient is continually playing to the social field, adjusting to the powerful waves she feels coming toward her, then it is necessary to see what these expectations require of the patient. This helps to clear the field of the wave distortions, allowing us to see what else might be there as well. But since waves keep coming, forcing and obliging responses from the patient, this activity of counter-projection is always necessary to renew.

If the patient is self-absorbed, like a hidden particle, then the search for her, the methods of active empathy, of putting oneself in the patient's place, are the only ways one is likely to get a view of how the world and her position actually look and feel to her. Therefore, given the priority of reliable observations, the methods of interpersonal and existential psychiatry, in some kind of alternation, become the principal tools for Havens. They serve the purpose of moving the "narrative flow" in directions more likely to be believable and reliable. This gives "successive approximation" as to where the patient lives. This is our principal job.

We not only find the patient this way, but also set her free. For the projected expectations force her responses, in a closed circuit, while her hidden self-absorption remains disconnected from the world.[7] For instance, Havens discovered of the young woman writer of the first conversation that he had to uncouple her from the force of three different projected expectations: that he too would expect her to be perfect; that he too felt sorry for her (was "touched"); that he too could alter the world for her. All three expectations would have kept her very passive. Her poor responses would have been forced. These massive forces uncoupled, she could begin to allow her feelings to flow. But they were so painful. They needed to be shared to be tolerable at all. She was so lost in this torment, how could she give back in writing to the world? The interpersonal methods help break the closed circuit, while the existential methods help carry the person in the transition back to the world.

Perhaps I can describe this kind of help best by describing my own experience. I am as sensitive as anyone to not fitting in. The animal out of step with his local environment does not feel well. That's what his nervous system is for, to let him know when he is out of step. This is to keep him from being killed, wounded, or humiliated. Therefore, when I am out of step, when I do not like what is happening in my faculty meeting or at a social gathering, I feel down or nervous. I often know only one more thing, which is how I am supposed to be reacting—like my smiling neighbor, or course, or my nodding colleagues. If I could get no farther than this, I would be in neurotic misery. Given my own nervous or discouraged feeling and the weight of social expectations, I would have nowhere to stand. But I have learned to talk to myself with the interpersonal or existential methods of inquiry described by Havens. I step back out of the force of the social field, giving myself the benefit of the doubt. Perhaps my colleagues and neighbors are forcing a response upon themselves that I do not want to force upon myself? In their light, my response is wrong, but what do I think of their light, anyway? Not so much. I begin to get some room to see what I do feel about the situation. I have uncoupled myself from the extreme force of social expectations. But now that I have some room, I must listen and accept and look after myself, or get someone to help me, for it is painful to feel situations all by yourself. We human beings are not well equipped for this. If I can carry myself along, with some help, I can begin to accept my own feeling about the situation. I can begin to find other people who could accept my feeling as well. I am making a transition, in my mind, to a niche where my response fits. Then, I feel fine.

In this perspective, neurotic misery is a *forme fruste*. You might have a response, which is not seen in your family, your neighbors, or your colleagues. But until they are pulled off your back, you will not be able to know the possibility. It cannot become a story. It is merely negative, an absence. The circuit is closed. The interpersonal methods of inquiry are necessary to allow the response its own room. Then the existential methods of inquiry nurse the response along, which is difficult to bear alone, until the response can discover its positive domain. This is what the "loose holding" methods can do.[8]

But notice that the "loose holding" inquiry about myself would not have been possible unless I had some faith in myself as a worthwhile person who is often right. I would never know there was something to look into. I just would have felt badly. Many of our patients do not feel worthwhile or admirable, and so they just feel badly. This is why Havens could get nowhere with his third conversation, why he was reduced to smiling at the young woman, since any comment by him was taken up as a new self-criticism. Why give her fresh ammunition? Finally, he saw a place which could not be taken away from her, a place to live from, as Winnicott would say, where Havens could begin a stand. She was not as garrulous as her mother the editor told her. She was brisk and to the point. He admired this in her. "Loose holding" now can make its discoveries, when he has fastened to what is admirable in the patient.

And one more thing. Some patients act foolishly when they are appreciated and understood. "Loose holding" could discover them, only to have them charge off and do something stupid. The megalomanic patient of the second conversation was this sort of person. "So much for hope!" Havens had to say to him, driving a wedge sharply between himself and any notion the patient might have that Havens approved of his great expectations. If one is going to use these "loose holding" methods to find the responses of the patient, one has also got to keep in mind that patients act on what they find. As Sullivan would say, the psychiatrist better find out what the "routinely futile operations" of the patient are likely to be and discourage them! Then it might be all right to get to know the patient better.

THE DOMAIN OF THIS TECHNIQUE

The greatest limitation on the domain of this technique by far is the extreme range of technical abilities required by the doctor and the demand for the utmost clarity of integration of these abilities. This is virtuoso playing. No doubt much of it will be dimly understood by the reader. I only hope that he or she will study Haven's texts for further understanding. Experiment and practice are also indispensable. With this technique, one can play about anything — almost. We'll come last to its limitations.

I have so far conveyed two crucial aspects of his technique. One is the central preoccupation with the problem of reliable findings. The second is the greater reliance on "loose holding," the interpersonal and existential methods, to control for the wave and particle phenomena which are the most powerful distortions. I have not yet described how all of the methods are brought in and integrated. Havens himself has described this integration of all of the methods of inquiry in psychiatry in four different kinds of languages. If we are to grasp the domain of his technique, we need to grasp what range of method it can integrate.

First of all, you could say that Havens is describing *history taking*. His *Lancet* article (1978c) takes this angle. History taking starts from the objective-descriptive tradition of medicine. But because patients become afraid, their fear must be *shared*. This sharing keeps patients from running away from their own overwhelming history. The technical possibilities for sharing are described primarily by the existential tradition.

But patients when frightened tighten up and forget, get confused, slip, stop, and start. For these situations, the *psychoanalytic* methods are necessary to underline the unconscious interference, allow free association, to *give room* for the unconscious to speak clearly what it is saying by its partial interference. Finally, patients have distressing or shameful things to tell, which are quite conscious, perhaps off to the side of attention, which will never be told to the wrong listeners. Therefore, the doctor taking a history also needs to *separate* himself from these projected hostile or negative aspects of other persons, utilizing the interpersonal methods.

In summary, Havens is describing how all of the schools contribute to the central activity of *reliable history taking*. The supplementary *activities* necessary to history taking are sharing, giving room, and separating oneself from "the other people in the room."[9] A fourth supplementary activity, *admiring* what is worthwhile in the patient, both separates oneself from the others in the room and shares the particular place from which the patient may live.

Of course, Havens, writing for the English medical profession in the *Lancet*, made objective-descriptive "history taking" the starting point and primary activity, to which the other activities are supplemental. Maybe for medical doctors this is well and right, enabling them to lead from their strength. For psychotherapy, Havens has made clear that the loose holding that comes from separating oneself from the other people in the room and from sharing takes over from the beginning in history taking.

Each of these activities of history taking (improving the narrative flow) uses different modes of the English language. Objective-descriptive history taking asks *questions*: "What brought you here today?" Sharing in the existential tradition depends on simple and complex empathic *statements*: "How frightening!" Separating oneself from the others in the room also depends on *statements*, those which point out there to the others in the room: "They have not wanted to listen to you." Admiring the patient is carried by *performatives*, such as: "You have courage!" As an expert, I recognize that quality, deem it to be so. Giving room comes from *commands*: "Tell me whatever comes to mind." The reader may refer to the different articles where an entire vocabulary of each mode is described. Havens provides for a lifetime of study.[10]

Each of these modes of the English language corresponds to a body language. As we say, we use different parts of ourselves with different situations. For history taking, we use our eyes. We look for gaps, contradictions, and so forth. For giving room, we use our heads, by suspending its rational use in favor of its capacity for free association. For sharing we use our hearts. For separating ourselves from other persons, we use our hands, to move us from "them." We seem to use our ears for all these activities, but in different ways: to hear contradictions, to listen for the unconscious slipping in, to catch the suspended sob which needs to be shared, to pick up (hands again) how one is being run together with mother or father or whomever. The tone has gone flat. One will hear this, before one sees it. Thus, the interpersonal methods are especially ear to ear, but so are the other methods to a lesser extent.[11]

Finally, the different activities necessary to history taking, each using different modes of the English language and different parts of the body language, each pull for different sitting positions in relation to the patient. The history taking in the objective tradition is across a desk. The existential sharing requires the desk to be put aside, nothing between doctor and patient. When the patient needs to be given room, in the psychoanalytic tradition, he faces away from the doctor, the doctor sitting behind him. When the doctor needs to separate himself from the other people in the room, both look out together in the same direction at the patient's social world.[12]

There are doctors from each tradition who hold literally to one of these four positions. Utilizing Havens' technique, one might literally shift position, or one might make *gestures* which approximate a shift of position. For example, I may begin taking notes, my yellow notebook being a kind of desk. The patient begins to cry. I put it down. The patient lapses. I say, so to speak, "go away from me, go into yourself," which is close to looking away (note also the command). The tone goes flat. We both gaze out into the social world to see who has entered the room while we were talking. So the shifts of position are there in subtle form, without getting out of one's seat.

Now, what is extraordinary is that many, many doctors are locked into one activity for advancing the narrative, one mode of the English language, using one part of their body ego, and stuck in one physical position in relation to the patient. This reminds me of the Marxist cartoons of the overspecialized worker glued to his machine. This is the kind of occupational illness one can get from being a member of one of the schools. But it is worse for the patient. If the doctor is using one-fifth of the possible equipment for making reliable observations, the doctor will be deceived more often than not. This is very bad news for the patient. The doctor is useless or even dangerous when he has poor information. His actions will not make sense, although accidental improvements may occur.

Havens has described a technique for increasing the likelihood of reliable findings. Because no patient can be helped (reliably) unless he or she can convey what he or she is up to, and up against, getting an accurate reading from the different angles to make sure of the findings is the single most important activity of the psychiatrist. It is the one necessary capability for helping a patient. The more widely one can get reliable findings, the wider one's effective domain for helping patients.

I see but two limitations to the domain of Havens' technique. One I have debated with him on many occasions, with little change in either of us! For him, most patients are like lobster traps, a small particle in the sea which is hard to find down there and which is buffeted by the waves. Hence, the search is always complex, and likely to be long. First interviews are invitations to blunder. For me, this is a familiar kind of situation, but I also think there are patients more easily found out. They have had less harm visited upon them. They have been loved and given room. Therefore, they come out of hiding more readily, because they can tell a hospitable environment from a predatory environment. These two capabilities—to connect and to be able to defend oneself—for which Havens himself has devised tests in the interview, tests of normality (1984b), make possible brief psychotherapy. The relatively normal patient can sense a doctor who can be trusted, but be ready to protect himself if proven wrong. This allows fast engagement, making use of the doctor to remedy some deficit and then leaving him. Havens thinks this is very, very infrequent, probably a fairy tale. Thus I think his technique *can* be overly cautious, and elaborate, when this is not so necessary. He thinks I am overly optimistic, like Candide. Maybe I have seen too few Bulgarian invasions, inquisitions, earthquakes, and shipwrecks.

The other limitation to Havens' technique is that he has not studied much about family therapy, so he is unfamiliar, by and large, with circular epistemology. His is still a linear world, although it is but a few steps into the circular world from his grasp of the power of "the other people in the room." We will see in later chapters how Bateson, Maturana, and the Milan tradition have adopted a new activity, to supplement "history taking" in the presence of the family, literally in the room or figuratively in the room. This activity is circular questioning. It develops a new mode of the English language, which is one of distinguishing the distinctions. It uses the body as part of a group body. Finally, it adopts an equidistant position between family members, which is called "neutrality," although this is quite a different meaning from "neutrality" in the psychoanalytic tradition. Here is an entire fifth world of technique, a revolution of perspective unfamiliar to Havens, which allows us to clarify the profound subordination of the individual to his niche in the family organization. Without this technique, without the reliable information *it* gives, I imagine Havens would have a difficult time or at least a slower time locating some of his patients enmeshed in the guts of a family situation.

ORDINARY USE: HISTORY TAKING OF
A CASE OF CHEST PAIN

Another way to describe Havens' technique is to say it is a kind of history taking which is receptive to opposing currents. The skill is to ride the opposing currents until they calm down, which allows the main drift to gather momentum again. The interviews are deceptively smooth, because the doctor never runs directly against any opposing force. He usually joins the opposing force until it is spent, or accepts it only to send it off elsewhere. One word of caution: keep your eye on the story. Havens slips back to the story, which is the main drift of the interview, whenever he can, without announcing that this is what he is up to. I am more likely to announce that I am getting a story, or have such and such an hypothesis, when I am working with patients who are relatively well in the Brief Psychotherapy Clinic. Indeed, I often begin with my pencil and yellow notepad, departing often into the opposing currents, and then back to getting the story straight. I am inviting these patients to help me get the story right, to be equals in that job. Notice how we trade back and forth, almost line for line. I have had to leave out all the noises back and forth, by which the patient and I accompany one another, for the transcript would be hopelessly long. I hope it will be evident that I am inviting correction, at every turn, at every phrase — and that I get it.

Sometimes there is an opposing current before I can even take a single step forward. In this case, the preliminary interview had upset the patient. Notice how I join him in his hostility to us, until he is able to tell me that it is important to him to be in control ("cruisin'"). Having gathered this, I wonder "where to start" and invite him to *tell me* where we start. He is more than willing to run things, and explains his "excuse" hypothesis.

We saw this young man in the Brief Therapy Clinic for evaluation for chest pain. In the first hour, we learned the pains had begun in the late summer, when his thoughts had turned to preparing to leave home for graduate school. They became extreme when he arrived here with his parents to set up an apartment. Extensive evaluations by his internist and cardiologist here had discovered no physical basis for the pains. In the first hour, we had found no suggestions of a major psychiatric disorder. Instead, we had been impressed by his vigorous and close relationship with his family and many close friends. He seemed to be deeply attached to his ethnic neighborhood in South Milwaukee. Given these findings, which are encouraging for brief therapy, we offered him a two-hour session of "trial therapy" to see if we could help him with his "problem" of pain.

THERAPIST So. Let's see where we should start? My recall of where we left off was that you told us some about what had happened between the summer and here . . . and you were already getting better. You had already discovered . . .

PATIENT Yah!

THERAPIST . . . already had discovered that you get over this. But we offered to see if we could help you make some sense of this. So that you might be stronger, for the whole pain of it all.

PATIENT Uh, huh. Well, since last Wednesday, I kinda had 'em again, stronger.

THERAPIST Oh, you did.

PATIENT Yah.

THERAPIST All right, so there's something to . . . Not only do we have to go over what did happen, we can perhaps help you get over this little bit you just had.

PATIENT I had an EKG Tuesday.

THERAPIST You did?

PATIENT I talked to the cardiologist who said there's nothing wrong, cardiac, so that's good.

THERAPIST But it was good to get the news about that. All right, so you had a bout of it between last time and now, which would have been on the weekend?

PATIENT Starting that night after I saw you.

THERAPIST Oh, thanks to us.

PATIENT Thanks to you guys.

THERAPIST It was nice of us to stir up your trouble and upset you. I'm sure you're grateful for the interview.

PATIENT Then a little bit over the weekend. But I felt a little better yesterday, and today though.

THERAPIST So it kind of comes and goes. It's probably sensitive to what's going on. Did you think the interview stirred something up?

PATIENT I'm pretty sure it did.

THERAPIST What did you think it was?

PATIENT I was a little nervous. I didn't know there would be four gentlemen here. But . . .

THERAPIST So maybe there was something about four doctors. . . . One is bad enough. . . . What makes four worse than one?

PATIENT I didn't expect it.

THERAPIST So maybe it was the surprise.

PATIENT Then going through it all again. For two or three days I was pretty much cruisin'.

THERAPIST That's one of the problems with treatments. They can make it worse for a while. Because they bring the whole thing right up.

PATIENT Yah.

THERAPIST All right, there's a lot of ways we could start. We've got . . . a couple hours here to make sense of this. Where shall we start. I think, . . . do you have any ideas?

PATIENT I was thinking about . . . if I'm possibly trying to make an excuse about not passing or failing. . . . I might not make it and this would be an easy way out. I'm guessing.

THERAPIST Could be.

PATIENT But then I'm thinking being here . . . seeing the caliber of the students . . . the part about me not belonging here. . . . I'm pretty sure I do.

THERAPIST You match up pretty well.

PATIENT Yah.

THERAPIST So if that idea's true, it would seem you wouldn't need the excuse . . .

PATIENT That seems logical to me.

THERAPIST So maybe there's something of that . . .

PATIENT It's a guess.

THERAPIST So what made you, brought you to that guess?

PATIENT I was apprehensive about coming here. Always wondered if it was the right decision. Whether you're biting off more than you can chew.

THERAPIST Sure. Sure.

PATIENT You don't know if you're kidding yourself.

THERAPIST Has that happened to you before? Where you bit off more than you can chew?

PATIENT No.[13]

THERAPIST But you thought maybe this time . . .

PATIENT Maybe I went over my head.

THERAPIST Okay, that would make sense that you would be anxious about that.

PATIENT Uh, But uh, pretty sure, yah . . .

Now I have a nice difficulty here, balancing two opposing currents which are about equal. I want to accept his thinking as useful, which it is, up to a point. But it is also demeaning, the notion that he is merely covering himself. So I suggest there are several possibilities. "Yes, the sequence is clear, but why the heart?" My eye suggests that this is unexplained.

Another denouncing current enters the room, suggesting, implying that pain is not pain. I say it *is* pain, but also "one of the common ways in which something painful in a person's life comes to his attention." For this man, what is common, need I say it, is acceptable. He is also a scientist, and a hardworking man, so a transition to a "hypothesis" and our "job" rides well with him. We are back to history.

THERAPIST Another ordinary possibility is that there are several things here, together . . .

PATIENT Yah, that might have been the start of it. Then having the pain and the anxiety about that. I think that may have contributed. . . . The whole thing bothers me more when I think about it.

THERAPIST Maybe you get apprehensive, think you're biting off more than you can chew, then maybe getting anxious, you start paying attention to this, and worrying about that.

PATIENT Right.

THERAPIST That's plausible. . . . Of course, then, we need to understand. . . . A lot of people are worried about graduate school, then focus on something, like their heart, then that becomes a big worry. The sequence would be clear, but then why would it center on your heart?

PATIENT I have no idea.

THERAPIST That part is obscure.

PATIENT Very.[14]

THERAPIST Okay.

PATIENT Does this happen?

THERAPIST Oh sure, it is one of the common forms that fear takes or worry or anxiety.

PATIENT I'm so mystified by the whole thing.

THERAPIST Oh I think we can find out . . .

PATIENT It *feels* like pain, I mean . . .

THERAPIST Yah.

PATIENT To me pain is pain.

THERAPIST Well, it *is* pain. . . . It is pain. It would be a mistake to say this is not real. Something painful is going on here. You wouldn't go to all this trouble for nothing.

PATIENT Right.

THERAPIST Sometimes, something very painful psychologically is experienced literally as a pain right here, or here. I don't think this is unreal.

PATIENT Okay, I just wanted to know how unusual or usual this is.

THERAPIST It's one of the common ways in which something painful in a person's life comes to his attention.

PATIENT Something I didn't know.

THERAPIST No, it's something that doctors see all the time. But for each person . . . what it is for each person that is painful is somewhat different. So maybe we can surmise that this period in your life, this transition in your life is . . . painful in some way. That would be our working hypothesis. Does that make sense?

PATIENT Uh huh.

THERAPIST So maybe our job right now is to see what would make this period of your life so painful.

PATIENT Right. That's what I've been thinking about for two months.

THERAPIST Okay.

PATIENT I'm not quite sure. My best guess is that excuse hypothesis.

THERAPIST You know yourself best.

PATIENT I'm the first person out of my neighborhood to get out of college, let alone graduate school. So when they say . . . I often answer their questions by saying, "I'll just see how far I can go."

Now comes a little period of mutual adjustment, as I try to get the patient's intentions word for word, his trying so hard to be a "good example." Notice how I finally declare myself with him, using the existential methods: "There *is* something good about that. You and other people could be quite hurt." And, later, "You've been a good example. You don't want to let people down about that." This is the active empathy Havens has described, reaching for the particular existence which is his, which might get otherwise lost among its relatives.

THERAPIST . . . so there's a lot riding on this.

PATIENT I didn't mean that. I didn't want to get everyone's hopes up.

THERAPIST I see. So . . .

PATIENT Including my own. If I understand the odds, I won't be too disappointed whichever way it goes.

THERAPIST I see, maybe it's a way of preparing yourself, and everyone else, for the possibility of a defeat.

PATIENT Yah, I thought that was good.

THERAPIST There is something good about that. You and other people could be quite hurt.

PATIENT Uh huh. But within a week that I got here, I saw how I stood with my class, and I'm pretty average. So that's good. I'm not way down on the scale and I'm not way up.

THERAPIST You're comfortable being in the middle there.

PATIENT Yah.

THERAPIST Some people are uncomfortable being in the middle, but for you that's a good place to be.

PATIENT Or even a little on the low side . . . might give me a little more motivation . . .

THERAPIST . . . to dig in there and do it. All right, so one idea you've had, why you wanted an excuse, is that some people have had high hopes for you.

PATIENT I don't know if that's the right terminology.

THERAPIST Put it in your own words.

PATIENT They've just been kinda supportive. What's the right word. Just a "good example." Not that my parents go around saying, "My son, the graduate student." That is not it.

THERAPIST It's more that you've been a good example. Not "The Best of Saturday Night Live," or something like that. It's more of a quiet pride. You've been a good example. You don't want to let people down about that.

PATIENT (Jaw set, nods with eyes, perhaps, welling)

THERAPIST (Also nodding) I sense there is a lot of feeling there.

PATIENT Yah, there is. A friend came down from Milwaukee last night. We were saying you've got to let yourself alone about this stuff. I push myself a little too hard. . . . I don't know. Sometimes, I seem to get the hang of it . . . but then this thing comes out of nowhere, and that's what worries me.

THERAPIST Okay.

PATIENT I'm stable for a couple of days, and then this thing comes out of nowhere. (Finger points accusingly at head (probably unconscious))

This finger pointing at the head is one of the most common signs of an accusatory, opposing current. One of the virtues of looking at many videotapes is that you get to see this gesture in crucial places, over and over. I had never noticed it before in polite society or in conducting interviews without the videotape. Let us call it Gustafson's sign, to be modest. So I now work the opposing current, that he "blames himself," while I pull the main current along, of his pain in his heart, especially with my unconscious gesture of my own hand over my own heart.

THERAPIST So then you blame yourself for that.

PATIENT Yah, maybe I do. A little bit (voice breaking).

THERAPIST In all probability, it's not nowhere. It seems like nowhere. You just don't know what hit you sometimes. But maybe we can see what nowhere is about because I think there is good reason for it, but you're not familiar enough with how this works.

PATIENT I'm pretty sure that's it.

THERAPIST You understand it in general. There is something painful about being a good example, and (hand on heart now unconsciously) being concerned that you'll fall short of it. . . . You can feel a lot of emotion about that.

PATIENT I think, I'm not sure that's what I'm feeling emotion about?

THERAPIST (Hand still on heart) You might be feeling emotion about something else. What are you feeling emotion about? You look full of emotion.

PATIENT I'm kinda tired of the whole thing.

THERAPIST It's important to you not to cry right now.

PATIENT I could, if I wanted to . . .

THERAPIST All right . . .

PATIENT No, I want to stay with it.

THERAPIST There's certain things that, if you thought about them all the . . .

PATIENT Hold it, I wanta say something. I wanted to say so many things you're supposed to put aside. Just to get through everyday life. Moving away from the house. Reminding myself that the parents are going to be closer to getting to retirement. I mean, there's like an unwritten law somewhere which says, you just gotta deal with it. Not getting overly sad about it.

THERAPIST So you're very sensitive to that stuff.

PATIENT (Voice breaking) lately . . . lately.

THERAPIST In this period, the folks getting older, and . . .

PATIENT It doesn't have to be something close. It could be something I read in the paper.

THERAPIST Like?

PATIENT Something that happens to some innocent person. Uh, people losing their jobs.

This interview, so far, has not called for much analytic technique, but here is a little bit, where I invite him to let in what is right there on the periphery, waiting to be invited — just giving a little room, for free association.

THERAPIST (Noting tears in his eyes) Who are you weeping about? Obviously you associated to somebody.

PATIENT (Grabbing Kleenex) I don't know.

THERAPIST Maybe you? . . . It hurts.

PATIENT (Now crying into hands.)

THERAPIST So you don't know why but you are very sensitive to these kinds of losses right now . . . folks retiring, somebody losing a job. You struggle not to, but it touches you. . . . You don't think it should.

PATIENT I wouldn't say that. I just think I should deal with it, but it shouldn't have that much effect on me.

THERAPIST Not that much. It bothers you that it affects you so much. You figure you should take it in stride. But that's not how it is. It's taken hold of you more than you would expect. I'm sure we can find out why that is.

PATIENT I like to think I've gone through tougher things.

After a little more of riding his opposition to his own sensitivity, I said that, while he feels he "should take it in stride," that's "not how it is." This brought us back to the matters of fact, to history. We then compared his transition from high school to college to his transition from college to graduate school. While he had thought the first *should* have been more difficult, he felt how the second "ripped him up." He was much more alone now. Should we have a look at where this bothered him the most? Yes, he was ready. On went the history, into the most painful episode of his arrival here, when he burst into tears in the supermarket, buying goods for his apartment, with his parents. I will leave off this history here of the young man with chest pain, returning to its conclusion at the close of Chapter 12 concerning the work of James Mann. We will see why this young man was in such pain about separating from his parents to become a big success in graduate school.

History is not given without riding the objections to its being told, without riding in to find that individual to whom the particular intentions mean so much. But most practitioners do not have the virtuoso talent of Havens for all the different ways to pose the opposing currents. The reader may turn with relief from the richness of possibilities in Havens and his companions, Sullivan, Winnicott, and Balint, to the diagrams of modern brief dynamic psychotherapy.

INTRODUCTION

Modern Brief Individual Psychotherapy

(CHAPTERS 11 THROUGH 14)

*E*veryone of us is a sea of opposing currents.
*The description of these seas can be very rich and complex in possibilities,
as we have seen in the work of Sullivan, Winnicott, Balint, Gedo, and Havens.
But the description could also be a simple diagram which draws a single distinction between opposed directions, such as south and north, or opposed
forces, such as the tide and the undertow. This kind of map is what we get
from the four modern brief therapists who are best known: Malan, Mann,
Sifneos, and Davanloo.[1]*

*Each of these modern diagrams can be identified by a central distinction,
while each also makes lesser distinctions, which are often shared with the other
diagrams. So they overlap on their margins, while the center is different for*

each of them. Roughly speaking, I would describe the centers of these four diagrams as follows: for Malan, the critical distinction is between duty and true feeling[2]; for Mann, between sincere trying and pain; for Sifneos, between childish regressive behavior and adult responsibility; for Davanloo, between walls of resistance and the flow of true feelings.

Now it is too soon for the reader to appreciate what is possible when you set up a diagram for representing the patient with one of these four distinctions. The following four chapters will attempt to demonstrate what is possible, but I would like to anticipate the conclusions very roughly here. Each distinction allows the patient and therapist to tell a class of related stories. For Malan, the stories are about patients who are devoted to their duty, narrowly, until the therapist helps them to discover their opposite true feelings. For Mann, the stories are of patients who have struggled so long and hard to be something worthwhile, but, in spite of their best efforts, they find themselves back in pain. For Sifneos, the stories are of patients who pretend to be children sneaking around with sexual interests, because they are afraid to own up to their powerful, adult, sexual demands. For Davanloo, the stories are of patients who sit passively behind walls of vagueness, until the wall is destroyed by the therapist, whereupon the patient has a breakthrough into true feeling. Obviously, it is possible to draw points of overlap between these four classes of stories, but it is remarkable how each of these four therapists generates his own class of story over and over again.[3]

A patient seeing any one of these men will have the opportunity to see if he or she can organize his or her own individual story as a variation of the therapist's class of stories. Maybe his or her sea of opposing currents, which is more inchoate than that of the doctor, can be described better with the doctor's map. Maybe the central distinction of this doctor will improve the narrative flow of the patient, so that the story can be better told than ever before. Maybe not; often yes, because the class of stories that each of these doctors allows is a class of stories that is very common in English or American society. Most of our lives are already *organized along the lines of these archetypal, cultural stories, but we think ourselves so individual that we are unaware of the simplicity of form which we share with our neighbors. I think this is what allows the doctor with one of these four diagrams to hear many moving tales. The narrative flow is improved for many neurotic patients.[4]*

These four methods have also been very useful for the progress of the field of modern brief individual psychotherapy. First they appear to be straightforward to learn.[5] Secondly, they appear to transmit across long distances, literally by reading the text of the author, or figuratively by watching a videotape of the author at work. Thirdly, the description and demonstration of standard technique have encouraged follow-up studies, which have secured the reputation of the field. Fourthly, the reproducibility, transmission, and reputation of these four doctors have invited a kind of commercial success which invites interest in the field set up around them. A little deification of the pioneers is therefore to be welcomed.[6]

However, the reader needs a few words of warning concerning the risks he or she will have to run in learning these modern methods. The chief danger I see is that the reader will actually *learn one of these methods, perhaps after a year or two of trial and error. Then what?*

Then he or she is in trouble. This is highly probable, because he or she will have some successes, which the method makes possible, and some failures, which the method makes likely. After all, each method is only one class of stories. Therefore, each has a limited domain of patients who can describe themselves well along the lines offered. The trouble for the doctor is that he or she becomes anxious after the early success begins to pale.

This situation invites dogmatism. Many of us like to learn only one trick. When this trick has its bad days, many of us become more insistent about its good days. We become devoted to a narrow school of practicing. We become apologists for the school of Davanloo, or whatever.

This is a shame. It is unfortunate for our patients, but even worse for ourselves. The richness of all the possible opposing currents becomes reduced to the same class of story over and over again.[7] *We lose connection with the fertility of the field. We stop learning. No one of these methods is worth the lifetime of a student. These teachers have already made that sacrifice. Therapists need a drift for their education which is good for a lifetime of curiosity and pleasure. Being locked in a snug harbor of dogmatism puts an end.*[8]

Fortunately, there is an alternative. This is to appreciate what distinctions are possible with each method, what stories can be told, what domain of patients is likely. Because some families are organized by the distinction between duty and true feeling, we do not have to look for all *families to be derivable from this rule. We can consider that each diagram of modern brief therapy is consistent with the rules of one class of families. We may allow ourselves to know many classes of families, which makes our lives much more interesting, which makes our ability to get the story much more wide-ranging. We may have the entire tradition of psychotherapy as our own private sea for our own education.*[9]

11. *Malan: Duty and True Feeling*

ALTHOUGH David Malan gave up his method in the late 1970s after writing very well about it for nearly 20 years (1963, 1976, 1979), I still think the method has much to recommend.[1] For a class of cases this metaphor tells very well what the patient will do and what the therapist needs to respond for progress. The most successful example of this kind of detailed prediction, in the second series from Balint's Workshop on Brief Psychotherapy, was the case of the Zoologist (1976, p. 267).[2]

THE CASE OF THE ZOOLOGIST

"The patient . . . was a young man of 22 with a previously successful career, who was studying zoology in order to become an ethologist, but who six months previously had suddenly thrown up his studies." The referring psychiatrist saw a "constant conflict" between this young man and his father, the boy having a "genuine desire" to be a zoologist, the father wanting the boy to do something of higher "social and financial status." The boy gave in to the father by smashing his new start in college.

He came in bitterness to the first interview at the Tavistock, saying how his parents, but more his father, had "no idea of his son's sense of vocation or his deep love of animals." He got the interviewer to try very hard to "understand," to ask many questions, and to interpret a connection between his hostility to his teacher, his father and the referring psychiatrist, "all without avail."

A "simple remark, based on a 'choked' quality in the patient's voice when he spoke of things that mattered to him, that 'he seemed to have a lot of intense feeling that couldn't come out,' . . . finally broke the deadlock. . . . At this the patient, suddenly opening up, spoke of an incident in which a little girl had put her hand in his and said, 'I like you,' which he said had been one of the proudest moments of his life" (p. 268).

So what does this "strange story" mean? "The patient's nuclear problem was that his love for his parents had become spoiled by his parents' lack of understanding and his own anger about it, and that — much as he longed to — he could no longer entrust himself to close human relations for fear he would be let down again." He therefore acted out his mistrust with the interviewer, but the interviewer could penetrate this by his intuitive recognition of the boy's need for expressing love. "The story of the little girl who loved and trusted him falls into place immediately." An extremely meaningful problem had reverberated between the relations with the parents, the interviewer (transference), and outside persons. When the perspective from each corner of the so-called "triangle of insight" is the same powerful and identical perspective, there is great hope that what is most wrong is found. The prediction of the research team was that this trouble with disappointment in love, and the self-destructive anger which would follow, would be gone over and over in the brief psychotherapy (pp. 270–271).

Indeed this held true, even sooner than expected, for the therapist went on a long holiday and therapy didn't begin for three months. The patient's love was thwarted even before he began. His response was to distance the therapist for the next nine sessions! He would punish the therapist, and himself, by not using the opportunity. Very much as he had punished his father, and himself, by throwing up the opportunity of college. The therapist knew the patient had gone "wandering" by session 4, and suggested that "perhaps he was feeling that he wanted to escape from the relation that had gone wrong with me" (p. 273). Although this "obviously meant a lot to him," for he could see now that this was the painful story of his life, he could not or would not forgive the therapist his absence.

Finally, by session 9, the patient went so far as to complain to the therapist that " . . . since he started treatment not only had his relations with human beings become worse, but now even his relation with animals had become spoilt" (p. 274). The therapist was more than ready for this and threw it right back at him. He told him that this was exactly what he did when disappointed and angry. He wrecked things and then said it was the fault of the person who disappointed him, whether it was his parents or now the therapist. "The patient became animated and admitted openly for the first time that he had thrown up college to spite his father. In the next session he said that his relation to animals had improved again."

The therapist was more than ready to catch the same hell over the termination planned for session 17. In session 16, an association to a complex dream was that "when doing his National Service in the Army, he had been transferred from a station that he liked to one that he didn't, and had deliberately done his work badly so that he had failed to get a commission." This allowed the therapist to tell him "that he was dissatisfied with what the therapist had given him, as he was dissatisfied with what his parents had given him, that he was now being 'transferred' from therapy to life, and that it looked as if he would deliberately sabotage his life in order to get his own back on the therapist. The patient smiled and said it was probably right . . . ." A dramatic upsurg of warmth and hope arose in the next and final session, including a dream of meeting a girl with whom the "barrier" had prevented any progress, memories of being a small boy with his father at Christmas, wanting to write a story about a "very motherly woman" he once knew and to write a "diary plus" to send to the therapist, "to which the latter readily agreed" (pp. 274–275).

This ending was a success in one way and not in another. He went back to college, and eventually finished. He made sustained attempts to pursue girls, which "previously the 'barrier' had always made. . . impossible." But the reader familiar with the "depressive position" will see trouble in the great hopes he entertained in the last, 17th session. As Balint wrote of such patients, " . . . behind every one of the many forms of object-relation there remains practically unchanged the eternal archaic wish: I shall be loved for every little bit that I am, by everyone of my objects for whom I need not care, whose interests and sensitivity I need not consider, who shall be just there when I want them, and shall not bother me after my needs have been satisfied" (1952, p. 263). This Zoologist had not yet accepted and passed through "the depression — caused by the realization that the environment is largely indifferent towards us (or as someone said to me recently 'has not been cut to fit us') and that we must renounce certain of our wishes if we want any favour from our environment." This had not been " . . . accepted as inevitable, and the attempts at circumventing it largely given up" (Balint, 1952, p. 259).

And so he was set up, still, for depression, which came and went over the next two years, and he was allowed to come and go from the therapist for another 15 sessions. Two years after session 17 he asked for a session because the "attack of depression and inner confusion was . . . worse than he had ever known before." This was traced by the therapist and patient to his having discovered an old diary of his girlfriend, where he found out that she had been going out with another man in the year before the Zoologist and the girl became engaged. The therapist gave the patient his usual interpretation about how he wrecked things when disappointed, and the "result was that he succeeded in talking over his feelings with her and their relation improved again" (p. 276).

The final, final episode of the therapy was that a year later the therapist got a letter from the patient complaining that the girlfriend, Barbara, had gone from being "full of life" to "apathy." When the patient came in to present Barbara's "case history," the therapist "brushed aside" this attempt and suggested that she was probably reacting to something in the patient. "Perhaps he had been less able to be affectionate since the diary incident" (p. 276).[3] Perhaps he "still hadn't forgiven" her? "Then, noticing something rather nasty about the patient's smile, the therapist suggested that the patient took some satisfaction in reporting to him that things had gone wrong." When the patient admitted satisfaction over a breakdown of his father, the therapist "then took the bit in the teeth and suggested that since he seemed to have been glad about his father's failure, perhaps he wanted to make the therapist fail too, by making a mess of his life. . . . Shortly after this the patient, near to tears, began to admit how cold he had been to Barbara over the past year."

A happy ending? Not quite. Follow-up three years and five months after the very final, final session (32 altogether) discovered he had married Barbara a few months after that session, had two children, and become successful in his work as an ethologist. While he had managed to fight off interference in his job, skillfully, and while he spoke of good companionship with Barbara, "his remarks suggested he handles conflict with her by avoidance, even indifference" (p. 243). The judges felt the criteria for "dynamic change" were "almost completely fulfilled" concerning work, but only half met with his wife. "He had never really been able to forgive her for what he felt, seemingly quite unjustifiably, to be her betrayal" (p. 277).

Balint describes this kind of falling short of complete success in psychotherapy as follows:

. . . the patients leaving analysis before the depressive state could be resolved usually complain a lot, try to raise guilt feelings in their environment (and in their former analyst) by exhibiting and even flaunting their shortcomings, but they hardly ever want to make real efforts towards a basic change. Apparently they cannot renounce their right to expect miraculous help from their environment—a clear remnant of the archaic object-love. (1952, p. 256)[4]

THE CENTRAL DISTINCTION FOR MALAN

Malan had less complicated ideas about psychotherapy than his teacher Balint. For Malan it always has been a simple diagram, with two opposed considerations.[5] But it is a powerful diagram for some patients, like the Zoologist. On the one hand, there is what Henry Ezriel of the Tavistock called "the required relationship," which has to be challenged. For the Zoologist this is the withdrawal. On the other hand, there is what Ezriel called "the avoided relationship," which has to be reached for, to find what Malan would call the patient's "true feelings." For the Zoologist, this was his love and his pleasure in punishing others when disappointed.

What is therapy? Very simple: the therapist is as vigorous as possible in challenging the "required relationship," to get as deeply as possible to the "true feelings." "The aim of every moment of every session is to put the patient in touch with as much of his true feelings as he can bear" (1979, p. 74). Of course, this aim has to be balanced by reckoning how accessible the true feelings are to being reached, how much anxiety or pain will come with them, and whether the patient has the capacity to bear them. "Rapport is the universal indicator by which the therapist may be constantly guided. If rapport increases after an intervention, the intervention was appropriate and appropriately made; if rapport decreases, his intervention was inappropriate (not necessarily *wrong*) and he must wait until he can try something else" (1976, p. 75).[6]

What are "true feelings"? Many American readers may not know what a "true feeling" is about. It is not the same as a "feeling," as opposed to "thinking," that is, is being emotional as opposed to discursive.

Readers of romances know better what a "true feeling" is about. Statements such as the following qualify: "It is my duty to love you, but I do not. I truly love another." "I ought to be kind, but I want to tear him to pieces." "I am supposed to respect him, but I hold him in contempt."

English readers know this distinction much better than we Americans do. They know its opposite term, which is more indistinct for us. "Duty" is everyday vocabulary for them, while for us it is an embarrassment, as if the individual using the word was confusing himself with his great-great-grandfather back in the nineteenth century. The English are explicit about what duty calls for in the family, the firm, and the country. They are very interested in stories in which someone is drawn into his or her "duty," only later to come forth with "true feelings" which are opposed to "duty." "Duty" is compelling, but it can be too narrow.

The power of Robin Skynner's method for family therapy (Skynner, 1981; Skynner, 1984) draws upon the interest of the English family in this kind of story. Robin falls in with the family, becoming a loyal member, until he cannot bear the feelings he is carrying from the interaction with them. He bets that this "bomb" in himself is the "bomb" in them set up by their interactions, which stimulate such feeling but do not allow it to be brought forward. The "true feeling" could be sexual excitement, destructiveness, envy, or whatever. He shows them it is possible to have the feeling, without wrecking things, by showing it in himself, often humorously, toward one or more of them. English families love this kind of ending, and so they learn from Robin how to integrate loyalty, which has been too constrained, with deeper feeling.

For us there are occasions which pull for the same construction, between duty and true feeling. One is practicing medicine. The doctor is to take care of the patient, whatever his true feelings are. This is his duty. All kinds of trouble derive from this essential distinction between the doctor's duty and his actual, personal, true feeling. One class of problems is generated by the doctor's locating himself at a distance from the patient, only thinking of what the patient, as an object, requires of him, not noticing his own responsiveness, which builds up and is sent back as unnoticed hostility, or whatever. The attempt to practice "pure medicine" backfires. Another class of problems is generated by the doctor's locating himself very close to patients, who may remind him of mother or grandfather or whatever, so the doctor is unable to stand back and make the ordinary, but tough, decisions that subject the patient to painful but necessary procedures. These classes of problems are so prevalent that the so-called "Balint Groups" or "GP Groups" have been set up for doctors to present their difficult working relationships with patients, by bringing both the objective requirements of the treatment *and* the true feelings of the doctor into focus *together*, the perspective standing back and the perspective standing in, the perspectives which are separated by the distinction between duty and true feeling.

Now, one occasion which puts us therapists in this central dilemma of the doctor is the occasion of first interviews with patients wanting psychotherapy.

We too are likely to be drawn into one of the two positions where doctors find themselves. One is that we get a very objective description of the patient's situation, from a distance, but do not move to get in touch. Often we'll miss the patient's ability to connect. This may leave us only with a view of what's wrong, which may give such a negative picture that we miss a chance for the possibility of brief therapy. Or, conversely, we may not notice our own annoyance with the patient, say, who's been whining or running on at excessive length, so we lose crucial data about how the patient is likely to wreck the therapeutic relationship by what he obliges us to feel about him. The other position we are drawn into, easily, is being so close to the patient, so anxious to help, that we do not stand back and survey the extent of the damage. We take on people with the best of intentions, in brief therapy, who need more than we could ever give.

I think the most lasting contribution of Malan's diagram of duty and true feeling is for this job of selection for brief therapy, where his "double description" keeps us entertaining both positions — standing back, and close in. His six chapters at the close of *Individual Psychotherapy and the Science of Psychodynamics* (1979) and his "Cautionary Tales" at the close of *The Frontier of Brief Psychotherapy* (1976, Chapter 16, "Some Contraindications") are about the necessity of both positions, the discoveries we make when we take up both, the calamities which befall us and the patient when we fail to consider from both positions. I will return to this at more length in Chapters 19 and 20, when I discuss our clinic's procedures concerning selection.

Getting back to the Zoologist, we find the same kind of situation. His duty is to do as his father says, to look for a field of "higher financial and social status." But when he goes along, there's hell to pay, because his need to express love is given up and his revengefulness is set going. He will wreck things. Of course, he goes along with the therapist, too, with three months of waiting for him on holiday, with ending at 17 sessions when he is not ready to end, and will take his revenge on the therapist — except that the therapist is ready for the whole pattern and can call him on it. Several lessons are necessary. Of course, he also goes along with his girlfriend, who becomes his wife, until she too disappoints him, and he withdraws as always. It is a shame she never got a chance to learn what the therapist knew about interrupting such performances! Perhaps his withdrawal fit some need of hers; we never learn.

The Zoologist is very much like many doctors I know, like many people in related "helping professions," such as social work, teaching, psychiatry, and so forth. We are supposed to help, but we feel the opposite inclinations. Malan's diagram is able to pick up these situations. It describes what we are "supposed" to be thinking, responding, and doing, while looking to describe our opposed "true feelings." This "double description," as Bateson (1979) would say, is perfectly tuned to those of us who organize our worlds along the lines of this distinction between duty and true feeling. It draws out the important events of our stories.

The Domain of Malan's Technique

Malan got overly hopeful about the potential of this point of view, which only ended up disappointing him.[7] We have seen what is right about making the distinction between duty and true feeling the very center. People who devote themselves to their duty, as sons or doctors or teachers or social workers or whatever, often do not notice when they are going one hundred and eighty degrees from what they want. It's quite orienting to find this out!

Some readers may have noticed that we are right back to where Freud started with his invention of psychoanalysis. Only instead of the awkward translation of German, we are getting a version in more colloquial English. Rather than people burdened by their superegos (in German, *Uber-Ich*), who do not know about the opposite urges of their id (*Es*), we have people lost in duty, not knowing their true feelings. So now it seems that Lucy, the good governess, devoted to the children, was hiding from herself her true feeling of wanting to possess the children's father (Breuer and Freud, 1895).

So this brief psychotherapy of Malan is essentially a return to Freud's original point of view. Notice that Freud's favorite therapeutic idea, that of demonstrating the Oedipus complex, depends entirely for its dramatic power on a comparison between supposed, conventional duty, and its opposite. One is supposed to honor one's father, but one would like to kill him and take his place. One is supposed to be taken care of nicely by one's mother, but one wants to take sexual possession of her.

So I think there is something useful here. People taken over by duty are often very excited by finding opposite desire. They recover their bearings. There is now east and west, where once there was only west. Our psychiatry residents have always gotten the biggest kick out of this sort of thing. Most of them have been in some derivative of "psychoanalysis," but they also love similar occasions in supervision or seminars, where they can share their hate or desire for patients they are supposed to look after, and so forth. So far, so good.

But then the trouble began for Freud, and much later for Malan. It could also begin for us, unless we learn something about the limits of this metaphor. After Freud's discovery of the usefulness of this distinction between duty and true feelings for many of his patients, he still had some very painful experiences in which he could not help certain people. Dora was one famous case. The Case of Homosexuality in a Woman much later was another. One line of response to such difficulty was to look for darker and more primitive content to bring to light. We have seen this attempt succeed in the hands of Ferenczi and Rank, concerning the Croatian Musician, who was boldly put in touch with her autoerotic obsessions (Chapter 3).

Malan followed the same line of solution as Ferenczi and Rank. His diagram could be as simple as ever: Be as vigorous as possible against resistance. Get as much true feeling as possible, as rapport will allow. Only the greater difficulty would be to ferret out more unusual, more complex, and more primitive content. *Individual Psychotherapy and the Science of Psychodynamics* (1979) teaches the novice to look first for ordinary, denied urges such as jealousy of a girlfiend, and gradually takes him or her deeper into the darker waters of more disturbed people. The diagram is still resistance, and true feeling.

Well, it works occasionally, even with very disturbed people, and then makes for the terrific English story of duty and emergent true feeling, but more often than not it does not work.[8] Why not?

Well, first of all, many, many people will not tell their so-called true feelings, even when invited to do just that, even when their resistance is well challenged. Something more powerful is needed. Indeed, two revolutions of perspective were needed to meet this difficulty. This has been the subject of previous chapters. Reich posed the "constant attitude" as a "wall" between therapist and patient. This was the first revolution, of character analysis. Alexander, Sullivan, Winnicott, and Balint posed the need for "strengthened contexts" which would make the patient's feeling bearable the second time around when received by the therapist. This was the second interpersonal revolution of perspective.

Although Malan bowed to Alexander and French (1976, p. 351)[9] and his teacher, Balint, he actually borrowed very little from them about relationships.[10] Thus, we need not be shocked that Malan found Davanloo's technique to be the answer to all his questions: "In summary: Freud discovered the unconscious; Davanloo has discovered how to use it therapeutically" (1980a, p. 23). After all, the revolution of character analysis *is* powerful. Reich was better at "getting through walls" than Freud, and Davanloo is faster at this than Reich. Malan seems to have been so bowled over by this revolution that he gave up the virtues of his own perspective.

The other major set of problems which cannot be handled by Malan's diagram is that many people know their "true feelings," but this is useless to them when they do not know how to act to get out of destructive interactions. As Gedo summarized, and as Alexander, Sullivan, Winnicott, and Balint showed so well, patients have to learn how to keep from sacrificing themselves. Most patients have their own kind of vicious circle with other people, wherein they lose their vital psychological functions: their potential for calm, their ability to defend themselves, and their readiness to tell actual capability from illusion.[11] If this occurs to an individual, knowing how he feels about the experience will only be the consolation of knowing his own misery very, very well. Indeed, the Zoologist reached through to his feelings of disappointment and revenge. Still, he could not altogether stop acting on his feeling.

Thus, Freud's great distinction, and Malan's English version of the same distinction, is a good thing for some of us duty-bound types, but it will only reach some few of us, who do not hide behind walls, and some of us it reaches it cannot deliver from painful interactions.[12]

A Daughter of Soap Opera

Perhaps the most common sort of problem to defy Malan's diagram of help is the hysterical patient who discovers true feeling every time she turns around. Her life is a romance, already, of such declarations. I do not mean to say that she will not be helped by this method, for certain histrionic defenses will be produced. Challenging them, as Malan would, often gives a useful beginning. The problem is that it is only a beginning, to know her true feelings. Then she will need help about what to do with them.

For example, a young woman who came to our clinic for spells of panic had had one the night before her trial therapy. I asked her if she did not want to look into this last episode, and off she went with a grand description of working herself into hyperventilation.[13] All I had to do was stop her and say that this sort of thing was usually a distraction from something else which upset a person. Her mother did it, but I didn't see why she had to follow suit, as it only made her think of herself as sick and weak. Right there she could tell me her "true feeling."

PATIENT I know what was bothering me now.

THERAPIST Okay.

PATIENT I just remembered it.

THERAPIST Okay.

PATIENT I was lying in bed, and I was trying to think about us having a party on Friday, and I was trying to think about good things and all of a sudden I started getting angry at Sam for writing me that letter and I was angry because I wanted to tell him how I felt and how he is . . . was being unfair to me, and it was so frustrating because I couldn't tell him and I wanted to and that's what I was thinking about last night and then after that it started to happen.

THERAPIST Okay, isn't that interesting? So what this suggests is that it is real hard for you to be angry at Sam.

PATIENT Yeah, I don't like to be angry at Sam.

THERAPIST Well, let's look at that, shall we?

PATIENT Yeah.

A little more work about her shame in being mad at such a nice person as Sam, and there she was "mad as hell at Sam," but, as the reader will soon see from her following remarks, this discovery of what was hidden by the hyperventilation episode did *not* take care of her difficulty:

THERAPIST So you're mad as hell at Sam and . . .

PATIENT Yeah.

THERAPIST But you seem . . . I can't tell whether you're comfortable with it or uncomfortable. I keep changing my mind. One minute I think, "Well, she seems really, you know, quite straightforward about this and she's mad as hell and hurt and damn it that's the way it is."

PATIENT Yeah. That's how it used to be with him.

THERAPIST That's how you used to be, hmm.

PATIENT And then he changed me I guess?

THERAPIST He did?

PATIENT Yeah, he did. I'd calm down where I wasn't such a hothead when he was around. I would take things and look at them before I'd get angry and see if I should get angry. Because a lot of times I'd get angry over things that in the end aren't . . . when you weigh the cost with the outcome it's just not worth that at all.

THERAPIST Well, that's an improvement.

PATIENT Yeah, it was a very big improvement but now I'm kind of caught in between.

THERAPIST Maybe you're going the other way.

PATIENT Yeah, I don't want to be extreme. I don't want to be weak. I want to be strong. I want to be like, here's the middle, here's this, I want to be right here.

THERAPIST Right, right in the middle. All right, so you have this problem about anger that you used to be something of a hothead and you could flare up over little things and it could even be destructive.

PATIENT But people would take it, men would usually take it.

THERAPIST Hmm. They did take it.

PATIENT Oh, yeah, they did and they'd come back for more. Ha, ha.

THERAPIST Oh, they did?

PATIENT Yeah.

THERAPIST They liked it.

PATIENT I don't know if they liked it. I always overpowered in every relationship I've ever been in until Sam.

THERAPIST I see. So now maybe you've swung too far the other way.

PATIENT Yeah.

THERAPIST Maybe you're acting. . . . Sam was right about that, in a way.

PATIENT Yeah, in a way.

THERAPIST Then you could be overpowering and knock men down.

PATIENT Right.

THERAPIST Now you're the one . . . now it's . . . you swung too far to the . . .

PATIENT I get knocked down.

THERAPIST Yeah, and you're knocking yourself down.

PATIENT I'm knocking myself down.

THERAPIST You're letting yourself act like your mother does, that kind of stuff. Huh?

PATIENT Yeah, I guess so.

THERAPIST You see, you're trying not to . . . it seems you're trying not to be destructive to something that's been good . . . but you go very far and then you act like you're not even allowing yourself to be made when you're made as hell, even to feel it, even when he's not there.

PATIENT I know and at home when I'll get mad at one of my roommates even — before I would just yell, but now I think and I don't say anything now. I just let it boil inside. I might say something to somebody else, but I won't say it to the person I'm mad at.

THERAPIST Really?

PATIENT Because I don't want them to think I'm a real bitch, and I don't want to . . .

THERAPIST Yeah, but you might go too far, and not tell somebody off when they ought to hear something from you.

PATIENT Yes, I know. A roommate of mine needs to hear it.

THERAPIST And she needs to be told off, I bet?

PATIENT She does, and I don't want to do it because I know what she'll say. She'll cut me down.

THERAPIST She will?

PATIENT She'll just level me. That's when I'm afraid people will level me when I criticize them.

THERAPIST I see.

PATIENT They'd level me because they don't . . . like I think a lot of people do that. When someone criticizes you, you tend to take the defense, instead of listening to that person and just saying . . . . You take the defense and that's what turns an argument into a real fight.

THERAPIST Exactly.

PATIENT That's because people take the defense when they should just listen and say either you're right or you're wrong.

THERAPIST They get defensive.

PATIENT I get defensive, so do a lot of people.

THERAPIST Sure, they do. Sure, they do.

PATIENT Sam never really got defensive. He'd listen, and he'd say, "you know, you're right, and I know I have to change that about myself and, you know, I'm working on it, but I don't appreciate you yelling at me or doing this or doing that."

THERAPIST Hmm. That helped you?

PATIENT Yeah, it did because it made me understand that I . . . you know, I can't run around getting defensive or screaming at people every time they criticize me because they're not perfect.

THERAPIST Right.

PATIENT But now I do feel like I'm down for the count.

THERAPIST All right, all right. You're pretty smart. You figure out things.

PATIENT Well, now that I . . . when I came in here I didn't have any idea what was wrong, but after sitting down and mapping everything out, it all fits in one way or another. It's like a big soap opera. You know, everything fits at the end.

THERAPIST Yeah, right. So, you're down for the count because you're concerned about being too destructive in your ferocity, and you tempered that before, but now you're knocking yourself out.

All right, so now we have a plausible picture of her swinging from one excess to another, from screeching like mother, to holding it all in and becoming sick like her mother. She still is quite a ways from getting somewhere. She is like the Zoologist in that she too wants to let go with all her true feelings, whether her environment can bear her true feelings or not. One way to tackle this setup for depression, this "depressive position," is to pose "the ordinary solution," since it invites the patient to see whether she can get what she needs without having to be so damn special. After all, *having* to be special only means you will often get disappointed, and depressed. Why not the ordinary solution?[14]

THERAPIST All right. Well, let's talk about that. You mean if somebody is mad as hell at their boyfriend, and they don't want to act precipitously, they're tempted to — boy, they'd really like to sock it to them — and so, they don't know yet. What do you think people ordinarily do when they're in that situation? What would be an ordinary way to handle that?

PATIENT Well, one percent beats up her boyfriend, but I don't think anyone deserves to be hit. I don't think that's the right answer. And then another person I know sits and takes it and gets abused emotionally because she does take it, and she gets taken advantage of and she gets abused and I am not to be abused by anybody and I won't put up with it.

THERAPIST Good for you. So, those are the extremes, aren't they?

PATIENT Those are the two extremes.

THERAPIST What would be in the middle? What would be a sort of middle ground, sort of sense about this?

PATIENT Sitting down and saying to the person, "I'm mad at you and this is why." And then they'll respond and then go from there. I would love to do that, but I can't because he's gone. How do I have a conversation with someone who's across the ocean?

THERAPIST Usually, one writes a letter.

PATIENT Yeah, I guess so. I guess that's the only way I'm going to be able to because I don't like to be in a fight with anybody because it makes me feel very bad inside.

THERAPIST I can see that, yeah.

PATIENT I don't like to fight.

THERAPIST *But being mad and being in a fight are not the same thing.*

PATIENT *I know they're not. They're different.*

THERAPIST *But you tend to run them together.*

PATIENT *Yeah.*

THERAPIST You're mad and you don't want to be destructive and have a fight. But you are mad and you don't want to be taken advantage of.

PATIENT Right.

THERAPIST And so, one thing to do, one ordinary thing to do, you're quite aware of. You can tell the person in a matter-of-fact way you're mad. You don't want to be destructive but you're mad. Huh? So why not that? Why wouldn't you do that? That would be the ordinary thing to do, I think. It would be, you know, the ordinary, constructive thing to do. Huh?

PATIENT Yeah, that would be the ordinary thing to do.

THERAPIST I'm not saying you should do that. I'm just asking a question.

PATIENT Yeah, I know. I'm not ordinary though. I get carried away, either to one extreme or the other in the letter.

THERAPIST I know. I see that, but *that either wrecks you or wrecks him.*

PATIENT Yeah, I know.

THERAPIST It's tempting.

PATIENT When I write a really good letter that's really in the middle of those extremes — but I haven't been able to do that — it makes me feel really good about sending it.

THERAPIST I bet it does. I bet your self-respect is very . . .

PATIENT It's very good. It's very high. The last letter I sent, the one, it was almost in the middle, except it was a little too destructive, but not so much where it was going to destroy anything if he really wants me. But still I do have a hard time keeping my anger in check. Either I just sit down and let it roll or else I'll just say, goddamn it, you're not going to do that to me.

THERAPIST Hmm. Sure.

PATIENT And if I could even it out, maybe that would help. I don't know how it would hurt. I don't know.

THERAPIST You're very clear. I say, "Well, why not tell him you're mad and not be destructive either to him or to you," and you say, "Well, I do that sometimes and I feel good about myself, but boy I feel like letting go. I want to let it roll." You're feeling such a load of it.

PATIENT I just want to tell him to . . .

THERAPIST Fuck off . . .

PATIENT Leave me alone!

THERAPIST Mmm.

PATIENT And just have him crawl back and just apologize, because once I can be so mad that I just want to kill something and if someone says they're sorry, it's gone. It's just gone. If they apologize and they're sincere about it. If they sincerely know that they're wrong, be it my mother or my father or one of my friends or Sam or anyone, I am no longer angry at all. I do not let it stick with me at all. It's gone.

THERAPIST Okay. So if they . . .

PATIENT I'm very forgiving.

THERAPIST All right but before you're forgiving you're very punishing.

PATIENT Very.

THERAPIST You'd like, "Oh, boy, crawl and beg!"

PATIENT Right.

THERAPIST And *what you're dealing with is not only anger. You want to punish him, until he says uncle.*

PATIENT Yeah. I think so. It's terrible but . . .

THERAPIST What's so terrible about it?

PATIENT You shouldn't treat another person like that, I guess.

THERAPIST *But it's tempting, isn't it?*

PATIENT Yeah, it is but I don't like feeling like that because then again it makes me feel like my mother.

THERAPIST Yeah, I guess she did a lot of that.

PATIENT She did unintentionally. She didn't figure on this. I could never tell her any of this because she'd take the defense and get all upset and I don't want to do that to her, but I think a lot of it, you know, has to do with her because she's just a bitch with men.

THERAPIST Yeah. So you're tempted to be like her.

PATIENT Yeah. I would because . . .

THERAPIST Children identify with their parents. They see their mother doing it and they think, "Oh boy, I'll do it too," even if it is destructive.

PATIENT Yeah.

THERAPIST So it's very strong in you, this urge to really sock it to him and punish him and make him crawl and beg and really, really be destructive.

PATIENT I've done that before with other people.

THERAPIST You've done it to other men.

PATIENT Yes.

THERAPIST So, and you've done injury that way.

PATIENT Yeah, my old boyfriend, I just abused him because he took it. The more he took it, the more I gave. I need someone who's going to be even with me and not succumb. . . . I don't want a man that I can push around. That's what, I'm testing them.

THERAPIST Right, you don't respect them then.

PATIENT I'm testing Sam and he tested out just fine.

THERAPIST Good. All right, but nevertheless he tested out, I mean, he's not somebody lacking in self-respect. He's a man.

PATIENT Yes, he is.

THERAPIST And, but boy, you're full of this urge to wreck him and so that's why this is what you're having trouble with. Right now.

PATIENT I think so.

THERAPIST It seems to me that you're getting closer to a solution but it's still a problem, *this urge to punish is so strong.*

PATIENT I know it is. I just wish that he would think of me instead of himself more while he's over there and let me know what's happening because he might be over there and have all these new things, but I'm still back here and I'm wondering about him everyday, and he's making me angry because he's not taking consideration that there's someone here that's worried about him. He's just going off in his own little . . .

THERAPIST Thinking of himself.

PATIENT And being selfish and letting me sit here and worry for the both of us.

THERAPIST And stew, yeah, really. No wonder you're mad.

PATIENT I'm mad. Yeah, I'm mad and then I'll get mad and then I'll think, well wait until the next letter comes. I'll wait until the next letter comes and then I'll see if he's nicer to me.

THERAPIST Right and then decide whether to cut off his head next week.

PATIENT Uh huh. I think it's on the couch [she points to my watch I was looking for].

THERAPIST Oh, there it is. Thanks. I was trying to check on the time. All right, so I think we have some understanding of what, what these episodes of General Hospital were about. It was really a way of your holding back this anger and destructive urge that you have. You know, it looks like there might be a better way to do it. You want a way that doesn't make you think, you know, you're some kind of hysterical woman or some such . . .

PATIENT Yeah, I hate hysterical women.

THERAPIST Well, I can see you've seen too much of that stuff. It does a lot of injury to the woman's self-respect.

PATIENT It does, it just makes us look bad as a whole race.

THERAPIST Right, I think you're right. So, you're struggling to find a way to deal with your anger *and* your destructiveness . . . when it's real strong.

PATIENT I don't want it to get out of check.

THERAPIST Well, it can do harm, you know. You know, you're growing up and so you know that this is a force that has to be taken seriously. Well, you and I have to stop in less than 10 minutes. So, it seems like we've come a long way toward understanding you.

PATIENT It does to me too, ha ha. I never really realized all that.

THERAPIST Well, it's easy to work with you. You're really able to do this kind of thing.

PATIENT Thanks. I enjoy it because I get it out, where otherwise I've never gotten any of this out before, I guess. I have in little bits and pieces but I've never, you know, told anyone and no one will ever sit and listen to me and tell me what they think either.

THERAPIST Sure.

And so we come to a close of another episode of General Hospital. Not only did this young woman find her "true feeling," which she was hiding from herself in hyperventilation, but she also posed an "ordinary solution" for herself, and got the distinction straight between anger and cruelty. Finally, she got the distinction between feeling cruel and acting cruel like her mother, however tempting it was to let go with true feeling. She had an "ordinary solution" which allowed for her feeling, yet was more likely to augment her self-respect. I had had to help her find a sensible way to defend herself, when this was being sacrificed to the soap opera relations she got into, like her mother. This is more of a job than locating true feelings.[15]

Think back finally to the Zoologist. He too was caught at wrecking things when disappointed. He too had this forcefully brought home to him. So what's the difference? Very little? Both the therapist of the Zoologist and the therapist of the Daughter of Soap Opera got through to a destructive position of their patient. I have only followed in my way what Malan did or described. This is true, but it is also misleading.

For to do what Malan did or described with the Zoologist is to go beyond the theory in which Malan locates his action. Isn't it interesting that I repeat something demonstrated by Malan by thinking in a theory like that of Sullivan? This is no accident. For no action is comprehended at the logical level in which it is occurring. The less complex may only be surrounded and seen by a map with one more logical level than it contains.[16]

12. *Mann: Sincere Trying and Pain*

MANN HAS CAUGHT ON TO one of the important stories of life in America so well that he arranges to find and enact this story with most neurotic cases. This is Mann's ritual of the 12 sessions. We need to pay attention, even if we would not want to arrange our own work according to his ritual, as this story is all around us.

A Fugitive from Georgia

I like this the best of Mann's cases for its dramatic quality (Mann and Goldman, 1982, pp. 131–165). The inexorable march of a tragedy was halted and reversed. The patient was a 54-year-old black woman who had come to Boston from Georgia four years previous. She had been referred by the primary care unit for depression and for numerous somatic complaints, including headache, backache, swollen and sore ankles, and chronic cough.

She was the mother of seven. She came to Boston with her youngest son when he graduated from high school. She left her husband in Georgia. Within a week of arrival she was hospitalized for ten days with a swollen ankle. Then she was followed by the arthritis clinic, although a definitive diagnosis was never made of her ankle complaints. For the two years prior to seeing Mann, she had made steady visits to primary care. So far, what have we got? One of the most common presentations seen in medicine: aches and pains for which little basis in physical disorder can be found. The next step, too often neglected, is for someone to take the trouble to see if a painful life might explain the pains in the body. For her the step was taken.

The interviewer in psychiatry felt that the following incident from ten years before had been decisive:

One of her brothers had come to her house in a drunken state and demanded the use of her car so that he could go to town to kill someone with whom he had been fighting. She had refused to give him the keys, whereupon he had opened fire on her and her house. She was successful in preventing injury to herself and her children. During the fray, she asked her husband to steal out and get the sheriff. He did steal out of the house, only to disappear and not return for help. For obscure reasons, the patient's sister, who had been a witness to the incident, said it had been all the patient's fault, and from that point on the patient's mother and other family members blamed her. Her relationship with her husband deteriorated so much that she eventually left him and moved to Boston, where several of her children were already living. (Mann and Goldman, 1982, p. 132)

The interviewer sent Mrs. R. to Mann in hopes of her being helped by Mann in brief psychotherapy. The patient began as directly with Mann as she had with the first interviewer. What did she most want help with? She could not understand why her brother had tried to kill her and why her mother had sided with the brother. What made her cry was that her mother died blaming her.

Mann told her that he saw how very lonely she was and how she always felt hurt. She had tried hard, but this is how it had come out. He offered: "Would you like to work on that problem to see if you can't find some way to handle it so that you'll feel better about yourself?" Mrs. R.: "I sure would" (p. 134).

Sessions 2 and 3 brought out several other loose ends to the story to be put together. Mrs. R. thought of her mother as being in hell for the unkindness to herself. Mrs. R. wanted to be in Georgia, but she was driven out by a hex of some kind when she tried to return. In her absence her husband was trying to take sole possession of their place. Finally, her chronic cough dated from the time of the shooting. As is customary for Mann, he offered to make sense of these confusing elements in 12 sessions.

The middle sessions 4 to 8 were concerned with Mann's asking Mrs. R. why she hadn't defended herself. "Why not the ordinary solution?" as Sullivan would say. In session 4, he asked her why, if her mother and family had blamed her for being shot at by the brother, hadn't she explained her own position? She told Mann she said nothing because they hadn't cared to ask her! Her passivity being so marked, Mann thought she must be terrified of her own anger. He found she had been beaten more than her brothers and sisters. How did she feel about that? "Did you take the whippings and say thank you?" (p. 139). The patient seemed to feel no hate. Since she only cried and looked at the floor, Mann told her she was the "goat of the family," someone who had endured all these injustices . . . and wouldn't she please look up at him? She lifted her gaze to his with great effort.

She came in for the fifth session not feeling well, with a new complaint of abdominal pain, ready to have surgery for what some doctor had taken to be gallstones. Mann figured that he had stirred her up by insisting that she look at him at the close of session 4. He thought he'd better settle her down if he could. Essentially, he got a very confusing picture of her feeling controlled by some outside force when she looked at Mann and when she went back to Georgia. Mann subsumed all of this very nicely by telling her she had been "frightened a long time." She agreed it was so, and cried. After session 5, Mann asked the surgeon to hold off. Both the surgeon and Mrs. R. consented, for the time being.

In session 6, Mann brought home to her as plainly as possible that, after what she had been put through by her family, Mrs. R. had to be angry. This allowed him in session 7 to say why she had had "funny feelings" around her family:

"Why are you still scared? . . . I'll tell you . . . you were scared and still are scared when you're around them because they hurt you so much you'd like to beat the hell out of them."
 Mrs. R.: "I guess I would . . (begins to cry)."

In session 8 Mann offered that her hate could not be gotten rid of, until she got it out of her by talking it out. She had to remember her hate in order to forget her hate. She agreed she once nearly put a pitchfork through a cousin's head after he had got her a bad licking by her mother, and she agreed her mother was in hell. The successive approximations of sessions 4 to 8 did come nearer her hatred.

 Session 9 was the beginning of the end of her time with Mann. She seemed to be "wandering off," more remote than before, which Mann could place as the beginning of her response to being dropped by himself. But she was also thinking of going to Georgia to defend her right to her property — only she was afraid that the return would make her sick again. Mann suggested she got sick there because of all the hurt and anger coming back to her when she got to her house. She came in for session 10 planning to leave for Georgia that night, again afraid to enter her own house. Mann supported her again, by telling her that her fear was of her own anger:

I remark that maybe she would like to put a pitchfork through her husband's head; that she doesn't actually have to do that, but that her anger has been preying on her mind for a long time. (p. 156)

Mann also brought up the fact of two more sessions. Did she think Mann was "beating it," just as her husband did in the hour of her being shot at by her brother? She said no.

 She came back from Georgia for session 11 to report that she had not gotten very far with her husband. Mann responded that she did fine under the circumstances. She cried. Since Mann has built in a disappointment so sharply by giving 12, and only 12, sessions, ending on such and such a day, he will see any obscure piece of action by the patient toward the end as a way to handle being left. So Mann saw Mrs. R. as appearing to be a failure in Georgia, to cope with being failed by Dr. Mann in Boston:

DOCTOR I don't think that's the whole thing . . . I think you feel that I'm hurting you too.
MRS. R. I don't feel like that.
DOCTOR Well, whose idea was it, yours or mine, that next week would be the last meeting?
MRS. R. You're the one said that next week would be the last meeting.
DOCTOR You wouldn't say it's the last meeting if it was up to you, would you?
MRS. R. I hope not.

DOCTOR Because if it was up to you we would keep on meeting . . .

MRS. R. We sure would.

DOCTOR So I must be hurting you too.

MRS. R. I couldn't really say that.

DOCTOR I think you're afraid to say that . . . I think you have the feeling that I'm kind of deserting you under fire.

MRS. R. No, I couldn't say that . . . because the way you feel after this long time I should have felt better than the way I do. . . . I could never say that you're deserting me . . .

DOCTOR So it's all your fault? . . . . You don't think I'm deserting you under fire the way your husband did, but you're saying that you should be much better than you are, so you must feel that you have disappointed me.

MRS. R. I've had so many disappointments.

DOCTOR Yes, but remember now . . . you're not disappointing me . . . I'm disappointing you.

MRS. R. I guess I have to pray harder. (p. 160)

She won't admit hate for Mann, but she will later in session 11 admit carrying a load of hate of her own, which they propose to discuss in session 12.

Well, the last dramatic turn came exactly 24 hours before her final appointment with Mann. She got herself readmitted at that hour by the surgeon, again for abdominal pain. This time Mann had to send two different emissaries to Mrs. R. before she would agree to walk over from the hospital to the outpatient department for the final session.

Mann went after her in session 12, as before, about her hurt, by himself and her family, and got little. He didn't get much, except more protestation by her about trying so hard. As far as she would go was this:

DOCTOR . . . and those angry feelings made you feel sick, sad and depressed . . . and hurting all over.

MRS. R. They really did and I never did know it. (She is crying). (p. 164)

I imagine what was most important about session 12 was that she came to face her problems rather than be operated on by the surgeon. She was acting on her own behalf, rather than being a victim.

Ten months later Mann saw her for follow-up; she was neither depressed, nor hopeless, but "animated" (p. 165). Her chronic cough of ten years had stopped shortly after her twelfth session. Her "gallbladder" trouble seemed to have abated after two weeks in hospital after her twelfth session. Nothing had changed about her property in Georgia, but she now got along well with her family, with the exception of the brother who had tried to kill her. She was making quilts and thinking of getting a housework job. Did she have any thoughts about Mann?

I thought about you right often. . . . I felt very good about you because I know you done a wonderful thing for me . . . overcome all that chokin' and everything else. . . . I was dying by degrees . . . it's gone. (p. 165)

Ordinary People

Many people go around with a painful description of themselves, as weak, fearful, stupid, incapable, unattractive, or whatever. This is what Mann calls their "chronically endured pain." They try hard to beat this rap, but they slip back into it quite often, so the pain is a "present and chronically recurring pain." When they meet people who might actually take care of them, they tend to experience a revival of hopefulness. This hopefulness is usually excessive, as with most revivals. But for a while, the enthusiasm will allow them to work hard again. When the new hope pales, they collapse, as before, into the chronic pain. This, Mann is betting, is the usual story of ordinary people, people like Mrs. R.

What Mann has set up for receiving this kind of story is a very simple but powerful diagram. The patient will be seen as trying very hard to be worthwhile, but slipping back into the recurrent painful view of the self, in the past, in the present, always. Is this familiar? A person from an evangelical background like Mrs. R. would feel at home when received like this by Mann.

Mann also sets up a ritual, in which this story is likely to be dramatized between the patient and himself. By describing the patient's trying very hard to do well, but falling back into pain, tailoring his diagram to the intentions and vocabulary of the individual patient, summarizing the whole life of that individual in one sentence, in one of the first several sessions, he arouses the patient's hopes to be completely understood. After all, this is very, very impressive, that this man could see the struggle of your whole life, and the pain of your whole life, in one breath. After all, you have never heard him deliver the same pronouncement, with small variations, to anyone but yourself!

Mann knowingly sets up great expectations. He utilizes the patient's capacity to work with this enthusiasm in the middle phase, to unearth the patient's capacity for an ordinary solution. We saw him getting Mrs. R. worked up to defend herself.

Then he readies himself for the deterioration of progress, which will come when Mann is taking his leave of the patient. He has made the end as clear as possible, so the timing of the falling apart will be shown to be a response to ending. Mrs. R. became a failure again, and a passive object for a doctor again, right on schedule.

The evangelical churches are familiar with this rise and fall: first the revival; then, hard work from the convert, while he or she is full of the love of God; but finally a backsliding. Mann is very astute about the time line of most relationships which offer to take care of people.

The Domain of this Technique

Mann's second and most recent book (Mann and Goldman, 1982) shows he has gotten more experience in his method than was evident in his first book (Mann, 1973), for he now sees more exceptions to his first offer to most neurotic patients. One category of exceptions is the patients who dare not take a chance on becoming so hopeful so fast. Schizoid, cautious types, passive obsessionals, hysterics who want to be compensated for what they have missed,[1] and narcissistic patients who feel they are owed much more than brief therapy will not be aroused by Mann's one sentence understanding and offer of 12 sessions. This defeats the ritual, for the drama of the end and the hard work of the middle depend on the great expectations of the beginning. Another category of exceptions is those who could get involved, but could not stop. Patients who have had profound early losses and borderline patients who must have their gratification, hell or high water, do not give up great expectations gracefully.

I see several other major categories of exceptions, besides these two outlined recently by Mann. First, many patients do not lend themselves to being organized along the lines of Mann's favorite story. Many are *not* trying hard but slipping back into feeling ill of themselves, common as that may be. For example, the Daughter of Soap Opera of the last chapter did not think of herself as such a virtuous person, in slippage, but rather as a person full of holy hell for others, needing to temper her ferocity. Not everyone loves the religious framework of trying hard but slipping into sin. So many won't become involved with Mann's message.

Secondly, many will sign up, but be much more difficult to liberate than Mann admits. He makes no reckoning of systemic loyalty, which may hold a patient into sacrificing the most vital, individual strengths. For example, if he had had a clinic in Georgia and seen Mrs. R. there before she fled from the context of her extended family, I doubt if he would have done as well in extricating her from being the family goat. Only because she had been driven so far out of this family, only because she had fled to Boston, were the ties of her family system weakened, so that Mann could give them little attention and yet succeed. Indeed, his most typical case is the kid who has left home for school in Boston, who is weakening ties with his family en route eventually to setting up his or her own family. In these situations, where the hold of the family of origin is at its weakest, at the apogee of independence, Mann can often get away with a minimum understanding of what the family of origin might require from the patient for its own continuation.

But many patients are needed very badly for the stability of the families from which they have fled. When the systemic requirements are still powerful, Mann's method is too weak, for he offers no way to look into these requirements.[2] We find in our clinic that many 19-year-olds can do very well in trial therapy, in facing their own difficulties with great emotion and thoughtfulness, although they are not able to enter brief therapy because their families would not approve or would be too upset. They are more loyal to their families than they are to their own needs. Only a systemic method can appreciate these ties that bind, such as in the Case of Chest Pain in Chapter 10, to which we will now return.

Only a few more words about the domain of Mann's technique, before we look at the systemic ties of the young man with chest pain. When the systemic ties are least compelling, it is possible for Mann to think of the young person coming to him as being undone only by his own needfulness. Coming to Mann is like having a visit to your uncle or grandfather for a holiday from the loneliness and hard work of the university (1982, p. 11). At first, it is terrific to be with him, because all your hopes of being looked after as a child are revived. Also, he is supportive. You get a boost for your strength, borrowing some from him. Mann's patients seem to experience this literally as a borrowing, as an "aug-Mann-tation" or becoming a "Mann" or learning to be a "great Mann-ipulator," and so forth. But the kid also gets less than his great expectations which have been revived, so he gets restless as the disappointment begins to become apparent. As the visit to Mann is coming to an end, the kid is tempted, in his hurt and anger, to throw out the "Mann" that he was borrowing, but Mann is quite ready to confront him about this child-ishness. Of course, I have just restated the ritual, from the religious version I first presented, here to a secular vocabulary. The metaphor works, when the kid's needfulness is more important than the needfulness of the family back home.

A Case of Chest Pain, Continued

But we do not have to follow Mann's procedure to borrow his vocabulary, which is so useful for receiving one of the most common stories we are likely to hear. Mann's diagram, of trying hard, but slipping into pain, picks up so many people so well, including the young man with chest pain to whom the reader was introduced in Chapter 10.

Some people try so hard, but, in spite of their earnest efforts, they feel as if something terrible and painful will happen when they have to go on their own. These two elements, trying and pain, are so common in American life stories. Perhaps it is because so much of the emigrant culture was built from the urge to brave things in the new world on your own, missing the union with the old place, and finding terrible pain in place of the great expectations.[3] Perhaps it also is because the migrations of groups from one region of America to another brought about a comparable great expectation, longing and pain, such as for the blacks from the South going to the Northern cities, like Mrs. R. Perhaps, the migrations of individuals in the twentieth century to one end of the country or another, to make their individual career or fortune, giving up the home town, is again the same story of great expectation, longing and pain.

We left off from the story of our young man in trial therapy when I had gotten the history that his chest pain had begun the summer before leaving home for graduate school, rising to a crescendo in the first week at the university. Also, I learned that he had burst into tears in the supermarket, buying goods for his apartment with his parents. It appeared that there was something terribly painful about proceeding with his career, apart from his parents. Why?

In the last half-hour of his two-hour trial therapy, the story fell into place, as I will relate. I knew from what I have told already that this young man saw a recurrent painful story, but he did not know why this story meant so much to him. He felt he should be "cruisin'," but he was feeling "ripped up." The story is a variation on Mann's drama of trying hard but falling into pain. What this young man saw everywhere in the world was that some people give very generously of themselves but get cheated of their reward.

This upset him tremendously, but he had little notion of why it did, and why now, as he set off on his career. There was one very significant detail that the reader should know, which I had gotten in the preliminary interview. When I had asked him whom he had ever known to have a heart attack, he, first, did not recall anyone, but then, with a rush of tears, remembered his favorite teacher in junior high school, who was also the father of one of his friends. He had been very generous to our patient, but died suddenly of a heart attack when our patient was 14. Here was a very giving man who got cheated.

We come back to the trial therapy where we are discussing why he had gotten so upset with his parents in the supermarket, where he was buying a few things to set up his first apartment away from his folks. What was so upsetting about setting up on his own? Well, what would life now be like for his parents? Both were close to retirement. The patient is talking about his father:

PATIENT He's got a file cabinet like with all these brochures from different places. I just . . .
THERAPIST That he'll eventually go to?
PATIENT Yeah.
THERAPIST You wish he would have a good time now, take it easy now?
PATIENT Yeah, and not worry about work so much as he does.
THERAPIST Do you think it could make him sick to worry so much?
PATIENT No.
THERAPIST Do you worry about his getting sick from so much worry in postponing his . . . ?
PATIENT Yeah. He's, ah, I look at him and I see, I mean, he's never been sick as long as I've known him, so ah . . .
THERAPIST So you're worried about his suddenly becoming sick?
PATIENT Yeah, a little bit (tearfully, voice breaking).
THERAPIST Quite a lot I would guess.
PATIENT I guess, I know that that would rip me up. Ding, ding, ding, ding, ding . . . (crying). I think we hit another one. Yeah, I'm pretty sure that ah, yeah, I think . . . I think, I think, you know, they deserve having a

good time, and it would really be a *cheat* if they got ripped off some. That would be like, ah, I don't know, one of those things that you're supposed to deal with, but . . .

THERAPIST But, it's unbearable?

PATIENT Yeah.

THERAPIST It's an unbearable idea that they would get cheated after . . .

PATIENT Yeah. I think we're hitting something big here.

THERAPIST Okay. We can take our time. When we get to something big, let's just sit and . . .

PATIENT No. Okay, go ahead.[4]

THERAPIST No, I'm not. I'm just acknowledging that it seems like there is something back here about your folks having really put themselves out so hard for you and your sister, postponed their pleasure, and put up with shit. And they could get cheated suddenly by getting sick like your teacher.

PATIENT Yeah (cries). Oh, boy! Yeah. Jeez, who would think that . . . ? Somehow all of this stuff ties together. I don't think I've thought of that guy's dad for 10 years, and I mentioned it that day, and oh my god, it fits like clockwork. Yeah. See, like I mentioned before, stuff like innocent people getting hurt or people getting ripped off—that's really bugged me lately. Really bugged me. Ah, yeah, all that stuff you're supposed to take like it's part of everyday life, like all those people getting laid off or stuff like that, is really hitting me, like . . .

THERAPIST All right, so . . .

PATIENT Yeah. There's a song . . . I'm kind of a Bruce Springsteen fan.

THERAPIST Mmm, hmm.

PATIENT Ah, the title song of his new album is about a guy who comes back from Vietnam, and well, he was forced to go because he got in trouble with the law and he comes back and there's nothing here and here that's happened. I don't know and it just rolls off so many people's backs.

THERAPIST But not yours.

PATIENT But not mine.

THERAPIST It's something you're very tuned into, that innocent people get ripped up.

PATIENT Yeah (voice breaks) . . . it seems like no one cares or something . . . (cries) (Long pause) Yeah, but then, yeah, I guess I just get kind of irritated when people say you can't take care of everyone or something like that—that really irritates me. (Pause, grasping for words) I just like to think that we have a responsibility for those who aren't as fortunate. I get kind of irritated when people ignore that, and I just thought of something. Ah, it might connect about my being up here, being pretty much for me, whereas, I think I'd like to be doing something for other people. Whereas this is my concern that this is too much of a selfish thing and I don't like that.

THERAPIST Yeah, I see.

PATIENT I think that . . . yeah, but, I mean, I look at my career goal and one of the reasons I picked this is that . . . I do have an opportunity to help a lot of people. First of all, there are a lot of kids in the country that, I mean, just people's attitude toward science isn't real healthy and I think one of my gifts is the ability to explain. One of my favorite things is the teaching part of things. If I have one kid and make him . . . I mean, I guess that's a goal of any teacher.

THERAPIST Especially you . . .

PATIENT Yeah, but I look at my long-range career choice and I see the potential there for a lot of help but I look at the next four to six years and that looks *all* toward me and that seems like a waste of talent or whatever.

THERAPIST Mmm, hmm. It feels too selfish even though in the long run you can give back what you've got. It takes so much, right?

PATIENT Does that make any sense?

THERAPIST Absolutely. It's clear as a bell. You're a very loyal person.

PATIENT I think that I just . . . it's like I don't want to be accused of being selfish which I hate myself . . . man, this is easy stuff.

THERAPIST You've been punishing yourself.

PATIENT (Smacks his hands together) Man, oh man (cries)! You were right before, that wasn't the whole thing . . . (sighs). So what do we do now?

Mann's vocabulary fits this story so well. This young man has struggled to be as generous as his teacher and his father, yet, in spite of his best efforts, he feels "selfish" about being allowed four to six years of graduate school for his own learning. He feels that his good fortune may be purchased by his father's giving, only to have his father become sick and be cheated of his reward. This is unbearable. This rips him up.

But I got this story from thinking that is different from Mann's thinking. I stayed with the current of what would happen to his parents when he left them, because I thought this young man was extremely loyal to the interests of his family. This got us to the dread of his father's being cheated. This is a little piece of looking into the systemic implications of independence.

But now, with 15 minutes left of our two hours, we get another twist to the story of generous men being cheated. The patient also dreads that it will happen to himself. He too will be cut down. This is a usual sequence. When the interviewer gets an appreciation of the patient's loyalty to his family, how deep and extensive the ties have been, then the patient is ordinarily free to say something about more selfish preoccupations.

THERAPIST Well, we've got about 15 more minutes today and I know you've really made a lot of discoveries, so the question now is if it's true that one of the reasons that you've been suffering so much up here is that this phase of your life, this four or five years, feels like you're being too selfish, that innocent people who are being . . . are suffering and just for the time being it's hard to give back what you've gotten . . . the way you want to.

PATIENT That's exactly right.

THERAPIST So then your problem is, your pain is, how can you give back, especially to your folks who are in danger of getting ripped off if they should die suddenly or sickness should hit them suddenly. So you really want to give something back to your folks before it's too late.

PATIENT Yeah. I think it's more, now that I think about it standing back a bit . . . I feel that part is I'm giving back, but I look at it again and I guess I realize that they have been pretty lucky, they've had like two lives, and they're a lot luckier than most people. They got a chance to do their own thing except like I wasn't around to see them do that, I guess . . . when they were young and everything, but I do know that they did it, so I guess, I realize that they probably. . . . Logically, I realize that they have been rewarded but it is like I want to be part of it. I want to be part of the rewarding process.

THERAPIST Well, yeah, I think maybe that's what you've got to figure out how to do.

PATIENT Yeah.

THERAPIST And I think when you figure out how to reward them, then you'll be okay.

PATIENT Yeah, I see.

THERAPIST So, you see, maybe that's something that needs to happen next. We can't do it all today. We get the lay of the land and we get it quite clear. Then the task ahead is clearer and you'll be able to do what you need to do.

PATIENT Umm, hmm.

THERAPIST And then your pain will be gone because . . . your pain is a very lucky thing.

PATIENT I know you can't tell me in terms of percentage, but is that overwhelming as compared to the career thing?

THERAPIST How do you mean?

PATIENT I mean in terms of like rewarding my parents and then just being here for myself. See, does that rewarding my parents have . . .

THERAPIST Is that more important?

PATIENT I mean, is that the whole thing?

THERAPIST No. It isn't. You know. *You* tell me.

PATIENT So I can get around that one it seems but how do I . . .

THERAPIST How can you tolerate being selfish for four or five years?

PATIENT Yeah, or is overcoming the other one enough to tolerate . . .

THERAPIST Well, maybe not. Maybe there are two things here. I think that is what you're telling me, right?

PATIENT Yeah.

THERAPIST Actually, you tell me when I'm a little bit off, which is good.

PATIENT Yeah?

THERAPIST I mean, it's good. You're revising what I'm saying.

PATIENT Okay.

THERAPIST So, there is something about rewarding your parents which is something unbearable, you know, which Springsteen's song brings up, you know, getting cheated, ripped off, but there is also something about your career here that doesn't have to do with your parents.

PATIENT It seems like that to me.

THERAPIST Okay, which is what? How would you put that?

PATIENT Maybe that seems just a more general case of the specific.

THERAPIST All right and how would you put it?

PATIENT (Pause) Um, how do I, I mean, get around just spending five years on my goals.

THERAPIST Okay, when you feel that that's not fair.

PATIENT Yeah.

THERAPIST Well . . .

PATIENT And there's something else too. (Pause) Ah, but there is still, I think, a fear involved of not getting . . . there's a fear of not getting to the place where I can pay back after being here, like if I somehow along the way they say, "Well I don't think he can cut it," then I'll feel lack of ability to pay back.

PATIENT Yeah.

THERAPIST Well . . .

PATIENT I don't know if that term applies in this case but I won't have reached my full potential (tearful).

THERAPIST It's upsetting to you?

PATIENT Yeah, a lot because I see a large need. I guess I consider myself pretty lucky . . .

THERAPIST What?

PATIENT I mean we're in deep trouble and we need some help. That's what I'm trying to say as far as . . . I mean just the more general kind of human thing.

THERAPIST Kids?

PATIENT Yeah.

THERAPIST Kids need help? You feel passionately about that?

PATIENT Yeah (voice breaks) . . . I really do. Or they can be given a some . . . I guess part of it too is, you know, you'd like giving someone else a better chance.

THERAPIST A break?

PATIENT Mmm, hmm because I like to think that I've gotten some breaks.

THERAPIST Right, you have.

PATIENT So, if those breaks have given me the opportunity to excel, well then, I'll give some other kid . . .

THERAPIST Right, so that's really big.

PATIENT That's *real* big.

THERAPIST Okay, so there are two things; there is something about your parents getting a fair shot which is real important and there is something about this four or five years and you being able to give back and to give other kids a break that you got. You see, you've got to figure out how to do that and to be confident that you'll be able to do that for them. What have we got? [Therapist asks resident for time left.] Are there about 10 minutes left then? Okay. So you and I have got to stop in 10 minutes. You've really put a lot of things together with just a little bit of help. I haven't done that much. What?

PATIENT A lot of help.

THERAPIST I've done my share anyway and so we need to . . .

PATIENT I couldn't have done it . . . I was trying for a long time (voice breaks) to put things together by myself.

THERAPIST So you needed a break.

PATIENT I needed a break, from somebody.

THERAPIST So I gave you a break.

PATIENT Umm, hmm.

Finally, we had to end our two-hour session, which had been astonishing to the patient in its force and clarity. He had depended on me to an extent which surprised both of us, I think. To me this was impressive, but I thought he might find it alarming, because his background of South Milwaukee was not exactly keen on psychiatry or on men depending on other men. Here was a fellow who liked to be "cruisin'," in control. So I put him right back in the driver's seat. Also, I put myself in alongside him as an equal. He accepted this, as the reader will see, as his shooting the basket and me tipping it in. But I still gave him a pain in the neck. He still hated himself for not having figured it all out himself. How come he needed a psychiatrist? Well, hell, he was a moron. This was a secret pride. Well, hell, I said, " . . . us morons don't do too bad." Again, we are back to equals. I wanted nothing of being the great man, who understood everything. I figured he'd have to run from that. As Balint has emphasized, equality is usually a safer bet, across the board.

THERAPIST So, the question now is: what do you need here further and the options are: one of our team could continue with you for some sessions, as much as you needed to figure out these two things, so you can keep this thinking going that we've begun. That would be one possibility. You could be in brief therapy with one of the doctors and to continue figuring things out. You might need more of a break here than the session that I've given you. You might not.

PATIENT I might not.

THERAPIST Maybe you've got the break you needed from this.

PATIENT Yeah, I mean, I don't know.

THERAPIST I don't either. What is your feeling about it?

PATIENT My feeling is I did have something pretty big and I think I need some time to see what happens.

THERAPIST All right. So why don't we give you some time to see what happens.

PATIENT It's not, I mean, I'm not saying, "Oh I've got it all under control now." I'm just saying, "Well I don't *know*."

THERAPIST Right. I don't either.

PATIENT Oh, okay.

THERAPIST That's where I'm asking. You know, we proceeded here by me getting an idea and you giving it back and seeing what you think and going back and forth here. Where we are right now is considering whether you need more from *us*: maybe you do, maybe you don't, maybe you've got enough. It appears that you need some time to see whether this is sufficient.

PATIENT You know, get a chance to work on something.

THERAPIST Sure, you'll see. We're here.

PATIENT I've got a feeling this stuff is going to go away pretty fast.

THERAPIST I think it is too.

PATIENT It's funny how the body takes care of itself.

THERAPIST Yeah, the wisdom of the body, as they say . . .

PATIENT Letting me know something was up.

THERAPIST Yeah. So you got a big message. Pretty amazing, isn't it?

PATIENT Yeah. Like I'm thinking back to July, nothing could have been further from my mind, I was having a great time.

THERAPIST Cubs were doing okay . . .

PATIENT Cubs were doing okay . . . wasn't working, felt great, see the friends . . . sit down and watch TV and my heart hurts . . .

THERAPIST Something coming up there.

PATIENT Being a scientist I think, why?

THERAPIST What's going on here?

PATIENT Got to have an answer. There's got to be a reason. Well, there was a reason. Yeah, but you like to think that you're on top of things.

THERAPIST Sure, we all do. Well, you're getting back there. Sometimes one needs to be on the bottom of things to get the message.

PATIENT Yeah.

THERAPIST Temporarily, but you'll get back on top of things once you've taken this into account, you see.

PATIENT That was pretty exhausting.

THERAPIST Yeah, it sure was. How do you feel about stopping with me? You and I . . . this is our last session. You can continue here with one of the residents and I'll supervise, but how do you feel about you and me quitting here?

PATIENT Um, I don't know. I mean I think, ah, like I don't feel the dependence always.

THERAPIST Okay, so you feel pretty much . . . you're not feeling a big tug like, "Please stay with me."

PATIENT Nothing like that. No, I mean you were right when you said, kind of like, just tipped it in . . . I made the shot, you tipped it in.

THERAPIST Mmm, hmm, right, like in basketball.

PATIENT I just like gotta rest for a while, I think that's what I need.

THERAPIST So you are feeling like this was exhausting, we did a lot, I'm ready to take a break.

PATIENT My neck hurts (rubs neck) (laughter).

THERAPIST I'm sure I'm partly a pain in the neck or maybe they're (the residents behind the mirror) a pain in the neck, I don't know. Something's a pain in the neck here. See, if you pay attention, it will tell you you're mad about something . . . as we end.

PATIENT See, it doesn't say nothing, it just kind of hurts.

THERAPIST Well, it will speak. (Patient laughs.) What could you be mad about at the end? What gives you a pain in the neck as we stop here? What do you think about that one?

PATIENT Ahhhhhhhh . . . logically, I just say, you know, "Okay, it's happened and it could have happened to anyone." The neck says, "You dummy."

THERAPIST You dumb shit, how could you . . .

PATIENT how could you do this?

THERAPIST Yeah, and how come you didn't figure it out yourself?

PATIENT How come you needed this psychiatrist? How come you didn't figure it out yourself . . . What a moron.

THERAPIST What a moron you are . . .

PATIENT That is kind of an inside joke because at school we were known as "The Morons," a sort of antifraternity, and you have to watch how you throw around the word "moron."

THERAPIST I've got to be careful . . .

PATIENT It's a sense of pride. What was our motto? Something in Latin, I don't remember, it goes something like, "In stupidity we are united, in stupidity we are one."

THERAPIST I see.

PATIENT Of course in being an antifrat you become a self-parody of the actual frat but you are only in college and you know you're stupid. You have some fun.

THERAPIST So you're trying to live with being a little stupid?

PATIENT Yeah, because, you know, we weren't nearly good-looking or athletic enough to get into the real frats so it's been one of our own. You got to be stupid. If you're not *stupid* enough to be with us, get out of here. That was fun.

THERAPIST Yeah, well I'll miss seeing you.

PATIENT Ah . . . thanks. It was pretty interesting for me too. I haven't done anything like this . . .

THERAPIST Yeah, yeah, well us morons, we don't do too bad.

PATIENT Yeah.

THERAPIST Well listen, we will leave it then that you'll see how it goes for a while with what you've got.

PATIENT Could you like give me a number?

THERAPIST Yeah, I'll give you my number and you call me and . . .

PATIENT I think I've got your number.

THERAPIST You do? I gave you that other sheet. So, you've got my number and you'll think about it for a while. Why don't you call me in, say, two weeks and tell me how you are doing, either way.

PATIENT I will.

THERAPIST Okay?

PATIENT Umm hmm.

THERAPIST And if you're progressing on your own, terrific, and if you want to talk to one of the residents for a session, fine. It doesn't have to be any big deal, like you have to do 20 sessions. If you want to have a consultation like you've got today to get a little more, you know, just putting your head together with another moron, that's fine. That's what us morons are here for. Okay?

PATIENT Yeah.

THERAPIST So you call me in a couple of weeks. Just leave your number — you know, you'll get my secretary — leave your number and I'll ring you back and you can tell me, you know, that you're fine or you're mostly fine or you'd like to consult . . .

PATIENT I think if the Cubs win the Series, I'll be pretty fine.

THERAPIST That will help, won't it? Us morons are going to beat the shit out of them in San Diego.

PATIENT Those wimps.

THERAPIST All those wimps from San Diego.

PATIENT It's hard about Detroit, 'cause they're nice and working-class. I like to think that, you know, I'm like them too.

THERAPIST Sure. It would be hard if the Cubs beat up on those Tigers, those working-class Tigers.

PATIENT I went to Detroit last summer. It is a pretty tough city. You can see that stadium. It is like corrugated aluminum nailed on the side. It looks like a prison, but it has got to be a great stadium, right?

THERAPIST Right.

PATIENT All that concrete and astro-turf.

THERAPIST Right, none of that upper-class bullshit.

PATIENT I just love Wrigley field so much. I almost get tears in my eyes reading the stories.[5]

Well, what is the end of this story? He decided to go into brief therapy with one of our senior residents before he left the trial therapy. This was stormy and quite brief. Four sessions. He was nearly over his chest pain after our long session. He presented twinges to the resident, but mostly what we saw in supervision was his competition with the resident, by presenting his own discoveries. The resident became tense about this. The more the resident wanted to see what was wrong, what needed help, the less the young man wanted to be there. He didn't show up after Christmas break.[6] According to Student Health records, there have been no presentations for chest pains since the trial therapy, a few for other minor complaints.

I take this sequel as another moral about keeping to the equal relationship, even being willing to admire the patient, even being willing to offer that he might be able to do it all on his own. This allows a little dependence. For many patients, the great doctor is a pain in the neck.[7]

13. *Sifneos: Oedipal Lessons*

Let us suppose that nearly all of us, at one time or another, are secretive about our sexual interests. It can get complicated, sneaking around. It could get simpler if someone called us on what the hell we are doing. Scary. But scary-exciting. We'll feel better about ourselves later, since sneakiness has been chipping away at self-respect. When we are summoned for this kind of lesson, we all look about the same—like children caught in the act. Therefore, the cases of Sifneos (1972, 1979, 1981) are a series of sketches with minor shades of difference, one from another.

THE CASE OF EVERYMAN

For example, a 28-year-old graduate student complained of having a "façade" which interfered with being close. Sifneos (1981) presented the dialog between himself and this patient for the third and fourth interviews. The man was a caricature of a graduate student, who ran on in broad generalities about his mask.

Sifneos began his approach in the third session by posing a question: Was the "mask" different with women than with men? Sifneos also told him four or five times to stop intellectualizing and be a little more specific. Well, the man volunteered that he did imagine himself to be Clark Gable with women. What did Clark Gable get out of taking out beautiful women? "Peer group status?" What? Now Sifneos will throw the fellow on his mettle:

DOCTOR Let me just point out something that you do. We drew a parallel between yourself and Clark Gable . . . you like to go out with beautiful women. I ask you what is the advantage of that? And immediately you go on to something tangential, like in social status and peer groups. Now there's something much more direct.

PATIENT OK. Well, if a woman goes out with me it means that I have some import to her, some value to her. You're really straining my brain.

DOCTOR Come on! There's nothing wrong with your brain! (Laughter)

PATIENT You probably already know this, but I am trying to use your vocabulary and I'm going to try to get out of that. Because I'm not that qualified to use it. I'll try to be spontaneous. Could you rephrase the question?

DOCTOR No.

PATIENT No you will not?

DOCTOR You heard my question. You don't need any assistance. You can do it, perfectly well. Carry on. (1981, pp. 54–55).

The patient now suggested he got "warmth" out of seeing beautiful women, being reminded of his mother nursing his sister. Sifneos replied that "warmth" was hardly "sexuality." He had been expecting this slip into pregenital pleasure. He had a question:

DOCTOR Now, don't run away. The question now is, what are you trying to hide from? Not from me, but from what is inside you, and from what some of these associations have stirred up. (p. 59)

The patient now told him about romping in the woods with his sister and cousins, and about his mother's crying when she told him of her disapproval. Sifneos has gotten past a little of the "coverup."

The patient came in for the fourth session having fallen 40 feet with his painting partner when their scaffolding collapsed. He had suffered only minor injury. Given the commands of Sifneos to be more "specific" about his sexual interests as a child which were shrouded in vagueness, he described sleeping in his parents' bed. "What was the arrangement and what do you remember of it?" (p. 70) He enjoyed sleeping in his father's position. Did his father punish him? No, but the patient remembered his father's being angry because the patient was being lazy up on the roof when they rebuilt the house. The patient felt very anxious. He felt imperiled up there. There was also a dream about this kind of elevated situation on a bridge.

Sifneos associated back to the patient's fall from the scaffolding. The four situations were close, yes? The scaffolding, the father's position in bed, the roof job, and the bridge in the dream.

PATIENT Well, I don't know. I suppose I could be thinking that my father was forcing me into a situation that would imperil me.

DOCTOR Yes, so why? (p. 74)

The patient could not summon any "competitive feeling." Sifneos suggested that he hid it. Sifneos asked more about the relation with the painter and discovered that the man regaled the patient with stories of his sexual exploits. So that's the secret! The patient replied that this was "funny." Sifneos asked: "Why funny?" This again hid his feeling. The patient now confessed that he had done more touching of his sister's vagina while romping in the woods, even after his mother forbade him.

The therapy with this patient lasted four months (13 interviews in all), and it was successful. In terms of outcome, the patient gave up his tendency to hide his feelings. When seen in follow-up, he was having a meaningful relationship with a young woman who was "unattached." . . . He had no symptoms, and had a good insight into his relations with his mother and father, which were the focus of his therapy. (1981, p. 79)

SHORT-TERM ANXIETY-PROVOKING PSYCHOTHERAPY (STAPP)

There is not much more to tell. Sifneos wrote:

From our experience, any young therapist who has an open mind, is well versed in psychodynamic theory, and has treated a suitable STAPP patient under intensive individual supervision can rapidly learn to practice this therapy, without a protracted period of training. What is needed is enthusiasm. (1981, p. 49)

You tell the patients to be specific. You tell them not to run away. They get anxious. You tell them they can carry on anyway. They slip into some guise of being a little child. You tell them that won't do either. They come out with it. They feel better, and act more like adults, less like sneaky children.[1] Follow-up shows that the success is continued (1968).

THE DOMAIN OF THE TECHNIQUE OF SIFNEOS

You take patients who are willing to circumscribe their complaints to a single, most important complaint, who have been able to sacrifice for others, who relate well to the interviewer, who are intelligent in the psychological sense, and who want to change (Sifneos, 1979, Chapter 3). Then you set up this little force field. Well, are you going to be a man (or woman) and own up? Or a child? You have made the arrangements, of selection and technique, which draw the patient to the likely conclusion. Sifneos himself says it is like positive reinforcement for being an adult, negative reinforcement for being a child (1979, p. 123). It is an oedipal lesson, for those who already have most of the qualities of being adult—except about sex. This oedipal lesson is just about what Lucy got from Freud, or Katherina got from Freud (see Chapter 2). It works, for the few individuals who are as well as we ever see in psychiatry.

So what is wrong? It would be easy to ridicule how silly it appears to reduce psychoanalysis to challenging someone whether he (she) is a man (woman) or a child, to positive reinforcement of the first, negative of the second. But it is sometimes a useful exercise. It worked fine for Lucy and for Katherina when Freud did it and I have no doubt that it has worked fine for Sifneos among his young charges. I could have used it myself when I was 20. Why get more complicated than necessary? More complex ideas could be evading the simple truth of someone's pretending to be a child.[2] As Alexander and French would say, more complex ideas could invite "couch diving."[3]

The trouble for the doctor is that once you have learned to do this (which, as Sifneos wrote, will not take you very long—one case well supervised! (1981, p. 49)), what then? You then have two roads. One is to look for the very few patients who are suited to this. The other is to learn something else to cope with the other 90 percent of your caseload.

The Case of the Modern
Passive-Feminine Character (Third Pass)

I have already taken the reader through this interview to describe Reich's point of view (Chapter 4) and Sullivan's (Chapter 6). This is the young man who believed he had no sexual feeling for women, hence no future as a married man. I believe the logic of the interview depends upon Reich and Sullivan all right, but the line-by-line back and forth borrows from this modern idea of Sifneos that some patients need your insistence to be *specific*.[4] When they become anxious, you do not relent. If you dog their footsteps, you will soon become the transference parent who is frightening.[5]

We take up the dialog where the patient has confessed he has had no sexual feeling for women, ever. He saw my head jerk up, so he thought that I thought he was "sick." I told him, "I was just paying attention. . . . Many young men are quite inhibited. We don't know how your sexuality got put away." So how were we to find out?[6]

DOCTOR   OK, well let's see, what would be the simplest way to explore this? One way to explore this would be to see what your experiences with women have been. You know, I mean what situations have you been in with women where one might expect that some sexual feeling might arise?

PATIENT   After dates, you know, taking them home, on the porch, in the car.

DOCTOR   How much dating have you done?

PATIENT   Not much.

DOCTOR   How much?

PATIENT   In high school I went regular with a girl for a few months and that was just about it.

DOCTOR   What was her name?

PATIENT   Sue.

DOCTOR   Sue, you went out with Sue for a couple of months.

PATIENT   Ya.

DOCTOR   Ya, so we could talk about what went on between you and Sue.

PATIENT   Not much, I really liked her, she is a nice person, you know, it, she might be the kind of person you might want to marry. She is really nice, I like her a lot. I think I still like her, if — I haven't seen her in a long time because I am from out of state. Well, she — we went out together, we had a good time, you know, went to concerts. She had a birthday party. I went to that and got her some presents. And, you know, I think we had a good relationship. We had a good time. We went well together.

DOCTOR   Describe this Sue to me, would you?

PATIENT   She was a little shorter than me. She was a little, a little flabby, not too much. Not as much as I was.

DOCTOR   Are you uncomfortable saying that?

PATIENT Well, I don't like, I wouldn't like to say, you know, something like that about someone.

DOCTOR She was though?

PATIENT Ya, a little.

DOCTOR Look, you and I have to get to how you really feel. This is not a social situation.

PATIENT OK.

DOCTOR Okay, she was flabby and your . . .

PATIENT But not very . . .

DOCTOR She was flabby.

PATIENT Well, OK.

DOCTOR OK, was she?

PATIENT Ya.

DOCTOR All right . . .

PATIENT A little, but it, I want to explain it, she was a little flabby, you know . . .

DOCTOR Right.

PATIENT She was sort of big, not very, she was short, but she was good-looking . . .

DOCTOR She was? You mean she had a pretty face.

PATIENT Ya . . .

DOCTOR She did. But she was flabby and short?

PATIENT Ya, shorter than me, that is.

DOCTOR See, I want to call your attention to this. You're really uncomfortable saying this, stating the facts here.

PATIENT OK, um.

DOCTOR What makes you nervous about this?

PATIENT OK, I don't know.

DOCTOR Well, let's explain it. Here you were just being a little critical of this . . .

PATIENT I'll start over.

DOCTOR No, no, hold on a minute.

PATIENT OK.

DOCTOR This is important because you start to describe this Sue to me and you tell me that she is flabby which is a matter of fact but you're real nervous being a little critical. You laugh and try to explain to me, and explain. . . . What makes you so nervous about criticizing Sue?

PATIENT I don't know.

DOCTOR Well, what do you think? What occurs to you?

PATIENT I really can't say.

DOCTOR You're acting like it is dangerous to say these things about women.

PATIENT I really couldn't say. You know . . .

DOCTOR What could be, what harm could there be in your being critical of Sue? You're being careful not to be.

PATIENT Ya. I can't think of why. It must be there . . .

DOCTOR What do you think right now?

PATIENT Just blank, I just can't think of what might make me not want to, I don't . . .

I sensed by now I had gotten on his nerves to a considerable extent, where, despite his inclinations to please me, he could discover that pleasing me was becoming more than he bargained for. It was time to bring up his relation to me.

DOCTOR Are you a little annoyed with me for stopping you there?

PATIENT Well.

DOCTOR You smile?

PATIENT I have been annoyed with you at various times, here when . . .

DOCTOR Right now.

PATIENT When you push me like that but I know it is necessary . . .

DOCTOR OK, but then you go and explain my behavior for me. I asked you how you felt.

PATIENT Ya, you annoyed me when you were pushing me.

DOCTOR I was annoying you just now.

PATIENT Ya.

DOCTOR OK, but you see, you smile when you tell me that, about your annoyance.

PATIENT Ya.

DOCTOR Right.

PATIENT Ya.

DOCTOR So you're a little uncomfortable. Usually when people smile at me like that, they are uncomfortable. So you're annoyed with my pushing but you're uncomfortable telling me you're annoyed. Right?

PATIENT Ya.

DOCTOR OK.

PATIENT We still on the same thing? I am still trying to think, I don't really know what would . . .

DOCTOR All right, look what we have found so far. For one, you're uncomfortable saying something critical about Sue and you're also uncomfortable saying something critical to me.

PATIENT Usually if I'm saying something critical about someone I will do it jokingly.

DOCTOR Yes.

PATIENT Ya, I do that a lot. Sometimes, when I do it, it is not really a valid criticism. I joke a lot and people realize that. But, I think, sometimes I criticize when I mean to and I do it jokingly but rarely do I criticize seriously . . .

DOCTOR Yes, I see. You act like criticism is dangerous.

PATIENT Ya.

DOCTOR Either of Sue or of me. What makes criticism dangerous in your life? As you have known it. If one does it seriously?

PATIENT And not just someone else . . .

DOCTOR The other person is upset.

PATIENT Hurting them.

DOCTOR Ya, what are you thinking? You look like you're feeling it.

PATIENT Right now, I just kind of feel upset. I don't know why.

DOCTOR OK, let's see if we can find out. OK?

PATIENT I guess.

DOCTOR Go ahead, you're doing fine.

PATIENT I don't think I can talk.

DOCTOR Tell me what you are feeling and what you're thinking. It is very important.

PATIENT I don't know.

DOCTOR Well, we can wait. Obviously we have come to something very important.

PATIENT I just don't know what is making me feel this way though. (Patient is sobbing.)

As I have explained in the foregoing descriptions of the interview (Chapters 4 and 6), the sobbing connected us to his past, in which a show of hostility led to terrible things, biting his best friend and losing him, his parents' fighting and divorcing. We both could see how it was that he would pretend to be a nice, little child. Being aggressive and big seemed to mean wrecking things. Once he became able to accept his being aggressive and big again, he began to experience his sexual desire.

So it's a simple idea to demand that the patient be specific and live through the anxiety. But it's a useful idea.

14. *Davanloo: Getting Past the Patient's Wall*

DAVANLOO PROCEEDS one step beyond his teacher Sifneos. The therapist can insist that patients be specific, and therefore, anxious, but many will still be vague. The next step is to make threats. But you must not only threaten; you must pound on the door through the wall, and you must also reappear on the other side of the wall alongside the patient, to imagine how this pounding feels from his or her side. You've got to be in both places.

THE LITTLE BLOND DUTCH GIRL

The entire interview is worthwhile as a technical achievement, so the reader may want to refer to my previous account (Gustafson and Dichter, 1983a). I want to emphasize here only the first third of the interview, where Davanloo exhibits what is original with him, what gives him his peculiar power to bring about "breakthroughs."

"The patient was a 22-year-old student complaining of depression, crying spells, a constant fear of rejection by other people, a pattern in relation to men characterized by passivity and a need to bend over backwards to please them, and problems with her parents" (Davanloo, 1980, p. 102). The patient opened by offering that her crying was unsuccessful: "I have an escape that I use, and this is crying. But that doesn't do anything except put it off for a while [problems with people]; and then you know, it crops up again. It is a vicious circle" (p. 102).

Davanloo opened like Sifneos, asking the patient to be more specific. Since she ruminated about all relationships, Davanloo asked her to tell what she experienced with her boyfriend. She replied that he talked her into feeling she was wrong.

Since "gentle" questions were obtaining only vague replies, Davanloo decided to "sting" her: "Then you were the passive person" (p. 104). All interviews of Davanloo discover the patient's "passivity." This patient was "stung" all right and offered that she was "afraid" to be more active. Therefore, she "contradicted" herself, which made her boyfriend furious.

Davanloo now got her OK to proceed with this: "Could we look at this issue of contradiction . . . that you say something, and then you say something opposite to what you said?" (p. 105). This explicit OK is important, and standard for Davanloo, because Davanloo will now catch the patient at agreeing to proceed, but behaving so this is impossible.

Immediately, she stopped him. "I just think it [contradicting myself] is ordinary" (p. 105). Now, Davanloo could demonstrate to her that she made the job impossible:

THERAPIST You said you were a contradictory person. How about right now here with me?
PATIENT Have I contradicted myself?
THERAPIST What do you think?
PATIENT Well, yeah, I do contradict.
THERAPIST You see, right now, we are looking into your difficulties. You said that you have some difficulties and that you want to look at them.
PATIENT Yeah. I suppose. (p. 106)

This vagueness will not be tolerated. "This is [another] standard situation with a standard response" (p. 106). "Therapist: Why do you say 'suppose'? Do you, or don't you?" Davanloo again got the patient to say she *wanted* to be helped (p. 107), but that she was acting to make this help impossible.

THERAPIST . . . You have not been specific in what you have told me so far. Do you notice that you leave things hanging in the middle of the air nowhere?
PATIENT I am being evasive; I know that. (p. 107)

The logic of the patient's position is exposed: You need to do x, right? You want to do it, right? But you are not, right? The situation is nailed down as an objective failure, obvious to anyone.

Now Davanloo could make his first threat:

THERAPIST And that is really the issue. Are you specific, or are you evasive? We are here to see what your problems are, your difficulties. But if you say there is, and at the same time you say there isn't and continue to be vague and evasive, then we won't be able to understand the problem, and we will not have further opportunity to get to the core of your problem. (p. 107)

But notice that this threat is followed by going over to her side of the wall. " . . . And the most important question for both of us is, "Why are you so evasive?" . . . you have given me the picture that you are very disappointed in him (the boyfriend). Obviously, you have difficulties in life that are a source of agony for you. . . . "

Now Davanloo set up and made his second threat. " . . . And I assume that you came on your own volition, or didn't you?" (p. 108). "Now if you continue to be evasive, you know you do, then I will be useless to you and this session will be of no value to you. If we continue to skate around we cannot get to the core of your problem, something we are here to understand. Do you see what I mean? Patient: Uh-huh (silence)."

Now Davanloo followed his second threat with a summary which offered to be objective:

THERAPIST You set up a goal for yourself . . . to come here, as you, yourself, put it, 'to understand' yourself, to understand your problems with people. At the same time there is a paradox: namely, by being evasive and vague you are in a sense defeating your goal. My question is, "Why do you do that?" Is this the way you are in every relationship? Is this your way with other people? (long pause).

Now there was another long pause after Davanloo asked, "What do you think? (long pause)."

Here was the final standard situation which was likely to precede the breakthrough. "The therapist knows that this silence is concerned with feelings aroused by his repeated confrontations, which must be brought out at once" (p. 108). Davanloo will now go over to the patient's experience of being hounded. Davanloo will now give her room: "What do you think (long pause). . . . How do you feel right now? In a way you didn't like what I said. . . . What do you feel inside? . . . Do you feel irritated or angry? . . . What do you think about what I said?" (pp. 108–109).

A beginning of a breakthrough now occurred:

PATIENT Well, about setting up a goal—putting up a wall, or whatever . . . well . . . that . . . uh . . . that has been for like . . . I have done it a lot. (The patient is crying.) This is a pattern of my life. I have done it in school because I have tried for an A, but I have always said to myself, "What the heck; I will probably never get an A and don't be surprised if you don't—so don't get upset." So I don't know if I have every really tried for an A. This self-defeating system is basically in every aspect of my life. I don't think I could really stand and really try for the highest. (The patient continues to cry.) (p. 109)

But Davanloo would not allow the tears to be the entire story, only an entry, for crying had also been used to "put off" her difficulty she had first told him. He wanted an accurate picture of her destructiveness, so he asked her to go back to the specific relationship with the boyfriend, and got quite a vivid account of her rages against him. "This completes the first phase of the interview, which has accomplished a very great deal—breaking through the patient's defensive vagueness and getting a true and living picture of her disastrous relations with men" (p. 113).

Like the other methods of modern brief therapy, this one is also a simple diagram, so there is not much more to say about it. First, you have to take care, if you are going to corner someone about making access to themselves impossible, that you corner them about something important to them and "specific." This patient said her crying was useless and that her boyfriend situation was where she was most at a loss. Thus, Davanloo begins in a specific place like Sifneos. I have seen many students try to break through the patient's wall over some vague, general difficulty or over some specific situation which is trivial to the patient. This is bound to fail, as the patient has no stake then in being reached.[1]

Secondly, you have to establish "objectively" that the patient *wants* to do what is necessary, but *behaves* to prevent what is necessary. Usually, the therapist will have to show the patient these behaviors in the rapid succession in which they appear. Often, the therapist will see a run of defense, related but different, perhaps five to ten which are to be pointed out as they occur. Defenses are not "interpreted." They are called as they occur, and summarized together as defeating access — access which the patient agreed was necessary and desired by her.

Once the "objective" picture of self-defeat is in place, the therapist may threaten while appearing to be "objective" himself. One threat will not do, but several, building up, one more stinging than another: If you do this, we will get nowhere. . . . If you do this, I will be useless to you. . . . If you keep up your wall, you will defeat me, but you will lose. . . . Perhaps we should stop?

But it is equally important for the threats to be followed by going over with the patient, to her side of the wall. When the threatening has become unbearable, the doctor suddenly is not the confronting doctor, but the one at her side, sensing how she feels about that confronting doctor. There are two of him: the outside doctor who tells the patient "objectively" what she is doing to prevent access; the inside doctor who shares her feeling about such objective hounding. Also, there are the summaries of the entire situation, which pose both sides, alternating between the outside eye and the inner eye, resonating between the two eyes of the "double description" (Bateson, 1979). Finally, the patient is exhausted, and a breakthrough begins.

THE DOMAIN OF DAVANLOO'S TECHNIQUE

According to David Malan, this technique is a "twentieth century miracle" (1980a, p. 18), for " . . . Freud discovered the unconscious; Davanloo has discovered how to use it therapeutically" (1980a, p. 23). Now it is true that there are too few patients like Lucy with Freud or the Zoologist described by Malan who will tell the "true feelings" opposed to their duty or get "specific" when anxious. Most put up "walls." Freud learned this to his great chagrin with Dora. Reich decided that most, if not all, neurotic patients have such neurotic characters wherein the "constant attitude" is a "wall" which prevents access (Chapter 4). Indeed, the attempt to "help" is very likely to bring about much feeling of futility in the therapist, when he or she is kept at bay outside the wall, waiting forever to be let in, like the housecat. Few of us enjoy this patience in the night. Therefore, we can appreciate Malan's point about passivity:

It needs to be stated categorically that in the early part of the century Freud unwitting-ly took a wrong turning which led to disastrous consequences for the future of psychotherapy. This was to react to increasing resistance with increased passivity — eventually adopting the technique for free association on the part of the patient, and the role of "passive sounding board," free-floating attention, and infinite patience on the part of the therapist. (1980a, p. 13)

But breaking down walls is no twentieth century miracle. It was Reich's principal objective and metaphor (Chapter 4). Davanloo is much more swift about it than Reich.[2] But neither invented the basic routine, which was well-known to nineteenth century religion, and long before that as well, as described by William James in his *Varieties of Religious Experience* (1902).

A religious breakthrough depends on the willful activity of the subject be-ing shown to be completely in vain. One subject described his plight as follows:

. . . the following impressions came into my mind like a small still voice. You have been seeking, praying, reforming, laboring, reading, hearing, and meditating, and what have you done by it towards your salvation? Are you any nearer to conversion now than when you first began. . . . It brought such conviction upon me that I was obliged to say that I did not think I was one step nearer than at first, but as much condemned, as much exposed, and as miserable as before . . . *for the ways I have prescribed to myself have all failed me*, and I am willing they should fail. (James, 1902, p. 177) (my italics)

This allows a surrender. Another subject described the giving up:

I committed myself to him in the profoundest belief that my individuality was going to be destroyed,that he would take all from me, and I was willing. In such a surrender lies the secret of the holy life. (James, 1902, p. 182)

When the willful, failing self is given up, something tremendous flows in, as described by a third subject:

I was there prostrate on the ground, bathed in my tears, with my heart beside myself, when M. B. called me back to life. . . . I came out as from a sepulchre, from an abyss of darkness; and I was living, perfectly living. But I wept, for at the bottom of that gulf I saw the extreme of misery from which I had been saved by an infinite mercy; and I shuddered at the sight of my iniquities . . . stupefied . . . overwhelmed with wonder and gratitude. (James, 1902, pp. 182–183)

James summarizes the transition as follows:

Revivalism has always assumed that only its type of religious experience can be perfect; you must first be nailed on the cross of natural despair and agony, and then in the twinkling of an eye be miraculously released. (p. 185)

But how to do it? There is a simple, powerful method here. James writes:

There are only two ways in which it is possible to get rid of anger, worry, fear, despair, or other undesirable affections. One is that an opposite affection should over-poweringly break over us, and the other is by getting so *exhausted* (my italics) with the struggle that we have to stop—so we drop down, give up, and *don't care* any more. (p. 173)

But the "opposite affection" which "should over-poweringly break over us," has to be nursed along, while the willful self is broken and exhausted:

When the new centre of personal energy has been subconsciously incubated so long as to be just ready to open into flower, "hands off" is the only words for us, it must burst forth unaided. (p. 172)

The subject's willful activity must appear to be as destructive and deceptive as possible, if it is to be suddenly dropped:

I saw at once that all my contrivances and projects to effect or procure deliverance or salvation for myself were utterly in vain; I was brought quite to a stand, as finding myself totally lost. . . . When I saw evidently that I had regard to nothing but self-interest, then my duties appeared a vile mockery and a continual course of lies. . . . (p. 174)

This breaks the will:

. . . it seems that the very last step must be left to other forces and performed without the help of its activity [the will]. In other words, self-surrender becomes indispensable. "The personal will," says Dr. Starbuck, "must be given up." In many cases relief persistently refuses to come until the person ceases to resist. . . . (pp. 170–171)

The final step is this:

What then must a person do? "He must relax," says Dr. Starbuck, — "that is, he must fall back on the larger Power that makes for righteousness, which has been welling up in his own being, and let it finish in its own way the work it has begun." "Man's extremity is God's opportunity" is the theological way of putting this fact of the need of self-surrender; whilst the physiological way of stating it would be, "Let one do all in one's power, and one's nervous system will do the rest." (p. 172)

Davanloo's technique is well-known to revivalism. He makes the vigorous challenge to the patient's willful activity, which is shown to make help impossible. This is maximum intrusion. Then he threatens to abandon the patient, forever. This is all performed in a framework of help, so that intrusion and abandoning are punctuated by empathic statements, objective summary of the situation, and the rationale of help. This brings out "breakthrough" in either the religious or the psychotherapeutic realm. Can the reader tell whether the following subject saw Davanloo or went to a revival?

I have been through the experience which is known as conversion. My explanation of it is this: the subject works his emotions up to the breaking point, at the same time resisting their physical manifestations, such as quickened pulse, etc. and then suddenly lets them have their full sway over the body. The relief is something wonderful, and the pleasurable effects of the emotions are experienced to the highest degree. (James, 1902, p. 201)

Another breakthrough needs only the substitution of the world "Davanloo" for "God":

All my feelings seemed to rise and flow out; and the utterance of my heart was, "I want to pour out my whole soul to God." . . . It seemed as if I met the Lord Jesus Christ face to face. . . . I fell down at his feet and poured out my soul to him. I wept aloud like a child, and made such confessions as I could with my choked utterances. It seemed to me that I bathed his feet with my tears. . . . (James, 1902, p. 203)

The best news of all is that the relief stays. A funny version of this is quoted by James from a fellow named Billy Bray about his post-conversion:

I can't help praising the lord. As I go along the street, I lift up one foot, and it seems to say, "Glory"; and I lift up the other, and it seems to say "Amen"; and so they keep up like that all the time I am walking. (p. 204)

There is no doubt this is a powerful method. I experimented with it for over a year after watching Davanloo at work in Montreal and I brought about a number of conversion-breakthroughs myself, one report of which will conclude this chapter. And they do hold up. We do not have to take David Malan's say-so. William James reports the same, 80 years before, based on the research of a Professor Coe (p. 193) and a Professor Starbuck (p. 206) who studied 77 and 100 subjects, respectively. Professor Coe anticipated Davanloo's preference for the "passive" patient, for the "passive subclass," as that to "which most of the subjects of striking transformations belonged" (p. 193). Professor Starbuck found that only 6 percent relapsed from their faith, although most showed a little backsliding. Malan may be exaggerating very little when he claims for Davanloo:

This method of therapy is applicable to severe and chronic conditions: as an example, fifteen weeks of treatment result in complete recovery from symptoms which have lasted for twenty years—a ratio of about 70. . . . this is the method of "duration ratio" carried to the limit. In this type of experiment, of course, the patients act as their own controls, and the result is virtual proof that it was therapy that caused the improvement. . . . As already mentioned, recovery is complete by the time therapy is terminated, and follow-up merely confirms that there is no subsequent relapse. (1980b, p. 346)

I myself do not doubt the converging evidence of several hundred years of conversion.

There are two major problems, however. First, while the techniques of Davanloo are more powerful than those of Malan, Mann, or Sifneos for getting through "walls," many patients will still defy the technique. Many patients will not give way to religious conversion, however vigorous, for they will not allow themselves to be subjected to its overwhelming influence. Those who are more desperate are more promising, when other methods of help have failed. The desperate often hope in secret that someone will really come after them.[3] Many do not want this, however. The trouble for the doctor is to use this technique with the patient and fail. You have committed yourself so forcefully that you now have no other alternative but to withdraw. You cannot do something else now, after declaring the first route is the "only way."

The other trouble is what happens between the "relentless healer"[4] and his audience of students and rivals. While his method may have strong advantages for reaching some patients, it has some disadvantages for the ecology of the great man who practices in this way as a lieutenant of God.[5] Evangelists become gods themselves by acting so profoundly, with such conviction, in His name or stead. Therefore, what Luther wrote about God becomes what is also true about his representatives, the evangelists or gods:

Therefore God must take this maul in hand (the law, I mean) to beat in pieces and bring to nothing this beast with her vain confidence, that she may so learn at length by her own misery that she is utterly forlorn and damned. (James, 1902, p. 196)

This man with "maul in hand" for the best of purposes also has a profound effect on his audience of students and rivals. Look at what happened to Malan. He went from "bewildering despair" (1980a, p. 15) to seeing Davanloo as a saviour, a "true research worker" and "profoundly guilty practitioner," although few from a distance would have thought on their own of Davanloo as outstanding in his reporting or guilt. Malan, however, saw the "crippled walk again," a "twentieth century miracle" (1980a, p. 18).

This has always been the great difficulty with an atmosphere which fosters conversion. It cannot be set aside. The evangelical atmosphere must be actively sought by the saved for new converts, to keep the sinful, destructive atmosphere, in themselves, now decimated, from returning. The saved are always in danger of falling back into their own bewildering despair. This makes them quite vigorous on behalf of the man with the maul. They rough up disbelievers in the audience, while the great man can sit in the back. Of course, he is always ready to come to the forefront to explain everything at great length, which will swamp any persistent objections.

Science is possible about conversion, as William James showed, but the student must be at one remove from the saving activity. If he is desperate himself to believe in the conversions, he will overlook weaknesses in the procedure or in the context or ecology which the procedure brings about. For example, Malan has been willing to overlook many of the criteria for first-class science about psychotherapy that he himself presented years before (1963, 1976). He appears to be untroubled that Davanloo is unknown for discussing any failures, for admitting errors in videotapes he is showing, or for being able to be criticized. Davanloo makes claims for research, but has never published any findings which we could scrutinize for what is weak, as well as for what is strong. All we get is his showings of the dramatic breakthroughs on video-tape, which are indeed impressive. Those will have to do for the faithful.[6]

A CASE OF MIGRAINE

I am not opposed to the would-be brief therapist seeing for himself if he or she too can bring about conversion-breakthroughs in the way of Davanloo. Those who have not wielded this power are apt to be envious of Davanloo having something over them. Who wouldn't like to be as powerful as possi-ble? Who wouldn't have a secret desire to lead a troop as an evangelist? Too many who hate to see a power they could not have for themselves will con-test or deride this power, while hiding from themselves their own envy. This is a shame, for the power ought to be granted.

Therefore, I am not opposed to learning this method. Once you can do it yourself, you are in a position to consider whether other methods could be of equal or comparable power, without the negative effects on the thera-pist's relations to his audience. My own opinion, which I will present at length in Part III and Part IV, is that this method, which is based on the revolution of character analysis, is less useful than the methods derived from the subse-quent interpersonal and systemic revolutions. It is more dramatic, but the en-thusiasm of conversion is often expensive for the patient's friends and fami-ly. There is quite a potential for negative effects on the audience of the patient, as well as on the audience of the therapist. The patient may feel reborn, but his audience may want to kill him. Sometimes they will be glad for him. The difference depends upon the consequent interactions between the reborn and his local environment. A difficulty with the revolution of character analysis is that the reborn have this mixed potential, which is apt to go unreckoned.

I would like to report a conversion-breakthrough of my own, if only to show there is nothing mysterious about it after all, except for the remarkable storm of the nervous system which is brought about. The method itself is one of these diagrams of modern brief therapy, which can be learned in a year if you have the feel for the obligatory role. My grandfather was a Protestant minister, so I do not find it so difficult to be conducting a revival. I never saw my grandfather conduct church, but our family has passed down some of his ways.

I will give excerpts from the final half-hour of a two-hour trial therapy of a patient with severe migraine. She had had almost daily attacks for several years, which were not being controlled by the usual pharmacological methods. Hence, she was referred by her internist to Brief Therapy Clinic. The most important observation from the first hour of the trial therapy was that I noticed a grimace or contortion or squinting on the right side of the patient's face, which seemed to appear when we were getting to something emotional. The patient also stroked this right side of the face, as if to comfort herself there. I asked her where her migraine attacks began, whereupon she pointed to this place under the right eye. I told her I was not surprised, as she continually tightened that area, which appeared to get rid of what she was feeling. She seemed to take this observation as a command to stop contorting her face.

But she was extremely vague about whether anything bothered her very much at all. She recited laundry lists of "little things," which annoyed her a little, which gave *me* a headache. I went out for a glass of water. I came back determined. If I were to help, I would have to have something which was worth talking about for *her*, something specific which was big for her, which mattered. I insisted.

She finally agreed there was an omnibus term paper the last semester which she hated, which seemed to bring on a particularly severe headache. Did she want to look into this experience? Yes, fine. I insisted on being told about the assignment, and what she felt about the assignment. I got specifics about what she did, finally, but little about what she felt. We enter the interview directly where I am summarizing our progress. Notice how the patient responds by a rapid series of evasions, how I call them, one by one. The patient wants to do what is necessary to describe her feelings, but is making this impossible by her behavior, which will be well described to her.

DOCTOR See here, we finally come to something that we agree is big, which is that you really hated this — that was your word — hated this . . .
PATIENT That's true . . .
DOCTOR This, uh, omnibus assignment that was much bigger than the credits warranted or the usefulness warranted . . .
PATIENT So far anyway, ya.
DOCTOR And you start, all right? So then you start to tell me about it but then it evaporates on you. Your resentment — you start to tell me and then you're shrugging and smiling and saying, "Oh, it's nothing," you see? That's how you lose your feelings.
PATIENT Well . . .
DOCTOR What?
PATIENT Is that bad?
DOCTOR And then you get apologetic, you see? I'm just trying to tell you as a matter of fact . . .
PATIENT Um, hmm.
DOCTOR It's not a criticism, it's just a statement of fact, but then you feel you have to apologize . . . (pause). And then you wait for me to take the lead. See, that's another way you do it, become very passive, you see?
PATIENT Ya. I know that.

DOCTOR Well, that diminishes you . . . (pause). You don't know what I want
  you to do?
PATIENT No.
DOCTOR So you get confused too.
PATIENT Ya.
DOCTOR I want you to stay with whatever you were feeling about this, this
  class that you resented.
PATIENT I don't, somehow I don't want to.
DOCTOR You don't *want* to?
PATIENT Well, that's what I feel.

This "objective" description of her preventing our success went on for a
half-hour, until I was sensing that she could bear my presence no longer. Then
I asked her how she felt about my pushing her so long and hard. I have to
describe "objectively" how she even prevents our success at getting to her feelings about me:

PATIENT I know. (Long pause) I don't know where to start. It's like, it's a
  very insecure feeling . . .
DOCTOR Go ahead.
PATIENT I know, I'm thinking. It's so strange, but it feels like you're attacking
  what I am, which is not real good. (Patient covers face with hands.)
DOCTOR Um, hmm.
PATIENT I don't like that.
DOCTOR How does it make you feel. (Patient sniffs.) You've just had a feel-
  ing, didn't you?
PATIENT Ya.
DOCTOR And you tried to get rid of it.
PATIENT I'm trying very hard to get rid of it.
DOCTOR Well, let's stay with it. You just started to have a feeling about me,
  you feel as though I'm attacking who you are.
PATIENT Um, hmm.
DOCTOR What does that feel like to you?
PATIENT I doesn't feel good.
DOCTOR You're trying to push off your tears, aren't you?
PATIENT Ya. (Pause) (Patient cries. Therapist hands her Kleenex.)
DOCTOR You don't want to look at me now do you?
PATIENT No.
DOCTOR Why not?
PATIENT Because.
DOCTOR Why?
PATIENT If I don't look at you then maybe I can be, remain *in control*.
DOCTOR But if you do this we're not going to get anywhere. (Patient barely
  suppresses grin, covers mouth with hand.)
PATIENT I know. But you asked *why*, and I told you.

DOCTOR See, there it is again. I'm not criticizing your response.

PATIENT I know.

DOCTOR I mean, you take my observation as an attack again. You're trying to stay in control, which is like a wall, just when you and I are starting to get in touch with who you really are and what you really feel. You really want to put up this wall.

PATIENT Ya. I do.

Having secured the "objective" agreement that she is defeating our joint work by putting up her "wall," I am well positioned to make a series of threats which will jolt her. She refuses to stop, even for a break in the interview!

DOCTOR Well, you certainly *may*, I mean that's your privilege, you see, but if you do, then we won't get anywhere. We'll start to get somewhere like we are right now.

PATIENT Um, hmm.

DOCTOR We're starting to see what you really do feel about our conversation, that you feel attacked in terms of who you are. We're starting to get to your feelings about that, but now you're defeating. You're defeating that endeavor right now by your present behavior of trying to resume control. I'm not going to lose, you see, but if you keep the wall up there, putting it back up, you're the one who's going to lose, because I *won't* be able to help you. You'll succeed, you will defeat me, you will have succeeded in regaining control and making sure that I don't upset you, but then you'll not be getting any help from me.

PATIENT I know. (Patient unconsciously sticks out tip of tongue.)

DOCTOR You *do*?

PATIENT Ya. But it's *not* easy. (Patient fingers necklace, smiling at me.)

DOCTOR I know.

PATIENT If I don't do that.

DOCTOR You don't what?

PATIENT Let down my wall. So . . .

DOCTOR Well, we could stop if you want. Right here. You don't have to let down your wall for me. We're trying to get behind your wall so we can get to what your true feelings are, but it's a difficult procedure, as you see . . .

PATIENT It is.

DOCTOR You don't have to. I mean we could stop right here.

PATIENT It's very tempting. (Patient plays with hair.)

DOCTOR Well, do you want to do that?

PATIENT No. Yes, but no.

DOCTOR It's up to you, I mean no one's making you come.

PATIENT I know, if I didn't want to *be* here, I wouldn't be here, which is not true. I mean I don't want to be here, but . . .

DOCTOR Well, I'm just saying you're free to stop at any time. We can stop here if you want. You see what we have to do.

PATIENT I know.

DOCTOR We're trying to get behind this wall that you put up. Why don't you think about it for a while, why don't we take a little break here for ten minutes, and you can think about it.

PATIENT *No, I* don't want to take a break.

DOCTOR *You* don't want to.

PATIENT No. Unless you guys want one, but I don't.

DOCTOR Well, I was thinking this would be a good time because it seemed pretty clear to me that you didn't want to go on at this point. You were just going to resume control, which would defeat what we were just starting to get to. You want to go on now?

PATIENT I don't feel like I have a choice because, I mean, I've got to get help.

DOCTOR You don't have to get help from us. There are other . . .

PATIENT I know.

DOCTOR This is just one.

PATIENT I mean, I've tried other things though.

After a little more rough handling, I go over to her side of the wall. I extend myself to gather what I can about what makes this "not being liked" so extremely painful. We fall down a deep hole of pain together when I say, "Yes, you're very sensitive. You're very aware of whether I'm liking what I find."

DOCTOR Um, hmm. So you really want to get help from me. Well then, let's go *back* to what you were just feeling, this feeling that my observations were attacks on who you are. You were starting to have feelings about that so tell me how that makes you feel.

PATIENT I'm just, well, afraid, of what I don't know. (Patient waves hand, as if to dismiss subject.)

DOCTOR Well see, there's that shrugging again, the moment you start to tell me something. But I believe you do want to tell me something, you see?

PATIENT Um, hmm.

DOCTOR You started to say fear; you're sort of gesturing, very vaguely. I think you could tell me more about your fear. This vagueness, you see, doesn't help. You have to say what your fear is like. You're afraid of me.

PATIENT Not of you, but of what you're doing.

DOCTOR Well, tell me what's scaring you about this.

PATIENT Maybe I'm afraid of what I'll find. (Plays with hair again.)

DOCTOR Maybe. You see, there's that vagueness again.

PATIENT Right. So I probably am. (Covers mouth again.)

DOCTOR Probably. There's that vagueness again. Are you or aren't you afraid?

PATIENT I am.

DOCTOR You are afraid.

PATIENT Um, hmm.

DOCTOR Tell me what you're afraid of.

PATIENT Of what I'll see, I guess, ya, I *am*. (Waves right hand to dismiss something again. Sticks out tongue a little unconsciously.)

DOCTOR See, there's "I guess" again.

PATIENT But I caught myself this time. Well, I'll tell you why I'm being vague, because . . . just a minute, I just lost my sentence (pause). Oh ya, I'm being vague because I don't want to be afraid of what I'll find.

DOCTOR But you are.

PATIENT But I am. I don't want to be so that's why I'm being vague.

DOCTOR All right. So that's another thing that you do to yourself.

PATIENT Um, hmm.

DOCTOR You're not supposed to be afraid; then you tell yourself not to be afraid.

PATIENT That's right. (Covers mouth again.)

DOCTOR But you are.

PATIENT Ya.

DOCTOR So let's go on.

PATIENT All right.

DOCTOR It's more than fear. You were starting to cry and that was painful.

PATIENT And it still is.

DOCTOR You mean, it's right there.

PATIENT Um, hmm.

DOCTOR What is that pain? There's something very painful about being attacked for who you are. That was your phrase. That hurts you a lot.

PATIENT Ya.

DOCTOR Okay, tell me how that hurts.

PATIENT Well, it's like what if I don't like what I find and that's what I'm afraid of. (Hand in front of face, waving something away, covering mouth, right side of face. Very shaky.)

DOCTOR That you don't like? (Pause)

PATIENT Well, ya, it doesn't really matter what anyone . . . no, it does matter to me what other people think.

DOCTOR Yes, you're very sensitive, you're very aware of whether I'm liking what I find.

PATIENT That's right.

DOCTOR So there's something painful here about not being accepted, not being liked for who you are.

PATIENT Ya. Probably because, um, when I was in, I don't remember, but elementary school, junior high and all that, people didn't like me . . .

DOCTOR Hmm.

PATIENT It really wasn't too nice.

Now I will try to stay with her as best I can. There will be mostly little empathic extensions[7] of my showing I get the picture, an occasional summary statement about what actually happens to some kids, which backs up her testimony. This reaches her pain, put behind the wall for over ten years.

DOCTOR That hurt.

PATIENT Ya. I mean it wasn't everyone 'cause I did have friends.

DOCTOR There you go, see.

PATIENT It wasn't everyone though.

DOCTOR All right, but you were starting out. I was just concerned that you were going to minimize it. It was something, it was. All right, go on . . .

PATIENT I was telling you the truth . . .

DOCTOR Okay, go on. So there was something about not being liked . . .

PATIENT I was getting to it.

DOCTOR Okay. I'm a little impatient, aren't I?

PATIENT Yes.

DOCTOR All right, go on.

PATIENT I'm just telling you the story. No, I mean some people *did* like me, but there, most people didn't. I don't even know if that's true, but I know that . . .

DOCTOR See, there it is, you just started to tell me something painful, you see . . .

PATIENT I'm trying.

DOCTOR Now this is important. You just started telling me something, that most people didn't like you, that was your phrase, in elementary school, and you started to cry and then you started saying *but*. You see?

PATIENT Um, hmm.

DOCTOR So there's some, there's really a lot of pain here about not being liked in elementary school which you're trying to keep me away from.

PATIENT Well, I don't like reliving it.

DOCTOR But we have to, you see.

PATIENT I know, I'm just, I'm telling you that I don't like reliving it.

DOCTOR Okay.

PATIENT Well, just, you know, I was not very attractive. It was *nothing* to do with my personality, and I still believe that. They couldn't get past what I looked like, so . . .

DOCTOR Well, what was wrong with how you looked? You're . . .

PATIENT Well, just I had a very large overbite (covers mouth) and wore glasses and just things like that so . . . (pause).

DOCTOR That was hard.

PATIENT Well . . .

DOCTOR The kid who looks, has the overbite and has to have glasses gets a lot . . .

PATIENT Yup.

DOCTOR Gets a lot of bad things, hmm? You feel it now.

PATIENT Yup.

DOCTOR Let's stay with that. What that was like for you? (Long pause, patient is crying.) It must have been, you were harassed then . . .

PATIENT Um, hmm.

DOCTOR As a child by the other kids. You were the kid in the class that they picked on?

PATIENT Yup.

DOCTOR This went on for years?

PATIENT Yup.

DOCTOR From the very beginning, from kindergarten on?

PATIENT No.

DOCTOR What grade did it start?

PATIENT Say, third I think.

DOCTOR It started in third. How long did it last?

PATIENT Oh, till about the end of my junior year.

DOCTOR In high school.

PATIENT Um, hmm.

DOCTOR That's a *long* time.

PATIENT Yup. (Patient cries.)

DOCTOR A lot of pain there. So that's when you wanted to put up your wall.

PATIENT Sure. Doesn't hurt as much. (Long pause)

DOCTOR I bet there were certain times that were really awful. What occurs to you? You were attacked essentially.

PATIENT Yes.

DOCTOR Okay, tell me about that. How were you attacked? (Long pause. Patient crying.)

PATIENT Well, you know, just the normal, they'd laugh at you, call you names . . .

DOCTOR See here now, you're trying to minimize it.

PATIENT I have to.

DOCTOR Yes, you really are. You're trying to make it normal when it was awful, hmm?

PATIENT Yes, I mean, I have seen it done since then too.

DOCTOR You know that, how kids are, how some kids are treated. You see, that's you trying to get a little distance on it and observe it from the outside, but you and I have to get into this because this is where your pain lies, you see? Which is terrible, hmm? What do you remember? What are the worst things they did to you?

PATIENT It was mostly the laughing. I hated it. (Patient cries out . . . cradles right side of face in hand.)

DOCTOR Tell me about it. (Long pause) Tell me about it.

PATIENT I'd walk past, people talking, hear them say things about how I looked and then they'd all laugh or . . .

DOCTOR What'd they say? You don't want to remember, do you?

PATIENT No.

DOCTOR Well you have to. Yes, you have to. We have to get to some of this.
PATIENT Just . . . (patient is now sobbing, waving her hand in front of her
   face). (Long pause) (Curled up as if to defend herself from bodily blows)

This is as far as I could go with her. I really couldn't bear anymore myself. I insisted she tell me what the other kids actually said about her, and
I threatened a little more, and I appeared to be willing to be with her. But
I was not. If I had actually been willing to be with her, I would have said
it was actually unbearable. I know I had tears in my eyes which she never
saw, for she was sobbing and looking down, waving her hands in front of her
face, waving off the cruel kids, curling up to protect her bodyself.

Holding a fish on the line is tolerable only when one can tolerate the extremity of feeling in the fish, and in oneself subjecting the fish to this terror.
I reached my limit and tugged too hard, when I needed to let her wind out
some line. Besides, this was no fish. This was like tormenting the kid in the
next seat.

So we took a break soon after. We had gotten far enough. The torment
in the face had been connected to an extreme sensitivity to not being "liked."
The migraine trigger was clear as could be to both of us, so the patient
began brief therapy with one of our residents. This went through two clear
phases. First, many more episodes of migraine were understood, because it
became apparent how threats of "not being liked" were coming up in many
areas of the patient's life. The patient could now feel how hurt she was by
apparently small details where she might be disliked. Second, there was more
than hurt. She wanted to torture people who hurt her only a little. She was
savage back, and now could allow herself to feel her own revengefulness in
place of hurt and pain in the face and head. Follow-up six months after
the semester of brief therapy showed her almost completely free of migraine,
an enormous shift from where she began with us.

INTRODUCTION

The Systemic Perspective

(CHAPTERS 15 THROUGH 17)

I *will be taking several more pages than usual to introduce the final revolution of perspective, the systemic perspective. This is a very difficult position to adopt. Selvini Palazzoli and her colleagues wrote: "We are convinced, after ten years of hard work, that we have only just begun. . . . Changing our linear way of thinking in order to acquire a new epistemology, systemic and circular, is a tortuous process. Sometimes we fall prey to the illusion, rather widespread, of having achieved this, only to discover ourselves, with some dejection, confronted with failure. Detecting our error, we realize the goal is still far away" (my emphasis; 1978a, p. x).*

In contrast to this modest warning by the Milan team, the reader may well know of many writers and family therapists who propose to explain systemic thinking which is "higher" and "better" than any other perspective. I have no doubt that these authors have a higher perspective, but I do doubt that the wider field they enjoy is better than all other perspectives for all other pur-poses. This would be like saying that the view from the forest fire tower is better for seeing everything that goes on in the forest with the animals. Such a "higher" systemic view is very grand, but it cannot be "better" if it triggers colleagues to bring you back down to earth by undercutting your perch. I hope the reader will bear in mind that this author will discuss an attack on prob-lems of a "higher" logical type, with no intention of suggesting that this perspective will make the actual work of the reader "higher" and "better." Adopting this perspective will make some therapists more stilted and worse! I hope the reader will also bear in mind that I appreciate that many, many authors have sought and found access to a systemic perspective by routes dif-ferent from that of the Milan team. I do not mean to slight anyone by my interest in the route taken by the Milan team, which merely happens to be a route which I have wanted to travel. There are many roads to Rome. There is no such thing as "the" systemic perspective, which is a class of possibilities. This perspective is no one's property.

Still, there is little doubt in my own mind that the systemic perspective is more difficult *to comprehend and sustain than any of the three previous perspectives I have attempted to present. Therefore, I will take a little time here to explain the difficulty which lies ahead in the next three chapters. The reader will have to decide for him or herself whether this difficult study is worth his or her while. This is entirely an individual matter. It may help to have had certain recurrent difficulties while working from the interpersonal perspective. Let us back up, momentarily, to that vantage point for observa-tion.*

Many have described interpersonal maneuvers which entrap and entangle. Most writers who have taken these dangers seriously have also proposed counter-maneuvers or counter-structures which could hold up against these wrecking operations. This armory has two regions. Most of us only know a little about one of the two. One region is the literature of "interpersonal" thinking about individual patients, which I have described from Alexander, Sullivan, Winnicott, and Balint (Chapters 5, 6, 7, 8). The second region is the literature about such operations by entire families or their subgroups, which comes under various names, including "strategic therapy," "structural therapy," "systemic therapy," and so forth, which comes from writers like Watzlawick, Minuchin, Haley and so forth. Taught from these two traditions to see the moves of our antagonists more swiftly, ready with our own guile, we may win more therapeutic combats.

Bateson provides a theoretical jump for handling something more than pathological moves, beyond what he calls Learning I, to learning about the class of moves *available to an individual or family, which is at a higher logical level than the* moves themselves. *Bateson was interested in how an individual or family might move from an entire class of operations to another, as from "threatening" to "playing." This led Bateson into the study of what he called "context markers," which could signal, for example, whether a given move ought to be taken as a "threat" or as "play." Bateson's idea suggested that these "context markers" might be a much more powerful object of therapeutic interest. Therapists might not have to work so long and hard if they could bring about transformations of "context," which would be what Bateson called Learning II (Rabkin, 1972).*

This is a very difficult idea for many modern minds, for whom everything is quantitative, for whom qualitative jumps to a "higher level" are little but mysterious talking (Schumacher, 1977). A traditional Catholic might get the idea more readily, but perhaps most of us have enough religious training to follow an analogy to Dante's Divine Comedy. *Those in hell have sinned, but are mired in hopeless, circular destruction. Those in purgatory have sinned, often identically, but are slowly ascending the mountain of Purgatory. How is the difference to be explained? Those in the inferno have not repented. Those ascending the mountain have repented. How could this "repenting" make such an enormous difference? For many this is puzzling or foolish. But "repenting" is no matter of words. Repenting admits the glory of God, a completely different world of His Creation, which is literally figured in a beautiful mountain versus a godless, murky, stinking inferno. The consequences of admitting, or not admitting, God are enormous in this perspective of Dante. Perhaps this gives the reader a glimpse in advance of the burden of Chapter 15 "Bateson and the Inferno," of an attack on problems of a higher logical order. Admitting the* class *of operations allowed to the family, admitting its creation, may have major consequence for individuals for altering their own context.*[1]

The Milan team invented a series of means for carrying out this theoretical possibility which Bateson had imagined, so that it might be possible to get access from the moves a family might make to its class of moves, to its "context markers," to its higher order rules, to its creation, for the potential of transformation.

The Milan team members were psychoanalysts who became interested in 1967 in the ideas of Watzlawick, Haley, and other colleagues of Bateson about recognizing and fighting pathological maneuvers. The first, smaller jump in thinking they borrowed was the idea that you cannot fight pathological moves so well by proposing better moves to a patient or patient family. Prescribing back to them their own pathological moves might make it more difficult for them to continue with the same moves.

But there is a hazard in such procedure: the "problem" for the family might indeed be "solved" while leaving the destructive apparatus of the family about the same as it was.[2] This would be like catching a minor criminal while missing the syndicate which employs him. The job which interested the Milan team was not only to win the preliminary skirmishes at the periphery, but to carry on to the center of the labyrinth (Selvini Palazzoli, Boscolo, Cecchin, and Prata, 1978a, p. 48).

The big jump they invented, I think, was the idea that access to a vicious game could be gotten by devoting themselves to studying this game as if it served some higher purpose. This "positive connotation" finds the red thread which leads to the center of the labyrinth where both children and parents are sacrificed (Selvini Palazzoli et al., 1978a, Chapter 5). Notice this appreciation in the following description by Selvini Palazzoli of the "discovery" which makes possible anorexia nervosa:

"She sometimes begins dieting with the approval of her parents. But very soon her parents' reaction to her thinning informs her of the great power *she has acquired through fasting. And, of course, she secretly thinks: 'I am the ruler now; nobody will succeed in making me change my behavior.' In trans-* actional contexts *like those described in this book, escalation becomes unavoidable—just as unavoidable as the reinforcement of the reciprocal behavior: 'The more you insist I should eat the less I will eat.' Once imbued with the erroneous belief that she has gained power* over *the others (*in game*), the identified patient is hardly ever willing to give up her symptom. (my emphasis; 1974, p. xi)*

The reader may see very well, intuitively, that an interviewer looking at a tangled up family in this way might have a chance of penetrating from its periphery, because the interviewer has an attitude of positive interest in how the moves go together to make up an irresistible game. This attitude of positive connotation is sympathetic to the players, who think to get advantages in the game.[3] Such an interviewer has a chance of being let in. Such an interviewer is friendly in the sense of appreciating that the girl has chanced upon an exciting move which appears to offer her unlimited power in some game of escalation yet to be defined.

But we will not be conducted to the center of the game only by a friendly interest in what makes it so compelling for the players. We may only become new victims, like someone who becomes curious about the game of drugtaking. One hebephrenic girl named Carla put most eloquently what else is needed after a successful intervention by the Milan team to her family:

"No one in the room had noticed Carla, who in the meanwhile had moved furtively towards the mirror. Only the two observers, speechless with amaze-

ment, saw her face, close to the mirror, beckoning to them, while her right hand moved as if shaking hands in a gesture of congratulations and her lips clearly formed the words: 'Well done.' Carla's message, in essence could be translated as follows: 'They play a tough game at home . . . and you've guessed it. . . . Well done! I congratulate you because you, too, know how to play rough.' " (Selvini Palazzoli et al., 1978b, p. 8)

How then do we play friendly and rough to infer the game from the moves? Even if we had had the last 18 years to study and practice, like the Milan team, I doubt that few of us could have made so many inventions. Bateson's theory is one thing; the inventions to carry out the idea are another. I have been studying how to do it myself, with my fellow team members, for three years only, but I have been saved many months and years already, not only by re-reading and rereading the Milan team and seeing them at work, but also from the descriptions and demonstrations of what they do from Karl Tomm (1984a, 1984b), John Burnham (1986), Peggy Penn (1982), and Lynn Hoffman (1981). I propose that I may also be able to save the reader some months, if not years, as well. I propose in Chapter 16, "The Milan Team: From Farce to Music" to describe what to do to get from moves to the game, from some skill at interpersonal interviewing to systemic interviewing. What I say is for interviewing of individuals, couples, or entire families. I attempt to describe what is not to be found, or was not explicit enough for me, in the previous authors.

I see three classes of technical inventions in which the reader will need to become adroit to get from a sense of certain pathological moves to the appreciation of the family game. The first class is that of the opening moves, for which the Milan team has offered many original inventions. Sullivan wrote very well about the necessity of locating a "worthy problem" for every interview. The Milan team has written about this as the difficulty of finding the "loose end" in the tangle which the individual or family presents (Selvini Palazzoli, 1985). How do we locate what they are in the room for at a given hour? There are many different crucial moves an individual or family can make to obscure this point of access, making the consultation pointless. The context is often decided before walking on the field or just as you look about for where to begin. Without the "loose end" of the thread there is nowhere to go.

The second class of technical inventions is for the middle game, where the skill is to get from the "loose end" to the other end of the "tangle" by inquiry. I see two major kinds of difficulties here. One danger is to get caught in a particular move which the individual or family appears to emphasize, a move which is highly distracting. For instance, the mother in the family may droop to the floor halfway through the interview, dragging the family and the family therapy team with her down a hole. This farce puts the contributions of other family members into the background, where they are more difficult to define. The converse kind of difficulty is getting the other members of the family to play out their parts in the music clearly so that the main lines of the score come through. Only when the inquiry has pulled out the hidden parts and powerful rhythms will the composition make much sense. The tangle hides the music. The farce of hearing one voice or two voices also hides the music. But hidden behind every farce is a set of ingenious contributions. After all, it takes tremendous dedication to keep a frace going. That hidden music is what we are after.

Chapter 16 is chiefly devoted to describing how to put the family game together. Here I am attempting to put together the game of the Milan team. Its individual moves for forwarding inquiry, such as circular questioning, observing of analogic dances, forming hypotheses, and retaining neutrality, are well-known and have been described by themselves and by observers commenting on their work. Most observers, however, cannot follow or explicate the sudden switches of direction in the lines of questioning or the messages that seem to come out of nowhere. This is what I am after — not their familiar moves, but their game.

The third class of inventions of the Milan team are for the end game, which, unfortunately, may come very suddenly in the opening game, at any time in the middle game, or in its own due time of concluded work. When an individual or family or other group with a history temporarily joins into an ensemble with a therapist or family team, they do so on a very provisional basis.[4] If their own closure or security, if you will, is threatened, they may end the ensemble in a matter of minutes, or seconds. The Milan team has a fine sense for this class of ending moves. I call them the "return to zero learning," which often occurs just as they are getting to the most decisive findings. Bang, you are back to zero. They had been facing you, now you see only their backs.[5]

Most of us tend to feel hurt or discouraged or destroyed by such sudden disconfirmations. The Milan team taught themselves to see these moves as the biggest help in appreciating the individual or family. These close-out moves show their organization best, being merely the negative aspect, seen from the outside or backside, the positive aspect being what is conserved as seen from the inside. Positive connotation of this is most critical, in order to receive its decisive significance and revelatory potential. Then we are ready to prepare our sudden countermove. Their ending moves help us the most, if we are ready for them.

But it is not easy to be tangled up, to be dragged down holes, or to have doors slammed in your face by people you are trying to help. How is one to receive these awful exclusions as the most helpful of revelations? No small work is involved here in reversing one's responses. For this reversal, I see theory as an invaluable pointer. For the Milan team, I think the pointer was Bateson's idea of appreciating moves, however vicious, as irresistible when you see the game.

We all have our own calamities of this kind, where we are rudely disconfirmed by our children or spouses, friends or colleagues. In ordinary life, this is very painful, for we like to know what's coming from those we depend upon. It is a bad day when friends ignore one's lecture or when medical colleagues don't show up for meetings — when both events are unexpected. For such occasional experiences, Bateson pointing to our neighbors as caught up in moves within their games may help us to be less injured and more forgiving, even enlightened.

But systemic inquiry brings this experience of the strangeness or otherness of others continuously. I have been continually tempted to give it up. The way I give it up, mostly, is to revert back to one of the interpersonal schemes for correcting interpersonal pathological moves that particularly upset me. I revert to "instructing" my patients.

For example, I did not like watching a family in which the stepfather and children battled each other over minor advantages, what our team called "the consumer product wars," while the mother acted as judge. I wanted to revert to Sullivan's idea of "ordinary solutions" for such situations to "help" the father regain his "normal" position of authority. Our team succeeded in crowning the father, at my instigation, which made the children more rebellious, the mother more miserable. The mother withdrew from the father, who stepped down, and we were back to zero again!

The temptation to "improve" the patient by "instructing" him or her in more successful solutions is much stronger in individual therapy, where it is much easier to side with individual "improvement" against the family restriction. After all, the invisible "other people in the room" can be ignored or dismissed.

For example, I have a young man who tortures himself in a hundred different ways away from home here at the university, so as to keep fit for going home, for thinking something positive about his place at home. When he came in during final exams, describing the perfect hell of extreme study he had forced upon himself, I found it very difficult to listen. I've never been very keen on people who wreck themselves studying, then go get drunk after finals. I very much wanted to instruct him to find a "better" way to handle final exams. This instruction would have been for my interests, to get him to stop something which distressed me more than him. I was just barely able to keep Bateson's point in mind: that this had to be a move to conserve his usual game. Then I could see that very little held him at home except *that his misery here in finals week made being at home the following week a* relative *relief. That was one contribution his family could make to him. He was determined to keep them helpful. Once I could see what he was up to, he was enormously relieved.*

Bateson's idea of seeing moves, intolerable to us, as indispensable to some other game, pointing to this possibility, seemed to be enough theoretical help to the Milan team to bear up. Thankfully, there is more theoretical help available to us now. This help is the theoretical biology of Maturana, which is the subject of Chapter 17. I find Maturana particularly useful for pulling myself back from these "instructive interactions" which I am inclined to enforce when my patients are making moves that distress me. The drift or pull into these "instructive interactions" is extremely powerful. This is a serious hazard because such interaction denies one access to seeing other persons operating in their own worlds, in their own games, in their own domains. They become someone or some others to be stopped from being distressing to me. I instruct them. Or I allow them to instruct me. How to overcome this inclination, which pulls us out of one systemic inquiry after another? This is the subject of Chapter 17, "Maturana: The Otherness of Others."[6]

Maturana's "topology of living systems" could include Bateson's idea about moves as part of games, but this is no occasional *trouble to ourselves. Living systems are* entirely *self-referential entities. We may perturb them or trigger them. We may discover a consensual domain with them. But they re-main* closed *upon themselves, like a pilot operating in the fog. They operate "autopoetically" to build the structures which reproduce the same organization.*

I call this the "otherness of others," which is very hard for us to tolerate seeing for very long. Our drift is to stabilize the medium for our interaction with others, which keeps us seeing something familiar from them which we need from them. One way of stabilizing relations is to have these "instructive interactions." At times Maturana speaks of "instructive interaction" as an error of epistemology. This is true in that we lose sight of the living system in its own right, which defeats systemic helping. But Maturana himself appears to be conducting "instructional interactions" about the error of "instructional interactions."

Why not? He needs to be comfortable too! This is an extremely successful way of relating, of structural coupling which stabilizes a medium between living systems. This "instructive interaction" is everywhere, while being known by many other names such as "the director culture" (Freire, 1970), or "bureaucratic authority" (Gerth and Mills, 1946), or "normal science" (Kuhn, 1957, 1962).

For us to get outside this extremely successful form of relating, of stabilizing relations, Maturana's description of entirely self-related, autonomous, autopoetic (self-regenerating) entities helps us to see the "otherness of others" to which we are otherwise blinded by our inclination to instruct them, by our inclination to confuse our map with their territory.

I believe it is no accident that an Italian team has gotten outside instructive interaction with very little theoretical help and that a theoretical biologist from the third world gives us further help in seeing the "otherness of others." We are living near the center of an equivalent to the Roman Empire, where we Instruct the World, where we do not see those who are ill from such instruction, at home or abroad.[7] Some of those on the periphery of this Empire recognize the Game, and may help us get out of it, to see our patients.

15. *Bateson and the Inferno*

BATESON was such a far-ranging fellow. I expected he would have written more than a few scattered paragraphs about ordinary neurotic problems, but perhaps he realized that things closest to home are hardest to see.[1] So I have given myself this job of bringing Bateson's thinking home to the neurotic worlds we visit in brief therapy and in ourselves.[2]

The idea of Bateson which seems to be most useful to me in neurotic worlds is the idea that all the moves *seen* are but members of a class, which is *unseen*. The unseen class is the eye of the needle through which we may pass. But my reference to the parable of the rich man (Matthew 19:21) may be no more help than my abstract statement of the idea of Bateson I want to bring home. Bateson's "Tale of the Polyploid Horse" (1979, pp. 55–56) is a contemporary parable for the successful modern man which may be more accessible to the reader. I find in this story a condensation of most of what I want to convey about neurotic worlds and about getting out of them. Here is the story, complete.

THE TALE OF THE POLYPLOID HORSE

They say the Nobel people are still embarrassed when anybody mentions polyploid horses. Anyhow, Dr. P. U. Posif, the great Erewhonian geneticist, got his prize in the late 1980s for jiggling with the DNA of the common cart horse (Equus caballus). It was said that he made a great contribution to the then new science of transportology. At any rate, he got his prize for creating — no other word would be good enough for a piece of applied science so nearly usurping the role of deity — creating, I say, a horse precisely twice the size of the ordinary Clydesdale. It was twice as long, twice as high, and twice as thick. It was a polyploid, with four times the usual number of chromosomes.

P. U. Posif always claimed that there was a time, when this wonderful animal was still a colt, when it was able to stand on its four legs. A wonderful sight it must have been! But anyhow, by the time the horse was shown to the public and recorded with all the communicational devices of modern civilization, the horse was not doing any standing. In a word, it was too heavy. It weighed, of course, eight times as much as a normal Clydesdale.

For a public showing and for the media, Dr. Posif always insisted on turning off the hoses that were continuously necessary to keep the beast at normal mammalian temperature. But we were always afraid that the innermost parts would begin to cook.

After all, the poor beast's skin and dermal fat were twice as thick as normal, and its surface area was only four times that of a normal horse, so it didn't cool properly.

Every morning, the horse had to be raised to its feet with the aid of a small crane and hung in a sort of box on wheels, in which it was suspended on springs, adjusted to take half its weight off its legs.

Dr. Posif used to claim that the animal was outstandingly intelligent. It had, of course, eight times as much brain (by weight) as any other horse, but I could never see that it was concerned with any questions more complex than those which interest other horses. It had very little free time, what with one thing and another — always panting, partly to keep cool and partly to oxygenate its eight-times body. Its windpipe, after all, had only four times the normal area of cross section.

And then there was eating. Somehow it had to eat, every day, eight times the amount that would satisfy a normal horse and had to push all that food down an esophagus only four times the caliber of the normal. The blood vessels, too, were reduced in relative size, and this made circulation more difficult and put extra strain on the heart.

A sad beast.

Dr. Posif is a busy man, more so than he ever imagined when he conceived of his polyploid horse. He reminds me of so many people that I know who have big plans. We race to carry out the unforseen implications of our polyploid horses. Actually, it is much easier to see the problems of polyploid horses which the busy Dr. Posif had to contend with than it is to see what most of us are up to. Polyploid horses get into exponential difficulty, as Bateson explains, because of their "divergent curves of increase":

In the case of the imaginary horse, length, surface area and volume (or mass) become discrepant because their curves of increase have mutually nonlinear characteristics. Surface varies as the square of length, volume varies as the cube of length, and surface varies as the 2/3 power of volume. (1979, p. 57)

The trouble with polyploid horses is easily summarized in this mathematics. The trouble with ourselves is not quite so easy to describe. Consider a very nice, well-meaning young doctor who came up to me after a lecture I gave about systemic thinking. I had suggested in the lecture that people often become "hostages" to contradictory systems. He presented himself to me as such a hostage. He said he could see his medical academic career was enough for 12 or more hours a day, perhaps 15 or all his waking hours, if he were to succeed and get tenure. He could also see that his wife wanted to be equally successful. So that she could spend 12 or 15 hours a day on her career, should he spend all his waking hours looking after their young children, since he was as devoted to his family as he was to his work? Or ought he to do half of what he needed to do for his work, half of what his family needed? A nice problem for the lecturer! How do people from the middle classes *not* get sick? That is the better question!

Now let us think about Dr. Posif and my young doctor together. Both are very skillful at handling feedback from their departments and their families. Both adjust nicely to quantitative measures getting out of line. Too much weight? Get the pulleys. Too much heat? Get the hoses. And so forth. They are adept at bringing the sources that measure success into line. They do that best. Indeed, there is a joke about this among the group of medical doctors that I work with every week, concerning what they call "U-boxic death." The joke is that patients have to die in University Hospital with the right numbers still prevailing on their laboratory box scores. The serum sodium, potassium, etc., are "U-boxic" to the very end. This becomes an enormous job. I doubt if it is very different for the young businessman and for the working-class family holding down three jobs.

What is wrong? In a way, everything is right. Every move is the right move. Dr. Posif and my young doctor are doing exactly the right thing, meeting obligations beautifully. Their inventiveness is ingenious, a kind of beauty.

For the child this meeting of obligations to do better begins auspiciously. The child who studies twice as much as his nextdoor neighbor could get the A. The child who practices his instrument or his sport gets the applause, and so forth. Redoubling the effort seems to be very worthwhile.

What later could be more logical than *"creating*—no other word would be good enough for a piece of applied science so nearly usurping the role of deity—creating, I say, a horse precisely twice the size of the ordinary Clydesdale" (p. 55, 1979) like Dr. Posif? What later could be more consistent than trying to live two lives in the time and space of one like my young doctor? All of these moves are consistent moves within the same logical class, which is that "double is better."

This is getting close to being explicit about Bateson's idea of our neurotic problems. Our "moves" are very responsive to "feedback." They are the "fast" adjustments. Adjustments are quantitative, more or less. But the "class of moves" is set, or "calibrated." It is "slow" to alter, if at all, this "qualitative" setting. For Dr. Posif and for my young doctor, the setting is the class of moves which are acceptable, namely that doubling is better.

But how to reset the calibration which is disastrous? The first problem is to see the problems, which is to see that every move possible is only more or less of the same qualitative idea. Most of us would be inclined to reject this idea of a jump to the higher logical level of qualitative ideas, for we live in a modern world in which quantitation decides the contests. The belief in a hierarchy of ideas has been decapitated (Schumacher, 1977).

But how to see the problem from within the problem? Another pair of stories from Bateson may show us the way out. Consider a poor dog and a fortunate dolphin. First, the dog:

The paradigm for experimental neurosis is as follows: A dog (commonly a male) is trained to respond differentially to two alternative "conditioned stimuli," for instance, a circle and an ellipse. In response to X, he is to do A; in response to Y, he is to do B. . . . When the dog is able to discriminate, the task is made somewhat more difficult by the experimenter, who will either make the ellipse somewhat fatter or make the circle somewhat flatter so that the contrast between the two stimulus objects becomes less. . . . At this point, the dog will have to put out extra effort to discriminate between them. But when the dog succeeds in doing this, the experimenter will again make things more difficult by a similar change. By such a series of steps, the dog is led to a situation in which finally he cannot discriminate between the objects. (1979 pp. 118-119)

Now the poor dog "may bite his keeper, he may refuse food, he may become disobedient, he may become comatose, and so on" (p. 119). Compare the fortunate dolphin in a related situation:

At the Oceanic Institute in Hawaii, a female dolphin (Seno bredanensis) had been trained to expect the sound of the trainer's whistle to be followed by food and to expect that if she later repeated what she was doing when the whistle blew, she would again hear the whistle and receive food. This animal was being used by the trainers to demonstrate to the public "how we train porpoises." "When she enters the exhibition tank I shall watch her and when she does *something* I want her to repeat, I will blow the whistle and she will be fed." She would then repeat her "something" and be again reinforced.

So far we have a dolphin set up like the dog. Now for the second half of the story, where the trouble is introduced. Notice that the dolphin gets more "help" with this "trouble."

The animal would experience a series of learning sessions each lasting from 10 to 20 minutes. The animal would *never* be rewarded for behavior which had been rewarded in the previous session. Two points from the experimental sequence must be added: First it was necessary (in the trainer's judgment) to break the rules of the experiment many times. The experience of being in the wrong was so disturbing to the dolphin that in order to preserve the relationship between her and her trainer (i.e., the context of context of contexts), it was necessary to give many reinforcements to which the porpoise was not entitled. Unearned fish.

Second, each of the first fourteen sessions was characterized by many futile repetitions of whatever behaviour had been reinforced in the immediately preceding session. Seemingly only by accident did the animal provide a piece of different behavior. In the time out between the fourteenth and fifteenth sessions, the dolphin appeared to be much excited; and when she came onstage for the fifteenth session, she put on an elaborate performance that included eight conspicuous pieces of behavior of which four were new and never before observed in this species of animal. (1979, pp. 122-123)

What is the moral of this contrast of stories? The dog did not get over the jump in logical type, from the "context for discrimination" (between the circle and ellipse) to "context for guessing." He kept faithfully to his original training, which made him wrong over and over again, in the new context. He became disturbed. The dolphin also kept faithfully to her original training for 14 sessions. She too became disturbed, but she was *nursed* along with unearned fish, until she suddenly made the jump. She needed the *array* of

14 previous disconfirmations of the original context, with the hint of a new regularity, before she excitedly jumped to a different definition of the context, as being a qualitatively different kind of situation. The dolphin jumps through the eye of the needle.[3]

Now let us go back to our disturbed Dr. Posif and our disturbed young doctor. Like the poor dog, they are faithful to their original training that "double is better." As trouble mounts to indicate a new context where "double is a nightmare," both carry on through an array of disasters. Hopefully, both have understanding wives or friends, who feed them unearned fish. Will either doctor make a jump like the dolphin? Probably not. Could we devise a brief therapy where such a jump would be more likely than in everyday life? Maybe.

Before we discuss how we might get more of our patients to the transitional zone of the dolphin waiting offstage for his fifteenth session, I believe we need to have a better description in language for how us humans experience and describe such predicaments. Language is likely to trap us more finally than the dolphin, but language may also get us out faster.

Dante is my favorite writer for the description of the trap of staying the same, of staying in disturbance, whatever it costs us, the *Inferno* being this terrible location. I like Cantos Twenty-One and Twenty-Two the best. The game of graft being played here seems wholly contemporary to me, a cousin to the game of "double is better." John Ciardi introduces the reader to this next descent in the Inferno, as follows:

The Poets move on, talking as they go, and arrive at the Fifth Bolgia. Here the Grafters are sunk in boiling pitch and guarded by Demons, who tear them to pieces with claws and grappling hooks if they catch them above the surface of the pitch. The sticky pitch is symbolic of the sticky fingers of the Grafters. It serves also to hide them from sight, as their sinful dealings on earth were hidden from men's eyes. The demons, too, suggest symbolic possibilities, for they are armed with grappling hooks and are forever ready to rend and tear all they can get their hands on. (Dante Alighieri, 1954, p. 182)

The poets witnessed a new arrival to this Bolgia, announced by one of the demons to his fellow demons as follows:

> "Blacktalons of our bridge," he began to roar,
>   "I bring you one of Santa Zita's Elders!
>   Scrub him down while I go back for more:
>
> I planted a harvest of them in that city:
>   everyone there is a grafter except Bonturo.
>   There 'Yes' is 'No' and 'No' is 'Yes' for a fee."
>
> Down the sinner plunged, and at once the Demon
>   spun from the cliff; no mastiff ever sprang
>   more eager from the leash to chase a felon.

Down plunged the sinner and sank to reappear
    with his backside arched and his face and both his feet
    glued to the pitch, almost as if in prayer.

But the demons under the bridge, who guard that place
    and the sinners who are thrown to them, bawled out:
    "You're out of bounds here for the Sacred Face:

This is no dip in the Serchio: take your look
    and then get down in the pitch. And stay below
    unless you want a taste of a grappling hook."

Then they raked him with more than a hundred hooks
    bellowing: "Here you dance below the covers.
    Graft all you can there; no one checks your books."
                                       (p. 184)

Notice how avidly both teams of players to this game go about it, the demons
in pursuit, the grafters in defying them even here, arching their backs in mock
prayer in the pitch. Later, one of the grafters even offers a bribe to Virgil
and Dante, the game being irresistible, even when most cruelly thwarted:

"If either of you would like to see and hear
    Turcans or Lombards," the pale sinner said,
    "I can lure them out of hiding if you'll stand clear

and let me sit here at the edge of the ditch,
    and get all these Blacktalons out of sight;
    for while they're here, no one will leave the pitch.

In exchange for myself, I can fish you up as pretty
    a mess of souls as you like. I have only to whistle
    the way we do when one of us gets free."

Deaddog raised his snout as he listened to him;
    then shaking his head, said: "Listen to the grafter
    spinning his tricks so he can jump from the brim."
                                       (p. 194)

And so on the game goes forever. The array of disasters for "Graft is rewarding" leads nowhere, in 14 versions, or 1400. It is a perfect circle of organization, always returning to zero, after each version. There is no getting out.

    Think back to the unfortunate dogs trying to tell ellipses from circles,
punished every time. Now think of these grafters trying to pull another fast
one, punished every time. Is there any difference between the dogs' hell and
the men's hell? I think so. To see what this difference is about, consider the
following story of my patient who experiences himself as a degraded confused
dog of the family and who also experiences this in his own words as his
hell.

The Case of "A Dog in Hell"

For several years before I saw him this young man was in analytic psychotherapy with a colleague, where he definitely got an interest in his feelings, fantasies, and dreams, but little movement. He was stuck, almost visibly in a relationship with a girlfriend who was very mean to him. But he was also stuck midway through college. He was unable to study, unable to hold a job, and unable to sleep until dawn, most nights, all because of extreme "anxiety." He was mostly confined to his apartment with his girlfriend there to criticize him, for he feared being laughed at outside. At night, he feared being attacked inside if he slept while it was dark.

The reader need not fear that I proposed brief psychotherapy to him. At best he was in a masochistic bog. At worst, he was quite paranoid. Torture was either self-administered or feared from the periphery of his world. His family claimed to be able to afford only once-a-week visits. So we began. His first year with me taught me about the overwhelming pattern he proposed for me to see, that he was, in his own words, a "dog trapped in hell." He might get angry at his girlfriend. He tortured himself with self-blame. He had other sexual interests. He tortured himself with whether to tell his girlfriend. He thought about being stuck. He tortured himself with contempt for being so weak. And so forth, and so forth.

In other words, he couldn't win. Like the poor dog we discussed before, there was punishment either way. If he stayed in his circle, he was punished. If he ventured into thinking about ellipses, of widening out a little, he was punished. His girlfriend appeared to assist him in this experiment. She tortured him for staying the same, for thinking the context was one of circles. She tortured him for trying out new things, for thinking the context was one of ellipses. He did the same thing to himself.

Is he merely the dog who is punished either way, with nowhere to turn? If so, perhaps some unearned fish and 14 trials of being in an experiment of psychotherapy in a new context might lead my patient "the dog" to jump like the dolphin into a new beginning? Not quite. Indeed, my giving him unearned fish did arouse little jumps of his feeling entitled to something better. But he always disconfirmed these moves. We always went back to zero learning, or worse. He could be more paranoid than ever, or more contemptuous of himself. This "dog" was more trapped than the dog. How?

To hear him talk you might be tempted to think his being "a dog" was literally the same as being a dog. He often visited with his parents and older sister, where his father took the lead in berating him, deriding him, poking at him, laughing at him, and calling him endearing, disgusting names, such as "my fat old thing." His older sister followed suit, his mother to a lesser extent. He got very little sympathy from mother, almost none from sister, none from father; no one would defend him against his running humiliation.

His only comfort was the memory of having been close to the actual family dog. The symbolic "dog" seemed worse off than the actual dog, who had been dead 10 years.

Actually, the "dog" was doubly trapped. He was not only literally put down, but he also symbolized himself as a "dog."[4] As Maturana might say, he coordinated his conduct with the family, like the dog, but he also coordinated his coordination of conduct by adopting a view of himself in language as a "dog," which meant he was trapping himself in language as well as literally. But the trap in language also gave me a way to spring him loose. I will explain how that has been accomplished.

After I had seen him for a year I was thoroughly familiar with this scheme for keeping him in a hopeless bog forever. Because I was getting interested in the Milan systemic perspective on such situations and because I had just put together a team for studying and working to rediscover for ourselves this Milan method, I invited his family to be seen by us. We saw them once a month for about seven months, while I continued to see my patient once a week. This family therapy was not a remarkable success, but I did find a way out for my patient, in part because I could see the family game better from these monthly sessions. A brief description of the fourth session will give the reader some appreciation of the talent of this family.

The older sister began by appearing to stand up to the old man. She berated the father for his lack of understanding of how to give support to either herself, the daughter, or to the son, about being unemployed. The father lectured back about the urgency for grownup children to take a job, any job, if they were ever to get anywhere. The son and mother sat observing this argument, as they had sat for most of the first three sessions.

I went out to confer with my colleagues behind the mirror, while my female co-therapist stayed in the room. I came back and told the family that we would like the father and the daughter to sit together because they are a team to keep mother and son from talking, which is very dangerous. We thought father and daughter could be a better team if they sat together.

The son then began to berate his mother for not responding to the flowers which the son had given mother on Mother's Day. I then left again. I felt we had a second team to help the first team which had entertained us for three sessions and a half. More of the same.

My attention was drawn to my own feeling that I wanted to sit near my other female team member behind the mirror, just to sit by a mother, quietly. This gave myself and my other male colleague behind the mirror the idea that the father, the daughter, and the son might also be wanting a mother to sit with. This was the bomb, as Robin Skynner would say, that they couldn't face without exploding the family; the need seemed enormous. The three of us behind the mirror then agreed that I would be replaced as interviewer by our second female team member from behind the mirror.

She went in and said: "We think that mother needs some help. She is spread too thin." The situation now seemed very fluid. We had accepted the father-daughter team protecting the mother-son team. Now we protected the mother, who had been berated by the son, and provided another mother, so that now they had three: our two female co-therapists and the mother herself. Now there was a mother for father, one for daughter, and one for son.

At this point we were astonished to watch the father burst into tears. He told the story of his childhood, in which no one had looked after him. He had been sent to work in a factory at age 12. He had tried to accept his father's inability to give him anything. Now mother began to cry, saying about the same about her father. Perhaps, we suggested, ending the session, everyone needs to get a little holding.

I hope the reader will forgive our naivete.[5] This was an interesting set of moves we had not seen from this family. My patient explained the final moves by father and mother the next week in his individual session. He said, sardonically, that they *always* talked about what they missed in their own childhoods when the son or daughter was threatening to do something different. They were terrific performers at what had seemed so moving to us. Since being reminded of the great holes from childhood would be so "upsetting," now the father and mother would have to keep the family away from us for several months! So much for our suggestion that all of them might get a little mothering! As for the berating, deriding, poking of the son, which he described as continual at home, we never say very much of this at all, as son and mother sat quietly on the sidelines! We never got near the scapegoating of the family "dog." Obviously, they were much too talented for us at that time two years ago.

But my eyes opened for the individual therapy which went on for the next two years and is not yet completed. What I saw was that the father felt all right about himself by deriding the son. The mother felt all right about herself by giving a little comfort to the humiliated son. The sister felt superior to her brother by following the footsteps of her father. The son, in his turn, was very skillful at eliciting or triggering all of these familiar moves by his father, mother and sister. He knew how to brag to set off his father's and sister's putting him down. He knew how to threaten staying away to get a little something from mother. And so forth. He was indeed a dog punished for staying stuck, but also punished for moves to get out: punished for discriminating circles, punished for discriminating ellipses. This was true enough. But he was also *playing* at being a "dog in hell" with all the skill of his partners. Like the sinners in the bog, he knew how to set off the Blacktalons, how to get a little sympathy from the Poets, how to keep on the perpetual hellish game.

All right, but how to get him out? The reader has waited long to learn how to jump through the eye of the needle, through the eye of the class of moves. Allow me to explain the principle of such jumping and then to describe several illustrations of how he has jumped. What I do every week is see every move he presents me as a different way to construct, again, the "dog in hell." All his moves are in this class. But, pay attention closely here. The class of moves, the construction of "dog in hell" is itself in the class of classes, namely, he constructs hell to help his family. Notice carefully this is not a trick. It is only a perspective from which to work. I have to *see how* his moves reconstruct himself as the dog in hell, which is often difficult to decipher. Then I have to *see* further, on the occasion of each hour, how this construction helps him conserve his family. This too may be very subtle. What is the upshot? "So what?" as Bateson asks at the end of *Mind and Nature* (1979). "So what?" is this: If his moves are different ways to construct hell for a dog, then any one move can be revised, if it is especially degrading, painful, or destructive for him. Gradually, he has given up many, many such moves, while still appearing to be constructing hell for a dog. Furthermore, if constructing hell for a dog is *a* way to help his family be conserved, then there must be *other* ways to help his family be conserved! One is to be a big success. That he is becoming. But all the while he appears to be the same, namely, constructing hell to help conserve his family! He is ambiguous about this. He is both in hell, and not in hell. Of course, that is what purgatory is all about! If there is only hell, a godless world, then there is only hell. When there is hell, and something else, namely the devotion to God, then there is purgatory. As he discovers his love for family, as he sees he can love his family by remaining degraded in hell, or by some other means, he wavers between both, but he slowly rises the mountain of purgatory, lifted by love and desire.

I hope the reader who understood little of that long paragraph will not despair but read of two sessions that follow, which are more down to earth, and then return to the abstract scheme I just provided.

In his session 134, he described "working his brains out" in finals week. He said it was a torture of continuous work without a break. What did I have to say about all this torment? I was sinking in this misery, swimming in it, to tell the truth, until I saw its advantage. He had been very down on his family of late. He anticipated that all his recent accomplishments would get 15 minutes of notice with his family, then back to being the servant-dog as usual this summer. Here he was one of the best students in physics this year, having been unable to study at all two years ago. I saw his brilliant move: If finals week was totally painful, then his next week at home would be a "relief." After all, his family could still give him *something*. Hell again served conserving his place in his family.

In his session 135, he described being disappointed by his new girlfriend. She seems to be an optimist. My patient has confronted her about several unpleasant situations with other people which she had, of course, overlooked. She, in turn, had been very unappreciative! My patient felt tortured by this. "See," he said, "no one appreciates me." This time I was more prepared. I asked him why he might be so naive as to introduce rain to his sunshining girlfriend and look for appreciation? He laughed. I suggested he had been brilliant again. If "nobody appreciates me out there," then the return to home after finals week, with 15 minutes of appreciation, would be all the more acceptable. He burst out laughing. He said, "Oh, the social equivalent of my academic proof of last week." I nodded.

Perhaps the reader now sees how this patient has steadily climbed from one success to another, from being "unable" to study, work, sleep, or have friends to being a major success in the university and sleeping relatively well and having a friend. If all of his moves are subordinate to reconstructing hell, then any one of them can be revised. You could make finals into hell. You could prove that no one out there appreciates you. Or you could build hell some other way. They are brilliant moves. He has steadily given up one such self-destructive move after another, which has allowed him to study, sleep and have a woman friend, while appearing to be continuing to torment himself! Thus, he rises up the mountain of purgatory, all the while mindful of hell. He loves his family, but he increasingly acts outside the class of moves which show love by self-torture. He shows love by capability. He has come through the eye of the needle. But purgatory is slow going and rising.[6]

HIGHER ORDER MAMMALIAN GAMES

Now you could say with Bateson that I have helped sort out a "message tangle" in the stories told to me by this young man. I have put in a few "context markers" so that the stories fall into place consistently. I do not only see stories of the usual mammalian showing and gesturing about emotion (Darwin, 1899). This is only the first logical level. I also see stories in which the emotions you would expect in a mistreated dog are carefully organized by a family game which makes "hell" for a "dog," which is a second logical level. But I then see this game as *a* way to show devotion, which is a third logical level.

I have been "classifying messages" (Bateson, 1979, p. 116). This is Bateson's idea of what you can do for patients in psychotherapy, if you ever hope to get them untangled.[7] From this perspective the reader may see why interest in "true feelings" is apt to make only a little sense of the stories, and why interest in "pathological interactions" is apt to make only a little more sense. The stories are coherent only with all three logical levels well demarcated. The first logical level allows empathy with a poor dog, the second astonishment at the hellish intricacy of the "dog" and his "partners," and the third admiration for how "hell" has been needed to conserve the family. True feelings *often* build a hell, and this hell is not a mistake, but a necessary place in a creation where there is love.

Bateson was worried about saying such things as this about "classifying messages," however. This fear of his had to do with what he called "vulgarization," which he described as "consciousness running around like a dog with its tongue out—literally cynicism—that asks the too simple question and shapes up the vulgar answer" (1979, pp. 213–214). It is all too easy to "rush in," as he wrote, hot for practical answers. Two such vulgarizations of Bateson are already well along on the march. One is to see his discussion of logical levels as a "trick" for solving "problems." A second is to see this discussion of logical levels as merely a "cognitive" activity. Both moves betray the complete misunderstanding of Bateson of which he was fearful.

The difficulty which Bateson discussed at the end of *Mind and Nature* is that any subject can only be comprehended when it is mapped onto something more complex than itself. "No, you see it's not possible to map beauty-and-ugliness onto a flat piece of paper. Oh yes, a drawing may be beautiful and on flat paper but that's not what I'm talking about. The question is onto what surface shall a *theory* of aesthetics be mapped? If you ask me that question today I could attempt an answer. But not two years ago when this book was still unwritten" (p. 210). Now there is the same problem of what surface is it possible to map "Bateson's thinking" onto? The reader may have thought it strange that I have mapped his thinking onto Dante's *Inferno*, but I think only something of that order will do to understand Bateson. Only some surface with that kind of clarity of logical levels will allow Bateson to be understood at all.

Now I think that the Milan team has succeeded in mapping Bateson's thinking onto a surface of sufficient complexity. I will attempt to explain this surface in the next chapter, "The Milan Team: From Farce to Music." I will describe how they gave care to their first steps with any family, or rather how they learned to take this first step with exceeding care. Bateson wrote that attempts to locate a theory of aesthetics and consciousness usually led the questioner off on "a wild goose chase" (p. 211). "Il n'y a que le premier pas qui coute. It's the first step that is difficult" (p. 211). A third of the Milan map is about first steps with families!

Secondly, the Milan team did not try to pull the "problems" out of the tangle, to straighten out one stretch of thread while throwing away what remained all balled up. No, they were after the entire tangle, so that the "problem" presented is an entry into that tangle of the entire family game. They followed Bateson's principle that the simple can only be understood by the more complex. The interaction of two people can only be understood if the interaction of the entire "n" of the game is seen (Ricci and Selvini Palazzoli, 1984). The moves of the entire "n" of the game only make sense within the entire class of moves which are allowed, etc. This is why I say they move from farce to music, because farce is a truncation, a comic abbreviation of something complete. The farce only is comprehensible if you can see the whole which is being parodied. This leads to the ingenious music in the background which is obscured by the farce. But how was the Milan team to describe ingenious music? Onto what surface could they map their own descriptions of ingenious music? The reader of *Paradox and Counterparadox* will miss much of what is going on if he or she cannot see how the Milan team has borrowed several literary forms to convey their appreciation of the music of families. What other surface could handle the complexity?

Thus, I think the Milan team is full of guile, but the reader who sees only "tricks" is only mapping them onto himself. The same is true for readers of Bateson who see only a chance to "paradox" people out of their "problems." This is one kind of vulgarization of Bateson.[8]

The other widespread vulgarization of Bateson is to see his message as merely "cognitive." Now it is true that Bateson was interested in an epistemology or grammar of such diverse structures as insects, embryos, schizophrenics, primitive tribes, universities, and evolution. You could get awfully abstract about what these "stories" have in common! But this would be a misfortune, an aberration. What Bateson said about Levi-Strauss being misunderstood could equally be said about Bateson being misunderstood: "I have noticed that Anglo-Saxon anthropologists sometimes misunderstand the writings of Claude Levi-Strauss for precisely this reason. They say he emphasizes too much the intellect and ignores the 'feelings.' The truth is that he assumes the heart has precise algorithms" (1972a, p. 139). So it is with Bateson. It is only when you fail to recognize the "precise algorithms of the heart" that you end up with the usual dichotomy of feeling and thinking. I believe that readers who see "only thinking" in Bateson are only mapping him onto themselves.

But I can appreciate why it is tempting to keep one's distance from Bateson in this "thinking" way. I do not believe it is possible to take Bateson seriously without getting badly wrenched, without pain. Bateson says this as follows:

In the fields of psychiatry and psychoanalysis — and even anthropology — one thing more than any other makes progress difficult. It is this: that to embark upon a new area of investigation is not merely to begin looking at a new part of the universe external to the self . . . : it leads to a very profound and irresistible discovery that the laws and processes of our perception are a bridge which joins us inseparably to that which we perceive — a bridge which unites subject and object. This means that, for everybody who would work in the sciences of man, every new discovery and every new advance is an exploration of the self. When the investigator starts to probe unknown areas of the universe, the back end of the probe is always driven into his own vital parts. (1958, p. 96)

What could Bateson mean here? Anyone who has struggled to follow the moves of families as the Milan team has knows how suddenly and rudely they disconfirm everything you are doing with them. Now, you can learn to learn the most from these sudden exclusions, from occasions when people turn their backs on you, but you cannot learn to learn about these disconfirmations without pain, especially when a new way to knock you down is being run on you. The unanticipated fall hurts.

It cannot but be even more painful to see how individuals and families have shut you out for months or years, by getting you off on "wild goose chases." To see how little one has known about opening moves, or first steps, has to be humbling.

All of this kind of pain can be stopped by stopping systemic inquiry. All you have to do is get a procedure you are comfortable with, get a supply of patients who are comfortable with your procedure, and forget those who don't fit in with your procedure. The patients fit you, and not vice versa. It saves much pain. You instruct them how to operate in your procedure. "Instructive interaction" (Maturana, 1984) will numb you very well.

But it will make you unable to see much about other people, what they are up to, why they have to have the pain that they do have, why they slam doors in your face. Such systemic inquiry is a rough business. If you think you can proceed from Bateson's biology to that of Maturana on a purely intellectual level, I say good luck. Perceiving what I call, in Chapter 17, "The Otherness of Others," how they are completely closed, autonomous, autopoetic, self-referential entities, you unfortunately are led to the same conclusion about yourself. "The back end of the probe" is driven into your own gut. Bateson describes the hazards of more "awareness" for either the psychiatrist or the patient as follows:

One starts by blaming the identified patient for his idiosyncrasies and symptoms. Then one discovers that these symptoms are a response to—or an effect of—what others have done; and the blame shifts from the identified patient to the etiological figure. Then, one discovers perhaps that these figures feel a guilt for the pain which they have caused, and one realizes that when they claim this guilt they are identifying themselves with God. After all, they did not, in general, know what they were doing, and to claim guilt for their acts would be to claim omniscience. At this point one reaches a more general anger, that what happens to people should not happen to dogs, and that what people do to each other the lower animals could never devise. Beyond this, there is, I think, a stage which I can only dimly envisage, where pessimism and anger are replaced by something else—perhaps humility. And from this stage onward to whatever other stages there may be, there is loneliness. That is as far as I can go in recounting the stages through which man progresses toward an image of God. (1958, pp. 99–100)

So much for "cognitive" messages from Bateson. The reader is warned.[9] To begin a long journey of systemic inquiry is a dangerous, painful business.[10] But it is also high adventure.

16. *The Milan Teams: From Farce to Music*

THERE IS no one right way to explain the Milan teams. Indeed, they began to explain themselves differently. Mara Selvini Palazzoli organized and led the Milan team from its inception in 1967. She has also been the principal writer. In the 1980s the team divided into two teams, one led by Selvini Palazzoli and Prata, the second led by Boscolo and Cecchin. Then there have been a series of teams around the world which have taken their leading ideas either from the first or derivative Milan teams: the Birmingham team in England, the teams in Calgary, Alberta, led by Karl Tomm, the teams at the Ackerman Institute in New York, our team here in Madison — all have their own emphasis. All are evolving in their own way. Therefore, I will use the plural, referring to the Milan teams.

I prefer to introduce the Milan tradition in a down-to-earth way. I show the action, in an interview conducted by Cecchin in April of 1984 in Calgary of four volunteers asked to be a "family." They appeared to be the first four individuals who came forward from an audience of several hundred family therapists to help with a simulation of family therapy. They were allowed no preparation. Cecchin just began to interview them. Several further volunteers helped Boscolo constitute a therapeutic team to assist Cecchin, while a number more helped Evan Imber-Black constitute an observing team to propose an alternative message (Boscolo and Cecchin, 1982). I choose the example, because I was there in person to observe the work and because I thought it was a technical achievement of a high order.[1] The reader will be led, gradually, from the deceiving simplicity of this action, to the complexity of the thinking behind the scenes, to how the game of the Milan teams is put together.

I suppose it is inevitable when you have a grouping of family therapists who become "a family," you get a game about "help," about the intricacies of who's superior at helping and who's the poor patient. So it was here. It is difficult to describe the fascination of such a game and its subtlety of innuendo, particularly about being one-up or one-down on the other people involved. The players moralize upon one another mercilessly, each wanting the others blamed, boxed and corrected. It is difficult to describe the bland, nonplussed way that Cecchin maneuvers in this field. He accepts the necessity of their moves to do this to each other, while not getting stuck in any one version at all. For this job, he shows a kind of bland even-handedness. The blandness will show especially in the final message to the family. How strange that bland equality might be a way out! How dull! How interesting! The following remarks are based upon my direct observations of the event itself, restudy of the videotape and restudy of a typescript of the videotape.

The Calgary Simulation

The little group of four defined itself very fast as a "family" with a "difficult" relation between the mother and the father, an older responsible daughter, Janine, age 25, and the "problem" daughter, Wendy, age 17. All of this within a few sentences after Cecchin asked: "I see you here today. Which one of you called this center in order to get this appointment?" Father said Wendy was the "problem," because "We can't get her to do anything that we think she ought to do and she doesn't listen to us at all. It makes it very, very difficult. You know, Jean and I have a hard enough time working out our own things without Wendy making things difficult for us." So this family offered a "loose end" to their tangle straight off. This allowed a fast beginning.

Now what Cecchin did was to follow what other family members actually *did* when Wendy was being a "problem." This led rapidly away from Wendy through all four members of the family, as each became "the problem."[2] Wendy didn't obey. But Janine lectured her mother. Father complained and took to his study. Mother was soon slumping to the floor in apparent "dejection," in the course of this interview.

Now Cecchin did not get drawn into this hole which mother offered. He did not let the family set into this fresh concrete. Mother seemed all too ready to make despondent, self-pitying, martyr speeches as she drooped. Cecchin rather looked away from her to the others. He accepted her move, but only to see what the others did in response. Now he asked a series of questions of the other three. Facing father, he said, "What is making her a little . . . no? . . . better sometimes? What helps her to feel a little better? Whose agreement does she hope to have mostly? Your agreement, Janine's agreement, or Wendy's? Which of you helps her the most?" Then he faced Wendy: "Do you succeed . . . sometimes lift her mood some way? . . . Your father is more successful than your sister or vice versa at making her feel better?" The picture offered back to Cecchin is that no one succeeds. "It's not much fun to be in the house."

But Cecchin will not accept this picture that they have concocted here together. He incites them to competition with his next question: "Well, the little life that is there, who brings it, the little life? Can I ask you who brings a little life in this family?" Father and mother both rise to this bait, Cecchin learning that mother attempted a college course and quit it after father complained about his cold suppers. Back to misery. Again, he will not accept this hole for all four of them. He asks: "Well, when was the last time that you remember that your family was ever in different spirits?" Now he learns they dropped into this hole when Janine left two years ago, all having enjoyed the foursome previously. All right, next step. "Obvious thing is that Wendy was not able to take your place . . . ," he says to Janine.

Another big hole looms, which is back to blaming Wendy, but no, mother wants to keep the hole for herself.

JANINE She's not like me.
CECCHIN What do you think that she should do in order to . . . ?
JANINE Well, she could go to school and everything. . . . I think Mom would feel better 'cause, you know, everytime Wendy keeps messing up then Mom gets more and more depressed and gets more worried about her, and if she didn't have to worry about her maybe she could do some of these other things she wants to do.
MOTHER Mom must be a pretty horrible mother to have a daughter that's acting like that.

But Cecchin is ready for her, ready in a few, small words:[3]

CECCHIN Somebody's telling you that too?
MOTHER What?
CECCHIN Somebody's telling you that you are a terrible mother?
MOTHER *His* mother (pointing to her husband).

Well, now Cecchin is off onto the contribution of the grandparents, both paternal and maternal, discovering that mother was once an "honor student." Mother has not drawn the inquiry down a black hole.

Two more moves by Cecchin conclude the interview. The first is in the series I have described which gets swiftly from mother's collapsing to others' responding. Cecchin: "Somehow you see yourself in a bad situation now, right? Do you have one person that understands your position? You don't seem to. Like you said, 'My husband criticizes me, like mother-in-law criticizes me, Janine scolds me all the time.' So you don't have anybody on your side?" He learns of the supportive teacher of the course again, dropped because of the husband's "bitching." Cecchin: "So you usually give up when somebody bitches at you? What about Wendy? Does she bitch at you also?" Now, an amazing thing. Wendy gives Mom the most support! The one for whom Mom has the most hope to fulfill Mom's dreams in the university! Not like Janine, the mere secretary! The interview has moved completely off from its beginning, which made Wendy the family "problem." She is now the heroine for mother. Cecchin concludes the interview with his second move, asking for their expectations from the family therapy team. Naturally, each one wants to be delivered from the onerous position each is in by having the others altered. Mother wants father changed, so he can't talk his way out of everything. Father wants mother to take responsibility for getting on with her own happiness, not blame him. Janine wants not to be called by mother all the time. Wendy wants to stop making mother miserable.

The interview is now concluded, having lasted about an hour, 35 minutes of actual interviewing, the balance for Cecchin's time-outs to get help from his therapeutic team. Now the team discusses its hypotheses, its findings, and its message back to the family.

Hypothesizing

What have they got? The family has offered a farce. To be overly crude about a subtle event, I could summarize this farce as a contest for moral superiority. The father and older daughter, Janine, mostly offer criticism and lecturing, from an elevated balcony. The mother and younger daughter, Wendy, offer failing and blaming themselves, from a hole in the ground. This is a perpetual game, like those in hell. The criticism and lecturing of father and Janine are managed by mother and Wendy by being even more failing and self-blaming, beating the critic-lecturers to the punch. This collapsing threatens to pull father and Janine down into the sinking hole, which they fight by climbing up in the balcony to be critical, and so forth. This is also a rough game, like those in hell, which erodes what little virtue each may locate in himself or herself. All begin to stink.

If Cecchin had only seen this farce, he would have little to say to them, for such a description as I just provided delves into hell with them, but there is no sign of a way to get out. Indeed, such a negative description is only likely to deny the interviewer access to this family. The players are beleaguered already, so they are not going to be interested in further judgment upon themselves. They get that from each other, perpetually. This is not an unusual family.

But the interviewer never did accept this farcical perspective, that Wendy was to blame, or father, or Janine. A major bid by mother to be the one to blame then threatened to take over the center of the stage. This was the loudest instrument. But Cecchin, as I have described, drew out the other parts, the "ungrateful parts" which, like second violins, are more difficult to hear, the responsiveness to mother's drooping moves. Like a conductor, Cecchin got mother to suspend her playing, so he could bring out the others. This will allow something other than farcical music. This will allow a music which reveals the coordination of all their moves, so this can be seen and heard. The interview is a kind of rehearsal towards this possibility. Now the message will be a performance by the conductor of the music he has elicited. I want to offer a few musical programme notes on its logical structure, before I quote the music.[4]

Cecchin has asked questions of the family to see what they do when mother is down, etc. This implies a perspective in which all four of them are playing together on the same level, despite the appearance of some being up, others being down, despite the appearance that the down claim to be truly up, and so forth. No, they are all making moves within the same class, within the same game. How to describe the game in such a way that all the players are seen as cooperating in an equal and positive way? This perspective will allow access to their fascination with this game. This is the perspective of positive connotation.

The positive contribution of this game to this family is seen in the context of several important discoveries which Cecchin made by eliciting the parts of the quieter voices. One discovery was that they were relatively successful until Janine left. Now Wendy might leave also, which could make matters even worse. Another discovery is that mother and father seem to have become worse on their own. Another is that this worsening of mother and father has made both Janine and Wendy indispensable. In what game, then, are the four players coordinated? A hypothesis which puts together these findings is that they are not ready to break up from a quartet into solo or duo playing. Therefore, the game of the quartet needs to be appreciated and prescribed.

Composing

The message which I will soon quote will go roughly as follows: You were a close family. What went wrong? A new phase came, of children growing up and ready to move out. But the family has needed to "help" one another with this transition. The parents help the daughters grow, to live without them, but not too fast. The daughters help the parents practice surviving on their own, but not too fast, by taking their time. Janine helps by lecturing, Wendy by misbehaving. Both say, "I am going, but not too fast. The parents help by saying, "Stay nearby to help us, so growing up will not occur too fast." All four work to slow down the unavoidable, to find the right pace. But they help each other too much. Therefore, outside help is a good idea. The team is unsure. They will see either the daughters for a given session, to help the parents, or the parents, to help the daughters. They can decide which. So long.

Notice how the quartet is orchestrated in this speech of Cecchin. All four are equal players in a game of "help," to slow down growing up which has been too fast. Janine and Wendy, grossly unequal in the farce, are perfectly equal from the perspective of slowing down the leaving of the parents behind. One lectures. One misbehaves. Both help the parents equally by staying around until the parents learn to survive. Father and mother, grossly unequal in the farce, are perfectly equal in helping the daughters stay back. So the quartet of helping has two new equal pairs, corresponding to the two generations. But "helping to slow down the unavoidable" places such helping in another, wider class of music, which is the march of the unavoidable. This march can be slowed down; it can be speeded up. Therefore, in posing the quartet as slowing down the march, they also imply that sometimes it could be speeded up, or varied, or whatever. In other words, the march has various possibilities. For now, they are committed to the adagio.

We have three logical levels here, or a class within a class within a class. The class of Janine and Wendy and the class of father and mother are in the class of the helping quartet. The quartet of helping by going slow is in the class of the marches of the unavoidable, which can be slow, fast, or whatever. This orchestration gives several openings or degrees of freedom for the musicians, which were not seen or allowed in the farce. Since Janine and Wendy are equals in slowing down leaving parents behind, both are free to reconsider how they accomplish this playing. Janine may look for some part which is more grateful for her than lecturing to a mother who gets worse in the lectures. Wendy may look for some part which is more grateful for her than being a failure like her mother. These are *only* moves within the *class* of helping parents not to be left behind. Other moves might get the job done. This is also true for the parents, who have bad moves in the class of helping the children stay near and not grow up too fast, a class for which other moves might get the job done. There are also degrees of freedom at the next logical level, that the quartet is slowing down the march of the unavoidable. Since slowing is only a necessary tempo for the time being, this opens up the realm of other tempos in the *class* of handling the march of the unavoidable. In summary, this orchestration of the quartet gives freedom for the players at two logical levels, while conserving the necessary relations of their logic, of their music.

Message-Giving

I would say only a few more remarks about the mode of the message, having described its logic, for the mode — the tone, the gesturing — is equally important to the logic. The music has to have these clear lines of orchestration, but it also must be conveyed so the tone and gesture fit the lines. The tone of this message is as bland as can be described. The reader may go to sleep reading the lines. It is hypnotic, in its rhythm of Cecchin saying every other sentence: "no?" "hm?" It is hypnotic in the parallel placement of the two pairs, the perfect symmetry of back and forth. It is hypnotic in the use of the bland words of "helping, slowing, growing, etc. This is the music drawn out, when the farce is quieted. Cecchin says:

It's about what we saw before, what you told us. Somehow we were thinking about this change which has been going on in the last years. Before, you were a very close family . . . hm? You enjoyed each other, you did many things together. Somehow in the last few years something went wrong . . . no? Everybody suffering, there's a lot of pain in the family, everybody is upset about something so we are trying to think, you know, try to explain to ourselves *why* this thing is happening . . . hmm? We come out with an explanation.

We have the feeling that you are a very *close* family. You've been very close and united family . . . hmm? Everybody close to each other, dedicated to each other. Somehow in the last few years a new phase started in your family life . . . hmm? Children growing up, getting ready to move out of the home . . . hmm? Find a new life . . . hmm? Organize it themselves . . . hmm? And now you are trying, all of you are trying to help each other very much. We see the parents trying very much to help the daughters, both daughters to grow, to learn how to live without the family . . . hmm?

Without the parents. To learn how to be autonomous, independent. So we see also the daughters, the two of you . . . hmm? Doing any efforts, somehow, to try to help the parents survive without you. Everybody is doing their own way . . . hmm? For example, Janine is coming by teaching, explaining, and trying to give support . . . no? Wendy is doing by misbehaving in school, by behaving like a . . . somehow . . . not . . . an independent person, a very dependent one, trying to make sure the parents see "Look I'm here. Oh, I'm here. I'm not trying to move away too far, too fast. I'm reassuring you now, 'don't take it easy, learn slowly how to be autonomous'." Well, in some ways both of them are working very hard somehow to help the parents to live without them . . . hmm? They are taking their time, Janine, by teaching, by her saying, "Look, I'm here. I'm not growing up. Don't worry for the moment. I'm here taking care of you" . . . hmm? We see the two of you doing the same with the children . . . hmm? You say, "Grow, but don't do it too fast" . . . hmm? "Because we are here and we have problems and we need you. Come back and take care of us." . . . hmm? So somehow all of you are helping each other to slow down this process of growth which somehow is . . . no? . . . unavoidable at the moment. You are helping each other somehow to find the right place in the direction . . . hmm?

So we feel you do the right thing to call a place like this one . . . no? . . . and try to look for help . . . hmm? Because I think the four of you are trying to help each other so much so now you are running into trouble . . . no? You reach a point where you know you feel you are helping each other too much, so intervention from outside can be very useful at this moment.

Our point is now we don't know what to choose. So we help now the two daughters, Janine and Wendy, to help the parents knowing this process of growing? Or shall we help the parents to help the daughters in their process of growing? So since you are doubtful which one we should help, the two groups, we decided that now sometime we see the parents . . . hmm? . . . and we try to help you to take care of the daughters to help them grow, and sometime we see the two of you . . . hmm? . . . and discuss about how to help the parents overcome these difficulties.

So that's our prescription today . . . no? So we'd like to see you next time in a month period . . . hmm? And you choose which of the couples would come the first time . . . hmm? Two parents or the two daughters. Okay, we'll stop here and now going out you take an appointment with the secretary.

The reader will please wake up, now that this family has been put to bed. For now, I would only like to add a few remarks about how the "family" members experienced the interview and the message. Father, Janine, and Wendy were all "relieved" that they were not blamed, and were all "relieved" that the interview did not sink into the hole mother was digging. All felt more hopeful, therefore, as the interview went along. About mother, I was not so sure of her feeling from what she said. She had set a huge trap revolving around her martyrdom. She had failed to get this confirmed. I didn't think she liked it, but she accepted her defeat well, even humorously. When all become equal, some are promoted a little, some are promoted a lot, some are demoted a little, some demoted very much! The effect of equal measure depends on your starting point.[5]

One final remark: After Cecchin had given the foregoing message of the therapeutic team, the observing team got its chance to deliver its message. At this point the father and mother unconsciously showed an extremely powerful nonverbal message. Father covered his crotch with both his hands, and mother her belly, as this message, with a sterner, more formal quality, was being delivered. I thought this was a dramatic confirmation of the previous message, which had not threatened the parents by bringing them closer together vis-à-vis each other, to wit, sexually. Instead, the pair had been pointed outwards towards the daughters, a music at which they were much more adept. You could say the sexual music was unplayable for this couple, so better to continue the quartet for whatever it was worth.

THE MILAN SYSTEMIC METHOD

The Milan method looks so much like other interpersonal and systemic methods that the reader may see only what it has in common with methods like those of Sullivan, Alexander, Winnicott, and Balint in the individual realm, or methods like those of Watzlawick, Haley, Minuchin, or Skynner in the family systemic realm. I have attempted to stay clear about the Milan theory and practice for the last two years, but continually found myself drifting into confusion with these neighboring interpersonal and systemic methods. I seem to have had a lot of company in this confusion. Hopefully, since I may have emerged from this more clearly than otherwise, I may help the reader to see what is shared with other interpersonal and systemic methods and what is different.

I explain this sharing with and difference from the interpersonal perspective most clearly by a comparison between the method of Sullivan and the method of the Milan teams. I presume that Sullivan's thinking and proceedings are representative of the class of interpersonal methods in most ways and might introduce a comparison between the Milan method and the entire *class* of interpersonal methods. I explain this sharing with and difference from other systemic perspectives by a comparison between the systemic method of Robin Skynner and the systemic method of the Milan teams. I presume there is much in common between Skynner, Minuchin, Haley, Watzlawick, Bowen, Whitaker, and so forth, however extreme their surface differences. A comparison to Skynner might introduce a comparison to the entire *class* of methods which see the family as a system. Since the latter subject is likely to concern only those well versed in family therapy, I offer the latter in comparison in my Afterword for Family Therapists at the conclusion of the chapter.

There is common to Sullivan and to the Milan teams shared interest in "problems" that occur between or with other people. The shared orientation is in "hypotheses" about why such problems continue to recur for those who complain about them. The shared method is to ask relevant questions. The shared hope is, as Havens would say, to "improve the narrative flow," or as

Sullivan put the matter, to "get an adequate account." The anticipated trouble is that the unseen "other people in the room" who have a large interest in what the patient reports to the doctor will influence the report mightily. They will make the patient "anxious" about giving himself or themselves away, so the doctor is likely to get confused reports or even an "extended bill of goods." There is a high likelihood of the doctor's being pulled into these "routinely futile operations."[6]

Therefore, Sullivan and the Milan teams agree that they had better come to any meeting with a patient or patient family with a strong procedure for working against these currents, if they hope not to be drowned themselves. Indeed, each offers a "special occasion," as Winnicott would say, for an "interview" or "consultation." There will be an informal formality. There will be an informal, sometimes offhand, sometimes colloquial, ease about the proceeding, but it will indeed be a proceeding conducted by the doctor, not by the patient or the family. Both Sullivan and the Milan teams are determined to keep their procedure very clear and strong in its lines, not to lose their bearings in the confusion or seduction attempted by the patient or family (Viaro and Leonardi, 1983). In other words, each prescribes a ritual for himself or for themselves, like Odysseus having himself tied to the mast to preclude temptation. For Sullivan, this "interview" includes: the "formal inception," which locates a "worthwhile problem"; then the "reconnaissance," which locates the relevant people involved in the problem; then the "detailed inquiry," which looks to confirm or disconfirm "hypotheses" which are already being entertained from the first two steps; finally, the "termination," in which a transition is defined to the next interview with a comma or semicolon or an end made with a period. The Milan teams have different names for the "formal inception," the "reconnaissance," "detailed inquiry," and "termination," but their procedure definitely includes these clear phases. So much for what is shared.

Now what is different? I may best explain what is different by grouping the moves of the Milan teams into three classes, as Freud did of psychoanalysis: namely, the opening, middle, and end games. I hope the reader who is studying these three phases of Milan interviewing will eventually see that these technical ideas imply a different construction of "reality" from Sullivan and from nearly every other school of psychotherapy. Especially for the Milan team led by Boscolo and Cecchin, there is no "single reality" out there of "hidden needs" in the family to "bring to light" (Cecchin, personal communication). There is no "brush clearing," as in Sullivan (1954, p. 238), which discloses the "truth." No, there are just different "constructions" which have different music, different drift. For both Milan teams, the constructions of a family are not to be underestimated. Like the whaling practices of the Nantucketeers described by Melville in *Moby Dick* (1851), the practices of families are stable over generations because they are rich in practical resourcefulness and build an entire cosmos in which to dwell. We are no match for them, unless we are equally ingenious and equally poetic. Only then may we comprehend the scope of their constructions. Only then are we likely to be of much use. Anything less is finagling.

Opening Moves

First, the opening moves. The Milan teams discovered through painful experience that they had to be very circumspect about the opening move by a family. The "family" I described Cecchin interviewing gave a relatively easy opening move, because they actually came in with the daughter Wendy defined as a "problem." However tangled up they were, they offered a "loose end" (Selvini Palazzoli, 1985, p. 32) to the tangle. Cecchin then could thread his way from the "problem" member through all the moves of the other family members. This got difficult only in the middle game, with the sinking mother I have described. But it is not unusual for individuals or families to be very troublesome at the outset. Often, they will be confused about why they came for the session, so they appear to make no move for help at all. Or, they appear to move for help, but it is extremely unclear who wants this help given.

Sullivan was also very circumspect about where to begin with a patient. He appreciated that there were endless topics which could be discussed, but many would be unprofitable, many could make the patient worse, and only a few had promise. He would refer to this as finding a "worthwhile problem." He knew very well that patients would often come to sessions in semi-total confusion or disarray about where to begin, or come to mislead the doctor into topics that were hopeless bogs.

So there are three possibilities for beginning a session. One is to be given a worthy problem. Two is to be given no place to begin. Three is to be given a place to begin which the interviewer should decline as dangerous, hopeless, or useless. About these prospects for the opening move Sullivan and the Milan teams would agree. Thus, both Sullivan and the Milan teams are quite deliberate about where the session is to begin, because the outcome depends on having a worthy "problem." Only one of the three kinds of prospects will lead anywhere at all. Therefore, do not get underway until you have such a problem. I will illustrate the critical importance of this idea in my Case of Bulimia which follows.

But the Milan teams go farther. Since they see an individual or a family presenting to a doctor as an incomplete arc of an unknown circuit, since the impetus for the individual or family to be in the room for the interview may have originated back in the circuit prior to the arc which is present, then the interviewer may often fail to see this impetus and therefore not address his interview to where the motivation is originating. This sets the interviewer up to fail. He accepts a "worthy problem" but fails to see to whom this problem belongs.

Therefore, they do not wait to receive the presenting problem, thereupon to exercise the circumspection which they would share with Sullivan. This would not take the system seriously. Systems are too powerful to allow an interviewer to be so passive. He would be misled into going to work for people and purposes of which he could catch no view — until too late. He would be like the man who is asked to fix a revolver by a nice lady, only later to discover that she needed the revolver for her boyfriend who needs it for his gang, whose gang is part of the syndicate. The revolver ends up in his shop because the syndicate is on the move.

No, they do not wait for nice ladies to put their jammed revolvers on the table when they come for their first session. They take two previous precautions. First, they have the lady telephone in advance about who referred her, what the problem is about, and who lives with her or is involved with her about the problem. Secondly, they have a pre-interview discussion about what seems to be the trouble, what is the scope of the system involved, what preliminary hypothesis might explain the difficulty, and what findings will have to be looked for.

This *preliminary* looking into the system before some representatives of the system arrive for consultation has afforded the Milan teams a readiness for an entire *series* of "snares" concerning the opening move by an individual or family. The opening move is a snare when it only appears to present a worthy problem. The interviewer without the preliminary view would set about his inquiry on this worthy problem. He would be fooled, because the purpose of the visit for the interview has been held back. There are a series of such maneuvers, which the Milan teams have reported. The "referring person" may have obligated the family to go for an interview, but the family will often fail to mention this. The interviewer proceeds on the worthy problem they offer for the visit, all the while missing that the purpose of the visit is to meet the obligation with the referring person (Selvini Palazzoli et al., 1980a). A prestigious sibling may be the "sibling as referring person," who has obligated the family to show up (Selvini Palazzoli, 1985). Again, this will often not be mentioned, so the interviewer misses that the entire purpose of the visit is to satisfy the sibling. The identified patient may be in individual therapy, or be getting drugs, and this will not be mentioned. A competition of therapies is the actual, covert purpose. The family may dawdle through most of the session, then come forward at the end with the "secret" they have been saving. They may call at the last minute before the session and offer a covert alliance with the interviewer (Selvini Palazzoli and Prata, 1982). The series is potentially endless with variations.

My point is this: Both Sullivan and the Milan teams appreciate how the entire interview depends on finding a worthwhile place to begin the inquiry. But the preliminary telephoning and pre-interview thinking give a better chance to see the machinations, from far back in the system, which tamper with the presenting move for consultation, which obscure its system-maintaining purposes. This is how the Milan systemic perspective alters the opening moves of the perspicacious Sullivanian interviewer.

Middle Game

Now for the middle game. Once Sullivan had his worthwhile problem, he would be onto the scent of an ordinary solution.[7] Why? Sullivan believed that most problems between people are solved by recognition of the simple needs involved. Lust, recognition, power, punishment, and so forth, are relatively straightforward. Most dogs know what is meant by these matters. They are just the mammalian inclinations. But for us humans, becoming "secure" is not like this at all, for we are willing to go to endless complications in arranging for our security, or at least for *feeling* secure.[8] For Sullivan, the various kinds of psychopathology were various, often complicated "security operations." Therefore, the technical problem of the inquiry by the psychiatrist came down to looking through all this complication to the relatively simple needs involved, to get a relatively simple history of what had gone wrong, about meeting these needs, and what relatively simple moves might get them met again. Also, the psychiatrist had to help the patient tolerate being seen like this, for the patient would be damned uncomfortable when he was not hiding in his security operations.

In a way the Milan teams might accept everything in Sullivan's perspective. They too want to find their way through a maze of complications to the relatively simple history Cecchin and Boscolo get. In the Calgary simulation, they get a history of great convolutions, since the older daughter left and since the younger daughter might also leave. This is usual for their histories. Someone coming or going, growing up or staying back, has become a problem for meeting needs in the family. The messages always have a simplicity about this kind of action.

The difference for the Milan teams is in how the complication will be addressed. The complication is not to be brushed aside, as with Sullivan. The complication is rather to be appreciated as a remarkable construction, having its own ingenious domain.[9]

Think of the farce of the family in the simulation. For Sullivan this loud maneuvering, this wailing and sinking of the mother, is a familiar "security operation," which hides the actual threats to security in the family: namely, the moving on of the daughters. Therefore the suspension of her loud operations was important for getting to these findings, which would otherwise have been obscured, lost in what he called "selective inattention."

The Milan teams share this determination not to be trapped by farces, like this one. But their determination is not only to get to the underlying history of needs met and unmet; they need these findings, but something else is equally important. As I have attempted to describe, they also want to capture the remarkable coordination of the family, the teamwork, the musical composition with its logical levels in which the family is engaged to bring about such a farce. The moves of the family for security are not to be brushed aside, but pulled together into the remarkable game they allow. The presence of a farce implies the presence, often unnoticed, of a skillful musical theatrical company, namely the family itself. When this amazing company is not looked for behind the scenes, it is often underestimated. The Milan team of *Paradox and Counterparadox* (1978a) wrote:

How many times we found ourselves literally routed by, for example, the family of a modest postal clerk, his wife an illiterate, his son the designated patient who had seemed completely deteriorated, only able to marvel, laughing over and over again, . . . realizing once again that great gamblers do not need academic educations. (p. 126)

When the amazing company of the family is not literally present in the room, it is even more tempting to underestimate its power for the individual patient who is being interviewed. We overlook the "other people in the room," as Havens (1976) has written, because we do not know how to look for them.[10]

End Game

Should we take the trouble to devote our inquiry of the middle game to studying the complications, the logical, musical composition of the family game, as well as the relatively simple history of met and unmet needs, we come to a different end game in the interview. We will not assume with Sullivan (1954, pp. 238–239) that the patient will get on with successful adaptation once he is relatively secure and the brush of obstacles has been cleared away. This frontier metaphor is not accepted in the Milan thinking about the end game. It underestimates the compelling power of the family game.

Sullivan would conclude an interview by demarcating where the journey led forward. This could be a summary, going over the route which led to the ordinary, successful solution located in the interview. A period could be put down then. The conclusion could also be more transitional, like a comma, noticing where the discussion left off, where it could be leading. The ending message from Sullivan, whether more explicit or more implicit, was always that the individual had a way to get through the dark forest.

The end game of the interview for the Milan teams is quite different. Often they will say, that, *for the time being*, there is no way forward. The forest is tremendously constructed so that everything must stay the same, so the patient must stay right where he is now staying. This is not to be underestimated. Indeed, it is better to overestimate the entanglement in the concluding description. Why?

I think this concluding description has to be more extreme than the actual situation for reasons which are explained well by Bateson (Chapter 15). The first is that you cannot map a complicated message tangle very well onto a structure which has fewer dimensions, that is, fewer logical levels, than the message you are trying to describe. As Bateson wrote, you cannot map a theory of aesthetics onto a flat sheet of paper as if it were only a drawing. A theory of aesthetics will only have the requisite dimensions if it is mapped onto a description of the mind which is more complex than the theory of aesthetics. The more complex is necessary to explain the less complex (Selvini Palazzoli, 1985, p. 32; Ricci and Selvini Palazzoli, 1984). This is the first reason why concluding messages to individuals or to families tend to overestimate the situation, so that they contain its lesser complexity.

The second reason for a concluding message which overestimates the difficult game is that this continues access through positive connotation to how the game appears to the players involved. For them the family game is fascinating, exciting, dreadful preoccupation. The interviewer who stays with this perspective is of continuing interest to the players. He will get an ear. This positive connotation may be the most important technical idea invented by the Milan teams.

Therefore, the concluding message will tend to be the opposite from what Sullivan might offer. Not a clearing away of the complications, showing a straight shot. But rather a fine appreciation of the complications, why the straight shot has to be slowed down or sacrificed altogether, for the time being. I have described such a concluding message from the Calgary simulation.

Many are reminded by these messages of the forms of dance, music, or literature. I would like to say why the dance, musical or literary *form* for the message-giving is not accidental, but necessary. This has to do with the two criteria I outlined for such descriptions: the requirement for mapping onto maps of greater logical complexity than the event mapped, and the requirement for positive connotation of the event to capture the ears of the players. Since our musical composers and writers have been working for hundreds of years on how to compose such messages which capture the ears of their audiences and place their preoccupations within structures of greater depth and range, since the successful versions of these compositions are passed down to us as our musical and literary tradition, then it is entirely clear, I hope, why the messages of the Milan teams are musical and literary. They are borrowing from what is most successful for giving the kind of messages they need to give. We end up deep in the humanities, from deciding how to give concluding messages to families!

I have said enough about the message in the Calgary simulation as a beautifully balanced quartet. I have indicated the degrees of freedom which are revealed to the players by the clarity of the logical levels in that arrangement. I would only like to cite several other examples from the Milan writing so the reader has a small array of the possibilities, from which he might see the entire class of concluding messages. Here is one of my favorites, a pair of love poems to be read to each other by the parents of an autistic six-year-old:

Luigi,
    I do not see you, I don't hear you, because I'm not even here, I'm with Dr. Selvini. I'm doing this for you, because if I were to show you how much I love you, I would put you in an intolerable position.

Jolanda,

I can't say that I have hostile feelings for Doctor Selvini because, even if I did, and if I said so, it would be the same as saying I love you, and this would put you in an intolerable position. (Selvini Palazzoli et al. 1978a, p. 133)

Consider the very different form of a long speech, which could have been taken from a historical play of Shakespeare. This one is addressed to a favorite son, Aldo, concerning the problem of his schizophrenic sister, Nina, for their parents:

Since it was you, Aldo, who brought your family here, it is to you that our conclusions are now addressed. The team has decided not to accede to your request for family therapy. We have decided to call it a day, to finish after today's session. Let me explain why. Family therapy could prove dangerous because right now, and very likely for some time to come as well, you, Aldo, are not ready to lose the crown passed on to you on the death of your brother Carlo.

That crown, which you were handed seven years ago, weighs heavily upon you at times . . . as any crown would . . . but it is also very useful . . . it is this crown that keeps you at home. And there at home is your sister, Nina, who, partly because of her depression and partly because of her strange behaviour, provides your justification, your authorization, for not moving out. You can tell yourself quite sincerely: "It is my duty to stay home because I have a sick sister." But if you look carefully you will notice something else as well . . . you will realize that it is only at home that you feel really important, admired, replete with all those gratifications that are so difficult to gain outside. I am thinking of work, for example. At work, it is easy to feel you are a nobody . . . but at home you are the sun, you are always the king, always adored by your parents and relatives. And Nina, your sister, provides you with an excuse for staying on. That is why we have decided to call it a day, for, you see, family therapy might help Nina to get better before you are ready for it, and then you might get more depressed than she is. . . . (Selvini Palazzoli, 1985, p. 27)

Thus, the concluding message maps the events onto something of greater complexity and emotional power, the map being derived from some dance, musical, or literary form. The form utilized for a given message depends entirely on what will carry its logic. A knowledge of the humanities may be practical for psychiatry, after all, by affording a large range of possible vehicles for mapping family games.

What if the interviewer fails to convey this kind of appreciation? If he is lost in the farce? If he cannot untangle the message, to find its logical levels and degrees of freedom? If he attempts to brush away the entanglement? Surely, he may keep his job. Surely, he may still be useful.[11] But all too often the individual or the family will suddenly turn their backs on him. He is out. He is excluded from their world. This exit may occur at any place along the way of the interview, in the telephone call beforehand, in the actual opening moves in the room, in the inquiry of the middle game, or in the message-giving and receiving. I call this the "return to zero" (learning). It is the most important message of all. If you can stay alert for this close-out message, if you are ready to hear yourself being totally disqualified or disconfirmed at any time, then you may catch such a message, so you have a little room to respond. You will appreciate that the end game in the interview often comes long before the scheduled end, perhaps even before the beginning! You are then ready for serious play.

MILAN THINKING FOR INDIVIDUAL THERAPY

If I take the Milan perspective for interviewing an individual rather than a family, I find little technical difference. Most of the thinking about the opening, middle and end game is nearly the same (Ferrier, 1986). I notice only two inclinations in myself when I am interviewing individuals which give a different emphasis.

One is that I do not have to be so strict about conducting the interview. When I see a family, I conduct the interview. I choose the questions. Often I leave the room to consult with my team or, in their absence, with myself. I do not allow the family much leeway to respond. When I see an individual, I have a much looser hold on the situation, which allows the individual to help me conduct the session.

Second is that I usually give families a job to do before the next session. I put a burden back on them to work on their problem together in a different way, which I prescribe for them. I will see their difficulties better if I see whether they can carry out the most modest of jobs: Can they keep the session confidential? Can they keep notes about their observations? Can they get together once a week for a half-hour? I give them a specific job which requires these general capabilities for cooperation, a specific job based upon my hypothesis. Their actions will tell me more than their words. When I see an individual, I am more interested in giving a message about how I see his or her predicament. When I do this well, the individual will conduct his or her own experiments in action. These experiments are better than I could devise or propose, often leading to many "independent discoveries" (Balint, Ornstein, and Balint, 1972).

A CASE OF BULIMIA

For several years I have been getting referrals of bulimic college women who appear to be relatively healthy. The usual story is that they are vigorous and attractive, good at school and/or athletics, and close to their fathers. Mother is often more difficult to locate in their existence. Father is very prominent, often resented for his directiveness. When we look closely to exclude any major psychiatric disorder, we find none. When we do a long and deep trial therapy to test the suitability of brief psychotherapy, we have usually gotten something very emotional about the father. Then the patient has talked over our offer of brief psychotherapy for a semester with the father, and he has decided against it. The family system has prevailed!

This reversal by the family, of what appeared to be a promising departure for the young woman, was one of recurrent experiences in our Brief Therapy Clinic which drew me towards a systemic method of individual brief therapy. It looked as if the family had to be taken more seriously. These 21-year-old women could not be taken as free-standing individuals. They were very much tied up in their families.

The present case of bulimia is like the 10 to 20 previous cases of bulimia that have come through our Brief Therapy Clinic. Only now the Clinic has changed: We no longer seek to bring about emotional breakthroughs like Malan or Davanloo. We no longer seek to find a route out of the entanglement with the family, boyfriends and girlfriends, like Sullivan. We are now appreciating the family game, and why bulimia has been an important move by the patient.

This young woman I shall call Susan was referred to me privately by her father. Over the Christmas holidays, she had confessed to him her bulimia of the past six years, which had been a secret to her family. The father was quite alarmed by this finding in his favorite daughter. Since she was about to get her master's degree in May, since there were only four months left of her financial dependence on him, she appeared very anxious to conquer her bingeing and vomiting while she could get father to pay for the brief therapy.

Her story was entirely familiar. She had been a confident and vigorous girl until junior high. Then she "lost confidence" in her athletic ability, in her diving. She was still a very good student, but in college she "lost confidence" about her ability in chemistry and dropped down into home economics. The bingeing and vomiting began when she left home for college six years before I saw her. The most striking clue to this bulimia was that it was "ten times worse on visits home." While at school she did it about once a week, while at home it was twice a day.

My message to her at the conclusion of her trial therapy was something as follows: We saw that she *could* compete and she *could* be well. She *could* be self-confident. But she was giving that up. We needed to appreciate why she needed to "distract herself" from her capability. I offered to see her for the semester. And so we began. I knew that so much of what I said to her got relayed back to the family. Evidently, I had not aroused father's anxiety, yet, for he did not halt the treatment. But neither had I allowed this farce of bingeing and vomiting to set into concrete. I accepted it as an important activity of hers, for the time being, while being interested in why it was so important to "distract herself" from her strengths. I wanted to get from this recurrent move of hers to the game with the family, very much as Cecchin had wanted to get from the wailing, sinking mother to the game of that family.

Now I do not propose to tell the entire story of this brief therapy. Allow me to glide over the first six weeks by saying that she seemed to come in each time to degrade herself about being clumsy with men, being less attractive than her roommate, being less intelligent than some men she knows, being an imposter at various sports, and, above all, having this disgusting inclination to binge and vomit. I began to see the bingeing and vomiting as only one of the many ways she lowered herself. Why this entire *class* of moves to appear less than worthwhile? Evidently, she was going to a lot of trouble to appear this way. Why?

The domain for this activity of hers came out more clearly in the seventh session, when I became interested in why it was that she was courting disaster in several courses, which could cost her graduation. Why was she running the risk of giving up her summer trip with her girlfriend to South America?

It appeared that the trip to South America would be a great liberation for her. She would be doing as she pleased. This would threaten her mother, extremely, who was devoted to her sacrifice for her ten children. Indeed, eating was about the same. Susan was also inclined to eat as she pleased. This would include *not* being willing to sit down with her parents, brothers and sisters at dinnertime. This upset mother enormously. So Susan would go along with mother, by sitting down, eating what mother wanted, and then going to the bathroom and vomiting, surreptitiously.

I told her in concluding the seventh session that I was equally prepared for her to go either way. She might need to screw up her graduation, and her eating, because she might need to continue not being a woman of pleasure. She might allow herself more confidence, by doing well in the courses and by eating naturally. We didn't know. I could accept either way.

She came in for the next session, the eighth, a different woman. She had taken back eating as her own natural territory, not belonging to her mother. She had gotten on with her coursework, so she would graduate. The next four sessions were about her sexual interests. I was very struck by her new posture on my couch, reclining languidly like Venus. She now had a boyfriend, for the first time in years. Now what we discussed for these four sessions was how she had previously adopted mother's entire position about sexuality. She had a terrific gesture with her hand that symbolized what she called "the even keel," which she shared with her mother. She simply moved her flat hand through a horizontal plane. This was a kind of perfection which she and her mother shared. Sexuality didn't go with this at all. After all, one might be upside down! Neither had the thrill of diving, which she had given up in junior high school. The trouble with these risks was that she was so full of excitement. How could she allow herself these ventures? She felt like she might let the horses out of the barn and trample people, especially her mother. My message to her was that her even keel was very important. This helped her slow the horses, those horses which could interfere with her relationship with her mother, so important to her. She appeared to have another way to keep her even keel. She and her father were so close in interests, in being able to talk to each other. This would provoke her mother, which helped to keep some distance between Susan and her father. She and her mother were a team to keep Susan on the even keel.

All of this was interesting to me, but the twelfth session was the most interesting, because the "loose end" was so difficult to find, so crucial to locate. These opening moves in an interview give as much technical difficulty as anything in brief therapy.

We had ended her eleventh session over her concern about having a big fight with her mother. Since she had been successful in attracting a young man, she was full of confidence, just waiting for her mother to provoke her into an outburst of candor about how wrongheaded mother had been about men, about eating, about religion, etc., etc. She was anxious. She also didn't want to do this. I had ended with the following message: I thought she had to have this fight on her visit home, because this would help her and her dad not to get too close. (Her Venus posture on my couch was more striking than ever this session, I could not help but notice!) They would make mother jealous, who would elicit the outburst from Susan, who would then feel awful about herself, who could then go back to being comforted by father. This game helped her parents not fight about what mother did not get from father. This game helped her modulate her relationship with her father. So the fight looked inevitable to me.

Now she came in for the twelfth session looking extremely well. She told me she had been a "basket case," over the weekend, however. The friend who was to accompany her to South America was gravely injured in a car accident. When she had tried to reach me, unsuccessfully, by telephone, somehow she had found the strength to carry on. Her new boyfriend had been no help at all. She had had to go through the disappointment that he was not going to be a true friend to her. Her mother had been all over her on the telephone about the terrible accident, about how upset she felt, etc., etc. Susan had had to keep herself from being swamped for not being such a feeling person as her mother. Meanwhile, she had had to continue studying and take three final exams. She had done just fine. Her report lasted nearly a half-hour. She was stretched out in her Venus posture. Now what was there for me to do?

I responded. I said that she looked like a woman who could stand on her own. She grinned, "Yes . . . I'm glad I couldn't reach you, actually. I did it myself." She went on quietly to say that her attitude of confidence was completely back. She said it was so interesting how other people were responding to this in her. They came to her. Men too, of late. She realized you don't have to sit around waiting. You can make things happen yourself. You don't have to depend on any one individual or any one capability. Then you can weather storms, like this most difficult week of her life.

Then she got red, pointed a finger at her head unconsciously, and said this "boasting" was not right. I said that was interesting, as I had not thought of her as "boasting," but rather as showing a "quiet pride." I thought I could tell the difference. It was very interesting that she was confused about the difference. Perhaps we needed to appreciate why she had to be confused about this? I had located the "loose end" of her concern, after a half-hour of reporting.

She explained that people who are cocky are brought down. I said I knew that, but she did not appear cocky to me. How did she explain her running quiet pride and cockiness together? Now she sat up, as if startled. She said she didn't quite know how this train of thought fit, but it seemed very important. Her mother seemed dead set against her getting really good at something, also against her going away in the summertime. Mother had put down a crucial veto against her going to several camps where her diving might have jumped to a new level through the fine coaching and competition and practice. Mother did not approve of such specialization. Mother liked "problems." This got her interest up. She loved to be of use when there was trouble, as in the last week. But if you got really good at something, really confident, mother would be less useful, and less powerful.

I replied that I could now see why it was important for her to stay confused about the difference between cockiness and quiet pride. After all, this confusion would make it difficult for her to enjoy her own pride, which would prevent her from going down the road of getting confident and very skillful and very independent. This way, her mother and I could both keep our jobs, our usefulness, and our power in her life. She smiled: "My mother would never *admit* she wants to hold onto her position of power with me." I agreed, "Yes, she might not admit it."

I saw her two weeks later for her last, thirteenth session. She had graduated. She was ready to set sail for South America. She was completely pleased with herself. Her question to me was what to tell her parents about her therapy?

She thought out loud, working this one out for herself. She would not try to explain what we had discovered to her mother. Her mother would only be hurt. She would keep it to herself. Her mother could be her way, Susan her own way. She seemed to be giving up the adolescent game of changing mother. As for her father? She thought a "first" was coming this week. She could tell her father that she could no longer please him by "going along" with mother. That had made her sick. This would put distance between her and father, but that was too bad. It was time.

Thus, she took her leave from me with two altogether different moves in her family game. It appeared I had helped her find some new degrees of freedom. I had put bingeing and vomiting as a move in the class of self-degrading moves. This gave her a degree of freedom about whether to binge and vomit or whether an equivalent weakening of herself would do. We began to see all the different ways she did this. I had placed the class of self-degrading moves in the class of helping her mother stay useful and powerful. Here she shows a degree of freedom about that as well, by refraining from taking her mother down, by letting her be. Finally, I had placed the moves for keeping her mother useful and powerful in the class of moves to keep herself on an even keel, especially with her father and with other men. Here she seems to have two new logical levels of freedom as well. She need not have her mother keep her from excessive stimulation with her father. She coolly takes this upon herself. The move to provoke mother to intervene to distance her and father is, therefore, no longer obligatory. Finally, she shows every sign of being ready to set aside the class of staying on an even keel.

An Afterword for Family Therapists

The reader who has followed this book through four revolutions of perspective about the individual patient in brief therapy may now see how we get from psychoanalysis to character analysis to interpersonal interviewing to Milan systemic interviewing. But for the reader who comes from the other direction, from one of the other systemic methods of interviewing, this narrative will not be satisfying. He or she will want to know about the relation of Milan thinking to the *class* of systemic methods. After all, nearly every prominent family therapist of our time attempts to apprehend the "family system." Most would say that their actions are cleverly aimed at improvement of the system, its hierarchy, its rules, even while tackling more modest problem-solving. Thus, Watzlawick, Haley, Minuchin, Bowen, Whitaker, and Skynner are systemic about perception and intervention. In general, their derivative schools, of strategic, structural, experiential, and group-analytic family therapy, are members, *with* the Milan systemic method, of the *class* of systemic methods.

So what's the difference? What is the difference between the Milan systemic method and the other systemic methods in the class of systemic methods? This is the subject for a book, rather than for a few paragraphs. But I could give a little light on this subject by comparing the Milan method to the other systemic method I know best, namely the group-analytic method of Robin Skynner (Skynner, 1976, 1981, 1984; Skynner and Cleese, 1983).

About opening moves, Skynner is also very careful.[12] As most of the systemic family therapists, Skynner wants to bring into the interview room the members of the system involved in the chief complaint. He calls this "the minimum network." The findings of the Milan teams concerning the *class* of "snares" set before the first words of the first interview would interest him very much. But Skynner is not anxious to discover these snares in advance, for his overall strategy is to be *captured* by the family labyrinth. Therefore, Skynner will not need the long telephone talk before the first interview nor the pre-interview discussion of what to be prepared for in advance.

The middle game for Skynner could proceed as a history-taking. Many families could have quite common troubles, for which Skynner could offer quite common remedies. Impotence in the husband, for example, could elicit from Skynner a prescription for how the husband and wife might proceed in bed for the next while (Skynner and Cleese, 1983). But what about apprehending the system, as it were, in which this sexual problem is embedded?

For this, Skynner will rely on the feelings building up in himself. If he should discover a "bomb" in himself, such as the desire to cut off the tongue of the yapping wife, if he should also discover that this family would find such a feeling incomprehensible or terrifying or morally reprehensible, then Skynner knows he has a systemic problem. He knows by having the two contradictory states within himself, at once. Holding the contradictory states together is a very difficult juggling maneuver, which can only be sustained against gravity for a short while (Skynner, 1985, personal communication). This is akin to what Bateson meant by double description. There is a terrific sense of depth of field, gotten by feeling both the tremendous feeling and the impossibility of communicating this feeling in this family.

Think about Skynner in the face of the wailing, sinking mother. He would want to go under with whatever unspeakable feeling this took him down with, with whatever impossibility he saw about bringing it out to them. He would apprehend the situation of the other family members by diving deep into the hole with them.

For the Milan teams this would be a mistake. The Milan view of the system depends on *not* being taken in by the farce, but in seeing all the background moves which are obscured by the prominence of the farce.

Skynner will perceive the leviathan by being swallowed, like Jonah in the belly of the whale. The Milan teams will keep clear of the thrashing beast, watching for all the remarkable interactions which give the whale its habitat. Both see a whale. Both have their favorite vantage points, which are entirely opposite. The reader familiar with other systemic methods of family therapy will be able to draw a similar comparison along these lines, concerning the place from which the system is gathered.

A very brief example may be helpful. Minuchin saw a family in our Department of Psychiatry at Wisconsin (videotaped) in which the daughter was anorectic. Commenting on some red shoes which the daughter would be unlikely to have picked out for herself, he saw that the daughter looked anxiously to her mother for approval. Minuchin made an enormous fuss about this. The idea, of course, is that the system impinging on her shoes would be the same which impinges on her mouth, so the challenge to the "minor item" also challenges the symptomatic item; indeed, the whole *class* of impingements is called into question. I am reminded of the witch trapped under a house in *The Wizard of Oz*. The edifice of this system also rests on this girl's foot. Minuchin insists on getting the damn thing off her foot, an apparently minor request with large implications. Whitaker might exaggerate the whole damn thing even more, risking a blowup of the house, relying on some alternative physics to preserve the plumbing. Skynner might experience the house on him, whatever feelings that might generate and forbid. Watzlawick might insist they leave the house on the girl's foot, so they decide, "Enough of that." The Milan teams would be interested, I think, in appreciating why this three-story house is so necessary, even though it keeps someone's foot pinned down.

Of course, none of these therapists is obliged to think any of this at all, which is hopelessly schematic. If they were so predictable, they would have been replaced. My point is only that the system may be hoisted from many different fulcrums. House-moving companies all have their own favorite devices.

Finally, concerning the end game. For Skynner, the problem of greatest importance is how to give the "bomb" back to the family. How to tell of his desire to cut off the wife's tongue while staying in good standing in a family that finds this incomprehensible, terrifying or morally reprehensible? Skynner's idea here would be that if he can pull this off, the husband could follow suit. The husband might not have to continue in his impotence to keep himself from the aforesaid act of savagery. The class of primitive acts might not have to be expunged to stay in good standing in this family. But how to pull this off? Skynner will do it by humor most often, locating the terrible urge in the context of his friendliness for them. Jokes have this kind of logical contradiction. Skynner puts the joke to its most crucial function, to comment on and integrate the most difficult of situations.

The Milan message-giving is a cousin, for it too relies upon the contradictions between logical levels. The message will not appear, however, as funny, not at all. Think of the message, again, from the farce. Wendy has been presented as the failure, Janine as the lecturing success, mother was the wailing, sinking martyr, father as her impatient critic. The message will group them as two pairs, one helping the parents, the other helping the children, to slow down the march of the inevitable growing up. The opposite daughters are the same as the opposite parents at the next logical level of helping. The two pairs are in concert at the next logical level of moving together to slow down the march of the inevitable. The Milan message will *not* bring out the explosion of laughter which comes from bringing these contradictory levels into rude juxtaposition. They will state the levels, allowing the degrees of freedom I have described, at each level, for other moves to appear within the same class. Skynner will bring out a tolerable explosion of laughter by his juxtaposition, say, of the class of primitive urges within the class of devotion to the family.

I think individuals and families always present "problems" which are insolvable within the class of allowable experiences, perceptions, and actions that make them loyal members of a family or organization. Therefore, the ending message always has to indicate the impossible: How someone can feel, perceive or act in some unallowable way, to show their devotion to their family or organization (at a higher logical level). Skynner and the Milan teams have found different ways to indicate the impossible, by which they close their interviews in concert with the individual or family. Of course, Watzlawick, Haley, Bowen, and Whitaker, and many others, have different ways to close on the same kind of contradictions. Systemic appreciation depends on recognizing this difficulty in the ending game.[13]

I have no interest in setting up a contest between the Milan teams and

Skynner, or the Milan teams and any of the other systemic methods. All of them have to reckon with the shaping of the opening game — should I say the "distorting" of the opening game? — by the gravitational force of the relevant system, with the difficulty apprehending how the players are stuck in their own system in the middle game, and with the difficulty of taking a position on these contradictions in the end game.

I adopt the Milan way of working, from the many worthy variations in the same systemic class, because it is a way that I work well. I have experimented with Skynner's method as well. I also find it very useful. But it does not suit me so well as it suits Robin Skynner. I am interested in sinking adventures, also, like Robin, but I am more interested in building these remarkable compositions. This is extremely meaningful to me.

I also come to the possibility of systemic interviewing from my previous commitment to individual work. I have been able to use my sinking feelings in situations with individual patients to get a feel for their being stuck in their families. This can throw a light in these dark situations, no doubt. The Milan method for bringing out "the other people in the room" in individual work is more congenial to me, less painful.[14]

17. *Maturana: The Otherness of Others*

T HIS LAST ONE OF my trio of pieces on the systemic perspective may have a calm surface, but it carries the most troubling of currents. Once you allow your patients to be caught up in their own labyrinthine games, you drift towards the same allowance for your students.[1] This is upsetting, for where is the stability? Everyone knows that Freud had great difficulty with the drift of his own students, but a glance around the various schools of psychotherapy may show the reader how typical it is for the leader to pull the followers into line and vice versa. We all want company in our own way of thinking.

But when I watch my students I do not see them carrying out my ideas at all. The conversation we have is entirely misleading. Because we share many of the same theoretical words, I could think their interviews will look like the Milan interviewing which I prefer. No, often not at all. Their interviews say back to me, "No, you can tell us about Milan, but we do not do this. We do everything but this. What we do still looks more like psychoanalysis, or the analysis of character, or interpersonal interviewing. We will range around the previous 15 descriptions of the previous 15 chapters in your book as we choose. Please do not confuse your map with our territory!"

So here is my dilemma as a teacher. The schools of psychotherapy all seem closed. My students are closed as well! They are on their own. So, therefore, am I.

If I can live with this, I find I have very exciting learning situations in the Brief Therapy Clinic with my students. This is where the thinking of Maturana has been a very big help to me. The closure of schools and the closure of students is most beautifully explained on a map of all living systems. All are "autopoietic." Allow me not to explain this evocative word as yet. I only want to suggest what is ahead. Two practical possibilities: One is help in seeing how closed students are unto themselves (Bateson, 1979, Varela, 1979). All are "auto-nomos," a law unto themselves. Two is help in seeing that there are very different ways to relate to a world of closed systems; these ways make them opaque or make them visible.

I like to have biology on my side in this difficulty. We in psychiatry have been borrowing from biology for over a hundred years to make ourselves more powerful. This is only fair so that we shall not be hopelessly outclassed by our patients. We need to be armed.

Our strength could be better or worse for our patients. We could be stronger at making them stronger. We could be stronger at making them weaker. Either could be. I am less convinced than most in psychiatry about which of these statements is more often the truth.[2]

Allow me to explain, borrowing an idea from E. F. Schumacher (1977). He captures the idea of jumps of complexity, of logical levels also, from the mineral world (m) to plant world (m + x) to the animal world (m + x + y) to the human world (m + x + y + z). There are discontinuous jumps from physico-chemical events (m) to living systems (m + x) to consciousness (m + x + y) to the capacity for self-awareness (m + x + y + z).

Now here is where I may indicate our difficulty in borrowing from biology. Since the less complex level is always operating in the more complex, since living systems, for example, must obey the laws of physico-chemical events as well as the laws of living systems, then there is always the possibility of reducing the complex level to a lower level of explanations. Reversing Schumacher's equation, a human being can be reduced to physico-chemical events by subtracting the phenomena of self-awareness, consciousness, and living systems: $m - z - y - x$. Therefore, it would be well for us in psychiatry to think about what level of biology we are borrowing when we say we represent "biological psychiatry." In the nineteenth century, we meant the animal level of complexity: $m - z$. Human beings were explained in terms of Darwinian ideas like the survival of the fittest, or Freudian ideas like the sexual instincts. Since we do indeed share this lower level of complexity of animals, much could be explained about us in this kind of reduction. In the twentieth century, we mean an interest in explanations from either the animal ($m - z$) or biochemical ($m - z - y$) level. But even the biochemistry which is the favorite subject of modern biological psychiatry often says nothing about living systems at all. Much of it is pharmacology, just variations in drug chemistry ($m - z - y - x$).

Thus I am continually amazed that psychopharmacology gets away with saying it is "biological psychiatry." This is the most reductive biology possible. What a poor idea of biology we have in psychiatry to accept such loose talk! What impoverished patients to be robbed of all the phenomena which make them living systems, animals, and human beings![3] This is why I am grateful for the biology of Maturana (Maturana and Varela, 1980), which is able to describe these higher orders of complexity (m + x; m + x + y; m + x + y + z) in their own terms as higher-order recursive systems.[4]

Matter (m) is organized by living systems (m + x), which are "autopoietic" and "recursive," because they have "an organization which produces the structures which reproduce their organization." Thus, living systems are autopoietic, or self-producing, and recursive, or recurring like mathematical functions. Consciousness (m + x + y) is an awareness of a living system about its own living. Self-awareness (m + x + y + z) is an awareness of conscious being of the content and form of its own consciousness. A higher level of organization is built by a circular, recursive organization of a lower level of organization. The lower level continues to operate its own circular, recursive organization, but may also be subsumed in the higher level.[5]

I apologize for this digression into the levels of biology. I did not want to alarm the reader about this biology I bring on my side. I also want the reader to know that this chapter is certainly not about Maturana's thinking, but only about my neighbor relations with his thinking. Since his thinking perturbs me in some ways, as his thinking perturbs himself, I have some consensual domain with him. This allows me to stay neighbors with him in some thinking realm, specifically about helping students as closed beings, who are trying to help other closed beings, called patients. He helps me with the otherness of others. That is all I propose to explain about him, or about me, or about something we may have in common.

But now let us plunge into the alien world of other people, students and patients, without any further ado, as the "alienists" we are! I like Lewis Carroll's story of "The Queen's Croquet Ground" (1865) best for orienting ourselves to the "otherness of others." I think it very interesting that a biology that is interested in all levels of recursion and complexity in human beings $(m + x + y + z)$ is able to give an explanation of something remarkable from our literature. This gives me hope that both may be convergent, after all. I am even more hopeful when I see how this helps me to provide a learning situation for my students in our Brief Therapy Clinic. This is where we will come out, for having taken this trouble. I can only apologize to the reader in advance for the difficulty of the conceptual discussion which follows "The Queen's Croquet Ground." It is the most difficult passage to make in the book, which could take several years of study. If the reader doesn't have two years to spend on that passage, becoming impatient, he or she may amuse him or herself by jumping to "The Game of the Carrot and the Stick" on page 249.

The Queen's Croquet Ground

Now let us follow Alice through her eighth adventure and as we go make a few observations which have something to do with the theoretical biology of Maturana. Alice passes into her eighth adventure from her seventh by wandering into a lovely garden belonging to the Queen of Hearts. What will this story be about? The context is marked well by the first sentence:

A large rose-tree stood near the entrance of the garden: the roses growing on it were white, but there were three gardeners at it, busily painting them red. (p. 82)

So we are introduced to the particular madness of this adventure, to a little garden which explores the interest and the difficulty in instructing living systems. The reader will have to remember that the "people" in this garden are all playing-cards, having only two dimensions, or this description will make little sense at all.

Alice is curious about why these three gardeners are painting the white rose tree red. They tell her the Queen of Hearts wanted a red one, not a white one, so they were hiding their error to keep her from cutting off their heads.

The Queen's procession now enters, and all her subjects fall upon their faces. Why do they paint white rose trees red? Why do they lie upon their faces, so they cannot see the procession?

The Queen now demands to know who this child is standing before her and who these cards are lying upon the ground by the rose tree,

... for, you see, as they were lying on their faces, and the pattern on their backs was the same as the rest of the pack, she could not tell whether they were gardeners, or soldiers, or courtiers, or three of her own children.

"How should *I* know?" said Alice, surprised at her own courage. "It's no business of *mine*."

The Queen turned crimson with fury, and, after glaring at her for a moment like a wild beast, screamed "Off with her head! Off — " (p. 84)

This little passage concludes when the gardeners are turned over, their deception of painting the rose trees is seen by the Queen, the Queen orders their heads to be cut off, Alice saves them by putting them into a large flower pot, and the Queen shouts at the soldiers:

"Are their heads off?" . . .

"Their heads are gone, if it please your Majesty!" the soldiers shouted in reply.

"That's right!" shouted the Queen. "Can you play croquet?"

The soldiers were silent, and looked at Alice, as the question was evidently meant for her.

"Yes!" shouted Alice.

"Come on then!" roared the Queen, and Alice joined the procession, wondering very much what would happen next. (p. 86)

A few observations before we go with the procession to croquet. What kind of little world do we have here? It is a little world in which individuals disappear by pretending that white is red, by falling flat into two dimensions, hiding their faces and showing only the backs of their membership. If this newcomer, Alice, should assert her individuality, then the Queen has a terrific way of changing the subject, which is to roar, "Off with her head." The King suggests she be let off since "she is only a child." The gardeners are now let off since "their heads are gone." What is important in this little world is *not* whether something is literally so or not so, only that it *appear* to be so. This is the relation which has to be satisfied for the instruction to go on, for this little society to go about its business.

So let us go with the procession to croquet, where we will see just how this pretense of instructing living systems can get extremely difficult for the players:

"Get to your places!" shouted the Queen in a voice of thunder, and people began running about in all directions tumbling up against each other; however, they got settled down in a minute or two, and the game began. Alice thought she had never seen such a curious croquet-ground in all her life; it was all ridges and furrows; the balls were live hedgehogs, the mallets live flamingoes, and the soldiers had to double themselves up and to stand upon their hands and feet, to make the arches.

The chief difficulty Alice found at first was in managing her flamingo; she succeeded in getting its body tucked away, comfortably enough, under her arm, with its legs hanging down, but generally, just as she had got its neck nicely straightened out, and was going to give the hedgehog a blow with its head, it *would* twist itself round and look up in her face, with such a puzzled expression that she could not help bursting out laughing: and when she had got its head down, and was going to begin again, it was very provoking to find that the hedgehog had unrolled itself, and was in the act of crawling away: besides all this, there was generally a ridge or a furrow in the way wherever she wanted to send the hedgehog to, and, as the doubled-up soldiers were always getting up and walking off to other parts of the ground, Alice soon came to the conclusion that it was a very difficult game indeed. (pp. 87–88)

How could such a game go on at all? Well, it did, as follows:

The players all played at once without waiting for turns, quarreling all the while, and fighting for the hedgehogs; and in a very short time the Queen was in a furious passion, and went stamping about, and shouting "Off with his head!" or "Off with her head!" about once in a minute.

This "Off with the head" remark is very, very useful, for all difficulties which appear are thus dismissed as out of bounds. They are sent off. Only later in the ninth adventure do we learn how this simplifies the game:

All the time they were playing the Queen never left off quarreling with the other players, and shouting "Off with his head!" or "Off with her head!" Those whom she sentenced were taken into custody by the soldiers, who of course had to leave off being arches to do this, so that by the end of half an hour or so there were no arches left, and all the players, except the King, the Queen, and Alice, were in custody and under sentence of execution. (p. 97)

The entire game returns nicely to its zero point, after this, as follows:

As they walked off together, Alice heard the King say in a low voice, to the company generally, "You are all pardoned." "Come *that's* a good thing!" she said to herself, for she had felt quite unhappy at the number of executions the Queen had ordered. (p. 97)

But let us return to the conclusion of the eighth adventure, where Alice is trying to manage an escape from this game, which is nerve-wracking:

Alice began to feel very uneasy: to be sure she had not yet had any dispute with the Queen, but she knew that it might happen any minute, "and then," thought she, "what would become of me? They're dreadfully fond of beheading people here; the great wonder is that there's any one left alive!"

She was looking about for some way of escape, and wondering whether she could get away without being seen, when she noticed a curious appearance in the air: it puzzled her very much at first, but, after watching it a minute or two, she made it out to be a grin, and said to herself, "It's the Cheshire Cat: now I shall have somebody to talk to." (pp. 88–89)

Alice now appears to have an outside observer with whom she may discuss the mad situation:

" . . . and you've no idea how confusing it is all the things being alive; for instance, there's the arch I've got to go through next walking about at the other end of the ground — and I should have croqueted the Queen's hedgehog just now, only it ran away when it saw mine coming!"

But this Cat is quite a provocateur himself. He replies:

"How do you like the Queen?" said the Cat in a low voice.
"Not at all," said Alice: "she's so extremely" — Just then she noticed that the Queen was close behind her listening: so she went on, " — likely to win, that it's hardly worth while finishing the game." (p. 89)

Even worse, when the Queen and King want to know to whom Alice is talking and Alice offers to introduce the Cat, the Cat continues to break the rule which forbids showing individuality, which is outside the game and the society here:

"I don't like the look of it at all," said the King: "however, it may kiss my hand if it likes."
"I'd rather not," the Cat remarked. (p. 90)

Only the Cat can get away with this. Alice could not, for she feared having her head separated from her body. The Cat is only a head appearing in the air. When the executioner is summoned by the King to cut off the Cat's head, there is a terrific argument about whether this is possible or not. The executioner says he cannot and will not, since there is no body to cut it off from. The King argues "that anything that had a head could be beheaded." The Queen "that if something wasn't done about it in less than no time, she'd have everybody executed, all round (it was this last remark that had made the whole party look so grave and anxious)" (p. 91). Alice proposes asking the Duchess, to whom the Cat belongs. The executioner dashes off. The Cat fades away. The adventure is over. All of this argument has worked very nicely, as usual, to get rid of the distress of the game for the players. We have forgotten when this brouhaha began, just when Alice was getting upset again:

The hedgehog was engaged in a fight with another hedgehog, which seemed to Alice an excellent opportunity for croqueting one of them with the other: the only difficulty was, that her flamingo was gone across to the other side of the garden, where Alice could see it trying in a helpless sort of way to fly up into one of the trees. (pp. 90–91)

"Off with the head" and arguments about "Off with the head" are perfect for ruling the distress of the living beings out of bounds.

COORDINATION OF COORDINATION OF CONDUCT

The little imaginary society of the Queen's Croquet Ground allows me to bring out one problem in education which I think is pandemic, from among all the possible problems that it would be possible to discuss here utilizing the theoretical biology of Maturana.[6] The reader who wants to map his discussion of social organization from *Autopoiesis and Cognition* (Maturana and Varela, 1980, pp. xvii-xxx) onto the Queen's Croquet Ground will find a correspondence between nearly every proposition there and the story. But that would be a little book and I must keep here to only one idea, which has to do with situations for learning about psychotherapy.

Allow me to explain several definitions from Maturana which I will need to make my argument. For him, the most important finding about living systems is their autonomy. If you break the word "autonomy" down, you get auto-nomos, or literally, a law unto itself (Bateson, 1979; Varela, 1979).[7] Maturana and Varela choose to describe this autonomy of living systems by a new word, "autopoiesis," which breaks down into auto-poiesis, or literally, the creation or making of itself. Maturana distinguishes living systems as autopoietic unities, which create or make the components (structures) which recreate or remake the same unity (organization) in correspondence to its domain. Autopoietic unities, therefore, close completely upon themselves in this circular recreation or remaking of themselves. They are perfect in their conservation of this same organization and in their conservation of correspondence to their domain of existence. They are entirely self-referential, since whatever they do is determined by their own structures. But since they are in perfect correspondence to their domain of existence, utilizing different structures to maintain their organization and correspondence, then different ones of their structures are triggered or set operating or perturbed by their neighboring relations (Maturana and Varela, 1980).

I will be more specific. Think of the child Alice in the Croquet Ground. She is an autopoietic entity, who is continuously remaking herself, utilizing different structures to conserve her organization and correspondence. When the Queen shouts at her the first time to demand who the cards are by the rose tree, lying on their faces, the Queen triggers in Alice, "How should *I* know? . . . It's no business of mine" (p. 84). Later, when the Cat asks her how she likes the Queen, the Cat triggers a similar frankness, "Not at all . . . she's so extremely . . . ," but noticing the Queen behind her triggers a different ending to her sentence, " . . . likely to win, that's it's hardly worthwhile finishing the game" (p. 89). Either the candid or the cagey Alice can be elicited, but what you get from her is entirely self-determined, self-referential, and closed. She operates like a pilot in the fog (Maturana, 1978). Different readings on her meters will elicit different adjustments made possible by the variations in structure which are possible for her, but you will only get a selection of *her* possibilities.

But an autopoietic unity, such as Alice, has the potential for being coupled to another autopoietic unity, such as the Queen, or to an entire set of such unities, such as the society in the Queen's Croquet Ground. This structural coupling occurs when each selects structures in the other *which stabilize the medium* between them. This is how the society itself becomes a closed organization of a second order. This is what Maturana calls the coordination of conduct or the creation of a consensual domain. The little society which plays this recursive Croquet Game, in which all but three are sentenced to execution, only to be pardoned, beginning over again, is a kind of structural coupling which is possible for autopoietic unities.

A parallel example is the society of termites (Maturana, 1984). Termites are individual autopoietic beings, but they are coordinated by the phenomenon of tropholaxis, which stabilizes their society as a closed organization. They feed each other. In feeding each other, they exchange hormones, which perturb one another with the same drug. They are a perfect drug culture, in which all are hopping to the same drug rhythm. They perturb one another into this synchrony. This is their coordination of conduct.

A still higher order is possible. When Alice and the Queen and the other characters talk to one another about their coordination of conduct in the game, they con-verse, or turn together, which is a coordination of their coordination of conduct (Maturana, 1978). The most striking device in this little society is the use of the recursive statement, "Off with his head" or "Off with her head," whereby the individual spoken to in this way leaves the field temporarily with whatever he or she has been carrying, until the pardon later. This is one of many possible kinds of coordination of coordination of conduct, but a very significant kind which Maturana (1984) has called "instructive interaction." In this pandemic form of coordination of coordination, described so well by Lewis Carroll in the Queen's Croquet Ground, we human beings act as if some individuals "instruct" other individuals about what to do and how to do what they do. This is one way to stabilize the coordination of coordination of conduct, i.e., to stabilize the use of language. This too is a closed unity, of a third order.

Now that the reader is provided with these definitions, illustrated from the Queen's Croquet Ground, I may say the one thing I want to say in this chapter. This concerns whether or not a little society is coordinating its coordination of conduct with "instructive interaction," as in the Croquet Game.

Now it is *possible* for Alice to use a flamingo as a croquet mallet, a hedgehog as a ball, and soldiers as arches. They *may* be coupled in this way, since they do have this structural possibility of stabilizing their relations in this way. This is one possible, however unlikely, coordination of conduct between them. When we or the participants observe this coordination of conduct, we notice how painful and awkward it is for them. Also, we observe how they try to get out of relations, the flamingo by twisting its head as it is about to be used as a mallet, the hedgehogs and soldiers by running off, the flamingoes trying to fly into the trees and Alice herself looking to get out.

But notice what happens with the discussion of this coordination of conduct, with the possible discussion of how painful it is to the different creatures. Every time it crops up, it is dismissed by the Queen's or King's shouting "Off with his head" or "Off with her head." The creatures so instructed leave the field until they are pardoned and may return. Of course, Carroll is referring to the "instructive interaction" of Victorian parents and their children, or the Victorian upper-class and their subjects, or Victorian educators and their pupils, wherein painful feelings about absurd, awkward, and cruel social conventions are dismissed out of bounds, out of sight, out of hearing, and out of mind. The greatest fury is visited upon those who attempt to make observations about how they feel or how others might feel, such as upon Alice or upon the Chesire Cat.

Now here is what I want to say. Organization of the individual creatures in this story is one level. Organization of the game of croquet, a coordination of conduct, is another level. Organization of the possible discussion of the game of croquet, of the coordination of the coordination of conduct, is a third level. All are perfectly closed unities. What concerns me here is what was comedy for Lewis Carroll, namely, the contradictions between these different logical levels. When the third level, of language, is this shared orientation called "instructive interaction" by Maturana, then the seeing and the hearing of what is painful in this strange coordination of conduct, in the croquet game, can no longer be seen and heard. The same for seeing and hearing the individual creatures. Flamingoes become one kind of croquet mallet, hedgehogs one kind of ball, etc. "Instructive interaction" is extremely stabilizing, but denies access to levels two and one, to seeing and hearing what is actually going on in the coordination of conduct and what is actually going on with the individual beings.

Now coordination of coordination of conduct will always be perfectly closed. It will stabilize, one way or another, into some recursion or circular path. Fortunately, it need not always be in the form of "instructive interaction." It is also possible to have a perfectly closed ritual for the coordination of coordination of conduct, which allows the coordination of conduct and the individual beings to be seen and heard. We may have lucidity or opacity concerning what is going on, depending on how we are organized concerning language, or "languaging" as Maturana (1984) likes to say, to point to the shared coordination of coordination. George Orwell wrote of this problem in his "Politics of the English Language" (1946b), describing how language may be used either to show or to hide. One of his metaphors about the latter is unforgettable:

When one watches some tired hack on the platform mechanically repeating the familiar phrases—bestial atrocities, iron heel, bloodstrained tyranny, free peoples of the world, stand shoulder to shoulder—one often has the curious feeling that one is not watching a live human being but some kind of dummy: a feeling which suddenly becomes stronger at moments when the light catches the speaker's spectacles and turns them into blank discs which seem to have no eyes behind them. (p. 166)

So there are many Queens who shout, who instruct, who see nothing.

Before I describe a different kind of coordination of coordination of conduct, which we utilize in our Brief Therapy Clinic to see what is going on in the coordination between therapist and patient and in these individuals, I want the reader to appreciate the enormous domain of "instructive interaction." I do not think it is any exaggeration to describe this game as *the* most powerful coordination of coordination of conduct in the Western world. It has been given many different names, which obscure the unity of this organization. Seeing its enormous domain, the reader may be in a position to appreciate how he or she is continually pulled into this kind of relation, how difficult it is to have some different kind of situation for education.

Think of the different ways we are led into this game, in which some living beings appear to "control" other living beings. Even Maturana himself "instructs" about the illusion of seeing other living systems in the farce of "instructive interaction." After all, he cannot "instruct" us to see such illusion; he can only trigger in us the possibility of such seeing. In this "instruction," he too is pulled into what Freire (1970) has called "the director culture." Freire noticed that peasants remained in a "culture of silence," when directed what words to learn to read and write. They were unavailable, except in the most minimal of ways. They were invisible and inaudible as beings in their own right. When the peasants were shown pictures of typical difficult situations in the country and asked to find their own words for such situations, they became extremely audible and visible in their excitement, with their own "generative words." But education is more often the prerogative of the "director culture." We agree to act as if learning can be deposited in us, as in a bank.

This agreement is a cousin to ideas which are prevelant in the enormous use of computers for social "control." Coding of a few relevant markers allows large organizations to "control" large populations, for example, in my university concerning entrance to the library, or in my hospital concerning entrance to the clinics for patients. Bureaucratic organization depends upon individuals' acting as if "instructed" by such context markers (Gerth and Mills, 1946). They are not controlled, but they agree to appear to act as if they were controlled. Their experiences in the director culture of their education has prepared them for this shared pretense.

They have also been prepared for how to relate to strangers in such a way as to deny the interaction and the beings involved. All empires depend upon this intimidation. There are many descriptions of this, such as Orwell's "Shooting an Elephant" (1946c). This mutual coercion works upon both the colonizer and the colonized. Many have described the brutalization involved in the recent years of the Vietnam war, the relations between black and white, the Soviet archipelago, and so forth. "Instruction" is rampant.[8] It is also ancient. Brueggemann (1977) has called it "royal consciousness," describing how stability works in a society of consuming.

Finally, the same game, by another name, occurs routinely in marriage, wherein it is also reproduced. The game here is to act as if marriage is a struggle to "control" your spouse. You seek what is missing in your own being, find it in a beloved, and then spend your life with that individual finding how to punish him or her for having the very qualities you sought (Dicks, 1967). You want what you miss, but you also want to control what you miss, since it is unacceptable in your own family of origin. Hence, the game of seeking the unacceptable, and punishing the unacceptable—round and round. Of course, the game may then be extended to the children. You "instruct" them as well as your spouse.

Of course, all I am saying is that stabilization of enormous mass societies is a terrific problem, which is solved by the same coordination of conduct in all its component activities, from education, to banking, to computers, to bureaucracies, to empire maintaining, to consuming, to marrying, and to bringing up children. We are in one enormous stabilization, which is this "instructive interaction" by many different names. "Normal science" is just another version.[9] The pull into this game is extremely powerful. Therefore, in our little Brief Therapy Clinic, we have a problem conducting a situation for learning about seeing the coordination of conduct and the individual beings involved. If we do not do something quite powerful and different, we will close our organization in the usual way of "instructive interaction," seeing and hearing almost nothing except the triggers for our own "instruction."

A final word about "instructive interaction" before we proceed to some of the practical consequences from this difficult theoretical discussion. Strictly speaking, "instructive interaction" is *impossible*, since no individual may instruct another individual. Such linear control is impossible. All an individual may do is trigger another individual to do what that individual is capable of doing. All an individual may do is select or pull for some structures in another individual out of the repertoire that individual has available. Then that second individual will trigger, select, or pull for structures in the first individual. Often, this will lead into a *mutual* selection which stabilizes the drift between them. This is their consensual domain, or coordination of conduct.

But this pair may *converse* about their coordination of conduct to *pretend* or act *as if* the first individual "instructs" or "controls" the second individual. This is one farce for stabilizing their relations, which I am describing as endemic to our Western civilization, which I am saying goes by the many names I have described. Because it is so endemic to pretend such relations, I take pains to locate some other relations with my students. If I do not locate some *other* way of conversing about our coordination of conduct, I will be pulled back into pretending myself that I am instructing my students. Then I will see and hear much less.

THE GAME OF THE CARROT AND THE STICK

How are we tempted into "instructive interaction" in our clinic? How do we sometimes do something more interesting? I want to tell the difference with the story of a single hour of "supervision" by our team of senior residents, with myself as its leader, with one of them presenting his difficulty with his patient in brief individual therapy.

The doctor began by telling the four of us helping him that his success in helping his patient with "growing up" had become stuck in the sixth, seventh, eighth, and ninth sessions he would report. He wanted us to help him see how this had occurred and to decide what to do about the situation. So we began to hear a 15-minute report, which became extremely recursive. The patient was a man in his thirties dawdling in graduate school, as if he might never get on further with his life. Our doctor would ask him the interesting question, "What would you like to be when you grow up?" Our patient would be intrigued, talk about his interests in making a more humane world through his writing, then revert back to zero by saying his parents and grandparents could be successful in this, but not him. For several sessions he showed humane concern about his roommate, who had attempted suicide in this interval, but then he faulted himself for not having pursued some hints beforehand of the coming disaster. He had a friend who admired his writing as a possible contribution to humanity, but this friend was a poor judge. Maybe he couldn't grow up, for all he had was negative thinking.

We now listened to 15 minutes of audiotape from the ninth session, where we heard more of the same recursion. He was very much loved by his family; he could always rely on them. The doctor asked, "All right, that's terrific, but why would you not be saying, 'Thanks, but now I go on'?" The patient replied that he was "infantile," that he had been a "goody goody kid" and a "spoiled kid." His family would allow him to grow up, but he could not. "Maybe," he suggested, "I need to be whipped?" He seemed quite excited, to my ears, as he reported getting "straightened out" in kindergarten, obviously inviting the same from our doctor. When the doctor kidded him about revealing himself, he responded that he "perverted" situations. When the doctor said he was not so sure of that, the patient responded that a bad student was an incomplete person. He had a sense of humor, he admitted, but this was only appreciated in his family.

All right, we had his report. Now to the question for the day! Why couldn't he "grow up" in this family? What help could our team offer? One of the team noticed that our doctor seemed to be pushing the patient uphill, like Sisyphus, only to have every gain nullified, as he rolled back swiftly to his starting point after inching a bit uphill.[10] Another noticed that this man's parents had been pushing him like this for 30 years, with comparable results. Also, his previous therapist had done the same.

I then added that the doctor was being pulled of late by the patient's excitement over being punished, which was the loudest section of the audiotape. I summarized the team's view of this game, of this coordination of the coordination of conduct, as "Carrot and Stick." Our patient was extremely adept at offering the hope of "someday," "eventually" realizing his promise in humane letters. I suggested he was "The Prince of Someday, Eventually." This elicited either the Carrot or the Stick from family, previous doctor, now our doctor. Like Aldo in Palazzoli's case of "The Sibling as Referring Person" (1985), he was not ready to give up his crown. At home, he was royalty. In therapy he was royalty. Elsewhere, he would be much more modest, if not nothing.

Our doctor looked a little grim. He asked us, "All right, I agree this is exactly what is going on. Do you guys think I should lay this out for him?" Our team seemed very hesitant. Something seemed quite wrong. We noticed his demeanor. We asked him about it. He replied that he was no better than the previous therapist, no better than the parents. He too was a fool.

I then made my final move. I said, "No, I don't agree with that proposition at all. Indeed, you have brought about the most striking movement in this man in many years. Your interest in his 'growing up' has actually gotten him going. What we are talking about is his being scared by your success. You are being pulled into being the stick, by his hurting your feelings, by his making you feel the fool. Now we see that *we too* could contribute to wrecking your success by giving you this description of 'Carrot and Stick' with which to hit the patient. If we instruct you to 'lay this truth' out to him, to set him straight, we indeed only bring about the punishment which he is trying to elicit from you, to stop the movement of your success with him." Our doctor seemed very relieved. We stopped.

I would only invite the reader to notice the overwhelming pull into "instructive interaction," from the patient to the doctor, from the doctor to his teammates, from the team to me. We are invited back to the Queen's Croquet Game! The patient is a hedgehog. The doctor ought to get out his flamingo and pound him through the next wicket. Of course, it is impossible. The doctor is a frustrated player. The team sees the game, the coordination of conduct here, which has been perpetual. The team is invited to help the doctor in his "instructing" the patient about the impossible game we had so cleverly described. More pounding, at the next logical level. Same game. Finally, the doctor is appearing to be the fool among his teammates. I am pulled to give him his comeuppance, his "instruction" to be a better player. None of this. I content myself with appreciating him, declining to participate in punishing him and instructing him, as the Croquet Game here seems to ask me to do.

So what do we have here? We have a different kind of coordination of the coordination of conduct. The patient may invite being socked. The doctor may "instruct." But the team need not do either. The team need not do anything but describe the game. This allowed the patient's moves—their beautiful coordination with the doctor's pushing—to come clearly into view. The doctor got out his flamingo. The patient inched forward like a good hedgehog, then rolled back into his original place in the turf. This also allowed the doctor's distress to come before us, as he felt the fool for missing our view of the game. This also allowed me to see his temptation to strike a new blow, using our description as "instruction." Finally, I could appreciate how this would hide the success of himself and his patient, and set it back.

That's all. Our coordination of the coordination of conduct is a very closed procedure. It is very strict. The patient behaves. The doctor describes the patient's interaction with him. The team describes the game it sees between the doctor and patient. I describe the difficulty between us and the doctor.[11] It appears that much can be seen when the team keeps from instruction, when I keep from instruction. That's what we're up to, seeing and hearing. As Bateson wrote, you need to map a game onto a structure with more logical levels than the game itself. Otherwise the contradictions between levels cannot be deciphered. Hence, we play a game with these clear levels of recursion of description. Our ritual is strictly closed, but it is designed to allow an appreciation of organization at all the different levels of description.[12,13]

The Nantucketer, he alone resides and riots on the sea; he
alone, in Bible language, goes down to it in ships; to and fro
ploughing it as his own special plantation. *There* is his home;
there lies his business, which a Noah's flood would not interrupt, though it overwhelmed all the millions in China. He lives
on the sea, as prairie cocks in the prairie; he hides among the
waves, he climbs them as the chamois hunters climb the Alps.
For years he knows not the land; so that when he comes to it at
last, it smells like another world, more strangely than the moon
would to an Earthsman. With the landless gull, that at sunset
folds her wings and is rocked to sleep between billows; so at
nightfall, the Nantucketer out of sight of land, furls his sails,
and lays him to his rest, while under his very pillow rush herds
of walruses and whales.

—Herman Melville, *Moby-Dick* or, *The Whale*

PART III

A Theory for a Method of Methods

. . . it is this sense of a limitless subject that gives the style its
peculiarly loping quality, as if it were constantly looking for
connectives, since on the subject of the whale no single word or
statement is enough.

—Alfred Kazin, Introduction to *Moby-Dick*

INTRODUCTION

*T*he reader who makes his or her way through an epic poem, a long novel, or a theoretical argument likes to see where he or she is along the way. For instance, the reader of the Divine Comedy *can always picture himself or herself at whatever step in the descent in the Inferno, or whatever step in the rise up the mountain of Purgatory. This is both a distinct pleasure and a reassurance against the fear of becoming lost on a long journey.*

Much the same argument could be made for the needs of listeners to long works of music. They too need to know where they are if they are to endure the difficult passages, knowing the resolution is on its way soon. Theory, being more abstract and less spatial, is perhaps more like music than it is like a story.

But it is impossible for me to present a theory which integrates the array of Chapters 2 through 17 with as much simplicity of form as in those single chapters. My dilemma is very much like those faced by the nineteenth-century composers with such a rich tradition preceding them. So many kinds of melodies, harmonies, and rhythms were available to them to show their own abilities, but they needed to construct pieces in which the listener could stay oriented.

I have borrowed one of their favorite formal schemes to carry my own theoretical argument with all of its diversity. This is the sonata-allegro form, which is an ABA form consisting of an exposition of the main themes, a development of these themes, and recapitulation.

Allow me to explain very briefly how this form is crucial to my theoretical argument. My preliminary theme is the scientific criteria of explanation for the situation of brief therapy. My main theme is that for living systems change multiplies explanations, while closure simplifies explanation. I illustrate this main theme of closure from the four different positions for observation: psychoanalysis, the analysis of character, interpersonal interviewing, and systemic interviewing. These give us our methods of brief therapy.

The development is more difficult to follow unless the reader understands that the theoretical problem is precisely one of how to modulate from one observing position to another. Various kinds of complicated music from our patients can then be appreciated.

The recapitulation returns to the main theme of closing to stay the same. The complicated ways in which patients do this may defeat the singular methods, but a method of methods is prepared for such defeat. The re-capitulation of the main lines for a method of methods prepares the reader for that subject in Part IV.

18. *How to Stay the Same*

I
    Preliminary Theme: Criteria of Explanation

    ask this clinical theory of brief psychotherapy to help us in two broad ways. I will be entirely explicit, so the reader may judge to what extent he likes the aims and the results.

First, the theory has to meet criteria of explanation for any scientific explanation (Maturana, 1978, p. 28): (A) "The observer specifies a procedure of observation, that, in turn, specifies the phenomenon that he or she will attempt to explain." (B) The observer proposes a model or mechanism to generate the phenomenon. (C) "The observer uses the model to compute a state or a process that he or she proposes as the predicted phenomenon to be observed." (D) "Finally, in the fourth operation he or she attempts to observe the predicted phenomenon as a case in the modeled system."

Secondly, these scientific explanations have to meet the particular demands of clinicians in situations of brief psychotherapy. I propose the following translations of the broad scientific requirements:

A) The procedure of observation of clinicians is that they listen to stories. "A story is a little knot or complex of that species of connectedness which we call relevance. . . . I would say that any (A) is relevant to any (B) if both (A) and (B) are parts or components of the same 'story'" (Bateson, 1979, p. 13). Stories are the phenomena to be explained, especially, to use Mann's phrase (1973), stories of "present and chronically recurring pain." I appreciate that stories may not be seen in psychiatry as worthwhile objects of scientific interest. Psychiatry is not very interested in explanations of the phenomena of self-awareness, but rather in reducing the complex level to lower level phenomena of consciousness, animal behavior, and biochemistry (Chapter 17). I propose, however, to explain recursion in stories from the array of Part II, Chapters 2 through 17. This recursion of painful events in individual stories is hopeful from a scientific point of view, because it suggests that there is extremely powerful organization which is evident in very complex levels of self-awareness.[1]

B) The hypotheses used for explanation are less interesting as an ad hoc series, more interesting as they fit simply together (Lakatos, 1970). Parsimony is important in all of science. For clinicians it is probably essential. An ad hoc series of explanations, a loose collection of equivalent notions, what is called eclecticism, works poorly. The clinician has to carry too much baggage. He hasn't time to sort through it all to find what he needs for a given occasion. He has to have an overall policy (John Scamman, personal communication), which requires some hierarchy of explanation. Then he is prepared to make the few moves which are possible in any hour he may have with a patient (Margulies and Havens, 1981).

C) Patients usually come demanding a change, being stuck or drifting in a direction that seems bad to them. They want movement in a different direction. What they never see is how their present position or drift is tied to a series of other structures, internal and external (Cronen, Johnson and Lannamann, 1982). Thus, they always ask for a change which is impossible within the system they operate onto themselves and with others. Therefore, an adequate explanation will not only generate an explanation of their present position, but also disclose what *other* phenomena are part of this complained-about situation. Also, what other phenomena will be altered if the patient adopts a different drift? What consequences, intended and unintended, will be likely to follow? This is the state or process we are asked to compute from our model as the "predicted phenomena to be observed." Of course, any given observing position will only afford a vantage point for seeing some consequences, while missing the chance to see others. Therefore, a theory is to be preferred which may allow the given observer to adopt the known observer positions that have been reliable for us. This helps to conserve the overall tradition. A new theory could generate new possibilities for observation, while losing others of proven value. It is better when the new retains the advantages of the old, while adding something further (Lakatos, 1970).

D) Finally, the criterion of tests: Of course, a practice aims to satisfy patients. This means they like the drift of their position after consultation better than their position before consultation. Extreme frustration, pain, or even tragedy seems to be averted. The stories improve. But the human capacity for self-deception and deception of others being so amazing, we need theory to explain what will obscure various unintended consequences. What will prevent looking against the grain of the patient's presentation?

What is often not included in the testing of theory is to see what operating with a given theory will do to the therapist over time. We are "part of the equation" (Skynner, 1981). What if certain kinds of useful helping erode the therapist? What if such helping makes the therapist more hateful to his students? Theory, therefore, will propose how best to read and reckon the difference in drift for both patients and therapists generated by a method. Theory will tell us what consequences may be worthy of our interest.[2]

Finally, any clinical theory will have its successes and failures. Sometimes the relevant structures tied to the desired direction of the patient will be seen; sometimes not. What is most important, therefore, is the method for situations when the method fails. This means a method continually inviting correction at every turn and proposing other observer positions when stuck. An observer with such a method is always ready to start anew, to pose the problem differently, to propose different hypotheses. This is a scientific method of methods.

Main Theme: Change Multiples, Closure Simplifies, for Living Systems

My problem is to explain the array of stories from Part II. My chief constrait is the need to be brief. My overriding concern is to have a method of methods which allows all of us to keep improving on our errors.

We will be misled into very many complicated and diverse answers from the different schools if we ask ourselves to explain the different changes described in the array. I propose we ask the opposite question: How do patients *not* make such sudden and profound changes? This is an interesting achievement. How do we close out the multiverse to stay ourselves?

It seems that the different schools observe this achievement of closure from only a few different positions. If the observing position of the school of the observer is able to afford an accurate appreciation of what is being held, then sudden and profound changes often occur along dimensions which are free to adjust. Students of sport will understand this instinctively. To become a good shooter in basketball, you must appreciate the few elements of positioning which have to be kept relatively stable. You have to be able to jump straight in the air, keep your eye on the rim and use, from the wrist, a light touch. Once you are able to keep these relatively constant, then you may begin to dodge, dart, stop suddenly, race forward, and what have you. You hold loosely to what is essential, which gives you the amazing grace of varying everything else about your movements. How do the different schools of psychotherapy arrive at such crucial observations in their own field? What are the decisive positions from which to observe?

The theoretical solution I offer here is an opposite to the solution of classical physics concerning the motion of physical objects. This appeared to be extremely complicated to the contemporaries of Galileo, Descartes and Newton, until Galileo noticed the "kinship between an object at rest and an object in motion is a straight line at constant speed" (March, 1970). This is the principle of inertia. Few such moving objects could be seen in those times, for they were not surrounded by a world gliding according to this principle, such as the railroad, the automobile, and so forth. "Thus it was quite a feat to come to the realization that it was not motion itself but deviation from simple constant motion for which a cause had to be sought. The essence of the experimental method is that when you finally get around to asking nature the right question she will give you a simple answer" (March, 1970, pp. 23-24).

For living systems the opposite is true: the concept of inertia in living systems leads to the complications, for then causes need to be sought for changes in motion and explanations of change in living systems become impossibly various and complicated. Living systems adapt or move continuously to fit their environments (Maturana, 1985). *This continuous change in motion can be assumed. What needs to be explained for living systems is how they stay put. The way in which they are organized to stay the same is what simplifies the field of living systems* (Maturana, 1985). Let us now see how this idea holds up in the face of the diversity of the array to be explained.

Closure from the Perspective of Psychoanalysis

Psychoanalysis began as an observation of secret desires which could be traced from hints, such as from Elisabeth von. R.'s pains in the legs (Chapter 2) or from the stage fright of the Croatian Musician (Chapter 3). A secret story could be put together after all of the allusions were tracked down, such as from the manifest elements of a dream.

I propose we think of the "return of the repressed" as one kind of insistent closure. The wishes will not go away. They stay put, they peak forth, they trip up the patient. The mammal will be a mammal, no matter how rudely or out of joint. Only when this is deeply appreciated by the patient, with the help of the therapist, is any other movement possible. Thus the Croatian Musician of Ferenczi is tormented until she can accept her own voluptuous outpouring. The Zoologist of Malan (Chapter 11) is stalled in his unseen revenge. The Fugitive from Georgia of Mann (Chapter 12) could not take her revenge either. Everyman of Sifneos (Chapter 13) is tied up until he can face his preoccupation with sexual possession. The body will come round. It cannot be stopped.

Patients become stuck, or driven down paths they decry, when they will not allow the animal in themselves expression. They oppose what can only be delayed, detoured, or displaced. Complications abound when the mammal is being dissociated, hidden during the daytime in the back rooms, or locked in the basement for years. Simple dissociations are possible behind these vertical or horizontal walls. Labyrinthine building projects may take up all the genius of the patient (Gedo, Chapter 9). Anxiety tells us when there is too much knocking on one of these walls, so we renew our repairs. But full relief only comes when the mammal prances forth.

Psychoanalysis sets up the possibility for observing this force of bodily need. Adaptations will be clumsy or fixed or destructive when the closure of the body is not appreciated. Sudden bursts of adaptiveness or steady improvement will follow the reconciliation with needs, for the continual clamor may relent. This is one kind of observation which is decisive for brief psychotherapy. The paradox is that no intrest in change is necessary for the therapist; he or she need only be interested in how the animal has to stay the same.[3]

Closure from the Perspective of the Analysis of Character

I hasten to say that psychoanalysts have long had many other interests than the "id" in us. They give equal or greater honor to what is set against the id, namely the "ego and its mechanisms of defense" (A. Freud, 1946) and the "superego" which stands in for the demands of society (S. Freud, 1921). They follow ever so closely the "resistances" which crop up from these two structures (Greenson, 1967). This often means an analysis which lasts an hour four or five times a week for five years or more.

Physicists lose interest when complications begin to abound, as they have in psychoanalysis. Their intuition is that a poor question is being asked of nature when the replies are so lengthy (March, 1970, pp. 23–24). I think Freud and Reich asked a better question, which is still asked in psychoanalysis but often forgotten. The question is: How might all these demands for defense and for meeting society close in a very single-minded way? Defense mechanisms and introjects may proliferate endlessly (Havens, 1984a). Perhaps this is because their unity has become a vanishing point.

Freud (1909) and Reich (1933) argue that the defenses may hide the class of defenses, as trees may hide the forest. So long as the class of moves is missed, the game may go on endlessly, because additional moves are always possible without threatening the game. The class of moves is the "constant attitude." Perhaps Reich confused his readers by calling this "the cardinal character resistance," as if the red thread were only one thread among the others. Rather, it is the cardinal who remains inviolate as he marshalls his troops in front of him. As long as he goes unrecognized, as long as he is not recognized as operating at a higher logical level than his defenses, then his game goes on. He will do whatever is necessary to maintain or close or shore up his "constant attitude," whether that attitude be one of resignation, or élan, or conniving. Adding moves, defenses or introjects — or subtracting them — is nothing for him. Any number of them may be borrowed or dropped, so long as this closure of the "constant attitude" is conserved. Seeing the defenses, introjects or desires, one by one, is relatively useless, as they are quite interchangeable when the constant attitude can be held back out of sight. This is an impenetrable wall which curves back for ever to its zero point, to resume.

The first great success of looking for a constant attitude was Freud's observation of the Rat Man (1909). Later followed his Wolf Man (1918) and a series of cases described by Reich in the twenties and thirties (1933 and 1948). The reader may remember Reich's appreciation of the passive-feminine attitude, my own of a modern counterpart (Chapter 4). Only when the utter determination of such an attitude is fully recognized, only when the amazing order of its contrivance is appreciated, will its hold be eased. Again, the paradox is that the therapist need have no interest in change, only in seeing what attitude has to be kept constant. This is the second kind of observation of closure which is decisive for brief psychotherapy. Davanloo (Chapter 14) is the modern brief therapist who takes this closure most seriously, although Malan and Mann and Sifneos also depend upon its recognition. The Little Blond Dutch Girl of Davanloo (Chapter 14) is such a tour de force.

Closure from the Interpersonal Perspective

Now the "constant attitude" is a transitional idea, for it may be posed inwardly or outwardly. Reich saw this but his emphasis falls more inward and bodily, as in how the child borrowed the defensive posture of an animal. A startling coherence may follow from such looking. Presently in my own practice I recognize a "rabbit," a "fox," and a "bullfrog." Each is very consistent in his or her own defensive posture. But many patients are difficult to characterize or put together in this way.

Many patients do not become coherent until we see what makes them worthwhile in relation to other people. Here is a third standpoint for observation, from which Alexander saw the desperate contributions of the Scientist (Chapter 5), Winnicott could hold out for the precious memory of childhood of Mrs. X (Chapter 7), Balint could see the "victory" of the Stationery Manufacturer (Chapter 8), and Sullivan could see the potential of the Housewife-Economist being held back (Chapter 6). Once the worthwhileness of the patient is found, the destructiveness falls into place, for the patient will do whatever is necessary to hold onto the worthwhile element.

The *feeling of security* is paramount, whether actual security is eroding or improving. Misconceived "security operations" now make sense as moves which give the right feeling (Chapter 6, Sullivan). This is how the patient must close him or herself, feeling secure therein, whatever disastrous effects this may have upon his or her actual standing. Sullivan and Alexander were extremely adept at appreciating this kind of situation (Chapters 5 and 6).[4]

Winnicott and Balint use the same idea but different terms. They borrowed from Melanie Klein the concepts of "the paranoid position" and "the depressive position." The paranoid position is a constant interpersonal attitude which holds that other people will never give you what you need, except to draw you in to hurt you. They are always, finally, bad or indifferent. You may only keep your security by keeping what is good locked away from their reaches. The constant interpersonal attitude of the depressive position acknowledges the good which can be gotten, but holds that one's own demands will destroy what is received — by insisting upon perfection, by taking revenge for slights, and so forth. Melancholy is a kind of security, therefore, since the attitude predicts the disappointment which will be inflicted by oneself.

Again, the possibility of seeing how security in relation to others is so coherently organized has little to do with being interested in change. The paradox is that this is a closure which has to be appreciated, which is allowed by the interpersonal perspective. You "meet the challenge of the case," as Winnicott would say, when you reach to the worthwhileness of the patient and to what destructiveness has been necessary on behalf of this security (Chapter

7). The road backward and the road forward are then appreciated; this allows the patient some latitude about how he or she will travel this necessary road when the way is well-known and accessible. Single sessions could open a way, as Winnicott and Balint and Sullivan and Alexander would often show.

Closure from the Systemic Perspective

Finally, a fourth position may simplify the wealth of possible observations. Often it appears that patients may put off the mammal in themselves forever. The body is rebuked. No constant attitude is discernible, no posture for hiding consistent. No security is obvious for this individual, who appears to have very little security in herself. But her apparent insecurity seems to keep the husband feeling superior and both children hovering about home. However the neighbors may be impressed by the imminent breakup of this cohort, it never happens. However the doctors try to improve her disposition, it is soon sour again. A fourth kind of closure may now be noticed by standing back to see the orchestration of the family game (Chapter 16). Such closure is all the more impressive when it is seen to recur through three or four generations. Therapists who take a stand against such a locomotive have given themselves a very, very long job.

Therapists who see the necessity of such a continuing closure, who can appreciate its conservation, offer degrees of freedom about *how* the individual or family members will meet this necessity. The reader may recall my Case of Bulimia, how a daughter had to wreck her body and confidence so her mother could feel herself a successful mother, so the daughter could be friends with the father, so the father could tolerate what was missing in his wife. Once this was appreciated, she looked for different ways to help her mother feel successful, to keep her mother from feeling threatened. She got her body and her confidence back in the bargain (Chapter 16).

TRANSITION

In summary, brief psychotherapy has become a technical possibility since we have had these four positions for observation from which closure or constraint on the diversity of adaptation in a given patient is evident. The patient can be seen to be organized in a singular way to come round to a recurrent powerful desire, to hold to a constant attitude, to defend something worthwhile from other people, to continue a family game. The appreciation of this sigular organization allows the patient latitude about how this necessity may be achieved. No patient needs help to change, only help to discern what has to be held at all costs.

If this much were understood, then there would be four different kinds of brief psychotherapy depending upon the observing position available to the therapist for recognizing the singular organization of the patient. Each kind would pose the necessity of closure in its own way, which would suggest a necessary class of moves, which would allow the patient to give up particular moves that he or she did not want to continue. Thus, we would see four different kinds of double description, specifying a necessary class, specifying variable moves.

Indeed, we have seen the success of such a viewpoint in the array of stories of Part II. To some extent, it is possible to see these four observing positions as relatively separable, as relatively successful and sufficient onto themselves. It is possible to hold strictly to the observing position of a psychoanalyst, an analyst of the constant attitude, an interpersonal interviewer, or a systemic one. Each will generate a double description, which will generate a degree of freedom for some patients.

But the stories of our patients are often more complicated. Think of the potential for complication in this way. The patient has to find some moves for bringing out his instincts. Psychoanalysis will see this difficulty. But the patient will be an observer of his own moves to do this. These observations must fit into a constant attitude, once adopted to allow the child-adult to feel right with himself. The analysis of character will see this attitude. But the patient will be an observer of his own attitude to see how this fits into being secure with other people. The patient has to feel right in relation to others, for which a certain class of security operations has been found to be successful. This will be seen by the interpersonal interviewer. But the patient will also be an observer of his own security operations to see how the security in individual relationships is contributing or not to the stability of the family game. This will be seen by the systemic interviewer.

Notice that the possibility of recurring observation of the previous level of organization generates a next level of organization, which then may be observed as well, and so forth until four different levels of organization or closure to stay the same have been generated. This is the capacity for complicated organization of the human being, which is made possible by his capacity for recursion of observation. This potential for complication is what makes explanation of recursion in stories so difficult for us. This is why our scientific model has to be able to generate complication in a relatively simple way, if we are to appreciate the "present and chronically recurring pain" in the stories of many of our patients.

Therefore, I will now propose how four different recursive levels of organization to stay the same will often bring about complicated situations which need to be appreciated. I pose four kinds of problems in appreciating complication: missing other levels of organization, eclecticism, fiction or continuous distortion, and contradictions between logical levels. Because of these common complications, our singular methods will often fail. This is the necessary development that I see for my main theme of closure. However, when we see how our methods fail, we prepare ourselves for such occasions, which may give us a method of methods. We will then have technical replies for complication, which I summarize in the recapitulation.

DEVELOPMENT

It may well be that there is no substitute for the therapist's having and showing respect and appreciation for his or her patient as an individual being. It may well be that various lines of research converge on this finding (David Kaye, personal communication). The "intentionality" of the interviewer is of very great importance (Karl Tomm, unpublished). But the ability to carry out such intentions is also necessary, and complicated in several different ways. "Every being cries out to be read differently" (Simone Weil),[5] but we have to know something about the difficulties of reading individuals. I see four kinds of complications.

How to Miss Closure at Another Position for Observation

Perhaps the most grateful part for a therapist to play is to be looking from the analytic position and find some tremendous feeling which the patient has been holding at bay, hoping to be found out. The catharsis is tremendous. The patient is amazed. The doctor is terrific. I envy Freud his Elisabeth Von R. (Chapter 2), Ferenczi his Croatian Musician, (Chapter 3). What a pleasure. We have had our few as well, including the Case of the Inadmissible Roar and the Case of the Murderous Medical Student, described in Chapters 2 and 3. A more complicated case is our Case of the Modern Passive-Feminine Character, described in Chapters 4, 6, and 13, but it too shares in this aspect of profound relief.

Mostly this will not happen. This closure of the animal proves weaker than closure in the other three ways. "The constant attitude" is an organization to be reckoned with more commonly, as shown in the very same case of the Modern Passive-Feminine Character. Only when such a constant attitude is appreciated will the flood come booming through the wall. Only then do you have access to these tides, for which a suitable bridge may be located.[6] If the fascination with true feelings could miss the closure of the constant attitude, then a fascination with any observing position could miss the other three positions equally.

The constant attitude of passive dependency may be gotten right, but the doctor may miss the skill with which the patient mobilizes so many helpers. Such a doctor may be asking his patient to give up her greatest talent. Of course, she refuses. A remarkable security operation is being demonstrated.

The doctor may see the power of a medical distraction, but fail to see how the "ill" daughter is helping her mother stay close, which keeps mother from being too disappointed in father. Such a doctor might interrupt medical distraction, only to worsen the turmoil at home.

Finally, the doctor may be quite astute about the family stability, but miss the roar of the patient, which can barely be contained. He is out of touch. Clever, but strange. So the patient feels no rapport and leaves.

In summary, the fascination with any one observing position will often lead to missing closure at a different level of organization which is decisive for the patient. The patient will feel misunderstood. Often that is the end of the relationship with the doctor.

Eclectism

If the doctor is to see closure from different levels of organization, he had better not be scattered. This is quite unnerving for most patients. Most patients like the feeling of "control" achieved from a routine which is easy to follow.

Most patients will become comfortable with a certain formal recursion in the interview. Most patients soon grasp that I will proceed from *problem* to *inquiry* to *closing message*. This is analogous to the *beginning, middle* and *end* of any formal scheme for a television program. Audiences become coupled to such routines.

Then it is possible to design or have degrees of freedom within this recursion. I will come to that element of surprise momentarily. But without the formal recursion, you are quite likely to get a content recursion, with the therapist varying the form of his struggling quite a lot. This will entertain the patient as a new regularity.

Fiction

If the time period of the interview has to have some minimal definition for both patient and doctor to be comfortable to proceed together, most patients will extend their control of that definition of time and space so that it becomes routine. Thus, we are subjected to the series of banal maneuvers described by Sullivan (Chapter 6) as the "stream of generalities," "the extended bill of goods," "the highly improbable accomplishment," the notion which is "off the beam," the "damaging admission," and "the routinely futile operation." If we allow this takeover, we become useless. The interview has become a farce, conducted by the patient.

Such a farce begins innocently. The patient purports to give an "objective" description of him or herself. The doctor falls for such a description, because he loves the objective landscape of breaking through walls of resistance, fording rivers of instinct and building bridges missed in development (Gustafson, 1984).[7] Most presentations by patients which purport to be objective point in a direction one hundred eighty degrees from the direction which will be useful for explaining the patient's behavior. The patient is so influenced by "the other people in the room" that he would orient the therapist as he has been oriented himself. This will make little sense. Both will stay stuck.

Just look again at the orientation offered to Alexander, Sullivan, Winnicott, and Balint by the four patients I have presented. Alexander was invited to see a generous Scientist who could not force himself to give even more;

Sullivan, a Housewife-Economist who was too lazy to run the household; Winnicott, a Mrs. X. who had never gotten anything; Balint, a Stationery Manufacturer who was being humiliated by defeat.

These were all fictions which were convenient, both for the patient and for the important persons in each of their lives. If we were so foolish as to take them literally, to reify these fictions as "walls" to be "broken through," much mischief could be set afoot, confronting such "constant attitudes," looking for the "true feelings" of the generous Scientist, the lazy Housewife Economist, the worthless Mrs. X, and the humiliated Stationery Manufacturer. The patient digs in against such enterprise, and a perpetual struggle may ensue. Often, such a struggle only continues what the important people in the patient's life have been waging with him or her already. They fight the patient. They tolerate him. Either way, they help to confirm the fictional battle. Such is a perpetual game.

This is routine in our Brief Therapy Clinic. Most of our patients offer such a game. For example, we see many hysterical patients such as the Daughter of Soap Opera (Chapter 11), who offer some amazing medical distraction, such as hyperventilation. Inexperienced residents are inclined either to let such an event run on and on, showing their empathy, or to confront the "defense," showing their vigor. Either way the fiction is made substantial, like a mountain. This is why residents are very surprised to see that such a "massive structure" can be given the slip in a few seconds or minutes. It is a mountain only when it is allowed to be a mountain. Actually, it begins as a small device to jog us from the conversation about the evening when our patient became upset, listening to her roommate and the roommate's boyfriend. Nothing more. It only points one hundred and eighty degrees from where we want to look further. It is only a device she has watched her mother use a thousand times. No doubt her mother would smile to see her understudy.

Contradiction Between Logical Levels

Here is the final and most difficult complication of all. While we are tempted to see a patient who has reduced herself or himself to a medical distraction, a second-class citizen, or an individual without confidence, etc., we are actually getting behavior which is rich in contradictions at several logical levels of organization.

The interpersonal observers with whom we have been concerned (Chapters 5–10) have often seen three logical levels in contradiction. Consider briefly a message from Davanloo to The Little Blond Dutch Girl (Chapter 14) and a message from Sullivan in consultation concerning the Housewife-Economist (Chapter 6). The Little Blond Dutch Girl complains of "depression, crying spells, a constant fear of rejection. . . . " Here is a first logical level. A second is that she behaves in such a contradictory, evasive and passive way with Davanloo that he will get nowhere with her. Here is her constant attitude about proceeding with him. A third is that she desperately wants him to get through to her. The Housewife-Economist of Sullivan has similar complaints at the first logical level. A second is Sullivan's idea that this is "more encouraging than otherwise. . . , "showing she is intended for more ambitious situations. A third is that her being stuck is quite convenient for upholding her husband's superiority.

Notice how Davanloo and Sullivan "work the opposing currents" (Havens, Chapter 10) differently, to move from the presenting complaints. Davanloo sees the patient as passive, evasive, and contradictory in her behavior with him in the interview, but also desperate to be found out. Sullivan sees the patient being bogged down as a sign of ambition, but also a convenience for the husband. My point in comparing the two messages is that there are several ways to break up the routinization of complaining and to break up the "objectivity" of a view which is merely convenient for staying the same. The second and third logical levels in both messages are completely contradictory.

Working the opposing currents is extremely powerful, one way or another. I find it nearly always fishes up some disturbances, for the two extremes are both acceptable. This gives the patient room to step forward. The trouble is that it is successful. Something important comes up between patient and therapist. This may be fine for the therapist, but it is usually not well for the other relations the patient wants to maintain. This is where the patient is likely to disconfirm the finding, taking the discussion right back to zero, where it began.

I am reminded of Ricci and Selvini Palazzoli's (1984) discussion of a very common but very commonly misunderstood sorrow. A young man is wooed by the director of a firm to join the management. So soon as he joins, the director appears to give him notice no longer. He is very hurt and angry. He is disconfirmed. No one tells him that the director has put him at a distance because this distance is convenient for the director's relations with all of middle management. He keeps from having favorites.

Something like this happens to therapists. They are allowed a special audience, until the patient turns around to face his other relations, whereupon this audience with the therapist is disconfirmed. The "return to zero" learning is extremely disconcerting for the therapist. But this is a move in many family games — to arouse outsiders in this way and then drop them. How may we be prepared to observe such events with equanimity? How may we see the necessity of such closure? Three logical levels will not suffice for mapping a family game which has three such logical levels. The therapist will need four, to map three, to retain his equanimity as an observer, to keep from being pulled in and under (Chapter 15, Bateson).

The reader may rightly ask what on earth is going on in such families. Selvini Palazzoli et al. (1978a) reply that families appear to deteriorate when they complicate themselves to hold together in conditions of increasing strain between the old way of one generation and the new way of another. The contradictions of the family double and quadruple.

The old generation may rule by direct intimidation: "Do it, or be left behind." There are only two logical levels here: the complaints, and the necessary constant attitude which organizes the complaints.

The middle generation, which has been wounded by having high hopes which collapsed, is often more overtly genteel. It will not insist. Rather, it will seek to control the definition of relationships, while disconfirming that this is going on. These people ask for help, but behave to make it impossible, while disconfirming that they do this. Davanloo and Sullivan catch these people at their game.

The third generation, defending itself against the middle generation, may be most devious of all. If the therapist catches them at the game they play, this threatenes to destablize them with their parents. Therefore, the job is to catch them, but to propose the necessity of this being obscured. This is a fourth logical level, which includes the complaints, the necessary constant attitude, the disconfirmation of its effectiveness, and the domain in which this operation is perfect.

If I propose that we often have to be introduced to such labyrinths with four logical levels, the reader may well complain that two logical levels, or double description, is quite enough difficulty already. Anthony (1976) describes this struggle in a parent of one of his patients in his essay called, "Between Yes and No":

The mother of a 16-year-old girl sought advice for her daughter who was dating a "mature" man of 24. . . . The daughter had asked whether she could visit this man in his apartment where he proposed to give her dinner. "Here I made a big mistake: I at once said 'no,' and as soon as I said it, I realized that it was a king-sized blunder. I had made it impossible for her to do anything but keep the assignation. Yet I could not have brought myself to the point of saying 'yes.' It would have stuck in my throat, and I would have simply choked. Why isn't there something one can say between 'yes' and 'no' which would have allowed us to go on talking and perhaps, who knows, changing one's point of view?" (p. 323)

Anthony proposes that the therapist of an adolescent needs to devise such a transitional area between "yes" and "no" which allows him and his patient to "go on talking and perhaps, who knows, changing one's point of view." I find this a very helpful idea, but an idea which has to be more complicated to be useful to many adults.

A story involving myself may explain my meaning. Recently I participated in a weeklong conference of therapists, which was said to be a series of "conversations." Actually, it was mostly a series of lectures by an individual of some considerable originality. He lectured and we asked questions. Our "conversations" consisted of meeting in small groups to think of what questions we would ask him. Naturally, this was somewhat galling for a very able group of therapists, but the atmosphere was pleasant. It was made more difficult by the difficulty of following some of this man's thinking, which eluded many in the group. An underground of discontent was brewing.

This broke out in the final evening, when one of the therapists purported to give a paper, but actually arranged something like a graduation mockery of the faculty. She directed a series of skits to illustrate the ideas of the great man. The atmosphere was hilarious, as the skits delivered a considerable punch at the great man, while seeming to be good-natured.

I did not find them good-natured, this being my own response, which I could not deny to myself. I backed out of the skitting, whereupon I was asked afterwards by one of the organizers just why I seemed to dislike the proceedings. By then I had been strengthened by several discussions with friends who had also resented the goings-on.

The organizer asked me if I did not think the event clever? I said, "Yes," it was extremely clever. He asked me if I did not think it was appreciated by one and all? I said "Yes," it was extremely popular, obviously meeting a great need of the gathering. He asked me then what was my problem with the event and why didn't I like it? I said, "No," I didn't like this way of fighting back against a powerful intellectual argument by storing up ammunition. Perhaps this was necessary to medical students concerning their faculty, but I did not like it in able therapists. But I had to agree with him, "Yes," that it had been necessary, since the group had indeed acted like medical students. They must have felt that way, whether I liked it or not.

Therefore, my answer to him was: "Yes . . . yes . . . no . . . and yes." My point is that such situations are common for us adults. If we are not to become lost in confusion, we may need to keep track of complex responses at different logical levels. I felt many of my colleagues to be very confused in this event, judging from some of the distorted looks on their faces as they were pulled into some sexual interpretations of the great man's ideas. It was funny, but humiliating, all the same, for themselves — closing with the group, with relief, but wrong for some attitude in themselves, hence the contortion. Surely, it was more complex than that.[8]

I am saying that adult life in our complex society often pulls us like this strange event. We have a feeling pulling one way, an attitude pulling another, a need to arrange our colleagues in another, and a family game which could be something else again. The "sea of opposing currents" can be turbulent.

Brief therapy can be relatively simple if but one of our ways of closure goes unappreciated. We therapists can then supply the missing appreciation — for some unrecognized feeling which will not go away, for some unrecognized constant attitude which defies us, for some unrecognized security operation which cannot be spared, for some unrecognized family game more powerful than a locomotive in which the patient has to ride. These are grateful parts for us.

But life events are often more twisting, like my conference of therapists. Hence, our job becomes more interesting and more difficult by far, to modulate between the several points of observation, to put together messages of three and four levels, to catch the patient in the place where he or she is actually twisting. I'm glad for this myself, because there is endless fascination in helping patients, in helping myself, out of such binds. If the patient has lived very long in such a twisting world as my conference, he or she will need no less.

RECAPITULATION: A METHOD OF METHODS

If most singular methods for observing how patients stay the same will often be defeated by the complications I have described, what then is the method of methods by which I propose to be in readiness for my continual defeat? I would like the theoretical lines of such a method of methods to be as clear as possible. Hence my recapitulation.

Becoming an Observer of How We Stay the Same

All along, I have relied on an idea which I understand most clearly from Maturana, which has been sketched in the background. I prefer this, for most readers will not understand the direct presentation of Maturana's thinking (Chapter 17). I find it better to keep this thinking to myself and use it by allusion.

But once I must bring it forward in this theoretical discussion. Maturana thinks we are drifting, as living systems, in perfect and continuous adjustment with ourselves as closed entities and with our environment, which is continuously triggering us to respond as our structure allows us to respond. We also drift in concert with others by becoming a medium for one another which is mutually stabilizing, which Maturana calls structural coupling.

From this way of thinking, I only want to draw out one implication from the many which are possible. If we do not like the drift which is carryng us along, we have already become observers of ourselves. But this "no" which we say to ourselves and which we sometimes bring to a therapist is usually less powerful than the course to which we are holding. We hold on without thinking, without being observers of holding on. Only when we observe what we hold onto is it possible to dislike some of the moves which achieve what is necessary, while liking other moves better. Therefore, the crucial observations in psychotherapy concern what must stay the same.

A trivial example from sports may make the argument more familiar. Most who play tennis know what it is like to become very tight with anxiety in important matches. If you have had that experience, you also know it is useless to tell yourself to "relax." The only way out of such a tense state is to become an observer. The most useful observation to locate, I find, is to notice some detail which contributes to the tightening. For example, I may notice I am not outstretched on my service, but cramping it, which makes the shot hit from a lower point, which makes more errors, which makes more cramping, etc. — a vicious spiral. Whereas, if I notice the cramping, and stretch out my toss again, I get more fine serves, which allows me to stay outstretched, which relieves my anxiety, etc. In other words, I have found a different drift for my game, for the time being.

All of this follows from my ability to observe myself serving, to see several different ways to serve, some of which I may dislike, some like. As Bateson would say, the class is serving, the high toss is one move, the low another move, within that class. But I have no access to these degrees of freedom if I do not have the presence of mind to watch or observe serving. I will serve automatically and the serve will drift in one way or another automatically. When a drift is poor, often one will not think of observing, which is not necessary to our activity at all.[9] However, it is the only freedom that we have, the freedom to train ourselves to become observers, so that we will think of observing ourselves when tight situations occur.[10]

I am proposing that we are in the strongest position as therapists if we are trained to observe the family game, to observe the interpersonal maneuvers which contribute to that game, to observe the constant attitude which follows from such maneuvers, to observe the animal feelings which are excluded by such an attitude and are constantly at bay. *For all of these continually tighten us up.* Once we become observers of these necessary kinds of closure, we have access to the different moves for doing what is necessary to us.

Formal Recursion in the Interview

If we must have access to the different positions for observation of staying the same, we must move in a sequence which is calming in its reliability. I propose that all interviews move from *problem* to *hypothesis* to *message-giving*, from *beginning* to *middle* to *end*. Chapters 19, 20, 21, and 22 will describe such a sequence in the beginning, middle and end games of brief therapy.

Working the Opposing Currents

If we see that understanding is only a momentary correspondence between a part of what is in the patient's mind and a part of what is in the doctor's mind, we will continually revise our understanding, sentence by sentence (Havens, Chapter 10). If distortion by the patient is continual to stay the same, then only an "ear to ear" method will be reliable when the patient purports to be objective, when "objectivity" is constructed in spatial metaphor. Only "sound" which is non-spatial will carry the accents which mark the context. Not quite — gesture will also comment silently on the text. But we cannot depend upon alone upon the eye and the ear. We pull with the flow and against the flow, to see and hear and feel the strength of opposing currents.

Complexity and Simplicity

My argument is for complexity, for being able to comprehend the logical relation of the four familiar kinds of closures I have outlined, for being able to comprehend "yes, yes, no, and yes" in unfamiliar situations. As Laing (1961) once emphasized, some patients are tied in very difficult knots. Perhaps it is better to emphasize that the knots are continually being tied all around us.

I find my long-term patients are all this difficult. I agree, therefore, with Havens and Gedo and many, many other writers about long-term therapy, that such labyrinths may take years to understand. I find many of my brief cases are also as complex (Chapter 16, A Case of Bulimia), while some, as Sullivan suggested (Chapter 6) are more like sketches. I like to be prepared for either extreme.

This complexity needs a little justification. After all, I began this discussion of theory by saying that physicists lose interest in complicated theories. I still agree with them. I am saying that complication is sometimes the only way to save tradition, such as the continuity of a family, of an organization, or even of an individual. To stay the same—to hold on to what was dear to our grandparents, our parents, and ourselves—sometimes we must complicate ourselves.

I am not saying that our theories need to be so complicated, only that they must be able to *generate* the complicated phenomena that are of so much interest to our patients. Unlike physicists we had better not lose interest when the going is tangled. We want relatively clear and coherent models for generating the phenomena of the tangle. We explain the patient's findings, how to stay the same in his world. This meets our first and second criteria for scientific explanation.

But we must also generate new findings with the same model. We must generate degrees of freedom from the very explanations of how to stay in the same tangle. Such explanations must be tested over sufficient time. Fine explanations of the patient's phenomena which leave him in the same place have failed our third and fourth criteria for scientific explanations. They have the poetry of science, but they are wrong. This may often occur, for we only make successive approximations to the relevant structures which hold the patient's closure in place. A scientific method of methods will recognize when an explanation is fine but has no effect. The hypothesis then needs to be revised, posed, and the response watched again. And so forth.

But such a method of methods will often have to reckon with something beautiful in structure which is not seen in the physical sciences—this complication in the human character which is passionate. I saw three examples together in the Hedley Smith Room of the Ashmolean Museum in Oxford University this past summer; these reminded me of what needs to be appreciated in our patients in psychotherapy. I saw Rodin's "Balzac," which has so many planes of depth in the face that the head seems half again longer. I saw Daumier's "Ratapoil," which has this fellow with so many angles to his gait that he points in all directions, ready for wits on all sides; I could see how such planes and angles could defend a man well. Finally, I saw Rodin's "Dancer Examining the Sole of Her Right Foot," with her body poised with all the angles of Ratapoil across the way, but ready to fly, gathered up before taking off. So I thought I could see how extraordinary defense and feats of flying depend on a sufficient number of planes, angles, or dimensions.

Saul Bellow has written:

I stand in awe of the genius of the race. But a large part of this *genius is devoted* to lying and seeming what you are not. We love when this man Ulysses comes back in disguise for his revenge. But suppose he *forgot what he came back for* and just sat around day in, day out in the disguise. This happens to many a frail spirit who forgets what *the disguises* are for, doesn't *understand complexity*, or how to *return* to simplicity. From telling different things to everyone, he forgets what the case is originally and what he wants himself. How rare is simple thought and pureheartedness. Even a moment of pureheartedness I bow to, down to the ground. That's why I think well of you when you tell me you're in love. I appreciate this durability and I'm a lover myself. (1953, pp. 484–485)[11]

I believe Bellow is entirely right about this danger, which is a serious hazard for those who may adopt a systemic perspective. One may indeed become lost in disguises. It is dangerous to spend too much time in labyrinths. One becomes richly joined to them. This is why I believe in coming round full circle to the analytic position, which is interested in the simplicity of the child and his dream screen, in himself or his family as the center of the world. I stay interested in the bodily attitude of the child defending himself as a rat or a trout. I want to retain the capacity for simplicity, even as I also need to find the capacity for deciphering the labyrinth — both. This is the complex secret, to keep this range of positions for observations. Now I have to describe a sequence, how I build up the necessary minimum explanation to appreciate my patient, to go as far as necessary.[12]

Every being cries out to be read differently.

—Simone Weil, Auden and Kronenberger, 1962

PART IV

A Sequence for a Method of Methods

Any system which is without its paradoxes is by the same token as suspicious as an exact correspondence of several witnesses in a trial at the Old Bailey.

—Samuel Palmer, Auden and Kronenberger, 1962

INTRODUCTION

There are many possible methods for choosing how to borrow from the tradition of psychotherapy. I call these the methods of methods. The reader of Part III will understand in a general way what I ask from my own method of methods. I ask for perspectives which locate convergence in the entire field, which I find in the concepts of closure. I ask for a sequence in interviewing which has a clear beginning, middle and end. Both of these principles bring about a relative simplicity. But I also ask for ways to reckon with the potential deceptiveness and diversity, contradictions and complexity of the human being. I want methods which allow me to work opposing currents. I want methods which allow me to generate the highly complex and contradictory systems or organizations which are possible in our patients. The two latter principles pull for continual self-revision, as opposed to self-reinforcement, of method.

The reader who accepts such general principles about how to use the tradition of psychotherapy may not know how to carry them forward. Here I propose to show one way to operate with the necessary simplicity and complexity. A survey of what lies ahead in the next four chapters may help the reader to see the broad outline of this method of methods.

I see a very consistent reply in the tradition of psychotherapy to the question about what is wrong or ill with our patients. They come to us because of some painful experiences or behaviors or interactions which they cannot control. They have not only pain, but, in Mann's phrase, "present and chronically recurring pain." What then do we do? We look for some rigid mechanism which could be triggered over and over again to generate such a recurrent pain.

I see four ways in our tradition to generate such a mechanism. Each describes a different kind of closure or conservatism as crucial. Rigidity occurs because of some desperate attempt to bring about closure in emergency circumstances. Such a successful, albeit rigid, move will later have unforseen consequences, since the rigid mechanism can be easily triggered, since this will become a present and chronically recurring source of pain.

We may become rigid in how we close out our needs or instincts. We may become rigid in how we borrow a constant attitude or gesture about ourselves. We may become rigid in the prevailing security operations we utilize with other people. We may become rigid in our loyalty to a vicious, circular family (or institutional) game. Any rigidity, such as in these four different kinds of closure, is both a great success and a great failing. The rigidity succeeds in protecting a crucial vulnerability. The rigidity fails in that it is continually triggered to bring about unforseen consequences which are painful.

The very first concern I have is whether or not to probe such a rigidity. This is the subject of Chapter 19, The Opening Game: Preliminary Interviews. I am most interested in the extremes states of the patient, when the patient has been in greatest pain, despair or terror, when the patient has been helped most by another individual. I seek to discover in advance what is likely if I probe into the rigid mechanism which is both protecting and limiting: whether suspending this rigid mechanism will put the patient into very dangerous circumstances; whether this suspension has potential for improvement.

When I am convinced I can probe the rigidity without undue risk, with probable success, I proceed to a trial therapy, usually two hours in duration. This is the subject of Chapter 20, The Opening Game: Trial Therapy. The aim for me follows that of Winnicott, to reach the illness of the patient and to reach his or her well-being. Access to these extremes in the patient will be gotten by finding the loose end of the patient's preoccupation, by positive connotation of the patient's attempt to conserve one of the crucial constancies, and by working the opposing currents back and forth until we reach both the worthwhileness of the patient and the rigidity which brings about such pain. A working hypothesis about what is getting triggered over and over again to bring about this pain will give some hope of improvement.

But the improvement will not be secure until the several uses of the rigid mechanism are identified. The working hypothesis has to be improved until it specifies how the mechanism works in the service of several crucial constancies to bring about the polyphony of the illness. This is the work of The Middle Game, described in Chapter 21. This work is analogous to poetic construction, in that many different elements have to be brought together with considerable concentration or intensity (Eliot, 1919). Change becomes possible when the patient sees what he or she has to hold onto or conserve. Then the rigid move utilized for such purposes is only one of many possible moves that will accomplish the necessary purpose. It will no longer be triggered automatically when such purposes are aroused. I describe a brief therapy which is brief by virtue of the economy of conception, rather than brief by virtue of limiting the time in advance. The "skill," as Sullivan wrote, "consists in very considerable measure of doing a lot with very little—making a rather precise move which has a high probability of achieving what you're attempting to achieve, with a minimum of time and words" (1954, p. 224).

Once a good result is gotten, the final technical problem is to gauge and reckon with the effects of subtracting the therapist from the equation of the successful relationship. This is the subject of Chapter 22, The End Game. There is a high likelihood of the patient's making a serious attempt to wreck his or her success in such a conclusion. Some of the common maneuvers are crude in their savagery, some very complicated and replete with contradictions. They are attempts to obviate the pain of breaking up a successful relationship. If unrecognized, they will continue as a kind of rigidity, which continues to be triggered, which continues the recurrent pain.

Just as the entire course of a brief therapy may be seen as having its opening, middle and end game, any particular session may be seen as a microcosm of such thinking. The opening is concerned with where to take hold. The middle is for getting different illuminations of this focus. The end provides a concluding punctuation. Condense, widen, and condense again. Exposition, development and recapitulation. This rhythm proposes a method of methods, allowing all of the different methods to have a say about the location of the problem, the hypotheses or the concluding message.

Finally, I would like the reader to keep in mind that I do not propose any attempt by the therapist to change the patient. No such finagling is described or necessary. My entire aim is to be clear about what the patient has to hold onto or conserve. Such appreciation will allow the patient many new moves. A moment's consideration of the usual difficulties of developmental transitions may make my final point clear. Individual histories are like the histories of entire peoples in that certain periods bring in many contingent, unforeseen situations, "only one emergency following upon another as wave follows upon wave" (Fisher, 1935, p. v). The usual response is desperate rigidity, as the in-

dividual seeks to conserve certain crucial constancies against erosion. This rigidity may make matters worse, since it is poorly adapted to the new situations. A vicious cycle sets in. However, if the individual is helped to appreciate what he is desperately trying to hold onto or conserve, then the moves for such ends will not be obligatory, but variously deployed to accommodate the new, disturbing circumstances. I believe such an appreciation of the patient also proposes to the patient a kind of scope or dignity which he or she may lose as he or she seems to fail. I do not suggest by such positive connotation that our patients are not involved in evil—not at all. Only that the circles of hell are perpetual without the discovery of better intentions.

19. *The Opening Game: Preliminary Interviews*

WE OFFER a semester of help in our Brief Therapy Clinic only after a two-to-three hour "trial therapy" (Davanloo, 1978, 1980, Chapter 14) appears to be helpful. The conduct of trial therapy is the subject of the next chapter. The purpose of a preliminary interview discussed here is to decide whether or not to invite the patient to take a leap into such a long and deep inquiry (Gustafson, 1984).

The doctors and nurses in the Student Health Service at our university know that the procedure of brief therapy is plausible for "relatively healthy" students with some recurrent distress who want to talk it over with us. Mostly, they refer to us plausible cases, since most of them have had five years of interaction with us and our Clinic.

How do we decide whether to go farther with the patient or not? Our thinking about this decision is very straightforward. We are interested in whether the patient is looking for the kind of help we are giving. Some are misguided towards us by their families, friends, acquaintances, teachers, doctors, or nurses. The referring person and the patient may share some unusual ideas about how to use us (Selvini Palazzoli et al., 1980a). Therefore, our first interest is: How did the patient finally decide to call on us?

If the patient appears to be after something we could give, then we are interested in two further questions. The order of these two questions will vary. One is how the patient has been able to get help or to allow others to help him or her. This is what we call the best news. The second is how the patient feels and thinks and acts at his or her worst. This is what we call the bad news. We want to reckon these two extremes.

If the patient is after something we might give, if the patient has gotten help in a serious way from other people, if the patient at worst has been in no serious danger, then we are likely to offer a trial therapy. If answers to any of these three questions are negative, we will decline to go further and propose some alternative kind of help to the patient. About half of our referrals are accepted for trial therapy, half sent elsewhere.

The reader will recognize that this policy concerning selection in the Brief Therapy Clinic is cautious. This is because I do not want beginning therapists and their patients to be taking unusual chances; rather, I want them to begin an exploration with a high likelihood of success. In my own private practice, I run some greater risks, hopefully with my eyes open and the patient well advised about his or her alternatives. I'll say more about that later.

While our aims for the preliminary interview in the Brief Therapy Clinic may be straightforward, the technical agility necessary to the job may be subtle. Yet I do not agree with David Malan (1979) that preliminary interviews are the most difficult interviews of all, requiring the most experience and skill in psychiatry. I have watched most of our senior residents who are quick and sensitive learn to be reasonably able at these interviews after one year in the clinic.

I therefore propose to explain first to the reader what I find reliable to teach about selection in a single year in the clinic. Secondly, I propose to explain the common errors, which a subtle knowledge might avoid. Thirdly, I end with a discussion of how we propose the trial therapy to the patient we accept, which will be a bridge to the next chapter on that subject.

A Reliable Procedure

First let me say a few words about the usual atmosphere for these interviews proposed by our shared attitude as a team in the clinic. I have always proposed a certain challenge to the residents about these first meetings, what Winnicott called "meeting the challenge of the case" (1965a). I give the interviewing resident one half-hour to find out why the patient has come to us, who has been most helpful to him or her, and what the darkest hours have led the patient to do, feel, and think. Then the resident is to present his or her findings to his or her peers and myself. The residents become keen about this challenge, which conveys something hopeful to the patient.

If this first meeting goes well, the patient feels it is a special occasion, as Winnicott wrote concerning his consultations with children:

. . . in explanation of the very great confidence which children can often show in myself (as in others doing similar work) on these special occasions, special occasions that have the quality that has made me use the word sacred. Either this sacred moment is used or it is wasted. If it is wasted the child's belief in being understood is shattered. If on the other hand it is used, then the child's belief in being helped is strengthened. (1971b, pp. 4–5)

I think this is equally true for adults, who might prefer the same idea as put in more adult language by Sullivan, who said that the patient becomes more hopeful when he or she is asked questions in an expert way (Chapter 6). If we provide these situations described by Winnicott and Sullivan, we will get views in the preliminary interview and the trial therapy which we are not likely to ever get again. Alexander and French (Chapter 5) put this best:

The analyst during this period may be compared to a traveler standing on top a hill overlooking the country through which he is about to journey . At this time it may be possible for him to see his whole anticipated journey in perspective. When once he has descended into the valley, this perspective must be retained in the memory or else it is gone. From this time on, he will be able to examine small parts of this landscape in much greater detail than was possible when he was viewing them from a distance, but the broad relations will no longer be so clear. (1946, p. 109)[1]

This attitude about an unforgettable view of the patient becoming available to us also contributes to the keen spirit of the inquiry.

A few words of a more mundane nature are necessary about our arrangements in the clinic. Before the resident meets the patient, he or she is oriented by three sources of preliminary findings. First, the medical chart gives some idea of the recent history between the referring doctor or nurse and the patient, including the stated idea for the referral to us. If this interaction has been very involved, the resident may be well advised to think of the interview which will follow as a consultation to the patient *and* the referring person. If the interaction has been brief, the interview may be addressed more to the patient. Secondly, the resident will study the symptom checklist just completed by the patient before the interview, which is an SCL-90.[2] Thirdly, the resident will look through a brief questionnaire,[3] also just completed by the patient, which includes a list of family members, a few medical questions, and a few questions about "What specific reason made you come to the clinic now? Describe your major problem or difficulty in your own words," etc.

All three of these written communications get the resident thinking in advance about the questions he or she must probe in the half-hour interview. I ask the resident to state these preliminary hypotheses in advance of meeting the patient. This is very useful for two reasons. One is that certain traps may be recognized from the written communications that would be mysterious if the resident were not alerted in advance. An involved relationship with the referring doctor or nurse could go unmentioned, when the medical difficulty or disappointment in that relationship had led to the referral to us. An overall symptom pattern might not be evident in a half-hour, which could be seen at a glance on the SCL-90, such as polyneurotic presentation of anxiety, depression, and insecurity which includes hysterical, somatic, obsessive, compulsive, phobic, and paranoid complaints. The questionnaire might hint of unusual hopes, which would not be spoken of directly in the interview. The doctor often is warned in these written communications, if he or she is alert to such possibilities.

The five, ten, or sometimes fifteen minutes spent here is like the preliminary meeting of the Milan team before it meets with a family (Chapter 16). They think in advance because they believe that doctors like themselves are usually not as clever as the families they will be meeting, so the doctors need to be more deliberate to catch up with the families. After all, the families have been in training for their first visit for generations! I see no reason to think any less of individual patients who come to visit us. In a way they have even more advantage over us, because their families are hidden from sight. We are quite tempted to underestimate them, since they appear to be visiting us on their own. Therefore, the survey of the written communications helps us to be a little less likely to walk into some of the common traps which will be set right away.

The reader may be concerned that preliminary written communications which are used to make preliminary hypotheses are prejudicial. Yes, we do run this risk. But it is less of a risk than the reader might think, since we hold our preliminary hypotheses in a very tentative way, looking to be proven wrong. We enjoy reversals. A patient who announces herself in advance in writing as unworthy of our interest may be much the more promising. And vice versa.

THE YOUNG WOMAN WITH NO SELF-CONFIDENCE

Let us walk through a preliminary interview which is of average difficulty. The medical chart on this 22-year-old young woman was a little unusual, because we learned she had been struck unconscious by an automobile a year before and had nearly died of complications in the hospital. Somehow, she had survived and now seemed to have no medical complaints at all. Who would complain after an experience like that?

Indeed, the SCL-90 only showed the usual findings of depression and insecurity in relation to people. Ordinarily, this is a good sign to see a disturbance which is bounded. The patient had written in the questionnaire: "No specific event—feelings of insecurity/low self-image that won't go away and are affecting interpersonal relationships. . . . I feel that I'm not interesting, not fun to be around, not a good friend. . . . I either think that I'm not good enough for them or that something is drastically wrong with them if they like me and consequently they're not good enough for me. . . . I am especially afraid that I will never be able to have a normal relationship with a man." This also is not an unusual presentation. However, the patient, in listing the family members, noted that her older brother had died several years before.

This particular interview was conducted by one of our residents with his three peers and myself watching, because we only had one patient at the appointed hour on that particular day.[4] I may, therefore, report the preliminary thinking. We were struck by two impressions. One was that this individual had been hit hard by two disasters, which would be very unusual for one so young. The second was that the symptom pattern and the chief complaint were routine, calling for the usual questions to differentiate relatively ordinary depression and insecurity with friends and with going out with men from the major disorders that could present in this sheep's clothing.

What emerged when we saw this patient? It did appear that this young woman was very upset about recent attempts to go out with men. She was trying and failing. She attributed this failure to her own insecurity and low self-esteem. It did appear that she was coming to see us under her own steam. The nurse who referred her had seen her only once. Her family was far away. Her friends did not seem to be shoving her through the door at us. It appeared that we were talking to the individual who wanted something done about the "problem" that she herself presented. This was essential.

For now the interviewer would not attempt to understand why this young woman had this problem. Inexperienced residents frequently use their entire half-hour in such a pursuit, but those who are well trained in our clinic will pivot midway, from following the story of how the patient came to us to seeing for himself or herself if we dare go any further.[5]

The interviewer, therefore, signaled an abrupt transition (Sullivan, Chapter 6) by getting out the SCL-90 and asking the patient if she would be willing to be asked a few questions. The transition signals the interviewer as well as the patient, for he or she must stand back and look with dispassion upon the extent of the patient's disturbance (Malan, 1979).

The usual first question is whether or not the present upset is as bad as the patient has ever felt or been? If it is not, then the inquiry has to go to that previous distress, for we must have as accurate a picture as possible of the patient in her most acute disturbance. What disturbed her then? What went through her mind when she was most upset? What was the strangest thing that she noticed in her mind then? What was the most dangerous thing she did to relieve herself? Notice we do not ask *if* her mind was strange or *if* her behavior was dangerous. We presume that *all* of us have some strange experiences and we all do things we would later think foolish when our lives are coming apart. We only want to know how *far* this patient got out of control. We also are interested in who was available to bring her back.

The job of the interviewer is a little simpler if the present distress is the most acute disturbance, for the SCL-90 allows the interviewer to track the shape of the cloud of disturbance. For a patient like the Young Woman With No Self-Confidence this shape of distress was relatively sharp, being confined to depressive and insecure items. This leads to some routine questions: "What did you have in mind when you checked 'Thoughts of death or dying,' 'A Little bit'? When you checked, 'Feeling that most people cannot be trusted,' 'Moderately'? . . . 'Feeling uneasy when people are watching or talking about you.' 'Moderately'? . . . 'Having to avoid certain things, places or activities because they frighten you.' 'A Little bit'?" For an individual like this depressed and insecure patient, these are obligatory questions. We are talking about telling how close the patient is coming to suicide and to being paranoid and phobic. Even if these items were not checked, we would have to lead into this mental territory. We would have to ask of her: "When your depression gets the best of you, what do you think of doing? What holds you back? Who would be most hurt or angry if you did such a thing? Do you get relief from your depression with drugs? With alcohol? What dangerous things do you do when depressed? What about when you get high? What do you do then? When you are insecure, what are other people thinking about you? How do they make you worse?"

The picture we got of this woman's worst moments was that she cried and withdrew and had had occasional thoughts of jumping in front of a car. She had never come close to acting on them, because she was bound to her family, friends, and to returning hope for her own prospects. The depression seemed to be well bounded. Her insecurity seemed not to lead into paranoia, but rather back to blaming herself. Her avoiding was this occasional keeping to herself when down, but not leading into a fixed phobia. In summary, we ruled out the dangerous complications of depression and insecurity. For us, classical psychiatry is a set of warnings which we take as seriously as possible. The medical history is the other set of warnings which we evaluate as seriously as possible.[6] The patient had been well before and after the accident and hospitalization.

Now the interviewer could take his final turn, again signaling to the patient and to himself, by becoming interested in the question of "Who has helped you the most in your life?" Here the distance between therapist and patient maintained during the middle section of the interview is no longer right. An interviewer who cannot go along with the feel of the patient's best relationships will not be told much about them. This patient was not difficult to go along with for the interviewer, nor for those of us who observed them. Who would not be filled with admiration for her strength when she talked about the death of her brother in Vietnam and about her own near death from the accident? She was a compassionate woman who inspired feelings in us. Hence, we were hardly surprised that she had been very close with another, younger brother and with several friends here at school, sharing apartments and confidences.

She passed our two tests of normality, so well described by Havens (1984b). She could connect. This was doubly verified by her relation to us and by her report of her friendships, which we found convincing. She could also protect herself, also doubly verified by her strength about her losses.[7] This is not to say her psychological healthiness was uncompromised. Indeed, it was troubled by this lack of confidence with men and by the inclination to blame herself. But she seemed sound to us. If she had trouble becoming connected with a man, she could connect in other situations. If she had trouble protecting her self-confidence against comparisons which were very unfriendly to herself, she could defend herself very well at other times. Thus, we found her troubled, but sound. This is very auspicious for brief therapy. Also, we found her having support in her own world, which would become necessary between hours with us and after she completed brief therapy. This is also auspicious.

In summary, this young woman answered well to all of our three concerns.

She had a familiar "problem" which *she* wanted to explore with us. The relevant dangers were excluded. Her well-being was found.

Common Errors Which a More Subtle Knowledge Might Catch

Before we conclude with the proposal of trial therapy to the Young Woman With No Self-Confidence, let us hold back and think about how the preliminary interview could have been more difficult. There are many false positive and false negative candidates for brief therapy. After all, if we disagree with the recommendations for brief therapy of our referring doctors and nurses about half of the time, other experts on brief therapy just might disagree with us. And they would be right to some unknown extent. So let us go over some of the subtle points of discernment.

Unfortunate Ideas About Using Us

The doctors and nurses who refer to us in our Student Health Service have gotten steadily better and more accurate in their referrals to us in five years. I would estimate that one in four sent to us five years ago would be suitable to us, while now it is one in two. Perhaps we are also able to take a broader range of patients now than before, but my point is still the same that some referral problems derive from unfamiliarity of the Student Health doctors and nurses with our clinic and have been ameliorated with time and discussions back and forth.[8] I regard one in two as a perfectly acceptable ratio of accepted patients to referrals. It is well when the specialists are a little more expert about their own field than the generalists.

One kind of subtle problem is the patient who is well enough to be a patient in brief therapy, yet the patient has an idea about using us which will make our job impossible. Some of these ideas the reader may find ridiculous, but the reader may be a little surprised to learn how long such ideas may go undiscovered by an alert team. It is impossible to refute an idea which you don't know exists!

I see three varieties all too often. One kind concerns the responsibilities of the patient. Many prospective patients imagine themselves to have none. For them, the free consultation of the first two visits may be followed by 20 more free visits. Alternatively, they may imagine that one or two hours of their time may be all that is necessary for reversing a vicious circle which has been going on in their family for generations. These patients may amaze the doctor with their selective inattention to his written description of the clinic which they received before the preliminary interview, which would contradict both of these opinions about money and time in brief therapy. They may also ignore the specification of both these responsibilities in the offer for trial therapy, which we will come to soon. Perhaps the only way to discover such ideas is to ask all the patients in preliminary interviews for their ideas about being in brief therapy. When it has never dawned on the doctor that the patient might be thinking of very free and very brief therapy, he will be quite shocked when the patient arrives in a temper for the third session saying she has just learned from the receptionist that she will get a bill and just how in hell did he perpetrate this trick on her![9]

A second variety of unfortunate ideas is derived from previous experiences with psychiatry or counseling. We may refute such ideas unwittingly by going about our business in a useful way. But some of these ideas refute *us* because we do not know the patient entertains a view of how we will be *later*. One man whom we managed in the preliminary interview to hold to answers of half the length to which he was accustomed had doubts about the worthwhileness of trial therapy, because he understood the free association which would come later would be useless to a man like himself who never stopped talking. We only stand a chance of separating ourselves from such foolishness if we ask about past experiences in getting help (Margulies and Havens, 1981).

A third and final variety of unfortunate ideas about using us is the most difficult of all to decipher. These are ideas in the patient's family back home about what will happen if their daughter or son gets into therapy at the university. Many young people at the university look more independent than they actually are of the needs of mother and father, sister and brother, and so forth. Many families are desperately dependent on this young person to come back, to hold the parents together, to rescue the younger siblings, and so forth. None of this is apt to be announced in first visits.

The resident sees the young person sacrificing independence, sexuality, and aggression for reasons which must be intrapsychic and which, therefore, call for some vigorous brief therapy. Such views get sent home in anxious telephone calls, triggering alarm about what is befalling the son or daughter. This begets sudden terminations. The patient will just fail to appear. A related version, which is more subtle, is that the parents and their son or daughter commune in advance about the visit to Brief Therapy Clinic, arriving at a joint idea about the patient's getting some kind of "support" which is quite idiosyncratic and which is, therefore, quite unknown to us. Most commonly, we learn of this concerning daughters who have very special relationships with their fathers. Often, they may complain of such fathers, getting us men who are therapists to think of ourselves as improvements. Often we fail to "work the opposing current," as Havens would say (Chapter 10). We fail to think or say, "Yes, this is upsetting, his being tight about money, but you seem to mean a lot to him . . . " or something of this kind. We fail to learn about the nice talk that father and daughter just had on the telephone about what kind of help might be comfortable for continuing their special relationship. Of course, they never did discuss such a thing directly, but an understanding was reached, nevertheless, in their negotiations. Therefore, I like to ask what mother and father think about therapy. They may think that some kinds of support would be all right. They may think therapy is hogwash. They may be insisting on therapy, which the son or daughter wants to prove is a ridiculous idea. I like to know these things in the preliminary visit. It saves us some rude shocks.

Ambulatory Disasters Nearly Always Present as Routine Problems: Cautionary Tales[10]

Before our referring doctors and nurses improved their acumen about the "relatively healthy patients" we proposed to help, we had many "relatively healthy patients" sent to us who were about to kill themselves or lose their minds. I was continually astonished that these desperate persons could have passed for normal in the medical office. I was obliged to think about this phenomenon, because one or two out of the four cases seen in an afternoon for preliminary interviews appeared to be on the verge of disaster.

How could they be missed? I reviewed all of the missed emergencies in the patients referred to Brief Therapy Clinic in 1983–84 in an attempt to understand this strange phenomenon. Three examples may give the reader an idea of what I found. A 29-year-old, single graduate student was referred to us for depression. He complained to us that his girlfriend had broken off with him, which was bothering him more than usual because the girlfriend would not allow him to see their one-year-old daughter. An 18-year-old freshman appeared on our last clinic day before Christmas break to discuss his trouble finding a girlfriend. A 24-year-old man in business school appeared a month before his graduation to complain of difficulty speaking in front of his class.

Notice that all of these are perfectly routine presentations. Notice also that all three are men.[11] Finally, I would emphasize that all three were capable and likeable men. The first was a poet of deep feeling and clear and vivid expression. The second was the kind of farm kid you often see in Wisconsin who is very conscientious and earnest. The third was an urbane fellow who could have been mistaken for a Kennedy, being so charming and well-spoken. All did well in their studies.

But all three were a step from a disaster. When I asked the first man what went through his mind when he thought of missing his daughter, he told me he thought of shaving his head so he could place it in a noose. When I asked him what kept him from this proceeding, he cried and said his little daughter was the only person he loved in the world. When I asked when he would get to see her again, he cried again and told me that his girlfriend had just proposed to leave the state in a few months.

A similar set of shocking replies came from the other two gentlemen from a few questions. When I asked the freshman what had happened the last time he had felt the absence of a girlfriend, he told me about getting the family shotgun out and seeing what it felt like against his own head. When I asked him what he would be going home to over Christmas, he described a lonely, cold and distant farmhouse with two parents to whom he had never been close. The shotgun could be found on the stairs to the basement.

Finally, the urbane business student about to graduate: He puzzled me, because he was altogether smooth with the resident, yet he had checked "Extremely" for nearly every category of disturbance on the SCL-90. I told him I had only one question in reviewing the findings with the resident. I just couldn't tell if he had a little or a big problem. He replied that that was interesting. He had the same question himself. When he looked in the mirror, his eyes looked to him like those of Van Gogh when the painter was going crazy. This terrified him, but more he could not say about this experience. This was all. Well, I knew from the indescribable effect of this report on myself that I was listening to a man who was quite unsure which side of the mirror was himself.

In the fall of 1984 I was asked to give a lecture on the recognition and management of psychiatric emergencies in medical practice for my annual presentation to the doctors and nurses at Student Health. Since I described the findings I have just summarized, we have seen only an occasional extreme situation. It appears that our referring doctors and nurses are asking a few more questions before they send along to us a routine depression or anxiety. I believe this may underline for the reader that there is a moral to these cautionary tales, which is not so difficult to practice once you are aware that ambulatory disasters always present as routine. You will ask the right questions once you know that they have to be asked. Your referring persons may or may not do your job for you.

Hidden Hope

A few words are important about the opposite situation. Many patients are quite sound who present themselves as all fouled up or as impossible to reach. What is for them but an opening move is often received by the residents as objective reality.

Some patients will check "Quite a Bit" or "Extremely" in nearly every category of disturbance of the SCL-90. Then they may fall apart within a few minutes in the interviews. Finally, they may tell the interviewer about all their relationships which have gone wrong, forgetting to mention everyone who is looking out for them. Some of these individuals are hysterical. Some are obsessive.

Now this polyneurotic presentation could be dangerous and could also not be dangerous. It is impossible to say from the description I have just given. The interviewer is warned, but he is not to be led to conclusions by the patients about their illnesses any more than he is to be led to conclusions about their well-being by the referring persons. The job is to tell whether one of these individuals is sound or is showing diffuse ego weakness. Is the patient a hysteric or an obsessive who is interested in seeing what the interviewer will do with exaggerated complaints? Is the patient a borderline who is continually falling to pieces? The job is to go over the pathology and to go over the most helpful relationships known by the patient. The interviewer will often need both reckonings to decide. Sometimes the pathology appears troubling, but the relationships seem reassuring. Sometimes the pathology seems to dissolve, but the relationships feel thin and unconvincing. Sometimes the team is evenly divided in weighing such findings. I will come back to how we proceed when we are divided when I conclude this chapter. For now, I only want to emphasize the possibility of exaggerated trouble, hidden hope.

Some other patients show no dangerous pathology but they make a poor impression on the interviewer. The interviewer finds the patient distant and wary, or dowdy and colorless, or shiny and superficial, or whatever. The resident who has such an experience of the patient is very likely to tell me that the patient has no substantial relationships. "Therefore, we must decline trial therapy."

The trouble here may be that the way in which the resident has conducted the interview has put the patient off. The patient does not like the doctor either or is scared by him. Therefore, the patient is not about to tell this doctor about his private relationships which mean so much to him. The job for me, when I have gotten such a presentation from the resident, is to come in from another angle. A little surprise is often very helpful. I recall most vividly one presentation from a resident years ago of a woman who seemed to him to be drab and flat, more like a worn-out woman in her forties or fifties than a young undergraduate. No trial therapy here he suggested; would I agree? I went in to meet the patient myself. Well, she looked at the floor and repeated to me she wasn't much at relationships. I just didn't think this was right sitting with her. I said, "Oh, is that right?" and she looked up and smiled at me. She was so pleased to be found out. We hit it off from there, and she went on to become one of the most successful patients I have ever seen in brief therapy.[12]

Routine Refusals

Nevertheless, we do end up declining to go further with about half of the patients who have a preliminary session with us. The last ten refusals in the clinic are typical. Three of the ten had made grave attempts at suicide in the past. We were obliged to decline brief therapy with all three of these individuals because the end of brief therapy would threaten to bring up the kind of loss which had previously led to despair—not only despair, but acting upon despair in a way which might not be stopped a second time. Three of the ten were polyneurotic borderline patients, with diffuse ego weakness and continuing chaos. We were obliged to predict this would be continuing well into the near future. Three of the ten had been let down enormously as children.

We were amazed they had gotten as far as they had gotten. They had survived by some string of minor miracles. We did not want to contribute to giving these three any high hopes, which we felt brief therapy could arouse. They obviously kept going by keeping their chins near the ground. The last of the ten came into her interview yelling about having to wait a half-hour and stomped out. I never learned what was ailing her. None of these ten patients was acutely disturbed in the preliminary interview, none like the ambulatory disasters I have presented. But all of them could be put into peril by brief therapy. Therefore, all but the last were referred to some other kind of help. The last may have gotten there with the greatest speed.

Running Risks

The reader would mistake my meaning to think that these last ten patients were unsuitable for brief therapy. No, I mean they were unsuitable for the Brief Therapy Clinic which is set up for relatively inexperienced therapists to be of help to relatively healthy patients. I share with my medical colleagues the belief that, "Above all, do no harm." *Primum non nocere*. I conclude that patients who are likely to become dangerously disturbed in brief therapy should not be subjected to the risk of being looked after by inexperienced residents, and vice versa. I appreciate that this pairing occurs all the time anyway on our inpatient services and outpatient emergency services, but the expectations of the patients there are apt to be low. They are more able to keep their distance; same for the residents. I appreciate that this pairing also occurs all the time anyway in our outpatient departments, but the atmosphere is also much more low-key and the continuity of care established. The patient is depending on the institution in all of these other situations, less on the doctor himself or herself. This is much less dangerous.[13]

The ten patients we declined for the clinic could all be suitable for some kind of brief therapy in some kind of setting. If Alexander could help the Scientist reverse his psychotic depression (Chapter 5), if Balint could help the Stationery Manufacturer reverse a slide into paranoid psychosis (Chapter 8), then it is possible to do brief therapy in grave situations. If Winnicott could give a single consultation which was very deep to Mrs. X (Chapter 7), then it is also possible to do brief therapy with extremely deprived individuals. If Davanloo could break through a vicious cycle of polyneurotic misery of many years standing for the Little Blond Dutch Girl (Chapter 14), then this too is possible in brief therapy. The reader might want to keep in mind that these are some of the most talented therapists ever seen in the tradition of Western psychotherapy reporting their most amazing, exceptional cases.

The reader who wants to take on challenges in brief therapy could proceed in several other, less hazardous directions. One leading possibility is that many patients who have been thought to require long-term therapy do very well in brief therapy. Nearly every case of mine own presented in Part II could be judged by analysts and other long-term therapists to require long-term therapy. I think especially of the Modern Passive-Feminine Character (Chapters 4, 6 and 13) or of the Case of Bulimia (Chapter 16). I believe such cases can be taken on in brief therapy when the three criteria of the preliminary interview are met and when the trial therapy is successful. It is right to tell these patients that long-term therapy is the usual recommendation, but that brief therapy has been successful as well. The risk they run is that the job may be incomplete. If the patients know this risk, then they may weigh their alternatives. It is best to be as evenhanded as possible in how we pose our offer. But I will return to that subject momentarily.

The other leading possibility for extending the therapist's range in brief therapy is in becoming able to adopt some of the other positions of observation. I am of the opinion that the strictly analytic method has less range than the analysis of character, which has less range than interpersonal interviewing, which has less range than systemic interviewing[14] — that is, when the therapist is myself. I have no doubt that the reverse is more probable for some of the therapists I know well.

But therapists like myself who *do* improve their range by shifting to more decentered perspectives for observation may set up relationships which are less destabilizing for their patients. The doctor is interested in how the patient is faring "out there." He is interested in disentangling those relationships which are more likely to unhorse the patient between sessions. He is interested in reckoning the vicious circles which are possible with any improvements out there; this reduces the turbulence of "being in therapy" between the patient and the crucial people in the patient's world. Such a doctor keeps himself less important. Therefore, leaving him is not such a big deal.

Therefore, there is some logic to make it appear that the interpersonal and systemic positions for making observations will allow more disturbed patients to succeed in brief therapy, and there is some evidence as well from the latter location of all the disturbed cases in the array of Part II. No one really knows how far and how extensively such experiments will go (Ferrier, 1986; Lerner and Lerner, 1983).

The two extremes of technique in brief therapy are very likely to have extremely different criteria for the selection of patients. At one extreme the methods of psychoanalysis and analysis of character will augment the patient's intensity which has been repressed. At the other extreme the interpersonal and systemic interviewing will disentangle contradictions of the "strange loops" (Hofstadter, 1979; Pearce and Cronen; 1980) of complicated family games. For some patients, an augmentation of intensity will allow breakthroughs. Such patients will find new simplicity with its own passage forward. For many patients, such augmentation would be foolhardy. They find that the greater intensity only puts them out of control on the "strange loops" of their roller coaster. Better for them to look over the course, carefully. Thus, more patients in difficult and complicated arrangements can be taken on for brief therapy if the doctor takes the interpersonal and systemic perspectives for his starting point. Fewer patients may be taken on in brief therapy if the doctor lacks such circumspection.[15]

About Taking Care of the Patient

I hope it has been evident during this discussion of preliminary interviews that we look after our patients all the while that we look for what we have to know about them. No method is worth a damn if it fails to help the patient feel hopeful. We will be obliged to put the patient through some difficult moments, but we will take care to help bring the patient back to his or her security (Chapter 6, Sullivan). Our concluding messages to the patients rest on the same principles.

If we must decline to go further than the preliminary interview, then we want to signal this transition as soon as possible and with as much time as possible to prepare the patient for the distress which is likely.[16] Sometimes we see a refusal is highly probable from our first glance at the medical chart, the symptom checklist, or the personal questionnaire. Sometimes we know when the patient walks in the room, or at some point along the way. There is time to cross-check this hypothesis in the several ways I have elaborated. False negative candidates are surely common. But once we have concluded that brief therapy would be folly, we allow as much time as possible for the transition to some kind of help which is in the patient's interest. The concluding message is very important in these situations. We attempt to be as matter-of-fact as possible. We say that it would be no favor to the patient to have brief therapy with us if it were quite likely to make him worse — better to have none. But we appreciate that this is disappointing, because the patient did come to a consultation about going on with us. Room is to be allowed here for crying, angry criticism of us, or perhaps relief. Finally, we propose several possibilities that we think could be more helpful than we could be, taking care to discover what the patient actually thinks about these alternative paths.

The concluding message when we propose trial therapy is also well considered. We say to the patient that we find her to be sound psychologically, although she is having troubles that may lead her to think or feel she is not at all. We may be able to help her. The way to find out is to have a long session, from two to three hours, with one of our team interviewing her, to explore the difficulty which she brought to us today. We see that she loses confidence in herself. We want to appreciate why that has been necessary. She will know at the end of the long session if she has been helped and we will know too. If she has been helped, it is highly probable that a semester of brief therapy will be constructive for her. So this is the way we recommend. Other possible ways would be a pharmacological treatment or a long-term therapy. So what does she think?

A variation is to pose the team as divided about what to recommend. We may say: "Some of the team are for proposing the long session. Some of the team say 'no,' better to send you to a long-term treatment, which will be more secure because it can last for several years." Or we may say: "Some of the team are for proposing the long session. Some say 'no,' better to wait for now. You seem to be getting better so fast already. Maybe you will succeed entirely on your own." Or we may say: "Some of the team are for proposing the long session. Some say 'no,' because you could change too fast. They are concerned that you are very important to your family just the way you are. So they advise leaving well enough alone. What do *you* say?"

Depending on the patient's readiness, therefore, we proceed to the trial therapy, which is the conclusion of the opening game of brief therapy. This is the subject of the following chapter.

20. *The Opening Game: Trial Therapy*

THE IDEA

The Aim

I LIKE Winnicott's aim for a therapeutic consultation: "To meet the challenge of the case" (1965a), to reach what is worthwhile about the individual and to reach the illness (Chapter 7).[1] This is in the right spirit, I think, so important to getting through to the patient.[2] I like a qualifier here which Winnicott himself would not need, but one that helps me very much. This is to say that the therapeutic consultation of the trial therapy also has to appreciate why the patient has had to be exactly as she has been. I would not like to change a single comma. This helps me to be ready for a major thrust by the patient, usually in the second hour, to return our conversation right back to zero learning.

The Situation

The "long session" which we offer after a preliminary interview is usually a very intense, meaningful event for the patient and for us. The structure has evolved over the last several years, after I borrowed the idea for "trial therapy" from Davanloo (1978, 1980). My idea from Davanloo was that we would take up to three hours, if we needed that long, to get a "breakthrough." If we got something so meaningful, then the success of the subsequent brief therapy would be nearly assured. I liked this trial by fire better than the lists of criteria proposed by Sifneos and better than the "trial interpretations" of Malan and Mann.

Our trial therapy is no longer this "relentless" attempt to outlast the patient (Davanloo, 1978, 1980). We have been more influenced by the long sessions of Winnicott and, later, of the Milan teams. Our trial therapy has evolved into a drama with a beginning, a middle, and an end. The first hour is the beginning, the history, the reaching to the worthwhileness of the person and to the illness, very much in the way of Winnicott or Semrad (Semrad, Binstock and White, 1966). The middle is the meeting of the team to deliberate upon what has passed and what is likely to be coming. The end is the second hour, in which there is a very high likelihood the patient will attempt to destroy the discussion, for which the therapist will attempt to be prepared quite like the Milan teams (Chapter 16). The setup in the room is private in a way and not private in another way, for the team is watching from behind the mirror, videotaping the session and very occasionally saying something through the electronic device in the therapist's ear.

Interestingly, we have evolved quite unconsciously into a drama very much as described by Aristotle in his *Poetics*:

Tragedy, then, is an imitation of some action that is important, entire, and of a proper magnitude, by language embellished and rendered pleasurable, but by different means in different parts—in the way, not of narration, but of action—effecting through pity and terror the correction and refinement of the passions (p. 14). . . . In general we may say than an action is sufficiently extended when it is long enough to admit of a change of fortune, from happy to unhappy, or the reverse, brought about by succession necessary or probable, of well connected events (p. 19). . . . Tragedy endeavors . . . as far as possible . . . to confine its actions within the limit of a single revolution of the sun or nearly so. (p. 13)

This change of fortune is best when "unexpected": a "discovery" and a "revolution" both "as in the Oedipus," or "suddenly and casually" as in the Tale of Alcinous in the Odyssey. The error is of "human frailty." The subject is "someone of high fame and flourishing prosperity." The story "lies in a small compass," consisting of the "complications" of incidents prior to the action and the "development" of the change of fortune itself.

For us, the beginning is this "complication" of incidents, the middle the anticipation of the action which is coming, the "unexpected" being the inevitable surprise brought forth by the patient in the end. The patient becomes someone of importance for us. The story certainly lies in this small compass. I usually feel that someone's fate is at stake. All of this parallel with Aristotle's description of tragedy has been quite unconscious.[3] I think there is something about such a structure which is fascinating, relatively timeless, considering that 25 centuries has passed between the height of Greek tragedy and the little height of our enterprise.

Aristotle explains ever so well the difference between the "epic plan" and a "tragedy," between, I would say, a long-term therapy and a brief therapy:

By an epic plan, I mean a fable composed of many fables; as if any one, for instance, should take the entire fable of the Iliad for the subject of a tragedy. . . . [Even an epic] should have for its subject one entire and perfect action, having a beginning, a middle and an end so that, forming like an animal a complete whole, it may afford its proper pleasure . . . widely differing in its construction from history. . . . Even in this, therefore, the superiority of Homer's genius is apparent, that he did not attempt to bring the whole war. . . . It would have been too vast a subject, and not easily comprehended in one view; or had he forced it into a moderate compass it would have been perplexed by its variety. (1934, p. 46)

A long-term therapy is a "fable composed of many fables." A brief therapy "should have for its subject one entire and perfect action, having a beginning, a middle and an end so that, forming like an animal a complete whole, it may afford its proper pleasure. . . . " I like that very much. That is what we're up to.

The Beginning: The First Hour

Our quick and sensitive residents usually learn how to cope with the technical problems of the first hour quite well. After watching in the fall, they mostly do quite well being the therapist in the spring.[4] They pick up the "loose end" of the patient's present concern without getting lost in the tangle of possible threads[5] (Chapter 16, The Milan Teams). They do not get pulled under in following such a "loose end," but find their way back to when the patient was relatively all right, when the patient started to go wrong. Mostly, they get a little history which is deeply felt. They reach to the worthwhileness of the patient and to the illness which has set in afterwards.

I would only mention two common technical problems. It is difficult to share some painful stories. I recall one of our residents backing away from a story of how the patient was subjected to cruelty by her two sisters. This held up the first hour, until we could tell him he had better listen. It is also difficult to *think* about the story which is being told, to see if it is actually making sense or to see if the story is some fiction. This is a fine ability, to listen, to think, to wonder, to put together a view of one's own, while accepting the view of the patient. This is what Bateson called the capacity for "double description." Havens calls this "working the opposing currents." It is lovely to watch.

The Middle: Discussion with the Team

This is the most difficult event in our clinic. The greatest restraint is asked of all of us. The therapist has to be given room to stay with his own perspective, with his own questions. Only when this first eye is clear do we allow a second eye to come into focus. If we do not have this restraint, the first eye is put out. Therapists who have been relatively well in the session may become ill by meeting with us — anxious, confused, and much worse in the second hour.

Now the second eye can be very, very useful, because it will be preoccupied with the reversal which is coming in the second hour, in the end. When the success of the therapist in the first hour is appreciated, when his own thinking is understood, then the time has come for this second eye, for helping the therapist be ready for the reversal. The timing matters.

The trouble with this meeting all derives from what the Milan team calls "becoming richly joined to the system" (Chapter 16). The team, which feels itself to be observing like gods on Olympus, is no more removed than were Zeus and Hera from Troy — always being pulled in, unwittingly. Therapists do well to put gods at arm's length, to listen warily, for the team is often all too ready to contribute to the trouble.[6]

A brief illustration may convey this folly. One of our residents had gotten a very clear little history of how the young man had been the most dutiful son, the most pleasing to his parents, but had little if any social life with women. The patient disliked his isolation. He was upset.

What then to look for in the second hour? Standing back, I may see now that we would be tempted to try to get this fellow to "take another chance." He was so appealing, the kind of fellow that girls feel sorry for in the high school band. We would become richly joined to such activities when we became interested in the therapist's "getting him going" in the second hour. This is the opposite of what you want to do in anticipating what is coming in the last act.

The End: The Second Hour

Often the progress of the first hour has disappeared when the second hour has gotten underway. The patient seems to be very unclear, in coming back, just where he wants to be in the second hour. Often, he has hopes for the second hour, but gets bogged down. Often, he uses the hour very well, until the very end when he suddenly has great doubts about continuing in therapy.

I think of this minor tragedy of the second hour as inevitable, sooner or later, because the patient has begun a different drift (Maturana, 1985) in the first hour than will fit with his current relations out there. The break has reminded him he will be leaving to face that world of his, which will be perturbed by his being any different. This will perturb him. Therefore, he will maneuver in the second hour to return his learning back to zero. The only uncertainty is just how he will attempt to destroy the relationship with the therapist which has gotten underway.

I have eventually learned to get ready for the final act. I like to face the end at the outset of the second hour by saying, "What do you need to get before we stop in one hour?" I like to face up to the different drift attracting the patient, versus the current drift. For example, one woman was contemplating having "more nerve." I was very interested in what would happen to her and to her family if she continued "with no nerve." What if somehow she "got nerve"? This gives me the crucial findings, often, for why continuing with "no nerve" is necessary. Finally, I like to know what would happen if the patient continued with no therapy or went into therapy? I like to pose all of these possibilities, because I have learned that in one way the patient is highly likely to destroy our working relationship: now, soon, or later; by not knowing what to discuss in the second hour; by knowing and getting in a muddle; by getting clear and then being in great doubts about therapy. I want to be prepared to appreciate the necessity of such closure by the patient, and to be able to explain my appreciation to the patient.

Finally, the reader may appreciate the technical problems of the team in the middle act with the therapist of the young man who disliked his social isolation. You may see how I might tell the resident to insist on some clarity about what chances the patient wanted to take in the second hour. What did he want to do next? How would he be more outgoing? Such advice is tempting because it is partly right. But it is mostly wrong.

The team is lost when it urges the therapist and patient forward. I may tell the reader how I like to pose various problems in the second hour, and I may tell the resident this as well, but the weight of my interest has to ride with how the patient will bring the discussion back to zero. I want to help the therapist get set for this, to help him think about why it will be necessary, this reversal.

It is a little like anticipating a tragedy which is coming in the third act.[7] In retrospect, it is quite necessary that this young man should *not* "take a chance" with the therapist in the second hour, if we appreciate the perfection of his relationship to his parents. What woman could compete with that? Of course, he took no chance, and the therapist only felt frustrated that he could not carry out my helpful and sensible advice with his "difficult" patient.

The Trial Therapy of the Young Woman with No Self-Confidence

The Beginning

The reader will recall from the previous chapter that this young woman complained of "feelings of insecurity/low self-image that won't go away. . . . I am especially afraid that I will never be able to have a normal relationship with a man." I knew little more about her problem, but I was confident in this strength because it came across right away to us and because we had taken pains to verify it in the several ways of the preliminary interview. This preparation allows a very fast start to this trial therapy because all three conditions for getting in deeply are met straight off. The patient provides the "loose end" of her preoccupation, namely, running herself down. We follow this thread down into her distress, but I am able to hold strongly to my conviction that she is a confident, worthwhile individual. This allows her to show me how she makes herself ill.

THERAPIST Where do you think we ought to start today?

PATIENT I guess what I really want to know is — I was hoping you guys would give me some good ideas on how to improve my self-image.

THERAPIST OK, then we need to have some idea of what you think is wrong with that. So that's what you'd like to get out of us today — how to improve your self-image?

PATIENT I guess that's my biggest problem. It's that I have a low opinion of myself.

THERAPIST You come across as a person with a certain amount of confidence, nevertheless, so I would imagine that at one time you felt pretty good about yourself.

PATIENT Well, no. I mean I do like some things about myself. I think I'm intelligent, I guess that gives me some confidence. I feel OK about my looks. I guess it's my personality I think is wrong.

THERAPIST All right, should we see about that? We can hardly make any suggestions unless we understand what is wrong.

PATIENT I don't know, like I said before I feel like I'm boring. I feel like what I have to say isn't worthwhile.

THERAPIST OK, so you feel you're boring and what you say isn't worthwhile? What do you mean?

PATIENT You know, like it's stupid. Like it seems like a contradiction because on the one hand I say I feel intelligent but I say stupid things so it's like I'm good at learning, I'm good at taking tests, I'm good in school.

THERAPIST School intelligent?

PATIENT Yeah.

THERAPIST But you don't feel smart outside?

PATIENT Right. Like I'm good at regurgitating—that's why I'm good in school.

THERAPIST Well, that's no mean talent. So you're good at that but you don't feel . . .

PATIENT But it's like I'm not really original.

THERAPIST You don't feel original? Compared to whom?

PATIENT I don't know.

THERAPIST Who's original?

PATIENT I don't know, some people just are.

THERAPIST Well, whom do you admire?

PATIENT I don't know, nobody in particular.

THERAPIST Well, one is always comparing oneself to other people and you look like you're comparing yourself with someone who is original, compared to you.

PATIENT Let's see. OK, like my friend Harry. It's like he is really funny. He just finds funny things to say.

For me there are two crucial statements here which catch this woman by surprise. "You come across as a person with a certain amount of confidence." She may have jumped in her seat when I said that to her. I thought she did. Here she was saying she had a "low opinion of myself," and I was saying I didn't think she did. But I also say that I accept her "low self opinion" and I am interested in how she arrives there: "You don't feel original. Compared to whom?" Here she may have jumped again. Again, I thought she did.

The eye for her confidence and the eye for her comparing herself badly, together, give a double description which brings depth of field and then depth of feeling. We drop down fast into what is most painful to her, because we have a hold on what is right about her. We are "working the opposing currents" (Havens, 1976). This gives a very fast slide, when both currents are gotten intuitively right away.

THERAPIST So Harry is funny?

PATIENT Yeah.

THERAPIST So you admire that in a man?

PATIENT Yeah, like at work it kind of bugs me because there's this man, but I feel really weird that it bothers me so much. (She begins to cry.)

THERAPIST Yeah, but it does, there's some Kleenex right here.

PATIENT He's just so friendly, everyone likes him. I guess I compare myself to him because he's just so comfortable with himself and it seems like he's just so friendly, he's just so like outgoing, just easygoing.

THERAPIST So this is painful to you by comparison to yourself. How would you describe yourself?

PATIENT Just really afraid.

THERAPIST So you criticize yourself for being too fearful? What are you fearful about?

PATIENT Like afraid of rejection.

THERAPIST Why shouldn't you be afraid of rejection?

PATIENT Because I'm so afraid that I don't take risks so I don't gain anything either. I'm always protecting myself and by doing that I don't get what I really need.

THERAPIST Like what?

PATIENT Like I'm afraid of people not liking me so I don't really try so they don't . . .

THERAPIST Sometimes a person learns to be a little cautious or protective and that's a good thing.

PATIENT But why is it good?

THERAPIST You can get hurt.

PATIENT Yeah, but I think it's better not to be afraid than to get hurt.

THERAPIST Really?

PATIENT No pain, no gain.

Now I'm leading into history. She proposes she "should not be fearful." I propose that she had to have had good reason. I propose we appreciate the necessity of his fearfulness. She tells me very clearly about her family:

THERAPIST It depends on what the experience has been. Some people have had an easy time of it or a pleasant time of it or a protective time of it. So you know, you've had some rough hits already. But you criticize yourself for your caution. I was quite impressed that you've already been through two terrible things.

PATIENT But they don't seem terrible to me.

THERAPIST They're a lot harder than what most people go through. There must be some reason why you're cautious and you don't take risks. I mean this just didn't . . . this must have a history.

PATIENT I don't think I ever have. Nobody in my family builds anybody else up; it's more like cutting down.

THERAPIST So your family doesn't give each other much appreciation?

PATIENT No. It's kind of weird. I don't know if that's the way I take it because I'm the youngest and so I was always called the baby of the family. I was always told that I was spoiled, and like my sister and two of my brothers always called me a little brat, and my other brother, Sam, I liked him because he was my favorite. My brother, Jim, and I, he's the second oldest, we always used to fight and I used to get him in trouble, like I'd do something to him and he'd do something back and I would start crying and my dad would yell at him. But my dad was like the head of the family so I always got the better end of it and like my dad would be yelling at my brother and my mom would tell me what a brat I was. And like now, those are the things I remember. Sometimes she would say, "Oh, you're such a good kid," but the feeling that I got was that I wasn't and like now she says, "When people called you a brat nobody meant it," she's kidding but it's like . . . you just don't say things like that.

THERAPIST Did she think you were a brat?

PATIENT If I was a bad person or how I interpret it?

THERAPIST What did she think was bad about you?

PATIENT That I was getting my brother in trouble and acting that way.

THERAPIST Your view is that she was siding with Jim and seeing you as being a troublemaker?

PATIENT I was, it was true but I think a lot of kids are like that.

THERAPIST That's not unusual, the youngest fights back. But your mother was pretty harsh, you felt.

PATIENT Yeah, she was. I don't think she realized. It was hard because I think she is very good at not remembering things that she doesn't want to. I'll tell her stuff she did and she'll say, "I said that to you and I did that? I don't remember that." On the one hand I feel like maybe I exaggerated it, but on the other hand I think that maybe she is just protecting herself because she really did do those things.

THERAPIST You certainly feel it very keenly from your demeanor. It sounds like we got into that because we were talking about this self-image of yours and you were saying to me why you might be afraid and might even be a devil.

PATIENT Yeah.

THERAPIST I mean the fight with your brother and ordinary things like that. Maybe it dates back to taking a lot of criticism from your mom for fairly ordinary things.

PATIENT I know she has a really low self-image too. I never thought she did but she has told me.

THERAPIST Maybe you got cautious somewhere back there. It sounds like you were actually taking some risks in the family there for a while, a fight with your brother and all that.

PATIENT How is that taking a risk?

THERAPIST You could have been sweet and nice instead you were having fights with your older brother. Isn't that taking a risk? You could have been a nice little girl.

She describes being run down by her mother, which allowed her to be close to her father. But she also describes her mother's disconfirming that she ran her down. I could see how she could have been quite confused, being disconfirmed about being a worthwhile kid, but also disconfirmed about being run down. This is why I am called upon to have a very good sense about what is fiction, what is to be believed. She will propose to me the fictions which have been proposed to her. I will say, no, I don't think that is to be believed. This will occur over and over, this having become the exciting new drift of our interaction.

THERAPIST Do you really think that at age five you started adopting this kind of . . . if your mother were telling you you were a brat you were quick to think so yourself? Do you think that started at that time?

PATIENT I don't know, maybe earlier, or later.

THERAPIST You're too spontaneous, this seems to me like something that came later. I could be wrong but you seem to . . .

PATIENT Yeah, if I started that early I'd really be in bad shape.

THERAPIST Yeah, you're in too good shape for that.

PATIENT That could be.

THERAPIST When do you remember sort of knocking yourself down a lot — what stands out?

PATIENT See I know I wasn't that young, grade school at least.

THERAPIST What really stands out in your mind when you really took yourself apart?

She proposes how she may have gotten to knocking herself down. I listen to whether such an event seems to be small or big. The proportions were gotten all backwards in her family, so she is very interested in seeing whether I can tell the difference. Somewhere in this woman with a latent confidence is a latent sense of what is help and what is harm, what is small and what is big. This sense has been sacrificed to get along in her family. She will now see whether I get pulled down into such madness. She is excited because she has the hope I will not be misled.

Her first move in our little history-taking is to propose that she has always been missing confidence. I don't believe it. Her second move is to propose she got shamed in a fourth grade class on one occasion. Since then she has lacked confidence. I don't believe it. Her third move is to propose she has been convinced she was an awful kid, since she socked a friend, Sally, in a card game. I hear she might have been a "touchy" kid. We are getting some "successive approximation" now. There is real trouble here with her peers.

PATIENT Other people were going through the same thing and they still had friends and they were still nice to people.

THERAPIST You mean you didn't have any friends?

PATIENT Not really. I mean I just wasn't fun to be around.

THERAPIST You were a real gripe, it sounds like.

PATIENT Yeah, I guess so.

THERAPIST So you really got isolated because of this. You didn't have any friends because of this?

PATIENT Well just acquaintances, no real close friends.

THERAPIST So the girls excluded you at that time?

PATIENT No, I wasn't really excluded, I mean I was kind of like, there was the popular group in grade school and stuff like that, seventh and eighth grade, and I was like on the fringes of it. I wasn't like right in the very center but I wasn't one of the duds in school. I was still invited to the school parties and stuff like that.

THERAPIST You were kind of marginal popular. But not in terms of having certain chums or chums you were really close with.

PATIENT No.

THERAPIST Zero?

PATIENT I would do things with different people but we weren't really close. For a while I was pretty close to this one girl named Virginia and she was probably the best friend I had in high school. I can't remember if we really talked. I think we did. We were pretty close. We talked about things that really mattered, which I never really did with anybody else. It was all kind of superficial.

THERAPIST So this was kind of deeper?

PATIENT Yeah. But she was kind of weird, she was kind of screwed up, her parents were really weird. She was the closest friend I had but it wasn't like we would always call each other up and always do things together. We were friends in high school too, on and off, and then all of a sudden we had this big blowup. She was really pissed off at me because I was doing certain things and so she decided to have a showdown and she invited two other mutual friends and she told me everything that was wrong with me.

THERAPIST She really ran you down, and that was very painful.

PATIENT Yeah.

THERAPIST That sounds important, this history of how you learned to run yourself down. What grade was that?

PATIENT That was probably my junior year, I think.

I feel something here is quite crucial. Here is a woman who is going to get herself hurt over and over again, in two different ways, both needing to be specified. She compares herself harshly. She also allows or even asks others to unload on her. After I hear about Virginia in high school, I hear about Judy who did the same to her in college. Therefore, I will close the first hour by a little summary of our finding, how we appreciate how he gets hurt.

THERAPIST It's about time to take a break for about 20 minutes but let me just summarize what you just told me because we have taken a history of how you might have become so self-critical. As a kind of reflex for any little thing. There are certain landmarks along the way, you know, like there was this thing that happened in fourth grade that wasn't all that bad. But then the thing that happened with Sally. You were really, really touchy and that became some sort of general condemnation of you in your own mind and it probably was not all that unusual you were so touchy at this time. And then this thing happened, you became close with Virginia but then she really let you have it. We need to know more about that. It was very painful but then you became afraid to talk to her, which is natural, but it might have gotten generalized. And then this thing with Judy is along the same line.

PATIENT Yeah, and then last night my roommate wrote me this long letter. She was really pissed off at me and she told me all these things that are bad about me.

THERAPIST So another person has unloaded on you. Who is this?

PATIENT My roommate.

THERAPIST What is her name?

PATIENT Karen. But the thing is, she's right.

THERAPIST I'm sure she is entirely right.

PATIENT Well, like with Virginia, she was screwed up and Judy is extremely insecure so I could see why she felt the way she did, but Karen is pretty easygoing and she just says I'm too uptight and it's like everything she does bugs me.

THERAPIST We'll have to come back to that. So there is a certain pattern here isn't there? People really let you have it and you feel terrible. That may explain why you are ready to criticize yourself at a moment's notice. And there was your mother. And so we are getting a little bit more idea of why you tend to be a little reserved and we are seeing a little bit why you tend to draw terrible conclusions about yourself. If anything goes wrong with a person this could be pretty damaging over the long run about how you see yourself. In spite of all of this you seem quite healthy, I think.

PATIENT I think basically I am.

THERAPIST Yeah, I think so. Let's take a break. This is the picture I have right now. Have I got it roughly what you've been saying to me?

PATIENT Yeah, I think so.

THERAPIST OK, we'll take a break until 4:00.

So we end our first hour. We have a picture of her illness, but we both agree she could be all right.

The Middle: The Team Discussion

The afternoon of this trial therapy was unusual because three of the four residents were away, which allowed the fourth resident and myself to have a quiet discussion. We discussed two technical problems which we both felt could become difficult. One was the missing history of what had gone wrong these last several months which had brought her to us. I could ask her to begin there. But that could be an error if she were preoccupied in the second hour with something completely different. She could go along with my interest in this missing history for most of the second hour, only to tell me in the end that she had wanted something else, only to tell me this was all very nice, but her family didn't want her in therapy.

I was particularly worried about the latter possibility. Here was a woman who had agreed to become confused to get along with family. Mother disconfirmed her being worthwhile and her being run down by her. She helped her by running herself down and by getting peers to unload on her as well. Here she was drifting in a very different direction with me, which would have to destabilize her relations with her mother and with brother and sister and father and her several friends. They were all used to her being someone they could run down, who would even help them by inflicting her own harsh comparisons on herself. She had to be anxious about going back to that world with confidence in her perceptions, which was building with her relationship with me. She had to stop what we were doing. I just didn't know how she would make the attempt. I wanted to see it coming as soon as possible and to appreciate it as entirely necessary.

I decided on a compromise. I would open the second hour with a summary very much like the summary I used to end the first. This would say, "Look, we have a clear picture. I haven't become someone else. I am still with you. I am interested to know what was upsetting you the most of late, which brought you into this room." If she went with this, I would follow. I had the feeling I could tell if it wasn't right. She was such a feeling person, I thought I could tell. However, I would be determined to get back to her family. I felt them at my back. If I did not set the right relation to them, she would quit. So I began with a summary of what was now familiar and I invited the history of what had gone wrong lately.

The End: The Second Hour

THERAPIST Hello, again. Ken and I were talking so let me share some of what we were thinking. The picture we have so far is that you came here to ask us what we thought about your self-esteem, your self-image, and how it could be improved and so far we have this picture that there are two things that have put holes in your self-esteem. One is that there is this kind of reflex to think you have done something terribly wrong on minimum evidence. And then there have been times where people have really let you have it. Both of those things would tend to weaken your confidence — both letting people hit you and what you're regularly hitting yourself with. That's so far. We've got another 45 minutes right now, you and I, and hopefully we can understand some more about you. So then, the question is: There are so many things we could talk about, so we have to choose where we take a look in the next 45 minutes. I have several thoughts about that. One is to look at what's been going on this fall when you chose to come in. Maybe we should attend to that. I mean you were distressed about it enough this time, and I don't have clear enough sense of what was so painful this fall that made you come here. Can we start there?

What she told me was that she met a man who impressed her. This was her undoing, lately. Her previous boyfriend she had dismissed after a year. He had been a little disgusting. She had not felt less than him. She had stood up to him very well. Now she had met a better man. This was trouble.

PATIENT I don't know, it was like, he's in graduate school and he's already experienced a lot and he wants to be a diplomat. So anyway I was really impressed that he knows what he wants to do and he just seems so secure of himself but not arrogant or anything. He was talking about these projects that he had worked on, like writing articles with some person who is supposed to be really good. It is like I start hearing these things and it's just like I feel that I can't live up to. I don't want to talk about myself because then this person will see that I am nothing and there is nothing to me when there is so much to him.

THERAPIST Twenty-four for him, zero for you, huh?

PATIENT Yeah.

THERAPIST I understand why you would admire him but why would you say that you are nothing?

PATIENT Because I haven't done anything.

THERAPIST You mean you haven't done any articles, and you aren't going overseas, and you don't know what you are going to do yet?

PATIENT Right.

THERAPIST So?

PATIENT It's like when I talk to people like that I feel like there isn't anything interesting about me.

THERAPIST Really. Do you believe that?

PATIENT Yeah, I do. It happened last week with this other man. I met him a while ago and he really liked me a lot and I wasn't that impressed with him and stuff.

THERAPIST You weren't impressed with him?

PATIENT No, so I didn't follow up or anything like that and then we just ran into each other the other day and we just decided to get together again and so we did and he's a dancer and he's really good and practices eight hours a day and he's planning to go to some school of dance out in New York in a couple of years and it's like I sort of started feeling like . . .

THERAPIST You're comparing yourself. You feel terrible by comparison because you don't have any big plans.

PATIENT Right. Whereas before I thought that I didn't really like him and I didn't think there was that much to him and now I've decided that he is so much above me.

THERAPIST Because he has these plans to go dancing?

PATIENT Yeah, because he can commit himself. There is something that he cares so much about that he spends that much time working at.

THERAPIST You admire that.

PATIENT Yeah.

THERAPIST You never committed to anything?

PATIENT No.

THERAPIST Really?

PATIENT No.

THERAPIST You're a big zero, huh? I doubt that. You've not yet decided what you want to do with your life?

PATIENT Yeah.

THERAPIST It's early, that's not unusual.

PATIENT Yeah, that's true.

THERAPIST But you draw a worse conclusion.

PATIENT Yeah, I've never been committed to anything. I never give all of myself to anything that I do because if I try my hardest and then I don't succeed then . . . I just couldn't handle it and so instead I never really tried my hardest at anything or committed myself to anything because if it doesn't work out I don't have to feel like a failure because I feel like I wasn't trying my hardest anyway and maybe if I would have tried harder it would have worked.

THERAPIST It's another thing that you are careful about. This implies that one time in your life you did try your hardest and it was very painful because you now obviously are avoiding trying to get hurt. So that means that one time you did put yourself into things and it was too painful. Now when did you stop putting yourself into things?

PATIENT I can't remember ever trying or being obsessed with anything.

Now I was in the difficulty I had known was coming, but now I knew how. Here she was making the most damaging argument against herself, the one which showed her determination to stay with her family, with their view of her. The argument to me is essentially this: "Look, you think I am worthwhile, I have confidence somewhere. You don't see me then. Don't you see that I cannot commit myself? That this *actual* weakness has terrible effects? You were too positive. I am not only self-critical. I am not only getting other people to unload on me. The criticisms are *justified*. I cannot *commit* myself. Therefore, this promising drift of our conversation is about to be over. Or maybe it could take forever, I am such a damaged person, as my family rightly knows!"

Well, I was not knocked over by this, having gotten myself ready in the team discussion. My reply back in plain English would be: "Oh, you're right. You have trouble committing yourself. *When* did you stop putting yourself into things? Let us appreciate why you *had* to do that. I see it has terrible effects. I also know there was once you could put yourself into things. Something very bad must have happened."

She disputed this with me for a while. She did not give her all to sports. She did not give her all to studies, etc. But I am stubborn. I trust my sense of her. Finally, I catch her by surprise again: She could not be crying about being uninvolved unless she had known how terrific it is to be involved. Her pain tells she knows, she feels what she is missing, what she once knew so well:

THERAPIST Little kids are very passionate if they're healthy. You know, they throw themselves into mud pies or whatever the hell they're doing, you know? You just strike me as a person who is not that detached. I've heard your story. I hear that you're being careful now, that you're very afraid to give yourself to some pursuit.

PATIENT Uh huh.

THERAPIST But your whole behavior suggests that you know what it would be like to get really involved in something. And that means that somewhere back when you were small you really were involved in things. And that's why this is so painful. Because you know the difference. We can feel the difference. I can see from your tears.

PATIENT Yeah, but how do you know that's not just because, um, because it's something that I see other people have so I think I want it? I mean, how do you know that I had it at one time?

THERAPIST Because, you feel it so painful, so painful to you. You've lost it at some point, you know. People who don't know what it is can hardly feel the pain of not having it.

PATIENT The only thing I can think of is, um . . . I was little and uh, my brother Sam was, he was really good at swimming in high school. And, um, I still loved to swim and I, and I remember, I don't know, going to a swim meet or something and seeing him do really well and saying to my mom that I couldn't wait to swim when I was older. (Crying) And uh, she said that I'd never be good (crying) because I'm too lazy (crying) . . .

Now she cried deeply. I could take the turn for home. I will give her a long message, which is a little more complicated than I would prefer. But it will be all right, because it takes care of two essential matters. I will appreciate how her eagerness has been actually hurt, which means that she *did* have to withdraw when she felt so eager with the new man. No doubt about it. She is right that she has an actual weakness about committing herself. She has to have that weakness. We see how. I will also appreciate how she has to knock down her own worth. She *has* to give herself a technical knockout. I do not oppose her bringing herself back to zero. I only see just how it is accomplished.

THERAPIST I'll just say what I get from this and you can correct me. I'll just say this so you can see what I get and what I don't get. We just came a little while ago to something very painful. This business of why your eagerness has been held back. The answer is that your mother, and what was probably the most painful thing that you talked about today in terms of your crying was your mother's meanness when you were eager. This has a background which you understand somewhat. All this understanding in a way could be a little academic, because if you feel that any time you are going to be eager about something, you're going to get it, you know, I can see why you held it back. That seemed to be because you have had to hold back really getting involved in something and you are really critical of yourself because you really would like to be very eagerly involved. That has been held up in your development and has something to do with your relationship to your mother. But then, because of that, you meet these men who have these qualities, particularly Hal, that you admire and then you feel crushed because he's been able to go ahead and commit himself to something and you actually have been held up in that. That's the picture I've gotten. Does that sound right to you?

PATIENT Yeah.

THERAPIST So then you have to withdraw from this relationship with Hal because you don't feel like a match for him. You feel really second and third class compared to him. The real problem appears to be that, well, there are several problems. One is that you really do have a problem with committing yourself fully, and somehow, if you have trouble committing yourself that becomes some terrible thing about you — you're nothing. It's almost like there are two steps there. Meeting Hal did allow you to recognize that there has been something held up in your development, that's correct. But then it's like he becomes great and you become nothing. That makes it even worse. So then you have to think that you don't belong because you haven't solved this problem and you have no business being with the man. That's pretty clear. That's what brought you here. So I mean you were partly right in that there has been something held up but it's abetted by some cruelty to yourself that you don't belong.

PATIENT Yeah, because he liked me when I start feeling bad about myself.

THERAPIST He wasn't ready to say that you were no good, but you beat him to the punch. You expect cruelty so you were cruel to yourself and then you quit the relationship.

PATIENT Well, I didn't, but it was like he never called me back. I figured the evening was such a bomb that I was going to let him make the next move and he never did.

THERAPIST The reason the evening was such a bomb was because you . . . do you know what a technical knockout is in boxing? A technical knockout is when the boxer lies on the ring on the floor and the referee is saying, one, two, three, . . . and then the guy finally gets up at the last minute and he starts wobbling around. You were a technical knockout by yourself. He just didn't call you back. You already pretty much knocked yourself out, it appears. So we come around to the same thing over and over again in different forms. In the first hour we were talking about, you asked us, for starters today, how you might improve your self-image and the problem is that you were actively attacking yourself or letting other people in so many different ways and that is the reason that your self-image has a lot of holes in it. So that's what we found out today. I would say the question now is where do we go from here. We've got ten minutes. We should spend a little time deciding how you want to proceed. That is the understanding that you and I have developed about what is wrong — namely, that there are these certain kinds of things that are happening that are damaging. So what do you think?

Well, her reply was that she hated to do this to herself. She accepted the offer of help.

From Problem to Relevant Hypotheses:
A Method

I would like to show the main lines of this trial therapy, before I go on in the next chapter to tell of the middle game with this young woman. I will be succinct, because a method of methods has to generate the actual complexity of the patient's mind, with as few ideas as possible.

All interviews that I do move from the "loose end" of the patient's preoccupation into the labyrinth of related findings. The preoccupation of this young woman is, "I have a low opinion of myself." I will now lead into the opposing currents which are most powerful in bringing her back, over and over again, to this backwater. As I go along, I will continue to revise my hypothesis about what has to stay the same with her and what moves are most crucial to this end.

She says she has no self-confidence. This is her preoccupation. I say, right away, that I sense confidence. I am making a mark the opposite of hers. I am saying: "Maybe you feel no confidence. Maybe you could have much confidence. Let's see." I do not pull in the dark for the opposing current of confidence. I got it in the preliminary interview (Chapter 19), and I get it now in the confident eye which she gives me when we meet again.[8] Sure, she takes herself down too. She says she is boring and not worthwhile.

I say, "You don't feel original? Compared to whom?" Here I am drawing out the "other people in the room" who stand over her. I get Harry who is "funny . . . friendly . . . comfortable . . . and easygoing." Whereas she is "just really afraid . . . of rejection." She says she "shouldn't . . . protect myself . . . by doing that I don't get what I really need."

I move in opposition again. I say, "Sometimes a person learns to be a little cautious or protective and that's a good thing. . . . You can get hurt." I propose she has to have good reason for being fearful. I propose we find out how she came to be fearful.

These two oppositions by myself set up the interview very well. The first says there is confidence here, as well as no confidence. She has signaled me she has both. I have signaled back I see both. I will draw out the opposing currents. This is hopeful for her. Therefore, she will become involved with me. The second opposition says that I do not agree this fearfulness is a wrong response. Somehow it is right, but we don't know how. This allows her to bring the current of fearfulness forward. We will see where it began.

Now my job is to finger the possible currents of fearfulness which she brings forward. Which ones seem small? Which ones large? Her disconfirmation by her mother feels important. Her being wrecked by age five feels doubtful. Her being humiliated in elementary school seems ordinary. Her hitting a friend over cards also ordinary. I make marks and I ask her to mark back.

Now she claims to have had no close friends, being marginal. I doubt this as well. I ask, "Zero?" I get her being very close with Virginia, in high school, who unloaded on her. "She told me everything that was wrong with me." I say, "That sounds important." She is crying. She says the same unloading occurred with Judy in college.

When I summarize our little history at the close of the first hour, I emphasize that her being self-critical is making more sense. There was her mother disconfirming her. There were her two closest friends, Virginia and Judy, unloading on her. I see why she tends to draw terrible conclusions about herself. She notes it has even happened again last night before the interview. Her roommate unloaded on her.

My hypothesis is getting some confirmation. I see a young woman who *has* to have little confidence, because she takes herself down at a moment's notice, because somehow, she allows other people to unload on her. The two recurrent moves seem clear. Both bring her back to zero learning about self-confidence. The reader will notice that her taking herself down is a move which can be observed from an analytic position, whereas taking herself down and allowing others to unload on her can both be observed from an interpersonal position. Both moves could be seen to be in the service of maintaining a constant attitude, which would be, "I am not good enough." I do not yet know the domain or system in which such an attitude is necessary to be maintained.

Since the patient is launching on a different drift with me in the first hour, a drift in which her possible confidence and necessary fearfulness are appreciated, I am confident she will have to bring this learning right back to zero in the second hour to continue the same in her constant attitude of "not being good enough." I do not know *which* move she will utilize to do this. Will she confuse the beginning, the middle or the end of the second hour?

I chose to go back to what brought her to us now, hoping, thereby, to keep clear about where she wants to go. She tells me, then, about being undone when she met this new man whom she admired. He is tremendous. She is nothing.

I see her admiration for him, but I do not see why she has to be debased.

"Why twenty-four to nothing?" Here, she moves to clinch her lack of worth. She actually has a difficulty "committing" herself. This man has the ability. She has the difficulty. Don't I have to concede that she is ill?

I do not want to concede to her here, for her argument puts herself down, down, down. She is "not good enough." If I concede to her being in this swamp, the climb up the mountain to being "eventually good enough" is very, very long. I will not agree to this picture of her situation and of her prospects. Actually, I do not agree. I think this is her demonstrating another move to pin herself down, by putting someone else way above her, by this admiration at her own expense.

Therefore, I say something like Sullivan's saying he is "more encouraged than otherwise by the patient's distress" (Chapter 6). If my patient is in such pain about being "unable to commit" herself, then this has to mean that she knows very well from the past about becoming involved: "You know the difference. . . . I can see you know it from your tears. . . . You've lost it at some point, you know. People who don't know what it is can hardly feel the pain of not having it." I have reached her ability to commit herself, for she gives this to me now, and I also reach to her deep crying about losing her ability in relation to her mother.[9]

The interview is now complete. As Winnicott would say, I have made a transition back to her being well and back to her illness (Chapter 7). The road backward having been reached, now I indicate the road forward is also open and more promising. I see she is an eager person, who *has had* to expect to be knocked down by someone she admired, who *has had*, therefore, to give herself a technical knockout first. She responds that she dislikes these two moves. She wants to give them up. She wants to receive help to give them up.

Notice the logical levels implicit in this message. She is an eager person. But she got disconfirmed in her family. Therefore, she has to have a constant attitude that she is "not good enough." Therefore, she has to have these several moves to maintain this attitude, especially getting unloaded on by people she admires, especially knocking herself out in advance. Notice that I do not yet have much of an idea of how her constant attitude is serviceable in her family. I assume it is serviceable, but I leave it to the middle game to become clear about this aspect of the working hypothesis. Somehow, I assume, her "not being good enough" helps others in her family.

But, for now, it appears to be sufficient that I see she is eager, that she was disconfirmed, that she has this constant attitude, that this attitude is maintained by certain crucial moves I have specified. Right away, there is a degree of freedom for her, for she may dislike the two crucial moves which maintain the necessary class, the constant attitude of "not being good enough." Perhaps there are other ways of "not being good enough" at one logical level, while "eager" at another. If we find out what this attitude of "not being good enough" serves in her family system, then perhaps there is some other attitude which may also serve her family, allowing her fundamental eagerness to shine through.

My *method* has been to move from her preoccupation, her "loose end," her "problem," to work the "opposing currents" which bring her back, over and over again, to her backwater of "no self-confidence." I conclude with a hypothesis which sketches in all four logical levels whereby an individual arranges to "stay the same." My *method of methods* is to be revising all along, since any finding is only a mark, against which other marks may be opposed. Reliable finding depends on continual revision. Even as I conclude the trial therapy with this young woman, I only provide a provisional view. The middle game and the end game lie ahead, for improving the sketch.[10] This is my method of methods: I am continually ready to be shown to be wrong. I am continually ready to take all four observing positions as relevant to seeing how the patient closes to stay the same. I will be more succinct about the middle game and end game in Chapters 21 and 22, insofar as both only continue to improve on the way of discovering where the patient lives, which I have shown here in the trial therapy. Like Winnicott, I see later sessions as first sessions which are given over as often as they are needed by the patient.

21. *The Middle Game*

Adjourney in a new direction will have fine morale when its first danger has been overcome. This is one of the advantages of trial therapy, that patient and therapist have come through a major reversal with confidence in each other.[1] The auspicious beginning will now run into a series of further hazards.

I think there is one danger most to be feared in this middle game of the journey of brief therapy. This is to lose the broad outline of what was successful in the trial therapy. Something about that long session was good enough to get the patient pointing or heading in a more hopeful direction.[2] That something will be blurred, no doubt, concerning many essential points which will have to be clarified. That something also has been stated in some ways which will have to be revised. It has only been an approximation to a useful map. But something is gotten right when the worthwhileness of the patient has been recognized, her illness reached, and a serious attempt to destroy this success has been appreciated. How could the broad relations of this success be lost?

Alexander and French thought that the broad relations were lost in the details of session upon session unless retained as memory. I quote my favorite passage from their book for the third time, this last because I think the final sentence is wrong.

The analyst during this period may be compared to a traveler standing on top a hill overlooking the country through which he is about to journey. At this time it may be possible for him to see his whole anticipated journey in perspective. When once he has descended into the valley, this perspective must be retained in the memory or it is gone. From this time on, he will be able to examine small parts of this landscape in much greater detail than was possible when he was viewing them from a distance, but *the broad relations will no longer be so clear*. (1946, p. 109)

I agree this is exactly what happens when you live with someone. Only if you are ingenious about separations can you retain the thrill and scope of first meetings. I agree this is exactly what happens in many relations between patients and doctors. The relations become routine when the connection is assured.[3] No longer standing back from one another, doctor and patient locate smaller points of interest. But what if the doctor has a method for meeting his patient many times as if their meeting were the first meeting? This was Winnicott's idea for brief therapy. You give a "therapeutic consultation," and then you repeat it several more times if necessary. The word "consultation" implies a single meeting. Winnicott's idea is that single meetings could be repeated and still be singular if they could be far enough apart.[4] This is how Winnicott contrived to keep that unusual openness which patients bring to first meetings. This keeps the broad relations before us. In this sense Alexander and French were wrong about subsequent meetings, about the middle of brief therapy.[5]

If the reader accepts that it may be possible to keep the virtues of first meetings in the middle game of brief therapy, then he or she will want to know the method.

I may say a few things about the method in the abstract, but I will do better to show my meaning in relation to a given patient. Very broadly, the technique could be stated in a few sentences. I will be clear in my own mind before the session begins where the patient left off in the previous session. A major swerve will tell me very much. Then I will not go a step until I have the "loose end" of the patient's preoccupation for today's meeting. Then, when I follow that "loose end" into the labyrinth to see where this hope will lead, I will always find the patient has contrived to close out her own hope. I will be ready to appreciate this necessity.

If this sounds very much like the logic for trial therapy, then the reader hears right, for I want to start over anew in all subsequent meetings, almost as if we met for the first time. But not quite. Yes, I want the patient to give me her preoccupation as it is now. Yes, I want to build an idea of her labyrinth as it is now. The shape of the labyrinth is always changing (Selvini Palazzoli, et al. 1978), so I do not think it is very useful to catch how it was last week. This is like catching last session's dream this week. But no, last session's dream is not irrelevant, if I got a glimpse of how the patient's world was put together. Maybe I can catch that world better this week in its latest form.

Now we come to something crucial. For an individual to shift her direction successfully, she will have to reckon with three or four variables shifting simultaneously. If the individual only sees one of the variables, the other three or four will pull her back to zero — as in juggling.[6] The individual fails if she can watch only one of the flying variables.

THE YOUNG WOMAN WITH NO SELF-CONFIDENCE IN THE MIDDLE GAME

An illustration may be more helpful. Think back to the trial therapy of this patient, from the previous chapter. The "loose end" of her preoccupation was her hope for being successful with a man. The tangle led back to zero, because she arranged to compare herself unfavorably with the man, because she arranged to allow people to unload whatever barrage of criticism toward her they happened to harbor. Therefore, she did have an actual weakness about committing herself, which was sustained by these continuing operations.

This long session gave her hope that she might not have to do herself in. I doubt if it would have sustained a new direction for very long. Too many elements of this construction remained in the blur, elements which would also pull her back to zero as well, without being recognized.

The middle game of brief therapy allowed the therapist to identify the other crucial elements which we look to put together, to sight simultaneously in their present position. A few words about the missing elements in the broad relations of the trial therapy, which came together in the middle game with this patient, might help the reader to imagine the augmentation. Since I am talking about the work of 25 sessions with this patient, only the broad outline can be indicated.[7]

We knew the headings she asked for. We knew the operations to make herself weak. What did we miss before, which we got now? Well, three large discoveries were to follow, which had been implicit in that blur of the trial therapy. The first was the coming difficulty with the therapist. We didn't know he would be tempted to occupy a pedestal way above the patient. The reader may have guessed that from the patient's lowering herself, but we didn't know in advance that the therapist would be heightened. Therefore, one major element of the middle game was the therapist's getting himself out of that position. Once he began to follow the patient more faithfully, line by line, no longer receiving and giving messages from on high, then one of the crucial new elements was in place.

Also, we had not known the domain in which it was important for this young woman to knock herself down. We were struck in the middle game with how she herself was behaving perfectly to survive in her family. If she demeaned herself, then she got the consolation of being close to her father, who also thought little of himself. If she did not try to be understood, she would not get mauled repeatedly like her brother who spoke up. If she were hurt, then this brother was very pleasant and her mother showed great interest in her welfare.

Finally, we did not know what would happen if she made a surge forward. When the perfection of her playing in the family was appreciated, she made surges which were quite out of control. She would walk in dangerous areas half hoping someone would waylay her so she could let loose her outrage. She would criticize her brother, who would then get very angry, coming close to physical blows. This loss of control in the new direction was the third new element in the middle game.

These three new elements came forward out of the blur in the sequence I just described. Now the therapist could become more and more exact about how the elements fit together in any single session. The working hypothesis was improving by successive approximation (Chapter 10, Havens). Five or six crucial variables could be read in a single constellation. When this is occurring, I think the patient stands a very good chance of staying on a promising new drift, because the five or six ways she could be swept back are all being held in view.

In summary, the therapist was able to observe this patient at several specific locations in which the following points could be seen: what she wanted to do next; how she weakened herself to undo this movement; how this helped put the therapist above her; how this allowed her to continue to survive in her family; and how she would surge too far and fast if she didn't undo herself.

In underlining three new elements sighted in the middle game with the Young Woman With No Self-Confidence, I do not want to oversimplify the reader's understanding of the methods used to reach these findings. I only want to specify the new findings which were unknown to us in the trial therapy.

A Survey of the Technical Means Necessary to a Reliable Method in the Middle Game

I do not see any new technical devices or concepts which emerge in the middle game. What is different is the recognition of many simultaneous and sequential maneuvers by the patient, which bring about closure at different logical levels. The therapist has to sustain an ear for increasing polyphony. In this way the middle game is much more demanding. Many can follow the exposition of a single theme, but few avoid confusion when such a theme seems to break up into many variations and modulations and contradictions.

Indeed, there is no method which can keep the most expert of us from becoming lost in some sessions. All we can achieve is a reliable method for revising our method as it proves imperfect or unsuitable as we go along.

I find some ideas necessary to my continual revision of method. Some of my confidence in this set of ideas derives from my being able to be more helpful to the residents and fellows who conduct the cases in our clinic. They seem able to use this procedure of thinking to revise their own methods very well. They seem able to sustain a very complicated technique necessary to the labyrinths provided by our patients.

I find the *minimum* set of technical concepts for revising the middle game to be as follows: location of the problem for every session; finding perspectives for relevant observations; clarifying and revising hypotheses which organize the problem and relevant observations; working opposing currents in conducting the interview; posing an appreciation of the necessary closure(s) to be conserved back to the patient so that new moves within such classes may be discovered.

The following survey of these technical ideas from the work in the middle game with the Young Woman With No Self-Confidence is deceptive in its simplicity. The reader must not suppose that he or she may borrow the thinking quite so fast as it is described.

About the concept of locating the problem for each session, I will say little more than to urge that it is indispensable. Nothing useful will occur unless the therapist can locate the "loose end" of the patient's current "preoccupation." Half of the sessions will be useless unless the therapist is determined to find this "loose end," unless he or she is willing to take 15 minutes or a half-hour to do what the patient is very unlikely to do on her own.

A small book could be written on this subject of "locating the problem." Indeed, several books are mostly about this subject, especially Winnicott (1971b) and Haley (1973). A little outline by myself for such a book may be of interest. I usually ask a patient what she hopes to get from me in the session. Sometimes she will not know. Then, I say, "Well, let's see if we can find out." Being explicit is very helpful, but I have to listen as well and watch the patient closely to locate her preoccupation. I may ask her to mention a number of possible preoccupations, probing them as we go through for depth (Winnicott, 1971a, Chapter 2). Thus, we may hit upon what the Milan team (Selvini Palazzoli et al., 1978a, p. 14) called the "nodal point, P_s." Still, we may not be able to tell for half an hour or even longer. I will not leave this subject. When locating the patient's preoccupation is this difficult, there is usually some disturbing feeling about myself which the patient fears to mention. I would not discover such a feeling, if I were not *determined* to wait for the "loose end" before going any farther. In spite of my dedication about beginning in this way, I occasionally plunge ahead with a patient into something which interests me about him or her. This usually means I have been captured by an obligatory relation.[8]

Of the relevant perspectives for observation for any problem, I have devoted the 16 chapters of Part II and the theoretical summary of Part III. Long study from each of these observing positions is also indispensable for using them well. The therapist with the Young Woman With No Self-Confidence depended upon crucial observations from all four perspectives presented in this book. He was able to continue from the trial therapy in reaching both her well-being and her disturbance: how she could be powerful, how she canceled herself out. This perspective on the closure against her own needs was continually observed in countless variations. Secondly, he and the patient reached a more accurate definition of her constant attitude, her barrier against being reached and found, namely her "wily ways" so well conveyed by the gesture of her mysterious smile. Thirdly, they reached a more precise definition of her crucial security operations, which she utilized with or against the therapist in their work together, especially an oscillation between being "buddy buddy" and putting the therapist back up on a "pedestal." Finally, they not only described the family game, but also the patient's part in triggering hostile moves towards herself, for example, in inviting "mental dentistry" by her mother.

All of these observations contributed to an improvement of the *hypothesis* which was sketched in the trial therapy, namely, that this patient could have considerable confidence, except for her arranging to bring herself down or to get others to unload on her. Her present and chronically recurring pain about lack of confidence was explained by such a mechanism being triggered so frequently that she herself could not see that she ever felt worthwhile. The trial therapy had reached her well-being and the mechanism of her illness. But such a hypothesis did not deliver her from her illness. It only gave hope that such a deliverance might be possible, since her well-being was found and the mechanism of its being confounded was seen in outline.

What the patient saw in the middle game was how this mechanism of her recurrent pain was triggered, specifically because of her necessary preoccupation with reducing her own arousal (especially of aggression), with maintaining her "wily" attitude, with balancing her security operations between being "buddy buddy" and getting the therapist back up on a "pedestal," with reinstating her family game, such as by triggering "mental dentistry" from her mother.

This specification of the mechanism of action of her recurrent pain gave the patient new degrees of freedom. If arranging to attack herself or to be attacked for being worthwhile was appreciated as a move within these several classes of necessary preoccupations, then the patient might experiment with comparable moves which would be less painful for her. Indeed, she found other moves for modulating her forcefulness, for being "wily" in her attitude, for adjusting her security about her actual strengths and weaknesses, for staying in relation to her family (see Appendix for follow-up interview).

Finally, the therapist kept access to her difficulties by a steadfast attitude of positive connotation towards the very mechanism of pain of which the patient complained. She did not put herself through such pain for nothing and for minor advantages. She continued such reductions of her confidence in the service of her most serious preoccupations. Such access also depends upon *working opposing currents*, which keeps the field of observation open to findings which are contradictory.

For example, just think of the specific observations which improved the working hypothesis from the trial therapy. They are quite contradictory in appearance, until understood. Here is a patient who is not only lacking in confidence, but in danger of surges of excessive confidence. Here is a patient who appears to have a constant attitude of "not being good enough," who may also have an opposite attitude of being "wily." Here is a patient who makes herself secure by putting the therapist on a "pedestal," but also can be "buddy buddy" with that therapist. Here is a patient who is victimized in her family game, who is actively triggering such moves by her family.

I hope the complexity of the method has been generated for the reader from these few terms. I hope also that it is evident why less sophistication could have led to failure. Working the emotional currents was necessary for reaching the patient's pain and for reaching her great forcefulness. But it is dangerous merely to augment someone's intensity (as by analyzing resistance). This is like speeding up a rollercoaster on a track with very strange loops.

Crashes are inevitable. For this patient, the mechanism of self-attack would loop her back to zero to conserve her constant attitude, her oscillation of security operations, and her family game. Yet it is not helpful to follow such strange loops from an excessive distance. Such sophistication could leave the patient feeling quite alone. She would rightly object, or reject the relationship. Thus, the therapist must be and stay with the patient, as well as becoming astute in improving the working hypothesis.

THE LONG MIDDLE GAME

I do not believe it is always possible to know the length of the middle game to be played. I believe it is desirable to estimate the length, when the therapist has an understanding of what is likely to allow a brief therapy, what is likely to prolong the discovery. I prefer to give the patient an estimate, while being quite prepared to be proven wrong. I do not like to underestimate the patient's dedication to very complicated arrangements. Often, this has been necessary to connect several generations, which are evolving too fast to hold together in any other way (Chapter 18). Therefore, I think Freud is right to say that the middle game can be very long. The middle game can become an epic, a "fable composed of many fables" as Aristotle said of the Odyssey. Then we have long-term therapy, from this extension of the middle game.

If we are modest enough to admit that the scope of the middle game may prove more elaborate than we thought in the preliminary interview and in the trial therapy, if we grant that the patient may only let us in on these necessary complications after a while, and if we still want to have estimates of the length of therapy which are reliable in most cases, then what principles will help us draw the distinction between a middle game which will be a single story and a middle game which will be a succession of stories?

I hope the reader has an idea of a brief middle game from the Case of the Young Woman With No Self-Confidence. To recapitulate in a few sentences, a brief middle game will discover the several different ways in which the patient has to stay the same, despite an inclination for different direction. The game to bring the patient back to zero, the pull of the therapist into this game, the domain in which such a game is perfect, the surge in a new direction which has too little control—if all of these ways to stay the same, to close as usual, are appreciated together, then the patient may find a new trajectory which is steady and reliable.[9]

Such a description allows us to imagine opposite of situations which will not allow the patient clear sailing on a new track. I see three kinds of "lengthening factors" (Malan, 1963). First of all, some patients dare not give us such access to a full view of themselves. Some will have been hurt too much. They will connect slowly. They will be quite unsure of being able to defend themselves against our failings. Although we believed they passed the two great tests of normality, they did not; they only seemed to pass. Therefore, they cannot swiftly come to the conclusion that they have found a hospitable place with the therapist. The predatory world cannot be excluded.[10] Therefore, the camouflage and posturing and the disguises will keep the patient's situation blurred. We will not appreciate how the closure to stay the same is actually being arranged — not in a brief while.

A second kind of lengthening factor is not so much a denial of access, not so much a problem of hiding and blurring, but rather a problem of the actual complexity of the patient's game. He or she may only demonstrate one piece at a time. He or she has devoted most of his or her life to perfecting a long set of performances. This set is appreciated for all its subtlety by the patient's family. No rough sketch by the therapist could possibly do justice to such a game. The therapist must appreciate all the angles, such as Freud did for the Rat Man (Gustafson, unpublished).

A third kind of lengthening factor concerns the possible stability of any drift the patient may adopt. There are environments in which it is possible to get along in a relatively simple and straightforward way. For example, a patient such as the Young Woman With No Self-Confidence may be able to choose new friends in college who will appreciate her strength. She may not need to undo herself for such friends, as has been necessary with her family. She may retain the subtlety for visits home, while maintaining a course with new friends which is reliable and which therefore lasts for a long time. But many patients are not so fortunate about the course of future interactions. They have to continue to live in a world of difficult diplomatic relations. What was successful last month is hit from the side next month. Foreign policy may only be successful when it has been hammered out over several years of trial and error with the therapist in consultation. The concept may be gotten right even in the trial therapy, but its implications for many difficult people and trying institutions may take some experiment. I suppose the most common example of such patients who stay in very difficult worlds are therapists who become patients. They put themselves into difficulties from which most other people would run, in the opposite direction. Therefore, given this fascination with trouble, they will have more versions of trouble than the average person to figure out. Consequently, they will tend to have an adventure in the middle game of therapy which is a much longer set of fables. This is also true for other diplomats of the labyrinth.[11]

THE MIDDLE GAME ON DEMAND, OR LONG BRIEF THERAPY

If the middle game may be brief or long, a single story or a set of stories, it may also be anywhere in between. But this "in between" need not be so grey and so lacking in shape as a category of "neither brief nor long." Sometimes the patient has some hopeful possibilities for reaching other people and for defending himself or herself, but the outcome is frequently in doubt. The access of the therapist to the patient, the complexity of the game, and the difficulty of the tests for a new direction are also in doubt. A useful third way to pose the middle game in such situations is to give sessions after the trial therapy "on demand."

Winnicott invented this possibility. When he gave "therapeutic consultations," which meant something very deep and meaningful to a child, he did not want to drop the child right there. His idea was that being able to come back was a kind of continuing with him which could be very sustaining. For some children, this meant much more than weekly sessions, which could become routine. It meant getting back, as needed. Winnicott wrote of only a few such arrangements with grownup patients, but I understand they were common with him (Chapter 7).

I find this possibility very useful as well for patients who are not obviously suited for brief therapy. There is hope for brief therapy, but it is clouded by the uncertainty of the ability to connect and the ability to defend, by the uncertainty of any of the three kinds of lengthening factors. The patient may also have little money or have a health maintenance plan which gives few visits. Long-term therapy cannot be supported, but it may become necessary. Brief therapy is a chance, but I want to be ready if the chance is not fulfilled. If the preliminary interview and the trial therapy are encouraging in these situations, I will suggest further sessions "on demand."[12] This is what the Milan team has called long brief therapy, because the few sessions are provided over a long time period of several years or more. An example follows.

THE CASE OF THE BUSINESSMAN ON PROBATION

This man came to me while he was in business school, because he was nearly failing. He claimed he was a "slow learner" and a "poor presenter." He was quite a forceful attorney in the case against himself. The average jury would have found him guilty as charged on both counts. I suppose I helped him in our four sessions in the first year by my unwillingness to accept the verdict. I became interested in the occasions when he was not slow, when he was not poor in presenting. I thought it impossible that he had always been slow and diffident. I sensed someone who could be very fast and bold. I didn't know why he had to hide such capacity, but I held out to him that this was my belief.

He gave me only a little evidence to back up my hypothesis. He did a little better, so he could pass.[13] He broke up with a girlfriend who was an albatross for him. But he was sly. He kept his distance like a poker player. So he did well enough, until he was just about to graduate the following year, when he appeared again. He said he was in dread of the new job he had secured for himself. In the last of these several sessions, he could hardly talk. He began in a vague way, but most of the two hours was an awkward silence. A week later he arrived in New York City for his job and he wrote me a long letter to explain the silence. The letter concerned his "Sam Against the World" stance which had always been in the way of our communications, especially at our conclusion. I understood the letter only a little at the time. What he wrote was not obscure, but I could not yet place its meaning in relation to his various difficulties. I will come back to the letter, as I got another chance with him.

After a year in business in New York City, he came back to me for two long sessions while on vacation. He'd survived, but he was on probation. It was difficult to tell if the probation were due more to a "marginal competence" or to his having been pegged as "difficult." I did learn he had told off an insecure boss. I was interested in why he had been unable to keep his mouth shut. Was he too "slow" with his mind? Was he too "quick" with his tongue? I may have helped him too much with his "slowness." Maybe I was seeing the consequences of that "improvement." This was my thinking at the end of our first two-hour meeting.

He came in for our second meeting tied up in silence, tears, and anger. For nearly an hour I could get almost nothing, until I asked him if I could reread his letter from a year earlier, when we had been stuck in a similar predicament.

The letter explained that he had survived by an attitude of "Sam Against the World" or "Ask For Nothing." His father hated him while his mother loved him for his self-reliance. All had gone well enough for him until business school, when he actually needed help with his study. He asked, but he felt wrong. He was giving in to his father, betraying his mother. But if he did not ask, he would fail school. He was a loser, either morally or literally.

Reading this letter while he sat crying and tossing himself about on my couch in frustration, I could imagine why he was now stuck. Again, he could not afford to give up his posture of "Sam Against the World" to ask for my help, but neither could he *not* ask for my help. So he did the next best possible thing. Neither. He stayed silent, while thrashing about in obvious misery.

I was glad to have kept where we had left off before in my mind, for my understanding of this led him now to pour out his present predicament. If he were "Sam Against the World" in his corporation, he would be attacked as "arrogant." If he were needful, he would be "too vulnerable." He recounted several versions, which seemed to provide evidence for such a double bind.

Now he asked me if I thought he was "paranoid" to think that his boss was after him. It appeared that his boss was looking for someone to pick on. He thought the junior executives would have a consensus about this judgment. This was why he had confessed his weaknesses to the boss when he was put under his supervision. He hoped to have less anxiety if he were not in dread of being found out later. Now he saw that this confession had identified him as a victim for a boss on the look for a victim. He had given this fellow quite an opening.

I doubt if our long brief therapy was over. I have only given him three little series of meetings on demand. All I am saying here is that such a schedule may allow someone with less security to make themselves known with startling clarity over several more years.[14] I think I now have put together several elements in his staying the same, so that I was able to imagine his complex activity in single crucial and telling meeting with myself. I saw how being "slow or fast" is a game in which he triggers others to put him down. Such a valve is a beautiful device to hold himself back.[15] This is perfect for his relation with his parents, for he is always able to include one or the other by making one pleased with him, the other denouncing, by either his slowness or his fastness. I got a terrific new variation, which was being neither slow nor fast, but stuck. I was able to appreciate the necessity of this position for him, because I saw that "slowness" was not improved when he got going "fast." The surge only gave him new trouble.

Now it remains to be seen what the drift is of being neither too "slow" nor too "fast" nor stuck. Since I see him "on demand" I do not worry about this possibility which remains in the blur. He will come for another visit when necessary. I will know where we left off here, so I will be thinking about it when he comes back. The intervening experiences may be seen as providing data about this "loose end," a kind of natural experiment.[16]

22. *The End Game*

RUTHLESSNESS

Finally, the patient subtracts the therapist from the course of his or her life. He or she says: "I cancel you, I delete you, I will do it myself." If the therapist has been recognizing this closure of the patient all along, the final, literal end will be similar to previous sessions.[1] The patient has always been playing the end game. While I will be very brief in this chapter, the reader will understand the entire book is about this subject, about closure.

But something is revealed more sharply, more poignantly, at the literal end of a relationship than could be seen anywhere along the way. What has been given is often recognized when it is being taken or sent away. I think here of Hart Crane's poem "Praise for an Urn, In Memoriam: Ernest Nelson":

> It was a kind and northern face
> That mingled in such exile guise
> The everlasting eyes of Pierrot
> And, of Gargantua, the laughter.
>
> His thoughts, delivered to me
> From the white coverlet and pillow
> I see now, were inheritances —
> Delicate riders of the storm.
>
> The slant moon on the slanting hill
> Once moved us toward presentiments
> Of what the dead keep, living still,
> And such assessments of the soul
>
> As, perched in the crematory lobby,
> The insistent clock commented on,
> Touching as well upon our praise
> Of glories proper to the time.
>
> Still, having in mind gold hair,
> I cannot see that broken brow
> And miss the dry sound of bees
> Stretching across a lucid space.
>
> Scatter these well-meant idioms
> Into the smoky spring that fills
> The suburbs, where they will be lost.
> They are no trophies of the sun.

As in this poem, the relationship between patient and therapist may become most clear before it is dispersed. Borges described this "moment" as follows:

A contemporary novel requires five or six hundred pages to make us know somebody, if it ever does. For Dante a single moment is enough. In that moment a person is defined forever. Dante unconsciously sought that central moment. I have wanted to do the same in many stories, and I have been admired for a discovery which actually belongs to Dante in the Middle Ages: that of presenting a moment as a cipher of a life. In Dante we have characters whose lives may consist of only a few tercets, and yet their lives are eternal. They live in a word, in a gesture; they need do nothing more . . .(1984, p. 15)

I think Dante sees so sharply with such characters because he is taking leave even as he meets them. Little blurring of himself and the object occurs.

Now when the patient drops the therapist, something very individual about that patient has a chance of standing out. This chance will be fulfilled, I think, only if the ruthlessness of the patient can be accepted by the therapist. Winnicott put this very well:

. . . growing up means taking the parent's place. It *really does*. In the unconscious fantasy, growing up is inherently an aggressive act. . . . If the child is to become adult, then this move is achieved over the dead body of an adult (I must take it for granted that the reader knows that I am referring to unconscious fantasy, the material that underlies playing). . . . In the total unconscious belonging to growth at puberty and in adolescence, there is the *death of someone*. . . . there is to be found death and personal triumph as something inherent. . . . But somewhere in the background is a life-and-death struggle. The situation lacks its full richness if there is a too easy and successful avoidance of the clash of arms. (1971a, pp. 144–145)

Now what is this "something very individual" about the patient which stands out when his or her ruthlessness is accepted in the ending?

I see the individual patient standing out sharply in the end in one of two ways. One way is in going too far. As the patient is dismissing me, he shows how he will *provoke* others in his own inimitable way to stop his accomplishment. A second way is to go all the way back to zero in his most characteristic gesture. He finishes himself off. These, I find, are the two great challenges of the last sessions. These are the two chief routes for not growing up.[2]

GOING TOO FAR: THE CASE OF THE POLICEMAN'S DAUGHTER

Revisited in Termination

The reader may recall this young woman from Chapter 10 who would get overheated like her mother, only to get cool like her dad the cop, and back again. After the intense meeting I reported, she, of course, had a cool and distant meeting in which she doubted if I could do more for her. For our final meeting, she began calmly. She felt less "illusional" about the lost boyfriend, but she felt apt to get "manic" in his presence. Could we talk over this agitation?

Soon the agitation found its vocabulary. She felt the boyfriend was a "schmuck" and she wanted her revenge upon him. Maybe someone else would hurt him? After all, she had been hurt further in trying four subsequent fellows. She would like to "decimate" someone. Yet she was scared because she saw she could be much too much for people in this way, even at work.

I agreed. I said her liberal use of the word "asshole" was indeed a problem. She inflicted it right and left as she talked with me. This startled her, for she had not given this usage any thought at all. She just talked offhandedly in that crude way. I thought she might not need to inflict, nor incur, "degradation" quite so much. She agreed, smiled, and left. Perhaps she will be less in need of bringing on the cops?

GOING BACKWARDS FAST: A CASE OF A SECOND-CLASS CITIZEN

Here we see the reverse, which is equally common. This man missed his second to last session after some hopeful improvements. He came to his last meeting, withdrawn, back to putting others on a pedestal, himself as second-class, as when I first met him.

How was I to appreciate the necessity of this ruination? Several large hints were available to me. One was that he reported he had begun to think much less of several important people in his life. He came close to dismissing them. A second was that he had not paid this bill for several months. When I asked him about this bill, he dismissed *me*: This was no concern of his. His mother would take care of it eventually. Why was I taking up *his* last session with *my* selfish interests? I told him I damn well was going to ask after my interests. He gulped and then finally allowed that I had a point.

Now I could tell him why he had arranged to put his important people back up on the pedestal of being superior beings in judgment of him. Then he could be cold, selfish, and bad again. I thought this necessary. This helped him survive. If he were well, he would take too many second chances with people. He would be offhand, as with me about the bill. It was better not to do this with people, better not to trust so much, better to nurse himself as a no-good person.

The following week I got paid after he talked with his mother. I think he felt better about himself again. Perhaps he could feel better more carefully?

AN EYE FOR AN EYE

The last session is an opportunity to put a stop to something promising, to a triumph in which the therapist is dismissed: the patient may either show a readiness to get others to stop him or do the job on himself. I like to receive these little murders with equanimity. I will only do a little, because I want to say, "Look, do yourself in if you must. I will not be pulled in to save you, because you're on your own. I will tell you what I see as your crucial move. This is how you bring yourself back to zero as you go out the door."

I think Sullivan's admonition about psychiatric skill is most apt in these parting shots: " I think the development of psychiatric skill consists in very considerable measure of doing a lot with very little — making a rather precise move which has a high probability of achieving what you're attempting to achieve, with a minimum of time and words" (1954, p. 224). The brevity is more important at the very end, because the patient is apt to make a ruthless move against him or herself, because the doctor may only make a single move back without becoming excessively responsible.

Therefore, the Policeman's Daughter shows how she provokes attack by her crude speech. Therefore, I give her a double description back. I say that I understand her urge to humiliate men and I also understand crude talk as *a way* to put men down and get herself hit back. I distinguish between the class and the particular move within that class. This allows her to reconsider: Is there some other way to enjoy savagery?

Thus, the Second-Class Citizen shows how he puts himself back in his place, elevating everyone but himself. Therefore, I give him back a double description. I say I understand that he is too self-concerned when he is feeling better and that being a second-class citizen is *a way* for him to stay mindful of other people. I distinguish, again, between the class and the particular move within that class. This allows him to reconsider: Is there some other way to be cautious?

The rule in my experience with brief therapy is that the patient makes a relatively simple, but powerful, thrust at himself or herself at the end, which calls for a relatively simple, but powerful, thrust back from the doctor, which is an appreciation of the move to handle a class of difficulties. The exception is a very complicated move by the patient at the end, which requires an equally complicated appreciation back from the doctor. I see this latter situation much more often in long-term therapy, where the patient and I have been describing a labyrinth of contradictions which hold the patient in place.

THE FOREST RANGER'S DEPARTURE

The reader may remember this patient, who had been in grave danger of suicide, measuring himself against his friend Jack as unable to be close (Chapter 8). I had seen this as an impossible aim for him, appreciating his (philobatic) need for wide open spaces. He responded very well in the year following by attenuating his relation with Jack, locating more accepting people in a new job, finding a girlfriend, and finally deciding to go back to graduate school in ecology. Evidently, my interpersonal perspective at that time helped him find a road which was possible for him, although I never did at that time understand why he had been trying to go the impossible road with Jack.

Now that he was leaving me, I got another shot at the disturbance I had seen before. This last time around I was more prepared for the complexity of this family game, which would allow me to appreciate the necessity of his interpersonal faults.

We reenter the story of this patient in session 232, the fifth from the last. He posed the problem to me of having gotten "a little weird" while I was away on vacation, listening to his friends about their miseries, saying none of his about his leaving. A "little weird" meant a few hours of despair, thinking if suicide were not the only way, etc. What would he do if that happened after he had left me? Could he talk to his new friends?

This session distressed me. I could see from my questions that he was determined to prove to me that he could not depend on friends. They didn't ask him about his troubles. If he had begun, and gone too far, too deep or too long, his friends wouldn't tell him. His gestures were very telling. His lips were closed like a book. His interpersonal maneuvers, his constant bodily attitude, and his anticipation of future loneliness all looked right to me.

I felt gloomy, not looking forward to challenging such resolute closure with so few sessions. Mapping three such closures onto a map with three levels left me as lost as him. I pondered whether a fourth level concerning the family game might throw the necessity of this session into relief.

For the 233d session, fourth from the last, he posed a variation on the problem of the previous session, "Perhaps I don't know how to criticize, when I am being ignored?" "If I ask for something for myself . . . and it goes no better . . . what do I do then?"

As before he seemed to have a reply against every avenue for addressing his girlfriend. It was an open and shut case — no way could he criticize her without making matters worse. This time I was ready for him. I told him that he was right that no one should be given disturbing feelings. His family had already settled that question. Indeed, he was a brilliant attorney for his family, proving that it was impossible to criticize without making matters worse. I accepted his proof. *Quod est demonstratum*. I waited for him here. He seemed thoughtful. "If it is impossible to criticize my girlfriend, haven't I chosen someone with a fragile ego?" he offered. "Haven't I chosen someone like myself, so the two of us fragile egos become more and more careful?"

I replied that I did not find him fragile. He argued so keenly. His argument must be entirely right, for such a proof about criticizing his girlfriend helped him maintain his attitude that being uncritical, undemanding, and unselfish is best. Although it may give the appearance of "fragility," this was one of the strongest possible doctrines. He was the best possible advocate for such a family doctrine.

He drew the conclusion: "But then I am left with all my feelings, always lonely." Yes, I had to agree.

Notice the degrees of freedom which have been introduced by a fourth logical level. Actually we are both freer. I do not have a struggle against overwhelming threefold closure of interpersonal argument, constant attitude, and painful, inevitable feeling. I may see all of these as in service of a fourth closure, namely the family game, even as perfect for that game, which relieves my distress of being caught in this juggernaut.

Now for him: now his doctor sees the necessity of going along with the family, whose organization has been well worked out over three, four or more generations. They live in a glass house pretending all are "fragile." No one must be given disturbing feelings.

But how to do this? I say the patient is a brilliant, fierce attorney for "fragility." This suggests a different view of how it is possible to conserve the "fragile" organization. One could swallow it whole, believing oneself fragile. One could be a fierce representative of fragility. One could, no doubt, make ten other different moves as well. Here is the first degree of freedom introduced, that any move, of any stripe, which backs the family as a "fragile" organization, is acceptable. Now the patient is free to see himself as the opposite of fragile, if it pleases him.

This need not disturb his constant attitude of being unselfish, uncritical, and undemanding. But such an attitude itself becomes more variable. He is fiercely uncritical. He is very critical of criticism. Here is a second degree of freedom of attitude, something more complex, like Indian pacifism. Of course, that is just how such traditions hold together over many generations, by such astonishing complexity of attitude. The same could be said of the Catholic church or of Judaism or any other complex tradition which has lasted centuries.

Finally, yes, he must be lonely. But since feelings states all fall in the class of acceptable states of mind for the constant attitude, then such a more complex attitude is apt to widen the set of acceptable feelings states. All, in some way, may contribute to the fragile spirit of the unselfish, undemanding, and uncritical, even by showing how episodes of gross selfishness, excessive demands, and harsh criticism show the wisdom of the virtues. After all, heaven is not appreciated without hell.

In summary, my reply to this young man accepts the necessity of certain difficulties when he has left me behind. Yes, he will have difficulty asking for help from friends, in place of me. Yes, he will be unable to be critical of them when they disappoint him. Yes, he will think of them and himself as "fragile." Yes, he will, therefore, be lonely. But all of these troubles are only moves. He may substitute different moves to stay the same in the several ways I have described.

We have seen many such simple currents soon lost in the
sand . . . Tradition is a matter of much wider significance . . .
if you want it you must obtain it by great labor . . . within it
the whole of the literature of his own country has a simultaneous existence and composes a simultaneous order.

—T. S. Eliot, 1919

PART V

Learning Problems

But the only way to apply something like the scientific method
in politics is to proceed on the assumption that there can be no
political move which has no drawbacks, no undesirable consequences.

—Karl Popper, 1957

23. *Autopoietic Students*

THERAPISTS have to close to stay the same in their method, but we forget this, as if we could instruct them. We cannot, any more than we can instruct patients, but we overlook this more easily because of the conventions of education.[1]

Actually, when a therapist borrows an idea, this may add or subtract from his or her capacity. A second eye may make the first eye better by allowing depth of field. A second eye may make the first eye worse by inducing the confusion of double vision.

We teachers are often seduced by the patient's predicament, so we feel compelled to persuade the trainee to carry out our therapeutic idea. If our rhetoric is powerful, the trainee may be induced to do something which fits very badly with his or her own inclinations. We act like Cassius or Mark Antony, inducing Brutus to think of the fate of Rome, losing himself down a fast slope in the dark. Even worse is our criticism, which makes the therapist feel small. We only set in motion some desperate attempt by the therapist to recover his footing and his height, which will take precedence over the needs of the patient.

Therefore, I say the main job of the teacher is to remember his place, which is to be given a chance at the dilemma of the therapist. The teacher has no access to the patient. The teacher may have a little access to the therapist, if he will listen to where the therapist is stuck, if he will remember he has only a chance to say one or two ideas.

If the teacher conducts a group supervision or consultation about cases in progress, as I do in our Brief Therapy Clinic, then he has no access to the patient or the individual therapist, but only to the relation between the individual therapist and his or her peers.

I do not expect what I say about access in individual or group supervision to be self-evident. Allow me to pose some of the routine problems which come up to me in teaching in our clinic.

THE LOOSE END

Before students get to know my ways very well, I most often get a presentation without a question, without a loose end. Why?

Often the trainee is pleased with a success, but he or she will not announce this to peers or to myself. The peers will then begin to search for something wrong. The report being intended as a success, the search will be futile. Hence, I always want to know right away if the therapist feels relatively successful. If this virtue can be confirmed, then the therapist will not need to use his or her time proving and defending what has been accepted forthrightly. He or she may pose a lesser difficulty or exception to the overall success, which the group could help think over.

Often the trainee will make a very long report because he or she fears to say that something about the session seemed wrong. I will not allow long reports. I interrupt. I say we understand such and such from what the therapist has reported and now what would the therapist like from us?

Often the trainee will have made his own assessment of his difficulty between the session and the group supervision, but he will act naively as if he is asking the group for their ideas about his mysterious difficulty. The group then shoots in the dark, not knowing the hypothesis of the therapist. The therapist smugly watches his peers be more foolish than he was in the session. Therefore, I always ask the therapist for his own hypothesis about what went wrong, before allowing the peers to attempt to be of help. If we know the starting point of the therapist in the supervision, we have a chance of helping him improve upon the position.[2]

AUDIOTAPE OR VIDEOTAPE SEGMENTS

When we have gotten the therapist's question about some difficulty, the therapist's hypothesis about that difficulty and the therapist's brief narrative report of relevant events, we get the therapist to play for us some segments of audiotape or videotape of the session.[3] Almost always, I will ask for the opening minutes of the session before we go on to later segments. Why? Often a crucial communication is missed straight off. The patient will suggest she is welling up with excitement about her progress, but veer in mid-sentence back to the usual list of complaints. The therapist will often follow into the complaints. The patient will give some small outcry of distress, which is lapped over by bland sentences. Often a small interaction at the outset will disqualify the therapist. A stubborn proud young man may get his therapist digging for something wrong. A hysterical young woman may get her therapist off on a wild goose chase about some complaint. The session may never recover.

LATER TROUBLES

More subtle are the problems of proportion. The patient offers a little problem, a big improvement. Can the therapist get the proportions right? If he jumps with both feet on the little problem, he will get nowhere. The patient speaks of her unwillingness to "carry all of her eggs in one basket," and her voice falters momentarily and strangely about "eggs cracking," only to rush on. The communication lasts a second or two, but it is more important than the other 60 minutes. Does the group have an ear for momentary faults which are enormous? For momentary pleasure which is a new departure? Proportions cannot be judged from the relative time of the report, but only by an ear which may imagine their meaning.

Mostly what the group hears are familiar games. Does the therapist have to be put on a pedestal? Does the patient have to blame herself? Is hysterical distraction going to be bought? Will the therapist be drawn into competition? The answer to all of these questions is usually yes. After a few months the group of bright and sensitive residents and fellows will get skillful at recognizing the therapist going under in one of these interactions.

The difficulty left to the teacher is often deceptive. How would the teacher have done something different? What would he do now that the error has been committed? With such questions, the teacher will often go under with the group. I recall my feeling ever so foolish on one occasion when I was asked to improve upon the lengthy remarks of one of the residents who was anxious with one of his patients. I gave a long speech on the importance of being brief. No one even smiled. So ridiculous. But this is the tidal pull of many patients upon us — upon the therapist from the patient, upon the group from the therapist, upon myself from the group.

The most powerful pull upon us occurs when the patient appears to be doing very well, but suddenly returns to zero learning. All of us want to do something to stop such misfortune. We would have conducted the session so this would not have happened. We would have found a way to right it at the time. We know what to do in the session which follows. In general, all of this call to action is foolishness. It means we are being pulled in. Thus, we learn gradually over the year of the clinic how to appreciate why these events have to happen. We become more and more interested in problems and hypotheses, less and less interested in doing anything about them. The following is the final consultation of the 1984–85 clinic, which may give the reader an idea of one of our better consultations as a group to one of the residents. The reader may come to understand why I say I have no access to the patient or to the individual therapist in such a situation.

THE CASE OF THE RAT EXPRESS

One of our bright and sensitive residents, let us call him Dr. Heinz, presented one of the favorite patients of the clinic for a final consultation. The man's way of talking was poetic, in a kind of offhand, Midwestern, lonesome way, which reminds me now of "Evening Song" of Sherwood Anderson:

> Back of Chicago the open fields — were you ever there?
> Trains coming toward you out of the West —
> Streaks of light on the long grey plains?
>   Many a song —
> Aching to sing.

I've got a grey and ragged brother in my breast —
That's a fact.

Back of Chicago the open fields — were you ever there?
Trains going from you into the West —
Clouds of dust on the long grey plains.
Long trains go West, too — in the silence.
Always the song —
Waiting to sing.

This appealing man, let us call him Mr. Larson, had found a very good ear in Dr. Heinz. Indeed, Mr. Larson spoke from time to time of his longing for a "co-pilot," someone to chart a new direction for him because he felt lost and unappreciated.

Dr. Heinz was obviously upset in presenting to the group for the final consultation. His distress was this. In the first of two sessions to be reported, he had appreciated Mr. Larson's bitterness about not being helped by his teenagers and by his wife. Larson had left feeling very much better about his relationship with his "co-pilot," only to come in feeling terrible the next session. Larson had protested to his family on the strength of his conversation with Heinz, only to be put down more meanly than ever.

Heinz now asked the group whether individual therapy was a bad idea with Larson. Was family therapy indicated? Heinz was discouraged. He had been uplifted by Larson in one session, and dropped badly in the next session. The return to zero learning had downed him.

The group was more removed than Heinz. They listened to his distress and to some segments of the audiotape of the two sessions. They heard a familiar story. Here was Larson getting himself knocked down again by his family. He breaks his neck earning a living, so his kids and his wife can run around as they please. When he asks for a little help, they ignore him or they put him down. When he gets bitter, they attack.

One of the group went to the blackboard and drew a cartoon of a milk truck with his family aboard, which was powered by a sidecar pedaled by Mr. Larson. "The Rat Express" was hilarious but it did explain the game between Larson and his family to some extent. Of course his family nailed him when he protested. They wanted him to keep pedaling!

Heinz was not so bemused. I noted his response to this consultation of his peers. He sank into deeper responsibility for Larson. While the group was proposing a look at this game between Larson and his family and the possibility of systemic family therapy through Larson as an individual seeing Heinz, Heinz was hearing that he needed to find better ways to suggest to Larson for getting out of his subjugation. Heinz was pedaling desperately alongside Larson. The co-pilot was right in there with the pilot.

Now I could contribute, having watched the interaction between Heinz and the group. I could say that Heinz and Larson had a terrific close relationship of co-piloting. This relationship gets Larson hopeful, so he accelerates his demands in the family. The family then put on the brakes. Then Larson brings his bitterness back to Heinz, where he renews himself again, which will allow him to start the cycle all over again. The more that Larson improved with Heinz, the more the family would have to clamp down on Larson.[4] Therefore, I thought that Heinz had to be very careful about his co-piloting with Larson. He did not really know why Larson's family was so set against Larson's acceleration. Somehow, their brake was necessary to him. But that was something which might be understood.

The reader may now step back to see the levels of this game of consultation. First, the patient: He is understood. He feels mirrored and accepted. He accelerates his complaints to his family and gets knocked down again. Second, the therapist: He is merged with the patient, rising and going down with the man. Third, the group: They see the game and describe it humorously. But the therapist can laugh only a little with the group, before he is back into pedaling desperately with his patient. Fourth, there is me watching the group's attempt to help the therapist. I watch their successful description, which reverts back to zero learning. This allows me to appreciate the complete course of the entire cycle, how the co-pilot game of Heinz and Larson fits in a perfect interlock with the accelerator-brake game between Larson and his family.

This is a relief to Heinz. He is no longer put down. The group's metaphor had hurt. It had been sharp in its caricature, but difficult to disavow, because it was right on the mark. I could stand back and see this, which would allow me to complete the picture of the cycle, in which Heinz could be more fully appreciated. Now he no longer had to pedal so furiously. He too could stand back and regain his interest in how this beautiful little system was being operated.[5]

Perhaps the reader will now understand why I say I have access only to the relation between the therapist and the group. The first level of the patient's difficulty and the second level of the therapist's difficulty with the patient are subsumed in the more powerful, present interaction of the third level of the group's difficulty with the therapist. If I stand back and observe this third level, I have the possibility of the fourth level of description, which is *my* difficulty seeing what occurs between the group and the therapist.

I find that many situations presented by our patients will need four levels of description, such as we get in our game of consultation, for us to get an adequate picture of how the situation is operated. As Bateson suggests (Chapter 15), you need a map with four logical levels to see a game which has three logical levels. If you only have three levels to your own map, you are pulled into the game. This is what happened at the third level between the group and the therapist. A fine, humorous description of the plight of the patient in the sidecar of the Rat Express seemed to help, but it hurt too much. Therefore, it accelerated the activity of the therapist again and furthered the game.

Thus, our team gives its view of the game in which the therapist is caught. This is a method. It is a kind of instruction. I watch the therapist respond to what the team is giving him, looking for a recursion of the game at the third level of observation. The method of methods is watching the response to the method.[6]

This is where I began and where I end this book. Any method, however intuitive and thoughtful, will only trigger in the therapist whatever he is apt to do in the situation described. Our group, by describing the sidecar of the Rat Express, only triggered Dr. Heinz to try all the harder to save Mr. Larson from his onerous role in his family. If we are modest enough to see that our best ideas are only ways to see what others do with them, then we can have a method of methods.[7]

WE ARE PART OF THE EQUATION

But Dr. Heinz will only be able to help Mr. Larson when he is able to see Larson as cooperating in his own degradation, when he no longer has to rescue Larson from such a predicament, when he can study and appreciate why Larson puts himself in the sidecar. This will be what Michael Balint called a "modest but substantial change in the personality of the doctor" (1954).

Heinz had closed against this possibility. Therapists always have to close against certain new directions in their work, ever so much as their patients. If they begin to act differently in their work, then they may threaten to act differently in their lives, with their friends, colleagues, and families. This can be destabilizing. Therefore, therapists may *not* be able to improve some of their relations with some of their patients. This is why we have to accept our students' failing in their own way, while we never know why they have to fail. We have to accept their autonomy, their autopoiesis within their own lives, which takes precedence over what they do with their patients.

I am no different from any other therapist. I, too, am held back by the threat of improvements in my work, which could make my life more difficult. I will close the book in Chapter 24 with a little story about myself, hoping that this will give the reader courage about him or herself. I am in no doubt that the greatest restriction in the ability of the reader to do this kind of work is derived from the threat to his or her own continuing relations. Improving can wake you up at two in the morning. It can be alarming.[8]

24. *Warriors, Farewell*

Familiar Weaknesses

WHY IS PROGRESS for the therapist a frightening adventure? I close this book telling a little of what I know of these dangers. I prefer to be clear eyed, for as Bertrand Russell once said, "Once you have accepted that the world is a terrible place, you may begin to enjoy it" (Robin Skynner, personal communication).

I do not want to say a word against staying home within a school of method. I have loved orthodoxy. I drew comfort as a resident feeling surrounded by the confidence of my teachers in psychoanalysis. I had the feeling of rightness, which comes from being a small fish in a school of fish. I slept well. My dream screen was perfect, when I was full of the faults of a beginner.

I do not want to say a word against a little eclecticism either. A little borrowing is also pleasant, to try some slants which are unfamiliar. I enjoyed this as well as a resident. Still, I really threatened no one.

Trouble begins when you become critical of your school so much that you leave home to go looking for something better. Like myself, you may become a young hood or highwayman. Affronted, you pay back the hospitality of your host with slashes. For their kindness to me in London, Montreal, and Boston, Malan, Davanloo, and Sifneos got back more criticism from me than thanks. If I benefited from Mann, I was more mindful of his limitations. If I saw something useful to borrow from Weiss and Sampson or Minuchin, I protested their dogma. When I recall my bad deeds, I think Freud knew something about young people, how terrible they may become on the road. I see why young people stay in the tent of their betters to worry about becoming like Oedipus.

Trouble also begins when you make a discovery of your own. You want to generalize your glory. You resent being confined by your tradition. You propose your own school, like Jung, Adler or Reich, or your own method of brief therapy, like Malan, Mann, Sifneos, Davanloo, and so forth. You see your favorite principle everywhere: your archetypes; your inferiority complex; your confrontation. You lose what religious restraint you may have once had. Either you give up the restraint of brief form or the restraint of being a small part of a larger tradition. Like Mahler in music, who wrote so perfectly when limited by the verse of the Kindertotenleider, you sprawl like a god into symphonies which fail to end. The demonic has gotten a hold of you—like myself, in my series of enthusiasms.

Trouble also begins when such a hero returns home with eyes closed like Agamemnon. You think your largesse will be received well. You return home recklessly, when you are in the greatest danger of all. Like myself, pouring out the riches I was finding on my travels to my students at home. I felt that the more I gave, the more I should get back. I lost for some while the ability to give a little, to watch to see the response. Maybe it helped, maybe it did not. Since I was not watching in this way, I was giving much which was unwanted. This begets hostility. Students then feel free to soak up as they please, not giving back.

All of these troubles I have brought upon myself, but I think I have gotten back home, nevertheless. I believe that some of this foolishness cannot be helped when the voyage is long and difficult. Whenever we depart from our school to look for something better, we cannot keep from becoming disturbed. When we have different arguments, we will wake up with them at two or four in the morning, because we only feel right accepting the usual argument in our daylight hours. Freud dreamt his argument for his theory of dreams in his Irma dream (Kuper and Stone, 1982). We wake up from such dreams in some fright, because we are departing from our comfortable relations with our colleagues.

Such voyages from comfort at home cannot be sustained, unless we have in mind those who went before us. I take heart from my array of forebearers. I think of Odysseus, the foremost of voyagers.

He learned well from others. He knew how appreciation of people opened their strongholds, their kindness. Thus the world lay open to him in all its diversity, as Hopkins wrote, (Gardner, 1972, p. 786) of the diversity of

All things counter, original, spare, strange . . .

He would be continually refreshed.

He also kept himself to the right size and the right distance, knowing his limits well. He left home for the great war only under protest. He had himself tied to the mast, because he knew his instincts could be drawn out by the Sirens. He came back to his home occupied by the superior force of the suitors as a beggar.

Yet he was fierce in his homecoming. He knew that giving may not yield getting back. His eyes were open. Those who soaked up his patrimony were paid back.

I love these virtues of Odysseus. There is some deep reliability here, which has held up well for nearly 30 centuries. Odysseus is entirely confident about his warrior society being at the center of the world stage. But it is impossible for us to be as sure as he was.

MODERN TIMES

As the world became larger, the virtue of a militant society or school or religion was called into question. Such ferocity of warring factions was seen as the recurrent nightmare of the Dark Ages. The claims of countless peoples overrun one another, unless all are subordinated to the City of God. Thus, Dante places Odysseus in the darkness of the Inferno.

Since the end of the Dark Ages, mankind has been protected within several great unifying ideas or constructions from the bewildering multiplicity of the larger world. The City of God came first, then, in the Enlightenment, the Brotherhood of Man. But both of these visions have lost much of their hold in the twentieth century. We feel the weakness of the comraderie of the scientific community, against the menacing of nations (Commager, 1985). We are again at sea, beset by a multiverse of interests. We could say of this dark world the same as Melville wrote of his book, *Moby Dick*: "A Polar wind blows through it, and birds of prey hover over it." (p. xi)

In such a modern world, it is difficult to have grace, to be full of oneself, yet to realize one's small position in the great order of all things which is falling apart: As Yeats (1920, in Gardner, 1972, p. 820) wrote,

> Things fall apart; the center cannot hold;
> Mere anarchy is loosed upon the world,
> The blood-dimmed tide is loosed, and everywhere
> The ceremony of innocence is drowned;
> The best lack all conviction, while the worst
> Are full of passionate intensity.

Who can keep their bearings and their proportions in such a deteriorating world? Indeed, this is the situation of collapse in Western civilization in which the new tradition of psychotherapy made its appearance with Freud.

But the tradition of psychotherapy has been subject to the same forces as all of Western civilization. Few have been able to keep their eye on the possibility of a greater architecture than the rival schools. The anxiety to have a place is too great. When the greater order of all things is weak, we run for protection into the smaller enclosures, of the schools, of family, of security operations, of rigid postures, of the deification of needs, or of sacrificing them. The smaller rigidities become more desperate.[1]

As the modern world runs into such enclosures, it becomes all the more necessary for the skillful psychotherapist to become more and more catholic in his or her understanding. Communication competence is only possible for those who can move freely in and out of countless different kinds of systems (Pearce and Cronen, 1980). But how are we to tolerate being at sea ourselves, when most everyone is narrowly enclosed in some special haven or another?

I believe our only reliable comfort is to take the entire tradition for our own use. Here we follow the main current of what has been most successful both in the arts and in the sciences. I see two great principles here, for us to keep as our poles for such a broad cosmos.[2]

The first principle is to take the entire tradition of psychotherapy as our province for learning. The point is not to amass knowledge. No, it is rather to become familiar with what is powerful and deep in the many different guises, genres, and schools which are possible in such a diverse tradition. Such an aim is akin to what T. S. Eliot (1919) proposes for the poet in relation to the tradition of literature. To ride the main currents, until they are a part of us, or we a part of them. Such an aim is akin to what every great history achieves. To relate a multitude of events in such a way that they hold together in the mind as single constellations.

I believe the field of psychotherapy would be much more convivial and more profound, if most of us were to undergo the great labor of getting a liberal education in our own field, which, I say, is a matter of putting it together for ourselves. We have had few teachers to help us along toward such an aim. Fortunately, Leston Havens has been my teacher and colleague for 20 years. Twenty years may be necessary to make such a tremendous field into one's own.

This is one great principle which is reliable for us, which is, thereby, a great comfort. We do not have to strive for originality, for special status, for being any bigger than we are—no, not when we can be part of such a great tradition. This is our glory, to have participated in such thinking. Indeed, I doubt if we can contribute very much to our field without becoming immersed in its most profound currents.

If the first great principle concerns the "poetry of science" (Maturana, 1985), then the second principle is its counterbalance. The poetic imagination, whether in literature or in history or in natural science or in our own field, proposes myths or stories or hypotheses to make sense of complex situations. Imaginative myths or stories or hypotheses can be extremely persuasive or interesting, but misleading and therefore dangerous. Only when such myths are discussed in relation to the findings they purport to explain is there a possibility of scientific explanation (Popper, 1949). But how best to *discuss* the myths, the stories, the hypotheses, as they are constructed in our field?

I do not propose to discuss the difficult subject of what kind of scientific methods are most promising for our field. I would only like to emphasize a single broad scientific principle which we must not lose sight of if we are to continue on a sound, reliable basis. This principle is as follows: A hypothesis is more interesting the more we have taken pains to prove it wrong (Popper, 1957). I believe the best way to do this in our daily work is continually to work the opposing currents. When we have a certain plausible story, we go pulling for a different story. When we have the patient appearing to feel one way, we probe to see if he or she might feel quite contrary as well.

We continually pull together the findings into a hypothesis, as parsimonious as possible. We continually take it apart. Thereby, we retain our bearings in relation to the two great principles of art and science. We stay faithful to both, in the broadest sense. If we can stay oriented in this way, we may venture out of our schools, bringing home the entire tradition of psychotherapy.

Appendix, Notes,
Bibliography

Index

Every evolutionary step is an addition of information to an already existing system. Because this is so, the combinations, harmonies and discords between successive pieces and layers of information will present many problems of survival and determine many directions of change. . . . But, as of 1979, there is no conventional method of describing such a tangle.

—Bateson, 1979

What is a feeling if not a world in thought?

—Balzac, 1835

Appendix: Follow-up Interviews of Cases Described in the Text

R EADERS OF PART III, A Theory for a Method of Methods, will recall the criteria of explanation for scientific explanations. The criteria include: (1) specification of the phenomena to be explained; (2) a model which generates these phenomena; (3) computation of states from the model to specify the predicted phenomena to be observed; (4) testing for these predicted states. Readers will also recall how these criteria of explanation were proposed for the specific field of brief psychotherapy: (1) The phenomena to be observed are recursive stories of "present and chronically recurring pain." The model proposes four observing positions for describing how people stay the same, namely those of psychoanalysis, the analysis of character, interpersonal interviewing and systemic interviewing. (2) The model which generates recursion in such stories utilizes both the singular closure which can be observed from one of the four observing positions and also the more complicated closure which can be generated by combinations of the four observing positions. (3) The computation of states to be observed depends upon seeing each kind of singular closure as a required class. Different moves within the class are possible, so long as the required class is conserved. (4) Testing of the theory may occur in follow-up interviews which search for whether or not such closure is conserved, whether new constructive moves occur within the closure which is specified.[1]

The reports which follow do not allow a sufficient interval between the original preliminary interview or the conclusion of psychotherapy and the follow-up interview. I would prefer an interval of five years or even longer, such as utilized by David Malan for his studies (1963, 1976). However, the psychotherapies conducted by the author or by trainees in the Brief Therapy Clinic were mostly concluded in the last year, a few longer ago.

The following reports are derived from interviews conducted by myself with the assistance of my current students in our Brief Therapy Clinic. Since I was the therapist who conducted either the trial therapy or the therapy itself, the detachment of the follow-up is compromised. No doubt most of our patients give a more positive view of our work to me that they would to a team of four therapist-researchers who have had no part in the treatment (Malan, 1963, 1976; Malan et al., 1975).

Nevertheless, I think that a recent follow-up interview by the treating therapist is of some interest, if the procedure is clearly specified. I have learned something from doing them and I believe the reader will learn something from reading about them. As long as the positive bias of such interviews is recognized, something is gained.

A few words about my procedure: In advance of all follow-up interviews or follow-up questionnaires I have committed myself to specifying in writing the closure to be expected in the patient and the previous moves known to the patient for achieving the closure, especially those moves which were disliked in some way by the patient. This allows me to judge whether new moves have been discovered during or after therapy. I present these *preliminary criteria* for all the cases evaluated on follow-up.

The follow-up procedure itself began with the patient's completing a SCL-90 symptom checklist and a one-page questionnaire called the Brief Follow-up Questionnaire, which included the following questions:

1. Your chief complaint when first seen for brief therapy, according to my records was: _____ (correct?) Would you comment on whether this complaint is about the same, improved or worse? (You may include any information on the ups and downs of this complaint, before, during, or after treatment, since the fluctuation could be complex, I realize.)
2. What did you learn in therapy, what stands out in your mind now, about how your complaint or difficulty is brought about, increased, or reduced?
3. How would your behavior be viewed by those who know you best, who are most affected by how you were before/during/after therapy? What would *they* comment?

These two paper and pencil tests allowed me to get some minimum data on all patients, especially concerning relief of symptoms, since I had the SCL-90 for nearly all cases from the original preliminary interview and a written chief complaint from the original preliminary interview as well.

A few patients could not travel to Madison to be interviewed. All other patients either had an interview privately with me in my office or a videotaped interview in our Brief Therapy Clinic which was observed and discussed by our residents and fellows.

The conduct of the interviews follows the method proposed by David

Malan in his essay, "Basic Principles and Technique of the Follow-up Interview" (1980a) up to a certain point, which I will describe carefully. I begin with a careful delineation of the patient's complaints, whether or not they have been relieved. I am assisted by the comparison of the SCL-90 before treatment and now, and by the written statements of the chief complaint before treatment and now. I make some judgment of symptomatic change.

Then I propose the various stresses specified in my *preliminary criteria* to judge whether or not the patient has new, constructive moves to handle the stressful situations which previously undid him. I make some judgment of dynamic change in relation to those "stress tests."

But then I depart from Malan. I become interested in the response of the crucial people in the patient's life to see if the patient's improvement has been purchased at the expense of a deterioration in the patient's social system. After all, if symptomatic change can be bought by avoidance or even worsening of dynamic ability to cope with stress, then dynamic change in the individual can be bought by avoidance or even worsening of patient's social system. Many have risen at the expense of their families. Therefore, I judge "systemic change" as well as "dynamic change" and "symptomatic change."[2]

The latter third of the interview returns to familiar themes explored in Malan's follow-up interviews: the patient's view of the therapy itself and the patient's questions of the interviewer in conclusion.

The evaluation of *results* also departs from Malan in several respects. I describe the essential data bearing on judgments of "symptomatic change" and "dynamic change" so the reader may compare my findings with those of Malan. I add the essential data bearing on my judgment of "systemic change," and I describe the patient's view of the therapy and the patient's relation to me, especially the final remarks or questions.

But then I describe the data bearing on my own predictions of required closure, both the necessary classes and the presence or absence of new constructive moves.

Notice the relation between the two different presentations of data: Malan assumes that certain classes of situations (the stress situations) will be difficult for the patient. He looks for new moves in these same classes. I assume that such a double description is interesting but incomplete. I assume that four kinds of closure or required classes are often necessary for an adequate description of the patient, classes at successively higher logical levels of recursion. Each class allows degrees of freedom which are possible to compute.

I also assume more complicated patients can improve from one perspective of closure while worsening at others. I assume contradictions between levels of recursion are frequent.[3] This has two practical implications for follow-up interviews. One is that I do not compute numerical values for symptomatic and dynamic change. After all, this makes "more" sound better than "less," when actually too rapid symptomatic or dynamic change can be more harmful than otherwise at other logical levels. Also, the assessment of patients with very contradictory systems depends upon a grasp of all four levels, for improvements at one level are often accompanied by deterioration or compensations at other levels, to conserve staying the same. These so-called "negative therapeutic reactions" are very common.

The reader may wonder how these constancies I predict in advance are required to stay the same. I predict they stay the same in *some* respect. For example, a constant attitude about the bodily self which must stay constant will be different when it has become revised to fit into the higher logical level of the patient's security operations with other people. The constancies change in the sense of becoming *subsumed* in wider operations, yet they will still be available to the patient and they may still be recognized to some extent by the observer.

The inherent reflexivity of the nervous system (Cronen, Johnson and Lannamann, 1982; Pearce and Cronen, 1980; Tomm, unpublished) allows one constancy to be revised by preoccupation with another constancy. The latter may acquire logical force over the former. But the reflexivity means that the former constancy will continue to have some logical force over the latter. The relative logical force will vary. In any event, I may use these constancies to assess the extent of the drift of the patient's mind from its previous position. Thus, the constancies are only *relatively* constant, given the revision which is possible in the moves which satisfy them, given that such revision gradually alters their quality. But since they are relatively constant, they provide useful and conservative perspectives on how much the patient has actually moved.

The reader will appreciate that the testing of my methods as reported here is not strictly comparable to the testing of a hypothesis in the natural sciences. There is no possibility of refuting my set of working hypotheses. Therefore, there is no strict testing.

All I am saying is that the tradition of psychotherapy has found it useful to look for what is happening in respect to these several ways in which people operate to stay the same. Therefore, I look at the patient in these ways as well. I cannot overlook such perspectives, which have been held to be of great potential importance. Such perspectives could be misleading, but perspectives which tend to be misleading tend to die out, for those who hold them will not fare well for long. Therefore, I think the convergence of the tradition upon these few perspectives is some assurance of their usefulness.

We cannot know what new emergencies will befall our patients (Fisher, 1935). We cannot know what they will do, either, for we do not know what knowledge and theories they will hold when such emergencies arrive (Popper, 1957). All we do is judge the well-being and faultiness of our patients according to what has been useful in our tradition in the past. This is our wisdom and our limitation. I believe the best we can do is to specify how we make our complex judgements, with what criteria of interpretation we judge the findings.

No doubt there are many other lines of interpretation for the findings presented here. All ways of interpretation have advantages and drawbacks. But some histories are better than others. All in all, I side with histories which pull as much together as possible into a single coherent story, yet continually work against themselves to find the opposing currents. All of our great novels, dramas and histories do this. Some enormous social world is conveyed in a single story. Even the complications of the story may be epitomized in some feeling in us that we cannot forget. H. A. L. Fisher begins his *History of Europe* (1935) with an argument against such a reduction:

Men wiser and more learned than I have discerned in history a plot, a rhythm, a predetermined pattern. These harmonies are concealed from me. I can see only one emergency following upon another as wave follows upon wave, only one great fact with respect to which, since it is unique, there can be no generalizations, only one safe rule for the historian: that he should recognize in the development of human destinies the play of the contingent and the unforeseen. (p. v.)

But his history becomes a story of such emergencies, which it makes it memorable for us. His story catches me, leaving me with a discernable feeling of fear in my throat.

I think that our minds are constructed in such a way that this is how we comprehend and remember social worlds. This capacity of our minds for condensation may be helpful to us, as long as we understand that many different ones are possible. But such single stories must be constructed with many different logical levels. Our minds are ensembles of great possible complexity. I agree with Bateson that measuring or reckoning the drift of such an ensemble requires a map with an even greater number of logical levels. There may be " . . . no conventional method of describing such a tangle" (Bateson, 1979, p. 20). I propose *a* method for the attempt, realizing full well that many others are possible.

We have one advantage in psychotherapy over our colleagues in history. Not only can we put together a story which explains the patient's difficulty and possible degrees of freedom, but we can also look to see if our interpretation seems to give the patient a better drift to his or her life. We can also estimate or propose the kinds of difficulties which have plagued him or her in the past to see how he or she copes with such difficulties in the future. We estimate the dire circumstances which have been catastrophic for him or her in the past. These may be proposed either as strains or strange loops, as emotional currents of great force, as contexts full of peculiar turns and contradictions. Thus, we look not only for symptomatic change, but also dynamic and systemic change.

But these judgments should not be taken as complete assurance for the

She could say to herself, "Too bad, if I'm not good enough for him!" This reversed the depressive thinking of "If only I were more perfect, this would not have happened." Able to yell at him, get it off her chest, feeling "lighter and better" (which would have been difficult before therapy).

B. Feeling deceived, cheated, unprotected: Same incident. Similar success with father's presuming.

C. New involvements: Yes, it has been difficult for mom that patient stayed on this summer to work in Madison for first time. Mom has been upset, comforted by patient, and able to get involved in many new activities across the board (quite busy). Patient dating, staying out nights, having fun. Able to be "mean" with a guy, declining to continue relationship because he will stay in "working class" and she wants to get ahead. Staying with him would have defeated her rising.

3. Systemic Change, Response of System to Dynamic Changes in Patient: The patient is still being called on to comfort mother and grandmother, especially as aunt gets competitive with mother, when aunt feels insecure. Since patient has been the "big hope" of the extended family, the first in a big university, this sets off aunt. Since patient is close to cousins, like brother and sister to her, she has not wanted to be "mean" to them by being successful. She seems able, nevertheless, to be successful, to separate gradually from her mother. This is not impossible in this family, I think, because there has been some hope for someone to rise above their class, on their behalf. In this sense, her separation remains loyal.

4. Patient's View of the Therapy: The trial therapy gave her hope that "maybe it all tied in," that she could "get to the source, not be scared." She recalls the "yellow blob, the color and the smell! . . . and the roar" which she equated with the "devil," with "complete meanness." She got the idea that she could let it out, "bit by bit." Indeed that is what she did. She learned in therapy "not to bottle herself up," especially through the dream analyses. She recalls the dream of the surprise of finding boyfriend with another girl and her "arm wouldn't move." She got the idea that such dreams would remit if she got out her feeling (viz., wanting to slug him). "It happened!" The resident asked her good questions; they went through different versions of the dream she first presented me in the trial therapy. What did she recall of the very final dream, of her teeth falling out? She laughed loudly. Yes, she really missed her doctor, someone to trust, someone to talk to. She still has not got a replacement. She hopes to. So perhaps her final dream was about frustration at losing him? Something to roar about there? Yes, she smiled, "but I was 'nice' then."

5. Relation to Interviewer: The patient was in a very attractive outfit, a striking improvement from two years ago when I first met her, but she was very diffident with me. There were a few moments of intense feeling, of laughter, of tears, but then she went back to her diffidence, her formality. What did she want to tell me or ask me at last? She wanted to emphasize it was a gradual shift for her. What if encouraging results had not come from bringing out her feeling? Then she might have gone back to the old way, but now she could take some bad results because she has confidence.

6. Summary of Findings in Relation to Criteria for Required Closure:

A. Needs: Impressive vigor here, with some diffidence.

B. Constant Attitude: Interesting. Very attractive, yet the diffidence and wariness of men is there.

C. Security Operations: Lessening of closeness to mom, very gradually, and ability to trust a man, her therapist. Misses this. Hasn't achieved it yet with another man. "Betrayed" by last boyfriend.

D. Family Game: Indeed, there is a very powerful matriarchal line here, but the patient is not enmeshed, but moving in a powerful way, towards a higher social class. We do not know if this drift will allow a man to become important to her or not. She does not know either. Perhaps that will have to be sacrificed for the line.

SUMMARY REMARKS, NOTEWORTHY FINDINGS

Powerful result, in symptomatic, dynamic and systemic terms. What interests me the most is how such a little help with "true feelings" in the classical way, from dream analyses, is "good enough" for a steady progress as here. I think this is possible because of the variation in her family system that she become their big hope. I would say that the augmentation of her ability to face her powerful feelings selected or elicited this powerful variation as opposed to the enmeshed variation she presented with at the preliminary interview. Both variations conserve the family, so that the brief therapy could set her on a different drift which emphasizes one variation over the other. Perhaps what Malan et al. (1975) mean by "star cases," patients who have these capabilities for being very responsible and very vigorous, are part of families in which such a variation is possible!

THE CASE OF THE MURDEROUS MEDICAL STUDENT
(Chapter 3)

THERAPY 8 sessions, 8 hours.
THERAPIST Author
INTERVAL Since original evaluation, 2 years, 8 months
    Since end of treatment, 2 years, 6 months
METHOD OF FOLLOW-UP Questionnaires

PRELIMINARY CRITERIA

1. Symptomatic change:
    A. Obsessional thoughts: including both aggression toward others, such as stabbing, toward self, such as in a heart attack, or both, such as in head-on collision ideas (chief complaint). Note that these have come and gone since high school.
    B. Dependent crutches: smoking, other variations? (second chief complaint)
    C. Anxiety, depression (mild to moderate on SCL-90)
2. Dynamic Change, Stress Tests for Dynamic Change:
    A. Being treated as a "mindless lackey," having serious objections to obligations, to demands, to being controlled.
    B. Having the opportunity to have crude aims himself, to dominate, to bully, to be attended to, to take revenge.
3. Systemic Change, Response of System to Dynamic Change in Patient: His previous position kept him in service, in a very restricted way, since he served so perfectly, since his objections only alarmed himself, which would send him back to try harder, serve more perfectly. Getting out of service might lead his parents to get busy, to pull him back in.
4. Patient's View of the Therapy: My idea in my report was that I got to his "crude aims," like Ferenczi with the Croatian Musician. If he could experience them in relation to me, he might not have to run to being so overly good when that only built up enormous tension. Will he emphasize this? Or something else?

5. Patient's Relation to Interviewer: Not relevant (questionnaires only for follow-up)
6. Summary of Preliminary Criteria for Required Closure:
   A. Needs: Can the crude needs, "the vile emotions," be owned and lived or not? Given his constant attitude of trying hard to be of service, some sacrifice is likey to continue of his needs.
   B. Constant Attitude: "I try very hard to serve, not ask or demand." Given his security operations of staying clear of archaic demands, some of this will continue to be necessary.
   C. Security Operations: Serving and trying very hard keeps him from the archaic demandingness of a depressive position, namely expecting too much and making holes in his holding environment when disappointed. Or at least, he could alternate accommodating with insisting on being accommodated.
   D. Family Game: His serving was a comfort to his mother which her demanding husband did not give. In turn, this comforted him to be her good son. Now what will he and his mother do?

RESULTS
1. Symptomatic change:
   A. Obsessional thoughts: "My original complaint is greatly improved, and in fact is almost nonexistent. I do have my good days and sometimes bad days, but for the most part I am very happy with what I am doing with my life."
   B. "I no longer smoke, nor drink alcohol or coffee to any great extent, and in general, I enjoy myself. I also keep in mind Emerson's words, 'That in any given day blunders and absurdity are bound to creep into your life, but try to forget them as soon as you can and begin each new day with calmness and serenity.' I also might add with a sense of humor."
   C. Anxiety, depression (mild to moderate on SCL-90): None. Only item checked of 90 items is "10. Worried about sloppiness or carelessness," "1, A Little Bit."
2. Dynamic Change, Stress Tests for Dynamic Change:
   A. Being treated as a mindless lackey, having serious objections, etc: "Before and during the early stages of my therapy, I managed to hide my internal turmoil from my fellow colleagues and employees, and was, amazingly enough, able to perform my job fairly well. However, my closer friends knew I was depressed and was not behaving in my 'usual manner.' At that time, this 'usual manner' consisted of being excessively rational, 'macho,' confident, and obsessed with my career. When I said that I was having problems, they were very supportive."

   "When the big change in reaction came was when I started making all the changes in my life that I felt were needed. These included starting a program of physical exercise, spending time in Church, quiting smoking, resigning my 'successful' position in the hospital, then receiving numerous job offers, getting married, moving to California, etc. One of my closest friends referred to my changes as a 'revolution.' Another said it was my 'Greek' ways beginning to express themselves. For the most part, most of my friends were totally amazed at the transition. Interestingly enough, I also learned that some of my closest friends, including my wife, went through a similar period(s) in their lives and benefited greatly from professional counseling."
   B. Having the opportunity to have crude aims himself: Patient has married, has one small child, a new job, is building a new house. Thus the situations for such aims

to be experienced seem to be there, yet he feels very happy. Nevertheless, this test is impossible to judge without an interview.

3. Systemic Change, Response of System to Dynamic Changes in Patient: Friends seem amazed by his "revolution," accepting of his "counseling," of having had to go through such difficulties themselves. Evidently less need to be "macho," "on top of things." No report on his parents. No report on nature of relationship with his wife.

4. Patient's View of the Therapy: This seems consistent with my idea of the therapy. I quote the patient:

"When I came to see you, I was very angry about many things. I was letting myself become stifled in my work and in my personal relationships. I deluded myself about a love affair that was unhealthy for me, and in which my self-worth became increasingly diminished because I let it do so. I was in no mood to deal with my father and his ways. I couldn't give up smoking, and everything I tried I got increasingly angry. In addition, I absolutely hated the idea of spending my life confined to being in a hospital that at that time did not really support medical student needs. In this regard, I was also angry about having to work in a lab for so many hours, which for me was particularly boring and was keeping me away from more important activities (at least for me). However, instead of taking steps to correct this situation, I became stressed out and fell into a rut of depression, anger, and loss of confidence. You might say that I was letting the 'child' in me with all its irrational fears take over. Therapy allowed me to communicate my fears, my anger, my emotional upheaval, and my frustrations to you in a manner in which I didn't feel judged nor condemned. I began to realize that I had choices and that I was worth something. I also felt that what I was going through under the circumstances was not unusual and that 'my feelings of going crazy and being obsessed' were understandable reactions. I also began to learn how to relax and to be far less critical of myself. I began to become comfortable with my emotions and to learn more about myself and my own personal level of sensitivity. I also felt more comfortable about communicating my feelings and personal problems with others and realized the difficulties that can occur when irritations are kept pent up without appropriate release."

5. Patient's Relation to Interviewer: Not relevant, questionnaire only.

6. Summary of Findings in Relation to Criteria for Required Closure:
   A. Needs: Appears to be satisfied. Degree of continuing sacrifice impossible to judge by questionnaire.
   B. Constant Attitude: Although he seems much more accepting of his needs, the SCL-90 still reflects a kind of perfection about not complaining.
   C. Security Operations: I cannot judge his "archaic demandingness," with the extent to which it has been buried, as Balint would say, "with full honors."
   D. Family Game: I cannot judge his relations with his parents, nor the extent to which his relation to his wife continues the parental pattern or diverges.

SUMMARY REMARKS, NOTEWORTHY FINDINGS

A modest technique yields a startling result, after all, for some patients like this one. This man has many of the characteristics described by Malan et al. (1975) of "star cases" who do very well with a *minimum* of help: namely, a determination to do better, vigorous attack on the difficulty, complete responsibility, etc. Of course, the follow-up is second-hand; hence it is less reassuring than an interview. Given the patient's character, I believe it to be reliable.

PATIENT'S COMMENTARY ON THE FOLLOW-UP REPORT

The patient's letter of October 19, 1985 indicates further improvements in relation to his family which had been unspoken in his first response: viz., that he and his wife are "passionate and emotional people . . . (who) trust and respect each other," that he and his father were able to talk about "the things that mattered" before his father died which removed "the major hostility that separated me from him," that he still has the "vile parts" which he can "laugh at," and that he advises on family matters to his mother, sisters and brothers without feeling "obligated to insure their happiness nor handle their affairs."

THE CASE OF THE
MODERN PASSIVE-FEMININE CHARACTER
(Chapters 4, 6 and 13)

THERAPY 14 sessions, 14 hours
THERAPIST Trial therapy, author; Brief therapy, fellow
INTERVAL Since original evaluation, 3 years, 5 months
Since end of treatment, 3 years, 1 month
METHOD OF FOLLOW-UP Videotaped interview

PRELIMINARY CRITERIA
1. Symptomatic Change:
   A. No sexual feelings
   B. Depression
2. Dynamic Change, Stress Tests for Dynamic Change:
   A. Being obliged to disagree, say no, criticize, assert self-interests against apparent interests of others.
   B. Being able to get involved, especially with sexual feelings.
3. Systemic Change, Responses of System to Dynamic Change in Patient: Little is known about this man's family system, since the work was conducted before this became uppermost in our clinic. Evidently, his parents' marriage broke up when he was in high school in some fights which were frightening. How his remaining without aggression (a nice child) may have helped his parents I can only speculate. How his becoming a man may destabilize his relations with his parents is also conjecture. I will have to set up this systemic hypothesis in the interview itself.
4. Patient's View of the Therapy: Since I have taken three angles on the trial therapy in the text, following the ideas of Reich, Sullivan, and Sifneos (Chapters 4, 6 and 13), the patient may be able to comment on *which* aspects of my method seemed most powerful to *him*: More the "challenge to the constant attitude"? More the line of inquiry finding matters in his favor? More the literal relentlessness about certain words ("flabby")? All three? How did the subsequent brief therapy work for him? Differently?
5. Patient's Relation to the Inverviewer: It should be evident whether the patient feels obliged to be the completely "nice guy" as before. I will have to be careful to give him much room, since he was so eager before to give a picture of himself which would please the doctor that I could be fooled. I went through five or six chief complaints in that trial therapy.

6. Summary of Preliminary Criteria for Required Closure:
   A. Needs: Some sacrifice of self-protective, aggressive abilities (Level II, Gedo) is expectable. Depending on the extent of that sacrifice, sexuality may still be held back as well.
   B. Constant Attitude: The nice guy, pleasing, pleasant and good-natured to a fault will be conserved, to an unknown extent. At what price? A man without edges?
   C. Security Operations: "I will give you what you want. Then perhaps you will take care of me." Again, some of this is necessary, useful.
   D. Family Game: All I know about this is that there is something important about being a nice, unaggressive, asexual child — perhaps even some crude demonstration of the opposite, of excessive edges and fights . . . which leads back to the first state. Perhaps the two opposite states work together?

RESULTS
1. Symptomatic change:
   A. No sexual feelings: Enjoys "sensual feelings" hugging and kissing girlfriend, and had a dream last week of sex with a 12-year-old girl fully clothed, and feels attracted to women when drunk, but continues to need fantasy of a man "younger, thinner, clothed, in jeans . . . a normal average guy . . . I wish I had been . . . " to have orgasm in masturbation. In other words, improving, but still inhibited. [See further discussion under Dynamic Change, item 2B.]
   B. Depression: The month of depression which preceded his coming for therapy, which included difficulty falling asleep, early morning awakening, appetite loss, and shaking in class to the point of having to leave on one occasion, has completely remitted. He feels he is less moody than he was before the acute depression. This improvement occurred gradually in the year and a half following therapy, he feels, as he found confidence in himself in a new field of study in the university. This decision was taken in the therapy itself. He felt good enough about the decision to decline the last two planned sessions, so the improvement actually began during the therapy itself.
2. Dynamic Change, Stress Tests for Dynamic Change:
   A. Being obliged to disagree, say no, criticize, assert self-interests against apparent interests of others: Many examples that he has become so comfortable with "having to say something" when he disagrees that he doesn't even think about it — as president of his political club, with lab partner/friend, with girls being dated, with his mother. This autonomy is very striking, in his haircut, in his occasionally daring clothes, compared to other inhibited students in his field of chemistry, compared to how he pleased his mother before.
   B. Being able to get involved, especially with sexual feelings: The progress with inhibition described previously concerning symptomatic change appears relatively clear to the patient and myself. He is able to be sensual with a woman, now, a large improvement for a man who only dated a "nice girl" in high school. But his dream last week of sex with a 12-year-old girl included her "urination" and his "disgust," which indicates to him and to me that he still regards being a sexual man as "dirty." Thus, he cannot picture a woman's face when thinking of her sexually and arousal and orgasm only occur when thinking of a young man as described before, a displacement from himself. He said he thought he needed further therapy to relieve this inhibition. I agreed.

3. Systemic Change: Because of the dearth of knowledge about the relation between this man's difficulties and his family system, I was obliged to construct a systemic hypothesis in the interview, as well as test the hypothesis. I learned he was the youngest boy among six children, the child "closest to his mother." His father and mother had several separations prior to their divorce when the patient was nine or ten. He felt "abused" by the yelling and hitting of both his mother and his older sister who replaced mother when she went to work. He took it "like a martyr," unlike an older brother who defied her by laughing. What then *if* he had fought back like his brother? When I asked him this question, he became much more lively, grinned at me, and advised me that "you're not supposed to yell at your mother." When I asked him how his father would have explained his submission, he said his father would have said that it was because the patient "loved her" (and wanted to please her). In summary, my hypothesis became that this youngest child became the comfort of his mother, the "martyr" who gave himself up for her.

So how was his apparent dynamic change towards autonomy and the beginning of sexual feeling being received as a perturbation in this relation of mutual comfort? The patient seems to have taken a stand for autonomy, not only in respect to his ability to speak up for himself, dress for himself, etc., but also by not going home to visit mother more than once a year. Mother seems to have told him she'd like him home, but he has told her that is not for him. She has gone through a difficult period, some perhaps related to this separation, some related to work difficulties, but is now emerging relatively well, running, talking again with his sister, etc.

4. Patient's View of the Therapy: He experienced the trial therapy as "I needed to be pushed. . . . I needed to endure abuse." Most he remembered how I "intimidated" him . . . because I "wouldn't quit . . . " He would think, "Isn't he satisfied yet?"

He did recall, when I asked him, my challenge about his difficulty calling the girl "flabby," as part of this difficulty satisfying me. The only content he recalled from me was my saying "that we needed to get at the reason for his crying." In other words, he experienced me as a very demanding, perhaps abusive, mother like his own mother. Since he loved her, since he thought she knew best, he tried to give in to her. This might explain the breakthrough in only a half-hour of trial therapy which was so remarkable.

The patient saw the fellow who was his therapist from here on as "a little more friendly." He recalled feeling "inhibited" with him as well, especially holding back his sexual feelings which he "didn't tell him." He was critical of the therapist for only "directing thoughts," for only "asking questions." He could not be open, because there was no "give and take relationship." But he suddenly backed off this criticism of his therapist by blaming himself, until I pointed it out to him, whereupon he laughed and agreed.

5. Patient's Relation to the Interviewer: The conclusion was telling. He wanted me to know, finally, about how proud he was in being autonomous, dressing as he likes, wearing his hair as he likes. Then when I asked him if he wanted to *ask* me anything, he turned full force toward me, sitting up very big, and said loudly, "Why? . . . " and burst out laughing.

6. Summary of Findings in Relation to Criteria for Required Closure:
   A. Needs: The self-protective, aggressive abilities have become vigorous, except in relation to women at close quarters, where he will not be "dirty."
   B. Constant Attitude: The "nice guy," the "pleasing child," the "martyr to pleasing mother," is still evident concerning sexuality.

C. Security Operations: In other situations, he is quite able to be vigorous, as in his final display of force with me in the interview. This was impressive, as he held it back and could be good-natured as well as bring home his point.

D. Family Game: I believe he is still demonstrating his attachment to his mother, his remaining potentially available for her, by sacrificing his sexuality, which might give him away to another woman. He holds his mother at arm's length, but he notes that his new field *could* allow him to work near home. Here is one of those bonds of mother with the last child to leave which is very deep. He had given up his aggression for her. He still gives up his sexuality for her, trying to be nice, not dirty. This could continue as he needs *some* way to continue to show his devotion to her.

SUMMARY REMARKS, NOTEWORTHY FINDINGS

Here appears to be one of those familiar stories from brief therapy which abound in follow-up interviews by Malan (1976). The patient makes a very big jump in assertiveness and in autonomy, while the sexuality is still compromised to some extent. Surely, the progress is remarkable, but the reader may think a longer-term therapy could have relieved the patient in both respects. Yet it could be equally said that the patient may now get a second brief therapy, to relieve him of his sexual inhibition, while saving three years of long-term therapy in between! Perhaps his close bond with his mother could go no faster in being loosened?

Finally, I am impressed by what a little systemic inquiry in the follow-up interview can do to elucidate the patient's continuing bind. Systemic closure is so powerful here it is difficult to see how brief therapy will be able to do without reckoning with such enmeshment if it is to be fully successful in cases which show such devotion.

POSTSCRIPT

I received a telephone call about two months after the follow-up interview from the patient, who reported that intercourse had come very naturally with a young woman for whom he had much affection. He hadn't even thought about it at the time, "but it is a very important thing in my life." Also, he had just graduated with a second degree in a new field. I congratulated him doubly.

THE CASE OF A
YOUNG BUSINESSWOMAN ON THE MOVE
(Chapter 5)

THERAPY 16 sessions, 20 hours
THERAPIST Author
INTERVAL Since original evaluation, 1 year, 11 months
         Since end of treatment, 5 months
METHOD OF FOLLOW-UP Private interview

PRELIMINARY CRITERIA

1. Symptomatic Change:
   A. Sore throat (chief complaint)
   B. Other somatic symptoms of tension, e.g., back pain

    C. Anxiety, insomnia

    D. Depression, especially early morning awakening

2. Dynamic Change, Stress Tests for Dynamic Change:

    A. Feeling alone, abandoned with difficult tasks, not understood or comforted. "No one else carries the ball" (Gedo's Level I disturbances).

    B. Being criticized, especially by tough guys, high-powered admired people or mentors. Being subjected to examination where right/wrong clearly evident, as in high school math. Having to say "no," even to her subordinates, having to give orders. Being able to "calculate" self-interest without guilt (Gedo's Level II disturbances).

    C. Having "great ideas," feeling very "big." Conversely, feeling left in shadow by others. Being able to control such swings of illusion, self-evaluation (Gedo's Level III disturbances).

3. Systemic Change, Response of System to Dynamic Changes in Patient: If the patient holds onto need for comfort and understanding (Level I), need to protect herself (Level II), need to be realistic about grand hopes and being in shadow (Level III), can new relations with spouse, colleagues, subordinates, family of origin be negotiated? How do these other people see these changes happening in the patient? In their relationships with her?

4. Patient's View of Therapy: What helped the most? What held the patient back the most? What stands out the most that the therapist did or said? How do these statements reconcile with description in text of therapist appreciating her "project" or "security operation" to build own medium, own mother? Of therapist grasping her similar attitude about "giving" to mother, grandmother? Of her courting overstimulation, to be sure not to feel abandoned?

5. Patient's Relation to Interviewer: This may provide another view of patient's capacities to stay calm, protect herself, be realistic, or not.

6. Summary of Preliminary Criteria for Required Closure:

    A. Needs: Sacrifice of Level I, II, III capacities as noted in the foregoing is expectable to some extent in view of "higher" goals.

    B. Constant Attitude: "Trying hard," as a "giver," or "guardian," or "good person."

    C. Security Operations: Willingness to be controlled by spouse's obsessive needs, to be passive in the face of these demands. Similarly at work with subordinates, colleagues, mentors: a muddy passivity; a working hard to fulfill such controlling expectations.

    D. Family Game: Conserving pride in herself as such a giving person, which retains a place or some notice.

RESULTS

1. Symptomatic Change:

    A. Sore throat: "Still a weak point, gets rough, irritating, but not interfering with normal functioning." Able to use it as a sign to back off (gathering too much tension).

    B. Back pain (no other physical symptoms): Stiffness, inflammation prevents biking, swimming, lifting since midsummer, but "steadily improving."

    C., D. Anxiety, Depression: "Hide is thicker. Not shaken to core as before (during various stressful projects)." Early morning awakening only around single major business project involving great risks. Depression which used to take the form of "existential anxiety" (despair) has not returned, but feels less "strong personal satisfaction" since back trouble, since disappointing vacation with spouse, both in midsummer.

2. Dynamic Change, Stress Tests for Dynamic Change:

   A., B. Has been attacked in a personal way by cynical board member, "number one on the guy's hit list," alone with this since other board members "can't stand tension and watch like little kids with parents." "Accommodated the guy . . . let it ride," but now will "take no more shit." Appears less worried about offending the guy, needing him, than in the past. Pulled to support project of another individual in the business, whom she does not want to offend. Giving minimal encouragement to keep the guy involved, but dislikes even this. Appears less accommodating, however, than in past.

   Wanted to rest on beach with spouse in Europe this summer, but accommodated to his "iron will" to travel, had an awful time, has withdrawn from marriage to become "consumed" in business for last several months. Now is tired of being consumed by business, but still "lives the job."

   C. Has not felt occasions of overstimulation or being nothing since therapy ended. Appears more confident regarding business ability.

3. Systemic Change, Response of System to Dynamic Change in Patient: Spouse would see "being consumed" as her main relation to the business, but would acknowledge her increased competence. He is seeking a better job for himself now. If she had *not* given into his iron will and yelling on vacation? This is unfamiliar territory for her. He might concede to her, which would improve relationship, but he might go "crazy." He did concede when she put foot down about his overeating. He has sought help. She respects him more. This improves their relationship. Yet she hesitates to put "risk capital" into the relationship. Views of her changes from perspective of business system and business colleagues, mentors and subordinates not discussed explicitly.

4. Patient's View of Therapy: Author's help stands out as "clarifying where I was: being in a central position, but not asking, not sharing, carrying load alone." "Didn't know how to tell people what to do." Negative effects? "Perhaps some appointments were a waste of time, showing up when not upset just to keep appointment."

5. Patient's Relation to Interviewer: Patient seemed composed, but slightly down. Clearly disappointed since midsummer holiday with spouse was so awful. I asked in conclusion if there was anything she wanted to tell me. She replied that she had gotten "one problem out of the way (sore throat), another shows up (back pain)." I decided to trace what would happen *if* she got released from back pain? She'd "feel better about (her) body . . . feel more confident, on an even keel . . . more spark with spouse, him more spark with her . . . more interest in relationship . . . relationship become more central." How might that be a difficulty? Spouse might "dwell on his physical difficulty." She might get hopes up again? Yes, she has been resigned of late. When I noted she might be better off with a back problem for now, her voice doubled in volume over the even volume of the interview and said, "Yah! There you may have something."

6. Summary of Findings in Relation to Criteria for Required Closure:

   A. Needs: Less sacrifice of calm, self-defense in work, but continues to do this with spouse, leading to back symptoms in place of throat symptoms. Mild improvement with spouse about his eating problem, increasing her respect for him. But continued difficulty with spouse leads to flight into being "consumed" in work, no sexual relation, fairly high tension level.

B. "Accommodation" and "giving" modified at work, but still crucial to maintain relation to spouse.
C. Still willing to be controlled by spouse's "iron will," quite unfamiliar territory to challenge this on vacation. Clearly has challenged this modestly, with success, about spouse's eating problem.
D. Family Game: Has not changed too fast with spouse or work so both relations are conserved by her giving, accommodation, etc. Clearly uses "being consumed" by work to lessen disappointment with spouse, which conserves relation to spouse, but builds up great physical tension.

SUMMARY REMARKS, NOTEWORTHY FINDINGS
This is one of those cases where several intrapsychic needs are being sacrificed to maintaining constant attitude, security operations, and the family game. If the patient improved too fast, the latter might indeed be jeopardized. Thus, she pays for slow improvement by carrying the tension in her body. Being "consumed" by work is still better than being terribly disappointed with spouse. In this sense, she is indeed still building her own medium, and she is getting much better at this job.

THE DAUGHTER OF A SAINT
(Chapter 7)

THERAPY 10 sessions, 19 hours
THERAPIST Author
INTERVAL Since original evaluation, 16 months
　　　　　　Since end of treatment, 6 months
METHOD OF FOLLOW-UP Private interview

PRELIMINARY CRITERIA
1. Symptomatic Change:
    A. Hurt, angry, lacking confidence, difficulty becoming sexually aroused with men
    B. Depression, anxiety, anger, somatic tensions, and obsessive self-doubt and jealousy (SCL-90)
2. Dynamic Change, Stress Tests for Dynamic Change:
    A. Feeling betrayed by men. Having to cope with rivals, with jealousy, with taking second place.
    B. Being criticized, attacked, put down.
    C. Feeling resentful, attacking, punishing.
3. Systemic Change, Response of System to Dynamic Changes in Patient: If the patient no longer oscillates between trying to be perfect, clinging to relations, and letting go with bursts of hostility, she will be less available to her mother and to her ex-husband. She will be more of a separate individual, which could be quite difficult for them. I doubt if they will let her do this without a fight. I doubt if she wants to give up such security either. In other words, her penchant for the depressive position is for such a "right" relationship. I imagine that this organization may only be given up very slowly, the system operating as a load against separation-individuation.

4. Patient's View of the Therapy: The emphasis in my story is on the fear of her own destructiveness making holes in needed relationships. Will that have stood out for her as well? The second emphasis is on loss of crucial men, father and grandfather, who could have helped her from sinking into holding onto mother so tightly. Will that stand out for her as well? In other words, did she feel we traversed the road from her destructiveness to her worthwhile relationships? Is Winnicott's map about right for what we did?

5. Patient's Relation to Interviewer: Will she have to give to me what I want to hear? Will she be able to go own way in the discussion, differ, criticize, take exception? Will she be depressed seeing me again, feeling some loss about not having a companion in her difficulties?

6. Summary of Preliminary Criteria for Required Closure:
   A. Needs: The major sacrifice has been about being able to defend and protect herself (Level II, Gedo), which has also compromised her sexual responsiveness. Some weaknesses are likely here, given constant attitude.
   B. Constant Attitude: Heroic, giving, being perfect, sensitive, understanding, vulnerable.
   C. Security Operations: "Now I give perfectly, etc. Now I am hurt, angry and punishing, and I let go, I threaten to make holes, I scare myself . . . so I can go back to being attentive, giving, etc. I put the lid back on." Essentially, I am discussing a very clear depressive position which is deeply held, which depends upon this archaic perfect self which demands a perfect responsiveness. (See Chapter 8, Balint, and Chapter 11, Malan.) I expect to find this is given up ever so slowly.
   D. Family Game: Patient continues heroic qualities of both parents, father the war hero, mother the saint, sacrificing themselves for higher purposes. Mother remarried an alcoholic to persist in her saintliness. Perhaps the patient has to do something similar. This is a romantic tradition.

RESULTS

1. Symptomatic Change:
   A. Hurt, angry, lacking confidence, sexual arousal: Definitely improved, but a little "uneasy, not completely good," fears "not loving enough." Only one occasion in six months of hurt, anger, jealousy for a day or two, resolved by discussion with the man who understood. "Things have been quite a lot better. I don't spend as much time thinking about myself and my problems. I am better able to accept myself and my emotions. I seem to be less blocked and more able to just live and not be so tied up all the time."
   B. Depression, anxiety, anger, somatic tensions and obsessive self-doubt and jealousy (SCL-90): Drastically reduced across the board to "a little bit" from "quite a bit" or "extremely." Only item which is "moderate" is "3. Repeated unpleasant thoughts" and "quite a bit" is "89. Feelings of guilt." This refers to feeling guilty several times a day in the last week for several minutes at a time about company telephone calls. A memo forbade local calls which are personal which she enjoys making. This "guilt" is worse than usual for last six months; the overall improvement has been stable.

2. Dynamic Change, Stress Tests for Dynamic Change:
   A. Feeling betrayed by men, having to cope with rivals, with jealousy, with taking second place: Feels much more "confident" about her position with new boyfriend

she has had since therapy. This "confidence" has several aspects. One is that she is not so involved with new boyfriend as with the boyfriend who sank her before. Therefore, "if something should go wrong, I'd be okay, on an even keel, not go down." Secondly, she has got the "ground rules" straight with this man, so that "unexpected bolts from the blue" are unlikely about rivals. The one occasion that threw her for a day was an "unexpected" absence of her boyfriend one evening, when he went out with someone else he had known from the past. Thirdly, she is able to bring out her feelings to this man, without him getting anxious and attacking back. Therefore, the incident described was relieved when he understood how she felt. Fourthly, the man reassures her well, "You're the one I care about." Thus, she was able to tolerate his hosting a party with his old girlfriend, being secure in her position, without jealousy. The only difficulty with this arrangement is that she is not wanting marriage or progression to more involvement, while the man is pulling her that way. Thus, her voice doubled in volume telling me she didn't want "enganglement" or "being married." When I asked to whom this defense was addressed, she replied that she felt "uneasy, not completely good, not loving enough" to the boyfriend because of holding him at arm's length.

B. Being criticized, attacked, put-down: Ex-husband nailed her vehemently about going out to a football game, when their daughter was ill, proceeding to broad, nasty generalizations: "You never took care of me either. You were always selfish," etc. She did not back down. She laughed telling me about this broad attack and her reply, but at the time she "wavered," until getting support from friends. Still, that is improvement.

C. Feeling resentful, attacking, punishing: One occasion of major frustration with boyfriend resolved well. Told him. He accepted her anger, apologized.

3. Systemic Change, Response of System of Dynamic Changes in Patient: Patient seemed in the dark about how she might trigger the attack from ex-husband, except to notice that ex-husband complained about not knowing her feelings sometimes, same complained by new boyfriend. I took this up with her directly (see Section 5. Patient's Relation to Interviewer) inasmuch as I felt this difficulty with her as well. It appears to me that she, unwittingly, provokes attack as from ex-husband, while pulling others to be closer as with new boyfriend. This conserves the "confinement" that she resents. She is getting more "distance" to be sure, more "room" for her own feelings, especially given choice of boyfriend, but this mechanism keeps her from moving too fast away from "confinement."

4. Patient's View of the Therapy: She emphasizes several lessons which were very specific for her: (a) That she could "have her feelings," without "swallowing" them or "confessing" them. This made them less powerful. (b) That "unwanted thoughts" did not have to be fought: for example, jealous thoughts of the "boyfriend with another woman" might be painful, but kept her from being "set up" by "unexpected" findings which would be more painful. This made the "unwanted thoughts" less powerful. (c) "Not to place expectations for sexual performance on myself when I'm not sexually attracted to the other person." These "lessons" from me suggested to me that she experienced me as a father helping her to differ from her mother. She emphasized that I tied early family experiences in well for her, but that I went on to helping her solve present difficulties. She seems to have taken from me a kind of interpersonal education.

She also emphasized the importance to her of two-hour sessions. Previous therapy in one-hour sessions had often left her "just getting going" after one hour, or "not bringing things up" which might not get resolved. She also liked the long interval — often a month — between sessions, since there would be time for something "significant" to happen, to bring back. She liked the regularity, for her, about once a month, which also left her on her own to do things.

5. Patient's Relation to Interviewer: This was most interesting. I felt she complied with my detailed questions about her symptoms with more and more restlessness and more and more of a cloud on her face. I felt she was getting angry. When she noted that her ex-husband and new boyfriend both agree they are provoked by "not knowing how she feels," I suggested I had a similar difficulty with her. I said that her face was extremely expressive, clouded or light, sending very strong messages, which she evidently was unaware of sending. If she were unaware of sending hints, then others might be provoked to oblige her to express her demands more directly. I found myself in a bind with her, even here, for I wanted to proceed with the interview, while she seemed from her face to want to stay with this interesting subject, but gave verbal consent to me to go on. I could go on all right, but I would be guilty of imposing my own purposes against her reluctant face. I could see where the ex-husband might feel very guilty, until he exploded at her. I presume such a confining interaction must have also begun and continued with her mother, the saint, but I did not have the time here for further discussion.

6. Summary of Findings in Relation to Criteria for Required Closure:
   A. Needs: Much better at defending herself, but "wavers" about this, securing others to support her, securing a new boyfriend who accepts her feelings much better than husband did.
   B. Constant Attitude: Heroic giving, being perfect, sensitive, understanding and vulnerable: This posture is somewhat revised but the pull back into the attitude is easily aroused. Interesting, she now pulls very strongly for this attitude in *others*, getting it from new boyfriend to a large extent.
   C. Security Operations: She is still deeply involved in sending nonverbal messages about giving perfectly, getting frustrated, etc., which she is unaware of sending. This little dance, which she pulls for from other people obscures what is a depressive position: the archaic perfect self which demands a perfect responsiveness (see Chapter 8, Balint, Chapter 11, Malan). Until this is explored and gradually given up, I would expect continued vulnerability to depression. A minor manifestation is the "guilt" about telephone calls which are now forbidden. I think she resents such infringement, but is less aware of her demands than her "guilt."
   D. Family Game: The sacrificing game of the family, which allows the patient to be either the sacrificing, giving person or the one who receives such perfect adjustment is still very powerful. Insofar as the "depressive position" continues unresolved, the perfect demandingness and the perfect reception of demands will be disappointed, generating recurrent depression, which will pull for redoubled efforts for perfection. This is a very powerful romantic tradition. There is some movement to reduce the game, based upon taking "lessons" from me about interpersonal relations, but the "wavering" suggests that the family tradition helps her to keep from moving away too fast.

SUMMARY REMARKS, NOTEWORTHY FINDINGS

I am interested here in two findings which are very powerful. One is that the accuracy of follow-up interviews depends on the interviewer being able to take his own response to the patient quite seriously. This patient reported major improvement, which is there to be sure, with this residual difficulty of being attacked by ex-husband, crowded by new boyfriend. If I had not noticed the powerful nonverbal pull upon myself of this patient's remarkable clouding and clearing of her face, then I would not have understood the residual difficulty she has with her most important relations. Second is the limitation of interpersonal "lessons." This patient used me to reduce enmeshment, to achieve arm's length from men, but the systemic closure is so powerful that such lessons can only give room. They do not resolve the difficulties which would occur if the patient got back into very close quarters. Thus, there is impressive symptomatic and dynamic change, but the systemic change may be very little or very gradual. Such changes have to go slowly. The nonverbal signaling helps to slow individuation, so the patient, her mother, and other important persons are not left out. Thus there will be no "unexpected bolts from the blue."

THE CASE OF THE FOREST RANGER
(Chapters 8 and 22)

THERAPY 236 sessions, 236 hours
THERAPIST Author
INTERVAL Since preliminary interview, 5 years, 9 months
                    Since end of therapy, 3 months
METHOD OF FOLLOW-UP Private interview

PRELIMINARY CRITERIA
1. Symptomatic change:
   A. Depression
   B. No self-confidence
2. Dynamic Change, Stress Tests of Dynamic Change:
   A. Disagreements, having to stick up for himself, say "no," defend himself against criticism, attack, etc. (Level II, Gedo)
   B. Loneliness
   C. Involvement
3. Systemic Change, Response of System to Dynamic Changes in Patient: If the patient becomes capable of getting on with his own life and setting up family of his own, this will be disturbing for the parents who look to him as the helpful child who will most available to them. Thus, there will be trouble for the patient and for them unless patient can, somehow, progress, while being gradual enough and while staying available.
4. Patient's View of the Therapy: I am particularly interested in the patient's recall of my final message, discussed in Chapter 22.
5. Patient's Relation to Interviewer: I understand patient has become ill with some virus which prevents his going to graduate school for now and he will be in Madison for a while. Thus, this interview may be part of a continuing relationship for the time being. Thus, the book chapters and this evaluation may be fed back directly into our work.
6. Summary of Preliminary Criteria for Required Closure:
   A. Needs: The Level II capabilities for self-protection have always been sacrificed to some extent.
   B. Constant Attitude: "I try to help."

C. Security Operations: "I merge into the wide open spaces" (philobatism; see Chapter 8, Balint)
D. Family Game: The patient is needed in case the parents fall apart, which is always possible.

RESULTS
1. Symptomatic Change:
   A., B. Depression; no self-confidence: Patient described overall change in questionnaire as follows: "The feelings of hopelessness do not occur as frequently as they once did. When they do, they do not last as long, nor are they as severe as they once were. Everything was always hopeless — I think it was built into my way of thinking. The feeling didn't come and go — it was always there.

   "My level of self-esteem isn't high, but I think some probably exists. I have days when I think I have really screwed up my life and everybody else's, but that idea is not a part of my self-concept anymore. Before treatment, I couldn't have imagined how or why I would ever think I was OK. Now I at least have some idea of how that might happen and feel."

   The SCL-90 shows "moderate" depressive and inferiority complaints and "quite a bit" of angry feelings, plus some somatization, which may be due to a viral illness diagnosed as "cytomegaly virus" by his internist. There is no SCL-90 from five years ago for comparison. Actually, the patient says that these depressive and self-esteem difficulties occur about once a week for a half-day or a day, when he feels "worthless" about something, but then they clear. He gets angry a couple times a week, probably an improvement over never getting angry before.

2. Dynamic Change:
   A. Disagreements, etc.: Several clashes have occurred, which test this capability. One was that the patient has decided to get married, eliciting the usual criticism of his gregarious, social friend. The patient listened, but then told the friend he didn't want to hear it anymore. "He knows I'll write him off if he continues," so the friend has laid off. The second was that the patient was told by an internist at the health service of the graduate school that his tiredness must be due to depression. The patient felt this was wrong, but was somewhat shaken in his confidence. He telephoned me long distance, whereupon I indicated some confidence in his instinct about his own condition. Thereupon, he asked his professor to recommend another doctor. The second doctor took note of the low-grade fever (about 100°) and chills and conducted some tests. He believes the patient has cytomegalic virus. The third test of some magnitude occurred the same day as the struggle with the internist, when the patient went to see the psychiatrist recommended by the internist. After a few questions, he pushed a prescription at the patient for antidepressants, despite the patient's objections. The patient has since written him a letter telling him he ought to listen to what his patients have to say.
   B. Loneliness: The patient felt "alone" driving out to the graduate school, but this was overtaken by excitement after a few days. Although he had feared being unable to depend on anyone for help but myself, he had become friends with a fellow teaching assistant whose office was across the hall and who showed some friendly concern about him when he became so tired after a week of being at school.
   C. Involvement: This new friendship was based not only upon the friendly interest, but also on some shared values. The patient felt pleased about starting a new re-

lationship with a "clean slate." He was also able to correct a misunderstanding of this friend, who recommended psychotherapy to him, by telling the friend he was entirely acquainted with psychotherapy. Since the patient was only in graduate school for a little over a month, this test of the capacity for involvement was only beginning to get underway. Still, he surprised himself in a pleasant new beginning, which he had not anticipated as possible.

3. Systemic Change, Response of System to Dynamic Changes in the Patient: The patient received daily letters from his parents, until he decided to return here because his illness made continuing in graduate school impracticable for the time being. Since then, there has been no correspondence. He sees this as entirely consistent, that being close again in a geographic way replaces the closeness of daily letters. He wrote as follows about how his family and friends have seen the changes in him before, during and after therapy:

"Those who knew me before therapy could not understand why I was always so unhappy. They would have said that I had everything going for me — family, friends, brains, sense of humor or whatever. I would not have believed a word of it. Some would have blamed themselves for my unhappiness, and were usually worried about me. I didn't discuss the details of therapy much with anyone. Most of my friends couldn't understand why I was doing it because I seemed like a happy person and they couldn't see anything wrong. I think my parents just hoped it would work. They would occasionally ask (indirectly) about it, or casually suggest that I 'seemed better.' I think they were kind of afraid of the therapy and of me. Since therapy, I think people would say that I seem less inhibited and more likely to do and say what I want to do. I'm probably not as 'nice' as I used to be. I think they would say that I seem happier and a bit more content than I was."

It appears to me that the patient is managing a gradual change in which he is freer to "be himself" while conserving the "closeness" important to his family.

4. Patient's View of the Therapy: The patient takes a very straightforward view of what I did that mattered to him. First, I helped him "keep control" when he felt lost. He would come in feeling terrible and I would take a different view of the findings. He would feel "all wrong" and I would disagree. Secondly, he began to get the idea from me that it didn't matter if he was different in his responses from others. "It was just what I think." In graduate school he found further confirmations of his views and values, whereas before he had felt as if no one was like him. Third, he had "never had anybody to talk to before . . . without it getting turned around or ripped up." He summarized this eloquently in the questionnaire as follows:

"I think some of my problems were brought about partially because I had never trusted anyone. I thought everyone thought my thoughts and feelings were unimportant (as I did), and were, therefore, not worth expressing. I was afraid of offending people or making them angry, because I assumed it would lead to their completely disregarding me. My inability to really communicate with others prevented me from bonding with them which kept my self-esteem low and feelings of helplessness high. I am probably better now because I don't think all of my reactions, opinions and feelings are intrinsically wrong. This makes it easier to communicate with people, which has allowed me to feel for them and feel their feelings in return. When I am not able to express myself, or dismiss my thoughts as silly, stupid or unworthy, the old feelings return."

How had he survived at all? He recalled being afraid of the woods in third or fourth grade, but gradually becoming more comfortable there, especially "up north" at the family cabin. This seemed to operate as a region of hope. Still, he came very close to killing himself in the darkest hours of the therapy. He "wanted to die . . . was actually going to do it by using the exhaust of the car . . . or cut wrists . . . ," but his friend and the friend's girl had been at his apartment when he came home with such an intention. Also, I had made it difficult for him to kill himself, because I kept saying I needed more time to figure it out, because I was more hopeful than he was about what might appear. Finally, how did he recall his departure from me? Two messages came through to him. One was that this didn't have to be the last time we met. Two was that he cared about at least two people.

5. Patient's Relation to the Interviewer: I never clarified this very well. I noticed he was a little agitated when I first met him. I noticed at the end this was evident again, and he confirmed being "thrown" by my letter proposing the interview. He ended up getting mad at his fianceé for being insufficiently interested in him or insensitive. I proposed he might have been angry at me. He denied this, but I still imagined he didn't like my inquiry. Rather, he only said he had been angry at me for making it difficult for him to kill himself.

6. Summary of Findings in Relation to Criteria for Required Closure:

   A. Needs: He defends himself better (Level II capacities), but it is much too soon to tell how steady this will be. A vulnerability probably remains here, as evident with the first internist. Perhaps the patient feels vulnerable to what I might want or expect from him, I don't know. It has always been important to sacrifice this capability for self-defense, for closure at subsequent levels.

   B. Constant Attitude: Despite his successful defense of himself, his ability to make a new friend and a new start, he still felt he "should" have been able to stay on in graduate school despite the viral illness. "Nothing should get to me," he said. He thought he got this attitude from his grandparents.

   C. Security Operations: The philobatism remains in place, I think, while he explores relying on other people to some extent to listen and take seriously what he feels and thinks.

   D. Family Game: The "closeness" to the parents seems to have some flexibility, some different moves, for example, by daily letters when far away, by being close in the geographic sense, by appearing to be okay, by being himself more openly.

SUMMARY REMARKS, NOTEWORTHY FINDINGS

Much more time will be needed to tell about the stability of the patient's new directions and capabilities. How do I reconcile the discrepancy between the patient's perspective of what he got from me and my own emphasis on the complications necessary to be appreciated (especially in Chapter 22)? I would say that my own hopefulness and my own confidence that the patient's responses made sense, which I could convey to him, which he says mattered very much to him, depended upon *my* not being tangled up in the contradictions that he was caught up in. *I* was helped by thinking that his turn to the "wide open spaces" had to be understandable, that his sacrifice of defending himself had also to be understandable, and so forth. This could come across more simply to him as hopefulness and confidence in him.

POSTSCRIPT

Several comments by the patient upon the text and upon the follow-up report seem to me of great interest. The first concerns the Summary Remarks, to which he replies, "Exactly." The second concerns his finding a "right" way to be in his own eyes: "I think you're right about that session (emphasized in the text as pivotal). It did make a lot of difference because I realized that there is no 'right' or 'wrong' way to be. I had always thought that because I didn't seem to be like most people, I was therefore wrong. You categorized me as a person who likes wide open spaces and independence as opposed to those who like closeness and confiding, which give me an identity other than 'wrong.' I think from there I could go on and become an individual. It gave me freedom which I hadn't felt before. . . . I think the reason I get along with (my fiancée) is because she shares my need for wide open spaces and for space in the relationship." The third concerns how we managed to get through the period of dangerous suicidal intent: "Also I was trying to think of what else you did which kept me from killing myself. One was simply the fact of our relationship. I always felt that nobody would even notice if I were no longer around, but I knew you would, since I was to see you every other day or whatever. Talking to you was also something I (usually) looked forward to. I guess it was the only release I had. Also, I think I knew from your obvious concern that you cared — at least, I thought, for the hour I was in there, which I didn't feel from anybody else. So when you asked me to give you a chance, I must have decided I would, for a while. The other thing which had an impact but which I don't think you had planned was when you suggested sending me to Kansas (Menninger's). That was a real slap in the face and made me realize this was serious. I never cared enough about myself to think that. I knew then that I had better either give up or give in to life and live with it, or I'd be in trouble. I knew enough about hospitals to know I didn't want to be there once because I'd probably be in and out forever."

THE POLICEMAN'S DAUGHTER
(Chapter 9)

THERAPY First brief therapy, 38 sessions, 38 hours
              Second brief therapy, 5 sessions, 6 hours
THERAPIST Author
INTERVAL Since original evaluation, 4 years, 2 months
            Since end of first treatment, 3 years, 9 months
            Since end of second treatment, 7 months
METHOD OF FOLLOW-UP Private interview

PRELIMINARY CRITERIA
1. Symptomatic change:
    A. Depression: isolation, sleeping a lot, vague suicidal thoughts, despairing
    B. Low self-confidence
2. Dynamic Change, Stress Tests for Dynamic Change:
    A. Disappointment in love, especially losing to rivals, being rejected
    B. Disappointment in work, not being a big success.
    C. Isolation, loneliness
    D. Involvement, becoming dependent or relying on someone deeply
    E. Feeling revengeful, punishing
3. Systemic Change, Response of System to Dynamic Changes in the Patient: This alternation between being the cop's cool daughter and the emotional daughter of an emotional mother conserves some kind of family game, which refuses to integrate

these two kinds of virtues. I really don't know or appreciate why this has had to be so. Therefore, I don't yet see how the patient integrating the two will destabilize the family of origin. Perhaps the parents stay close by battling over her identity? Perhaps she stays close by keeping this in doubt, keeping both hopeful she will be like only one of them?

4. Patient's View of the Therapy: I will be able to test my idea that the first brief therapy, which went fishing for "true feelings," set her up as her father the cop would predict, while the second brief therapy appreciated the two sides of her, cool and feeling, how each depends upon the other, how an exaggeration of one side only proves the necessity of the other side. If this second view were more correct, she ought to have felt a much greater sense of equilibrium from the second therapy. I will also be able to test my idea of the second termination, being a confrontation with her punishing inclinations, her unconscious degradation of those who disappoint her.

5. Patient's Relation to Interviewer: She has tended to alternate in her relation to me, being very cool and detached and minimizing our relation of her "cop" states, while being very intense about our relation in her "emotional" states. So whatever I get has to be evaluated according to the state in which it is given.

6. Summary of Preliminary Criteria for Required Closure:
   A. Needs: Can she connect and still look out for herself well? How much must these needs be sacrificed to her alternation?
   B. Constant Attitude: *How* will she alternate between her two attitudes, cool and warm, cop and mother? Will they be compartmentalized? Or can she get back and forth more easily (more integrated)?
   C. Security Operations: The two attitudes are also describable as two security operations which work as an alternating team, which keep her from having to revise what is essentially a depressive position (the archaic manifesto of Balint, see Chapter 11 on Malan): "I should have whatever I want."
   D. Family Game: How the alternation conserves the parental relation I will need to discover in the interview. Usually, the depressive position prevents growing up and separating, which somehow must be avoided in this family.

RESULTS
1. Symptomatic Change:
   A. Depression, etc.: The "acute" disturbance for which I saw her the second brief therapy has not reappeared in the last seven months. But "the basic underlying loneliness" can be "triggered" by seeing parents as not living forever, by seeing a man who is attractive but unavailable, etc. This lasts a few minutes, until she "marches myself out of it." Having roommates now helps give her company.
   B. Low self-confidence: Quite successful in school last two semesters and summer school, definitely bolder with me as well (see 5. Patient's Relation to Interviewer).
2. Dynamic Change, Stress Tests for Dynamic Change:
   A. Disappointment in love: Untested. Has definitely kept a distance, since "stood up" by a man who was "a pain in the ass" anyway, two months ago.
   B. Disappointment in work: Untested. Has been a steady success in school.
   C. Isolation, loneliness: Has improved her solution here, "marching myself out of it" when feeling such pain, finding good company, humor, stories, action, with roommates. On the other hand, the vulnerability to this pain is still evident, as she feared a discussion of the subject, feared being plunged "back" to the disturbance of a year ago.

D. Relying on someone deeply: Essentially, she has broadened her network to include the three new roommates, conserving a number of previous friends. This is constructive, keeping her out of the big hole she was in a year ago. But, on the other hand, you could also say she is still not ready to risk falling in love and weather its ups and downs.

E. Feeling revengeful, punishing: Two tests of this difficulty passed well, one when "stood up" by a man when lost in a crowd from him at a big rock concert, another about me being late for the interview. Feels punishing, but is "giving more room to be human, for others to mess up." "Less harsh, more lenient." So long as the other "kowtows," i.e., apologizes or bows to her, then she forgives and understands. She is still proud, asserts her pride, but with more restraint.

3. Systemic Change, Response of System to Dynamic Changes in the Patient: The patient still oscillates between the two states described in the text, between the "cool" independent state and the "need for security." This figures now in her recent dilemma about graduation, whether to go into corporate business, which is more secure but makes her the "same" as everyone else, or to risk a more independent venture, which is more exciting. Depressed by the former prospect in job interviews, she has deferred the decision until spring. Thus, I see more integration of this oscillation, but the oscillation remains between the stance of the father and the stand of the mother. She feels closer to them. They, getting older, ask for more respect for their autonomy from their kids, give more respect to the autonomy of the patient. Would they recognize the improvement of the patient in "looking out for herself"? She is "not sure they are that sensitive." They would see her as "happier." In other words, I see the patient as conserving her oscillation which keeps her in tune with her parents, yet allowing a slow movement to autonomy, which, paradoxically, makes her feel closer to them.

4. Patient's View of the Therapy: She saw the first therapy as "a cookbook of how to deal with your feelings," how to "recognize the forces and find a way to satisfy them." She saw the second therapy as coping with "much more powerful forces, more acute difficulty" than the first. She seems to see little difference in what I was doing differently between the first and second therapy. This is interesting, for she, indeed, seems to have greater equilibrium from the second as I predicted, while being completely unaware of what might have allowed this result to be different from the first result. The termination seems to have hit home, although she did not recall what I did, in that she is definitely better about being "stood up," feeling "revengeful" or "degrading."

5. Patient's Relation to the Interviewer: This was more striking than in any follow-up interview I have conducted. I stood her up ten minutes, fortunately catching her walking out as I walked towards my office. I had also "given no thanks" for her willingness to come in "to help *me*." Therefore, she had not been willing to do the SCL-90 for me! She wanted more respect. I apologized, for I felt she was right. She relented, because I "kowtowed" to her. I was impressed. In the past, she might have tolerated what was wrong to her, only to be very punishing later. Here, she let me know straight away, allowing me to apologize, allowing her to forgive me, allowing her not to have builtup revenge. Also, she was clear about fearing the interview as "opening up Pandora's Box," the feelings of "being out of control" from a year ago which were still frightening. Indeed, she went into these feelings some, but kept out of deep water. I was also impressed. Acknowledging the fear, the actual difficulty which remains, helped her to negotiate well with me. Here was less of the previous bravado and coolness, which would only be a setup for a crash. Again, I saw more integration of

the "cool cop" and the "needful girl." She was bringing the two together better.
6. Summary of Findings in Relation to Criteria for Required Closure:
   A. Needs: She connects and looks out for herself well. But she has to be careful about excessive depth and reliance upon some single individual such as could occur in "falling in love." A vulnerability remains. Her "broadening out" her dependency is constructive. Her ability to stick up for herself, as with the man who stood her up, as with me, is impressive. This allowed her, then, to come closer to me.
   B. Constant Attitude: The alternation between cool and warm, cop and mother, is still striking, but better integrated as I have described.
   C. Security Operations: I see a little taming of the archaic demandingness, but "falling in love" and settling into a line of work will be the ultimate tests of the progress.
   D. Family Game: I see a gradual separation to more "autonomy," which is quite constructive. The ultimate tests of love and work remain. Will she be able to continue to integrate better this oscillation of hers in some line of work, in some deep relationship with a man? This is unknown, although the movement is in the right direction.

SUMMARY REMARKS, NOTEWORTHY FINDINGS
Two findings interest me very much here. One is how the follow-up interview is an enactment of the previous difficulty. If the interviewer catches the right angle, he can see how the patient is showing her improvement and her remaining concerns. Two is how the systemic interest allows the slow evolution which is crucial to finding new versions for the closure required with the family game. This individual is deeply involved in this oscillation between coolness and warmth, cop and mother. There is no way this remarkable oscillation will be given up. The acceptance of its power (a necessary *class* as Bateson would say) allows different variations and more integration (new *moves* within the *class*).

Am I right that brief therapy is enough help? In his letter to me of September 28, 1985, commenting on the description of the brief therapy of this patient, Dr. Gedo did not recommend analysis. The follow-up I find inconclusive about brief therapy versus analysis. The patient is moving in a more constructive direction. Would analysis over the past four years I have known her allowed even deeper progress? Would she now have a deep, loving relationship with a man because of such an experience in analysis? This is possible. But only time will tell if she gets there with what she has gotten.

A CASE OF CHEST PAIN
(Chapters 10 and 12)

THERAPY 8 sessions, 9 hours
THERAPIST Trial therapy, author; Brief therapy, resident
INTERVAL Since preliminary evaluation, 1 year
          Since end of therapy, 9 months
METHOD OF FOLLOW-UP Videotaped interview

PRELIMINARY CRITERIA
1. Symptomatic Change:
   A. Chest pain

B. SCL-90: Moderate to quite a bit of anxiety, depression, other somatization
2. Dynamic Change, Stress Tests for Dynamic Change:
   A. Getting too far from parents, who sacrificed, who gave their hearts for him, especially "permanent separation": e.g., being successful, being selfish, new friends, girlfriends.
   B. Perhaps failing and losing heart, confidence, in himself.
3. Systemic Change, Response of System to Dynamic Changes in Patient: How are he and family seeing closeness/distance between them? How are they managing? His success means more separation, which is apt to be threatening and which will have to be countered by some other reassurance.
4. Patient's View of Therapy: What will he emphasize from the interaction between us?
5. Patient's Relation to the Interviewer: I basically expect a continuation of our positive relationship.
6. Summary of Preliminary Criteria for Required Closure:
   A. Needs: Chief sacrifice has been of forceful, aggressive, selfish interests, which I expect to continue to some degree.
   B. Constant Attitude: "You have to give back what you got, to give a break where you got a break."
   C. Security Operations: "You identify with the less fortunate, the innocent who are victimized. Yet you do not wear your heart on your sleeve. The pain of life becomes the pain of the body to reduce its intensity."
   D. Family Game: How to progress, but not so fast that you leave the less fortunate behind?

RESULTS
1. Symptomatic Change:
   A. Chest pain: "Exponential decay" until Christmas. Free of it for two weeks of holiday. Came back almost daily or every other day January to June, but he "didn't care," it was so trivial. Worse in May and June when mother's cancer discovered. Went away August 15 since he moved into "permanent place" with 10 or 12 guys — "always someone around."
   B. SCL-90: Not returned. I judge from his comments, reported in Dynamic Change, that his anxiety and depression have run in parallel to his chest pain.
2. Dynamic Change, Stress Tests for Dynamic Change:
   A. Getting too far from parents, etc.: He has established himself here, which is a kind of separation, by doing "all right, in the middle, in graduate school," by making friends, "yes, not soulmates," but fallen into a "gang." "1000 will be at his graduation party!" "Not as tight" as previous mates, but it's "OK." No girlfriends now, "no time now." Mother's illness has been the most difficult test of his ability to tolerate separation. Indeed, he got chest pain again for two months. He phones a lot, got a car to visit her every other weekend. But he realizes he has ambition, for "bucks" as well as for "science," so he persists with school.
   B. Failing, losing heart: "We (as a group) often joke that if we didn't lose heart once in a while, something would be wrong."
3. Systemic Change, Response of System to Dynamic Changes in Patient: When I asked the patient about how his old friends would see him, he said they would say he's the same, "Mr. Social Director." Evidently, he has conserved these relations well. When I asked him how his family would see him, he allowed his sister would see him as more

"selfish . . . disappointing." His parents would see he's for a "balance," being a "rocker" like mom who danced four nights a week, a "Mr. Old Country" like dad. Evidently, he can draw upon his mom's having been full of herself. This is a borrowing I was not aware of before. Thus, he stays close, by drawing upon a different potential of his family.

4. Patient's View of the Therapy: Our trial therapy was "constructive interference." We connected. I said he'd be OK. This reminded him of his mentor in college, who got him going in his field. On the contrary, he did not connect with the resident. He told him less than he would tell his friends. Perhaps it was his being young, perhaps inexpert, perhaps he couldn't quite catch the importance of what the patient talked about, perhaps because he only "categorized" things.

5. Patient's Relation to Interviewer: He seemed anxious to discuss with me his response to his mother's illness. Why was he not more upset? What was wrong with his priorities? I allowed that some denial was usual for now, but was interested in what he was doing about the trouble. This led nicely into his being divided between sticking to his own bent in school and doing something for mom. I was impressed he could ride both currents well.

6. Summary of Findings in Relation to Criteria for Required Closure:
   A. Needs: He seems much more accepting of his forceful, aggressive, selfish side. This is surprising.
   B. Constant Attitude: "Giving back" is still strong, but balanced.
   C. Security Operations: He seems now to identify with winning, with "making bucks," as well as with "contributing to science."
   D. Family Game: He progresses, but he does not leave family behind. Holding back on finding a woman will help slow down his separation. Indeed, I think that is now the chief device.

SUMMARY REMARKS, NOTEWORTHY FINDINGS

A powerful result, in symptomatic, dynamic and systemic terms, on this recent follow-up. A fascinating story of "being ripped from the womb," but seeing his devotion (the class of moves) has perhaps helped him to recreate his own "new gang" up here (a new move). He stays the same, not by illness, but by a new constructive move. It is quite clear that the establishment of the new gang, the new home, is exactly timed with the relief of symptoms, which were exacerbated by his mother's illness.

POSTSCRIPT

The patient comments on my final remarks concerning the timing of his recent improvement: "I don't understand how this can be when I admit that this new circle of friends is an inadequate match for the first." The patient comments on his not getting a girlfriend: "I initially wanted to talk about my lack of having a relationship in the last couple of years but was thrown a curve when you mentioned it. I backed off for some reason. It really had bothered me in the week preceding our last talk." In his letter, he describes two very powerful experiences since our interview, one about an argument with his roommates about the apartment being too cold, which made him "very angry at their lack of consideration." Telling his father about the argument over the telephone, he "began to sob uncontrollably." Then he had a similar experience watching Jessica Lange in "Country" "berate this auctioneer, screaming at him to get off her land. It was everything I could do to stop from bursting into tears. In general things since these incidents have been very good in terms of balancing things." So far it appears he is doing very well. He seems to go through the necessary emotional passage on his own, which the two of us had negotiated in his trial therapy.

THE DAUGHTER OF SOAP OPERA
(Chapter 11)

THERAPY 8 sessions, 9 hours.
THERAPIST Trial therapy, author; Further therapy, resident
INTERVAL Since original evaluation, 10 months
              Since end of treatment, 7 months
METHOD OF FOLLOW-UP Videotaped interview

PRELIMINARY CRITERIA
1. Symptomatic Change:
   A. Hyperventilation
   B. "Panic" thinking about "death"
   C. Polyneurotic complaining including somatization, obsessional complaints, depression, anxiety, low self-appraisal, etc. (all but paranoid items and phobic items positive on SCL-90 at original evaluation)
2. Dynamic Change, Stress Tests for Dynamic Change:
   A. Threat of being left: separations of all kinds, including parents, boyfriend, when dying grandfather leaves grandmother, etc.
   B. Anger at important people, where she might injure or destroy the relation: parents, boyfriend, girlfriends, etc.
   C. Disappointments with ideal relationships
3. Systemic Change, Response of System to Dynamic Changes in Patient: The dangers in becoming different from her mother (the star of soap opera relations) and more like her father (the so-called rational one) are several: She could lose her closeness with her mother, which could be difficult for both of them. She could become closer to father, only to become very disappointed in his weaknesses, only to discover aspects of "rationality" in him or in herself which are overly constraining, less fun, less lively, etc.
   Certainly, her boyfriend may decline a relation with her if she is not a girl to look after in a fatherly way, if she is too able and capable. This could be difficult for other men too. Certainly, she may have more difficulty with previous girlfriends, if she drops the hysterical female game which is so typical.
4. Patient's View of Therapy: I am supposing the trial therapy helped her by seeing medical complaining as a distraction from difficulties with disappointment, anger and being left, by posing the "ordinary solution," which keeps from the hysterical extremes of saying nothing/say everything. Since such an ordinary solution seemed within her reach in the trial therapy, once the distraction and exaggeration were put to one side, it could be that such observations were all that were needed, viz., the observation of how she sacrifices her needs, the observation of carrying on with an attitude like mother (the soap opera) — essentially observations of closure of needs and constant attitude. It could well be, however, that there was insufficient appreciation of the closure in her security operations and family game, which would be upset by improvements in

getting her needs met, in sorting her own attitude from mother's attitude. I could have put her into some sort of crisis about these kinds of closure. This is what I want to see about the trial.

The brief therapy was terminated by her for reasons which were unclear. I thought the resident was getting caught in one of two tangles: (A) being distracted with her in her medical complaining; (B) pressuring her to knuckle down. Will she confirm this or not? I suspect she lost hope that he could help her, and ran from the disappointment, anger, and fear of becoming mean and punishing.

5. Patient's Relationship to Interviewer: My chief difficulty, I suspect, will be in separating myself from being critical of her and her mother for their soap opera methods — which would only work to pull me into father's job. I will want to be clear about this, especially in giving her the chapter to read when we finish.

6. Summary of Preliminary Criteria for Required Closure:

   A. Needs: Can she be disappointed, angry, vindictive, and fear being left . . . with more constructive ways to meet these needs, with less medical distraction, hysterical exaggeration, etc.?

   B. Constant Attitude: Can she keep something of dramatic talent, of soap opera? Something of rationality? Without becoming lost in either? Without alternating between the two? Without being rational in work, while hysterical in personal relations? Some combination of these two attitudes of her two parents is to be conserved, but how?

   C. Security Operations: Dramatization, exaggeration, idealization will be present, but how constructively?

   D. Family Game: I really do not yet understand the family game here of grandmother, mother and patient all utilizing talents to be "weak creatures," so to speak. This could have been nursed along to support or to prop up various weaknesses in the men. If patient departs from this family game, she could feel quite lost and mother, grandmother could feel quite left behind and father could feel more insecure with her. But parents could already be on a different road, given their divorce 14 years ago, and welcome her individuation. We'll see.

RESULTS

1. Symptomatic Change:

   A., B., Hyperventilation, "panic about death": Fewer episodes of less duration: e.g., breakup with second boyfriend led to three-day siege instead of the nine months with first boyfriend, e.g., minor half-hour episodes, perhaps only four this past summer which "I can control now, since I accept dying as a natural part of life," whereas before they were much more frequent and tended to last two or three hours or all night.

   C. Polyneurotic complaining (on SCL-90): New SCL-90 shows drastic reduction in number and frequency of complaints (compared to original SCL-90 10 months ago) but same broad pattern of some anxiety, some depression, some somatization, some obsessional and some self-esteem concerns. She says this is typical and stable for her since she completed therapy. The only complaint worthy of note, she thinks, is her feeling self-conscious about being overweight. She weighs about the same as a year ago when I first saw her, but had gained eight pounds this summer, and has now begun aerobics to bring it down.

2. Dynamic Change, Stress Tests for Dynamic Change:

   A. Separation threats: Went through three days of hyperventilation, fears of dying, etc., at grandmother's house when breakup with second boyfriend appeared imminent at end of summer. Felt "nauseated, sick inside" when boyfriend wouldn' talk, until father, mother, told her to "knock it off. . . . This isn't that serious. Don't let this guy do this to you."

B. Anger, destructiveness: She had complained to this boyfriend a month earlier about him neglecting her, whereupon he had accused her of "not appreciating all I do for you." She was mad, but didn't yell or back off. Sat down and talked about her anger with him. She is clear she didn't repeat past savagery here. She is clear he tried to blame her, when indeed his outburst followed his not getting into the University this fall. He has gone downhill since, at home, with drugs; she is determined not to be blamed by him. She appears firm.

C. Disappointment: This second boyfriend had been more of an equal for her than the first, who was discussed in therapy. She felt appreciated by him, she felt she could be herself, she could stand her ground, she could keep her friends. The relation with the first boyfriend had been very "dependent," clinging, and left her feeling very helpless when she appeared to be losing the relation. Now when the second boyfriend appeared to have built up resentment, suddenly, at the end of the summer, perhaps comparing her good fortune with his loss of fortune in the university, she seemed to weather this well, despite the three-day crisis. She feels she can do better, if this is how he behaves, and looks forward to new relationships with men. She described being called "fat" at a fraternity party, and standing her ground well. She told the fellow, in front of many bystanders, that at least being fat was something you could do something about, whereas he was just plain ugly, which was hopeless. She laughed with good-natured pleasure in telling me about this incident. She seemed to put her dramatic ability to a new use here.

When discussing the faithfulness of men with her mother this summer, she learned that her father had been grossly unfaithful on the honeymoon of her parents and thereafter. She has a much lower view of him but still accepts him. Their relation has actually improved (see Systemic Change, next category).

3. Systemic Change, Response of System to Dynamic Changes in Patient: Despite my concern that closeness would be lost with mother if patient became less hysterical, the mother seems to have welcomed the patient's being less intense, less hysterical, more matter-of-fact. Mother too is less hysterical now. She seems to "follow" the patient in this regard and in other ways, such as in her kind of haircut. Mother likes to "keep up" with the younger generation, especially with her daughter. Patient says mother "looks about 30."

Indeed, she has become disappointed with her father, as I predicted would follow from a more clear-eyed stance. She has discovered how he cheated her mother; she has seen how he spoiled her but didn't give of himself. When he yelled at her late this summer about a medical bill, on the third day of her upset with the second boyfriend, she yelled back for the first time that he was unreasonable and selfish. "He admitted it" and has been trying to do better. He has been visiting her instead of just sending money, and their relation is "the best in about eight years." She still dislikes his putting down her mother, but she accepts him with his limitations. In other words, the idealization seen a year ago has been revised.

The same appears true about men who are her peers. Her first boyfriend had been idealized like her father had been. Now she sees that many men do not like strength in a woman, but she is hopeful about finding a new man in her life.

4. Patient's View of Therapy: She "enjoyed" the trial therapy, found it "interesting" and was relieved I was interested in her. The trial therapy gave her "hope" to "get out of the hole I was in," so she was very "anxious to get started with her therapy" after the trial. What did she remember that I did or said that helped her? Whereas she had felt "scattered," "grasping for straws," I had made circles (on my notepad, literally, but also metaphorically), which made her feel that it all "connected, fit together, came to a single point." How or what was that? The point was that "I was letting my important people get to me. . . . They were running me." From this she could see that *she* could be *in charge*. When I asked her how she would be in charge in the future, she joked with me that she might start a "male escort service." She laughed good-naturedly about this. More seriously, she said she had decided not to go into psychology and "end up driving a taxi." She had begun a medical field and was enjoying herself very much and felt "together" in school for the first time.

In other words, the clarity she had gotten from me seemed to have been enough to get her well underway, to begin the recovery from hysterical "scatteredness." I am reminded of Sullivan's observation (1956) that what hysterical characters need is to learn to make life a little simpler, not to muck it up with complications. Evidently my fear that I had not appreciated her security operations for their use in the family game proved unfounded. For her, this was not necessary. I think this is because she is a very strong, capable and likeable individual, not a pure case of a Daughter of Soap Opera, but having many rational strengths as well. I am reminded of Zetzell's (1970) description of the better prognosis of hysterics who have both hysterical and obsessive capabilities, who have both mother and father strong in themselves. They may borrow well from both, with a little help. Also, her mother and father both seemed to need her no longer to remain a "weak creature." The pull for this closure of the system proved to be relatively weak, at least for now.

The brief therapy with the resident also seems to have been much more positive than I had thought from her sudden unexplained departure. She felt it had been a "great help" to her. The resident had "acted like he cared," had listened well, had pointed out his own "hypotheses" without enforcing them, allowing her to make up her own mind. This meant a lot to her. It appeared, in retrospect, that it was this kind of relation which mattered most to her, not the content of what he said to her, for which she had little recall. So why did she leave suddenly? One day, she thought, "I'm going to be fine. Staying in therapy would be a waste." So she quit on this impulse. Various hints about what led to this "irrational impulse," as she put it to me, could not be confirmed with her. The impulse *did* follow telling the first boyfriend to go to hell, after nine months of pining for him, did follow taking up a better, more equal relationship with the second boyfriend. She felt terrific. She felt she didn't need her doctor any more.

The best I can make of this is that she found a different way to relate to a man, with more equality, with her resident doctor. Then she discharged her first boyfriend, to have a more equal relation with the second boyfriend. She kidded me about my looking into this, saying that she knew I'd be looking for her being in love with her resident doctor, that she knew I'd be looking for her being angry with him. In this way, she was acting as an *equal with me*. Perhaps this is the message? She's quick! She kidded me that I was overalert, like "the coffee generation."

5. Relation to Interviewer: Her bid for equality, which I have just described, was impressive and enjoyable. My concern not to be too critical of her and her mother for involvement in "soap opera" proved unfounded. She seemed more than prepared for

coping with critical men. She knew, already, that she was much more than hysterical. Indeed, she kidded me that I was doing well to be writing such a big book, but I was still wearing the same funny tie I had worn a year ago. She was eager to see the videotape from a year ago, which I provided for her, "to see myself when I was a blubbering idiot" (laughter). She didn't mind at all if her case was recognized. She seemed quite proud of herself. She seemed to be putting her dramatic capability to better use.

6. Summary of Findings in Relation to Criteria for Required Closure:

   A. Needs: She seems able to go through disappointment, anger, vindictiveness and fear of being left much more constructively. She still utilizes the hysterical mechanism, but much more briefly, much more under control.

   B. Constant attitude: The "dramatic attitude" is retained, for much better effects. The "rational" attitude appears to have been integrated with the "dramatic attitude," without oscillation, without compartmentalizing one from the other.

   C. Security Operations: Dramatization and exaggeration both very much present but revised. Idealization much reduced, but also present constructively.

   D. Family Game: It is much too soon to see if the patient is able to depart from the female line of being weak and dependent, although a strong start is underway. She appears to depart, yet to keep a good relation to both mother and father, indeed a better relation. This is impressive. But it is too soon to judge whether the pull of this family line does not, indeed, return, when she chooses her husband. The closure may be repressed, or put out of sight, only then to return.

SUMMARY REMARKS, NOTEWORTHY FINDINGS

We seem to see a very fine result of brief therapy in a case of "good hysteria" (Zetzell, 1970), but only long-term follow-up will show if this is the truth. We still do not know if the technique used in such a case, which is limited to observation of closure concerning patient's needs and constant attitude and security operations, which neglected the systemic closure, will hold up well enough when the time comes for the patient to choose a husband and bring up a family. This will test the limitations of such a method more deeply.

A CASE OF MIGRAINE
(Chapter 14)

THERAPY 48 sessions, 65 hours
THERAPIST Trial therapy, author; Brief therapy, resident
INTERVAL Since original evaluation, 3 years
            Since end of treatment, 2 years, 4 months
METHOD OF FOLLOW-UP Videotaped interview

PRELIMINARY CRITERIA

1. Symptomatic Change:

   A. Migraine headaches: Since age 12, worse in the semester prior to treatment
      Frequency at worst: daily
      Frequency at best: a few days a year

   B. SCL-90 showed almost no complaints, much less than the average patient, and the patient in the trial therapy recited a laundry list of very small annoyances. Improvement might have allowed her to complain more, to have more complaints on SCL-90 than before.

2. Dynamic Change, Stress Tests of Dynamic Change:
   A. Being rejected: "Not accepting who I am."
   B. Being treated unfairly, e.g., the omnibus assignment.
   C. Being angry, revengeful.
   D. Being close enough to risk being known, being hurt: "Letting down my wall." Has she been able to risk a close relation with a man?

3. Systemic Change, Response of System to Dynamic Changes in Patient: Somehow the patient could not get her family to help her cope with being victimized in school as a child. Evidently, her mother would say: "Ignore it." So the patient, unassisted, got into the victim rut with peers. I would presume that the mother could not listen to hurt and rage because it might destabilize some of her relations with her husband. Therefore, the patient could get no assistance in defending herself, because such assistance would destabilize the family somehow. The "victim in school" problem is usually corrected by the sensible support of a helpful family.

   This was never looked at in the therapy, as far as I know, since the therapy was conducted before the clinic got involved in systemic interests. Nevertheless, I would think that this patient could *not* introduce her feelings of hurt and anger back home, unless the parents underwent some major change of their own. I predict either more distance from the family, or a major change in the parents, or the patient backing down from major changes when at home.

4. Patient's View of the Therapy: Here is a chance to get both positive and negative evaluation on the Davanloo method. I did get to her in trial therapy, to her pain. Did the tactics prejudice her against being gotten to by others? By the resident? Did the rough handling help her to get in touch with her own roughness? Her own hostility? What was the difference between the trial therapy with me and the brief therapy with the resident (the first reaching pain, the second also the rage and revenge)?

5. Patient's Relation to the Interviewer: I recall getting a headache before from the patient's tendency to recite a laundry list of minor annoyances. I will see if she makes me feel the same way! I will also see if the patient has her "wall" up as before, whether feeling can be gotten readily.

6. Summary of Preliminary Criteria for Required Closure:
   A. Needs: I would expect some restraint about close relations, which could meet a need to be accepted, which would risk unfairness, hurt, rage, revengefulness. An intimate, sexual relationship would be very surprising.
   B. Constant Attitude: "Nothing bothers me very much." This attitude, with the characteristic gesture of waving away difficulties with the hand, with the characteristic gesture of stroking own face ("I will comfort myself") will be conserved in some ways.
   C. Security Operations: The crucial ones were twofold, I think: "You can't get to me, just try! I will be superior behind my wall." And "I know I will be put down, victimized, treated unfairly." In other words, she had ways to live with moral masochism, with being the victim, the teasee (Brenman, 1952) which would insulate her but perpetuate the relations. Some revision of this security would probably risk being hurt, being revengeful (sadistic).
   D. Family Game: Almost nothing is known about the fit of the previous levels of closure into this woman's family.

RESULTS
1. Symptomatic Change:
    A. Migraine: The past history of migraine, which I enlarged upon in the interview, was that she had migraine since about age seven or eight, consisting of a day of nausea and headache a few times a year, which began to come in clusters of days in college, until it became daily in sophomore or junior year. A six-to-eight-month trial of amitriptyline and imipramine made no noticeable difference except to give undesirable side effects. Thereupon the referral to Brief Therapy Clinic was made, at the same time propranolol was begun. Following brief therapy, she had "migraines of four to ten days every one or two months compared to a pretherapy frequency of every day." Since she dropped an aggravating thesis four months ago in favor of comprehensive exams for her master's degree, she has had "only one or two mild migraines which lasted less than a day." She believes, however, that the propranolol cannot be dropped below 240 mg. per day without bringing back the problem. Thus, she sees the improvement from brief therapy as allowing migraine to be "medically controllable."
    B. The laundry list of small annoyances: The SCL-90 shows almost no complaints as before, except for flu symptoms of last week. There is no laundry list of minor complaints, so *I* do not end up with a headache as I did when I first met her.
2. Dynamic Change, Stress Tests for Dynamic Change:
    A. Being rejected: This has not occurred.
    B. "Being treated unfairly, being angry, revengeful": 1. Impressive example here of professor who is well regarded failing to teach his class anything of value. Patient describes being "infuriated," shows old squint of right face. Patient describes plans to go over the chair to dean, because a "bunch of people," past, present, and future, are being cheated by this man. Yet, she is able to see this man as having some good, concerned qualities as well. Fascinating recurrence of her old phrase, "not at me personally," to describe the injury sustained. 2. Second impressive example of being scapegoated by the athletic team she coaches for recent losses. She was able to fight back against the blaming, not being willing to take it all on herself, whereupon the team got behind her again rather than replacing her as threatened.
    C. "Letting down my wall": 1. Describes a "failure" to do this with a continuing woman friend who receives her confidences with telling her what to do, with criticism of how she "should" be responding. I thought this caution was sensible, but she thought that I and the resident were in favor of complete openness. 2. Dated one man for six months, another recently for three months, but has only found these to be occasions for "going out" with someone "nice," not occasions to fall in love. 3. Another woman friend has been nonjudgmental, accepting of her confidences, about these troubles. They go out together, give each other company when neither has a date.
3. Systemic Change, Response of System to Dynamic Changes in Patient: Patient has succeeded in introducing her differences with parents in a gradual way, being accepted as an adult. She noted that she had to be careful, as "mother can get irrational" and father is reactionary in his politics. Father was never around, but now acts more available despite their political differences. When I looked into the family more deeply to consider a systemic hypothesis for why this young woman had gotten no help with being tormented as a child, the answer came with startling rapidity. "I have to explain my mother," she said. "For her, everything has been black and white . . . right or wrong."

Therefore, there was a "right" way to cope with being teased unmercifully. That was to ignore it. That was that. Grandmother was even more rigid, mother somewhat "diluted" in her "attitude": "This is your cross to bear." When I asked the patient if she did not continue to share this attitude herself, she replied that she now had the freedom to choose. "I don't have to, but I can," citing her refusal to take the professor's failure in silence, citing her refusal to bear the scapegoating of her athletic team. When I asked if migraines were still not a "cross to bear," she found that a very interesting idea. "Some," she said, but not every day.

4. Patient's View of the Therapy: She was obviously pained to recall the trial therapy, as her right face tightened in the characteristic squint. She felt the "pushing" might have been necessary, but she feels an "aversion" to ever going back into therapy. She would not, unless "desperate," because it was "too painful."

She felt the long brief therapy with the resident to have both painful and pleasant feelings. What she didn't like was losing the summer to all this pain in therapy, when she was having the last chance to be with some friends. She feels she lost three months of her life. She liked the resident better than me, found her more gentle. Yet she was critical as well. She never knew if the resident found her only to be "a screwed-up person." She resented pouring out all that feeling, getting so little back in reply. Yet she "got the OK" to experience and feel about anything. When I asked about the importance of being able to feel fierce and revengeful, she confirmed that this was important to her, to "use the feeling, without striking the person."

5. Patient's Relation to the Interviewer: When I asked her if she finally had anything she wanted to ask, I got a powerful challenge: "Was this an experimental program?" "Were you a guinea pig?" I replied. I told her this was one of many methods of brief therapy, which are all widely debated. The only experiment was my making up my own mind about this Davanloo method. I was glad she could help me with that, inasmuch as I too had many doubts about the Davanloo method. She responded that this was too much pain for an individual *without support between sessions.* She had made it through, but she would not advise such a procedure. Surely, we could have done better to tell her how bad it would be. I replied that some of this pain would have been inevitable, some would have been alleviated.

6. Summary of Findings in Relation to Criteria for Required Closure:
   A. Needs: Patient doing quite well about being close with woman friend, being able to cope with unfairness, hurt, rage, revengefulness, constructively. But "some restraint" as predicted. Dating, but not falling in love, so far.
   B. Constant Attitude: This is fascinating, as the characteristic gestures of right facial squinting, waving away with hand, stroking own face, appear when she brings up the most difficult situations. But they subside as he describes managing her feelings well.
   C. Security Operations: I do not see the previous superiority behind the wall, the expectation of being victimized, the moral masochism. Yet something is conserved here, the attitude of "bearing the cross" of the migraine itself.
   D. Family Game: Again, some fascinating findings, as I learned of the religious line of "bearing the cross" from grandmother to mother to himself, although "diluted" at each generational step. The "migraine" may be necessary to "stay in touch" with mother and grandmother, as a kind of valve, or "choice" as she put it, for what to bear/what not to bear, so that some continuation of this symptom may be necessary to the family line.

SUMMARY REMARKS, NOTEWORTHY FINDINGS

Again, I am amazed by what a little systemic inquiry can do to allow appreciation of the systemic closure which is so powerful, which had been altogether hidden before. Here is a family line which depends on "bearing the cross," which, therefore, calls for the security operations of moral masochism, the constant attitude of stoicism, the profound sacrifice of self-defense. Finally, I believe the patient is eloquent about the limitations of the Davanloo technique, at least for her, at least when there is little giving back by the therapist for all the outpouring of the patient. Davanloo himself would do better than that, I think, but I am inclined to think a systemic method would have been less painful and more profound. Still, the result is impressive, concerning symptomatic, dynamic and systemic change. The residual difficulty at close quarters, especially with the opposite sex, may resolve further, may be held up by the systemic closure which requires her to continue to "bear this cross" to stay in touch with the previous generations of her family. Sexual gratification, orgasm, might make this too difficult, because the orgastic discharge might make migraine discharge no longer necessary. Therefore, this may have to be sacrificed, for the time being.

THE CASE OF THE DOG IN HELL

(Chapter 15)

THERAPY 162 sessions, 122½ hours
THERAPIST Author
INTERVAL Since preliminary interview, 3 years, 6 months
          Since end of treatment, still in progress
METHOD OF FOLLOW-UP Private interview

PRELIMINARY CRITERIA
1. Symptomatic Change:
   A. "Anxiety"
   B. Inability to go outside apartment with some exceptions. Agoraphobia.
   C. Inability to sleep until dawn. Extreme insomnia.
   D. Inability to continue in schoolwork.
   E. Inability to talk with women, date, etc.
2. Dynamic Change, Stress Tests of Dynamic Change:
   A. Success: school, women, anything.
   B. Failure: being criticized, second-best, inferior, betrayed.
   C. Involvement with other people outside family.
   D. Being angry, revengeful.
3. Systemic Change, Response of System to Dynamic Changes in Patient: Any new capability threatens to remove patient from being used by family, so the patient can never use a new capability unless he is confident he can suspend its use with the family as necessary. He must advance under the cover of darkness. When he blows his cover, he has to retreat or he will provoke dangerous disturbance in family. Since he is the healthiest, most vigorous family member, he will take the disturbance upon himself.
4. Patient's View of the Therapy: I do not know whether he will see the therapy as coping with these many levels of contradiction or not. Maybe he sees it more simply?

5. Patient's Relation to Interviewer: Since we are in progress, the chapters and the report will become part of further discussions in therapy.
6. Summary of Preliminary for Required Closure:
   A. Needs: The question will be *which* needs are being sacrificed now. In the past, the sacrifice has been nearly complete.
   B. Constant Attitude: "I am the family dog, available for comforting all of us."
   C. Security Operations: Essentially, this is a "paranoid position" (see Chapter 8, Balint) in which love is one's willingness to be used, in which the users show indifference to the used at best.
   D. Family Game: Evidently, mother has needed patient as pawn in her uphill battle against father's tyranny. Patient has been willing to be that pawn given his love for his parents.

RESULTS
1. Symptomatic Change:
   A. "Anxiety": The SCL-90 is about the same, showing many 3's and 4's in nearly all categories (polyneurosis).
   B. Agoraphobia: The patient was quite limited in trips out of the house for three years here, but has been going to school again for a year and a half, riding buses, etc.
   C. Insomnia: For three years the patient could not sleep when it was dark, but now goes to bed between 12:30 and 1:30 and sleeps until 7:15 during the semester. At home during breaks, he tends to stay up later and get up later. Progress has been gradual in a series of steps.
   D. Inability to continue in schoolwork: After three years of incapacitation, the patient resumed one class in the fall of 1984, and has taken a full load the last two semesters and summer school in between. He received a 3.9 (of 4.0) in the first semester and a 3.5 in the second.
   E. Inability to talk with women, date: Since breaking up with his girlfriend between the fall of 1983 and the spring of 1984, he joined a brief group for a few months for people going through breakups. He made several friends there, including one woman who has been his best friend for nearly two years.

      Overall, the symptoms appear the same, but the interference with functioning is greatly reduced. He complains of the same, great anxiety, but operates with much greater latitude.
2. Dynamic Change, Stress Tests of Dynamic Change:
   A. Success: The school success is the most powerful instance of success. He finds it "unbelievable." Whereas in the past such success as with sports or his girlfriend led to him "choking" and feeling "I shouldn't be here," this feeling is present but not stopping him.
   B. Failure: The breakup with the girlfriend was the worst instance of "failure," but the usual tendency to "fall apart" and derogate himself altogether has not occurred. He continues to be "obsessed" with her, but has not been calling her. Rather, he has been determined to show his abilities in school.
   C. Involvement with other people outside family: The friendship with his new girlfriend of the last two years is "less intense" than with the girlfriend previous, less "wildly attracted." On the other hand, the new girlfriend is more "compassionate," listens about his family and his difficulties elsewhere. They never yell and never torture each other. She is "a friend," not a romance.

    D. Being angry, revengeful: The previous girlfriend and he were in a "hell," in which "no matter what I did I was punished." "I would get so angry, I would rip up my clothes." Now he feels in a "purgatory," having such revengeful feelings, but not going around in vicious circles of interaction about them.

3. Systemic Change: The patient sees a double response by the family to his evident improvement. On the one hand, they applaud the school success. On the other hand, they show no interest in what the patient is learning or accomplishing. He explains this as follows: Insofar as he can work hard and earn a living and make it easier for them, then this improvement is terrific. Insofar as he is no longer a little boy at home, this is bad. He gets on well with them if he is "knocking himself out," e.g., staying up all night working on a term paper. He gets on badly if he disagrees with them. Nevertheless, he quietly differs more than before. In other words, he is moving slowly with them, "under cover over darkness," showing the one aspect of change they find most agreeable, not showing the aspects of change they find most threatening. All in all, the policy seems successful, while obliging him to be under heavy strain while at home (cf. discussion of Patient's Relation to Interviewer under item 5).

4. Patient's View of the Therapy: The patient emphasizes first my personal qualities, with which he can identify himself — intelligent, athletic, and a good guy. He contrasts his psychiatrist in high school, who "sat back, nodded, and made analytic interpretations: 'You punish yourself for anger, so stop it.'" This he found useless. But my personal qualities do not quite explain the results, since he found just these qualities in the resident he saw before me for two years. "He pulled for me, when I needed it very badly." He seems quite grateful to this young doctor for his involvement. What he sees as the further help I gave him has to do with the "complexity" of the "game" he has been involved in. As a kind of "Karpov" himself, he has needed a worthy antagonist, a very experienced player rather than a newcomer to such games. "I've been laughing the whole time. It's an unbelievable game." I asked him what I had actually said to him that stands out for him now. He remembers my comments on his previous girlfriend "jacking him around" and his parents "saying x and doing y." He emphasizes that he feels "safe" with me because he will not end up "feeling like a jerk" when he presents some difficulty.

5. Patient's Relation to the Interviewer: The patient seemed tense until we could discuss his questions at the conclusion of the interview, which were threefold. Did I think he was an idiot for his current obsession with his former girlfriend? Did the interview mean he should get out or be over with therapy? Did I like him? My replies were as follows: I thought that his obsession with his former girlfriend was a great help just now, inasmuch as he could not be a sexual man without losing his mother or exciting her too much (Siberia, hot or cold). The obsession allowed him excitement, which would be quickly followed by self-abasement, threatening no one. I did not think we were at the end of our work, as I could see both his success and his limitation just described. I liked him. There was no way to be involved in the way we had been if I had not liked him. He seemed very relieved about all three fears.

6. Summary of Findings in Relation to Criteria for Required Closure:
    A. Needs: The chief sacrifice now is of his sexuality.
    B. Constant Attitude: The patient continues to adopt this posture at home of the "family dog," but this becomes increasingly difficult, since he discovers how his mother's seductiveness had obliged him to curtail his own sexuality, so he could be her little boy, so his father could punish him for being so special for mother.

He continues to tolerate the role, however, which has evolved to some greater dignity for himself as a "hard worker" at school who can object a little to his father.

C. Security Operations: As his part in being used has become clear, he has felt less used by his new friend and by myself, the two latter relationships being better sorted out from the confusions of the family game.

D. Family Game: The variation of his being a "hard worker" in school has allowed him to conserve his role of being available to mother, father and brother, since he gets some support or acknowledgment for his success, yet accepts the relations which keep him in his place. The dawning "sexuality" is destabilizing to this arrangement. The possibility of a new variation here is unknown.

SUMMARY REMARKS, NOTEWORTHY FINDINGS

A remarkable demonstration indeed of holding certain difficulties constant, which allows "advancing under cover of darkness," which secures necessary interim support (for an individual with little enough of that outside family) for both patient and for family. The patient continues to have the same symptoms (and even feel the same way, namely, working extremely hard with great pain in hell), while making impressive dynamic changes. The patient continues to be available to the family as family dog, while becoming a different kind of family dog as well, a very hard worker in school, who can feel some pride in himself for his intellectual abilities as well as for protecting the entire family. In a way, he was a "Karpov" before in the genius of his play in the family game, but now he gets recognition for his intellect in school as well.

A CASE OF BULIMIA
(Chapter 16)

THERAPY 13 sessions, 15 hours
THERAPIST Author
INTERVAL Since original evaluation, 8 months
               Since end of treatment, 4 months
METHOD OF FOLLOW-UP Private interview

PRELIMINARY CRITERIA

1. Symptomatic Change:
   A. Bulimia
   B. Anxiety and depression (SCL-90)
2. Dynamic Change, Stress Tests of Dynamic Change:
   A. Sexual excitement
   B. Aggressive tension
   C. Pulled into dependency and eating by mother.
   D. Pulled by dad into pleasing mother.
3. Systemic Change, Response of System to Dynamic Changes in Patient: As discussed in Chapter 16, three classes of change are possible which would conserve the closure required, if other moves can be found to weaken her force, "keep an even keel" herself, and help her mother and father feel all right. Otherwise, change is apt to be too perturbing, and set in motion negative feedback loops to stop the change.

4. Patient's View of Therapy: Since the method was addressed to the several different levels to her bind (closure), I may see which aspects impressed her.
5. Patient's Relation to Interviewer: We shall see what a holiday in South America has allowed!
6. Summary of Preliminary Criteria for Required Closure:
   A. Needs: Sexual and aggressive needs sacrificed to some extent.
   B. Constant Attitude: Even keel.
   C. Security Operations: Comply. Hide rebellion in toilet. Stay close to father.
   D. Family Game: Daughter and father unite to help keep up mother's belief in herself as a mother.

RESULTS
1. Symptomatic Change:
   A. Bulimia: Only one or two episodes in nine weeks in South America. None for the first weeks on return home, then once a day for some weeks when "bored, no friends around." Some "panic" about some weight gain. Cornered by mother to confess a lot of difficulty. Decided to "break out" by coming to see me, calling me just when I called her for follow-up interview. This is what is different. This determination to "break out," to catch herself sliding back.
   B. Anxiety and depression (SCL-90): about the same (moderate).
2. Dynamic Change, Stress Tests of Dynamic Change:
   A. Sexual excitement: "Fell in love four or five times, once a day!" Intimacy still unexplored, however.
   B. Aggressive tension: Did "break out" with mom, knowing that staying was vicious cycle, did "put foot down" with fellow traveler: "I've been visiting museums and churches with you for five weeks! It's time to have some fun at night!" Surprised by friend's accepting this. Did "put foot down" with guy who only wanted sex, despite a week of tears about losing him. "Easier with a lot of different guys coming by!"
   C., D. Pull by parents: "Breaking out" described. See also next section on Systemic Change.
3. Systemic Change, Response of System to Dynamic Change in Patient: Mother sees her as "sharper" in own views, which is negative for mother. Mother sees therapist as having bought patient's view and that we are "in cahoots." Mother would like to defend herself to me, but admits an improvement in eating disorder and accepts patient's liking to come see me for help. Father would see change as mixed for him. He is glad patient is "happier, independent, self-confident, able to use therapist's authority," but this is a "loss" for him who was her "only authority" before. Perhaps there is a gain for him and his wife if patient is less "in cahoots" with him.
4. Patient's View of Therapy: She got something from my attitude about risk, my asking "Well, what can happen if you . . . ?" Not "Oh my god." She got something from my understanding "why" she did something. This would make her think, "I don't like that . . . "

   When I asked why she laid off studying to keep from graduating and going on her own, she thought, "Oh no, I don't like that at all." She got something about "being able to be myself, not sweat it if someone knew if I had to ask for help." She got something from my proposing her fear of success, which made her think, "No, I want it!" The chief setback was when I "took off her rose-colored glasses for ten days," she had thought bulimia was *her* problem, but I suggested it was only a way to cope with difficulties in relations. She took this, for the time being, to mean "I have only myself to blame."

5. Patient's Relation to Interviewer: "They (my parents) *say* they want independence, they've got six other kids . . . as if I could be a different person overnight." I believe she was wanting me to appreciate her evolution as a gradual event. Indeed, I felt that it was coming along very well and needed time to unfold. I could tell her exactly this.

6. Summary of Findings in Relation to Criteria for Required Closure:
   A. Needs: Much more expression, especially in assertion, some in sexual excitement.
   B. Constant Attitude: Even keel retained. This is crucial, to "not let out the team of wild horses."
   C. Security Questions: "Breaks out" from compliance trap, but still careful not to be too difficult for mother or father.
   D. Family Game: Some greater distance from father in borrowing from myself, but the alliance is still strong. Notice how mother sees therapist "in cahoots" with patient, whereas before the emphasis had been on father "in cahoots" with patient. Thus, the system stays the same in this sense, but the slightly different move has a different drift.

SUMMARY REMARKS, NOTEWORTHY FINDINGS

A lovely example, if I may say so, of why symptomatic and dynamic change have to go slowly enough not to threaten close relationships. In this sense, *more* symptomatic and dynamic change *too soon* would be worse. The patient is modulating the pace with great cunning.

THE CASE OF THE CARROT AND THE STICK
(Chapter 17)

THERAPY 11 sessions, 12 hours
THERAPIST Trial therapy, author; Brief therapy, resident
INTERVAL Since preliminary evaluation, 8 months
　　　　　 Since end of therapy, 5 months
METHOD OF FOLLOW-UP Questionnaires

PRELIMINARY CRITERIA

1. Symptomatic Change:
   A. "Can't get schoolwork done. Unproductive."
   B. A wide range of other symptoms, including migraine, absence of sexual activity, overeating, low self-esteem, depression, anxiety, paranoia, and prevailing obsessional activity without fixed obsessions, compulsions or phobias.
2. Dynamic Change, Stress Tests of Dynamic Change:
   A. Advancing in school, in becoming capable, in being able to have a successful career of his own. To allow himself "conquering force."
   B. "Growing up" in other ways as well, e.g., being able to have a sexual relationship with a woman.
   C. Being able to be less responsible for what goes wrong around him, to cope with being blamed, criticized or not appreciated.

3. Systemic Change, Response of System to Dynamic Changes in the Patient: All of the capabilities described as indicative of "dynamic change" would risk destabilizing the close relation of this patient with his family, leaving behind his mother, father and sister. He was feared it might kill them, so the need not to "grow up" has been considerable. Whether he can move slowly on this without setting the family back very badly, or not, is the crucial question.

4. Patient's View of the Therapy: Confirms or disconfirms my view of the Carrot and Stick Game?

5. Patient's Relation to Interviewer: Not relevant in absence of interview.

6. Summary of Preliminary Criteria for Required Closure:
   A. Needs: Massive sacrifice of sexual and aggressive expression, of Level I, II and III capabilities for calm, self-defense, clarity about illusion and capability. Only need which has been allowed is to be looked after as a casualty or very limited person, and to give something similar to others. I would think any progress here has to be slow, because of required closure at subsequent levels.
   B. Constant Attitude: "I will appear to be a weak, neurotic, little boy as a comfort to my family."
   C. Security Operations: "I tempt you to inveigle me, to push me, out of my great sacrifice" (the Carrot and Stick Game).
   D. Family Game: "We may all stay close if we all seem unfit for the world."

RESULTS
1. Symptomatic Change:
   A. Unproductive: "The immediate complaint was an approximately month-long period of intermittent and extremely painful and dizzying headaches that would persist for up to 24 hours. Since their pattern and nature were unprecedented, I was scared, and went to University Health Services, where they were tentatively diagnosed as migraines. Since these are often attributed to stress, it was suggested that I inquire about brief therapy. Interestingly, these particular headaches disappeared *before* I began therapy, and never returned. However, the longer-term, underlying problem *is*, as you say, *lack of productivity*, and the consequent (or causative??) feelings of stress, frustration, self-hate, inferiority (due to my failure to complete my work like a 'decent' person), despair and panic. Compounded by loneliness due to a too quiet social life. The feeling of *entrapment* in a vicious cycle was very real. I have been a procrastinator — especially when writing assignments were due — and a slow (but thorough) student ever since I can remember, but throughout high school and undergrad years I would always be able to buckle down, concentrate and complete my work. However, as a grad student, I permitted myself to become completely paralyzed mentally, because I convinced myself I knew nothing (how then, could I write anything?), so even 11th hour efforts were impossible. Technically, there is no improvement in the 'complaint,' because even though I did make some feeble efforts at work during therapy, I did *not* regain my 'nerve' enough to finish my degree before leaving Madison. *However*, I believe my feelings of self-hate have moderated somewhat. Although I fully acknowledge all my past failures and present deficiencies, I am less likely to dwell on these and to translate discrete negatives into a wholesale self-condemnation. I've begun to believe, simply, do not do unto *yourself* as you would not do unto others, or as you would not have others do unto you."

B. A wide range of other symptoms: SCL-90 shows the same polyneurotic pattern, but in most instances shifted about two categories to the left: e.g. from "extremely (4)" to "moderately (2)."

2. Dynamic Change, Stress Tests of Dynamic Change:
   A. Advancing in school, etc.: A modest improvement here as described under 1A. Also, patient writes in accompanying letter: "Actually, I left Madison permanently in mid-August, and am staying with my family until I find a full-time position. Although no positions are currently available, I have received encouraging responses to many of my 25 applications, and I have an exploratory interview this Friday. It feels good trying and having tried, so morale could be worse."

      Given that he was stuck here before in neurotic misery, this appears to be a dynamic improvement.
   B. "Growing up," sexual relationship, etc.: No data.
   C. Coping with blame, criticism, not being appreciated: Patient's comments on the therapy (item 4. which follows) suggest strengthening along these lines, but no "stress test" for this kind of capability is known to me except the job-seeking, which he is tolerating well for now.

3. Systemic Change, Response of System to Dynamic Changes in Patient: Patient responded to "How would your behavior be viewed by those who know you best, who are most affected by how you were before/during after therapy? What would they comment?" as follows:

   "This is difficult to answer because I'm not sure whether 'would' refers to actual past, customary responses and comments, or to hypothetical future ones. I'll answer both ways. Also, my answer may not be too helpful, because I don't believe there were any significant, visible differences in my behavior before, during, or after brief therapy. There was no detectable change in the way family, friends, and co-workers responded to me. Response from nonfamily members has usually been positive, because I am, I believe, a basically sociable person, and though I'm unhappy with myself, I enjoy other people and external things. For example, the people I worked with in Madison, as well as friends there, said they enjoyed talking with me — and it was usually reciprocal. However, even though I do complain to my family (quite often), and to my friends (less often), I'm sure that I also *unconsciously* convey — in expression, nervous mannerisms, etc. — the basic sadness, tension, and frustration I feel about my situation and myself. (After all, I think I can often detect whether or not *others* are confident, motivated, content, and relaxed.) My family and some friends have, in fact, let me know that I sometimes appear uptight, self-conscious, or sad."

   I take this reply to mean that the patient has skillfully managed to *appear* the same, which is crucial to the stability of his relationship, even though a modest improvement and movement to a job is afoot.

4. Patient's View of the Therapy: Patient replied to "What did you learn in therapy, what stands out in your mind now, about how your complaint or difficulty is brought about, increased or reduced?" as follows: "We generally agreed that some of my attitudes and responses could be described as 'adolescent' — for example, being too concerned about the opinion professors or supervisors have of me. I think that now I'm *more* aware of ways I am immature — excessive self-pity, egocentricity, deficient self-confidence (which has a direct bearing on the major 'complaint') — even though I was not specifically charged with these offenses. I also learned — or rather, was reminded, indirectly — that it is beneficial to: 1. Systemically refute sweeping destructive generali-

zations about oneself (e.g., 'I am self-centered'), and 2. Replace or modify the negative statements with at least some true positive ones (e.g., 'I am not without compassion'). Apparently, the method of brief therapy includes: (at least as I experienced it): First, the therapist continually counters the therapee's statements with questions, etc., which challenge the therapee to defend or amend the original statement. (The *method* resembles a Socratic dialogue – but there the resemblance ends.) I found this worthwhile. Second, there seemed to be 'positive reinforcement' – that is, encouragement to elaborate – if the therapee said something self-congratulatory. I found this helpful too, naturally." I take it the patient did not get too much of the "Stick" from his therapist – quite the contrary.

5. Patient's Relation to the Interviewer: Not relevant, questionnaires only.
6. Summary of Findings in Relation to Criteria for Required Closure:
    A. Needs: Patient appears to be somewhat less self-blaming and derogatory, which allows a modest improvement in self-assertion, job-seeking, etc.
    B. Constant Attitude: Interesting ability to continue to project "the basic sadness, tension and frustration I feel," while moving ahead with a little vigor.
    C. Security Operations: No data.
    D. Family Game: Basically still very, very protective of family, but perhaps he may move on a little bit in the work realm if he can continue to project the same constant attitude, security operations.

SUMMARY REMARKS, NOTEWORTHY FINDINGS
An interesting, positive, modest result for a patient "richly linked" to family of origin, for a patient previously stuck in several years of long-term therapy. The simple constancy of the focus of "growing up" cut through much of the richly connected complexity of the patient's operations to stay enmeshed with his family. Here is another one of those cases where symptomatic and dynamic change *must* go very slowly, because the systemic closure is so powerful that it must not be disturbed. The result suggests that brief therapy can be helpful for deeply enmeshed patients (who have to appear profoundly neurotic) if the systemic closure is appreciated. Of course, only a long-term follow-up will allow us to judge the result.

POSTSCRIPT
It would be impossible to convey the countless suggestions made by the patient concerning the text and follow-up report. Many are remarkable, as illustrated by footnote 13, Chapter 17. Concerning the observation that the "patient appears to be somewhat less self-blaming and derogatory," he notes in red: "This is the key."

THE YOUNG WOMAN WITH NO SELF-CONFIDENCE
(Chapters 19, 20, 21)

THERAPY 27 sessions, 28 hours
THERAPIST Trial therapy, author; Brief therapy, resident
INTERVAL Since original evaluation, 11 months
    Since end of therapy, 3 months
METHOD OF FOLLOW-UP Videotaped interview

PRELIMINARY CRITERIA
1. Symptomatic Change:
   A. Confidence collapses
   B. Depressive symptoms
   C. Difficulty committing herself in work, in love
2. Dynamic Change, Stress Tests for Dynamic Change:
   A. Feeling powerful
   B. Being involved, committed
   C. Eagerness
   D. Being criticized or put down
   E. Dating
3. Systemic Change, Response of System to Dynamic Changes in Patient: This patient sacrificed the capability for meeting the difficulties of life just described, helping to stabilize her entire family, mother, father, and brothers. Here is a powerful sacrifice, the healthiest child looking as if she were as troubled as everyone else in the family. I would think her emergence from such a job would be taken very badly by her family, which would hit hard back.
4. Patient's View of the Therapy: What will patient emphasize out of the complex set of moves in the trial therapy? Out of the several themes of closure in the brief therapy?
5. Patient's Relation to the Interviewer: This patient has been so engaging I should be able to tell readily about her confidence from her relation to me here.
6. Summary of Preliminary Criteria for Required Closure:
   A. Needs: A certain volatility is expectable, from overeagerness and from slamming people.
   B. Constant Attitude: Some working at "modesty" is expectable.
   C. Security Operations: Getting others to admire and be above her, to knock her down, to unload on her, will still be useful.
   D. Family Game: Willingness to take it from mother and brother, to be depressed with father.

RESULTS
1. Symptomatic Change:
   A. Confidence collapses: She "amazes" herself with positive compliments, e.g., for "sticking neck out," for "not taking safe route" of choice of term paper, e.g., for being able to make business calls assertively.
   B. Depressive symptoms: Yes, "lonely, blue" for a couple weeks at start of school, roommates off for Labor Day, but recovered, no longer thinks she's bad to be feeling like that, not "wrong" but having reasons.
   C. Difficulty committing herself, in work, in love: Untested with men, but she no longer puts them on pedestal, giving herself no credit, not "zilching" them. No more of "I can't compare." So she feels "the road is open" to become involved.
2. Dynamic Change, Stress Tests for Dynamic Change:
   A. Feeling powerful: Yes, the dream of feeling helpless before an "indestructible" man, pushing head through screen door, frying his face in batter, and . . . waking up eating the eye!" (Savage?) No, that's not what bothers her; what bothers her is thinking this is the "whole truth" about her feelings for men: "Deep down it's hate," being "consumed" by it, turning into a "militant feminist." (I can see what she is afraid of.)

B. Being involved, committed: Friendship with Hilda, even when Hilda is not a good friend, being depressive, selfish, blowing patient off — able to discuss it, either fix it or give up. Also, involvement with politics course — able to be "excited" when feared it before, but holding back a little as counselor this fall, not going "head first."

C., D., E. Eagerness, being criticized or put-down: Just discussed in examples A. and B.

3. Systemic Change, Response to Dynamic Changes in Patient: She reported an amazing series of events in which she declined previous role with each of family members, which held her down. When I asked how each of the family members would see this shift of her position in relation to each of them, she replied that none of them would recognize any difference, being so self-preoccupied. So how did she feel that no one in the family could recognize her achievement, her remarkable change? She felt it was OK. Her expectations were low. She had distanced them all. She accepted them as they were.

4. Patient's View of Therapy: She had no memory of the trial therapy. She felt that the resident, her therapist, "frustrated" her a lot by "not saying 'this is your problem, this is the answer.'" But this gave her confidence, "I can change myself." She dreaded quitting but then felt a triumph. "I *did* it. I can do it." How did she think the resident saw her? As "on the ball, a lot of things going for me." Yet it was "awkward" when they did not discuss patient's problems. Perhaps the resident needed the distance?

5. Patient's Relation to Interviewer: Very engaged, very quick, anticipates questions, emotional, fun, e.g., final remark: "So, if you get paid for the book, how much is my cut?" In other words, she was quite equal here in many ways. Interesting how she "recalls" nothing of trial therapy (in one minute I gave to the subject or less), yet her grasp of the content is perfect, her dynamic understanding close to my own account in Chapter 20.

6. Summary of Findings in Relation to Criteria for Required Closure:

A. Needs: She is modulating herself, but not having to knock herself down, or get others to unload on her. Several examples here of braking herself — with politics, with men, with Hilda, etc. Excitement, eagerness flowing, but not out of control. Still worried though — see dream (Item 2A).

B. Constant Attitude: This "I am not so good" attitude really seems altered. She really shines, but she is being careful.

C. Security Operations: The clinging to the admired protector, or vice versa, seems to have yielded to much more equality. The equality, however, risks the depressive position of discovering own savagery, fearing being consumed by it — this is an ongoing current dream work for her. I recognized it, but left her with it, implying, as Sullivan would, "I can see why you *think* you're all hate down deep, but I don't think you are. I have confidence in you."

D. Family: No longer victimized by mother, brothers, no longer merged with father in depression. Parents' game with each other, brothers, seems to stay the same.

SUMMARY REMARKS, NOTEWORTHY FINDINGS

Really, we do not get a full test of her resolution of the depressive position, until she falls in love with a man. Really, we do not get a full test of the remarkable shift of position in relation to the family until she marries and makes a family which is different or similar to family of origin. Given these reservations, the result so far is very powerful, in relation to symptomatic, dynamic and systemic assessment. I was particularly impressed with the patient's facing such a dream as she reported with deep feeling and thoughtfulness. I have not often heard a patient come up with such a bold statement of the depressive position in a dream. Her whole demeanor, spirit, eagerness and involvement were unthinkable a year ago. Quite amazing.

The Case of the Businessman on Probation

(Chapter 21)

THERAPY 12 sessions, 21 1/4 hours
THERAPIST Author
INTERVAL Since preliminary interview, 2 years, 2 months
             Since end of treatment, 5 months
METHOD OF FOLLOW-UP Questionnaires

PRELIMINARY CRITERIA
1. Symptomatic Change:
    A. Failing to learn, procrastinating.
    B. SCL-90: depression, anxiety, low self-esteem; mild somatization, compulsive symptoms.
2. Dynamic Change, Stress Tests of Dynamic Change:
    A. Feeling criticized, put-down, inadequate ("slow").
    B. Feeling critical, angry, frustrated, revengeful ("fast").
    C. Depending upon others at work.
    D. Becoming involved with a woman.
3. Systemic Change, Response of System to Dynamic Changes in the Patient: What concerns me here is the ability to go "faster" in the business world may have a drift in his personal world which is too fast for the "slow" relations, which must be maintained, with mother, sister, ex-girlfriend. Actually, the difficulty is more complicated in that he must be able to appear fast and slow, independent and dependent, in his personal life. If he negotiates this in business well, he may lose patience with many of his personal relations, which are so contradictory.
4. Patient's View of Therapy: Since I see the interaction as a struggle with various paradoxical binds, I doubt if he can tell me much about this in a questionnaire.
5. Patient's Relation to Interviewer: Not relevant, questionnaires only.
6. Summary of Preliminary Criteria for Required Closure:
    A. Needs: Weaknesses in self-protection (Level II, Gedo) lead to various states of overstimulation (Level I) and to wide variations in self-evaluation (Level III). Some of this is inevitable given the constant attitude.
    B. Constant Attitude: "Sam against the world."
    C. Security Operations: "I blame myself better than anyone could blame me." "I get others to nail me." This is essentially a "paranoid position" (see Chapter 8, Balint; Chapter 11, Malan).
    D. Family Game: "If I am self-reliant, father hates me, mother loves me; if I am not vice versa. I will draw the fire in the center, either way, because I can take it like no one else in the family."

RESULTS
1. Symptomatic Change:
    A. Failing to learn, procrastinating, etc.: "I think the problems learning are pretty much gone with the synthroid (thyroid hormone). Hopefully, I am not being premature – but except for the first month or so with starting it I have been pretty happy with my thinking (still feeling behind, but learning curve is much steeper), and in general people who evaluate me are not saying that I'm hard to get along with and not very interested in business anymore (which is reassuring because telling them that I am *too* interested never really convinced them). This is not to say that I don't procrastinate when faced with a body of material I expect to have trouble getting through – but that is old, and although an imperfection, I'm comfortable with it. (And, breaking it down into more manageable segments does work by the way – but letting it go until there is enough pressure built up works too.)"
    B. SCL-90: depression, anxiety, low self-esteem, etc. Same pattern but reduced to minimal level (1. "a little bit,") across the board.
2. Dynamic Change, Stress Tests for Dynamic Change:
    A. Feeling criticized, put-down, inadequate ("slow"): "I am less likely to let myself be manipulated by someone else's anger (and specifically my ex-wife and my mother were very good at this)."
    B. Feeling critical, angry, frustrated, revengeful ("fast"): " . . . but also less likely to fall into the pattern of manipulating someone else with anger (I think I used to do this to my sister to some extent)."
    C. Depending upon others at work: "My sister thinks I was helped by therapy – more willing to trust the world and more relaxed. She might be right – in general I do feel more relaxed – the actual process of having to ask someone for help was a fairly *monumental* experience and sort of a forced choice: I didn't do it until I was on pretty shaky ground but having made that choice and actually getting emotional support has somehow made a difference" (my italics).
    D. Becoming involved with a woman: Unknown.
3. Systemic Change: Response of System to Dynamic Changes in the Patient: "My mother, unfortunately, thinks I have become an ungrateful, selfish son, because I do not take personal responsibility for her happiness (or unhappiness – which is more the problem). She also, apart from that, (I think) feels stabbed in the back somehow because I sought 'outside help.' I am not as close to her as I was (needless to say)."
4. Patient's View of the Therapy: In addition to previous quotations about the "monumental" experience of asking for and getting help the patient also adds: "I think (besides the above) that it helped to be able to get assurance from a (presumably impartial) person that I wasn't psychotic; that it helped to have some recognition at least that students are occasionally abused (I don't know why this is denied so completely but it certainly seems to be), and that it is not as frightening to think about myself as it used to be."
5. Patient's Relation to the Interviewer: Not relevant, questionnaires only.
6. Summary of Findings in Relation to Criteria for Required Closure:
    A. Needs: Self-protection seems more capable, hence more calm and self-confidence.
    B. Constant Attitude: Some revision of "Sam against the world."
    C. Security Operations: Some revision of "paranoid position."
    D. Family game: Move to self-reliance has, indeed, drawn heavy fire from patient's mother, which has led to some distancing from her.

SUMMARY REMARKS, NOTEWORTHY FINDINGS

A fine result for the short run, for the time being. Again, the five-year follow-up will tell the story. Also, a very interesting confirmation of the systemic closure which holds a "paranoid" interpersonal security operation in place. I am inclined to think that the systemic understanding of the family game was invaluable in understanding the patient's double bind, which allowed the patient a jump forward.

The patient is inclined to think that the correction of his hypothyroid condition allowed him the jump forward. It is impossible to tell which of these explanations is the most powerful and it is not necessary. Both are important: I think that's the point. As Engel (1980) argued so well, many behavior patterns are triggered by biological, psychological and social levels of organization. The challenge is to keep all of these important possibilities before us.

This case is also of theoretical interest. If we take biopsychosocial theory (Engel, 1980) seriously, then we look for the possibility of reflexive interaction between cybernetic subsystems. It is possible that a family social system in which "slow" versus "fast" is of decisive importance could trigger a biological system in which "slow" versus "fast" is regulated by the thyroid — and vice versa.

THE SECOND-CLASS CITIZEN
(Chapter 22)

THERAPY 17 sessions, 32 hours
THERAPIST Author
INTERVAL Since original evaluation, 2 years
     Since end of treatment, 6 months
METHOD OF FOLLOW-UP Questionnaires

PRELIMINARY CRITERIA

1. Symptomatic Change:
   A. "Feelings of alienation and coldness which prevent me from having a fuller, more vital life" (UWPD-1, Chief Complaint).
   B. "Extreme paranoia because I'm so wrapped up in myself" (UWPD-1, second Chief Complaint). This patient announced himself in his first session as a "narcissistic paranoid." What he meant was that he was very self-conscious, very alert to any rejection, very anxious to be liked. He scanned others continually for their judgments of him. He implied that he jumped to conclusions (paranoid projection), but it was also true that others often jumped to conclusions about him. Thus, he could never quite tell what others did to him, what he did to himself.
   C. The SCL-90 at the time of the preliminary interview showed considerable to extreme symptoms of depression, anxiety (as well as paranoid symptoms and symptoms of low self-esteem).
2. Dynamic Change, Stress Tests for Dynamic Change:
   A. Being treated meanly, or with indifference or with inconsideration. Becoming angry, frustrated.
   B. Becoming in love, spontaneous, trusting, believing in someone.
3. Systemic Change, Response of System to Dynamic Changes in the Patient: The pa-

tient's father died while his mother was pregnant with him. The patient's sister died when he was four. Hence, his mother was quite depressed when he was young. The patient has never quite sorted out what is *his* difficulty, what is *faulty* in the response to himself. This keeps him stuck in his "paranoid position." But it also keeps him from leaving his mother behind. I suspect that his moving on might be very difficult for his mother, yet his mother probably complains that he is stuck.

4. Patient's View of the Therapy: This will be difficult to evaluate by questionnaire, as it brings up the usual confusion between what is the patient doing, what is the other person doing. The report will be more reliable the more the patient can sort out this kind of mixup. If he is still stuck, I may get some considerable devaluation or he may give himself some considerable devaluation.

5. Patient's Relation to the Interviewer: Not relevant as the only follow-up is by questionnaire.

6. Summary of Preliminary Criteria for Required Closure:
   A. Needs: The patient gives up his need to be close, to trust, to be comforted, but also his need to defend his boundaries clearly and sharply, to be sensible (less illusional) about his strengths and weaknesses (Gedo's Levels I, II and III, are all compromised).
   B. Constant Attitude: "I am second-class. I must be doing something wrong." But the other side of this coin is an opposite attitude not often seen, which is that "I am perfect."
   C. Security Operations: "I will put others up on a pedestal, my self way below, so I can watch them. This distancing helps me to stay vigilant, to keep from becoming spontaneous, excited and overly hopeful." Essentially, this is the "paranoid position" described by Balint.
   D. Family Game: "The 'paranoid position' keeps me available to mother and her to me. Nevertheless, we both complain about my being stuck."

RESULTS
1. Symptomatic Change:
   A. Alienation, coldness: "I still hate myself severely at times, but all in all, I feel a sense of myself which I didn't have when the complaint was first made. And that sense can feel quite nice."
   B. Extreme paranoia: "I don't know where I learned this, but I notice myself accepting my faults which is a lot less painful than castigating myself for them. I can't 'psych' myself into a self-confident frame of mind — as a matter of fact, the more pressure I put on myself to be a certain way, the less likely I am to succeed — but I generally feel good about what I'm doing if I am being true to myself. This 'trueness' is what eludes me, and I still don't know what happens to make me not myself. I really don't have a clue. It's hard for me to say, because I've always twisted what others say to fit my own perspective. This is hard to answer, a million different answers pop into mind, depending on the person. I think most people would say I seem happier, but that's as far as I can take this one."
   C. SCL-90, depression, anxiety, paranoia, low self-esteem: The same items, but all reduced from "extremely" (4) and "quite a bit" (3) to "moderately" (2) and "a little bit" (1).

2. Dynamic Change:
   A. Being treated meanly or with indifference or with inconsideration: The patient responded to my three letters asking for his help with the follow-up (he had been

away so they were not forwarded) by an outburst of contempt ("your final whiney appeal to my selfish soul. . . . I don't exactly feel that I am obligated to treat you as a good buddy"), tempered by some friendliness after he "cooled."

   B. Becoming in love, spontaneous, trusting, believing, etc: Unknown.
3. Systemic Change, Response of System to Dynamic Change in the Patient: Unknown.
4. Patient's View of the Therapy: As previously quoted, patient seems more self-accepting, less self-castigating, and the patient seems to understand that "pressure" on himself to "be a certain way" makes him worse and less "true" to himself. But what occurred in the therapy to help with these new trends is unknown.
5. Patient's Relation to the Interviewer: Not relevant, given questionnaires only.
6. Summary of Findings in Relation to Criteria for Required Closure:
   A. Needs: Less sacrifice of comfort and acceptance of self, but still "hates self severely at times." Still indicates some confusion between what is in him, what is in other's response to him.
   B. Constant Attitude: Some lessening of this conviction of being second-class.
   C. Security Operations: Some lessening of the "paranoid position."
   D. Family Game: Relation to mother unknown.

SUMMARY REMARKS, NOTEWORTHY FINDINGS

Time will tell better whether such a brief therapy here will make a difference to this individual stuck in a "paranoid position." There is some improvement, but its drift is unknown. Balint (Chapter 8) has given a single demonstration of an extremely powerful effect from brief therapy with such an individual, but such attempts are few and far between. Therefore, the long follow-up in five years or so will be of interest. There are two strong opposing currents here, one which is hopeful, but which can expect too much, throwing the patient back upon the "paranoid" current. It appears to me that the therapy helped to revive the first current, but its drift and stability remains to be seen.

THE CASE OF THE RAT EXPRESS

(Chapter 23)

THERAPY 56 sessions, 56 hours
THERAPIST Resident
INTERVAL Since original evaluation, 1 year, 7 months
         Since end of treatment, still in progress
METHOD OF FOLLOW-UP Videotaped interview

PRELIMINARY CRITERIA

1. Symptomatic Change:
   A. Depression
   B. Will have to ask him to describe himself at his worst (since no SCL-90 completed at original evaluation). I believe it has been a feeling of alienation, isolation, despair. Other symptoms? Complications of controlling his rage, revenge, too?
2. Dynamic Change, Stress Tests for Dynamic Change:
   A. Insubordination from his kids. Generosity unappreciated.
   B. Blame from his wife.
   C. Feeling alone, not understood, no co-pilot, abandoned

    D. Urges to take revenge, be harsh
3. Systemic Change; Response of System to Dynamic Changes in Patient: Do we see family "braking" his acceleration of change, his insistence upon "being understood," "being appreciated" (as by co-pilot therapist)? Does he have "tunnel vision," as All-American unappreciated veteran, about how he triggers mean responses?
4. Patient's View of the Therapy: Does he take the "co-pilot" view of therapy? What does he see of interaction between subsystem of himself-therapist and subsystem of himself-family?
5. Patient's Relation to Interviewer: Interviewer determined to separate himself from derogatory slant of metaphor (Rat Express) of the supervision group (as *their* problem, *their* difficulty hearing the case), i.e., doctors fear being rats-in-service, etc.
6. Summary of Preliminary Criteria for Required Closure:
    A. Needs: What is he doing with his longing to be understood, his hurt, his anger/hate/revenge when disappointed? Is he still alternating between suppression/inviting suppression?
    B. Constant Attitude: Is he still the good guy who, somehow, is put down?
    C. Security Operations: Does he provoke the brake? Does he inspire the co-pilot? Does this allow a paranoid position to be maintained?
    D. Family Game: Do we still see this interaction of being rat in Rat Express which mobilizes co-pilot, which mobilizes brakes in rat express, etc.?

RESULTS
1. Symptomatic Change:
    A., B., Depression and Rage: His SCL-90 is very rich in depressive, anxious and anger complaints, obsessional ones, somatization also. Comparing Item 59, "Thoughts of death or dying," to one year ago, he says "Let's get it over with" and chuckles. Comparing Item 63, "Urges to run self down," "It's gone from intensity of 3 to 7–8 [where 1 is doing it], from 5–6 times a day to 1–2 per week."
        [Note: He came for therapy a year ago after an overdose following an argument with his family. He thought "Piss on it" [sic] and took a handful of diazide pills. He was alternating between fits of shouting, throwing, etc., and feeling guilty and depressed. Felt hopeless.]
2. Dynamic Change, Stress Tests for Dynamic Change:
    A. Insubordination from kids: Being kept waiting several hours by family: "boiling . . . daughter angry back . . . able to talk it out." Would have had chip on shoulder for a week before.
    B. Blame from wife: definitely stuck, worse he says . . .
    C. Feeling alone, misunderstood: Not by therapist who does understand him, but no one to replace therapist yet. He hopes wife will improve.
    D. Urges to take revenge? Be harsh? Better with kids. Same with wife.
    E. Additional test not on list: When he fails to do a job perfectly, e.g., yesterday, he couldn't make an electrical repair although he followed the protocol and was called away, he still *blames himself*: "If I had done the best I could I would have fixed it." "I couldn't stand it if someone else could do it before I did." He was able to see that such "perfection" sets him up for continual depression, as today, and laughed heartily, coming out of the depression he brought to the session. (Impressive) He was also clear about his following his Norwegian grandfather in "perfectionism/*without* using iron fist . . . ," which also set him up for depression.

He told me a poignant story about washing the steps to the lake 17 times before being allowed to swim.

3. Systemic Change, Response of System to Dynamic Change in Patient: Son and daughter, improved relations, but wife worse. She is seeing psychiatrist again. She seems to act as if his needs are not legitimate, but he seems to trigger this by his insisting, yelling, etc. (a vicious circle which remains in place). He thinks wife may be worse because the buffer of kids is being lost now, as kids leave home, leaving only the two of them.

4. Patient's View of Therapy: He appreciates the calm, low-keyness of therapist (Gedo's Level I), being talked to, and the therapist's not having all the answers. Most useful interpretation has been: "You can't be Mr. Perfect," linking this to perfection of grandfather. He spontaneously linked difficulty with this to early deaths of younger brother in forties, older brother in fifties, father in late fifties. He feels his family has helped him survive — "something to live for."

5. Patient's Relation to Interviewer: Didn't want to "bare my soul," he said, so he did not fill out Brief Follow-up Questionnaire — a little restraint there — but was extremely forthcoming, emotional, and thoughtful, as I had heard him be on audiotape with therapist many times before.

6. Summary of Findings in Relation to Criteria for Required Closure:
   A. Needs: Longings to be understood: Well with therapist, improved with both kids, a bit with co-worker in argument. Hurt, rage: Still inflicting on wife, but reduced in frequency; quite intense.
   B. Constant Attitude: Still the good guy who is put down? No, not quite. He sees he triggers wife, by insistence . . . sees he is afraid to be "unsettled" by being merely firm.
   C. Security Operations: Still tends to be either insisting or asking nothing: "unsettled, as if feet would be cut out from under him" if he were firm and got what he wanted (which he thinks is likely) Still struggling with getting beyond "paranoid position" here I think. Actually, he seems to be making clear statements of depressive position (perfection of archaic self).
   D. Family Game: Still locked in with wife as noted. Not clear if co-pilot relation with therapist . . . triggers the brake from wife. Note, also, the grandfather, father, brothers pattern — he is struggling to break the tyrant-victim game.

SUMMARY REMARKS, NOTEWORTHY FINDINGS

Team anxious he might interpret interview as signal he ought to be done with therapy, when, in fact, he needs a long while to build relations like the one he has with the therapist. Team worried that he could get much worse to prevent being dropped, unless this was appreciated. Perhaps explains some of SCL-90. I suggested he might need therapy until May (8 more months). Shorter separations, such as vacations, could also pose difficulty. I was also very impressed by the helpfulness to him of thought-experiment questions:

"What if he just thought he did the best he could on the job, . . . *if* someone did it better sometimes, so what? *If* he were not perfect and accepted it?" (This brought him out of depression he came in with, but it was not rhetorical; I meant it to lead deeper and it did.)

"What *if* he didn't insist to wife . . . *not* acting as if he didn't care, but instead was just matter of fact? And she responded well? Where does this 'unsettled feeling' lead? What if he felt that way?"

Finally, his staying identified with the perfectionist grandfather, father, brothers, etc., helps him to stay in position of *demanding/not asking*, which he must be very careful about, since asking must have such painful associations. He ought to move very slowly about any change in this security operation. (Michael Moran, M.D., personal communication).

Notes

1. A Proposal

1. I am indebted to Philip Booth (1983) for drawing my attention to the usefulness of the idea of tradition, which Booth borrows from Karl Popper (1949), for thinking about psychotherapy, and to Fred Wamboldt for drawing my attention to "the method of methods."
2. I like the concept of General Wavell, described by Dyson (1984), for testing new artillery. If the field gun is dropped from a hundred-foot tower and it still works, then it is worth further study.
3. Malan proposed a universal method (1979), which he soon dropped. Others have been more stubborn. That is the rule.
4. Conversing with many patients may pull the therapist towards a common language, while the poet need only talk with himself. Conversing with followers is like talking to oneself, only worse. This begets jargon.

Thus, the language of psychotherapy is subject to pulls in opposite directions. Orwell wrote that the purpose of language may be to show or to hide (1946). Thus, we get a range of languages in psychotherapy, from the perfection of a common speech to official newspeak.

5. Mt. Zion Psychiatric Clinic ended its residency in 1984. Psychoanalysis has lost its sway in psychiatry.
6. I appreciate that my opinion here is controversial. I think Freud backed off the analysis of character, while Reich continued what Freud began, while most of psychoanalysis followed Freud's retreat. I realize that psychoanalysis gives a minor bow to Reich. I do not think his central idea, of the analysis of the constant attitude, has been taken very seriously (Gustafson, unpublished manuscript).

2. Freud and Breuer: Double Appreciation

1. Here is an accidental moment of family therapy.
2. More family therapy!
3. See Chapter 15 on Bateson, especially footnote 9, for more discussion of the concept of "double description." I also utilize this concept to organize all four of the

modern methods of brief dynamic therapy in Chapters 11, 12, 13, and 14.

4. We will see later, with the Milan school, how the "positive connotation" of loyalty is very powerful (Marianne Wamboldt, M.D., personal communication).

3. Freud, Ferenczi, and Rank: Return to a Childhood Structure

1. Unfortunately there are few extant case reports of the brief, classical analysis. Malan (1963) found a few. Gustafson (unpublished) discusses all of Freud's eight published cases at length. Four are from the earlier technique discussed in Chapter 2 in the *Studies on Hysteria*, two are classical (failures), namely Dora and the Case of Homosexuality in a Woman, and two are the

analysis of character, the Rat Man and the Wolf Man, which I will discuss as technique in Chapter 4. See Freud's "Recommendations to Physicians" (1912, 1913, 1914, 1915) for the most explicit technical discussions by him of the classical technique (Gustafson, unpublished). Ferenczi and Rank (1925) are restating the logic of the treatment espoused by Freud between 1912 and 1915 so clearly. Rank become occupied with his myth of the hero (1924) after his technical contribution with Ferenczi to the classical restatement.

2. A long note here for would-be experts to anticipate what lies ahead in Chapters 4–17: Freud, Ferenczi and Rank invite the enactment by providing what would now be called a "frame" for its repetition. The "standard technique" will cope with "resistance" to the emergence of "free association" and "transference" (repetition). Strupp and Binder (1984) add the idea that the therapist will be caught up in this "enactment," if only in his feelings of "countertransference." They "interpret" the relationship being enacted between patient and therapist by stopping the action to allow its discussion. They feel that this more dyadic or interpersonal perspective widens the domain of patients who can tolerate the classical method, because they can catch those enactments that would destroy the analysis. They think that the other nonspecific qualities of the therapist also help when there is a good fit between patient and therapist, which strengthens the therapeutic alliance for weathering the strain of the inevitable enactment.

Alexander and French (Chapter 5) introduced an entirely different line of development when they suggested that the "enactment" is only possible for many patients when there is a "strengthened context" of a new relationship, which *specifically* designed to counter the relation seen in the enactment. Often, the nonverbal "holding environment" of the new relationship is more important than anything the therapist could say. Here is the line followed by the interpersonal methods of Sullivan, Win-

nicott, Balint, Gedo, and Havens and by the systemic methods, such as the Milan team (Steven Stern, personal communication).

The next step beyond Alexander and French is to see that the "enactment" or "pathological current" is not to be dismissed in the new relationship or new beginning. Rather, "pathology" contains capacities which are valuable for the patient. For example, Winnicott sees that destructiveness is a sign of hope, an attempt to force the environment to pay attention, to make up the loss. This is a "positive connotation" of a dark current (Chapter 16, the Milan team). The aim of interviewing is "working the opposing currents" to get a reliable reading of the river. In this view, the destructive envy of Case B, the Scientist, of Alexander and French, would not be merely an enactment to be caught within an appreciation of his actual superiority. Rather, this would be something to understand, why he has to win every battle, why he has to admit no weakness. Doggedness had to be useful somewhere. If this can be appreciated, the Scientist may retain the virtue, which only appears "pathological" from lack of perspective. This is what gets lost in Alexander and French's "strengthened contexts." For Havens, the pathological mother who edits her daughter's conversations (Third Conversation, Chapter 10) is not merely pathological, for the daughter wants to do well by this mother. Mother must be "given her due" (Steven Stern, personal communication), if only to allow what is admirable in the daughter to be recognized as well. Enactments depend upon "working the opposing currents."

4. Freud and Reich: The Constant Attitude

1. For the most graphic description of the telling gesture, see Reich's "Character Formation and the Phobias of Childhood" (1930).

2. Freud's greatest case is conducted strictly along these lines of the analysis of the constant attitude, namely the case of the Rat Man (1909). See Gustafson (unpublished) for a full description of what Freud did with the Rat Man. I argue there that Freud slipped back into the classical description of technique in his "Recommendations" to physicians (1912, 1913, 1914, 1915), where-

as Reich continued Freud's advance by making a system of the analysis of the constant attitude or character. Most of psychoanalysis followed Freud's lead, rather than Reich's, of course, so that Reich is honored more in the breach than in the observance. But Freud should get the major honor for the discovery of this method. Hence, I have placed his name first. Reich is second for recovering the method with such clarity, so that it would be more difficult to lose again. I have expounded Reich rather than Freud, only because Reich is more clear about the technique as a strict, coherent method.

3. I am indebted to Myron Sharaf for calling these two aspects of the technique to my attention in his reading of an earlier draft. The reader may want to see Sharaf's book on Reich, *Fury on Earth* (1983).

INTRODUCTION / *The Interpersonal Perspective*

1. Cronen, Johnson and Lannamann (1982) describe this kind of shift in perspective very well. Instincts and defenses do not disappear in an interpersonal perspective. Rather, the interpersonal perspective gives a stable platform for observing their operation in relation to another individual. What is unduly complicated and fixed in an intrapsychic perspective is simpler and fluid in an interpersonal perspective, because the two elements of instinct and defense are seen in relation to the third element of managing interpersonal relations. The third element alters, as Bateson (1972a) would say, the *punctuation*: no longer do we have "instinct, defense" but "(instinct, defense), security operations." In such a different punctuation, "(instinct, defense)" become "(moves)," which makes for much greater fluidity of both instinct and defense.

I appreciate that this discussion may be puzzling for readers who are unfamiliar with Bateson. If this is the case, forget it for now and perhaps come back to it after reading Chapters 15, 16 and 17. Not everything may be understood at once. A telling example from *Pere Goriot* is the following: "Eugene was bent upon deluding himself; he was ready to make a sacrifice of his conscience for his mistress. In the last two days everything in his life had undergone change. Woman had introduced various disorders, had eclipsed Family, and confiscated everything to her own profit" (Balzac, 1946, pp. 255–256. Original text in French, 1835). This is the power of interpersonal relations swiftly to alter the punctuation or proportions of our components. Even more powerful are interpersonal relations organized as systems. This is the subject of Balzac's interest in Paris.

5. *Alexander and French: With the Grain, Against the Grain*

1. See Chapter 10 on Havens for a continuation of the idea of "working the opposing currents." Havens borrows the method for finding the patient rather than for changing the patient, which he eschews. See footnote 6 for a very long discussion of those who "work the opposing currents" to change their proportions. These are the two main currents which flow from Alexander and French. I regard the first as more reliable. See Chapter 23 for my discussion of this preference.

2. The metaphor of the jigsaw puzzle continues in Strupp (1981), who poses brief therapy as the technical problem of locating the "missing piece." See also Gustafson (1984) for further use of the metaphor. Now I would say that it is equally important to appreciate why and how the missing piece has been sacrificed. People will make up holes in their development (Skynner and Cleese, 1983) unless the hole is needed. The systemic perspective (see Chapters 15, 16, and 17) suggests how to look for the system in which the individual gives up his or her potential.

3. I find this is one of the most difficult skills to teach young family and individual therapists. See Chapter 23.

4. Later, French would shift his terms in what I think was an unfortunate direction. Rather than writing of weak points in an "ingrained pattern," French would write of "focal conflict." His latter idea is very misleading, I think, because it makes the two terms of the "conflict", the impulse and the feared consequence, relatively equal, and because it makes the problem into an intrapsychic event, between an impulse and a fear. I believe it is far stronger to think of the ingrained pattern as the dominant structure of adaptation, which is now showing a weakness. The weakness *may* involve an impulse, such as the urge of this Scientist to destroy his competition. But the impulse is not "the" problem per se; rather, the problem is the weakness of his adaptation, which brings about a desperate impulse.

Thus, the impulse-defense model misleads us from centering on the problem of adaptation. That is, French in later work is backing off the interpersonal view back into the classical psychoanalytic paradigm. No wonder he did. There was enormous pressure on Alexander and French to recant. French did it for them. Much of current psychoanalytic theorizing is an attempt to cope with interpersonal ideas such as those of Alexander and French while trying to minimize the excesses or repair the damages of such thinking to the classical mode of psychoanalytic activity. Thus, ego psychology locates interpersonal relations back within the intrapsychic structure of "object relations." Thus, self psychology will acknowledge primitive security operations in relation to "selfobjects." A positive connotation of such operations by Kohut (1971) gives him access. Thus, Weiss and Sampson (1986) will call attention to the "testing" of the object, and Gedo (Chapter 9) will emphasize what the "holding environment" will supply for the repair of developmental deficits in psychic structure.

5. See Balint's Case of the Stationery Manufacturer for a comparable offer of relationship, which controls for related past dangers (Chapter 8).

6. I would mention briefly here that there are other variations of these ideas everywhere in the history of psychoanalysis, but no other writers have come close to working out such careful plans for retrieving the patient's losing battle until the Milan team which came along in the 1970s. Leon Saul, one of Alexander's team, subsequently wrote several books with some terms of his own, which are similar to those of Alexander and French (Saul, 1977). Reider (1955) had a similar talent for shoring up the patient's strength. In the first case of his paper, he described a businessman who became devastated by a positive Wasserman test (for syphilis). Reider put him to work on menial tasks for which he was given no special praise. Indeed, he was treated as a hired hand. This put him back to the Biblical "inexorable atmosphere" of his childhood, from which he could draw strength. Reider describes a small set of such brilliant intuitions, for making the patient able to bear the strain of a current setback, which augment those described by Alexander and French. The main idea is to be very attentive to what makes the patient become more capable. One has to take the history in this way. This is a very nice contribution, but Reider disclaims any attempt to construct a general plan like Alexander and French.

More recently, Weiss and Sampson (1986) have argued not only that the doctor does the planning—the planning as to how the patient will be strengthened to bear a warded-off feeling or difficulty, the planning as to how the relationship with the doctor will be decisively separated from the traumatic relationship to the parents—but also that the *patient plans, unconsciously*, to bring about these "conditions of safety." How does the patient plan unconsciously? An example of the first type is "crying at a happy ending." The patient will allow himself to cry, when he is reassured that the ending is happy and secure. The context is strengthened by the ending, so that the feared feeling can be borne. An example of the second type occurs when the patient provokes the therapist to do what has been traumatic in the past. If the therapist is clearly helpful rather than hurtful, despite the provocation or the "test," the patient may then revise his "pathogenic idea" about how he needs to curtail his own feelings and movements.

It is possible to describe Case B, the Scientist, of Alexander and French, in these terms of "unconscious planning." The scientist tempts Alexander to see him as weak and helpless, as he appears "weeping, agitated and exhausted" in the first session. Alexander was being provoked in an extreme way to take the position of the man's family. Alexander took the opposite position, that the man was very powerful and worthy of respect. This allowed the man to face his own decline, safely, without the unbearable strain of his childhood in which weakness earned him contempt. This is what Weiss and Sampson call a "direct transference test." The reverse occurs when the patient gives the doctor the problem he cannot bear, to learn from the doctor how he carries the difficulty through. For example, the scientist puts Alexander in the position of making a bold scientific demonstration, which contains the fear or dread of defeat. When Alexander succeeds in carrying this off, the patient follows him to do the same. This is what Weiss and Sampson call a "passive into active" test.

The reader may wonder, as I have, whether there are any technical advantages to thinking of the planning as coming from the patient as well as from the doctor. I doubt that our understanding of what Alexander did with the Scientist, Case B, is altered by thinking that the patient was planning, unconsciously, from his side. I think that Weiss and Sampson often use their ideas of "unconscious planning" by the patient so that the doctor has less planning to do. He may keep to his classical neutrality, waiting for the patient to separate him decisively from the traumatic parent, by the patient's unconscious experiments (provocations). Neutrality will pass most of these tests, according to Weiss and Sampson, which is very convenient for defending traditional analysis. It is no difficulty to them that it takes one hundred analytic hours, rather than one or two, when almost all the planning has to come from the patient's side, for they are interested in this unconscious activity of the patient from a scientific point of view that is anxious to make a minimum departure from traditional psychoanalysis. Perhaps their careful studies do show that it is possible for patients to improve by such gradual testing of their unconscious theories.

The metaphor implicit in Weiss and Sampson's theory is that the patient is a kind of *unconscious scientist*, holding and testing unconscious theories. This leads them to a kind of *optimism* about the patient doing what he needs to do to revise his own pathogenic theories, with some accurate and right reactions from the analyst, which are consistent with classical neutrality. This metaphor is misleading, I think, in cases just like Case B, the Scientist, of Alexander and French. If Alexander had only listened to the man's "weeping, agitation and exhaustion" in the first session, acting in the fashion of the neutral analyst, not being drawn into taking care of the patient as a weak man, I doubt very much whether the man would feel convinced in a decisive way that Alexander was different from his family, just because he had remained neutral. I doubt whether the patient would have waited around a hundred hours, to see that the analyst wasn't provoked by a hundred hours of weeping, agitation and exhaustion. This is undue optimism? Many patients are not very talented at being unconscious scientists!

Alexander and French have a more boldly experimental attitude than Weiss and Sampson. For them, every patient's adap-

tation is different. Each case needs its own tone and atmosphere and language to shore up the strength of the ingrained pattern and separate the doctor decisively from the negative past (transference). In each case the doctor needs to look for the developmental weakness hidden by the prominent ingrained pattern, so that the patient is brought round to amend the weakness. So every case is an experiment to find the differences which are critical to the individual adaptation. In this way, there is no standard technique, but a series of experiments guided by a general theory. Perhaps it is no accident that the first case in their series was that of a scientist. What better patient to appreciate a beautiful experiment and proof by a doctor! Milton Erickson also had an unusual talent like Alexander and French for gauging strengths which could be brought forward, weaknesses which could be overcome (Haley, 1973). Several schools of "strategic therapy" follow this line from Erickson (Watzlawick, Weakland and Fisch, 1974; Fisch, Weakland, and Segal, 1983; De Shazer, 1985).

Still, there is something to be said for Weiss and Sampson against the strategic experiments of Alexander and French and their successors. By seeing the individual patient as already having his own plans for revising his pathogenic beliefs, by asking the therapist to assist the patient in continuing to make tests to overcome such grim restrictions, they are careful not to take over. Strategic therapists often presume the best interests of the patient are served by their stratagems. This may violate the beginning efforts of the patient which are underway. The strategic therapists may be overly impressed by their own drama.

Weiss and Sampson risk being conservative and boring, sometimes, to be sure of being reliable in their assistance. For some lovely examples of unconscious planning by patients, see especially Chapter 7, "Dreams and Their Various Purposes" (Weiss and Sampson, 1986), concerning warning dreams, blissful dreams, and traumatic dreams. Weiss and Sampson may be said to have a fine eye for hopeful currents which are barely underway, which they augment. I myself would not attribute "unconscious plans" to such currents, but such an attribution is at least respectful of the autonomy of the patient. I like that very much about their work. My reservation is that this attribution may leave too much of the work to the patient, allowing the analyst to sit comfortably in the classical analytic seat.

7. Perhaps this experimental attitude is so important that schools of brief therapy are only successful so long as the attitude is vigorous. Then the school fades. See Malan (1963) and Gustafson (1981) who pose

this problem of the secret of brief therapy being continually lost.

8. See Chapter 10 on Havens for the technical requirements for fully "working the opposite currents." See Chapters 17 and 23 for my preference for getting an accurate picture over acting upon the patient (or trainee).

6. *Sullivan: Dependable Hypotheses*

1. I find Sullivan less trouble for students than Alexander and French. Both invite fine disregard for the classical rules, but Sullivan tempts them to be a little daring about getting an accurate picture, while Alexander and French tempt them to correct the patient. I also find that the work of the clinic team in giving consultations to its members is better when inspired by Sullivan than when inspired by Alexander and French. There is less mischief in helping a colleague improve his hypotheses than in trying to prescribe actions for him to carry out (see Chapter 23). Prescribing pulls for disciples, which usually means a deterioration from the advisor to the advised. For an interesting version of such a comedy, see the *Gospel According to St. Mark*.

2. I like this inclination of Sullivan to leave the experimenting to the patient. Here again is less presumption by the doctor. See also Weiss and Sampson (1986) for another version of leaving the activity with the patient.

3. Sullivan's sensitivity to the unseen audience derives from his small town upbringing in upstate New York. See the moving biography of Sullivan by Helen Swick Perry (1982). I find this small town boy from New York very congenial to my middle town experiences here in the Midwest. The poetry is related.

4. Cf. Havens (1984) on what are essential tests for being well.

5. This suggestion for taking the *Psychiatric Interview* in reverse order I got from Craig Johnson, M.D.

6. Cf. Sullivan (1976, p. 163) for a fine description of why the patient presented in the seminar could not remedy where his family left him short. It is not so much what your family cannot give you, but whether you then take a posture which prevents anyone outside the family from making up what is missing in your education. For example, a child who is obliged to act as a little grownup cannot let other children or adults see how far behind he is. "You are so childish you don't dare talk to anybody." This posture which prevents being helped or educated is the "constant attitude" which Reich first discussed so clearly, the "ingrained pattern" which Alexander and French have described in more interpersonal terms.

7. I would have no appreciation for Sullivan if it were not for my teacher, Les Havens, whose own work is described in Chapter 10. Havens (1976) suggested that Sullivan could be read for his technical ideas, rather than for his theorizing. This makes Sullivan much more accessible, for his technical ideas are very clear and sharp, while his theories become woolly and prolix. His *Psychiatric Interview* (1954), *Case Seminar* (1976), and *Clinical Studies* (1956) are very accessible for me, while I get nowhere with his other books.

7. *Winnicott: Therapeutic Consultations*

1. "The Antisocial Tendency" in Winnicott (1958).

2. "The Antisocial Tendency" in Winnicott (1958).

3. See Case XIII, Ada, age eight years (1971b) for a lovely series of moves by Winnicott which take him deep down, especially his

interest in the missing hands in the child's drawing. "I said, 'I would very much like to see what the lady looks like from behind'" (1971b, p. 226, 1971).

4. "Anxiety," according to the classical work of psychoanalysis on this subject by Anna Freud (1946, Chapter V), divides into

three kinds: "super-ego anxiety" or fear of the conscience taken in from the family; "objective anxiety" or the anticipation of signals of danger from the environment; "instinctual anxiety" or fear of having one's own control overrun by one's own instincts. Sullivan, in the light of this scheme, is almost entirely interested in "objective anxiety," although he knew about "instinctual anxiety" as a fear of breakdown and continually dealt with "super-ego anxiety," when the patient ascribed his own views to Sullivan. But this is to misunderstand Sullivan. His argument is that you do not understand human beings apart from their niche. You locate the animal at home defending threats to his territory, so that "super-ego anxiety" and "instinctual anxiety" are aroused *in the context* of interactions between the animal and the environment. Look there first. Winnicott is close to Sullivan's view, but the emphasis on "playing the internal onto the external" ends up with more definition or resolution of the internal aspect in Winnicott than you get in Sullivan. The map is better defined at its internal pole. Sullivan's map is more one of survival, getting through all right, something of more concern in upstate New York, while Winnicott's map is more interested in the quality of what is inside and between, something of more concern in Cambridge.

5. Winnicott also recognized an even less primitive, but also primitive, kind of anxiety, namely "talion anxiety," which was the fear of losing parts of oneself in retaliation for one's interests, such as losing one's penis, or hand. See "Hate in the Countertransference" in Winnicott (1958), for the most graphic description of both talion and annihilation anxiety occurring in the therapist. This is perhaps the best single clinical essay Winnicott wrote.

6. "The Antisocial Tendency" in Winnicott (1958).

7. See Chapter 14, "Primary Maternal Preoccupation" in Winnicott (1958).

8. In *Therapeutic Consultations* (1971b) the word "resistance" appears only twice, in passing, and the analysis of resistance has nothing to do with technique. There are only a few more references to the word, one to say that this work has nothing to do "in terms of transference neurosis samples." Rather, this book is a report of "communication with children" (p. 8). This was exactly Sullivan's position about his work,

that resistance and transference were not of interest per se, only occurring in his text a few times. His interest was "reliable communication" with adults. For Winnicott, psychoanalysis is not to be denied importance: "Psychoanalysis remains for me the basis of this work" (p. 1). But even here on the first page of his book, he writes: "I do believe, however, that selection is the most important of the psychoanalytic training. . . . One would rather have a really suitable person for doing this sort of work than an ill person made less ill by the analysis that is part of the psychoanalytic training." In brief, the *person* of the analyst makes all the difference. Thus, Winnicott shows his usual position about analysis. On the one hand, he bows to the tradition, on the other he says the person of the doctor is crucial; then he leaves the two statements side by side. He did not want this kind of paradox resolved. It gave him his room, his transitional area to work from. Thus, psychoanalysis is there in what he did, and penis envy, oedipal aims, resistance, and transference make occasional appearances in passing, with occasional bows to Freud and Melanie Klein and so forth.

9. This kind of work will strengthen three fundamental capacities,the "underpinning," as Sullivan would say, necessary to handling most problems of adaptation in life: the ability to connect to what is good, the ability to protect oneself, and the ability to control one's own destructiveness or at least make reparations for destructiveness.

10. I use this tracing of the transitions in most interviews, especially in the conclusion, but also along the way when the patient feels lost about how we got to something difficult or how we got out of something difficult.

11. Cases in Chapters 2, 4, 5, 10 (1971a).

12. Ada, the most beautiful of the cases, Chapter XIII.

13. Robin Skynner suggests to me that it is even better if the therapist has been ill before with the difficulty the patient is having, but has "tunneled his own way out" (personal communication). Skynner knew Winnicott well and suggests that his enormous capacity as a therapist came from his being so at ease with the patient's being ill. Winnicott had been quite ill himself, but somehow managed to become well — hence his accessiblity, his ease with disturbance.

8. *Balint: Regression for the Sake of Recognition*

1. I am more and more inclined to see that "hitting it off," in Balint's phrase, is essential. Without this, nothing. How to set up this intuitive relationship is one subject of Chapter 24.
2. I am alluding here to Havens' excellent discussion of the case (1982a), where he attempted to move the discussion from an overly cognitive description of the technique by describing how Balint used "head, eye, heart and hand." I have added the "ear," which is implied in Balint's own language of the "sounding board."
3. See the discussion by Meissner (1982) in the Massachusetts Mental Health Center debate of the case. His point is that the man's weakness and inferiority drive him to cruelty and grandiosity, and vice versa, in a never ending cycle of borderline activity, which Balint's treatment was successful in interrupting.
4. See the fine discussion by Avery (1982) in the Massachusetts Mental Health Center debate of this case, concerning how the patient's problem is structured by the limitations of the previous generation.
5. If there are these "opposing currents" (Alexander and French, Chapter 5; Havens, Chapter 10), then Balint will keep from being pulled under by the destructive currents, while riding the constructive drift. This is nearly a literal description of Maturana's concept of "structural coupling." The patient triggers various structural possibilities in the therapist, for either pulling him down into the undertow or having a fine ride together, while the therapist triggers back these structural possibilities in the patient. Becoming a medium for each other, they share a "consensual domain" which has a "drift." There is no "instructive interaction." The requisite structures are already there in the patient and in the therapist. *Which* structures are elicited depends on the wit and skill of the therapist. See Chapter 17 on Maturana, Chapter 18, and Chapter 24.
6. See the excellent discussions by Myerson, Morrison and Havens in the Massachusetts Mental Health Center debate (1982), about the patient's loneliness from childhood, about the need to help him extend himself from one extreme to the other, to go with him in this transition. Havens is very close here to Winnicott's notion of the road backward and forward.
7. See the fine discussion by Myerson (1982) of how Mr. Baker would have had a disastrous course if invited into such a regression.
8. "New Beginning and the Paranoid and the Depressive Syndromes" (1952) is one of the best and clearest short statements by Balint of his clinical theory.
9. See the opening quotation of this book and the closing Chapter 24.
10. Avery (1982) has a fine discussion of this in the Massachusetts Mental Health Center debate of the case.
11. I think that what saved his life in this period was Haven's idea about "counter-introjection," which will be described in Chapter 10. He was being "beat up" by his own introjects. I found some ways to oppose this, along the lines described by Havens. It would be irrelevant to my discussion of Balint to enter into the technique of "counter-introjection" here. See patient's comments in Follow-Up Interview (Appendix).
12. My colleague, Joseph Kepecs, M.D., suggests that "philobatism" is a "defense" against dependency, that my acceptance of this stance, paradoxically, allows the patient to depend on me to a deeper extent. I think this is partly right, but a little misleading, for his philobatism is a deep (true) relation to his environment. If I accept this meaning for him, we have some drift together which has more depth and reliability. If I see this meaning as a "defense" against (true) involvement, I accept or back Jack's view of involvement, which is a disaster for my patient. I believe Kepec's argument illustrates the usual (ocnophilic) bias of psychoanalysis which Balint believed to be hazardous for some patients. See also Balint (1959).
13. See Chapter 18 for "The Forest Ranger's Departure."

9. *Gedo: A Hierarchy of Personal Aims*

1. I have been asked on several occasions, by experienced therapists, why I do not include a chapter on Kohut (1971) in my book. They find his thinking so useful. My reply has been the following. I myself experimented with Kohut's thinking about

ten years ago, and did indeed find it to be of some technical help (Gustafson, 1976), but I also became aware that it had many misleading implications. First, the access to the so-called "mirror and idealizing transferences" was often very difficult, not something patients just fell into, the way Kohut described. The trenchant "constant attitudes" stood in the way, as Anna Ornstein (1974) observed, so we were back to the technical problems of character analysis after all. Secondly, I found it extremely limiting to confine my analysis to the disruptions of our primitive self-object relationships, as Kohut advised. This left me quite passive, standing by, for long periods, with some patients, when obvious deficits were being paraded by my nose, which I could have helped with. Thirdly, as Gedo has emphasized, this technical business of arousing self-object relationships and analyzing the "narcissistic injury" reactions to their disruption is based on a mistaken theoretical hodgepodge, which elevates these protective archaic possibilities into objects of central concern and therapeutic activity. This leads us away from the developmental deficits described by Gedo for which the patient needs our help. When this latter help is given, the self-object relations fade on their own. Fourthly, Kohut's description of primitive, useful object relationships is very biased. Mirror transferences and idealizing transferences are only half of the territory, that is, the half of primitive relating which has to do with closeness and clinging and merger with other people. The

other half of the territory, as Michael Balint (1968) has emphasized, is primitive relating to the lovely, wide open spaces. This too can be extremely protective, and calming, and crucial to the well-being of some children and adults, especially from families where enmeshment can wreck the child. Turning out into distant lovely worlds saves them. The case of the Forest Ranger, described in Chapter 8 on Balint, was of this latter kind. Kohut's map of useful protective primitive relationships is half right and half wrong. It is biased towards the close merger kind, which Balint (1968) has rightly suggested is a bias in all of psychoanalysis. It is very destructive to patients who do not want clinging and enmeshment, when their therapists suggest they are "resisting" such things. This is the kind of thing that was destroying my Forest Ranger, when his friends took the same tack. He was giving up hope for himself because of it. I was glad for Kohut's useful observations about these phenomena but I found as much trouble as help in his technical ideas. Hence, I have not included a chapter on him. I think Gedo has put Kohut to a sounder use. Therefore, my chapter is about Gedo's thinking.

2. The most moving and exact account of this kind of alternating identification between the cold world of men, and the warm world of women, and of its tragic consequences is to be found, I think, in E. M. Foster's *Howard's End*. (1910).

3. See Chapter 22 for a discussion of the termination with the Policeman's Daughter.

10. *Havens: Reliable Findings*

1. Borges (1984) sees in Dante what Havens sees as the technical possibilities of all the schools of psychiatry: Variation of intonation and accentuation for a music which fits all the emotions; intensity; tenderness and rigor; a narrative so clear to follow; characters defined forever in a moment; an author who is present in his own *Comedy*. But the parallel between representation in literature and representation in psychiatry is too large to freight this chapter on Havens with. I will return to it in Part III, Chapter 18.

2. Winnicott's ideas about "interpretation" are similar. One makes remarks in order to be corrected.

3. For an interesting set of hazards to be expected in first sessions, see Margulies and

Havens (1981). I will return to this in detail in Chapter 19.

4. Offhand moves of massive structures are also essential to the Milan method. See Chapter 16.

5. The argument is *not* that objective-descriptive methods are useless, only that forcing precision by the use of routine categories, such as the mental status examination, costs the interviewer reliability about other findings. For example, the patient might have to hide some bizarre experiences for fear of the official categories of disordered thinking. The analogy is to physics. When measurement of the position of very small particles is more precise, the measurement of velocity becomes more indeterminate. The argument is in "The Risks of Know-

ing and Not Knowing" (Havens, 1982b). Also, Havens is more positive about objective-descriptive methods when he writes for physicians, as in the *Lancet* article (1978c), or in the splendid ones of the 1960s (1965, 1967, 1968). After all, physicians are most at home with such methods. We shall see from David Malan in Chapter 11 that even more can be gotten from objective-descriptive measurements when other methods are used to control for the objective" distortions that are possible. Havens (1978c) and Malan are very close.

6. The argument is *not* that psychoanalytic *methods* are useless, only that the *framework* of a standard technique for getting pure versions of the past is a mistaken idea. The methods are terrific for giving the patient room when this is what the patient needs to recover something on the margin of consciousness. Havens has a very high regard for free association as a method when the method is called for.

7. This language of the "closed circuit" is the transition from the linear world of Havens to the circular world of the Milan team. The responses of the patient follow from the projected expectations of the family, while the responses of the patient, in turn, draw for more of the same expectations. These "closed circuits" hide other possibilities.

8. "Loose holding" is also vital for writers. A rule of thumb for me in writing is that a passage that will not flow forward should not be *forced*, but waited on, until I can see what in the passage is not fitting in. The longer and more frustrating the delay,

the more significant is the hold-up and the more revealing.

9. The phrase "the other people in the room" refers to those presences which are dimly or keenly felt by the patient. Most of them are not *literally* there in the room, insofar as an external observer would see only a patient and a doctor there in individual therapy.

10. In my opinion, the best of Havens' articles on the existential methods are "Explorations in the Uses of Language in Psychotherapy: Simple Empathic Statements" (1978b) and "Explorations in the Uses of Language in Psychotherapy: Complex Empathic Statements (1979). For the interpersonal use of statements, see "Explorations in the Uses of Language in Psychotherapy: Counterprojective Statements" (1980), and "Explorations in the Uses of Language in Psychotherapy: Counterintrojective Statements (Performatives)" (1984a). Fortunately, Havens' new book is devoted to the subject of *Making Contact, Uses of Language in Psychotherapy* (1986).

11. For a little more discussion by Havens of using different parts of ourselves, see 1978c and 1982a.

12. For more discussion of sitting positions of the schools, see Havens' "The Interpersonal Perspective and Techniques," Chapter 6, 1976.

13. On reading this text, the patient recalled feeling very frustrated here. Indeed, I needed to help him separate two currents which were canceling each other out. I do this next.

14. The patient recalled feeling angry at me here, again. He wanted me to do more. I probe the pain.

INTRODUCTION / *Modern Brief Individual Therapy*

1. Actually, they are presented by their authors as diagrams but I propose to see them as "double descriptions" in the following four chapters. See Chapter 15 on Bateson for a discussion of this concept.

2. Malan dropped his center of thinking after 20 years to adopt the related center of Davanloo's thinking. See Chapters 11 and 14.

3. See Bateson (1979) on stories, pp. 13–17. For further discussion of stories, see Chapter 15 and Chapter 18.

4. Balint used to say and write (1957) that the patient's illness is "organized" by the doctor from a relatively unorganized presentation of unhappiness. He ought to organ-

ize the illness which has the best prognosis for the patient! From this perspective, I would say that Malan, Mann, Sifneos, and Davanloo offer relatively promising illnesses to their patients. Simplicity is usually more workable than complications, as Sullivan would say. But it is better to have a large domain of possible ways to organize the illness in a simple way. This is the great virtue of Sullivan, Winnicott, Balint, and Havens. They have been complex in possibilities, simple in their assignments to the patient.

What kind of simplicity is best? Well, this is a deep question. Notice that an isomorphic distinction may help expand the story. We return to these problems in chapters 15, 16, and 17, concerning the systemic perspective.

For the more intellectual reader I might offer here the idea that each of these diagrams generates a different *language*, with different story possibilities. This is very close to Whorf's hypothesis (1956), concerning the relevant, central distinctions in a language, and the necessary actions in which its users are engaged. For example, Eskimos distinguish many different kinds of snows, because many critical actions derive from such distinctions. Whereas, for those of us who sit indoors in winter, snow is snow, i.e. the occasion for staying indoors. I find as I cross-country ski every day that I am more of a mind with the Eskimos!

5. Not exactly. As Strupp (1981) has suggested, the personality of the therapist in training may lend itself beautifully, swiftly, to one of those four modes. For others, the learning of any one of these may be painstaking and endless. I am indebted to Dr. Stephen Stern for this observation.

6. There are unfortunate side effects of this deification of a few, however. The indebtedness of the "pioneers" to their context is not appreciated. For example, Malan was very dependent on Balint and Balint's range of technique was far superior, yet Malan is the better known (Gustafson, 1981). The same is true for Mann, in relation to one of the greatest interviewers ever seen in Boston, Elvin Semrad (Semrad, Binstock, and White, 1966). Also, an emphasis on these "pioneers" gives too little recognition to newer contributors, such as Strupp (1981) and his colleagues (Binder, Strupp, and

Schacht, 1983; Strupp and Binder, 1984), Horowitz et al. (1984), Klerman et al. (1984), and Beck et al. (1979). There is little justice about such matters. Even history is fickle and self-interested.

7. Jung described very well the response of some patients to a doctor with a narrow scheme: "The more schematic the treatment is, the more resistance it — quite rightly — calls up in the patient, and the more the cure is jeopardized" (pp. 19–20, 1957). I am indebted to Craig Johnson, M.D., for this reference.

8. Even here there is hope, as described by Jack Prelutsky (1970), even for those who confuse the map ("cake") with the territory (cake):

> Uncle Bungle, now deceased,
> ate a cake of baker's yeast,
> then with an odd gleam in his eye
> consumed a large shoe-polish pie.
>
> His dinner done, it's sad to say,
> that Uncle Bungle passed away.
> Uncle Bungle, now deceased,
> still shines and rises in the east.

Incidentally, the drawing which accompanies the poem is worth looking up the book.

9. The situation in the field of family therapy is about the same as that in brief individual therapy. The "pioneers" are followed, with more or less intelligence. There too, progress depends upon appreciating what these pioneers actually *do*, what distinctions are critical to their thinking, what is the successful domain of their techniques. This work is farther underway for family therapy than for individual therapy. For example, see Karl Tomm's (1984a, b) exposition of the Milan technique.

11. *Malan: Duty and True Feeling*

1. Since my book is about contributions to technique, I will be unable to give Dr. Malan the honor he deserves for his overall contributions to the field of brief psychotherapy. Of the three areas necessary to the field — technique, selection, and follow-up — Malan has given least to technique, most to selection (1976, 1979) and follow-up (1980c; Malan, Heath, Bacal, and Balfour, 1975). In the latter two areas, he has given more than anyone. Also, he has been the best modern writer on the subject. His prose is bluff and vigorous, often using the meta-

phors of medicine in a convincing way. Yet the poignancy comes across as well. As I will describe later in this chapter, the power of Malan's vision comes from a "double description" (Bateson, 1979), both standing back and being close in. This vision has been extremely useful to Malan for solving the problems of selection and follow-up, and for writing well. We will see it is useful for technique, but to a lesser extent. The reader may refer to my history of the evolution of the Workshops on Brief Psychotherapy, from Balint to Malan, for a broader appreciation of Malan's contributions (Gustafson, 1981).

2. The therapist for the Zoologist is unknown. Malan wrote about the case as the leader of the research team. Nevertheless, his enthusiasm is unmistakable for the technique, which is very close to his own.

3. Notice the interpersonal interest in how the patient *triggers* his girlfriend's "apathy." This interest is quite crucial at several junctions in this treatment, but it has no place in the intrapsychic diagrams of Malan's theory.

4. The duty/true feeling distinction improves Malan's telling of the story of and by the Zoologist but it offers little way out of the depressive position which is in place, whether hidden or truly stated, rewarded or punished, rewarding or punishing. For a way out, see my case of the Daughter of Soap Opera later in this chapter. For a theoretical discussion of this problem and solution, see Chapters 15, 16, 17, and 18.

5. The usual diagram for Malan's presentations of technique has been the triangle. The "triangle of conflict" has corners of "defense," "anxiety," and "hidden feelings." The "triangle of person" has corners of the "other," the "transference," and the "parent" (1979, p. 80). The "triangle of conflict" is like Ezriel's triangle, of "required relationship," "avoided relationship," and "catastrophic relationship" (1976, p. 259). I am presenting Malan's triadic description as a double description, because I think the latter is closer to how it is used. The challenge to "defense" or "required relationship" is to be as deep as possible. These two are the powerful thrusts. The third eye is on "anxiety" or the "catastrophic relationship" so that "rapport" is not lost.

6. Notice that my presentation of Malan using Ezriel's terms is more interpersonal than Malan's own theoretical presentation of himself using the intrapsychic triangles.

7. Malan's despair and conversion to Davanloo's approach were stated by him in a chapter called "The Most Important Development in Psychotherapy Since the Discovery of the Unconscious" (1980a) as follows: "It needs to be stated categorically that in the early part of the century Freud unwittingly took a *wrong turning* which led to *disastrous consequences* for the future of psychotherapy (my italics). This was to react to increasing resistance with increasing passivity . . . " (p. 13). "The result of all the foregoing is that dynamic psychotherapists may be forgiven for be-

ing in a state of *bewildered despair*" (p. 15). Having described his dream that psychoanalysis might yet find a forceful and successful technique, having described how Davanloo is the answer to this dream, Malan concluded: "As the reader will see, I am thus stating as a sober truth that there has occurred a twentieth century miracle: the wish-fulfillment fantasy described above has come true" (p. 18). I will describe in Chapter 14 why I think Malan has had a midsummer night's dream.

8. "The result is that the patients with whom this type of (brief) therapy is attempted represent fewer than 10 percent of those referred to the Tavistock Clinic—and since by no means all such therapies are successful, patients who are actually suitable are even fewer" (Malan, 1980, p. 15). "What is the truth about the effectiveness of dynamic psychotherapy? More than 20 years of systematic follow-up work have convinced me of the following four-part answer: 1. On the whole, dynamic psychotherapy as usually practiced is ineffective. 2. On the other hand, in certain patients dynamic psychotherapy is extremely effective. 3. This effect occurs through the operation of certain factors, which can be identified and have been understood for decades. 4. But such patients represent a very small proportion of the general psychotherapeutic population" (1980b, p. 319).

9. "But really priority must be given to Alexander and French. Anyone who reads their case histories can see the clinical (not, of course, the statistical) evidence for the great majority of what has been written in the present work; to generalize, the use of all the basic psychoanalytical principles, especially interpretation of the transference and transference/parent link, in a radical technique of brief therapy leading to radical outcome" (1976, p. 351).

10. I have described before (1981) how Balint had the capability for the range of relationships represented by all the schools of psychiatry, whereas Malan reduced this potential to the psychoanalytic relationship.

11. The clearest and best venture of Malan towards an interpersonal paradigm occurs in his research on follow-ups, especially "Psychodynamic Changes in Untreated Neurotic Patients" (Malan et al., 1975). Here is a fine picture of how patients succeed or fail in making use of their environment, whether it is the therapeutic environment or the personal environment. This is very close to Winnicott's perspective on brief psycho-

therapy: the job is to make it possible for the patient to make use of the environment again.

12. Nothing I say here about the limitations of this idea of treatment should be construed as taking away from my appreciation of Malan as a very skillful therapist. I have seen this myself in visiting him in London and seeing some of his videotapes in 1982. I am grateful to Nancy Coalter-Lathrop, M.D., for bringing this possible misunderstanding to my attention.

13. Upon reading this text, the patient points out correctly that it was I, the doctor, who asked for her description of the hyperventilation. I get what I ask for. My tone may give the unfortunate impression that I deride the hysterical elaboration. Actually, I believe it has been useful and necessary, until she could get some help with what is obscured. The concept of "true feelings" tends to depreciate the hysterical elaboration. Nevertheless, the latter is felt very keenly by the patient. A positive connotation of the defense needs to be kept clearly in mind.

14. Malan's "Psychodynamic Changes in Untreated Neurotic Patients" (Malan et al., 1975) is a catalog of examples of the remarkable effectiveness of posing "ordinary solutions" to patients in first interviews. See especially the case of the Polish Refugee, but many of the others are equally fine. It appears that these moves, especially for patients who have already begun to take responsibility for their lives before the first interview, have a dynamic power of change which holds up for years. Malan himself was astonished, as he started out thinking he was studying "spontaneous change" of patients who were denied psychotherapy. Rather, the single interviews for some patients were as powerful as most brief psychotherapy, perhaps even most long-term therapy.

15. I hope the reader understands that the job has only begun with the trial therapy which is reported here. Such a patient is not yet fully understood, not by any means. She is very likely to continue like her mother; to act as if her learning has returned to zero, until she is fully appreciated about why she has to stay the same. See Chapter 18.

16. See Chapter 15 on Bateson, Chapter 17 on Maturana, Chapters 18 and 23 for more discussion of mapping and logical levels.

12. *Mann: Sincere Trying and Pain*

1. Mann has a useful discussion of a subtle problem of selection with hysterical patients, which I have not seen elsewhere. "They begin therapy, but instead of attending to the central issue, they concentrate on the qualities of the therapist, i.e., his capacity to listen, to care, and to understand" (1982, p. 56). They proceed to devalue the therapist for not "understanding," and the therapy ends in failure (pp. 56–58).

2. In other words Mann can operate with a theory of separation-individuation which attends to the individuating young person while neglecting the actual pull of the young person's family. I am indebted to Dr. Steven Stern for this clarification.

3. Rolvaag's novel, *Giants of the Earth* (1929), is one story of this genre.

4. In reading this text, the patient recalls "feeling slowed down and not liking it." My adjustment being wrong, I sped up again.

5. In reading this text, the patient recalls feeling "worked on," like "something was up." "The tone was different" in these last several pages. Although I actually did admire his "moron" stance and its double meaning, and I was glad to join such a club myself, I think he found this hard to believe. Therefore, it was a strain on his credulity.

6. We see an advantage of the two- to three-hour trial therapy over the single hour of Mann. The hopefulness of the first hour will be followed in the second by an attempt of the patient to destroy this learning. This young man made his attempt by tempting me to put myself above him. Thus, we see in the trial therapy of two to three hours what Mann sees in his first and twelfth hours. See Chapter 20 for further discussion of our method. I only want to note here that the resident who takes up the case has to be duly warned by the close of the trial therapy. He or she will be put to a similar test.

7. Speaking of disappearing in the great man, there is a second author of *A Casebook in Time-Limited Psychotherapy* (1982), Robert Goldman. However, the book is mostly written in the first person, as if James Mann were writing or speaking, so it is difficult to tell where Goldman came in.

13. *Sifneos: Oedipal Lessons*

1. Notice the grammar! Did you notice? Sifneos is all comments and questions (1979, p. 111). For discussions of the limits of this grammar, see Chapter 10 on Havens and Havens' own articles, especially 1978a, 1978c, 1979, 1980, 1984a.
2. For Sifneos, the "unconscious" speaks like a book. Once he has the "truth" he has no misgivings about reiteration (1979, p. 124). His student, Davanloo, gets the truth directly from the unconscious through the eyes and ears. Their "findings" are constrained, however, by the language distinctions that are possible in their "receivers," by the "punctuation" of the situation as child behavior/adult behavior. Sifneos and Davanloo teach the "punctuation" of child activity versus adult activity, which is a kind of second-order learning, not a first-order "reinforcement" of adult against child behavior (Bateson, 1972b).
3. The central distinction for Sifneos is regressive behavior versus adult behavior. For example, fondling under the table is regressive (1979, p. 138), while facing up is adult (1979, p. 133). The first gets pounded, the latter applauded. But the "double description" here (Bateson, 1979), the eye for "regression," the eye for "being a man" (woman) is used incompletely, as if the first were always negative, the second positive, as with Alexander and French. A more imaginative use of this "double description" is to read it backwards as well as forwards. Sometimes "regression" is positive, for "being a man" or "being a wom-

an" could lead to disastrous activities in an individual with foolish notions about the latter, like Don Quixote. Why go forward, to get killed? Better to hyperventilate, and pretend to be incompetent. I used this kind of "double description" to comprehend the Daughter of Soap Opera in Chapter 11 (Malan). The Milan team is the most original along these lines, in its "positive connotation" of regression by the family (Chapter 16). There is a back and forth between appreciating regression and appreciating that the family is speeding ahead with ordinary development. This is a full use of the "double description" inherent in the distinction which is central to Sifneos.

4. This insistence on *specific* descriptions was important earlier in the history of psychotherapy. Read Freud's description of what he demanded from Lucy and Katherina (Breuer and Freud, 1895), or read back in Chapter 2 in this book for my description of Freud's method. But it was forgotten for 60 years. Freud just did it, emphasizing other interests of his own, so getting the patient to be "specific" was not posed as central to technique. Therefore, it was forgotten. Sifneos saw it as critical. This was the modern discovery.
5. Many readers may be surprised to see that much of Davanloo's technique is here in Sifneos. Well, Sifneos was Davanloo's teacher.
6. Notice the grammer of *this* interview! It is all commands and questions, like Sifneos. See Footnote 1.

14. *Davanloo: Getting Past the Patient's Wall*

1. The most famous literary version of breaking through walls is John Donne's sonnet, wherein the oppressed but passive individual shows a great stake in being reached. I am indebted to William Wilson, M.D., for recalling this poem to my attention in connection with Davanloo's method:

Batter my heart, three-personed God, for you
As yet but knock, breathe, shine, and seek to mend;
That I may rise and stand, o'erthrow me and bend
Your force to break, blow, burn, and make me new.

I, like an usurped town to another due,
Labour to admit you, but O, to no end.
Reason, your viceroy in me, me should defend,
But is captived and proves weak or untrue.
Yet dearly I love you and would be loved fain,
But am betrothed unto your enemy.
Divorce me, untie, or break that knot again,
Take me to you, imprison me, for I,
Except you enthrall me, never shall be free,
Nor ever chaste except you ravish me
(Gardner, 1972)

If a doctor wants to take towns like this one, he had better begin by finding some help from within the town, some weakness in the walls where the subject wants to be found out.

2. Reich was slowed by his vehicle of conversation with the patient, the classical method of free association. Davanloo will make a direct focal inquiry into a specific occasion for which the patient seeks relief. Reich was willing to take weeks and months to describe and confront the patient's "constant attitude." Davanloo will set out to do this in one long session of two or three hours. Reich would make a steady series of consistent descriptions of the patient's constant attitude, not allowing himself to be distracted to any other object of analysis. Davanloo will not only describe the patient's constant attitude, but also frame the attitude as destructive behavior in the way of what is objectively needed. Reich gave the patient time to see what he was doing, to recover from each assault upon his "attitude," while Davanloo will exhaust the patient's defenses, until the breakthrough occurs. Both, however, utilize the same metaphor for the patient's plight and their own activity: the need to break through the patient's wall.

3. T. S. Eliot alludes to this passive hopefulness in "The Wasteland" many times, but especially:

. . . I have heard the key
Turn in the door once and turn once only
We think of the key, each in his prison
Thinking of the key, each confirms a prison
Only at nightfall, aethereal rumours
Revive for a moment a broken Coriolanus.
(1930, lines 412–417)

Robin Skynner and John Cleese (1983, pp. 214–218) have a fine description of less desperate but passive individuals who defeat others while hoping to be confronted by them. Mostly they are not confronted, because the helpers try to be patient. This is a common error, for example, with children with so-called "learning difficulty." Passivity is a challenging problem. For an opposite approach, see Erickson's use of the reflexive question in Haley, 1973, p. 247.

4. Davanloo is known for referring to himself as "the relentless healer." For several years he has referred to a book in preparation by that name, which will be definitive. For another description of Davanloo's method which is consistent with this chapter see Rosenberg (in press).

5. For an amusing portrait of the related types who adopt "The God Complex" see Ernest Jones (1923).

6. For a description of the pilgrimage of myself and a group of colleagues to Montreal, see Gustafson and Dichter (1983a). We were very impressed by four or five videotapes of different trial therapy sessions, but the one brief therapy by Davanloo, from which he showed excerpts from beginning to end, was very weak. Malan and most of the audience seemed to think the emperor was wearing amazing clothes, and Davanloo himself strode to the front of the hall on many occasions to explain everything at great length, but I and my colleagues could not see these clothes. The reader may refer to our description, especially footnote 3, p. 626 (Gustafson and Dichter, 1983a).

7. The best description of empathic extensions is by Havens (1978b, 1979).

INTRODUCTION / *The Systemic Perspective*

1. Yes, I am saying that "admitting the existence of God (Dante) is analogous to admitting a higher logical order — both get you out of circular destruction." Yes, this is "a way of passing through the eye of the "needle" (Michael Moran, personal communication).

2. A dramatic example from the Milan team is the case of the "Casanti" family (Selvini Palazzoli, Boscolo, Cecchin, and Prata, 1977), where a "cure" of the anorexic daughter left the family game as it was, and a serious suicide attempt followed the cure.

3. The positive connotation would see the dis-

covery of a powerful move in an *irresistible* game, but also the *sacrifice* of the players to the continuation of the game. My favorite example from literature of this positive connotation of the players in a vicious game is by Borges, "The Lottery in Babylon" (1962).

4. See Selvini Palazzoli (1984) for a devastating discussion of the difference between "coevolution" (of a family) and the very temporary "ensemble" of the family with the family therapy team.

5. In her letter to me of June 18, 1985 concerning this Introduction to the Systemic

Perspective, Dr. Selvini Palazzoli offered two clarifications which are very important. The family may "disconfirm" the team by its sudden "return to zero" learning, or the individual patient may do the same to the individual therapist. What is essential to understand is that this is *not* a dyadic interaction. The team or individual therapist is disconfirmed to maintain certain relations with a third party, such as the extended family. The patient or family baffles the individual therapist or team that can only see the disqualification as aimed strictly at themselves. We will not be baffled if we see the domain or audience for which our disconfirmation is necessary. By definition, a disqualification of a second party for the benefit of relations with a third party is a disconfirmation (Ricci and Palazzoli, 1984). Once this definition is clear, Dr. Selvini Palazzoli's point about the ending moves of the *team* being "interruptions," not "disconfirmations," should be self-evident. Her second clarification to me was to say that she stopped working with Boscolo and Cecchin in 1980, that she and Giuliana Prata began a completely different method of working and program of

research with families presenting psychotic members, and that she formed a new team in 1983. She prefers not to call the article of Boscolo and Cecchin (1982) the work of the Milan team. I shall refer to them henceforth as plural, the Milan teams.

6. Is there a "right" time or place to "revert" to "instruction" (Michael Moran, personal communication)? I would say therapists can get away with being helpful via "instructive interaction," as has happened so often using the schemes which involve interpersonal interviewing, analysis of character, or psychoanalysis. All instruct. All imply a right way versus a wrong way, a healthy way versus a pathological way. My objection to "instructive interaction" is not that it may not be helpful, but that it is less likely to see the "object" of its instruction. Hence it works more in the dark.

7. Fanon recognized this problem in *Black Skins, White Masks* (1967) and elsewhere. I hope I do not alarm the reader by such references. I mean only to say that "others" are difficult to see. I do not mean to imply a political program. Orwell discusses this problem of seeing in "The Politics of the English Language" (1946b).

15. *Bateson and the Inferno*

1. The most explicit, extended attempt at a discussion of neurotic problems by Bateson which I have found is "Communication Theories in Relation to the Etiology of the Neuroses" (1966). This essay seems to me like a preliminary sketch for a painting which was never commissioned. I have worked from this sketch for building this chapter. Several of Bateson's essays on pathological relationship, namely schizophrenia and alcoholism, are in *Steps Toward An Ecology of Mind* (1972a), while the list of "The Published Works of Gregory Bateson" at the end of that book may contain some other finds besides this essay.

2. I have only attempted to map Bateson's thinking onto the problems of neurotic patients. I have not attempted to represent his thinking in general. After all, he did that very well himself in *Mind and Nature* (1979), which pulls together his thinking on living systems, the "pattern which connects" them, the different kinds of "double description," the "great stochastic processes," and so forth. I felt tempted to write an entire book about Bateson, but he

seems to have written that book himself, which will stand beautifully on its own. It is very difficult, I think, but extremely deep. He knew how to set up his own enduring pattern. He spent his life studying how living systems do exactly that, among other things. I thought I could present Bateson to my own readers by following one of Bateson's principles. A paraphrase is only a "single description," which gives little more than itself and sometimes less. A mapping of Bateson onto the *Inferno* gives a "double description" which may yield some depth of field, as in binocular vision. In carrying forward this "double description" of neurotic worlds, I have used many of Bateson's most vivid ideas just in passing, such as "stories," "arrays," "calibration" and "feedback," "digital" and "analogic" coding, "the ensemble with mental characteristics," "spatial" and "temporal" context shaping, and so forth. I will return to some of these ideas in Chapter 18.

3. When I presented some of this chapter in the "Oxford Conversations" in July of 1985, Cecchin and Boscolo proposed an

interesting question for which Maturana proposed an interesting answer. Cecchin and Boscolo suggested that there is something quite powerful about the apparent need of the dog and the porpoise to be "right." Maturana agreed. This feeling of "rightness" with others is the experience of relations necessary to coordination or structural coupling, the hook in us which allows us or drives us to some logical jumps. My wife, Ruth Gustafson, had an interesting commentary on this discussion afterwards, when she noted that the search for "rightness" in the dolphin described by Bateson, which led to "eight conspicuous pieces of behavior of which four were new and never before observed in this species of animal," could have been a disaster for this dolphin. The porpoise might have become a genius because of her structural drift with the experimenters, but failed thereafter to conserve the necessary relations with her fellow dolphins and become ostracized and died of a broken heart. What if all elephants put in captivity and trained in the circus learned to be geniuses also? Since they reproduce in captivity at a rate less than their death rate, they would perish like intellectuals who don't marry or cannot carry a pregnancy. I could reply that they might propagate by publishing, but everyone knows how unlikely this propagation is likely to be. All I mean to say here is making logical jumps is a mixed blessing, if one is not mindful of the "unintended consequences." After all, a genius could conserve the "necessary relations" and feel "right," or she could be "right" like Dr. Posip for her environment and go privately nuts. Finally, she might "learn about the context for new learning" of the logical jump and confine her displays of genius to visits with the experimenters (Bateson's Learning III). Learning III could be necessary for surviving with Learning II.

4. The idea of representing oneself as an animal shows up over and over again in Freud and Reich, where patients organize their world as if they were a horse, a rat, or even a fish. In my own practice, I have the "dog" I mentioned, a "rabbit," and a "bullfrog," perhaps others if I thought about it more. This totemic representation is of theoretical importance, I think, which I will return to in Chapter 18, concerning these higher mammalian games.

A very fine review of Geschwind's work on the brain by Rosenfield (1985) suggests a parsimonious way to describe the differ-

ence between most mammals and man the mammal, between a dog and human being acting like a "dog." Mammals have "association areas" for each of the senses, such for visual, auditory and tactile sensations, which directly trigger the characteristically mammalian emotional patterns of the limbic system. Human beings also have such triggering possibilities, which are seen in emergency or high stimulation situations, but by and large human beings send their responses from the "association areas" to "association of association" areas, where "crossmodal" comparison of different sensory possibilities allows us to become observers of our own sensations and of our own inclinations without being forced to act upon them. Thus we have the Learning I capabilities and sensations and inclinations of mammals, but we also have Learning II and Learning III capabilities for classifying our capabilities and sensations and inclinations and for classifying our classifications. Thus we are mammals, and we are observers of ourselves as mammals, and we are observers of ourselves being observers of ourselves as mammals.

5. When we began our team we were more than a little confused about the difference between the experiential family therapy (of Whitaker or Skynner) and the Milan method of interviewing. Hence this peculiar interview. We got interesting findings, but it was difficult to keep our bearings.

6. Necessarily so. It would have been impossible for him to jump suddenly into a different way of showing love. If he had become suddenly capable and unwilling to be humiliated by his family, because of experiences in the context I set for him, he would have rejected his family, who need him for the family game. They would have assaulted him far worse, and he would have been out a family. Well, then he could have been capable and self-respecting elsewhere? No way. He had so little experience at being loved in that way. Most of his talent had been given to studying love along the family lines. He would have been clumsy and gotten hurt far too much.

I hope it is evident why he is slowly ascending in the best possible way. He appears to offer moves in the same class as always, of self-torture, which keeps him fitting into his family. He still needs them very much. But since the class of self-torture is subordinate to the class of showing love, he also shows them love by being capable. He shows love both ways. The latter way gives him more and more experience which makes it possible to get along with people outside his family. When you have to keep a foot in two worlds, you have to move slowly. My colleague, Joe Kepecs, M.D., put this very succinctly: "He advances under cover of darkness" (personal communication).

7. Perhaps this needs to be added. If animals can recognize shifts of context, as from "play" to "threat," they are also subject to confusions of context which make them ill (1979, p. 125).

8. Bateson seemed to want his last word to be against this vulgarization, which might also be called an attempt to reduce matters. Indeed the last chapter of *Mind and Nature*, called "So What?" is presented as a daughter asking that question over and over of her father, in one way or another. The father evidently wanted to take his stand against the cruel reductions of the future. Who can be more cruel than children, who go on as they like in their own way? Bateson did not have much faith in the university holding onto the "pattern which connects," in the face of vulgarization. See his Appendix: "Time is Out of Joint."

9. For another warning, see pp. 125–126 in *Mind and Nature* where Bateson discusses the terror in getting outside of "single descriptions." "Double descriptions" give too much depth of field on the universe, on our own paltry finitude in such a field. Few can stand it, Bateson thought. My friend Robin Skynner (personal communication,

May 16, 1985) suggests it is only possible for *moments*, like juggling, keeping a view of oneself and others both up in the air at the same time. Gravity intervenes. The personal difficulty then comes *both* ways: in tolerating these terrifying depths of field; in tolerating the cruel, inevitable return of gravity, which destroys the momentary vision. One has to learn to see, and learn to fall or be brought down, easily. This is a rough business. We will see in the next chapter concerning the Milan team that various epic heroes are invoked for this systemic journey. For me, Odysseus is most apt.

10. If I "warn the reader too darkly of the danger that we cannot explore these labyrinths without unless we stumble around in the labyrinth within" (Michael Moran, M.D., personal communication), then I am gladly corrected. Bateson's *Mind and Nature* (1979) is full of light, with some dark allusions in the beginning and in the end. If "we rhyme with what we perceive" (Michael Moran, M.D., personal communication), there is hope when we perceive the creation. As Hopkins wrote:

And for all this, nature is never spent;
There lives the dearest freshness deep
    down things
And though the last lights off the black
    West went
Oh morning, at the brown brink eastward,
    springs— . . .
                    (Gardner, 1972, p. 786)

I return to this theme in chapter 24.

16. *The Milan Teams: From Farce to Music*

1. Why do I present a simulated family as opposed to an actual family seen by one of the Milan teams? For several reasons: One is that I was present. I report better what I saw happen. Two is that there are too few extant reports of interviews by the Milan teams. I want to add a new interview. Three is that I thought the job by Cecchin and Boscolo with this case of simulation was first-class. Four is that the simulation shows the extremely rapid "structural coupling" which occurs between strangers to bring about such a profound story, triggering elaborations from one another which are beautifully coordinated. This is evidence for the power of systemic circuits. Evidently, Norman Mailer came to a similar con-

clusion, which he describes in his introduction to his film script, "Maidstone." Actors do better being given a very loose plot/situation and roles than they do playing "themselves" (Michael Moran, personal communication). The latter is tightly coordinated. The former obliges the actors to discover a coordination, which is more exciting. The Milan method is like acting, in that people are invited to discover new coordination.

2. For description of the "circular questioning" which leads from one family member to the others, see Selvini Palazzoli et al. (1980b) and Tomm (1984a,b). Family members are invited to talk about what they see going on between other family members,

to "gossip in the presence." This is enjoyable, disarming, and revealing, as they will trip over large unmentionable subjects inadvertently, which will show in prominent, nonverbal, analogic behavior. Such tripping up also shows the rules about what can be discussed, what cannot, how the family classifies behavior and experience, allowing some, disallowing others. For an extremely powerful example of this, see Penn (1982). It is difficult to follow, however, since the crucial events observed in the questioning were analogic subgrouping.

3. Here Cecchin uses the "little words of English," the "inner voice — the language within a language" of English (Barnett, 1962) with considerable power. According to Barnett (p. 34), there are about "850 volatile, versatile words that can say just about anything" in English, which are combined in endless complexity, making for the "masked complexity" of English. Somehow these suit this remarkable combination of complication and simplicity which runs through the work of the Milan teams. This is its vocabulary, which runs very deep.

4. Nothing I say here should be construed as a suggestion that musical or literary form or illusion is worthwhile in itself in therapeutic situations. As Selvini Palazzoli (1984) says so forcefully, such "higher" or "virtuous" pretension is farcical, only inviting its opposite absurd claim, that only solving problems counts. Psychoanalysis has indulged itself with this idea of "higher" and "virtuous" (literary, musical, etc.), therapy about as far as it is possible, but new occasions for this farce are continually being reinvented. It seems a favorite one for us. For example, "systemic" therapy may claim to be higher and more aesthetic. I am saying, with the Milan teams, I think, that musical and literary form is useful or foolish, depending on the messages it can carry. That's all. Either it's practical, or forget it.

5. For a devastating, powerful case of equality bringing about unequal effects on the family members, see Selvini Palazzoli (1985). When you level out a teeter-totter, those sitting at the extremes rise a great deal or fall a great deal. Those nearer the center of advantages and disadvantages move through less of the change.

6. I have not cited chapter and verse for these references to Sullivan and Havens that follow, all of which can be found in Chapter 6.

7. There is a fine description of Sullivan the bird-dog by Mary White (1952): "One patient described this as follows: 'I would suddenly become aware of a change in him, like the alertness of a pointer who has spotted a bird. It was a certain wave of thoughtful, kindly alertness, totally nonverbal. That knowledge of his already being where I didn't know where I was going, made it possible for me successfully to go through a number of rough spots'" (p. 132).

8. Walter Jackson Bate (1975) describes a similar capacity to Sullivan's in Samuel Johnson: "His honesty to human experience cuts through the 'cant', the loose talk and pretense, with which all of us get seduced into needlessly complicating life for both ourselves and other people" (p. 4).

9. This also means a difference in tone, not the irony of Sullivan saying, "It takes a great deal of competence to entertain as complex a mental disorder as you do," or "You have copied your mother's paranoid psychosis with some improvements on it." (White, 1952, p. 132). *Irony* can indeed be helpful, but *appreciation* by the Milan team has a different intonation and slant. I find myself sliding back and forth between the two intonations, if I am not careful, between an interpersonal and systemic perspective and attitude.

   This brings up a very substantial theoretical problem which I will address more fully in Chapter 18. What I am talking about here as the *appreciation* of "the necessary complications" has been recognized by all the previous perspectives. In psychoanalysis, this is seen as "severity" of the superego. If not reckoned with, improvements lead backwards, to "negative therapeutic reactions." I do not see that Reich admitted this problem until he had battered against the collective superego of psychoanalysis and of communism through the 1920s. He seemed to act as if he did not recognize the enormous power of the collective, conservative apparatus he was up against. Sullivan seemed to want to think that complications of "security operations" can be cleared, must be cleared, if help is successful. Havens has recently introduced much more of the necessary appreciation of the complications introduced by the "introjects" (see Chapter 10). In this way, Havens comes as close to the Milan school of thinking as any have before. See especially Havens' paper on counterintrojection (1984a). All of this is just introduction to what is coming later. A simple way of summarizing this is as follows. Freud recognized the individual Uber-ich (superego) as built upon shared introjection of the patriarch. The work of the Milan teams suggests that the logical structure of the Uber-ich and the operations of teamwork to build it in one another have been greatly underestimated. Shared introjection is pale compared to what we actually do together. When what we do together is appreciated, then brief therapy is much altered.

10. I say to the team of five or more residents in the Brief Therapy Clinic: "Do not think we have outnumbered this poor 18-year-old who has come to be interviewed by us. He or she is only a scout for an army of five generations — *we* are the ones outnumbered!"

11. Many, if not most, therapists would agree with Haley and Watzlawick, or Robin Skynner, that "problems" can be helped, without tampering with the system in which they are set. Even divorcing them may be indicated. The MRI group and David Malan use the same metaphor of the automobile. It may go wrong with needing the carburetor reset. Why go over the entire automobile? I believe they are right that therapists may be very helpful fixing carburetors, crank shafts, steering or what have you No doubt. The difficulty is that such tampering is apt to be *in the dark* about the implications for other elements in the system, for whom it could be worse *or* better. To utilize Bateson's idea of logical types, some moves by patients can be substituted without threatening the *class* of moves required to sustain, for example, a particular marriage. Some new moves, improvements in a certain respect, are disasters for maintaining the necessary class of moves. Therefore, fixing is quite an uncertain business. The Milan teams would be curious about why the family or individual was not repairing itself. The difficulty fixing its own defect implies a higher order systemic problem. As Maturana would put the matter, living systems are "autopoetic," not automobiles! They continually reproduce themselves.

12. My friend, Professor Yi-Fu Tuan, describes the attraction of outsiders in many cultures, where the stranger and the foreigner and the forest (LL *foranus*; forest) are more desirable, fascinating, or even saving. Winnicott (see Chapter 7) describes relying on this "very great confidence which children can show in myself . . . on these special

occasions (of first interviews), special occasions which made me use the word sacred. Either the sacred moment is used or it is wasted. If it is wasted, the child's belief in being understood is shattered. If on the other hand it is used, then the child's belief in being helped is strengthened. There will be those cases in which deep work is done in the special circumstances of the first interview (or interviews) and the resulting changes in the child can be made use of by parents and those who are responsible in the immediate social setting, so that whereas a child was caught up in a knot in regard to the emotional development, the interview has resulted in a loosening of the knot and a forward movement in the developmental process" (1971b, pp. 4–5). I believe the Milan first interviews also have this quality of the "special occasion" which depends on the sacred quality that strangers may have. Elsewhere, Winnicott called this "meeting the challenge of the case" (unpublished memorandum from Winnicott of September 1965, for his seminar on "Therapeutic Consultation," obtained from Robin Skynner). Professor Tuan points out that depending on strangers in a profound way is built into our complex culture: "In complex societies, A is helped by X, Y, Z — total strangers (e.g. fireman, hospital orderlies, etc.). A pays, of course, but what A pays is minute, compared with what he receives. What A receives is the cumulated labor and skill of strangers, most of whom are dead" (Yi-Fu Tuan, lecture, University of Wisconsin, spring 1985, "A World of Strangers: An Ideology"). All of this is a long way of saying that the "raw" (Levi-Strauss, 1964) has great potential and interest, as well as threat. The trick is to inspire the first rather than the second, the helpful forest rather than the dangerous forest of strangers.

13. Fred Wamboldt, M.D., previously a colleague on our "Milan" family team here at Wisconsin and now an Assistant Professor in the Center for Family Research at George Washington University Medical Center, puts a different emphasis on the comparison between the Milan and other systemic methods as follows in his letter to me of August 21, 1985 about this chapter: " . . . The family's 'farce' has extreme importance but only by its being enacted in a larger context. This premise of course is shared by a number of differing therapists. The Italians are in a smaller class of ther-

apists who not only look for meaning in 'farces' but who are never disrespectful towards the 'farce.' One of their most consistent communications to the family is that in their view the family is equal; no one is more to blame for the 'farce.' Still how can they get away with this radical departure from more linear traditional morality, let alone good old talion law? . . . I think they succeed because they don't thrust a new meaning, a new morality on the family. They simply understand the need for what currently is (appears to be) in the family and take a Kierkegaardian 'leap into faith' that the family can provide their own new meaning/morality over time. Their positive connotation has backbone. . . . So the midphase (as well as the final message) as I see it has two crucial moves: One, keeping the blame from coming to rest via circular questioning/logic; and two, an almost religious restraint fostered through an inquiry into communication of how the present problem has meaning in terms of family loyalty." Such discussions

with Dr. Wamboldt, with Karl Tomm, and with Cecchin have helped me shape this chapter.

14. The same is also true for me in consulting to small work groups, such as Balint Groups for medical doctors. I have struggled for 15 years through many different theoretical angles on small working groups with histories with my colleague Lowell Cooper. A series of our papers in *Human Relations* culminates in 1981 (Gustafson et al.). We have been stuck since then with various technical problems which defied solution, until recently, when Bateson's theory of logical types and the Milan systemic inquiry have been discovered to be enormously helpful in this small group domain as well (Cooper and Gustafson, in preparation). What I am saying is that the Milan systemic method suits me very well, as I can cross over from individual to family to small working group problems readily and successfully. Perhaps the other systemic methods allow this as well, but I haven't seen how.

17. Maturana: The Otherness of Others

1. Naturally, the allowance extends to family, friends, colleagues, etc. As Bateson described (1958) concerning Frieda Fromm-Reichmann, you end up very much on your own, when you adopt this perspective. You *are* anyway, but you might not want to see it is so.

2. See Main (1957) for a description of "pharmacological traffic" to shore up nursing staff going under with difficult patients. The patients must be weaker, or weakened, to keep the staff from sinking altogether. I think this is the necessary virtue of "pharmacologic psychiatry," the more exact name for so-called "biological psychiatry."

3. Schumacher is eloquent as usual about this "decapitation" of higher order levels in modern "reductionist" thinking: "From the point of view of philosophical mapmaking, this meant a very great impoverishment: entire regions of human interest, which had engaged the most intense efforts of earlier generations, simply ceased to appear on the maps. But there was an even more significant withdrawal and impoverishment: While traditional wisdom had always presented the world as a three-dimensional structure (as symbolized by the cross),

where it was not only meaningful but essential to distinguish always and everywhere between 'higher' and 'lower' things and Levels of Being, the new thinking strove with determination, not to say fanaticism, to get rid of the *vertical dimension*." (1977, pp. 10–11) And: "Self-awareness is the rarest power of all, precious and vulnerable to the highest degree, the supreme and generally fleeting achievement of a person, present one moment and all too easily gone the next. The study of this factor *z* has in all ages—except the present—been the primary concern of mankind." (p. 23)

4. Parsimony is often reduced in social science to reductionism $(m - z - y - x)$. This is a very debilitating confusion.

5. Maturana chooses to say that "autopoiesis" is the organization of living systems, such as cells and collections of cells which become organized as plants or animals. Furthermore, consciousness and self-awareness are also part of self-production or "autopoiesis," of the individual animal, as I have just described. However, Maturana chooses not to describe *social* organization as "autopoietic," even though it too seems to have a kind of recursive, circular organization, described so well by the Milan teams

and other writers. Maturana (1985) chooses *not* to call this "autopoiesis" because he sees social organization of many different animals as having many different properties from the individual animal's organization of its cells. The social body and the individual body are not strictly analogous.

6. As Maturana says, his theory is a "cosmology" which is "complete," closing upon itself. Its success as a map depends upon what you can map onto its descriptions (Maturana and Varela, 1980, p. xviii).

7. Bateson spelled this out previously in *Mind and Nature* (p. 126, 1979). For a fine discussion of the relationship between Bateson's thinking and Maturana's thinking, see Dell (1985).

8. This came through to me most urgently, of late, from the movie, "The Killing Fields," where "instruction" by the Khmer Rouge is terrifying. A fine local description of the same from our side is to be found in "Beneath the Roof" (Bradley, 1985), which describes the difference in view of the roofs of Saigon from U.S. Army helicopters and from under such roofs with a Vietnamese family.

9. See Varela (1979) for a description of the normal science of the "computer" applied to both mind and body and of what has been obscured by this thinking.

10. See Selvini Palazzoli (1985, p. 31) for a fine discussion of the difference between inching and flying forward: " . . . we move forward more quickly when attracted by desire than when pushed by guilt. In other words, Nina and her father, spurred on by the wish to live, would have moved more briskly than Aldo and his mother, fueled by regrets alone."

11. This is oversimplified. I will offer descriptions at levels to which I have no direct access — what the patient is doing, what the doctor is doing describing the patient — but I stay clear as I can that I have no direct access to these levels of description. The level I must *retain* is my description of the team's relation to the presenting doctor, since we may very well need this level to comprehend the game, which has contradictions at three or four logical levels. For a more comprehensive description of this method and for an example of a supervision needing four logical levels, see Chapter 23. It is essential that we not collapse the potential levels of the group's capacity, for we then lose our ability to read many family games.

12. The reader might want to ask what became of this patient and this doctor. Indeed, they began moving briskly again after this supervision. I hope the reader may have a glimmer by now of the solution to the paradox that an individual is a perfectly *closed* autopoietic organization, yet the individual may *change*. How is this possible? It is simply because there are many possible structural solutions which may conserve the "same organization." Other individuals or circumstances may then trigger a different structural drift in the individual in question from among his or her repertoire of structures. The paradox is more complicated when you consider that there are several possible levels of organization, based on the several possible recursions of consciousness and self-awareness. The "organization" of an individual *stays the same* at several different levels of organization or recursion. As I have argued in Chapter 15 on Bateson and will argue again in Chapter 18, this set of logical levels introduces *degrees of freedom* at each *level* of organization which must be held the same, since *many* moves or structures will satisfy the class of moves or structures which must be held constant at each level of organization. The more logical levels, the more possible degrees of freedom.

13. The patient deserves the last word. He points out that etymology of the Latin for instruction, namely *instruo*, means "to erect, build up; (military) to marshal, array, equip, provide, prepare; (figurative) teach, train." This constructional-military-pedagogic practice was quite successful for many centuries of the Roman Empire. Indeed, it has been an extremely successful coordination of coordination of conduct for the power elites. This ought to be admitted. I do not wish to be misunderstood. It is indeed possible to get "instruction" in building colliseums and Roman roads, in constructing speeches according to the best rhetoric or thoughts according to the correct Stoic philosophy. I may watch my teacher and try to discover similar structural possibilities in myself. "Structural coupling" as a circular interaction between us may elicit a structure in me which is very similar to the structure in him. Instruction may be *very* effective for those who want to duplicate their teachers. My argument concerns what is lost in such an interaction: namely, what is *different* about the student or patient from the teacher.

Our patient also points out that *The Little Prince* (Saint-Exupery, 1943) is a nice parallel to The Queen's Croquet Ground. The child sees the elephant swallowed by the boa constrictor, but the adult sees only the external outline of a hat. Such an adult is very much like the Queen who only sees compliance and no compliance. All else is invisible to her.

Finally, I would append the patient's astute observation posed in the form of a question: "Would you say that 'instructive interaction' can also describe the way some individuals communicate with *themselves*?" Indeed.

18. *How to Stay the Same*

1. My proposal concerning stories as objects of scientific interest reinvites a relationship between the humanities and psychiatry which was severed when psychoanalysis was replaced by objective-descriptive psychiatry in the leadership of American psychiatry. I realize that loose and dogmatic interpretation contributed to this downfall. A reduction of stories to the recursion of sexual themes was extremely presumptuous. This only invited other interpreters to see stories of archetypal gods, still others to see stories of superiority and inferiority, and so forth, and so forth. The Tower of Babel invited its own destruction. I think we brook less danger in allowing the humanities to be of help to us in psychiatry if we do not attempt a conquest of the subject, if we do not attempt to reduce the tradition of Western literature to our few ideas. (Jones, 1967) This tradition is much greater than psychiatry.

2. Surely this reckoning will always be approximation, since any method is tied to a host of structures which influence its influence: the nature of the patient cohort to whom it is applied, the quality of the therapist cohort who attempt to use the method, the economic prospects of both the patients and the therapists, and so forth and so forth. All tests of clinical methods are pulled and twisted by all the neighboring relations. All are experiments in the context of a shifting local ecology. Malan (1963) notes this well in his first follow-up study of brief therapy at the Tavistock Clinic (Gustafson, 1981, p. 92). He describes the study as being an experiment in nature in which two populations were brought together—analysts who wanted to make analytic interpretations, and chronic neurotic patients who were willing to listen to them. The study concerns the drift of such a "structural coupling" (Maturana, 1985).

3. A remarkable passage by Jung (1917, pp. 132–135) anticipates the difficulty that many patients will have with accepting the closure of the body. For many, this is no help. They become mired in the findings. A different appreciation of a different kind of closure will be necessary to them. In Jung's example, a woman lost in transference love began to bring dreams of being swayed by a nature god. Appreciation of this "transpersonal control-point" allowed her to grow out of the stuck relationship with Jung as a "pointless personal tie." If it were only a single example from the enormous class of the manifestations of the deity, then it need not be so compelling. The patient could hold onto the god, rather than to Jung. This kind of thinking by Jung anticipates the power which will be derived from other possibilities for decentering the therapist's and the patient's perspective on necessary closure: namely, the necessity for conserving a "constant attitude," or an interpersonal "security," or finally "the family."

Jung poses another possibility which I give little further discussion, namely the necessity for conserving the deity. In my discussion of Davanloo (Chapter 14), I do relate Davanloo's activities to a discussion by William James of the activities involved in religious conversion. This line for decentering is extremely powerful, as we see from the popularity of evangelical religion. I do not neglect it because I think it of minor importance. When I worked in the Indian Health Service in Montana and Wyoming, I found it was the most important therapeutic idea of all (Gustafson, 1975). The reader may refer back to Chapter 14 for a discussion of my misgivings.

4. Sullivan's idea that the patient operates on the *feelings* of security, not upon some objective map of actual prospects for security, anticipates Maturana's idea that *all* living systems operate in this closed way from internal computations. We operate like pi-

lots looking at their instruments in a fog (Maturana, 1978). Our job as therapists, therefore, is to appreciate how the patient's instruments are constructed. They are perfectly closed systems.

5. I am grateful to Myron Sharaf, Ph.D., for this sentence from Weil. (Auden and Kronenberger, 1962, p. 91)

6. What, then, if we allow that patients are not fortified towns awaiting assault and deliverance? If such towns only offer Don Quixote years of dedicated adventures? Not to mention the years of diversion for the spectators. Interpersonal closure is most impressive. Will the observers who hold to the psychoanalytic interest or to the interest in constant attitudes not be lost in the details?

Not necessarily. The analytic tradition has built in a way for backing off from its preoccupation. For example, Asch (1976) describes a series of failing cases, where the attempt to get the patient better by seeing his unconscious desires only made the patient worse. These are called "negative therapeutic reactions" in the analytic tradition. One such man, a Mr. B., only became more burdened to see the "disrespectful" feelings he might have to his long dead, depressed mother. Indeed, she was located "some place above, in the ceiling (where he usually fixed his gaze while on the couch); she was observing and approving his rejections of my interpretations." "It was only after it was accepted that he was doing this to show mother—who was watching—what a good son he was, how much he protected her against even a skilled adversary, that he was able to gain some distance from the conflict and to appraise it more objectively" (1976, pp. 389–390). The reader may see how Asch literally borrows the interpersonal perspective when he is in trouble with his analytic perspective. This is indicated for him when the "negative therapeutic reaction" tells him that the usually analytic interest has run up against an exception to its usual success.

Now it is also possible for those who conduct a vigorous analysis of the constant attitude to notice when "progress" will jeopardize relations with "the other people in the room." If the therapist thinks that the maintenance of the "constant attitude" is the very constancy which endears the patient to the important people in his or her life, then the therapist will be alert for "negative therapeutic reactions" to breach-

ing this constant attitude. He will expect such a counter movement for every serious thrust forward. Of course, the reader may object that analysis of the constant attitude has become thereby entirely social or interpersonal in its perspective. Not quite. The challenge to the constant attitude remains the favorite interest. The interpersonal perspective is a fall-back position for occasions when the trouble from the favorite activity is jeopardizing its success. For example, patients who have a powerful experience in trial therapy in the first of two hours will come back very different after a half-hour break for the second hour. They will routinely be much more cautious, trying to look ahead to the effects of the powerful experience on their social world. They will be preoccupied. They are thinking, "If this is what I may expect in therapy, what will happen to my relationship with my father who will be paying for such help? What if I find how much I hate him?"

Thus, the analytic interest and the interest in the analysis of the constant attitude may be tenable positions for the therapeutic observer if he or she is ready to fall back to the interpersonal position for making observations when there is trouble stirred up.

Notice also that the interpersonal position may generate excessive intensity and turbulence—witness Balint's Case of the Stationery Manufacturer (Chapter 8). I believe such cases may be less tormenting for the doctor and for the patient if a suitable systemic perspective for their awful interaction can be achieved.

My theoretical argument several years ago (Gustafson, 1984) was located in the perspective of the analysis of the constant attitude. I described looking for "fault lines," "breaking through walls," finding "floods of feeling," and "building bridges" over them. At that time, I was aware of the interpersonal snares and systemic games which confounded my method. I was attempting to get free from a linear world of walls, floods and bridges to a circular world of interaction. The reader will see now that I am located in such a circular, systemic world, proposing to take up "loose ends," "work the opposing currents," and "appreciate the sacrifices" necessary to the family game. I believe such location allows me the most latitude for observation, since the previous positions remain accessible from the systemic position. I admit that I have to be careful about retaining such access. There is a pull implicit in the systemic position away from the loops into the past, the loop behind the wall of the constant attitude, the loop of the transference relationship. In general, systemic positioning may weaken access to emotional currents by taking so much distance. As Cronen, Johnson and Lannamann (1982) argue so well, *any* emphasis will alter one's relationship to previous positions. The mind is an ensemble. When one plays a powerful systemic music, one has got to be careful not to lose the capacity for the music of intense feeling. Different musical emphasis alters the drift of the mind.

7. I see two powerful explanations for the pull into "objectivity." The first was offered by Whorf (1941). He suggested that the shared operations of the English language as a Standard Average European (SAE) language get us thinking in the terms of spatial objectivity: "Latin terms for nonspatials, like educo, religio, principia, comprehendo, are usually metaphorized physical references: lead out, trying back, etc. . . . In the Middle Ages the patterns already formed in Latin began to interweave with the increased mechanical invention, industry, trade, and scholastic and scientific thought. The need for measurement in industry and trade, the stores and bulks of "stuffs" in various containers, the type-bodies in which various goods were handled, standardizing of measure and weight units, invention of clocks and measurement of time, keeping of records, accounts, chronicles, histories, growth of mathematics and the partnership of mathematics and science, all cooperated to bring our thought and language into its present form" (1941, p. 157).

Such a tendency is exacerbated by the spatialization of time: "Just as we conceive our objectified time as extending in the future in the same way that it extends in the past, so we set down our estimates of the future in the same shape as our records of the past, producing programs, schedules and budgets. . . . No doubt this vast system once built, would continue to run under any sort of linguistic treatment. . . . It is clear how the emphasis on 'saving time' which goes with all the above and is very obvious objectification of time, leads to a high valuation of 'speed,' which shows itself a great deal in our behavior. Still another behavioral effect is that the character of monotomy and regularity possessed by

our image of time as an evenly scaled limitless tape measure persuades us to behave as if that monotony were more true of events than it really is. That is, it helps to *routinize* us. We tend to select and favor whatever bears out this view, to '*play up to' the routine aspects of existence.* One phase of this is behavior evincing a false sense of security or an assumption that all will always go smoothly, and a lack in forseeing and protecting ourselves against hazards" (italics supplied; 1941, p. 154).

Kundera (1984a, 1984b) suggests that such objectification becomes even more reductive of the individual, when empires like ours and the Soviet Union are on the march. This is augmented by the broadcasting of "identical simplifications" across the globe by the omnipresent media. Le Corbusier (1947) has a similar discussion of the loss of limits for such civilizations.

8. Two related theoretical statements about the grammar of complexity are worth discussing. One is the revision of Bateson's epistemology by Pearce and Cronen (1980) and Cronen, Johnson and Lannamann (1982). They argue against the use of logical inclusion, that is, against the idea of seeing classes and moves within classes, etc. They argue for a hierarchy of the mind which is similar to my proposal for seeing closure of needs, of constant attitude, of security operations, of family games—that is, for seeing a kind of cybernetic regulation of unities of increasing scope. They propose that this entire ensemble is "reflexive," which means that change in one level of organization will increase or decrease the "logical force" of that level on its neighbor.

Difficulty comes from "strange loops" (Hofstadter, 1979), wherein a kind of progress at one level leads directly into a contradiction of that progress at the next level, e.g., if gratification of sexual desire makes someone feel like a bad family member, which leads back to increased sexual tension and activity, which leads back to feeling bad, etc. Extrication from such "strange loops" is only possible if subsequent levels for observation give a stable platform for observing them.

The second theoretical statement is one which has only been hinted at by Chomsky (Rieber, 1983, p. 33) concerning the likelihood of a cognitive system which gives us "our ability to make sense of the social structures in which we play a role." Such a social relations "mental organ" seems to have a grammar such as that described by myself or Cronen, Johnson, and Lannamann. We propose the places where the "switches" governing the grammar are set: e.g., concerning needs, concerning a defensive posture, etc. We propose that there is great latitude in how these switches may be set, but they must be set one way or another and they do have great "logical force" once they are set. We ignore their setting at our peril, like the Romans neglecting key boundaries in their empire. It appears to us that the social relations "mental organ" is a "reflexive" hierarchy of cybernetic unities of increasing scope. Such a theory has many neighboring theories, as diverse as Popper's theory of tradition (Popper, 1949; Booth, 1983) or Northrop Frye's theory of literary forms (1957).

9. A similar example from baseball was described in a sports column recently. For several months Keith Hernandez went into a batting slump which he could not help. His father, an astute observer of the game, then got out and looked at videotapes of his son batting at the height of his success. The father then watched his son batting in his slump on television. Comparing the two views, he noticed that could he no longer see the second number on his son's back when his son completed his swing. Thus, he inferred that his son had opened up his stance, facing the pitcher more. He telephoned this finding to his son, who had been completely unaware of this drift in his stance. When he went back to his previous closed stance, his batting recovered its previous effectiveness. Hernandez commented, afterwards, that such a drift of stance, even though more and more ineffective, becomes more and more comfortable.

10. Another trivial example from daily life may clarify my meaning. Almost everyone is familiar with the feeling of being trapped by a ringing telephone. One finds oneself saying yes to proposals posed suddenly over this device. This is because we coordinate ourselves with other people in the automatic way described by Maturana without thinking or observing. The possibility of freedom comes in being an observer of such coordination. Thus, I always go to a ringing phone with the word "no" in mind. My routine answer to any proposal is "No . . . in all probability, but I will think about it." This gives me the time to observe and think about what I actually want to do.

11. If Bellow is right about the dangers of guile, Kundera (1984a,b) is right about the dangers of reduction. I am grateful to Myron Sharaf, Ph.D., for the first reference, Michael Moran, M.D., for the second and third.

12. My students in the Clinic in the fall of 1985, Drs. Huggins, Johnson, Johnston, Moran, Seator, Sigrist, Smith, Thompson, and Wonderlich noted in one of our theoretical discussions that one level of observation tends to *lead* into the next higher level of recursion. The narrowing of the instincts leads into the awareness of a constant attitude, the constant attitude about the body into the constant attitude about security operations, the dyadic security operations into the family game, and the family game back to the exclusion of certain instinctual trends, which then become a preoccupation! And so forth. I hope the reader will also appreciate my debt to Selvini Palazzoli concerning theory. Her discussion of how "loose ends" (1985, p. 32) provide the only access to complicated systems and her discussion of how the more complicated systemic construction may explain simpler constructions like those of psychoanalysis have been extremely helpful to me. As she writes, " . . . this broad approach helps us not to become lost in details or bogged down in arbitrary reductions" (Selvini Palazzoli, 1985, p. 32).

INTRODUCTION / *Part IV*

1. I am indebted to Myron Sharaf for these references.

19. *The Opening Game: Preliminary Interviews*

1. I agree with Alexander and French that this first view is invaluable for seeing the broad relations, but I do not agree that such a view is always lost later in therapy. It may be lost from many observing positions taken up by therapists. I certainly

have had the experience they refer to about being caught in the smaller details. I believe they write accurately about their own experiences as well. But the method of the middle game of brief therapy which I espouse and describe in Chapter 21 suggests that it is possible to position oneself to retain a view of the broad relations—indeed, that this is a principal objective.

2. SCL-90-R, Copyright by Leonard R. Derogatis, Ph.D.

3. Form UWPD-1 (Series T), July, 1974.

4. Ordinarily, we divide up the team of four to nine trainees and myself into two or three interviewing teams so that we can conduct two or three preliminary interviews simultaneously. We may see up to five new patients in an afternoon clinic of three hours.

5. Malan (1979) has been most influential for me about this technical requirement for first interviews. See especially Chapter 17 of *Individual Psychotherapy and the Science of Psychodynamics*; Chapters 18–22 are also very worthwhile. If residents are to be examined concerning their clinical skill in psychiatry, this would be the subject matter I would choose to challenge them.

6. Koranyi (1979) reports from the Outpatient Department of the Royal Ottawa Hospital that *43%* of 2,090 psychiatric clinic patients suffered from one of several physical illnesses. *Half* of these illnesses were undiagnosed! A university department like ours is likely to see many fewer diagnosed and undiagnosed physical illnesses in our psychiatric clinic patients, if only because our patients are much younger. Still, we are meticulous about ruling out undiagnosed physical illness *before* we proceed with trial therapy. We would hate to miss a brain tumor in a young person complaining of depression. For the relevant differential diagnosis of physical etiologies for depression and anxiety, see especially Hyman (1984). Given our precaution, I can think of only one outstanding physical illness in the last five years which we later learned we had missed. This was hypothyroidism in The Young Businessman on Probation (Chapter 21) who presented with being a "slow learner." See my note about this in the follow-up report in the Appendix.

7. I also like the idea of Sifneos (1979) that it is useful to ask what sacrifices the patient has made for the person he or she (ostensibly) loves. This tests for the strength of the ability to connect, but also for the ability to protect one's own interests. The two abilities are balanced here, one against the other. As Havens (1976) would say, you "work the opposing currents" to gauge the strength of each of them.

8. Letters from myself to the referring doctor or nurse on every patient referred have helped our mutual understanding, as have annual presentations to the medical staff on brief therapy which include a videotape of a trial therapy from the previous year.

9. The arrangement for students in our university is that visits to Student Health, including to our consultations at Student Health in Brief Therapy Clinic, are free, while visits to specialists at University Hospital are fee for service. Many students purchase low cost medical insurance which covers much of this fee for service, but many do not.

10. Malan included "cautionary tales" in his book (1976), about a few of the memorable disasters and near disasters which occurred in his clinic concerning missed and overlooked findings. Few writers about brief therapy or any kind of psychotherapy have been so candid. I was and remain grateful to him for such a report. He may have saved me from some comparable misfortunes in my own clinic. If he had glossed over such experiences, I might have had less caution than I have needed, such as in the cases which follow.

11. When I worked as area psychiatrist for the Indian Health Service in Montana and Wyoming, I reviewed the charts of 15 completed suicides of Indian men. Nearly all of them had visited doctors in the months before the suicide, and no mention of psychological difficulties could be seen in the medical record.

12. See Margulies and Havens for a comparable set of common mis-connections in first encounters (1981).

13. See Reider's interesting discussion of the "transference to institutions" which patients use to comfort themselves when their doctors in training are less than steady (1953).

14. The limited domain of analytic brief therapy technique looks very narrow, when you think of all the criteria required by Sifneos (1979). Malan (1976) seemed to suggest wider possibilities for analytic technique, but later (Malan, 1980a) suggested this was only possible with the Davanloo technique of confrontation (analysis of character). Strupp (1981) suggests that

wider possibilities are likely for an interpersonal method.

15. Haley (1973) puts this argument for narrow and broad selection very well in his Chapter 8, especially the footnote on page 268: "Freud's personal solution for his inability to deal with the family is a curious one. He says, 'In the years before the war, when the flux of patients from many countries made me independent of the goodwill or disfavour of my native city, I made it a rule never to take for treatment anyone who not *sui juis*, independent of others in all the essential relations of life. Every psychoanalyst cannot make these stipulations.' (Sigmund Freud, *Introductory Lectures on Psychoanalysis*. New York: Norton, 1929, p. 386). Such a stipulation essentially eliminates everyone involved with other people in any dependent way."

16. See Malan (1979) for some terrifying stories about getting in too deep in the preliminary interview and having to be responsible for the interview triggering a desperate mental state in the patient. See especially Chapters 17, 21, and 22.

20. *The Opening Game: Trial Therapy*

1. Semrad's consultations were very similar in aim, although the reader would have no idea from his only writing on the subject (Semrad, Binstock, and White, 1966). I saw 20 or 30 of them when I was a medical student at Harvard in his seminar on brief therapy.

2. Karl Tomm is writing a useful essay on this subject, which he calls the "intentions" of the interviewer (Tomm, unpublished).

3. I got interested in the *Poetics* three or four years ago when writing my book on Freud (Gustafson, unpublished manuscript), because of the importance for Freud and Breuer of the idea of catharsis which is derived from Aristotle. I forgot the subject for several years, until I noticed our trial therapy has drifted into this form of the tragedy.

4. We have come in the spring of 1986 upon a new variation for trial therapy conducted by trainees, which is related to the training exercise described by Boscolo and Cecchin (1982). The trainee who conducts most of the interview is assisted by myself at the conclusion of the first and second hour. I get a chance to probe something left aside and a chance to sum up and appreciate the work of the trainee and patient. I am also there in the room if the trainee falls into a deep hole along the way and needs a hand. The two of us are the therapeutic team. The other trainees are asked to be an observing team, that is, to confer, to attempt to put together a hypothesis about what they see between the therapeutic team and the patient. In the mid-session break, the therapeutic team and observing team meet separately for a while, then meet together to compare hypotheses. I am grateful to Dr. Hugh Johnston for working out this variation with myself and his peers.

5. The less difficult patients give the trainee therapist a good "loose end" to work from in trial therapy, although they may be more difficult in the middle game (Chapter 21). The more difficult patients give everyone a difficult time about the "loose end" in the trial therapy and in the middle game and in the end game. Not only may the therapist find it difficult to locate the patient's preoccupation, but the therapist may also be pulled deftly into a hopeless position. We have had many discussions in our clinic about remarkable "intuitive interactions" which occur within the first few minutes of interviews. I have gradually come to be a little informal with the patient before I ask the patient what he or she wants from me for the day. I have experimented with being somewhat offhand like Winnicott. Consider the following exhange which preceded the trial therapy of the Young Woman with No Self-Confidence:

AUTHOR Why don't you sit down. We're going to be on camera this time. Let me see from Dr. Robbins here, this is our fishing line (cord to electric device in my ear). Dr. Robbins, are we OK on sound? Maybe I can get this thing to work. Ken, I don't get any . . . he's going to explain something. It doesn't work. This is like psychology courses, everything is terrific except it doesn't work.

PATIENT You're a psychiatrist, not a psychologist? Do psychiatrists get any training in psychology when they're in med school?

AUTHOR (to Dr. Robbins behind mirror) I don't know. Try the other one . . . to hell with it, it doesn't work. (to patient) What did you have in mind?

PATIENT I was just wondering because I was talking to my friend who is going into med school and he said it was really strange because psychiatrists don't receive any training in psychology when they are in med school. They just learn about medicine and stuff like that, drugs.

AUTHOR Yeah, there's a lot more of that too. It's getting worse.

PATIENT I was really surprised.

AUTHOR What did you think?

PATIENT I thought they'd have training in counseling or whatever they want to go into.

AUTHOR Some of them. I don't know. There's some, it depends on where you go. Some places it's all drugs and chemistry and other places it's not. I think this will work somewhere along the way. We've got a couple of hours now to see about you. Now, where do you think we ought to start today?

PATIENT Well, I guess what I really want to know is . . .

This back and forth helped me in two ways. One is that I could get down off the height she might want to propose for me. Two is that I could get a feel for her confidence as an equal. Both moves seem promising from my little experiment.

Therefore, I could meet her proposal of no self-confidence with doubt. Yes, it seems true, but, no, it seems you also have confidence. Without this counter, she could have sunk us into a bog of evidence about her weaknesses.

I believe that many, many difficult patients sink the therapist in their first move, as if they get him in a hold around the neck and take him down with them. I think much of what is interesting in Erickson's work (Haley, 1973) is his adeptness for seeing such moves coming, for getting off on the right foot. Once he gets off right, the drift (Maturana, 1985) is very different. Erickson is supposed by some to be mysterious, but I see an algorithm in his openings which seems very consistent. I see Erickson as very adept for getting out of obligatory relations which go around the same worn circuit. He sees very fast what moves by the patient will compel the spouse, child, parent or himself into the obliging role. He proposes to go along, but asks for a small variation. This variation sets the relation on a new path or drift. The husband who is hounded by the wife at their restaurant is to be sent there a half-hour early by the wife (Haley, 1973, p. 226). Once she arrives, it is too late for hounding. The daughter who shouts at her parents, the parents who shout at their daughter, are asked to think for ten minutes before they shout as they please (p. 273). Thinking over what they will say, they no longer feel free to rant.

Recently, I saw a young woman whose security seems to involve being at every one's beck and call. In graduate school, her peer group of about 15 people always proposed something for her to do. She felt overly used, often, but she had an importance. In Madison where everyone is paired off as they get beyond school, she was left on her own. Like a teddy bear left in the snow, she waited in gathering darkness for no one to come after her. This kind of opening is dangerous for most of us, as we will be pulled into becoming responsible for her. Quite a hopeless prospect. She is quite prepared to lie hopelessly in the snow for a very long time, until *someone* will feel obliged to take care of her. She *might* even be willing to die in such an attempt:

Bums, on waking,
Do not always find themselves
In gutters with water running over their
    legs
And the pillow of the curbstone
Turning hard as sleep drains from it.
Mostly, they do not know
But hope for where they shall come
    to. The opening of the eyes is precious,
And the shape of the body also,
Lying as it has fallen, Disdainfully
    crumpling earthward
Out of alcohol.
Drunken under their eyelids
Like children sleeping toward Christmas,
They wait for the light to shine
Wherever it may decide.
(Dickey, 1958, p. 159)

In summary, I see three reliable ways for not being pulled under by such patients. One way is to be informal to get a little room and time to sense the obligatory response. Two is to wait until the patient asks for something—not to shine one's light around "wherever it may decide." Three is to have an algorithm for generating something other than the obligatory response. Not to have to lift up this teddy bear who weighs a ton. Better, perhaps to study how long she proposes to hold out. Once you break out of the compelled cycle, there is hope.

6. While the team must be put at arm's length by the therapist, yet they have something very useful to provide. They introduce whatever currents are dissociated from the relation between patient and therapist. The difficulty using such dissociated currents is that they are often introduced destructively. For instance, I enjoyed seeing a young woman who was her father's favorite. Since he was felt by her to be over-powering, I gave her much room, which she enjoyed. The team became full of the dissociated feeling of the neglected mother. They were extremely critical of myself and the patient. At the time, I found this difficult to use since it was so hostile and overpowering. It was a swift, dark river that often overwhelmed the patient herself into "black depressions." Since this awful interaction with the observing team, I have been very careful to propose to them that they are often carrying something of great importance. This makes them a little more merciful to me; therefore, more helpful. I also advise myself, by using such punctuation of their relation to me and the patient. I get myself ready. I may receive quite a rush of destructiveness as a contribution.

7. My finding of relatively high hopes in the first hour of trial therapy and attempts to destroy the work in the second hour of trial therapy is parallel to what Mann (1973) has seen in the course of twelve sessions. For him the most crucial events are the appreciation of "present and chronically recurring pain" in the first hour and the readiness for destruction of the success in the twelfth hour. I am seeing a comparable intensity in two hours, given the beginning, middle and end to which our trial therapy has evolved.

8. The residents and psychology fellows in the Brief Therapy Clinic in the fall of 1985, Doctors Huggins, Johnson, Johnston, Moran, Seator, Sigrist, Smith, Thompson, and Wonderlich, who discussed this videotape with me then, emphasize that what is most striking for them is the intuitive back and forth between the patient and myself at the outset of our interaction, the Winnicott informality about how we tune in to each other. They would not be making marks, as I do, quite so fast. They are surprised by my opposition to her "no self-confidence." They would be "taken down" into this pain. They would be more gullible. I believe this could be a tenable route, but a longer one, very much the route advocated by Greenson (1967) for psychoanalysts who want to risk being a little gullible to be taken in. They are also surprised by my holding fast to what feels ordinary, what feels much larger. I believe this is also crucial, for I separate myself thereby from her family, which has been *very* confusing and disconfirming, about what is large, what is weak, what is strong, etc. I will not fight the generalizations against her in general, but with my feet in the river. But I am no fisherman. Both the patient and I are fishing for each other, showing possibilities, showing dimensions. We are having a talk. She is a scout for an army of five generations which has not yet come into view. I am someone she met in the woods. I return to a view of this informality in Chapter 24.

9. I like the word "probe" to describe what I do in trial therapy. I probe what is right and what is awful. If Geschwind is right about the brain of the human being (Rosenfield, 1985), then the emotional force of the limbic system is triggered by the "association of association areas," where "cross-modal" associations from the different sensory "association areas" are conjoined. I *feel* this woman's pain. I *see* her latent confidence in her eyes. I *hear* her mother telling her she is not worthwhile. The senses are conjoined (Chapter 10, Havens). Such "condensation," as Eliot argued (1919), is a poetic construction: "For it is . . . the pressure, so to speak, under which the fusion takes place, that counts" (p. 1975).

10. I prefer to be "working the opposing currents," not finding *the* "conflict" or "focal conflict." The latter ideas, for me, reify a temporary sketch of the currents into something which is quite definite. Soon, I would be talking to the patient about "her" conflict, as if it were actually *hers*, not *our* sketch which is continually being revised.

21. *The Middle Game*

1. A possible complication should be noted. The trial therapy in our clinic is often conducted by myself in the fall semester, while the subsequent therapy is conducted by one of our senior residents or psychology fellows. Usually, the trainee who will be

carrying on with the patient has been the one to establish a relationship with the patient for the clinic in the preliminary interview. Therefore, the trainee is getting the patient back after a long consultation with myself. Still, this is a complication for the patient which prolongs the opening game to a third movement, namely whether or not the therapist and patient can find a way to continue the trial therapy in their own way. This often takes three or four sessions. I find that the present form of our trial therapy leaves less trouble for the trainee than before. When I only saw the patient for an hour to give an understanding of his or her "present and chronically recurring pain" (Chapter 12, Mann), when I saw this patient for up to three hours to get a "breakthrough," I was more often idealized for such magical performances, while the trainee was left to a more devalued follow-up. Now I too get the attempt of the patient to bring my work back to zero in the second hour of the trial therapy. I too live through the difficulty which will come to the trainee. This makes us more equal, which makes the transition back from myself to the trainee less difficult for all of us. Also, since the trainee shows his or her work to the entire team in the Brief Therapy Clinic, which includes myself, then the transition is also less absolute. In a sense the patient is asked to be in therapy with the team, represented by the trainee, then myself, then the trainee again. If there is a positive "transference to the institution" (Reider, 1953), this helps speed along the work. I am often struck with how some patients will be obviously delighted to be of interest to our whole group. No doubt, others are not. This is probably a limitation to our success in the clinic, for it is obviously the work of a team.

I see several problems here which are better decided by empirical study than by theory. Malan's study (1976) suggests that patients who do not improve by the tenth session will not improve later. Could this be extended to say that patients who do not improve in the long session of the trial therapy do not improve later in brief therapy? Is the method of trial therapy which brings on the attempt to destroy the work in the second hour a better predictor than the method of trial therapy which contents itself with a "trial interpretation" of the "present and chronically recurring pain"? Are there indeed patients who prosper more

in the group context of the clinic? Whose motivation is increased by group interest? Patients who are less accessible in the clinic? Less motivated? My predictions are clearly stated from my theoretical argument. If studies show me to be wrong, I will be glad to do some further thinking.

2. I like Winnicott's phrase, "good enough mothering," as descriptive of the aim of the trial therapy. It balances his other favorite phrase, namely, "meeting the challenge of the case." The intention or attitude of the therapist helps to set up an atmosphere which makes all the difference (Chapters 7 and 8).

3. See Maturana's discussion of "structural coupling," especially pp. xxiv–xxx (Maturana and Varela, 1980) and my discussion of Maturana in Chapter 17.

4. Masud Khan told me in an interview I had with him in 1981 that Winnicott would often see adult patients for three hours about once a month, perhaps three or four times in all. I began using this schedule myself when I returned from that trip to England. Now I vary the schedule according to what suits the patient and myself. I like two-hour meetings once a month, hour-and-a-half meetings every two weeks, and hour meetings once a week. I suppose that every patient has his or her own rhythm about getting help. If this is located, then the meetings do not get routine. Selvini Palazzoli et al. (1978a, p. 14) call this periodicity "t_s" or "the nodal time of the system." I think the same of relations with friends. If the right distance and frequency can be found, then the meetings are very refreshing.

5. Mann confirms Alexander and French about the routinization of the middle of brief therapy because he arouses an idealization at the outset. This would have to be worn down as doctor and patient become involved in structural coupling (Maturana and Varela, 1980). This is the usual drift of relations, unless measures are taken to prevent becoming fitted to one another.

6. I am indebted to Robin Skynner for this metaphor, from his letter to me of May 16, 1985.

7. I would like to be able to name the therapist of this patient who did a very fine piece of work, with some help from the team in the Brief Therapy Clinic. Unfortunately, this would compromise the confidentiality of the patient. The description which follows is based upon my notes from our

supervision of the resident, which were based on the reports of the resident and his selections of audiotape or videotape for each supervision. The succession of themes described here is a summary of the broad relation as they appeared in our discussions. Some repetition of the cycle of the three new themes also was evident.

8. See footnote 5, Chapter 20, for more discussion on staying clear of obligatory, hopeless relations. That is the other half of this subject of how to begin. As usual, Mike Moran, M.D., (personal communication) drew my attention to the need for greater clarity about this problem.

9. What emerges is that subject described by Aristotle (p. 4, chapter 20) which is "one entire and perfect action, having a beginning, a middle, and an end so that, forming like an animal a complete whole, it may afford its proper pleasure."

10. This idea may be restated in several different theoretical languages. The closest is the one of Melanie Klein concerning strength of character (1959). Such strength depends upon the child having been well protected. This, in turn, depends upon clear boundaries concerning hostility. Mercy can be relied upon when hidden in a woman's skirts, in a man's tent, or in a religious sanctuary (pp. 262–263). Dante represented this most acutely when he described the very darkest sins in hell as betrayals of confidence and loyalty. Patients who have often been betrayed along these lines have been badly injured. Brief therapy is quite unlikely because they dare not trust in the skirt, the tent, and the sanctuary. They do not show them what Winnicott called "the very great confidence which children often show in myself (as in others doing similar work) on these special occasions, special occasions that have the quality that has made me use the word sacred. Either the sacred moment is used or it is wasted" (1971b, pp. 4–5). The same idea could also be described in Haven's tests of normality (1984b) or in Gedo's description of Level I, II and III capabilities (Chapter 9).

11. I refer here to all those people who would not feel at home or in an interesting situation if they were not beset by contradictions in their social relations. Writers, historians, housewives, househusbands, and people from all walks of life can be diplomats of the labyrinth.

12. If the patient is obviously quite vulnerable at the outset, but has some capacity to connect and to defend and has but slim resources, I am likely to offer sessions "on demand" after the trial therapy. This helps to keep us out of great expectations which might build up in weekly meetings. In the setting of the health maintenance organization, I find this schedule very useful for more disturbed patients.

13. I only learned later that the patient's "slowness" about learning was also being triggered by his being hypothyroid. Both his internist and I missed this. The diagnosis was subtle, as there were no other signs, but an important lesson. Therefore, his improvement was also due to the thyroid hormone he began to take later when the deficiency was discovered by his internist in New York City. The patient believes this was the most important help he got. He managed to get by with the help of our sessions, but he jumped forward in his capacity to learn when he got the thyroid. See the follow-up in the Appendix.

14. General practitioners also have learned to make use of long brief therapy, given their context of a lifetime for a relationship. See especially Balint (1957).

15. I like Keeney and Ross's metaphor (1983) of the valve effect of a symptom, such as a headache for regulating relations with a system, which I have borrowed here. From this point of view, symptoms are *not* to be gotten rid of, as they give access to the patient's world. Symptoms will improve as that world is gotten on a more secure drift.

16. Most biological systems have many complicated levels in a reflexive interaction. Thus, the effects of large changes may not be calculated. As Popper (1957) suggests, they have "unforseen consequences." The idea of "going slowly" is sensible, often, to allow reckoning with the consequences, one by one, as they appear.

22. The End Game

1. If I see the relationship in brief therapy as a situation in which I am to become as nothing, in which the patient is to triumph, then there is less difficulty in being myself. I give myself away freely, then, as Winnicott would say (see Chapter 7).

2. Thus, the end for the way in which I work is very different from the end in the other methods. The reader will see quite a contrast in Mann (1973), for the great illusion in his opening game will need a very big ending. The reader will also see much more diverse endings in Malan (1979), because a relationship which invites transference to become as powerful as possible will take some trouble to disentangle. I do not make myself very important. I am the one dismissed, not the other way around. I see one indication for a sharp, clear ending which is set well in advance. When the patient is having difficulty getting over a ma-

jor loss, then the best access to that difficulty will be gotten when the patient has to lose the therapist as well. Losing the therapist will arouse losing the parent, child or girlfriend, if the treatment is set up clearly to demarcate the end phase (Malan, 1979, pp. 198–201). For such patients, I will spell out the number of sessions and the exact date that we end (Mann, 1973). For a discussion of the various moves to circumvent loss in the termination, the reader will enjoy Malan's (1979, Chapter 16) discussion of "flight into health," "premature withdrawal," and of a psychiatric emergency.

23. Autopoietic Students

1. See Maturana (Maturana and Varela, 1980) (Chapter 17) concerning the farce of "instructive interaction" and Freire (1970) concerning the "banking method of education."
2. Sullivan's brilliant case conference (1976) suggests that instruction may be possible after all, at least for the readers. I find that instruction may appear to be successful, but it is unreliable.
3. Audiotape will suffice when the group is familiar with the patient from having met him or her in the preliminary interview or trial therapy. Videotape is better for the crucial gestures.
4. This is what Hofstadter (1979) and Pearce and Cronen (1980) call a "strange loop." An improvement in the patient-therapist relation leads to a worsening in the patient-family relation, which leads to a worsening of the patient-therapist relation, etc. The "strange loop" is a figure eight or even more complicated figure in which two or more different levels in the hierarchy of social relations operate to reverse one another. According to Pearce and Cronen (1980), this is the shape of most difficulty in social relations. See Ferrier (1986) for another illustration.
5. This success could be described in the theoretical framework of Cronen, Johnson and Lannamann (1982) as well as in that of Bateson which I have used. The "strange loop" from Heinz-Larson to Larson family and back again will tend to pull new observers into its path. Thus, the peer supervision group is able to observe the interaction cleverly, but the cleverness hurts

Heinz too much, which only exacerbates the strange loop. Only when there is a level of observation which provides a "platform" for observing the strange loop is it possible for participants to keep from going under and around the loop themselves. My job is to set up such a platform by staying apart from the relation between the therapist and the peer group, which allows a "higher" level of social organization to be constructed. It is fascinating how such a level allows the observer to stay calm (I), to stay able to defend his boundaries (II), to stay able to tell illusion from capability (III), for these are the three levels of ego organization described by Gedo (1979) as necessary to well being. It may be that well-being in modern times depends on the capacity for generating levels of observation in a lucid way. See my discussion of this in Chapter 18, "Contradictions Between Logical Levels."
6. The categories which we use in our clinical notes are primarily: *problems list* and *list of hypotheses*. Two lesser but also important categories are: *the game* and *its domain*. I believe these categories keep us in mind of a method of methods.
7. I am indebted to John Follet, M.D., Ken Robbins, M.D., Joel Streim, M.D., and Fred Wamboldt, M.D., for this shared piece of work, especially to Dr. Wamboldt for his metaphor of the Rat Express.
8. I am indebted to Robin Skynner (1981) for his emphasis on the therapist as "part of the equation." He has helped me the most with this reality.

24. *Warriors, Farewell*

1. For a discussion of the common difficulties of *The Sciences and the Humanities*, Jones (1967) is very clear. I like very much his story about what happens to rats jumping for rewards toward white or black cards when the experimenter gradually merges the extremes of white and black into a common grey. Often, then, the rats "jump high and to the right" (p. 1). We become rather foolish when our success is threatened, unless we have a tradition for helping us to interpret our failures (p. 32), for helping us to put them in perspective (p. 7). Thus, Jones also sees how deeply we depend upon a method of methods.
2. If the discerning reader should say, " . . . but there is yet much difficulty to be borne in your cosmos" (Mike Moran, M.D., personal communication), I am gladly found out. Yes. If the reader eschews standardization of his or her method (Jung, 1957), he or she will have to tolerate much more of being alone. Standardization is the local rule. "Autonomy of the spirit" is a different rule in a "republic of letters (which) is inhabited by individuals" (Finkielkraut, 1985, p. 10). Committees do not come to thank one daily for his or her existence. This means some bitter defeats are to be borne by oneself. This means more occasions for terror at the way everything is arranged, or not arranged. This means more occasions of being poorly understood. But the great potential of the human mind which has access to the various levels of the great architecture is that a reduction at one level is seen anew at another. Have I not said anywhere in this large book that being delivered from a neurotic vicious circle will have its own pain? (Miller, 1979). I meant to. Both the pain of delivery and the pain of being in the world.

Appendix

1. The technique described in the text also tests theory, line by line, hour by hour, since the predictions of closure help the therapist to appreciate such necessity. When the relevant closure is recognized, the patient will often discover new moves for such closure.
2. It would be better to evaluate "systemic change" by interviewing the significant people in the patient's life directly about their observations of the patient before, during or after therapy. "Circular questioning" of the patient is second best. (See Chapter 16, The Milan Teams).
3. My theory of complications also predicts that the interviewer must have a calm sequence to his own interview and many ways to revise fictions presented by the patient in the follow-up interview, to get reliable findings. Malan also makes these assumptions about being well prepared and being ready to check findings from several angles.
4. The residents and fellows whose work is alluded to in these follow-up notes include: Nancy Barklage, John Follet, Ken Robbins, Steven Stern, Joel Streim, Fred Wamboldt and Jeffrey Winston.

Bibliography

Alexander, F. & French, T. M. (1946). *Psychoanalytic therapy, principles and applications.* New York: Ronald Press.

Alighieri, Dante. *Inferno.* (by J. Ciardi, Trans.). New York: New American Library, 1954.

Anderson, S. (1976). Evening song. *America is not all traffic lights, poems of the midwest.* (Alice Fleming, Ed.). Boston: Little, Brown.

Anthony, E. J. (1976). Between yes and no: The potentially neutral area where the adolescent and his therapist can meet. In S. C. Feinstein & P. L. Giovacchini (Eds.), *Adolescent Psychiatry,* Vol. IV. New York: Jason Aronson.

Aristotle. *Poetics.* (T. A. Moxon, Ed.). New York: E. P. Dutton, 1934.

Asch, S. S. (1976). Varieties of negative therapeutic reaction and problems of technique. *Journal of American Psychoanalytic Association, 24,* 383–407.

Ash, T. G. (1985). The Hungarian lesson. *New York Review of Books, 32*(19), 5–9.

Auden, W. H., & Kronenberger, L. (1962). *The Viking book of aphorisms.* New York: Viking.

Avery, N. C. (1982). A family perspective. *Contemporary Psychoanalysis, 18,* 480–489.

Balint, M. (1952). New beginning and the paranoid and the depressive syndromes. *International Journal of Psychoanalysis, 33,* 214. Reprinted in Balint, M. (1953). *Primary love and psychoanalytic technique.* New York: Liveright.

Balint, M. (1954). Method and technique in the teaching of medical psychology. II. Training general practitioners in psychotherapy. *British Journal of Medical Psychology, 27,* 37–41.

Balint, M. (1955a). Friendly expanses—horrid empty spaces. *International Journal of Psychoanalysis, 36,* 225–241.

Balint, M. (1955b). The doctor, his patient and the illness. *Lancet,* April, 683–88 (abridged version). Longer version in Balint, M. (1957). *Problems of human pleasure and behavior.* New York: Liveright.

Balint, M. (1957). *The doctor, his patient, and the illness.* New York: International Universities Press.

Balint, M. (1959). *Thrills and regressions.* London: Hogarth. New York: International Universities Press.

Balint, M. (1968). *The basic fault, therapeutic aspects of regression.* London: Tavistock.

Balint, M., Ornstein, P. H., & Balint, E. (1972). *Focal psychotherapy, an example of applied psychoanalysis.* London: Tavistock.

Balzac, Honore de. *Pere Goriot* (1835). In *Pere Goriot and Eugenie Grandet.* (E. K. Brown, D. Walter, & J. Watkins, Trans.) New York: Modern Library, 1946.

Barnett, L. (1962). *The treasure of our tongue.* New York: New American Library.

Bate, W. J. (1975). *Samuel Johnson.* New York: Harcourt Brace Jovanovich.

Bateson, G. (1958). Language and psychotherapy—Frieda Fromm-Reichmann's last project. *Psychiatry, 21,* 96–100.

Bateson, G. (1966). Communication theories in relation to the etiology of the neuroses. In J. H. Merin & S. H. Nagler (Eds.). *The etiology of the neuroses.* Palo Alto: Science and Behavior Books.

Bateson, G. (1972a). *Steps toward an ecology of mind.* New York: Ballantine Books.

Bateson, G. (1972b). The logical categories of learning and communication. In *Steps toward an ecology of mind.* New York: Ballantine Books.

Bateson, G. (1979). *Mind and nature, a necessary unity.* New York: Dutton.

Beck, A. T., Rush, A. J., Shaw, B. P., & Emery, G. (1979). *Cognitive therapy of depression.* New York: Guilford.

Bellow, S. (1953). *The adventures of Augie March*. Greenwich, CT: Fawcett.

Binder, J., Strupp, H. & Schacht, T. (1983). Countertransference in time-limited dynamic psychotherapy. *Contemporary Psychoanalysis, 19*, 605–623.

Bion, W. R. (1959). *Experience in groups*. New York: Basic Books.

Booth, P. J. (1983). Traditions, rules and homeostasis. *Journal of Strategic and Systemic Therapy, 2*(4), 29–48.

Borges, J. L. (1962). *Labyrinths. Selected stories and other writings*. New York: New Directions Books.

Borges, J. L. (1984). The Divine Comedy. In Borges, J. L. *Seven Nights*. (E. Weinberger, Trans.) New York: New Directions.

Boscolo, L., & Cecchin, G. (1982). Training in systemic therapy at the Milan Center. In R. Whiffen & J. Byng-Hall (Eds.), *Family therapy supervision: Recent developments in practice*. London: Academic Press.

Bradley, D. (1985, May 10). Beneath the roof. *Isthmus*. pp. 15–16. Madison, Wisconsin.

Brenman, M. (1952). On teasing and being teased: And the problem of "moral masochism." *Psychoanalytic Study of the Child, 7*, 264–285.

Breuer, J., & Freud, S. (1895). *Studies on hysteria* In *The complete psychological works of Sigmund Freud, The Standard Edition, 2*. New York: Norton.

Brueggeman, F. (1978). *The prophetic imagination*. Philadelphia: Fortress Press.

Burnham, J. B. (1986). *Family therapy: First steps towards a systemic approach*. London: Tavistock Publications.

Carroll, L. (1865). *Alice's adventures in wonderland and through the looking glass*. New York: St. Martin's, 1966.

Commager, H. S. (1985, November–December). Science, nationalism and the Academy. *Academe, Bulletin of the American Association of University Professors, 71*, 9–13.

Cooper, L. & Gustafson, J. P. *Unconscious planning in small groups*. Manuscript in preparation.

Crane, H. (1976). In praise of an urn, in memoriam: Ernest Nelson. In R. Ellmann (Ed.) *The New Oxford Book of American Verse*. p. 650. New York: Oxford University Press.

Cronen, V. E., Johnson, K. M., & Lannamann, J. W. (1982). Paradoxes, double binds and reflective loops: An alternative theoretical perspective. *Family Process, 20*, 91–112.

Darwin, C. (1899). *The expression of the emotions in man and animals*. New York: Appleton.

Davanloo, H. (Ed.). (1978). *Basic principles and technique in short-term psychotherapy*. New York: Spectrum.

Davanloo, H. (Ed.). (1980). *Short-term dynamic psychotherapy*. New York: Jason Aronson.

Dell, P. F. (1985). Understanding Bateson and Maturana: Toward a biological foundation for the social sciences. *Journal of Marital and Family Therapy, 11*, 1–20.

De Shazer, S. (1985). *Keys to solution in brief therapy*. New York: Norton.

Dickey, J. (1968). *Poems, 1957–1967*. New York: Collier Books.

Dicks, H. V. (1967). *Marital tensions, clinical studies toward a psychological theory of interaction*. New York: Basic Books.

Dyson, F. (1984). *Weapons and hope*. New York: Harper and Row.

Eliot, T. S. (1919). Tradition and the individual talent. In M. H. Abrams (Ed.). *The Norton Anthology of English Literature, Major Authors Edition*. New York: Norton, 1962, pp. 1971–1977.

Eliot, T. S. (1932). Dante. In *Selected Essays*. New York: Harcourt Brace and Company.

Eliot, T. S. (1934). *The waste land (1930) and other poems*. New York: Harcourt, Brace and Company.

Engel, G. L. (1980). The clinical application of the biopsychosocial model. *American Journal of Psychiatry, 137*, 535–544.

Fanon, F. (1967). *Black skin, white masks, the experience of a black man in a white world*. New York: Grove Press.

Ferenczi, S. (1921). The further development of an active therapy in psycho-analysis. In Ferenczi, S., *Further contributions to the theory and techniques of psychoanalysis*. New York: Brunner/Mazel, 1980.

Ferenczi, S. and Rank, O. (1925). *The development of psychoanalysis* (Caroline Newton, Trans.) New York and Washington: Nervous and Mental Disease Publishing Company.

Ferrier, M.-J. (1986). Testing the limits in Milan systemic therapy: Working with an individual. In D. Efron (Ed.). *Developments in strategic and systemic therapy*. New York: Brunner/Mazel.

Finkielkraut, A. What is Europe? *New York Review of Books 32*(19):10.

Fisher, H. A. L. (1935). *A history of Europe*. London: Eyre and Spottiswoode. Reprinted by Collins, Fontana Library, London, 1960.

Fisch, R., Weakland, J. H., Segal, L. (1983). *The tactics of change, doing therapy briefly*. San Francisco: Jossey-Bass.

Forster, E. M. (1941). *Howards end*. Harmondsworth, Middlesex, England: Penguin Books.

Freire, P. (1970). *Pedagogy of the oppressed*. New York: Herder and Herder.

Freud, A. (1946). *The ego and the mechanisms of defense*. New York: International Universities Press.

Freud, S. (1909). Notes upon a case of obsessional neurosis. *Standard Edition, 10*, 153–318. New York: Norton.

Freud, S. (1912). Recommendations to physicians practicing psycho-analysis. *Standard Edition, 12*, 109–120. New York: Norton.

Freud, S. (1913). Further recommendations in the technique of psychoanalysis: On beginning the treatment. The question of first communications. The dynamics of the cure. *Standard Edition, 12*, 121–144. New York: Norton.

Freud, S. (1914). Further recommendations in the technique of psychoanalysis: Recollection, repetition and working through. *Standard Edition, 12*, 145–156. New York: Norton.

Freud, S. (1915). Further recommendatons in the technique of psychoanalysis: Observations on transference-love. *Standard Edition, 12*, 157–171. New York: Norton.

Freud, S. (1918). From the history of an infantile neurosis. *Standard Edition, 17*, 3–122. New York: Norton.

Freud, S. (1921). Group psychology and the analysis of the ego. *Standard Edition, 18*, 65–144. New York: Norton.

Freud, S. (1937). Analysis terminable and interminable. *Standard Edition, 23*, 216–253. New York: Norton.

Frye, N. (1957). *Anatomy of criticism, four essays*. Princeton: Princeton University Press.

Gardner, H. (Ed.). (1972). *The new Oxford book of English verse*. New York and Oxford: Oxford University Press.

Gedo, J. E. (1964). Concepts for a classification of the psychotherapies. *International Journal of Psychoanalysis, 45*, 530–539.

Gedo, J. E. (1979). *Beyond interpretation, toward a revised theory for psychoanalysis*. New York: International Universities Press.

Gedo, J. E. (1981). *Advances in clinical psychoanalysis*. New York: International Universities Press.

Gerth, H. H., & Mills, C. W. (Eds.) (1946). *From Max Weber: Essays in sociology*. New York: Oxford University Press.

Goffman, E. (1959). *The presentation of self in everyday life*. New York: Doubleday Anchor Books.

Greenson, R. (1967). *The technique and practice of psychoanalysis*. New York: International Universities Press.

Gustafson, J. P. (1975). The group matrix of individual psychotherapy with plains Indian people. *Contemporary Psychoanalysis, 12*, 227–239.

Gustafson, J. P. (1976). The mirror transference in the psychoanalytic psychotherapy of alcoholism: A case report. *International Journal of Psychoanalytic Psychotherapy, 5*, 65–85.

Gustafson, J. P. (1981). The complex secret of brief psychotherapy in the works of Balint and Malan. In S. Budman (Ed.), *Forms of brief therapy*. New York: Guilford.

Gustafson, J. P. (1984). An integration of brief dynamic psychotherapy. *American Journal of Psychiatry, 141*, 935–944.

Gustafson, J. P. *Freud's unsolved problems*. Unpublished manuscript.

Gustafson, J. P., Cooper, L., Lathrop, N. C., Ringler, K., Seldin, F., & Wright, M. K. (1981). Cooperative and clashing interests in small groups. Part I: Theory. *Human Relations, 34*, 315–339.

Gustafson, J. P., & Dichter, H. (1983a). Winnicott and Sullivan in the brief psychotherapy clinic. Part I. Possible activity and passivity. *Contemporary Psychoanalysis, 19*, 624–637.

Gustafson, J. P., & Dichter, H. (1983b). Winnicott and Sullivan in the brief psychotherapy clinic. Part II. *Contemporary Psychoanalysis, 19*, 638–652.

Gustafson, J. P., Dichter, H., & Kaye, D. (1983c). Winnicott and Sullivan in the brief psychotherapy clinic. Part III. *Contemporary Psychoanalysis, 19*, 653–672.

Haley, J. (1973). *Uncommon therapy, the psychiatric techniques of Milton H. Erickson, M.D.* New York: Norton.

Havens, L. L. (1965). The anatomy of a suicide. *New England Journal of Medicine, 272,* 410–416.

Havens, L. L. (1966). Anatomy of schizophrenia. *JAMA, 196,* 325–331.

Havens, L. L. (1967). Recognition of suicidal risks through the psychologic examination. *New England Journal of Medicine, 276,* 210–215.

Havens, L. L. (1968). Some difficulties in giving schizophrenic and borderline patients medication. *Psychiatry, 31,* 44–50.

Havens, L. L. (1973). *Approaches to the mind, movement of the psychiatric schools from sects toward science.* Boston: Little, Brown.

Havens, L. L. (1976). *Participant observation.* New York: Jason Aronson.

Havens, L. L. (1978a). The choice of psychotherapeutic method. *Journal of the American Academy of Psychoanalysis, 6,* 465–478.

Havens, L. L. (1978b). Explorations in the uses of language in psychotherapy: Simple empathic statements. *Psychiatry, 41,* 336–345.

Havens, L. L. (1978c, January 21). Taking a history from the difficult patient. *Lancet.*

Havens, L. L. (1979). Explorations in the uses of language in psychotherapy: Complex empathic statements. *Psychiatry, 42,* 40–48.

Havens, L. L. (1980). Explorations in the uses of language in psychotherapy: Counterprojective statements. *Contemporary Psychoanalysis, 16,* 53–67.

Havens, L. L. (1982a). Discussion (of the case of Mr. Baker). *Contemporary Psychoanalysis, 18,* 511–522.

Havens, L. L. (1982b). The risks of knowing and not knowing. *Journal of Social and Biological Structures, 5,* 213–222.

Havens, L. L. (1984a). Explorations in the uses of language in psychotherapy: Counterintrojective statements (performatives). *Contemporary Psychoanalysis, 20,* 385–399.

Havens, L. L. (1984b). The need for tests of normal functioning in the psychiatric interview. *American Journal of Psychiatry, 141,* 1208–1211.

Havens, L. L. (1986). *Making contact, uses of language in psychotherapy.* Cambridge, MA: Harvard University Press.

Hoffman, L. (1981). *Foundations of family therapy.* New York: Basic Books.

Hofstadter, D. R. (1979). *Godel, Escher, Bach: An eternal golden braid.* New York: Basic Books.

Homer, *The Odyssey.* (Robert Fitzgerald, Trans.) New York: Anchor Books.

Horowitz, M., Marmar, C., Krupnick, J., et al. (1984). *Personality styles in brief psychotherapy.* New York: Basic Books.

Hyman, S. E. (Ed.). (1984). *Manual of psychiatric emergencies.* Boston: Little, Brown.

James, W. (1902). *Varieties of religious experience.* New York: *New American Library,* 1958.

James, W. *Pragmatism* (1907) *and other essays.* New York: Washington Square Press, 1963.

Jones, E. (1923). The God complex. In *Essays in Applied Psychoanalysis.* London: International Psychoanalytic Press. Reissued, London: Hogarth Press, 1951.

Jones, W. T. (1967). *The sciences and the humanities, conflict and reconciliation.* Berkeley: University of California Press.

Jung, C. G. (1917). On the psychology of the unconscious. In C. G. Jung, *Two essays on analytical psychology.* (R. F. C. Hull, Trans.) Princeton: Princeton University Press, 1972.

Jung, C. G. (1957). The plight of the individual in modern society. In C. G. Jung, *The undiscovered self.* Boston: Little, Brown.

Keeney, B. & Ross, J. (1983). Learning to learn systemic therapies. *Journal of Strategic and Systemic Therapies, 2,* 22–30.

Klein, M. (1959). Our adult world and its roots in infancy. In M. Klein, *Envy and gratitude and other works,* 1946–1963. New York: Dell, 1975.

Klerman, G. L., Weissman, M. M., Ronseville, B. J., et al. (1984). *Interpersonal psychotherapy of depression.* New York: Basic Books.

Kohut, H. (1971). *The analysis of the self.* New York: International Universities Press.

Koranyi, E. K. (1979). Morbidity and rate of undiagnosed physical illnesses in a psychiatric clinic population. *Archives of General Psychiatry, 36,* 414–419.

Kuhn, T. S. (1957). *The Copernican revolution, planetary astronomy in the development of western thought.* Cambridge, MA: Harvard University Press.

Kuhn, T. S. (1962). *The structure of scientific revolutions.* Chicago: University of Chicago Press.

Kundera, M. (1984a, April 26). The tragedy of Central Europe. *New York Review of Books.*
Kundera, M. (1984b, July 19). The novel and Europe. *New York Review of Books.*
Kuper, A., & Stone, A. (1982). The dream of Irma's injection: A structural analysis. *American Journal of Psychiatry, 139,* 1225–1234.
Lakatos, I. (1970). Falsification and the methodology of scientific research programmes. In I. Lakatos & A. Musgrave (Eds.), *Criticism and the growth of knowledge.* Cambridge: Cambridge University Press.
Laing, R. D. (1961). *Self and Others.* London: Tavistock.
Le Corbusier. (1947). *When the cathedrals were white* (Francis E. Hyslap, Jr., Trans.) New York: McGraw-Hill, 1964.
Lerner, S., & Lerner, H. (1983). A systemic approach to resistance: Theoretical and technical considerations. *American Journal of Psychotherapy, 37,* 387–399.
Levi-Strauss, C. (1964). *The raw and the cooked.* New York: Harper and Row, 1969.
Main, T. F. (1957). The ailment. *British Journal of Medical Psychology, 30,* 129–145.
Malan, D. (1963). *A study of brief psychotherapy.* New York: Plenum.
Malan, D. H. (1976). *The frontier of brief psychotherapy.* New York: Plenum.
Malan, D. H. (1979). *Individual psychotherapy and the science of psychodynamics.* London: Butterworths.
Malan, D. H. (1980a). The most important development in psychotherapy since the discovery of the unconscious. In H. Davanloo (Ed.), *Short-term dynamic psychotherapy.* New York: Jason Aronson.
Malan, D. H. (1980b). The nature of science and the validity of psychotherapy. In H. Davanloo (Ed.), *Short-term dynamic psychotherapy.* New York: Jason Aronson.
Malan, D. H. (1980c). Basic principles and techniques of the follow-up interview. In H. Davanloo (Ed.), *Short-term dynamic psychotherapy.* New York: Jason Aronson.
Malan, D. H., Heath, S., Bacal, H. A., Balfour, F., (1975). Psychodynamic changes in untreated neurotic patients. II. Apparently genuine improvements. *Archives of General Psychiatry, 32,* 110–126.
Mann, J. (1973). *Time-limited psychotherapy.* Cambridge: Harvard University Press.
Mann, J. (1981). The core of time-limited psychotherapy. In S. Budman (Ed.), *Forms of Brief Therapy.* New York: Guilford.
Mann, J., & Goldman, R. (1982). *A casebook in time-limited psychotherapy.* New York: McGraw-Hill.
March, R. H. (1970). *Physics for poets.* Chicago: Contemporary Books.
Margulies, A., & Havens, L. L. (1981). The initial encounter: What to do first? *American Journal Psychiatry, 138,* 421–428.
Maturana, H. R. (1978). Biology of language: The epistemology of reality. In G. A. Miller & E. Lenneberg (Eds.), *Psychology and biology of language and thought.* New York: Academic Press.
Maturana, H. R. (1984, April). Calgary lectures. Unpublished. Audiotape available from Professor Karl Tomm, University of Calgary.
Maturana, H. (1985, July). Oxford Conversations. Unpublished.
Maturana, H. R., & Varela, F. J. (1980). *Autopoiesis and cognition, The realization of the living.* Boston: D. Reidel.
Meissner, W. W. (1982). Discussion. *Contemporary Psychoanalysis, 18,* 487–498.
Melville, H. (1851). *Moby-Dick or, the whale.* Edited with an Introduction by Alfred Kazin. Boston: Houghton Mifflin, 1956.
Miller, A. (1979). *Prisoners of childhood, The drama of the gifted child and the search for the true self.* New York: Basic Books.
Morrison, A. (1982). Introduction, the case of Mr. Baker. *Contemporary Psychoanalysis, 18,* 474–480.
Myerson, P. G. (1982). Discussion. *Contemporary Psychoanalysis, 18,* 490–511.
Ollman, B. (1971). *Alienation, Marx's conception of man in capitalist society.* Cambridge: Cambridge University Press.
Ornstein, A. (1974). The dread to repeat and the new beginning. A contribution to the psychoanalysis of narcissistic personality disorders. *Annual of Psychoanalysis, 2,* 231–248.
Orwell, G. (1946a). *A collection of essays.* New York: Harcourt, Brace, Jovanovich.
Orwell, G. (1946b). The politics of the English language. In *A Collection of Essays by George*

Orwell. New York: Harcourt, Brace, Jovanovich.

Orwell, G. (1946c). Shooting an elephant. In *A Collection of Essays by George Orwell*. New York: Harcourt, Brace, Jovanovich.

Pearce, W. B., & Cronen, V. E. (1980). *Communication, action and meaning, the creation of social realities*. New York: Praeger Publishers.

Penn, P. (1982). Circular questioning. *Family Process, 21*, 267–280.

Perry, H. S. (1982). *Psychiatrist of America, the life of Harry Stack Sullivan*. Cambridge, MA: The Belknap Press of Harvard University Press.

Piaget, J. (1967). *Six psychological studies*. New York: Random House.

Popper, K. (1957). *The poverty of historicism*. London: Routledge and Kegan Paul.

Popper, K. R. (1949). Towards a rational theory of tradition. In K. R. Popper, *Conjectures and refutations*. New York: Basic Books, 1962.

Prelutsky J. (1970). *The queene of eene*. New York: Greenwillow Books.

Rabkin, R. (1972). Rabkin on books. *Family Process, 11*, 507–510.

Rank, O. (1924). *The trauma of birth*. New York: Harcourt, Brace and Company, 1929.

Reich, W. (1930). Character formation and the phobias of childhood. In R. Fliess (Ed.), *The psychoanalytic reader*. New York: International Universities Press.

Reich, W. (1933). *Character analysis*. New York: Farrar, Straus and Giroux, 1949.

Reich, W. (1948). *The Function of the Orgasm*. New York: Orgone Institute Press. Reissued, Farrar, Straus and Giroux, 1973.

Reider, N. (1953). A type of transference to institutions. *Bulletin of the Menninger Clinic, 17*, 58–63.

Reider, N. (1955). A type of psychotherapy based on psychoanalytic principles. *Bulletin of the Menninger Clinic, 19*, 111–128.

Ricci, C., & Selvini Palazzoli, M. (1984). Interactional complexity and communication. *Family Process, 23*, 169–176.

Rieber, R. W. (Ed.). (1983). *Dialogues on the psychology of language and thought, conversations with Noam Chomsky, Charles Osgood, Jean Piaget, Ulric Neisser and Marcel Kinsbourne*. New York: Plenum.

Rolvaag, Ole Eduart. (1929). *Giants of the earth*. New York: Harper.

Rosenberg, S. E. (in press). Brief dynamic psychotherapy for depression. In E. E. Beckham, & W. R. Leber (Eds.), *Depression: Treatment, assessment and research*. Homewood, IL: Dow-Jones-Irwin.

Rosenfield, I. (1985, Nov. 21). A hero of the brain. *New York Review of Books, 32*, 49–55.

Saint-Exupery, Antoine De. (1943). *The little prince*. (Katherine Woods, Trans.). New York: Harcourt Brace Jovanovich.

Schumacher, E. F. (1977). *A guide for the perplexed*. New York: Harper and Row.

Saul, L. J. (1977). *The childhood emotional pattern*. New York: Van Nostrand Reinhold.

Selvini Palazzoli, M. (1974). *Self-starvation: From individual to family therapy in the treatment of anorexia nervosa*. London: Chaucer.

Selvini Palazzoli, M. (1980). Why a long interval between session? The therapeutic control of the family-therapy suprasystem. In M. Andolfi & I. Zwerling (Eds.), *Dimensions of family therapy*. New York: Guilford.

Selvini Palazzoli, M. (1984). Review of *Aesthetics of change*. *Family Process, 23*, 282–284.

Selvini Palazzoli, M. (1985). The problem of the sibling as the referring person. *Journal of Marital and Family Therapy, 11*, 21–34.

Selvini Palazzoli, M., Boscolo, L., Cecchin, G., & Prata, G. (1974). The treatment of children through the brief therapy of their parents. *Family Process, 13*, 429–442.

Selvini Palazzoli, M., Boscolo, L., Cecchin, G., & Prata, G. (1977). Family rituals: A powerful tool in family therapy. *Family Process, 16*, 445–453.

Selvini Palazzoli, M., Boscolo, L., Cecchin, G., & Prata, G. (1978a). *Paradox and counterparadox: A new model in the therapy of the family in schizophrenic transaction*. New York: Jason Aronson.

Selvini Palazzoli, M., Boscolo, L., Cecchin, G., & Prata, G. (1978b). A ritualized prescription in family therapy: Odd days and even days. *Journal of Marital and Family Counseling, 4*, 3–9.

Selvini Palazzoli, M., Boscolo, L., Cecchin, G., & Prata, G. (1980a). The problem of the referring person. *Journal of Marital and Family Therapy, 6*, 3–9.

Selvini Palazzoli, M., Boscolo, L., Cecchin, G., & Prata, G. (1980b). Hypothesizing-circularity-neutrality: Three guidelines for the conductor of the session. *Family Process, 19*, 3–12.

Selvini Palazzoli, M., & Prata, G. (1982). Snares in family therapy. *Journal of Marital and Family Therapy, 8*, 443–450.

Semrad, E., Binstock, W. A., & White, B. (1966). Brief psychotherapy. *American Journal of Psychotherapy, 20*, 576–579, 1966.

Sharaf, M. (1983). *Fury on earth, a biography of Wilhelm Reich.* New York: St. Martin's.

Sifneos, P. E. (1968). Learning to solve emotional problems: A controlled study of short-term psychotherapy. In R. Porter (Ed.), *The role of learning in psychotherapy.* London: J. and A. Churchill.

Sifneos, P. E. (1972). *Short-term psychotherapy and emotional crisis.* Cambridge, MA: Harvard University Press.

Sifneos, P. E. (1979). *Short-term dynamic psychotherapy.* New York: Plenum.

Sifneos, P. E. (1981). Short-term anxiety-provoking psychotherapy: Its history, technique, outcome and instruction. In S. Budman (Ed.), *Forms of brief therapy.* New York: Guilford.

Skynner, A. C. R. (1976). *Systems of family and marital psychotherapy.* New York: Brunner/Mazel.

Skynner, A. C. R. (1981). An open systems, group-analytic approach to family therapy. In A. Gurman & D. Kniskern (Eds.), *Handbook of family therapy,* New York: Brunner/Mazel.

Skynner, A. C. R. (1984). Group analysis and family therapy. *International Journal of Group Psychotherapy, 34*, 215–224.

Skynner, A. C. R., & Cleese, J. (1983). *Families and how to survive them.* London: Methuen.

Strachey, J. (1934). The nature of the therapeutic action of psycho-analysis. *International Journal of Psychoanalysis, 15*, 127–159.

Strupp, H. (1981). Toward the refinement of time-limited dynamic psychotherapy. In S. Budman (Ed.), *Forms of brief therapy.* New York: Guilford.

Strupp, H. H., & Binder, J. (1984). *Psychotherapy in a new key: Time limited dynamic psychotherapy.* New York: Basic Books.

Sullivan, H. S. (1953). *The interpersonal theory of psychiatry.* New York: Norton.

Sullivan, H. S. (1954). *The psychiatric interview.* New York: Norton.

Sullivan, H. S. (1956). *Clinical studies in psychiatry.* New York: Norton.

Sullivan, H. S. (1976). *A Harry Stack Sullivan Case Seminar.* R. Kvarnes & G. Parloff (Eds.) New York: Norton.

Tomm, K. (1984a). One perspective on the Milan systemic approach: Part I. Overview of development, theory and practice. *Journal of Marital and Family Therapy, 10*, 113–125.

Tomm, K. (1984b). One perspective on the Milan systemic approach: Part II. Description of session format, interviewing style and interventions. *Journal of Marital and Family Therapy, 10*, 253–271.

Tomm, K. Reflexive questioning. A generative mode of enquiry. Unpublished manuscript.

Varela, F. J. (1979). *Principles of biological autonomy.* New York: Elsevier.

Viaro, M., & Leonardi, P. (1983). Getting and giving information: Analysis of a family-interview strategy. *Family Process, 22*, 27–42.

Watzlawick, P., Weakland, J., & Fisch, R. (1974). *Change, principles of problem formation and problem resolution.* New York: Norton.

Weiss, J. & Sampson, H. (1986). *The psychoanalytic process: Theory, clinical observation and empirical research.* New York: Guilford.

White, M. J. (1952). Sullivan and treatment. In P. Mullahy (Ed.), *The Contributions of Harry Stack Sullivan.* New York: Science House.

Whorf, B. L. (1941). The relation of habitual thought and behavior to language. In B. L. Whorf, *Language, thought and reality.* Cambridge: MIT Press, 1956.

Winnicott, D. W. (1958). *Through pediatrics to psycho-analysis.* New York: Basic Books, 1975.

Winnicott, D. W. (1965a). Outline for a seminar on therapeutic consultations, September. Unpublished. Copy obtained from Robin Skynner.

Winnicott, D. W. (1965b). *The maturational processes and the facilitating environment.* New York: International Universities Press.

Winnicott, D. W. (1971a). *Playing and reality.* New York: Basic Books.

Winnicott, D. W. (1971b). *Therapeutic consultations in child psychiatry.* New York: Basic Books.

Zeig, J. K. (1980). *A teaching seminar with Milton H. Erickson.* New York: Brunner/Mazel.

Zetzell, E. (1970). *The capacity for emotional growth.* London: Hogarth.

Index

INDEX OF CASES

GENERAL INDEX